MOTOWN
THE HISTORY

SHARON DAVIS

MOTOWN

THE HISTORY

GUINNESS BOOKS

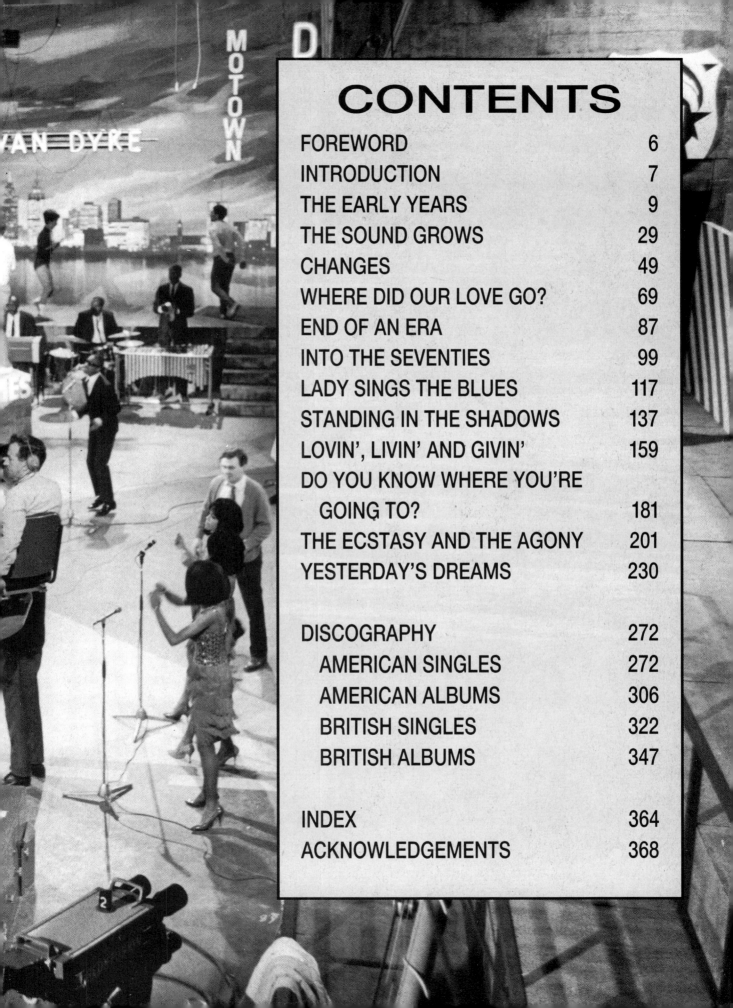

CONTENTS

FOREWORD

When I first decided to write the history of Motown little did I realise at the time, over two years ago, that it would cause me so much heartache, sleepless nights and re-writes. The book started its life as a labour of love until it became an obsession when it took over my life. Motown and its artists dominated my teenage years and like every starry-eyed fan I avidly consumed the music, collected newsclippings and diligently and happily attended all the British concerts. I then became involved in 'Motown Ad Astra', the Motown fan club, before writing about the company's artists in *Blues & Soul* and other magazines during my adult life. I've been fortunate in that I've interviewed all the artists who enjoyed British record releases, except Tammi Terrell and Florence Ballard. Now I must confess to being relieved that this manuscript is finished – I feel that I have now got the Motown Bug out of my system.

As my research got under way in 1969, different versions of certain situations emerged. To overcome these I've printed what I, and knowledgeable people in the business, consider to be the most likely. The majority of Motown's artists have been included but information on some of the lesser known acts couldn't be found. To add a more personal touch, interviews I and other journalists have conducted have been included; otherwise the result could well have been entirely self-opinionated.

I could not have completed this project without a great deal of encouragement and support. Firstly, my grateful thanks to *Blues & Soul* magazine for allowing me to use their resources so freely, particularly John Abbey, Jeff Tarry, Roy Daniell and John Hassinger, and Bob Kilbourn for allowing me off work to complete the book. And thanks to the other British magazines including *Echoes*, *Record Mirror*, *New Musical Express*, *Melody Maker* and *Sounds*, whose coverage of Motown helped put the picture together as well as the American publications like *Billboard*, *Cashbox*, *Record World*, *Rolling Stone*, *Ebony*, *Soul*, and those whose identities aren't known, having been misplaced in the course of research. I would also like to acknowledge certain authors – Gerri Hirshey (*Nowhere To Run*), J. Randy Taraborrelli (*Diana Ross*), John Swenson (*Stevie Wonder*), Randall Wilson (*Forever Faithful*), Don Waller (*Motown*), Mary Wilson (*Dreamgirl: My Life As A Supreme*), Nelson George (*Where Did Our Love Go?*) and David Ritz (*Divided Soul*).

Talking of research, a big thank you to my researchers and assistants who gave their time eagerly and freely – Gary Byrd, Noreen Allen, Veronica Jones, Bryan Tyrrell, Paul Williams, Keith Russell, Jim Hegarty, Peter Scotney, Barry Murphy, Kevin Melville, Carl Feuerbacher, Peter Duelling, my sister Hazel Eagle, Graham Canter, the MACMA staff and facilities in Brixton and those who supplied information by letter and telephone. While burning the midnight oil for the past two years, there are certain people without whom I would never have completed this mammoth task and who I feel deserve a credit for their unwavering support and love – Sandy Philpott, Susan Smith, Sandy Pattison, Kay Rowley, Debbie Bennett, Taloolah Box, Michele Fellows, my parents Joan and Douglas, Daniel and Carly, Paul Eagle, Richard Hartley and Gill Trodd for rescuing many bouts of exhaustion in her inimitable style. Finally, in these personal credits, a special thanks to Ingrid Maus for her unenviable and thankless task of keeping body and soul together during the last two years.

I would also like to thank Guinness Books for having the faith in me to take on this project in the first place, my editor, Honor Head, whose constant and patient persuasion and rigidly-enforced deadlines eventually brought out the best in me and Michael Stephenson who originally took up the challenge.

Finally, I lovingly acknowledge Motown's staff, Peter Prince, Karen Spencer and Nick Denato, for their co-operation and help over the years and Gordon Frewin who spent an excruciating few months preparing the UK and USA discography – the very first time it has been published.

This book is dedicated to my mentor and life-long friend Dave Godin.

SHARON DAVIS
1988

INTRODUCTION

The Motown Record Corporation as we know it today was the result of a young black man's frustration arising from his problems in producing music in a white man's world. The youngster, Berry Gordy Jnr, turned his desire to make a name for himself in American music into the first major black owned and run record company. From humble beginnings Gordy and his handful of staff forced the industry to accept a raw, earthy sound which was to become known as 'The Sound Of Motown' throughout the world. Little did he realize his shaky start would not only introduce a distinctive, multi-million selling musical trend, but many international artists as well – like Diana Ross, Stevie Wonder, Marvin Gaye, The Supremes, the Jackson 5, the Commodores, Smokey Robinson, The Temptations, Lionel Richie, Martha and the Vandellas, the Four Tops, Gladys Knight and the Pips – and these are just the cream of the crop.

From Berry Gordy's run-down offices on the rough side of Detroit, Michigan, Motown's early music was born. Based on a simple beat complemented by a handful of repetitive arrangements and verses, against a tight, disciplined sound, Motown music was instantly recognizable. Gordy readily admits that he didn't set out to manufacture a particular 'Motown Sound', it just happened. What is clear though, is that the music churned out on his conveyor belt produced hits. As recording techniques changed and advanced, and as money poured into his company, Berry was able to experiment and introduce more sophisticated, non-black sounds, while retaining the essential melody and lyric of his early recordings. Thus the Motown hallmark was stamped – however slightly – on every record released. Never before in the history of music has a company made such an impact on the world's record-buying public and retained that impact. Other companies have followed in Motown's footsteps but failed to reach the international status and selling power that was attached to the little blue 'M' on Motown's record labels.

The Marvelettes (this page) were Berry Gordy's first female group to give him a number one single with Please Mr. Postman. However, they soon became second league to The Supremes (left) who went on to enjoy a string of chart-toppers.

seeing the movie. So I was inspired by her and Danny Thomas of all people.' The same year that Terry was born, Thelma Gordy filed for divorce proceedings citing her husband's infidelity and violence.

By this time two of his sisters, Gwen and Anna, were working for The Flame Show Bar, having secured the cigarette and photography franchises. Berry frequently visited the Detroit nightclub, to watch local artists perform. It was then he realized that the city held a wealth of raw, untapped talent. Working at the Show Bar were the in-house bandleader, Maurice King, and saxophonist, Thomas Bowles, both of whom would eventually work for Motown. Berry Gordy: 'In those days when you were really broke, you didn't have time for love or anything else and in trying to write a song I wanted to start off writing something that was very unique and different. Everybody was writing love songs. I was basically a dreamer of love songs, and that's what I wanted to write too. But wanting to write love songs and also living in the real world and listening to the earthy problems of life, I tried to mix that in with the love and the feeling.' His sister, Esther, recalls Gordy was a positive, aggressive and totally confident person: 'He had a job shining shoes in downtown Detroit where he would often be run off the street by older and larger competitors. But the positiveness of him made me want to help the force along in whatever he wanted to do. Whatever he did, we knew we had at least nine genuine supporters who would go up with you or down with you. Mom and Dad were the most substantial supporters we had.'

Around 1957 boxer-turned-singer Jackie Wilson was looking for songs, so a determined Berry Gordy left his trimmer's job to follow his deep-felt ambition to write songs. Jackie Wilson: 'I admired his nerve and will to get on. I had just left the Dominoes and my manager at the time, Al Greene, introduced us and there was this little guy with a briefcase crammed full of tunes. There must have been at least fifty songs in that little bag. I was the first named artist to actually record one of Berry's songs, and we must have recorded close on twenty at our first session in New York. Sure, there were some I didn't record at that time.' One in particular was *You Got What It Takes* which became a huge hit for one of Gordy's protégés Marv Johnson, who was also a partner in the ill-fated 3-D Record Mart.

Berry Gordy's sister, Gwen, introduced him to composer Billy Davis, aka Tyran Carlo, and together they wrote numerous songs with Jackie Wilson in mind. Gwen Gordy: 'I always wanted to be in the record business and I knew Berry was interested, so I was constantly asking him if he was ready to venture into the business full-time, but at that time he wasn't.' Although Berry didn't want to commit himself totally to the business at this time, he wrote several songs for Jackie Wilson including *Reet Petite, To Be Loved, Lonely Teardrops* and *That's Why I Love You So.* Berry: 'Dick Jacobs at Decca Records would always call me when they recorded a song for Jackie: For *Lonely Teardrops* they actually flew me to the company to be in on the session. I enjoyed working with Dick Jacobs, he always gave me a lot of credit which built up my ego quite a lot. But I didn't actually make any money from those songs that I was writing, because by the time I got my royalties I owed everybody in town, especially my family.'

Jackie Wilson recorded *Reet Petite* on Decca's Brunswick label; it sold over a quarter of a million copies. In a Seventies interview the singer recalled: 'It was a funny record. I loved it on first sight, so that shows how nutty I was. Berry wrote it in the way I sang it, so if I hadn't come along, God knows who could have recorded it.' (Twenty-nine years later in 1986, the single was re-issued to become Britain's number one single over Christmas.) Wilson also remembered his first meeting with Berry Gordy; 'He was a little man with a big dream. I always said he was under-rated as a songwriter and even at that time he could see what the future held. He was more into publishing than recording because at the time I wasn't even signed to a record company. He was far more interested in getting his songs recorded.' Wilson enjoyed a flourishing career until he suffered a heart attack on stage in October 1975. He spent the next eight years in a coma, and died on 21 January 1984.

It is thought that Berry Gordy wrote and produced his first record, *Ooh, Shucks,* in 1957. It was released by The Five Stars on George Goldner's Mark X label. C. P. Spencer and Walter Gaines, two future members of The Originals, fronted the Stars. This single was one of several compositions Gordy would produce for Goldner. Not only did his musical career now look promising, but also his personal life. Berry met a fellow music enthusiast Raynoma Liles in 1958 after she won an amateur singing contest in a Detroit club. Liles: 'The emcee recommended I go and see Berry, who had some acts. I went by his place and auditioned with my sister. I had about one hundred songs written, most of them were lousy, but they were songs. I'd been writing since I was twelve. I guess Berry thought the songs could have been better, but I went on to work with him and his talent. Basically, I set up the harmonies for the vocals, wrote the lead sheets, worked on continuity, the hooks of songs, that kind of thing.' Together they also formed and fronted the Rayber Voices ('Ray'-Raynoma, 'Ber'-Berry), adding backing vocals to singers Gordy was associated with. The first single to carry a label credit for the Rayber Voices was Herman Griffin's *I Need You* for HOB. It was also the first song to be published by Jobete, the publishing house Gordy set-up during the Sixties and named after his children. Raynoma used a hairdressers called House Of Beauty (HOB) which at one stage opened its own record label. For some reason after Griffin's 1958 release it closed down, although the premises would later be used as a rehearsal hall by Motown acts, including The Supremes.

Raynoma Liles became Gordy's second wife in 1959. They had a son, Kennedy, before divorcing in 1964. Gordy later had another son, Berry IV, as a result of his marriage to Margaret Norton in 1965. In 1984, Kennedy recorded under the name Rockwell to enjoy a major hit with *Somebody's Watching Me*.

Producing records was Berry Gordy's quickest way of earning money (royalties from songs took a long time to materialize) and production meant he was responsible for the song's arrangements, harmonies, mixes and overall presentation. With a second-hand disc-making machine, a rented studio and, occasionally, non-professional musicians, he charged $100 to anyone wanting to use his facilities. He also offered to promote records on local radio, but when this became too difficult he hired Alan Abrams to work as his first white plugger. Money was slowly coming in, but he still didn't own his own record company. Producing his own master discs meant he still relied on white companies (e.g. United Artists) for distribution and promotion. In 1958 the Detroit based Kudo Records released four Berry Gordy productions including Marv Johnson's first *My Baby-O* and Brian Holland's *Shock*. Brian's brother, Eddie, also recorded a Gordy composition for Mercury in Chicago. The Holland brothers were destined to join Motown, but now Eddie was pursuing his solo career. Berry's own brother, Robert, using the pseudonym Robert Kayli, recorded *Everyone Was There* in '58 for Carlton. Three years later he was the first of Gordy's family to release a single on Berry's Tamla label, *Small Sad Sam* in reply to Jimmy Dean's *Big Bad John*.

Around this time Berry Gordy decided to work regularly with his protégé, Marv Johnson; real name Marvin Earl Johnson, born in 1939. A native Detroiter, he started his career in local amateur shows when he was 13, as lead singer of his own group, The Serenaders. Singing wasn't Johnson's first ambition. His instructors at Detroit's Cass Technical College advised him to become an aeronautical engineer, a path he was quite keen to follow. However his destiny changed when, as a part-time clerk in the 3-D Record Mart, Gordy heard him playing the piano. He suggested they talk and ended up recording *Come To Me*. Although Johnson reputedly wrote the song, Gordy is credited as composer.

While visiting Jackie Wilson's office during 1957, Berry Gordy met the man who was to encourage him to open his own record company: William 'Smokey' Robinson. Robinson, born 19 February 1940, was raised in Detroit's slum North End area. His mother worked for the local government and his father was a

truck driver. From the age of six, Robinson had experimented with songwriting, and wrote tunes for a school play in which he portrayed Uncle Remus. He also became an avid lyric reader of the popular song books of the time. Robinson was educated at Hutchins Intermediate School and graduated from the Northern High School. While still at school Smokey (so nicknamed by an uncle) formed his first band, The Matadors, whose sister group was The Matadorettes, led by Claudette Rogers who later left to join The Matadors when her brother Sonny joined the Army.

In 1957, instead of enrolling for college, Smokey Robinson with Ronnie White, Bobby and Claudette Rogers and Pete Moore, decided to audition for Jackie Wilson's manager instead. The audition, featuring five Robinson compositions, failed because Wilson's manager felt Robinson and Rogers should branch out as a duet. However Gordy, who was present at the audition, was interested and persuaded Robinson, with his re-named group The Miracles, to start working with him. Robinson and Gordy worked together in all areas of the recording business and their first publicized collaboration was

Berry Gordy wrote Reet Petite *for Jackie Wilson.*
Wilson: 'Berry wrote it in the way I sang it, so if I hadn't come along, God knows who could have recorded it.'

The ever-changing
Smokey Robinson.
(Below) the original
Miracles line-up with
Claudette Rogers,
(above) Smokey
Robinson and The
Miracles (minus
Claudette) and (right)
Smokey the solo artist.

A partner in Berry Gordy's ill-fated 3-D Record Mart, Marv Johnson became Gordy's protégé and hit-maker in the early days of Motown.

Eddie Holland, who was to become a member of the legendary Holland-Dozier-Holland songwriting/producing team, first recorded Berry Gordy's compositions as a solo artist, and as Jackie Wilson's demo singer.

the recording Insane sung by Wade Jones.

Working with Berry Gordy was an adventure in itself for Robinson, but it also presented some unusual dangers as he explained: 'We were going to release Marv Johnson's Come To Me in January or February (1958) but we didn't have any records to distribute to the radio stations. The weather was so bad, ice and snow all over the highways. The company wasn't going to truck them down to us, so as Berry and I had this old car we started up to Awaso to get them. The maximum speed on the highway was fifteen miles an hour. We're driving on a four-lane highway, there were no guard rails separating the roads and there were roads leading back up into farms and so on. Berry's driving, we're slipping and sliding all over the highway, when this car suddenly darts out in front of us from a side road. In order not to hit him we skidded in the middle of the highway and faced the oncoming traffic. Finally we manoeuvred our way off onto the soft verge. We started up again and we're probably ten miles outside of Awaso when a truck and two trailers come down our side of the highway. The only thing we could is go into the ditch. They had to call the snow plough to get us out. After all this we picked up the three hundred records and eventually returned to Detroit and got the records out to the stations.' Come To Me, licensed to United Artists, featured the Rayber Voices as backing vocalists, and sold well.

Encouraged by her working relationship with composer Billy Davis, Gwen Gordy ran Checkmate Records with him for a time, a R&B subsidiary of Chess Records. This dabbling prompted her to open her own label, Anna (named after her sister) in 1958, the same year as The Miracles recorded Got A Job leased to George Goldner for his End label. Got A Job was the 'answer' record to Get a Job by The Silhouettes. Robinson: Get A Job was really the national anthem all over the world at the time. So I wrote this answer song and showed it to Berry. We changed a few of the spots, he put another bridge in there and we recorded it on The Miracles. At the time America only had Top 60 R&B charts and the Top 60 pop – only the contemporary people were on that one like Elvis Presley, Fats Domino and people like that. Other than that you still had Frank Sinatra and Patti Page on the pop charts. Our record Got A Job had gone to number one on the R&B charts. We were performing at a state fair in Michigan and Berry came up to present us with a gold record. There have been so many great moments in my connection with the company but when you are a recording artist, you dream of having a gold record. It was a great day for Motown too, it put the company on the map.'

Due to radio airplay restrictions during the late Fifties and early Sixties, the number of black acts achieving chart status dropped for the first time in four years, as whites were more keen to record a black song which was then re-released and given the airplay not granted to the black version. However, the Anna label made some progress and recruited future Motown artists, producers and writers like The Voice Masters (featuring Walter Gaines, C P Spencer, and Ty Hunter). David Ruffin, (Jackey) Beavers and (Johnny) Bristol and Lamont Anthony (Dozier). As the first rumblings of the Mersey Beat Sound stirred within Liverpool, England in 1960, Gwen was joined at Anna by singer/writer Harvey Fuqua. He was lead singer of the doo-wop group The Moonglows – previously known as The Crazy Sounds – signed to the Chance label. Chess Records had bought the group's recording contract from Chance and released their first single Sincerely in 1954. The Moonglows enjoyed a run of hit singles for four years before they disbanded. Fuqua wanted to keep the group and sound going and on discovering The Marquees, whose 'occasional' member was the young Marvin Gaye, he reformed The Moonglows but failed to repeat his former success. So Fuqua joined Gwen Gordy and Billy Davis at Anna, and eventually Marvin Gaye left Washington DC to follow in Fuqua's footsteps. Although he was signed as an artist, the young singer never recorded but was confined to the role of session musician. When the Anna label folded, Fuqua opened his own Harvey and Tri-Phi labels, and married Gwen Gordy in 1961. Anna's biggest-seller was the Berry Gordy/Bradford composition Money (That's What I Want) for Barrett Strong. Gordy: '(That was) the first popular song I wrote. I was very broke at the time. I was embarrassed because when people asked me what I did for a living I would say "I write songs". They would have sons and daughters that were becoming doctors and lawyers, and my mother and father were always somewhat embarrassed when I would tell their friends I wrote songs. Even though I had many hits, and there were other writers who had many hits, we just didn't have any profits. And coming from a business family, my father and mother always talked about the bottom line, and the bottom line is profit.' For Money and The Miracles' Got A Job Berry Gordy received $3.19 cents!

The Tri-Phi and Harvey labels boasted a number of future Motown artists like Jr Walker, The Spinners and Shorty Long, but both labels were shortlived and Fuqua was destined to become record promoter and head of stage presentations for his wife's brother. (Years later, when Fuqua left Motown, he was the major force behind the gay superstar Sylvester, who in 1978 released the multi-million seller You Make Me Feel (Mighty Real).) Gordy, meanwhile, became increasingly depressed by his reliance on major record companies to expose his product and the way other people treated his songs: 'I wrote songs because I love writing.' He explained in an Eighties interview: 'The reason I produced songs was because I didn't like the way (the majority) were being produced. Through my experiences as a writer, I found that songwriters were not getting what I considered was a fair shake. They were not making money. So my idea was that if songwriters could make money, how wonderful, and how big a company could grow.' He also developed an extremely cautious attitude to spending the little money that was coming in. On his promotional trips to Chicago and New York, for example, he stayed not in hotel rooms but with friends, and it was upon such economies that his future company was eventually founded. Smokey Robinson was aware of his friend's professional anguish and urged Berry to stop 'messin' with majors' and start his own recording operation.

This was all the encouragement Gordy needed. He borrowed $800 from his family and in 1959 opened Tamla Motown: 'Tamla', a spin-off from Debbie Reynolds' hit of the time *Tammy's In Love* and 'Motown', an abbreviation of Detroit's nickname: 'motor town'. Gordy really wanted to use 'Tammy' but it was already registered as a label. (Although Gordy acquired the names Tamla Motown, he used Tamla first as a record label in 1959. Motown started as a record label in 1961. Tamla Motown does not exist as a label in America, but does in Europe. Tamla Motown will be referred to as Motown hereafter even though the official name-change did not occur until 1976.) Its probably true to say that Motown was as much Robinson's company as it was Gordy's, and during the following years the two ran Motown as one, although Gordy was unquestionably the head of the company.

Motown's progression was slow because the early singles still had to be leased to major companies, and Gordy's time was split between writing and producing for numerous artists on other labels. He was in debt and represented the struggling yet dedicated business man. Gordy could not have envisaged that thirteen years later he would be reputed to be the richest black man in America, with a yearly salary of $10 million.

Money (That's What I Want) has always been credited as Tamla's debut single, but it wasn't. The first single was *Come To Me* by Marv Johnson (Tamla 101) in January 1959. *Money (That's What I Want)* was given to the Anna label because of its already established selling power. The record shot to number two in the R&B charts. Eddie Holland's *Merry-Go-Round* and Nick and the Jaguars' *Cool And Crazy/Ich-I-Bon-I* followed on the Tamla label. An error in the matrix numbering of *Solid Sender* and *Snake Walk (Part 1)*, the next two Tamla singles, occurred as they were both given the same five-digit prefix record number, 54024, in error. The label colour also changed from green to yellow. In 1961 a globe was added to the top of the label, and a brown strip replaced the globe five years later.

By the early Sixties, Gordy was exhausting his supply of record companies to distribute his product, and with Tamla being black-owned and operated, he was unwilling to negotiate further non-profitable agreements like those he had been forced to make in order to get his records in the shops. Taking gambles was almost second nature by now, so he took another and pressed *Way Over There*, by The Miracles, himself. The gamble paid off and the single eventually sold a remarkable 60,000 copies.

Gordy was now confident of his future in the music business, so the next step was to find cheap but adequate premises for his

Harvey Fuqua, ex-lead singer with The Moonglows, later became a guiding influence on Marvin Gaye.

The original five member line-up of The Miracles featuring Claudette Rogers, Smokey Robinson's future wife, looking rather worried as they wait to appear on the Sixties British television show Ready, Steady Go!

As a solo artist David Ruffin failed, but as a later member of The Temptations his distinctive voice became an integral part of the group.

Marvin Gaye became a session musician for Anna Records. When the label joined Motown, Berry Gordy was at a loss as to how to record him.

(Right) Jamie was Eddie Holland's debut hit as a singer for Motown. As a writer/ producer he faired much better although his early recordings are very much in demand today.

company. This was left to his wife Raynoma who transformed 2648 West Grand Boulevard (in a row of run-down houses in a once affluent neighbourhood) into a pulsating music concern. Gordy's most immediate staff had to be enthusiastic, supportive and trustworthy, so who better than his own family? Pops Gordy took on the role of consultant and became irreplacable in the running of the company. Berry's sister Esther – married to local councillor George Edwards – handled the daily administration while another sister, Loucye, was the company's first head of sales. Married to musician Ron Wakefield, Loucye was also responsible for collecting money owed to Motown. In July 1963 her husband became a copyist in the arranging department, moving to artist co-ordination a year later. Loucye Wakefield had worked for the government with shrewd business woman Fay Hale prior to her move. Once Loucye was installed she persuaded Hale to join her, saying 'you don't have to like the music, just remember the names!' Loucye was invaluable, keeping Motown solvent during the first years. Unfortunately, she died in 1965 without seeing her struggles come to fruition. Berry's brother Robert left his post office job to work as an apprentice studio engineer for 65 cents an hour. He became Motown's first stereo engineer, producing several artists but receiving no credits on record sleeves.

The small upstairs bedrooms at 2648 West Grand Boulevard were turned into offices, one of which served as Berry's bedroom cum office, where a much-used dartboard hung on the back of his door. Several members of his staff lived at West Grand Boulevard, too. Apparently Pops Gordy and David Ruffin (Anna recording artist) converted the basement photographer's studio into the first Motown recording studio, known as the snake pit. It was well named, too. The room was poky and claustrophobic, and the soundproofed walls did little to contain the music. A cubicle big enough for one lead singer stood near the console board, where the producer or producers would oversee the recordings, leaving backing vocalists to fight for spare microphones. A toilet which doubled as an echo chamber was annexed to the studio. It was a musical sweat shop. Author Nelson George reported: 'The control room had two Ampex 8-track machines near the wall next to the door. Engineers like Mike McClain and Lawrence Horn and some of the other producers had, through trial and error, built the original 3-track recording machine into an 8-track by the mid-Sixties. Microphone cables hung from the ceiling like branches of black licorice sticks. Looking over the main 8-track console into the studio, you'd see chairs positioned there for guitar and bass players. The piano was to their immediate left and the drums diagonally across from the piano. ... Side rooms had been built into the wall next to the piano after Berry Gordy had purchased the

building next door. There vibes, organ and percussion instruments were usually stationed. There was no room for large amplifiers in the studio, the guitar and bass were right into the console, and were heard through the room's one speaker.' Before a session, guitarists would be expected to adjust their volume to a level not to be exceeded once in the studio, George added, and should a guitarist regularly play above the accepted level he was sacked. An electronic device which controlled volume levels was later introduced into the studio. Called a 'limiter' it saved valuable time in sessions by regulating musical highs and lows. In time, expensive and intricate equipment was installed to combat human error, but should a mistake become apparent it was erased in the final mix which, writers moaned, could sound little like their original song. In 1963 Gordy bought a disc cutting machine as he felt much spontaneity was lost in the lengthy transferral of music from master tape to record. This machine transferred directly from tape to record.

Motown's early musicians, writers and producers were hand-picked. The musicians were mostly Detroiters with jazz backgrounds, while the writers either respected Gordy's ambitions or wanted a permanent base to work from. Most of them couldn't read or write music. Writer/producer William 'Mickey' Stevenson was put in the trusted position of overseeing the entire A&R (artists and repertoire) department run by Clarence Paul. Stevenson handled every step from the song's conception to the choice of artist best suited to record it. In time he became a very powerful figure within the organization. When he wanted Motown's releases to have an edge over competitors, he persuaded Gordy to introduce string accompaniment on records. It wasn't an easy transition and Gordy argued with the Detroit Symphony Orchestra on several occasions: 'Sometimes when I asked them to play a particular riff they were insulted. They said the music wasn't right and

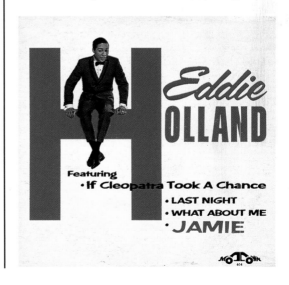

you couldn't do this or that. They'd say "but you can't play this chord against that chord" and I'd say "it sounds right and I don't care about the rules because I don't know what they are". Many of them would play it anyway and mostly they would all enjoy it.' Another Symphony grievance was the absence of sheet music. Gordy, like his writers and producers, used to hum songs to them, then explain the requirements. He cared little how a song was recorded as long as the result was a winner. These amateur techniques of the early Sixties dissolved when Gordy and the musicians insisted writers outline their songs on paper. The musicians then developed the music.

Brian Holland, whom Gordy had met as a teenager, began as a recording engineer before moving into writing and producing. Holland's talent for commercial sound did not peak until he was joined by his brother Eddie, and Lamont Dozier. After recording for Mercury and United Artists Records, Eddie Holland sang demos for Jackie Wilson. He joined Motown as a singer, where his debut Jamie, (US, Jan '62) was his only success. Dozier was the last recruit to the famous Holland-Dozier-Holland trio (circa 1963).

From 1959 the studio musicians were more important in Gordy's operation than the artists although none was given any recognition or credit. This experienced group of musicians ran the studio in their own way and guided the inexperienced creative staff. One such musician, keyboardist and bandleader Earl Van Dyke, joined Motown in 1962. Born in 1929, he took piano lessons at the age of eight and studied a variety of instruments until he was 16. After being drafted into the US Armed

Forces he worked in New York clubs before returning to Detroit. Van Dyke headed a touring group known as 'Earl Van Dyke and the Soul Brothers' or 'The Earl Van Dyke Sextet'. The keyboardist actually recorded his own work although much was left in the can (recorded, unreleased and stored). On his first four singles Earl Van Dyke was joined by The Soul Brothers and the fifth Six By Six (with The Motown Brass) was a big seller on England's specialist northern soul scene. Van Dyke then appeared as a soloist on the 1969 single Runaway Child, Running Wild. Four years earlier an album – now a collector's item – titled That Motown Sound was issued containing backing tracks of several of his Sixties hits.

Keyboardist Johnny Griffin, guitarist Robert White and bassist James Jamerson (who joined Motown in the early days after working with Jackie Wilson and Raynoma Gordy) formed a band called The Funk Brothers led by Earl Van Dyke and saxophonist Eli Fountain. For various reasons the line-up would change over the years. Musicians like Joe Messina and Eddie Willis (guitarists) and Jack Ashford (percussionist) made up the numbers, while saxophonist Choker Campbell worked both in the Motown studios and on the road heading up the first Motown touring band. Like Van Dyke, Choker Campbell and his 16-piece band recorded an album in 1965 Hits Of The Sixties which, once again, contained backing tracks of released singles. Joe Hunter was one of several in-house group leaders. When the musicians were in full swing they could record six singles a day. Joe Messina told Don Waller: 'First we'd play a song as it was written, then we'd start messing around with it. We'd do three or four takes and that would be it. We never did anymore than that. The whole thing would take about twenty minutes. Then we'd take a ten minute break and go on to the next tune.' The Funk Brothers' sound can be heard on almost every Motown record released during the early Sixties.

William 'Benny' Benjamin, drummer extraordinaire, was also hired when Motown started. He was probably the most famous of all the musicians using Motown's Studio A and his ability to play numerous rhythms simultaneously earned him the respect of his contemporaries. He was a total professional in the studio, yet his personal life was in turmoil. Benjamin had a drug and alcohol problem and when his health worsened his work suffered and two drummers trained by him (Richard 'Pistol' Allen and Uriel Jones) were brought in as his replacements. Benjamin died following a stroke in 1969.

A musician's basic wage at Motown was well below existing union rates and the temptation to work for Gordy's competitors became irresistible. Many moonlighted for Ed Wingate's labels Ric Tic and Golden World, leaving Gordy little option but to match outside offers. Apart from insisting his musicians

(Top left) Where would Berry Gordy have been without Earl Van Dyke? Keyboard wizard and band leader Dyke can be heard on the majority of Motown's early recordings before he worked as a soloist and with The Soul Brothers and the Motown Brass.

remain loyal to him, Gordy became agitated at the number of soundalike Motown songs being recorded in outside studios. Author Don Waller recalled an example of Gordy's annoyance: 'He fined The Funk Brothers $1,000 a piece for playing on *Agent Double O Soul* by Edwin Starr. When Ed Wingate found out he paid all the fines.'

Ed Wingate's studios were used to record the hit single *Hungry For Love* by Motown musicians working under the title The San Remo Golden Strings. This single appeared on the 1968 album (UK, '73) *The San Remo Strings Swing* with instrumentals like *Festival Time, People, Lonely One* and *Home Coming* produced by Gil Askey and Larry Maxwell. In 1968 Gordy got his own back on Wingate by buying Ric Tic's product but not the label and the Golden World name for a reputed $1 million. Gordy integrated the labels and the artists (The Fantastic Four, Edwin Starr, J.J. Barnes, Al Kent) into his operation. Ten years later James Epps (member of The Fantastic Four) told *Blues & Soul* about his regrets at having to leave: 'We was just like one big happy family and I think that's why those records were so different from anything else. Everyone was involved in the music and that was what really mattered. I think we were all upset when the company closed, it was like closing a page of your life. We were the last that Ed Wingate kept but when he arranged that we join Motown he felt we would stand the best chance of succeeding.' The group wasted two years with Berry Gordy: 'We never felt the company was interested in us and we were never able to concentrate on what we should have been doing.'

Jimmy James 'J.J.' Barnes was born on 30 November 1943 in Detroit, and spent his teenage years singing in local church choirs until 1959 when he led his own choir, The Halo Gospel Singers. Two years later he moved into R&B to record his first single for Ring Records. His self-penned *Poor Unfortunate Me* and *Just One More Time* brought him local attention but financial problems led to Ring folding in 1962. After working at Chrysler Motors and singing part-time at weekends for two years, Barnes signed to Ric Tic. His first release there was *Please Let Me In* (RT106), which was a flop, but its follow-up *Real Humdinger*, released in 1965, became an American top twenty R&B hit. Barnes' third single was a cover of The Beatles' *Day Tripper* which marked his British debut release via Polydor. The last Ric Tic single *Say It* was produced by Barnes and Don Davis (who also worked with Major Lance, Johnnie Taylor and The Dells). When Berry Gordy bought Ric Tic's product a wealth of Barnes' work was canned and he spent a year with Motown. Barnes: 'They had me in the studio almost every day with one producer or another. I cut things with Richard Morris, Sylvia Moy, Dean Weatherspoon, Clarence Paul and Norman Whitfield. And some of that material was good. I never really knew what they were doing. When they took us over, I was doing okay but they seemed to ignore Edwin and me. It was as if they weren't interested so I got the hell out as soon as I could.'

Edwin Starr, real name Charles Hatcher, was born on 21 January 1942 in Cleveland, Ohio, and began singing in 1956. He won first prize on a television programme *Uncle Jake's Talent Hour* and formed his own band The Future Tones. His circuit singing ended in 1960 when he was drafted into the Army where he performed for servicemen at bases in Germany and America. Once discharged, Starr toured with organist Bill Doggett for three years. While playing in a Detroit club, a Golden World Records' representative offered him a deal. Two days later *Agent Double O Soul* was recorded. As a promotional tool for this single Starr appeared in a short film with actor Sean Connery, then famous for his James Bond character. The film was called *00 Soul Meets 007*. Starr went from strength to strength with his single success and toured with artists like Jackie Wilson, Sam and Dave and Wilson Pickett.

It wasn't just Gordy's attitude to his artists' work that generated bad feeling. Unlike his competitors Gordy refused to allow his account books to be audited and therefore exact record sales figures couldn't be ascertained. As a result his artists were denied officially-recognized awards of the music industry for charting singles. The Supremes' Mary Wilson: '(Motown) made it difficult for outside people to ascertain the accuracy of its earning reports, since according to contract, there were two auditing periods, but an artist was only allowed one audit per year. In other words, even the most astute artist could only know the details of his finances for half a year. Without seeing the second period's figures, there was no way to know exactly what was going on, how much money you had earned, or how much your were entitled to.'

Earl Van Dyke, on the other hand, held no grudges against Motown 'because the opportunities were there to do more and I didn't take advantage of them. I just got locked into the fact that I was playing music and making a living. It was not what I wanted to play but it was good.' He also considered the salaries to be above average so, in his opinion, if a musician left Motown empty-handed it wasn't Motown's fault. During 1965 he said he earned $60,000; a year later (with freelance work) his salary soared by another $40,000. However, by the mid-Sixties Motown's session musicians could earn up to $3,000 a week.

When musicians left Motown amicably they were sworn to secrecy about recording techniques. Rightly or wrongly, Gordy assumed competitors would pay generously for information. Motown music was, after all, a unique, distinct sound which to this day nobody has been able accurately to dissect. However, certain fundamental guides were used: the strong bass line would pick out the original melody.

Percussion, lashings of tambourines and keyboards would develop that guideline until a tight beat set the pace for the singer. Saxophone breaks were liberally used; in fact, a listener could almost identify a Motown single by the way that instrument was used. The back-up voices were sharp and shrill using the call and response technique with the backing singers responding to a question posed by the lead singer. When strings were introduced, the arrangements were sweeping, suggestive and low keyed. Berry Gordy probably came the closest when he said the sound was 'a combination of rats, roaches, talent, guts and love'. Once a winning formula was discovered the riffs would be used time and again, which is why during the Sixties records would sound almost identical. Holland-Dozier-Holland compositions from the early Sixties sung by The Temptations and The Supremes are a fine example.

Detroit-born Lamont Dozier, as a member of the short-lived Romeos, recorded for the Fox label. As a teenager he wrote a local hit for them titled *Fine, Baby, Fine*. After a nine-to-five job in New York, Dozier returned to Detroit where he joined The Voice Masters, later recording as a solo artist using the pseudonym Lamont Anthony. In 1962 he became a Motown artist where, after one single, *Fortune Teller Tell Me*, he teamed up with the composing partnership of Freddie Gorman and Brian Holland. Gorman, previously a Ric Tic artist, worked with Holland and Dozier until he left Motown in 1963 to lead The Originals. Mickey Stevenson, meanwhile, was aware of the potential of three writers working together and persuaded Eddie Holland to take Gorman's place. The team of Holland-Dozier-Holland was born. Working for a basic wage plus royalties, Dozier was responsible for creating the song, with Eddie Holland assisting on lyrics and melody. Brian Holland engineered the song's structure and overall sound. None could write chords, so fellow writer/producer Hank Cosby invariably did it for them. Bassist, James Jamerson: 'Holland-Dozier-Holland would give me a chord sheet but they couldn't write it for me. When they did, it didn't sound right. They'd let me go on and ad lib.' Jamerson would then build up his bass line around the melody, often intricately so, which presented problems on stage when the touring guitarist was unable to repeat his sound. Jamerson died from a heart attack in August 1983. Several musicians – Paul Riser, David Van De Pitte, Hank Cosby – were also prolific writers and arrangers. In time they were able to develop their talents, with Riser, becoming an integral member of Motown's horn section.

Berry Gordy's paranoia in keeping a tight rein on his staff was typified by his introduction of a fines system, for below-standard work, absenteeism and so on. He detested bad time-keeping and, as Lamont Dozier told *Melody Maker*, he introduced a punch clock and

(Top left) Hardly James Bond, but Edwin Starr did appear in a short film with Sean Connery, 00 Soul Meets 007, to promote the classic single Agent Double 0 Soul.

(Left) Left to right, Lamont Dozier, Brian and Eddie Holland, Motown's hit-makers of the Sixties who, with the musicians, discovered what the world called 'The Motown Sound'.

THE MARVELETTES

LA 54097

The original membership of The Marvelettes who recorded Motown's first national number one single Please Mr. Postman *in 1961. The Beatles later recorded this song on their album* With The Beatles.

card system similar to that at Ford when he had worked on the assembly line. Gordy was a strict boss and his demands were excessive, yet he could be generous with money and gifts to employees he liked. He was also a stickler for perfection; the standards he set and demanded were high. For instance, he turned down one hundred Smokey Robinson compositions, and hundreds of other songs costing thousands of dollars to produce were canned because they didn't come up to standard. His policy was simple – every record released had to sell. During the Eighties many canned tracks had the dust blown off, were re-mixed and scheduled for release. Gordy never knowingly modelled Motown on any existing company, but when a competitor, such as United Artists, had a string of hits, he would look closely at its formula for success.

At the start Gordy had more songwriters and producers than he really needed, so it wasn't unusual for three or four producers to be working in the studio at the same time. With most of the recordings taking place at night, local residents complained bitterly and frequently. Eventually, Gordy purchased the adjoining properties, evicted the tenants and thus owned several houses in a row. He joked he owned the only seven-storey building going sideways!

All the creative staff worked in cramped conditions which were considered ideal by Gordy for his family of music. A song could be conceived in one of the small rooms then passed for opinion and alteration throughout the building until completed. It was then left to Gordy to decide whether the result should be recorded and by whom. When Motown expanded, the A&R director would make the

final decision. Gordy: 'The people at Motown had a choice of sitting in studio creating something that would make them feel good and proud, or they could be out robbing somebody's house or taking dope or doing some of the things that people do when they're bored.'

Part of Gordy's regular working routine was based around three meetings. The first held on Monday attended by songwriters and producers who chose new songs for release and shelved sub-standard work. Tuesday's meetings were chaired by Esther Edwards, head of ITM (International Talent Management Inc), where proposed tours were discussed and planned. The third was the Quality Control discussion on Fridays in Gordy's office. All key staff were required to attend this. The Quality Control division in those days was a harrowing experience as The Temptations' Richard Street told Gerri Hirshey in *Nowhere To Run*: 'On a Monday or Tuesday I would get about twenty records. First we would judge them from one to ten, and then on Fridays we'd take all the records into Mr Gordy's office. Twelve people would then vote on them. If we gave something an eight or a nine, it usually turned out to be a million seller for Motown'. The only office meetings Gordy didn't attend regularly were the sales meetings chaired by Barney Ales.

Once records were chosen for release, sessions would be held in local dance halls where punters would be asked for reactions. Car radios were the main route by which punters heard a single for the first time, and indeed many songs were recorded with the radio's 'tinny' reproduction in mind. Needless to say many proposed singles were returned to the studios for re-working as a result!

Looking for artists for his record company proved no problem as Berry Gordy was inundated with potential talent. He had, of course, acquired many from Detroit's nightclubs like The Twenty Grand Lounge and had sent scouts to high school talent shows and into the streets where youngsters used the pavement as a stage. He later introduced Saturday morning auditions at his offices which also proved fruitful.

In September 1961, by which time Tamla had released over twenty singles, Gordy opened his second label, Motown, with The Satintones' *My Beloved*. This group was probably his first vocal group; membership included Chico Leverett, James Ellie, Robert Bateman and Sonny Sanders. Under the Motown label prefix 1006 the group is credited with two singles. *Tomorrow And Always* was their 'answer' record to The Shirelles' hit *Will You Still Love Me Tomorrow*. Gordy hastily withdrew this single when he was threatened with an infringement suit and replaced it with the safer *Angel*.

The most successful act on Tamla at this time was a relatively short-lived outfit, The Marvelettes. These girls formed Gordy's first female group and gave him his first number one single with *Please Mr. Postman* (US, Aug '61/UK, Nov '61). Their original line-up was Gladys Horton and Wanda Young (both lead singers), Georgeanna Tillman (Dobbins), Katherine Anderson and Juanita Cowart. (Young married The Miracles' Bobby Rogers; Tillman married Billy Gordon, leader of The Contours.) All girls were born within months of each other in 1944 in Detroit and sang together in Inkster High School at about the same time as Gordy was opening his record company. Katherine Anderson: 'The school was having a talent show where part of the prize was that a representative from Motown would be at the show. He selected different acts and we went down to the company.' They were probably known as The Marvels then and sang a Chantels' hit for their audition. By the time of their second single *Twistin' Postman* (US, Dec '61/UK, Mar '62) the line-up was reduced to three. After constant ill health both Tillman and Cowart left. (Tillman died from sickle cell anaemia in 1980.) The trio continued until 1967 when Gladys Horton left to get married. Ann Bogan replaced her. The Supremes' Florence Ballard became a Marvelette temporarily when Rogers was pregnant and couldn't work. The girls used the in-house session group, The Andantes' vocals to pad out their recordings and had a variety of writers and performers at their disposal. For example Brian Holland, Robert Bateman, William Garrett and Marvelette Georgeanna wrote *Please Mr. Postman*.

Lamont Dozier and Eddie Holland joined Brian Holland to produce further Marvelettes' songs. H-D-H were in constant demand as Dozier told NME twenty years later: 'If we didn't complete an average of two or three songs a day, at least we would start them. We would have parts of the songs or maybe parts of a verse done, so that at the end of the day we would have something accomplished. I guess that was primarily the reason for the success we had in such a short time. Berry Gordy trusted us to do what we wanted to do. We had a free range to pick and release what we felt was proper or would be a hit for the company.' Unfortunately, the expanding artist roster's demand for repertoire, contributed to The Marvelettes drop in status as songs were either not available for them or were of inferior quality. However, all was not lost for waiting in the wings was Smokey Robinson who re-established them with a catchy *Don't Mess With Bill* (US, Nov '65/UK, Jan '66) followed by gems like *The Hunter Gets Captured By The Game* (US, Dec '66/UK Feb '67), *My Baby Must Be A Magician* (US, Nov '67/UK, Jan '68) (with Melvin Franklin's spoken introduction) and *Here I Am Baby* (US, May '68/UK, Jun '68). Also, in November 1963 the girls recorded *Too Hurt To Cry, Too Much In Love To Say Goodbye* under the name The Darnells.

Even with Robinson's contributions the sound that made The Marvelettes superior to their competitors vanished. Yet despite the loss of originality the girls maintained their popularity and contributed success and wealth to Gordy's expanding empire. Their talent reached Europe when The Beatles recorded *Please Mr. Postman* on their second UK album *With The Beatles*. John Lennon double-tracked the lead vocal with George Harrison and Paul McCartney providing back-up vocals. On the same album they covered *Money* where Lennon again took lead vocals and *You Really Got A Hold On Me*, featuring Lennon and Harrison on lead. The Beatles and singer Dusty Springfield were instrumental in exposing Gordy's music throughout the world by recording his songs and referring to his artists in interviews.

Five months before The Marvelettes' debut single, another female group released their first title, and in time they would take precedence over every other Motown act. The three girls called themselves The Primettes – later to become The Supremes – and the story of how they joined Motown has varied over the years. The most likely version seems to be that two Detroit friends Florence Ballard and Mary Wilson sang in their local church and attended the same school. Wilson, one of three children, born in Greenville, Mississippi in March 1944 to Sam and Johnnie Mae, was raised in Detroit by an aunt and uncle. Like other future members of The Supremes, Wilson moved to the Brewster Projects (where low-salary families lived in small but decent houses). Ballard, one of thirteen children, was born to Lurlee and Jesse Ballard on 30 January 1943. While a teenager at school she wanted to form her own group. Wilson was her first recruit and another school friend Betty Travis was the second. As quartets were popular in those days, they searched for a fourth member. A young singer, Paul Williams, lived in the same neighbourhood and, with his singing partner, Eddie Kendricks, suggested Diane Ross be the fourth member. Diane Ross was one of seven children born to Ernestine and Fred Ross in March 1944. She became

obsessed with music during her last two years at the Cass Technical High School where she graduated with fashion illustration and costume design awards. She jumped at the chance to complete the all-female quartet. Williams and Kendricks sang with their own outfit. The Primes, with whom Florence Ballard was soloist, would later become The Temptations under the management of Milton Jenkins. The four girls decided to become The Primes' sister group, hence the name The Primettes.

Ernestine Ross wasn't keen on her daughter wasting time singing and rehearsing and insisted that Diane remain in high school. The mothers of Ballard and Travis were also anxious about their daughter's education and both eventually pulled their offspring from the group. Wilson and Ross continued as a duet. Eventually the two mothers relented and the four Primettes (with Barbara Martin replacing Betty Travis) rehearsed in earnest, working their way towards a recording deal. Smokey Robinson once again came to the rescue. He lived near Ross and as he wanted their musician, Marv Tarplin, for himself, he auditioned The Primettes. He was unim-

pressed with the girls' performance, but got Tarplin! To prove him wrong the quartet auditioned for Robert West who had just opened his Lu-Pine label. West signed them to work with his in-house writers/producers Richard Morris and Wilmar Davis. The result was two singles *Tears Of Sorrow* and *Pretty Baby*; Ross sang lead on the former and Wilson the latter. The girls also did session work for signed artists like Eddie Floyd. Wilson told *Blues & Soul* in the 1970s: 'I don't believe the records were ever released outside of Detroit although the label was quite hot with The Falcons, etc., and we sold enough records locally to start getting a few little gigs.' The Lu-Pine deal ended in failure as did Milton Jenkin's management of the girls.

Later on, Robert Batemen saw their performance at a talent show in Canada and arranged a Motown audition. Berry Gordy wasn't present, as Wilson explained in that same interview: 'I remember we sang The Drifters' *There Goes My Baby* and Ray Charles' *What'd I Say*. They seemed to like us but put us down gently by saying that the company was new and that they didn't feel they could take a chance on having another girl group. Their experience with girl groups had been rough, and in comparison with a male group he's completely right.' The Primettes were told to return to school. Undeterred, they visited the offices every afternoon – watching, listening and hoping. In time Gordy relented and allowed them into the recording studios to hand clap for about two dollars a time. He then hired them as session singers. (In 1962 Barbara Martin became pregnant, married and left the group, although she can be heard on their early singles.) It gradually became obvious to the producers that Wilson and Ballard had the best voices, yet Ross had a strong personality and young determination that attracted Berry Gordy. Robert Bateman and Brian Holland had recently written I *Want A Guy* for The Marvelettes, but when Ross heard it she wanted to record it. Gordy conceded and took The Primettes into the studio. The song became their first single when they signed to the company in January 1961. Nobody liked the name Primettes so Ballard was handed a list of fifteen names: she chose The Supremes. As the youngsters were still at school, future recording sessions were slotted in between lessons. The girls were primarily all potential lead singers and each one was tested on numerous demo recordings. At the instigation of Gordy, Ross was promoted to permanent lead and songs were written with her voice in mind. She also changed her name from Diane to Diana, maintaining there was an error on her birth certificate.

Mary Wilson: 'Diane was very sharp and ambitous. She always wanted to be more than us. We wanted to be stars, but that wasn't enough for her. She had to be THE star. To begin with we all had turns being in the middle of publicity shots. But Diane soon

The original line-up of The Supremes in an early publicity still c 1960. (Left to right) Barbara Martin who replaced Betty Travis, then later left herself, Mary Wilson, Florence Ballard and Diana Ross on top.

pushed us out because she discovered the importance of being the focal point. It was the same with her singing, she wasn't the best. Florence Ballard was more powerful and soulful but Diane made sure she had the leads. Just like everything else, whether it was clothes or boyfriends, she would try to pinch one of ours if she thought we had something better. Diane was so vulnerable and jealous she had to assert herself over us to prove she was so powerful, more attractive. In the early days Diane's aggressiveness was a help, but it was a pity she had to be that way. It's strange because people just see Diane as being a very beautiful woman, which she is. But they don't see how ruthless and abrasive she can be.'

In her autobiography Wilson also outlined her first recording contract which, she said, was fourteen pages of double-spaced typing detailing her obligations to Motown as a singer and/or musician for a year: 'Somewhere in all that legalese were some revealing terms – no advance, no salary, and permission for Motown to recoup any monies they'd advanced to us or spent on our behalf from the royalties we would be entitled to.' Each girl signed a separate contract and Mary presumed each contract was identical. Her royalty was 3 per cent of 90 per cent of the suggested retail price for each record, less all taxes and packaging costs. 'What was especially interesting about that was the 3 per cent royalty applied only when I cut solo records. Based on my figures this meant that as a solo artist I would get approximately two cents for every 75 cent single sold. If I, or any of the other Supremes, recorded a million seller as a solo, that person's net would be around $20,000 before other expenses were deducted.'

When The Supremes recorded as a group, the 3 per cent royalty was split between them. Writer/producer Clarence Paul: 'Just about everyone got ripped off at Motown. The royalty rates were sub-standard. Motown had their own songwriting contracts which were way below the rest of the industry. Tunes were stolen all the time and often credit wasn't properly assigned.' Motown's recording contracts were in essence no different from those offered by other companies at the time. However, when an act signed a Motown document it was invariably incomplete and did not guarantee a record would actually be released by the signatory. British record companies, too, paid meagre royalties. For instance, when EMI signed The Beatles in 1962 to its Parlophone label, the one year contract paid one (old) penny for a double-sided single to be shared between each Beatle!

It's interesting to note here that when artists signed a recording deal, Gordy also secured them to his other companies. He controlled all their publishing rights with Jobete (his writers and producers also signed away their rights) and handled their careers via ITM. For a 10 per cent fee ITM would act as a tour

agent and ensured that personal finances, like mortgages and taxes, were paid regularly. Jobete earned Berry Gordy a fortune in sheet-music sales, mechanical royalties and re-recording of songs, not only by his own artists but by third parties. Jobete eventually held a catalogue of approximately eleven thousand available songs and earned in excess of $10 million annually.

I Want A Guy (US, Mar '61) written by Gordy, Freddie Gorman and Brian Holland for The Supremes was released on the Tamla label in the US only. Buttered Popcorn (US, Jul '61), a Gordy/Barney Ales composition with Florence Ballard on lead, was also a US only release. If this single had been a hit Ballard might have continued as the group's lead singer. Both flopped. For their third single, Your Heart Belongs To Me (US, May '62), the girls switched to the Motown label where they were to stay for the rest of their career. Let Me Go The Right Way (US, Nov '62) also bombed out. However, it did have the Holland, Dozier and Bradford slice of brilliance Time Changes Things on the flipside. (The song had staying power because it appeared again on the B-side of the group's twenty-fifth single Forever Came Today in 1968.) By their seventh single, When The Lovelight Starts Shining Thru His Eyes (US, Oct '63/UK, Jan '64), and after they had failed with Smokey Robinson's songs, The Supremes association with Holland-Dozier-Holland (H-D-H) had begun. Sources suggested it was Diana Ross' affair with Brian Holland that led to the working relationship. Whatever the reason, they worked so well together that success was unavoidable. It started with Where Did Our Love Go (US, Jun '64/UK, Aug '64) followed by Baby Love (US, Sep '64/UK, Oct '64), a number one single on both sides of the Atlantic in 1964. With this success behind them The Supremes re-signed with Motown and ITM for a further three years.

Generally speaking at this time, standard recording contracts were for one year, with four one year options, allowing the record company the choice of not picking up an option should an act fail in the first year to enjoy recorded success or was unable to fulfill its recording commitments (ie, one/two singles and/or album). It is thought The Supremes 1964 contract was similar in content. Another clause in their contracts stated that Motown owned all master recordings by the group (irrespective of whether records were released or not) and owned the name The Supremes, and not the individual group members. To this end their 1964 agreement stated 'We (Motown) shall have the same right in the collective name (The Supremes) that we have to use your name pursuant to paragraph 6 (which dealt with Promotion) and you shall not use the group name except subject to the restrictions set forth in that paragraph. In the event you withdraw from the group, or for any reason cease to participate in its live or recorded performances, you shall have no further right to use the group name

The Supremes' line-up might have changed but the necklaces haven't! In this early publicity shot the group's founder and shortlived leader Florence Ballard is featured centre. Mary Wilson (left) and Diana Ross (right) look on.

for any purpose.' It was these two clauses that would, in later years, cause Mary Wilson and Florence Ballard immense problems when embarking on solo careers.

The Supremes' live performances were covered by separate contracts. Florence Ballard: 'I never saw any contracts that we had for different clubs (where the group performed) only the recording contracts. I didn't receive any royalty statements either.' The income from the group's live performances was credited to a fund in the joint name of The Supremes and Motown. The trio's record royalties were also paid into a fund and they were paid a weekly salary of $50 in 1964. Ballard: 'Then we received an allowance of $225 dollars a week in 1967 and the other money was supposedly placed into savings accounts, stocks and bonds.' Diana Ross: 'We really don't know where our money is.'

Mary Wilson: 'Our success was really almost by accident. We were becoming disenchanted with the company so we started to demand more interest from them. The company in turn gave us Eddie, Brian and Lamont, and they played us a whole bunch of songs and we didn't like any of them. Brian told us to believe in them and that *Where Did Our Love Go* was a hit. I remember the night we recorded the *Meet The Supremes* album (their first) I went straight home and cried myself to sleep because I was so disappointed.' Interestingly, H-D-H wrote *Where Did Our Love Go* for The Marvelettes, whose lead singer, Gladys Horton, had already recorded the vocal in a lower

key than Ross was used to. However The Marvelettes weren't happy with the song, so it was recorded by The Supremes instead, with Diana Ross singing in Horton's style.

H-D-H knew precisely what they were doing, as Lamont Dozier told *Melody Maker*: 'We got ideas for songs from watching soap operas on tv, reading magazines or just dreaming up situations. Our songs were generally slanted towards girls as they made up the biggest market. We deliberately tried to be as commercial as possible and always used a very simple approach because we believed that simplicity was the key to being commercial. Another point is that our numbers were very melodic as well as having lyrics with which girls could identify. We enjoyed taking other people's songs and doing them with our own arrangements. We did this on several albums. When we were producing albums we never threw on old tracks that were not good enough for singles.' If The Supremes were H-D-H's lucky charms, then The Temptations belonged to Smokey Robinson. And like their sister group, The Temptations had to wait for that all important hit.

Paul Williams and Eddie Kendricks were born in 1939 in Birmingham, Alabama. After an abortive attempt to earn a living as a singer in groups like The Cadillacs and The Teenagers, Kendricks heard about Berry Gordy's company. He cashed in a tax credit belonging to his brother Robert and left his three best suits as re-payment, and travelled to Detroit to join up with Paul Williams. The two, with

C. Osbourne, were members of The Primes and met Otis Williams (real name Otis Miles, born in Texarkana, Texas in 1941), Melvin Franklin (real name David English, born in Montgomery, Alabama in 1942) and Richard Street (born in Detroit in 1942). The three youngsters, with Albert Harrell and Elbridge Bryant, became The Elegants, later The Questions, finally The Distants. As such they recorded Come On – with Street on lead – for Northern Records. When Street left The Distants, Williams and Kendricks joined. The five were re-named The Elgins, and performed anywhere that commanded an audience. (Street rejoined The Temptations during 1971, after working as a Motown session singer and heading Motown's Quality Control Division, then formed The Monitors – a short-lived vocal group.)

The Elgins' introduction to Motown was via Jackie Wilson, as Otis Williams remembers: 'We were asked round to his house to sing for him. Jackie must have liked what he heard because he got in touch with Berry Gordy.' So, with the line-up of Kendricks, Williams, Franklin, Williams and Bryant the group was signed. In 1961 they recorded two singles on the Miracle label – Oh Mother Of Mine (US, Jul) and Check Yourself (US, Nov). When the Gordy label replaced Miracle in 1962, The Temptations (so called by Otis Williams) moved too. Dream Come True was the first which touched the R&B charts, followed by Paradise, I Want A Love I Can See and Farewell My Love within a year. All featured lots of vocals against a sparse musical backing, and were typical of the rawness of Motown's early releases. All were nonsellers. They also recorded Mind over Matter (I'm Gonna Make You Mine) as The Pirates on the Melody label in September 1962. Smokey Robinson and Berry Gordy's input didn't produce hits until early 1964 with The Way You Do Things You Do, which was written by Robinson and The Miracles' Bobby Rogers. Elbridge Bryant left the group weeks before the release of this single, to be replaced by David Ruffin. The Way You Do The Things You Do gave them their first taste of success but the best was to come when Robinson suggested Ruffin sing lead on My Girl, a song he'd written for his daughter. It earned The Temptations a gold single, the first of many. Robinson actually taped the song's rhythm track while The Temptations were performing at The Apollo and intended to record it with The Miracles. Otis Williams: 'He came to the theatre to rehearse the song. At the time he ran the track down it didn't really hit me. Then we recorded it, Smokey put strings on it and it sounded like a number one. Lucky enough for us it was.' It was The Temptations' first British hit, reaching number forty-three in March 1965 on the Stateside label.

Claudette Rogers, now Smokey's wife, still toured with the group at this time. During the four years she was on the road, she suffered eight miscarriages. Once the strain of living from a suitcase ended in 1967, their son Berry (named after Gordy) was born a year later. She wasn't replaced in the group.

David Ruffin, born in Whyknot, Mississippi in 1941, brought a distinctive, soulful voice into the group, perfectly complementing Kendricks' falsetto and Franklin's deep booming bass. Ruffin's father was a Baptist minister, his mother a college professor. 'My brothers Jimmy and Quincy, and my sister Rita Mae were known around Mississippi as the Ruffin Family. When I was thirteen I left home to practice in the ministry in Memphis in 1955/56 but ended up singing. I sang with Elvis Presley on the same talent shows, then joined a

The Primes, aka The Temptations, wearing the fashion of the early Sixties. After line-up changes the group settled down to become hit-makers. (Left to right) Paul Williams, Eddie Kendricks, Melvin Franklin, David Ruffin and Otis Williams.

The Temptations, known for their tight and innovative dance routines, went on to stun audiences with The Temptations Walk.

gospel group The Dixie Nightingales.' When he was 17, Ruffin worked his way to Detroit and, after a brief relationship with Chess records, he signed to the Anna label. There he recorded *Hope And Pray* with The Voice Masters together with some solo work. When Ruffin joined The Temptations his brother Jimmy was already a signed Motown artist, chosen to replace Elbridge Bryant. However, being a member of a group didn't appeal to Jimmy, and as his brother needed a perma- nent job he turned the offer down in favour of David. Jimmy did have a run of hit singles, mostly in Britain, but nothing like that enjoyed by The Temptations!

Berry Gordy now had a stable of acts to work with and he also had a supportive and enthusiastic in-house working team of musicians, producers and writers. The 'Motown Sound' or 'The Sound of Young America' that was to become known inter- nationally was in its early stages.

THE SOUND GROWS

'Berry liked to play mind games . . . a manipulator who loved stoking competitive fires. Everyone was out for number one. Berry first and foremost. He established himself as king. He owned us. We were all a bunch of ghetto kids looking to break out and Berry was the cat with the key to the recording studio. The object of the game was to get in that little studio.'
Marvin Gaye

Two months after The Supremes' minor hit single I *Want A Guy* was released, Marvin Gaye, a former member of The Moonglows, issued his debut single *Let Your Conscience Be Your Guide* on the Tamla label. Born on 2 April 1939 in Washington DC, Gaye's future career with Motown was to be rife with disagreement and frustration. His father, a Pentecostal minister, ruled his son with an iron rod, and his mother, Alberta, spent much of her life keeping the peace between father and son. Marvin spent much of his early life singing in his father's church and was heavily influenced by the power of their religion. He was educated at Randall Junior High and Cardoza High School, and despite his father's objections to any form of physical education, Marvin was a natural athlete and excelled in swimming, football and track teams. Naturally, music formed a large part of his young life and he participated in many school entertainment activities. When he was 15 Marvin joined a local doo-wop group, The Rainbows, who performed in and around the Washington area. Occasionally the band members – who included Don Covay and Billy Stewart – would let him sing lead. They recorded *Mary Lee* on the Red Robin label during 1956. At 17 Marvin Gaye graduated from high school and at his father's insistence joined the Air Force: 'It was a horrible experience. It was the worst thing I have ever done. I hated the discipline and was always getting into trouble because I was a frustrated member of the ground staff.'

When Gaye left the Air Force he returned to what was left of The Rainbows. They later became The Marquees and recorded *Wyatt Earp* for the Okeh label as well as backing Bo Diddley on I'm *Sorry* for the Chess/Checker label. After his association with The Moonglows, Gaye followed Harvey Fuqua to Detroit to work with him on the Anna label, although he never actually recorded as a solo artist. Instead, he became a session singer and drummer for artists like The Spinners. When Gwen and Harvey Fuqua's labels joined Motown, Gaye followed: 'I worked at whatever they asked me to do. That was mainly drumming. I did sessions with The Miracles and The Marvelettes. I also toured as a drummer, especially for The Miracles and sang on most of the early Motown records.'

Gordy faced a dilemma with Gaye because his voice was jazz-based and Gordy felt that the market wasn't ready for another jazz singer. Meantime, he knew Gaye was rapidly becoming restless and frustrated with his session work. He had little choice but to experiment, so wrote and produced *Let Your Conscience Be Your Guide* for him and released it in May 1961. Gaye: 'It was a real disaster. I'm not trying to discredit Berry by that statement but it was one of the few lemons he'd had!' A month later Marvin's first album *The Soulful Moods Of Marvin Gaye* – Tamla's second album – was issued. It contained middle-of-the-road and standard songs such as *My Funny Valentine* and *How Deep Is The Ocean*. It was with the release of this album that Marvin decided to add an 'e' to his surname. Neither record made him a star so he returned to session work. Two singles followed, *Mr Sandman* and *Soldier's Plea*, and both had disappointing sales results. The records were not released in Britain.

However, Gordy had other plans revolving around a young singer named Mary Wells. Born in Detroit, it was Wells' intention to write as a career and she had composed *Bye Bye Baby* for Jackie Wilson. She sang it for Gordy who insisted she record it for his new label, Motown. The song stayed on the US charts for over a year. Wells recalled her introduction to Motown some years later: 'I met Berry through Robert Bateman, who was the engineer at the time. I started out as a writer, but once I got into recording it took all of my time to get into learning how to perform, walk on stage and walk off. I stopped writing to get more into being an artist.' When she recorded *Bye Bye Baby* (US, Feb '61) Motown had a one-track recording system, she said, and no-one could make any mistakes. 'The singer, the musicians had to come out perfect. And we did (the song) in twenty-two takes so I was pretty hoarse. The result was a gospely blues track. The twenty-second take was released as the single. The other tapes were wiped down.' This session was an exception to the rule according to Hank Cosby, known for his occasional speedy sessions: 'A real producer, when he hears something, he knows its good. And to go over and over it again like a lot of people do is a waste of time and money in the

(This page) Originally a song writer, Mary Wells was pushed into singing by Berry Gordy. Wells was a one-time partner to Marvin Gaye but is best remembered for her number one single My Guy in 1964.

(Right, top) The Contours, whose line-up at one time included future Temptation Dennis Edwards and Four Tops' Levi Stubbs' brother Joe. The group created a storm on stage with their fast-paced dance routines.

(Right, below) The original membership of Martha (centre) and the Vandellas. The group was born when Mary Wells twice failed to keep an appointment in the recording studios.

Smokey Robinson song because invariably it was a hit and hits meant attention and promotion. Smokey's unique writing style led Bob Dylan to call him the world's greatest living poet and Gordy too was quick to honour his friend's importance. He promoted him to vice-president of the company which meant that Smokey was almost on a par with Gordy himself. Robinson: 'Originally my office was designed for the induction of new talent. Most of the people signed in the early Sixties were signed by me.'

With the My Guy hit, Wells became Motown's Queen Bee and, according to sources, acted the part. She admits Motown spoilt her. For instance, she was the first of Gordy's acts to wear elegant gowns on stage and tour with The Beatles, and she changed her appearance to separate herself from his other artists. Needless to say, none of this helped in-house working relationships. My Guy was her last 'official' single; it seemed success had gone to her head. There are several versions of why she left Motown, but the most likely theory is that she tried to get out of her Motown contract by claiming she was underaged when she signed it. Motown had spent a fortune on promoting Wells, but when her case went to court the outcome was in her favour. Berry Gordy was furious and, it's said, was determined that the singer would never enjoy further success. She was at the height of her career and other companies were anxious to sign her. When 20th Century Fox courted her with a sum reputed to be between $50,000 and $100,000, plus an offer of a film deal, she accepted. Her stay at 20th Century was unsuccessful; the film never materialized and further deals with Atco, Jubilee and Warner Brothers pushed her into even greater obscurity.

Competing for those all-important chart placings with Wells were The Contours, Gordy's most exciting visual performers. The original members (Sylvester Potts, Billy Gordon, Hubert Johnson, Billy Hoggs, Joe Billingslea) first got together during 1959, performing in Detroit, their hometown. The line-up changed regularly over the years to include the future Temptation Dennis Edwards and Joe Stubbs (brother of Levi, lead singer with the Four Tops). Once again Jackie Wilson had a hand in pushing the group to Motown. Berry Gordy recorded Whole Lotta Woman with them during 1961 which, with its follow-up, The Stretch (on the Motown label), meant little outside the studios, so in an effort to start again they transferred to the Gordy label, which opened in March 1962. There, Berry wrote and they recorded the popular dance number Do You Love Me (US, Jun '62/UK, Sep '62), thus earning them a crossover hit. The song was covered by the British group Brian Poole and The Tremeloes who had a UK number one with it in 1963. Prior to this Brian Poole and The Tremeloes took their cover version of The Isley Brothers' Twist And Shout to

studio. You have to know what you're looking for, and it's hard to say what it is. I've seen producers at Motown work on one project for months and not be happy with it, and I've seen them work on a song for half-an-hour and be very happy with it.' In 1961 Wells' Bye Bye Baby album (UK, Aug '63) was the first to be released on the newly-formed Motown label followed by The One Who Really Loves You album in 1962 and Two Lovers (UK, Jul '63) and a Live! On Stage album a year later.

Mary Wells teamed up with Gaye in April 1964 for his ninth single Once Upon A Time (UK, Jul '64) written by Clarence Paul, Dave Hamilton, Barney Ales and William Stevenson. It was a good seller in America and reached number fifty in the British charts. The track was taken from the duo's only album Together (US, Apr '64/UK, Oct '64). Gaye: 'Mary was the biggest artist at Motown and Mickey Stevenson cut an album of us duetting but there weren't that many strong songs. The whole thing seemed to be a watered-down version of my style and her style.' Before this Gaye's solo work was doing well – he had recorded Hitch Hike (US, Dec '62) in order to cash in on the current dance craze, followed in April 1963 by Pride And Joy (UK, Jul '63) – a tribute to his wife Anna Gordy whom he married in 1963.

Meanwhile, Wells became Smokey Robinsons protégée and enjoyed a series of minor hits until hitting the jackpot in March 1964 with My Guy (UK, May '64). Motown artists fell over themselves for the chance to record a number four.

Gordy label mates with The Contours were Martha and the Vandellas, a three-piece female group which started nearly a year after The Supremes. Alabama-born Reeves, one of eleven children, was raised in Detroit. Her father Elijah was a Methodist minister who, with her mother Ruby, raised their children in a God-fearing manner. When she was six-years-old, Reeves sang in church with her brothers Benny and Thomas (nine and seven) as a trio. While at school the young girl excelled in poetry and represented her class in amateur reading contests. Her first ever recording was Bach's *Allelujah* which she sang at her graduation and which a colleague taped as a memento. Although Reeves loved music, she had to take regular work to help support her large family. She did shift work and sang at weekends using the name Martha Laverne. Her professional debut was in Flint, Michigan, where the gospel-singing Reeves was forced to sing blues because that was all the in-house band knew. Some time after this discouraging debut, Reeves joined Jo Ann, Shirley and Bernadette in The Fascinations, and worked with Curtis Mayfield for a while. When that outfit broke up, she was asked to join The Delphis comprising Gloria Williamson, Annette Beard (Sterling) and Rosalind Ashford. They recorded *Won't You Let Me Know* for Chess/Checker, and although Williamson sang lead on the single, it was Reeves who was to front her own hit group. The girls weren't successful so decided to audition for Motown. They were turned down! Wandering through the A&R department after the audition, Reeves spotted an advertisement for a secretary: 'I applied and took the job for about eight months or so. Part of that job was getting acts into the studios as quickly as possible as there was always something waiting to be recorded.' Her boss was Mickey Stevenson but she ultimately worked for everyone in the department. As well as secretarial duties, she was also asked to cut demo recordings for other artists.

When Mary Wells failed to turn up for a recording session, Reeves and the girls were asked to stand in. They recorded *There He Is At My Door* (again with Gloria Williamson on lead vocals) as The Vels because The Delphis name was owned by their previous record company. The result of the session was so discouraging that Williamson left. Reeves took her place. When Wells once again ignored a recording date, the girls went into the studios for a second time. This was the start of the trio's career, as they recorded their first official single *I'll Have To Let Him Go*, written and produced by Mickey Stevenson. When it was released in September 1962 it sold about three copies which, according to Reeves, were bought by the girls themselves!

Around this time Saundra Mallett and the Vandellas recorded *Camel Walk* for the Tamla label. (Mallett née Edwards later became a

31

Martha (right) and the Vandellas performing in London during the Sixties. The British public took the trio to their hearts.

Murray the K (far right) was one of New York's top DJs who staged spectacular shows that included pop and soul acts. His most adventurous was probably a 1965 special which included British artists.

member of The Elgins.) As it was the practice for artists to work on each others' records and issue singles under a variety of pseudonyms, *Camel Walk* was scheduled again by the Vandellas under the name La Brenda Ben and the Beljeans on the Gordy label.

Motown's publicity machine devised an elaborate explanation about the origin of the name Vandellas, and achieved plenty of media mileage by declaring that Marvin Gaye had chosen the name. He had heard the girls' finished tapes and in his enthusiasm used them as backing vocalists on his recordings. The publicity sheet proclaimed he nicknamed them 'vandellas', the female equivalent to 'vandels', as they stole the vocal limelight from the lead singer. His *Stubborn Kind Of Fellow* (US, Jul '62/UK, Feb '63) is a good example of this 'vandelism' as Gaye's vocals were almost drowned by their backing vocals, so they might have had a point. However, the real name change emanated from 'Van' – Van Dyke Street where Reeves' mother lived, and 'Della' in tribute to the singer Della Reese.

Unlike other acts, Martha and the Vandellas were spared the long wait for success. Their second single *Come And Get These Memories* (US, Feb '63/UK, Apr '63) was a hit. Written by

H-D-H, it charted early in 1963, and was the first of many. Reeves: 'I was a musical junkie after that. I just couldn't get enough music out of me. I was hooked on the business and knew I wasn't getting out. I'm sure that if I had wanted to be a secretary, I'd have been the best secretary in my particular office. Being the best, doing my best, is important to me.' She also confessed that she was extremely naïve about the business: 'I had to learn very fast, but the business made me a stronger woman than I would be had I chosen some other profession.'

However, with success came upheaval. Annette Sterling retired from the group and music itself in 1964 to be replaced by Betty Kelly. She in turn left in 1968, leaving Reeves' younger 18-year-old sister Lois to take her place. Martha sacked Rosalind Ashford in 1968 and Sandra Tilley replaced her. These replacements rarely recorded on a regular basis because by the late Sixties it didn't matter who provided back-up vocals in the studios so long as the lead singer was present. Additional vocalists were required for stage work only. Martha Reeves told author J. Randy Taraborrelli: 'The biggest misconception about the Vandellas was that we were a group like, say, The Supremes. My decision to have vocal back-up was a result of my need for companionship on the road, as opposed to a need for serious background singers. I've had more background vocalists do sessions for me and have their names be Vandellas than the world would know.'

Throughout the existence of the group Reeves' role was one of mentor, adviser and employer, and against heavy odds she guided her girls through one hit after another. Reeves, a strong-willed and determined woman, was one of the few artists to stand up to Berry Gordy and question the way he ran his company. As a result their relationship became strained, although invariably the singer had a valid axe to grind, particularly when it became obvious that Gordy's enthusiasm was for The Supremes. While other groups secretly seethed, Reeves expressed her resentment publicly. Gordy's manner with non-hit groups was off-hand. Years later Rosalind Ashford explained the group's feelings to Taraborrelli: 'We were always told that we had to wait until The Supremes opened the door and then when that door was opened they'd let us through too. That was fine and good because Diana Ross opened up a lot of doors for our group and other groups. But the question we always asked was "why can't we open some doors?" We felt we were a pretty strong act and had a lot of untapped potential and we were at Motown before The Supremes.' Ex-Motowners reveal that the need to have hit records was more to gain Gordy's attention than revel in personal success. Marvin Gaye summed up the situation as such: 'Berry liked to play mind games . . . a manipulator who loved stoking competitive fires. You can't imagine what a hotbed of competition that little bungalow on West Grand was like. It was beautiful because we were young and talented and willing to help each other. But people being people, everyone was out for number one. Berry first and foremost. He established himself as king. He owned us. So there was this mad scramble for position. We were all a bunch of ghetto kids looking to break out, and Berry was the cat with the key to the recording studio. The object of the game was to get in that little studio.'

Martha Reeves also had another job as part-time baby-sitter for the blind black youngster Little Stevie Wonder. He used to wander around the studios making a nuisance of himself, yet with a potential talent that even Berry Gordy could not envisage at this time. Today, Wonder is hailed as a musical genius, yet his rise to fame was from his own hand and not ultimately through Motown's hit-making machinery. In an Eighties interview Wonder said: 'I was born 13 May 1950 in Saginaw, Michigan, but the life of Stevie Wonder began in 1971. Shortly after my birth my family moved with my two older brothers Calvin and Milton, and myself then just born, to Detroit until 1971. We lived on Breckinridge Street, which is on the west side with very beautiful people. There was a warm atmosphere and I did all the things that the normal boy did. Going up trees, or we used to hop barns; they were where you would keep different parts of a car or whatever. They were at the back of the house like small shedding places. We had enough to get by but I didn't know what being poor was like. We were very appreciative of what we received. Sometimes we would go without eating. I can prove that by the pain I felt in my stomach, but my mother raised us in the early part of that time by herself. She was fortunate enough to meet my second father, who then with them being married, my mother gave birth to three other children, Timothy, Renee and Larry.'

Stevie's mother, Lulu Mae Hardaway, called him Steveland. His natural father's surname is Judkins, although his birth certificate shows Morris. Stevie wasn't born blind. He was born prematurely and too much oxygen was pumped into his incubator thereby destroying his sight for life.

Lula Mae worked as a cleaner at Motown and her 8-year-old son used to go along with her. Wonder: 'When I first met Berry I didn't know he was the same guy I'd heard a lot about. But I did know he was a black man and someone who was making a good, positive direction in the black community. Anybody who would let me come into their studio and let me play drums, vibes and piano, guitar, bongos and so many other things, had to be a good person.' During 1960 his mother signed his five-year recording contract which stipulated Motown handle all his business affairs and that money earned would be held in trust for him until he was 21. Meanwhile he was given an allowance for his upbringing. He had to receive special schooling so recordings were fitted in where possible.

Berry Gordy rapidly became aware of the youngster's special talent as a writer and singer, so Clarence Paul was instructed to guide him. Paul wrote and produced Stevie's first singles, and with Hank Cosby, he wrote I Call It Pretty Music But The Old People Call It The Blues (Part I), Stevie's debut single in August 1962. Little Water Boy (US, Oct '62), a duet with

Paul, and Contract On Love, with The Temptations on back-ups, followed (US, Dec '62). Although Wonder had a special appeal because of his youth and blindness it was a live recording that gave him his first number one single. Gordy recorded his performance at Chicago's Regal Theater and the song that caught everyone's attention was a seven-minute version of Fingertips. Gordy wanted none of the spontaneity and atmosphere of the performance to be lost, so it was spread across two sides of a single. Fintertips Part II was the side that took Wonder to the top of the American pop charts in 1963.

Wonder: 'In 1971 I moved to New York and the life of Stevie Wonder began through a very close friend of mine with whom I had formed a group about two years back. Through him I had the pleasure of meeting Ronnie White of The Miracles. John Glover who was a cousin of Ronnie's introduced me and Ronnie asked did I sing? I said "yes" and that John and myself had formed a group called Steve And John. I would play bongos and sing, and John played guitar.'

Business was good and by 1964 Berry Gordy's roster of labels had expanded to include the Harvey and Miracle labels (to which The Valadiers, his first white band, was signed), Divinity (his first gospel outlet), Workshop Jazz, Melody, Gordy, Motown, VIP and Soul. Gordy realized he had to introduce more labels if his business was to expand further. It was difficult for his promotion staff to get airplay on singles bearing the same label and should a radio DJ regularly play records with the same label he might be accused of payola (bribery). (A club DJ could, and still can, be paid to play a record without fear of payola convictions because they don't use airwave frequencies.) Although Motown was often linked with payola over the years no evidence was found.

Unfortunately, as more records were being released so the standard dropped. The top selling acts continued to record the best material to ensure their popularity, yet Motown's music slowly became a lukewarm version of the black/soul music that was its foundation. This diluted music enjoyed white radio exposure and white record shops began selling the product. Berry Gordy was selling out to the dollar. By the mid-Sixties that dollar numbered 100,000 a year, most of which was ploughed back into his company.

With his artists now making progress on vinyl, Gordy needed to present them to the public. Touring would not only increase company profits but also benefit the artists financially. However, before any artist could step on the public stage Berry Gordy ensured that they were properly prepared.

Shortly after opening his company, Gordy introduced a choreography and grooming department which was initially situated in his father's flat. Eventually one of the houses Gordy bought was split into three

Little Stevie Wonder caused havoc in Motown's recording studios in his quest to become an artist. In 1963 he proved he was more than a nuisance when Fingertips Part 2 *became an American number one single.*

departments – choreography, musical arrangement and wardrobe design. Each act was trained to perform an original stage show, with dances and dialogue worked out for them. Even the adlibbing was rehearsed. The choreography was painstakingly thought out, right down to holding the microphone and the many ways of using it effectively. Meeting the press was not encouraged but nonetheless learning how to hold interviews was an important factor. Artists were taught stock answers to questions and, according to sources, the questions were usually vetted beforehand.

Harvey Fuqua was originally in charge of artist grooming. In 1964 he was joined by Maxine Powell, who opened Motown's own Artist Development School which operated for six years. Powell was a friend of Gordy's and had run her own modelling school. The personal grooming included artists being taught how to walk, the proper way to smoke a cigarette, the graceful way to walk up and down stairs and jump on a piano and the correct way to enter and alight from a vehicle. Powell explained her role to author David Ritz in 1985: 'I taught them discipline and also how to handle people. My philosophy was, don't antagonize the enemy, obligate them. The kids had three main teachers. Maurice King taught them music two hours a day. Cholly Atkins taught them dancing for two hours and I taught them manners. . . . I explained that body communication is an art.' Powell also acted as chaperone to The Supremes and toured as their wardrobe mistress. Gordy's ambition to merge black entertainers into white society was now being realized as he produced professional acts that appealed both to blacks and whites. All the artists were expected to attend the school which offered its tuition free of charge. Marvin Gaye, however, was an exception. He resisted the training and years later regretted his decision as he lacked the on-stage dance repertoire that made The Temptations and the Jackson 5 such visually entertaining performers.

Cholly Atkins became a freelance coach during the Fifties, and was engaged during 1965 as staff choreographer. It was his job to train artists in stage routine: how to emphasize a song's lyrics visually in the most dramatic way. Maurice King (from the Flame Show Bar) was also hired in 1965 as musical director. King: 'We didn't stand for a bit of nonsense. No drinking, no pot. We worked the kids until they became pros. When we were through with them, they could play any supper club in the country and shine.' Artists were trained until they dropped from exhaustion and this lasted week after week until Berry Gordy was completely satisfied with the result.

Mary Wilson: 'As beneficial as our grooming lessons were, there were some things that makeup and poise just couldn't help. Padded bras and falsies were all the rage, and even

Mary Wilson (right) of The Supremes: 'Padded bras and falsies were all the rage, and even Flo (left) who definitely didn't need anymore, was wearing them.' (Note: Diana Ross is now centre Supreme.)

Flo, who definitely didn't need any more, was wearing them. Diane and I, still being beanpoles, used anything we could. Diane added hip pads, and I padded my backside.' Martha Reeves said the training was a revelation: 'I didn't know what to do with a wig when I first got it. But it was part of the costume. Under the lights those wigs could poach your brains. We had recorded, we were professionals, but we had never been in show business before. We had to adjust to it and hurriedly get in the right frame of mind.' Martha and her girls were also chaperoned. 'They were also elderly ladies that basically sat and watched and taught us poise and how to use our knives and forks correctly. We were doing fine before all this. I don't think I ever offended anyone with my eating habits!'

Originally very few booking agencies were interested in handling black artists so Berry Gordy had to find an alternative means of exposure. He decided to put together a touring package of his major acts. His staff collated and finalized the details and late in 1962 he convinced certain promoters to book his package which he called the Motown Revues. Dates were booked on the 'chitlin' circuit which comprised venues catering for black audiences.

Some of the acts only had a couple of days

to prepare a show, and the shortage of stage clothes presented a major problem as a female group closing a show couldn't be seen wearing the same gowns as the opening act! The first Motown Revue kicked off at the Howard Theater in Washington with The Contours, Singing Sammy Ward, The Miracles, Marvin Gaye, Mary Wells, Little Stevie Wonder, The Marvelettes and The Supremes (who were the only hit-less group on the bill). As Diana, Mary and Florence usually opened the show, Ross would then sit out front to watch the others and use the best from each act in future Supremes' performances. This continued until she was reprimanded after numerous complaints.

Before leaving Detroit Gordy insisted his artists should act with dignity as they represented Motown. He instructed male performers to sit in the back of the bus, with girls in front. Once the battered bus – a relic from a scrapyard with 'Motor City Tour' blazoned along its sides – was out of the city, the occupants mingled. Despite chaperones in attendance, Mary Wilson remembers people were pairing off before the bus had crossed the Michigan state line. Others gambled, smoked pot, slept or rehearsed. They usually dressed for the stage *en route* or in a public toilet. Wilson: 'Every few days we would stop at a cheap motel to bathe and wash some clothes. We seldom got to sleep one in a bed, but compared to sleeping sitting up on a hard bus seat, being able to lie on any mattress was

heaven.' Artists weren't allowed to stay at certain hotels because of their colour and should a white touring manager check in for a night, he wasn't allowed black visitors. (A white manager would accompany the touring artists to divert possible conflict, especially in the South.) Also some restaurants refused to let them eat on the premises and they had to order their meals at the back of the establishment for a takeaway. Martha Reeves angrily recalls the situation: 'It's an awful insult when you walk around and you got money and you can't eat.' She also accepted the touring was tough yet it did, she said, benefit the music. 'It was the promotion that put us all on the map, so I can't say it was a bad move. Motown knew what they were doing. It might have been tough but we made it. People died on those tours, just getting worn down, getting in the station wagon after playing on stage, then trying to drive three hundred miles.'

The Motown Revue tour took in about twenty one-night stands, through the mid west, down south and back to New York to Harlem's Apollo Theater. Performing in the South was a history lesson for the performers. Segregation still operated in Southern states, which meant blacks were often confined to theatre balconies. Weapons were openly carried into the theatres by both races, yet when the music began, both were united. A typical Motown Revue in the early Sixties went something like this. The show would open with

The Miracles, the closing act on the successful Motown tours, perform at an EMI Records reception in London early in the Sixties.

Little Stevie or The Supremes, followed by The Marvelettes whose act lasted for twenty minutes. The Temptations would take over, then The Contours who held the audience in raptures with their fast moving show. It was usually left to Mary Wells to calm down the hysteria. The finale was reserved for Smokey Robinson with the Miracles, then all the acts would return to the stage for the closing number. An album *Recorded Live At The Apollo Volume* I captured moments from the first tour.

'Touring back then was murder,' Thomas 'Beans' Bowles (who doubled as musician and road manager) told David Ritz in 1985. 'Berry packed far too many people on the bus. We were always overcrowded. And he booked way too many dates. The strain was bad. We had a bad accident in November '62, my driver was killed and we were lucky not to have others (killed). There might have been a little weed around but no coke. Who had the money? The pay stunk. In order to protect the singers and musicians, we'd put part of their money in an escrow account. Most of them were under eighteen, and if we hadn't done that, they'd have blown all their bread before we'd get back to Detroit. The problem was that Berry kept those accounts going for too long. He didn't know when to stop treating people like kids. They wanted to be respected as adults.' The Temptations' Melvin Franklin recalled the touring bus as holding a minimum of forty passengers. 'I used to sleep in the luggage rack. Wasn't any of us under 6ft 1in. I can't climb like I did then, got rheumatoid arthritis. Maybe it's from being a 6ft 1in sardine all them years.'

By 1964 artists were travelling further afield. In October The Supremes visited Britain for the first time. It was a two-week promotional visit for *Where Did Our Love Go* which included a taped spot on the tv music show *Thank Your Lucky Stars*. It was an exciting and interesting time for the trio who found themselves in constant demand by the British press. Being referred to as 'negresses', however, did tarnish the glitter until they were told it wasn't a derogatory term. Marvin Gaye was equally upset when, on his first visit, he read headlines referring to him as a negro. Barney Ales, a Motown executive, on the other hand, was overjoyed with the response they received: 'When I first started going to England we were as successful overseas as we were in the States. In fact, it was a tremendous compliment when I went there and they would tell someone I was from Detroit. They would say "oh, that's where Motown's at". In the States if you said you were from Detroit they'd say "that's where Ford or General Motors are, that's where they make cars". People used to come back and tell me they heard Motown over in England or as much of it, as they did in America.'

During 1964 six British pirate radio stations emerged, the most popular being Radio Caroline, which broadcast from a ship moored in

the North Sea. These stations were instrumental in promoting black music (particularly DJ Tony Blackburn) and it is quite possible that without their existence black hits would have taken a lot longer to make the UK charts.

With Motown's big selling acts touring outside Detroit recording became difficult. For instance, should Martha and the Vandellas need to record a new single, the musical and vocal backing would be completed, then Reeves would return to Detroit to lay down the lead. If an act was staying in Detroit for a while, most of the time was spent recording future singles and album tracks. The material was then canned and issued whenever needed. In emergencies, previously released singles were pillaged for riffs and choruses. Once recording sessions were over, the artists were then referred to Cholly Atkins to learn a new routine. Interestingly, some new stage routines were actually memorized before a single was released, so, should a new single be issued while an artist was on tour, that could be included in the act!

As Motown's product continued to cross over from the black/soul market into white/pop, record shops were unsure how to display the material. Motown's incongruous and unimaginative album sleeves rarely featured pictures of the artists. Instead a montage or a single picture relating to the hit single the album contained would dominate the front sleeve and sketchy sleeve notes would appear on the back. However, in the Sixties, the

Motown travels abroad in 1964. Pictured here from front to back: Berry Gordy, his sister Esther, Florence Ballard, Barney Ales, Mary Wilson, Diana Ross and Butch Edwards.

covers were not a priority and the problem of exposing a product was being overcome by recruiting white personnel like Phil Jones, responsible for promotion, Al Abrams, head of the publicity department, Barney Ales, head of the sales section, and lawyer Ralph Seltzer. Motown's main problem now was how to achieve regular television exposure. Twenty years on, Ales explained the transition from stage to screen: 'In those days it was a gradual step. You went from hit records to Vegas. Concerts weren't a big thing in those days. You went to nightclubs. In those days we used to call it the chitlin circuit starting in the east and working down south to New Orleans and Texas and then back up. Very seldom did they get out to the West Coast because it was too costly. When an act enjoyed a certain amount of success, they were capable of holding down a performance at the Copa. Outside of playing Las Vegas, the Copa (in New York) was the next best thing. The Supremes and The Temptations were among the first to appear but all the acts eventually played at the Copa at one time or another.' For promotion purposes, he added, costs were kept to a minimum and gave this example: 'We couldn't afford to send The Marvelettes to San Francisco for a concert at The Cow Palace. So we just sent Gladys Horton and picked up three girls in San Francisco.'

During 1965, when The Supremes opened at The Copa, New York, three significant milestones were achieved. The first was in New York where one of America's top DJs, Murray The K, staged one of his rare and spectacular shows at the Brooklyn Fox Theater. This show, featuring both American and British acts, broke all previous box office records by earning $204,000 in business. Dusty Springfield and The Searchers performed in the show alongside The Dovells, The Shangri Las, The Ronettes and Little Anthony and the Imperials. The Temptations enthralled the audience with their brisk and dazzling foot work. Two drummers on stage introduced one of the years' biggest hits *Where Did Our Love Go* and The Supremes, dressed in striking red, stepped into the spotlight. 'Nineteen Sixty Four an' we're gonna dance some more' launched The Contours on stage. Their wild act of high-flying, leg splits and fast routines delighted the audiences. Martha and the Vandellas then stormed on stage with *Heatwave* and *Dancing In The Street*. They were more popular than The Supremes at this time because the youngsters identified with their street level sound. The Vandellas provided back-up vocals when Springfield performed *Wishin' And Hopin'*, while she joined them to support Marvin Gaye. Reeves: 'Dusty became one of the gang, and you really couldn't tell the difference between her voice and mine. We struck up a friendship when I wrote to her thanking her for promoting our career in her interviews.' The Miracles appeared next with their highly-polished act, showing why they won the title of top group over the years. Closing the show was Marvin Gaye, the epitome of cool soul. For the finale all the acts joined Gaye and Murray on stage.

The second milestone was probably the riskiest in terms of money. Berry Gordy decided to send a specially-compiled Revue to Britain in March 1965. Taking part were The Supremes, Martha and the Vandellas, Stevie Wonder (who arrived three days before the others on the 12th), The Miracles, Earl Van Dyke and his Soul Brothers, with British artist Georgie Fame adding (so-called) credibility. The tour was a financial disaster, as Mary Wilson explained at the time: 'It was a flop. What's the use in denying it. The audiences were good but they were kinda thin. We didn't get too many people along. So, it's like being wise when it's too late, but in my opinion the show was too specialized for British audiences. We should have had a few more British groups with us. Another thing is that the British people wait until the end of a number before they show their appreciation. We found that a bit strange at first, but then we got used to it. Other times it's disappointing. You might be feeling good and you want everyone to be happy and sing.' Stevie Wonder, and indeed The Supremes, had been to England before, but this was the first time a full package toured. (In August 1963 Wonder's *Fingertips Part* II was issued in Britain; four months later he appeared on two pop music programmes, Rediffusion's *Ready Steady Go!* and ABC-TV's Saturday night's *Thank Your Lucky Stars*.)

The Revue did, however, give the audiences a chance to see face to face the artists behind the music, but as one promoter explained; 'By the time people got to know how good the show was, the Revue had moved to another venue. I didn't make any money at all but I have to admit those Motown people know how to put on a very good show.'

Critics who reviewed the shows were of one mind. For example a Scottish newspaper printed: 'In terms of impact on Britain's pop scene the American influence is becoming stronger with every release from Detroit.' Others were more colourful: 'I have just seen one of the best shows to be staged in Bristol. Yes, I'm referring to the Tamla Motown show. And I was appalled to find such a small audience. What's the matter with the British public when they won't support such brilliant artists'. And: 'Because of the poor reception given to Tamla Motown artists in Leeds recently we are forced to the following conclusion that the English audiences are either stone deaf or cabbages in disguise. How live human beings could sit through that talent-loaded show and not be moved escapes us!' The tour began on 20 March and finished on 12 April.

Motown enthusiast Dave Godin ran The Tamla Motown Appreciation Society from Bexleyheath, Kent, and Berry Gordy actually

invited Godin to Motown to meet his artists. The Society was superbly operated by Godin with Motown's help and was a powerful promotional tool for artists, most of whom knew Godin personally. He had actually forewarned them about British audiences after seeing their shows in America: 'The audiences there (in America) are much more exuberant, they dance and sing and make a lot of noise. If this happened here I think the theatre manager would pull down the curtain.' Their visit was also long overdue he said: 'Both the label and the sound should have broken through a long time ago. But cover versions like Brian Poole's did a lot of damage. I think the breakthrough could have been made with The Contours instead of Mary Wells. I was told the sales of The Contours' disc were very good but too spaced out to make the charts.'

The final milestone was a British television show *The Sound Of Motown* organized and presented by Dusty Springfield. After working with the artists in America, she persuaded Rediffusion to build a show around the acts she loved so much. The tv executives eventually agreed and a show starring The Supremes, Martha and the Vandellas, Stevie Wonder, The Miracles and the Earl Van Dyke Sextet was screened on 28 April at 9.40 p.m. It was not only the first of its kind to be screened on British television, but the only one devoted to a particular style of music or record company. With the demise of Rediffusion the show's tape was thought destroyed, however, when Dave Clark (of the successful Dave Clark Five group and, in the Eighties, behind the London stage show, *Time*) bought up the *Ready, Steady Go!* footage he also

Motown Revue hits London in 1965. Official line-up included (left) The Temptations, (middle) The Miracles, (kneeling) Stevie Wonder, Martha and The Vandellas (dressed in white) and The Supremes (front).

One of Britain's finest singers, Dusty Springfield loved Motown's artists. She persuaded a British television company to screen 'The Sound of Motown' which she hosted.

acquired the rights to this Motown show and it has since been released as a commercial video under the title *The Sounds Of Motown*.

Meanwhile, back in Detroit, Motown continued to work as a twenty-four hour operation. Daytime was reserved for the business side, night-time for the studio work. Barney Ales: 'Because most of the guys worked either at Ford or Chrysler or one of the factories, they worked during the day and had to come in at night to record, so usually the studio had more activity from eleven o'clock to four in the morning than it did during the day. Usually during the day Berry would just be playing piano and writing songs or playing ping pong and darts.'

It became apparent at this time that strange effects could be heard on Motown's singles. For instance on *Where Did Our Love Go* the introduction featured people walking from one side of the studio to the other, and large chains clanging together were used on *Dancing In The Street*. Producers' ambitions were satisfied with pipes, cans – anything that produced an unusual sound. If fuller backing vocals or handclaps were needed secretaries and clerks would be called into the studios. Before recording in her own right, Diana Ross was paid $2.50 per backing session for Mary Wells, Marv Johnson or Marvin Gaye. Other artists like Martha Reeves were paid $10 for singing, with a reduced rate for clapping and stamping their feet. 'People did whatever it was necessary to do,' Raynoma Liles Gordy said. 'Everybody did something, from maintaining the exterior of the building, painting and so forth, to what we called 'snack time' when someone had to cook and serve lunch. My speciality was chilli, so I usually did the cooking. Smokey usually was the one who had to mop up. This was how interested everyone was in just being part of it and watching it grow. It was fun, something that was in our blood, not just a job. It was a bunch of people who really believed, working together with a specific goal. It was a happening.'

Motown music was really making the headlines by 1964 with three-quarters of its sixty or so releases in the charts. The company enjoyed four number ones: *My Guy* (Mary Wells) and three from The Supremes *Where Did Our Love Go*, *Baby Love* and *Come See About Me*. These acts made Gordy a very rich man – and changed him in many other ways, too. He was known to his employees as Mr Gordy and a year later banned casual visitors to his office, isolating himself from the media and the daily workings of his company, while author Nelson George reported that Gordy 'was getting big-headed over success'.

With the continued success of Motown, Gordy was soon earning a small fortune, and could indulge in his love of gambling. George also wrote that it wasn't unusual for Berry Gordy to blow $50,000 to $100,000 a day in bets. Gordy's interest in Motown acts playing Las Vegas was, ex-Motowners speculated, partially prompted by his desire to be closer to the gambling tables. Gordy also organized football and baseball matches for his staff. Bets were made on the teams and Gordy always expected to win.

Selected Motown records had been released in Britain from 1959, the very first being Marv Johnson's *Come To Me* on the London American label. In November 1961, Motown's releases moved to the Fontana label with The

Stevie Wonder appeared in two films during the Sixties, Bikini Beach and Muscle Beach Party. The singer is shown here in a clip from Bikini Beach. Wonder was unhappy at the material he had to sing and neither film was a credit to him or his reputation.

Marvelettes' *Please Mr. Postman*. In September 1962 Motown's releases were transferred to the Oriole label with *You Beat Me To The Punch* from Mary Wells. Motown and Oriole stayed together until September 1963 when Stateside (an EMI Records subsidiary) took over with Martha and the Vandellas' *Heatwave* in October 1963. The music attracted a cult following which didn't buy sufficient records to chart them. This was to change early in 1965 when, following a European visit by Gordy, his sister Esther and Barney Ales, EMI secured a licensing deal to open the Tamla Motown label in Britain, combining the names of two of Gordy's American labels, and catering for UK releases on all his labels. The first single *Stop! In The Name Of Love* by The Supremes, released in the UK in March 1965, reached number seven. This was the start of Motown's climb to fame. The music was no longer black/soul based and aimed at a particular market, therefore EMI could promote much of it as pop music. Not every record was successful but on average Tamla Motown held its own. Through EMI's international network the product was available in most territories of the world and the Tamla Motown label was used consistently around the world. America was the only country to use the various other Gordy labels on a regular basis.

By 1964 Little Stevie Wonder was 14 years old and had released five singles and four albums – *Tribute To Uncle Ray*, *The Jazz Soul Of Little Stevie*, *Recorded Live – The Twelve Year Old Genius* (Wonder was in fact 13) and *With A Song In My Heart*. All were produced by Clarence Paul, except *Genius* which credits Gordy. For these albums Wonder adhered to his producers' wishes although he suggested songs he liked and worked on their arrangements. He also released three mediocre sellers in 1964 – *Castles In The Sand*, *Hey Harmonica Man* and *Happy Street* – and attended the Fitzgerald School for the Blind where he learned Braille until Ted Hull, a white man, was hired by Motown to act as Wonder's teacher, manager and chaperon. Clarence Paul meanwhile, continued to be his mentor, guardian and music director, and was responsible for the youngster's early career.

Wonder toured with the Sixties Motown Revues, where he used the nights to compose. His formal education ended in 1969 when he graduated from Michigan's High School for the Blind and Hull was dismissed. Wonder then devoted all his time to his career. *Stevie At The Beach* was released in the US in 1964 (UK, '65) and was produced by Hal Davis and Marc Gordon. Gordy decided to push him into the current beach music craze with this album, but it failed. However, the singer went on to appear in two films *Muscle Beach Party* and *Bikini Beach* although he was unhappy with the choice of material. *Uptight* (US, May '66/UK, Sep '66) followed, produced by Clarence Paul,

Sylvia Moy co-wrote with Stevie Wonder during his early career. She is also credited on other artists' work and was one of several unsung Motown heroes.

Hank Cosby and Mickey Stevenson. This album hotly followed the same-titled single which shot to number three in the American pop charts. *Nothing's Too Good For My Baby* was next early in 1966 (UK, Apr '66), and a change of style emerged with the semi-ballads *Blowin' In The Wind* (US, Jun '66/UK, Aug '66) and *A Place In The Sun* (US, Oct '66/UK, Dec '66). Both reached the American top ten. Wonder: 'There weren't too many people around doing white folk stuff like I was which is the reason for their success.' More importantly, Bob Dylan's *Blowin' In The Wind* was the first of several political statements Wonder would make on record. His writing expertise flourished as he composed with his mother, or Hank Cosby and Sylvia Moy. Wonder: 'I usually had things worked out. Hank would come up with a chord pattern for my melody, then maybe he'd help Sylvia with the lyrics. I would come up with the basic idea, maybe a punchline, and she would write the story.'

New artists were continually being added to the Motown roster. Some had 'star' potential like Brenda Holloway, Motown's first signing from the West Coast. Prior to this, the Californian-born singer recorded for the small Donna label, so was delighted to join Motown: 'It was like going to Disneyland for the first time! They were trying to push the Motown sound out there, they wanted every song that we put out to be a hit, not just a song to listen to. And they wanted me!' Holloway's Tamla debut single, *Every Little Bit Hurts* (US, Mar '64/UK, Jun '64), was a hit, and is one of today's evergreen tracks. However, she had heavy competition at the time from Kim Weston, Mable John, The Miracles and Little Stevie. Born on 21 June 1946 in Atascadero, California, Holloway was one of three children raised by her mother. Holloway: 'I was desperate to become a star and earn money to support the family. I had studied the violin so my ambition was to be a concert violinist. Then I started singing with my sister Patrice. She

Berry Gordy's first West Coast signing, Brenda Holloway, enjoyed one major success at Motown with You've Made Me So Very Happy in the mid-Sixties. Her distinctive, soulful voice delighted her European fans, while the Americans appreciated her sexy stage act.

recorded a single The Del Viking when she was 12 years old. She was on the chubby side so I used to demonstrate the dance for her. When the chance came for me to sing, I said I'd do it if I could make money out of it. So it was this that got me singing!' Patrice was also to become a singer/songwriter in her own right, and the two sisters later wrote together for numerous artists including The Supremes.

When Brenda took a day trip to Detroit to audition for Berry Gordy, who was looking for another Mary Wells, he personally signed her to his company. Gordy was attracted to her youthful beauty. Holloway: 'Berry treated me differently to the other artists. Sure, he was a womanizer and he was suggestive in his approaches to me. I told him either I had to be his woman or I sing. After that he never pushed me. But a lot of the other girls at Motown were jealous of me because I would stay with Gwen, Berry's sister, and his parents.' The young instrumentalist/singer/writer was engaged in session work until she recorded her first single. Holloway was not capable of singing a bad song and enjoyed success with her debut Every Little Bit Hurts and I'll Always Love You in 1964, and the 1965 releases When I'm Gone, Operator and You Can Cry On My Shoulder. The much-needed big seller arrived with You've Made Me So Very Happy (written by the singer, her sister, Gordy and Frank Wilson) two years later. This classic was later re-recorded by a variety of acts, including Blood Sweat And Tears in 1969. Holloway: 'Motown didn't encourage singers to write. There was a lot of competition, and they didn't want to bother with me. I was able to make money both as a writer and singer but it

caused a lot of problems because they just wanted me to sing. Motown didn't believe women could cut it alone, but if I got a male co-writer I was alright!' In September 1964 her only album Every Little Bit Hurts was released. Holloway: 'I was a black singer with a white voice, a perfect pop voice. When the company marketed me they de-blacked me, so that no-one could tell I was black.'

Holloway yearned for fame and did everything asked of her, believing this to be the quickest route to success. On stage she dressed elegantly in shimmering, tightly-fitting gowns and she toured North America with The Beatles in 1965. However, towards the end of her four-year stay with Motown it became apparent she was being ignored by the Detroit offices. She had reverted to a second class priority because she said 'Motown's policy was to build one act at a time. When The Supremes were taking off, the company would pull in records so that The Supremes could go for a million. When I asked why my records were being pulled, Berry Gordy just kept telling me "wait your time". My records would go out of stock, and stores were told to re-order. It was usually at a crucial point when the singles couldn't be got, so they weren't played and didn't go into the charts. I feel Motown really exploited me. For instance, they let The Supremes study my tapes and take songs from me. And as I came from a different cultural background to the others – I liked to play the violin and cello – it made me appear strange to them.' Holloway was also labelled as a trouble-maker because she was outspoken on occasions. This put a strain on her working relationship with writers and producers, like Holland, Dozier and Holland. Holloway: 'I was treated like dirt because I felt they didn't want me to be as big as the others. A lot of times I came across as too masculine to men, and when they couldn't handle me, they stayed away.'

Her singles were released in Britain although none produced hits. However that didn't prevent Motown/EMI issuing one compilation album The Artistry of Brenda Holloway in October 1968, where the front cover showed the singer with a violin apparently growing from her chin! The singer didn't visit the UK at this time because it was said her stage act was too daring for British audiences. In a 1987 interview, Holloway smiled as she commented: 'I was very sexy at the time. My skin couldn't breathe unless it was exposed! My costumes were made for sex appeal, and not for women. In fact, women wanted to pull me off the stage and knock my teeth out because they thought I was flirting with their men. I was influenced by Tina Turner. But when I was touring the Southern States, trying to be like her, Smokey Robinson told me not to do it again. He said "you have a voice, you don't need to act like her". So I tried to tone down my act after that but it didn't work for me.'

Holloway's decision to leave Motown

stemmed from frustration: 'I just walked out. I was actually in the middle of a recording session with Smokey Robinson when I ran away to Los Angeles. He later called me there and I told him I didn't want to be with Motown anymore. There was no future there for me because there was a long span when I was doing nothing. Then when Gladys Knight came in to do my songs that was the straw that broke the camel's back.'

When her contract expired, Gordy wanted to pick up the option. Holloway refused to re-sign. Holloway: 'Success meant getting out of that contract in one piece. I was afraid to go to Detroit for five years after I left because I wanted to wait until Berry Gordy had forgotten me.' When Holloway's departure was announced, Motown's press release stated she had decided to quit the business to sing for God. That was not true. Holloway: 'I told them to print that. However, I did sing in the church, but that wasn't the reason I left.'

Holloway was the first artist to take Gordy to court to ascertain her financial situation in 1969, the same year that she married preacher Alfred Davis. That marriage produced four children – Beoir, Unita, Christy and Dontese. In 1987 Holloway visited London for the first time to record for Ian Levine's Nightmare label.

On Motown's V.I.P. label in 1965 there was another songstress with a difference. Chris Clark was one of the company's first white singers, with long blonde hair: 'I joined in 1963. I was essentially a blues singer, that's what I wanted to be, but Motown didn't really know what to do with me', she explained in the 1980s. 'I started in the reception at Motown's offices and after two years cut a demo. Then I had to go back in reception for a further year before anything happened. I recorded my first single Do Right Baby, Do Right (US, Dec '65) which was written and produced by Berry Gordy. It also featured the background harmonies of The Lewis Sisters.' The single was followed by Love's Gone Bad (US, Jul '66/UK, Jan '67) which became her only R&B chart entry. With this success Clark was required to promote the record, presenting Motown with a problem – that of admitting she was white! 'With the record coming from Motown the stations thought I was black and then when I went on television they almost had a heart attack!' Clark co-wrote her third single I Want To Go Back There Again (US, Feb '67/UK, Jan '68) with Gordy although she's not credited on the label: 'Initially I did work in the background so I didn't really worry about it. I was in the learning process. Just working with Berry was a lot more important, but we changed that later on.' The singer then transferred to the Motown label. Although she never enjoyed national British acclaim, Clark was very popular with the cult followers who nicknamed her 'The White Negress', a title previously reserved for Dusty Springfield. During the Seventies Clark left her singing

career behind to work in Motown's film and television division.

The V.I.P. label signed on several talented acts. The first was The Velvelettes (Bertha McNeal, Mildred Gill, Carolyn Gill, lead singer, Norma Barbee, Betty Kelly), who before recording for Berry Gordy released the Mickey Stevenson production There He Goes for IPG Records in 1963. McNeal, a Western Michigan University student, formed the group in Kalamazoo in 1962. They performed at parties and college functions. Their name came from a colleague when he said their sound was as smooth as velvet. As it was popular at the time to add 'ettes' to a name, the girls became The Velvelettes. After winning a talent show, they met Gordy's nephew, Robert, who told them to audition for Motown. It was then the girls re-met Mickey Stevenson who signed them. Their initial sound was created by producer/writer Norman Whitfield in the studios during 1962 when the group recorded Should I Tell Them. This song is probably the earliest recorded work available by The Velvelettes, and the beginning of a style that was to become popular with soul fans and that was quite distinct from Motown's mainstream sound. It was the flipside of their first single Needle In A Haystack released in the US in September 1964 (UK, Nov '64). Betty Kelly left to replace Annette Stirling in Reeves' Vandellas as the single reached the American top fifty.

With the release of its follow-up He Was Really Saying Somethin' (US, Dec '64/UK, Feb '65) The Velvelettes were backed by another group, The Andantes (Motown's in-house vocalists – Louvain Demps, Jackie Hicks, Marlene Barrow). The single reached sixty-four on

The comings and goings of Motown's daily life in Detroit. Pictured left to right: The Lewis Sisters with Mrs Esther Edwards and Chris Clark.

The Velvelettes, whose singles attracted much attention, are pictured with Sandra Tilley as a member (right). Tilley later became one of Martha's Vandellas.

the pop chart. A mould had been set although some songs written for the group went elsewhere. For instance, Norman Whitfield and Eddie Holland wrote *Too Many Fish In The Sea* for them, yet The Marvelettes recorded it. *Lonely Lonely Girl Am I* (US, May '65/UK, Jul '65) was The Velvelettes' third single and died, whereas their fourth was scheduled and numbered V.I.P. 25021 yet not released until November 1965 under a different prefix. The A-side remained the same A *Bird In The Hand (Is Worth Two In The Bush)* (US, Nov '65) and their next *These Things Will Keep Me Loving You* (US, Aug '66/UK, Oct '66) was released on the Soul label. Around this time Sandra Tilley joined the group. The instantly commercial *These Things Will Keep Me Loving You* (produced by Harvey Fuqua and Johnny Bristol) was the last single and bubbled under the pop listings. Because of public demand it was later re-issued in England in July 1971 when it reached thirty-four in the charts. The girls final appearance seems to be on Jr Walker and the All Stars' *Live* release in 1967 when McNeal, Mildred Gill and Barbee left the business to concentrate on family life. Carolyn Gill kept the group together, hiring numerous replacements until 1969 when she married Richard Street and the group was disbanded at his request – 'one star in the family is enough,' he said. Twenty years would pass before The Velvelettes reformed and recorded for Ian Levine on his British Nightmare label.

Hot on the heels of The Velvelettes were

The Monitors with its three male, one female line-up, who had been singing together since the 1950s. In a *Blues & Soul* interview member John Fagin explained how they met: 'In the earlier years we all knew each other but were singing in various other groups. Richard Street, later to become a Temptation, was our lead singer. He first started out as a pianist but when our regular singer left we found that Richard was a very capable lead, so we formed a new group.' Fagin's wife, Sandra, was also a member although the group was four years old before she joined, and the fourth was baritone Warren Harris who joined in 1958. Their debut single on V.I.P. was *Say You* in November 1965; *Greetings (This Is Uncle Sam)* and *Since I've Lost You Girl* followed a year later. They transferred to the Soul label and continued to record excellent singles until 1968 – notably the song *Step By Step (Hand In Hand)* – then disappeared.

The Lewis Sisters, who provided backing vocals for Chris Clark among others, debuted on the V.I.P. label with *He's An Oddball* (US, May '65), but it was their second single, *You Need Me* (US, Aug '65/UK, Oct '65), which became much in demand. Helen and Kay Lewis were originally school teachers but turned to songwriting. Their compositions were many, including *Just Walk In My Shoes* and *Where Were You*. It was assumed for many years that Clark was also a Lewis Sister, but this was disproved when pictures of the singers were featured on Continental releases.

Sammy Turner was another Motown artist recording at this time. He was born Samuel Black in Paterson, New Jersey, and joined a local church choir when he was three. On leaving school he joined the US Air Force and fought in the Korean War. Herb Lotz signed him to his Big Top label where he recorded with The Twisters. He joined Motown in 1964 and left a year later. Amos Milburn was another short stayer. His career began on the Alladin label where he enjoyed a hit with *Chicken Shack Boogie*. He moved to Imperial to become a city blues singer and pianist.

Glancing down the Gordy listing during the early Sixties, names like Lee and the Leopards, The Valadiers, The Stylers and Hattie Littles could be found. Other acts recording at this time included a solo La Brenda Ben backed by The Andantes and Liz Lands, a gospel singer who worked closely with Dr Martin Luther King. Her debut was *We Shall Overcome* (US, Dec '63) with the Voices of Salvation, with Martin Luther King's solo I Have A Dream on the flipside. Another artist, Hattie Littles, was a blues singer of considerable repute. Born in Shelby, Mississippi, her family moved to Detroit in search of work. Littles modelled her singing style on Ruth Brown and Bobby 'Blue' Bland. She worked in a nightclub owned by Bill Lee and it was there that Gordy heard her. Littles' singles included *Here You Come* (US, Jan '63).

One of Marvin Gaye's singing partners, Kim Weston, was a regular feature on the Tamla label. Born Agatha Natalie Weston and raised in Detroit's Paradise Valley (also known as 'the Bottom' by the black people who lived there), she started singing in church at the age of three. As a teenager she played piano and directed the church choir. At school Weston wanted to become a professional swimmer, but abandoned that to study cosmeticology after graduating from high school. As a teenager she joined the gospel group The Wright Specials and gained valuable experience performing with The Staple Singers, The Caravans, The Mighty Clouds Of Joy and others. From gospel Weston moved into popular music which she felt was very much akin to the gospel field. When she became one of Gordy's artists, Mickey Stevenson was asked to work with her. The two eventually married.

Weston's records might have been scarce but the quality was second to none. She excelled on ballads where her rich voice turned storylines into pictures. Before recording with Marvin Gaye her solo work included the powerful It *Should Have Been Me* and Just *Loving You* during 1963. A year later *Looking For The Right Guy* was issued. In October 1964 Weston's debut with Gaye, *What Good Am I Without You* was released in the US, followed by *It Takes Two* (US, Dec '66/UK, Jan '67). The single was a semi-hit in the States and reached number sixteen on the British charts. Their only album was *Take Two* (US, Aug '66/UK, May '67).

Weston actually toured as Gaye's co-star

45

Motown's three ladies of soul. Nicknamed by her fans as 'The White Negress', Chris Clark (this page) caused promotion problems for Motown who were reluctant to admit she was white. Nonetheless her soulful voice equalled that of her contemporaries. (Right) Brenda Holloway's passionate yet sensitive voice melted the hearts of record buyers, while Mary Wells's sweet vocals appealed to mainstream fans.

were in the studio and we used them for background vocals.'

Five Gaye solo American albums (*The Soulful Moods Of Marvin Gaye* – 1961; *That Stubborn Kinda Fellow* and *Recorded Live! On Stage* – both 1963; *When I'm Alone I Cry* and *Greatest Hits* – both 1964) were issued prior to the *What Good Am I Without You* single with his second singing partner Kim Weston. Gaye: 'She'd been with Motown for quite a while but though she'd had a small hit or two she hadn't got away. We did that single but it didn't make it.' An album *Side By Side* was scheduled but canned and two years later in 1966 *Take Two* was released (UK, May '67). At the end of 1964 *How Sweet It Is (To Be Loved By You)* was issued with *I'll Be Doggone* in the New Year. 'I was very happy with *How Sweet It Is* because I nearly cracked the number one spot. It went to number five (in the US) and I hadn't had a record go that high in the charts previously. I had been going through some kind of personal rebellion, I guess, with myself and I was trying to find myself. I didn't quite know where I was or where I wanted to go. And Smokey Robinson pulled me out of my depression. We used to talk a lot and Smoke said "I think I'll do some things on you". So he came up with *I'll Be Doggone* in 1965.' For his July 1966 single (UK, Sep '66), *Little Darlin'* (*I Need You*) Gaye returned to H-D-H. Gaye: 'It was quite different from the earlier things they'd cut on me. It was a much more melodic thing. Similar to Smokey's things but it was still a dance record. And a big dance record at that!' As the Gaye/Weston combination was hitless it seemed logical for Marvin to concentrate on his solo career. But no, lurking in the wings was his next female duettist, Tammi Terrell, and together they were a hit combination. . . .

In between releases by The Monitors and The Velvelettes on V.I.P., The Elgins (not the Temptations' group) debuted with *Put Yourself In My Place* (US, Dec '65/UK, Feb '66). Three singles and one album totalled their Motown career. Not much of a success story, granted, but when the group did achieve semi-success Motown never followed it up. The original all-male line up of The Elgins included Johnny Dawson, Robert Fleming and Norman McLean. Known as The Sensations they released *Uncle Sam's Man* on Flip during 1958. As the Five Emeralds they recorded for State, and four years later, as The Downbeats, joined Motown to record for Tamla. Dawson: 'Then Berry Gordy suggested we try out a girl singer as at the time there was a great demand for female singers. He suggested Saundra Edwards (Mallett) who had been working at Motown for some time. And then he suggested we changed our name because he didn't think The Downbeats were very appropriate. So we changed the name to The Elgins hired Saundra and made our first record

Marvin Gaye, who never learned to dance, released Hitch Hike *in 1962, one of the year's top dance singles! Gaye: 'The dance was simple, you made like you were thumbing a ride.'*

which we cut with Holland, Dozier and Holland.'

With the line-up of Dawson, Miller, McLean and Edwards, The Elgins debut was followed in August 1966 (UK, Nov '66) with the dazzling *Heaven Must Have Sent You*. Their last single was *It's Been A Long Long Time* released in June 1967. Their only album, *Darling Baby* (US, Aug '66/UK, Sep '68), produced by Holland and Dozier, was lacking a photo of the group while the writer of the sleeve notes omitted Norman McLean from the line-up! Johnny Dawson was the only member to stay in the business and worked with producer/writer Norman Whitfield.

Heaven Must Have Sent You was re-issued in England during 1971 to reach number three in the charts. The Elgins re-formed to cash in on the success and toured the country. Yvonne Allen replaced Saundra Edwards, who had married and wanted to stay with her family. Dawson: 'We'd completely give up the idea of ever being successful and had got deep into the things we were doing. But we still all loved showbusiness and entertaining people, that's why it only took one phone call to get us all together again.' Prior to The Elgins, Yvonne Allen worked as a solo artist and session singer for acts like Wilson Pickett and Terry Lindsay. She also recorded *Bad Boy* with The Donays. British audiences were unaware of the change in female vocalist because Yvonne was instructed to sound like Saundra. With renewed British interest in group, plans were made for it to be re-signed as working and recording artists. However, after *Put Yourself In My Place* became their second UK hit, the group was heard of no more.

As Motown expanded with local talent, Gordy began signing acts who had already

The original line-up of The Elgins. Their 1966 single Heaven Must Have Sent You *was re-released in England in 1971 to become a number 3 hit. Yvonne Allen replaced Sandra Edwards.*

The Isley Brothers were already an established group when they joined Motown.

Dr Martin Luther King's publicist, Junius Griffin, joined Motown as director of publicity.

moved to United Artists in 1963 where their T-Neck label was opened, but it was to be several years before the label came into its own.

This Old Heart Of Mine (Is Weak For You) reached number twelve in the American pop listings (number 47 in England). The follow-ups were *Take Some Time Out For Love* (US, Apr '66/UK, Jun '66) and *I Guess I'll Always Love You* (US, Jun '66/UK, Aug '66) (the latter charting in Britain at number 45 in September 1966). *Got To Have You Back* and *That's The Way Love Is* were 1967 releases (only the former was a British release) with *Take Me In Your Arms (Rock Me A Little While)*, *All Because I Love You* in 1968 (only the former was a British release) and their final American single *Just Ain't Enough Love* in May of the following year. Fellow artists felt the brothers were getting most of Motown's best products, yet they were also criticized for sounding like the Four Tops, releasing a slew of secondhand H-D-H songs as album tracks like *Who Could Ever Doubt My Love*, *I Hear A Symphony* and *Stop! In The Name Of Love* (The Supremes), and *Nowhere To Run* (Martha and the Vandellas) doubtless with the original backing tracks! So when their contract wasn't renewed in 1969 the Isleys re-formed their T-Neck label to release *It's Your Thing*. Prior to this in 1968 they enjoyed their biggest Motown seller to date with the British re-release of *This Old Heart Of Mine*, when it reached number three. Motown/EMI continued to compete with the new material with the re-issue of *I Guess I'll Always Love You* and releases of *Behind A Painted Smile*, originally the flipside of the American single *All Because I Love You* and *Put Yourself In My Place*.

In 1966, three out of every four Motown releases reached the American national charts, a success ratio no other record company of the time could match. New white management might have contributed to this market success, although two black executives were hired for key positions. Dr Martin Luther King's publicist, Junius Griffin, became director of publicity, while Ewart Abner, ex-president of Vee Jay Records, became director of ITM (International Talent Management) which now handled over one hundred signed artists. Subsequently, many working procedures were altered to become more efficient and cost effective and the marketing was streamlined. Motown's operation expanded with offices in Los Angeles and New York. Recording took place at both, where local musicians were used for demo recordings. The tapes would then be sent to Detroit for completion or mixing. As early as 1966, and unbeknown to record buyers, Detroit's claim to 'The Motown Sound' was weakening as it was no longer contained within the Detroit studios and recorded by in-house musicians, although this was not reflected in sales. From the mid-Sixties Motown's gross record sales rose from $5 million a year to a staggering $62 million ten years later. With the signing of

enjoyed chart success, like The Isley Brothers, who had two huge selling singles *Shout* and *Twist And Shout*. Once signed they worked with H-D-H to release *This Old Heart Of Mine (Is Weak For You)* (UK, Jan '66/UK, Mar '66) on Tamla. (Note: *I Hear A Symphony* by The Isley Brothers was scheduled and canned on the V.I.P. label in 1965.)

Ronald Isley was born on 21 May 1941; Rudolph on 1 April, 1939, and O'Kelly on 25 December 1937, and all lived in Cincinnati, Ohio. Their parents sang in local churches and the youngsters toured with them. During 1957 the trio left Cincinnati for New York where they found plenty of club work. Prior to securing a three year contract with Gordy in 1965, they recorded for the Teenage (to release their first single *Angels Cried*) and Gone labels, before working with Hugo and Luigi, producers at RCA records, to release *Shout* which reached number forty-seven in the American charts. From RCA the brothers spent some time with Atlantic to release four singles (including the first version of *That Lady* which became an international success over ten years later) before signing to Scepter/Wand in 1962. There they cut their version of The Top Notes song *Twist And Shout* (a number seventeen hit) which was later covered by The Beatles among others. Following this, the trio

Gladys Knight and the Pips to the label more prestige was added to the star-studded operation. Knight, widely considered to be the world's most soulful lady, is one of the few singers who possess a rich, warm heart-breaking voice that can be manipulated to express every emotion. Knight fronted the Pips which included her brother Merald (Bubba) and cousins William Guest and Edward Patten, who are well-known for their tight choreography and harmonies.

As a child Gladys Knight (born 28 May 1944) was luckier than most having had a private tutor to teach her to sing. At the age of four she sang for the congregation of the Mount Morian Baptist Church, Atlanta, before joining The Morris Brown Choir to tour the South Americas. With this experience behind her, Gladys' mother arranged an audition for the Ted Mack Amateur Hour. The 8-year-old won the first prize of $2,000 by singing *Too Young*. She then moved to the Wings Over Jordan choir where she stayed until the Pips were formed.

At a 1952 birthday party for her older brother Bubba, Gladys, her sister Brenda, and two cousins (William and Elenor Guest) provided an impromptu entertainment. So entertaining was this one-off show that cousin James 'Pip' Woods urged the youngsters to stay together as a group. Woods was appointed their manager and christened them after his nickname 'Pips'. A succession of local appearances followed leading to the Pips' first national tour with Sam Cooke and Jackie Wilson. Their very first record was *Ching Chong* for Supersonic Productions in 1957, released when Gladys Knight was 13-years-old! Soon after this, another Knight cousin, Edward Patten, joined the group, and they then recorded *Whistle My Love* for Brunswick. When the single died Brenda and Elenor left and Langston George joined, only to leave again four years later.

The Pips' first break came with the evergreen *Every Beat Of My Heart* as Bubba Knight explained: 'We recorded the song as an experiment demo for the Huntom company in 1961 when it first went into business. We were performing at a club run by one of the owners. After the show he asked us if we'd test the sound quality of some new equipment they had. It sounds dumb but we even said OK when they said they would rather test something original. Sonny Woods, one of The Midnighters, had given as a new tune written by Johnny Otis called *Every Beat Of My Heart*, so being very green we put on the tape. Next thing we knew people were coming up to us saying "that's a great record you got going". We said "what record?" Meanwhile the song got so hot, Huntom felt they couldn't handle it, so they sold the master to Vee Jay. At the same time we had decided to sign with Fury. Each label had us covered and the only thing we got out of it was $2,000 advance from Vee Jay which was considered a loan, not pay-

ment. It makes me sick every time I think about the money, but as far as the record is concerned, I'm glad it did well because we worked off it for quite a while.' When Fury released *Every Beat Of My Heart* the record label read Gladys Knight and the Pips. Gladys Knight: 'We recorded *Letter Full Of Tears* and *Operator* there. I then left the group to start my family but the Pips had a mild hit in the South called *Darling*. By the time my second baby was due, I knew I'd have to keep on singing to support my first. I happened to be married to a saxophonist (James Newman) who was married to his music. Anyway, my husband and I left Atlanta to go to New York, because that's where all the business was centred.' She rejoined the Pips in 1963 to play local venues booked by their new manager. Knight: 'If we got to a gig and the man was talking funny about money, our manager, Marguerite, would want it in advance. And if he didn't come up with it, she'd tell him to kiss her behind and take us home. Our financial situation didn't change that much because she came on with the thing that she was the fifth Pip. Whatever we got, she got. Just ain't no way it should have been like that when she didn't sing a note. But management is a trip all its own!'

From Fury, they went to Larry Maxwell's Maxx label to record *Giving Up*, produced by (the late) Van McCoy, but before their contract expired the company folded. It was about this time that Gladys Knight was

Gladys Knight and the Pips added prestige to the Motown label. The family group, already hit-makers, struggled for nearly two years at Motown before enjoying further success.

approached by Smokey Robinson. 'When I was singing alone with a band Smokey asked me to join Motown, but I didn't feel I was ready then because they had so many female acts. I was still hesitant about signing with the Pips in 1965, but we have this thing where majority rules and I was out-voted. Outside of Motown I think we were the only group doing anything. I felt we'd just be into a whole lot of company politics and wouldn't get a fair shake while waiting in line to get over. In some ways I was proven wrong. Being with an establishment and not knowing what things are like, you have to learn. The main thing the four of us agreed on was that we wanted to sell records and if we could accomplish that we would worry about the rest of it later.'

Regardless of her reluctance, Gladys Knight and the Pips' debut *Just Walk In My Shoes* (written by Mastor and Miller, produced by Harvey Fuqua and Johnny Bristol) was released in the US in June 1966 (UK, Sep '66). Years later, in a *Blues & Soul* interview, Gladys Knight recalled: 'Our career didn't take off for about a year and a half. We were doing a whole lot of cutting (recording) and going into the hole. We really felt out of things, but maybe we were just out of place and they didn't have anything for us. Then Motown appealed more to the pop market because rhythm and blues was in the lightweight stage. It didn't have that deep down thing going. Our records went very well once R&B became heavy.'

Take Me In Your Arms And Love Me (US, Mar '67/UK, Apr '67), was Gladys Knight and the Pips' second American flop, but was a number thirteen hit in England in June 1967. *Everybody Needs Love* followed three months later in June 1967 (UK, Sep '67). 'At the time we didn't have any say in what we recorded, or who we recorded with' the group once said. 'We're the type of people who like to be co-operative and whatever was set up, we'd do our best and make it work. Since it was Motown's procedure to assign a producer to an artist, we left it up to them. We must have worked with every producer they had, except Holland, Dozier and Holland, who were reserved for the suppies (superstars). But we started working with Ivy Hunter who did *Dancing In The Street*. Ivy had the gutsiest things but they didn't get any further than the shelf.'

Despite the group's reservations on the quality of their releases, the million-seller was in sight. Written by Norman Whitfield and Barrett Strong, *I Heard It Through The Grapevine* was issued in the US in September 1967 (UK, Nov '67) and sold over two million copies in the US to become a number two pop hit. It had been previously recorded by Marvin Gaye, The Isley Brothers, and The Miracles for their *Special Occasion* album. Edward Patten: 'But we took it home, worked hard to give it a new treatment and Norman hardly had to do anything. That one wasn't nothing until we took it.' Gladys Knight: 'I really believe that that was the key to our whole future. Records can

determine your future and I believe that this was the major record that started our career moving over the fence and it opened the door for Gladys Knight and the Pips.' Motown's attempts to mould Knight into a Diana Ross clone, failed. She wanted nothing to do with being glamorous for the media, preferring to develop a style of her own. Whitfield was the first producer/writer the group met and claim they had a lot of fun in the studios: 'He'd turn up in beat up clothes, hippies weren't in then. It turned out that Norman was the one who could really put out the biggies. With our type of set up, though, the only way we could really make it financially was to get a string of best sellers. Otherwise, whatever your current release brings you out of, if your next record is not a smash, it sets you back.' Their recording relationship with Whitfied began to sour when he insisted they re-record songs released on his other acts, like *That's The Way Love Is*, *I Wish It Would Rain* and *Cloud Nine*.

Gladys Knight and the Pips continued with their hit run for several years despite the growing artist roster and with established acts taking priority. On the Motown label, for example, The Supremes and the Four Tops competed for chart places which gave little hope to Motown newcomers like The Spinners. Originally a quartet (Bobby Smith, Billy Henderson, Henry Famborough, Pervis Jackson) The Spinners treated Detroit as their home town, although none was born there. During the Second World War their families moved to the city to work in the munitions factories. Like other ghetto children the boys attended Lincoln High School where they formed their first quintet, The Domingos, a name inspired by The Flamingos whom they admired. In 1957 Bobby Smith was drafted into the Army and was replaced by George Dishico. When he left, Chico Edwards was recruited and when Smith returned the group settled down to establish a name for themselves. Harvey Fuqua signed them as his first act to Tri Phi in 1961 and insisted on being their lead singer as well as writing and controlling their material, a formula which was relatively successful for a short period until The Spinners left Tri Phi and joined Motown in 1963. At Motown The Spinners, minus Fuqua, were relegated to session singers for artists like Marvin Gaye, and their own debut single, the Mickey Stevenson song *Sweet Thing*, was not released until a year later (US, Oct '64/UK, May '65) on the Motown label. The single sold sufficiently well for the group to be added to the Motown Revues and on the Marvin Gaye Revue they became an audience attraction not for their music but for impersonations. Their act prompted *The Detroit Courier* to print: 'The Spinners' take-off of The Beatles, complete with long-haired wigs and instruments, will fracture you. Even in the take-off they are better than The Beatles.'

The Spinners released *I'll Always Love You* and *Truly Yours* – two of Motown's finest soul

singles – in 1965 and 1966 respectively, although only the former was released in England. A quiet year passed until the next single, *For All We Know*, and their first album, *The Original Spinners*, were issued in 1967. In Britain the album title was altered to *The Detroit Spinners* because there was already an established British folk group called The Spinners. Their last American single on the Motown label was *Bad Bad Weather (Till You Come Home)* in October 1968, although *In My Diary* was scheduled for the following year. That song became the group's first for V.I.P. followed by the controversial *Message From A Blackman* in 1970 (US release only). By this time Chico Edwards had been replaced by G.C. Cameron who sang lead on *It's A Shame* (US, Jun '70/UK, Oct '70) written by Stevie Wonder, his long-time friend Lee Garrett, and Syreeta. Wonder then co-wrote it's follow-up *We'll Have It Made*, but it failed to repeat its predecessor's success.

When G.C. Cameron left the group to sign up as a solo Motown artist, Phillipe Wynne replaced him. The group's seven Motown years ended in disappointment at their lack of chart success as they explained: 'We're not bitter but we hoped for a little more than we got. It was an experience and one that we will not forget lightly.' As The Detroit Spinners they secured a deal with Atlantic Records to enjoy international success with singles like *I'll Be Around*, *Could It Be I'm Falling In Love* and *Ghetto Child*.

Soul recording artists, The Originals, also became disillusioned with Motown after a relatively unsuccessful stay. The all-male group comprised Walter Gaines and C.P. Spencer (from The Five Stars), Freddie Gorman and Henry Dixon. The Contours' Joe Stubbs was a one-time member, and Ty Hunter replaced Spencer in the early Seventies. The band was the brainchild of Gaines in 1965 although Gorman told *Blues & Soul* that 'forming the group had a lot to do with Lamont Dozier who was a mutual friend of us all'. Gaines and Dixon created the nucleus of the band, later recruiting Gorman, who was already writing with Lamont Dozier. Ty Hunter was previously contracted to the Anna label as a solo artist, then he moved to Chess, later Invictus.

Gorman originally worked with Ed Wingate on the Ric Tic label. 'I had two singles out that did alright but I really wanted to get with a group,' he explained. 'I'd written The Supremes' *I Want A Guy* then I left in 1963. I went back to Motown with the group after my one year with Ric Tic. The first thing we did for Motown and The Originals was with Lamont Dozier, called *We've Got A Way Out Love* and it did fairly well. Then with the departure of Holland, Dozier and Holland we were left with no producers until Clarence Paul cut some things on us like *Goodnight Irene* which did nothing. Then came Ron Miller with *Green Grow The Lilacs*. In between and after that we worked as background singers for Stevie, Marvin, Jimmy Ruffin and even the girl groups.'

The band stood back and watched other

The Spinners, minus Harvey Fuqua, were session singers before recording their own work when they were added to the Marvin Gaye Revue.

Marvin Gaye with his third singing partner, Tammi Terrell. Together they recorded some of Motown's greatest love songs like Your Precious Love and Ain't Nothing Like The Real Thing.

Motown artists getting superior material from the writers and producers. Nothing had their name on it until their old friend Marvin Gaye approached them. Gorman: 'He just came up with the idea of writing and producing for us. He has a fabulous ear for harmonies and the session was fabulous.' The result, *Baby I'm For Real* (US, Aug '69/UK, Mar '70) topped one million sales in America. 'And then came *The Bells* and both records crossed into (American) pop for us. It was good for the group because it meant we got the chance to get out and work.' A slack period followed until *God Bless Whoever Sent You* (US, Nov '70/UK, June '72). Gorman: 'It broke simultaneously pop and R&B and it was around Chrismas time so it was a monster record for us. Then we had a mild hit with Joe Hinton called *Keep Me* in July 1971 but it was nothing too crazy. Then we began to have problems.' The Originals were destined to enjoy one more hit but it took five years to happen.

On the Tamla label Marvin Gaye and Tammi Terrell were delighting record buyers with their love duets. It wasn't a move Gaye relished as he preferred to concentrate on his solo career, yet he conceded because, as he said, 'Some people who were on their toes dug Tammi's sound and realized we may possibly make a good duet. I hadn't had a chance to hear her sing before I met her and had no idea she was as good a singer as she of course turned out to be.' Born Thomasina Montgomery on 24 January 1946 in Philadelphia, Tammi Terrell was encouraged by her actress mother to become interested in show business. Working through school the young girl decided to ditch her entertainment tutoring to study medicine, and spent two years at the university of Pennsylvania. While at school she won first prize at a talent contest held at the VA Club in Camden, New Jersey. Music was now in her blood so during 1961 she signed to Scepter/Wand where her first single *If You See Bill* was released under her real name, Tammi Montgomery. The following year she recorded *Voice Of Experience*. (These tracks were featured on *The Early Show* compilation released during the Sixties.) Terrell then joined The James Brown Revue before recording *I Cried* for his label in 1963. After a reputed stormy love affair with Brown, she married and divorced, although her husband wasn't identified.

Prior to signing with Berry Gordy she recorded *This Time Tomorrow* and *If I Could Marry You* for the Checker label. By 1965, and now known as Tammi Terrell, she was touring with Jerry Butler when Gordy spotted her. Her first solo single, *I Can't Believe You Love Me*, released in November 1965, reached the American R&B top thirty. In England only *Come On And See Me*, her second US single, was released in April 1966 although she did appear on the *New Faces From Hitsville* EP with her debut release, *I Can't*

Believe You Love Me. For her third single she duetted with Gaye on *Ain't No Mountain High Enough*.

Composers Nickolas Ashford and Valerie Simpson had recently joined Motown and, with Johnny Bristol and Harvey Fuqua, were assigned to Gaye and Terrell whose first duet was Ashford and Simpson's *Ain't No Mountain High Enough* taken from their debut album *United*. Ashford and Simpson presented Gaye and Terrell with some of Motown's biggest love songs, yet little was made public about these talented composers at the time. Valerie Simpson commented in 1982: 'I thought it was really strange because Motown wanted to keep you in the dark. Everything was Motown; that was all that was supposed to be there. At least we got our names on the records, they couldn't stop that. But you never really knew who was playing what, or anything.' The Terrell/Gaye relationship lasted longer than Gaye's previous two and was much more successful. Hit upon hit kept the world's lovers happy – *Your Precious Love* and *If I Could Build My Whole World Around You*, (US/UK '67) *Ain't Nothing Like The Real Thing, You're All I Need To Get By* (US/UK) and *Keep On Lovin' Me Honey* (US only) (all 1968); *Good Lovin' Ain't Easy To Come By, What You Gave Me* (US only) and *The Onion Song* in 1969 and 1970. Six singles were British hits, the highest being their last, *The Onion Song*, an album track, which Motown/EMI initially lifted for the British market. The gamble paid off as the song soared to number nine.

Tammi Terrell had a tremendous effect on Marvin Gaye yet they were never lovers. In fact, despite warnings from friends, Terrell fell in love with David Ruffin (of The Temptations) and once again found herself in the middle of a stormy affair. The couple argued continually and the mental and physical strain resulted in Terrell suffering from severe headaches. At this time no-one knew that the young singer had a brain tumour. During a show in Virginia in 1967, while onstage singing *Your Precious Love* with Gaye, Terrell collapsed in his arms. The tumour was later diagnosed as her health deteriorated drastically. Her weight loss was severe, her memory vague, and she became partially paralysed. As it was now imperative for Gaye to have a singing partner on stage, another Motown signing, Barbara Randolph, joined him. Meanwhile, so determined was Terrell that Gaye wouldn't suffer professionally because of her illness, that she continued working when possible, and was often seen in the studios singing from a wheelchair.

Towards the end of 1967 another solo Terrell single *What A Good Man He Is* was scheduled but not released. Meanwhile, Gaye issued the H-D-H track *Your Unchanging Love* (US, Jun '67/UK, Aug '67). Two months later the next Gaye/Terrell duet *Your Precious Love* was issued (UK, Oct '67) coinciding with the Detroit riots. Just when Berry Gordy was confident the trouble was over, he received a phone call from the rioters threatening

Tammi Terrell.

Young songwriters/ producers Valerie Simpson and Nickolas Ashford were Motown's most important backscene stars. Their greatest success came with Marvin Gaye and Tammi Terrell, and later Diana Ross.

Motown's destruction because of the company's powerful connections with white commercial enterprises. It was then he vowed to move his operation into other Detroit premises. Martha and the Vandellas were performing when the riots broke out and urged their audience to dance in the street rather than fight. Reeves: 'This was a bad time all over the United States, with the riots in different cities and I think the writers were inspired mainly because of this. Instead of fighting in the streets we wanted to get people to dance and be happy.' Reeves was later criticized for aiding the fighting with this single, although how the lyrics could be misinterpreted to support this was never explained.

As it became evident that the Gaye/Terrell partnership was a musical and financial success, the two returned to the studios to record a further album *You're All I Need* for 1968 release. Ashford and Simpson wrote *Ain't Nothing Like The Real Thing*, *Keep On Lovin' Me Honey*, *You're All I Need To Get By*, and *You Ain't Livin' Till You're Lovin'* while Bristol, Fuqua and Gaye, among others, were responsible for the other eight tracks. The album was a delight to listen to and possibly represents their greatest work together.

By now The Temptations had joined the regular touring acts. Since their number one *My Girl* in 1964, *It's Growing* and *Since I Lost My Baby* had kept them in the public eye on both sides of the Atlantic. By the end of 1965 they had even invented their own dance routine 'The Temptations Walk' (a series of basic steps in a high-strutting routine) which was adopted by fans and contemporaries alike. Their final release of the year, *My Baby*, seemed to end the run of ballads. With the start of 1966 Smokey Robinson wrote their next hit, a dance track entitled *Get Ready* (UK, Apr '66), while Norman Whitfield co-penned and produced *Ain't Too Proud To Beg* (US, May '66/UK, Jun '66) and *Beauty Is Only Skin Deep*

(US, Aug '66/UK, Sep '66). As the group was now constantly touring, its future recordings were prepared in its absence, and invariably released without the singers being aware of the final mix. This annoyed Eddie Kendricks: 'I never got the opportunity to digest all the material I recorded. Often the tracks would be completely ready and I'd just go in and lay down my vocals sometimes without having seen the material ahead of time.'

Once more with success came unrest. David Ruffin wanted his name to front the group; Motown refused. To further aggravate the situation, Ruffin travelled around in his own limousine while the rest of the group used the bus. He hired his own entourage to travel with him and stayed in separate hotel suites. The situation grew worse and eventually his ploys backfired with the band voting him out of the group in 1968. Nonetheless, he continued to follow them on tour and invariably invited himself up on stage to join them, much to the group's embarrassment. Meanwhile, although he had been sacked from the group, he was still under contract to Motown, and filed a lawsuit against Gordy and his company requesting a financial accounting and release from his contract. Ruffin lost and, much against his better judgment, remained a signed artist. He was then offered a solo recording contract by Motown which he eventually accepted. With million selling records, sell-out tours and public acclaim, The Temptations earned a lot of money. An American publication detailed some of the band's earnings as follows: $52,000 in 1964, $119,000 in 1965, $275,000 in 1966 and $561,000 in 1967.

When he was sacked from The Temptations in 1968, Ruffin was replaced by ex-Contour Dennis Edwards. Born in 1943 in Birmingham, Alabama, Edwards came from a religious background as his father was a church minister. His family moved to Detroit when he was still a youngster, and after graduating from school Edwards joined the Army and was stationed in Germany for three years. Once discharged he joined The Fireworks, then The Contours. Edwards: 'It was tough settling into The Temptations particularly when David had been such an idol. You'd appear somewhere and David's fans would be there and you could tell they weren't too sympathetic. All I could do was try . . . the best I could.'

In 1971 the health of the group's founder member, Paul Williams, began to give cause for concern. He was an alcoholic and a drug user, and started missing performances. Those he did attend saw Richard Street, his future replacement, standing in the wings singing his lines and learning his dance routines. Street told author Gerri Hirshey that he felt like a buzzard waiting backstage, and when Williams failed to perform in New Jersey, Street sang his lines for the last time anonymously: 'Muhammad Ali came backstage and said "I saw four guys (on stage) and could

The Temptations during happier times on a trip to London. By the late-Sixties/early Seventies the group's line-up changed when David Ruffin (wearing glasses), Eddie Kendricks (middle) and Paul Williams (right) left. Tragically, in 1973, Paul Williams, the founder member of the group, committed suicide.

have sworn I heard five voices".' When Street was recruited (his first single was the ballad It's Summer (US, Jun '71/UK, Aug '71), Williams worked behind the scenes for a time. He then opened a Celebrity Boutique in Detroit which specialized in theatrical make-up. The business failed and on 17 August 1973, the thirty-four-year-old, dressed in swimming trunks, parked his car a few streets away from his beloved Motown and shot himself dead. He left a wife and five children, plus $80,000 in unpaid taxes. Ironically, upon leaving The Temptations, Williams recorded an unreleased single called I Feel Like Giving Up. Williams' presence in the group was missed and the void he left would never be entirely filled. His sweet, soulful voice played a vital role in the group's harmonies and his solo work was emotionally aggressive and highly-charged. He not only acted as their first choreographer but also guided and encouraged his friends to persevere when times were rough.

Eddie Kendricks, too, left the group in 1971. This was prompted by continual aggrevation between him and the rest of the group regarding musical differences. By this time, of course, they had more or less left Smokey Robinson's mellow songs behind them to record with Norman Whitfield who, apart from a handful of slow numbers, excelled in hard, funky music. Kendricks explained: 'I must admit I don't dig those weird, freaky sounds, they're not my type of thing. The direction the group is going in is not for me. I like the old sounds we used to record, sounds that have good melodies and I wish we'd do some stuff like that again.'

Californian-born, Richard Owens (of The Vibrations) took Kendricks' place, but failed his probationary period. Although he never recorded with them, he did perform. Damon Harris (born in 1950 in Baltimore, Maryland) replaced him in 1971. He stayed four years before forming his own band, Impact. Harris: 'I think my biggest complaint with The Temptations was that I was never allowed the opportunity of performing as a real lead singer. My other problem was that I was never given the chance to establish myself except as the replacement for Eddie Kendricks and that can get you down after a while. Now I'm out of the group I can look back on it and be more appreciative. After all, this was the greatest group of them all; a group that has sold thirty-five million records. Even after all that success, though, they still have their financial problems because they typify the trap that so many entertainers let themselves fall into.' In 1978 he left Impact for a solo career.

Glenn Leonard, born in 1948 in Washington DC, and a veteran of four groups, replaced Harris. While a student in Washington, Leonard studied guitar before joining The Chancellors. He then teamed up with Instant Groove, The Unifics and finally The Reflections, based in Toronto. It was there that he

Although Norman Whitfield and Barrett Strong were known for subdued melodies and lyrics, all that was to change in the late Sixties with The Temptations' Cloud Nine album.

heard that The Temptations were looking for a new member and applied. Interestingly, both Leonard and Harris were staunch Temptations fans before actually joining them.

Prior to the group changes and Street's arrival, personal friction and professional discontent plagued the group both onstage and in the studio. Melvin Franklin: 'I knew what was happening but thank goodness the public didn't. I was worried too that when we made the changes if they would accept them. It was also the same time as we had a few flops, but our track record was comparable to no-one except possibly The Beatles in the States, so I figured it would be just a matter of time.' Of their performances, he commented: 'In the whole time we had just two bad reviews and they of course had to be in key cities. But those reviews just made us work a whole lot harder to tighten up.'

Although Norman Whitfield had taken over The Temptations' recording activities from Smokey Robinson, there wasn't a clear take-over point as the latter explained: 'Norman just started banging out one hit after another after Ain't Too Proud To Beg. That was, I suppose, the main reason why I left them because I felt they were in good hands.' Whitfield, had of course, been associated with the group prior to this, but it was Gordy's policy to avoid any producer having exclusive rights on an act for too long. He preferred to demonstrate his theory that competition breeds champions.

Born on 12 May 1940, in New York City, Whitfield began his musical career playing tambourine for Popcorn and the Mohawks. However, it was the theatrical side of recordings that attracted him, and when Don Davis became head of A&R at Thelma Records, Whitfield worked with him. In 1959 the label released Whitfield's first song, Alone, by Tommy Stone. He continued working for independent labels before joining Motown in the early Sixties as an exclusive in-house writer and producer and was immediately assigned to Marvin Gaye. Together they wrote Pride And

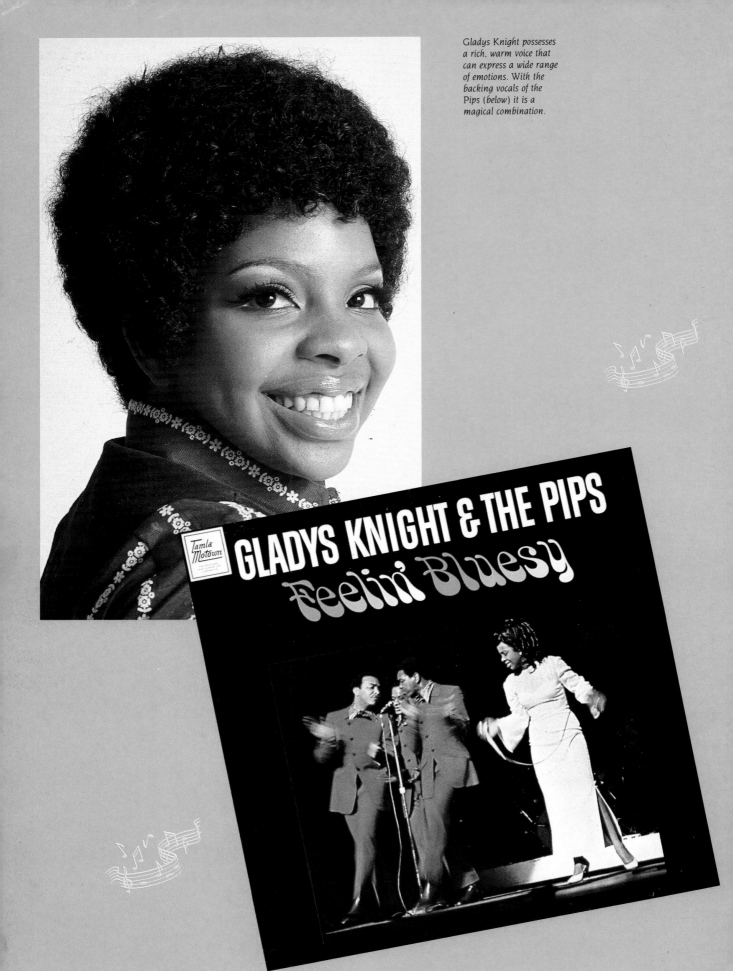

Gladys Knight possesses a rich, warm voice that can express a wide range of emotions. With the backing vocals of the Pips (below) it is a magical combination.

the Pips proved to be a hit formula that stayed with them from *The End Of Our Road*, and the powerful ballad *It Should Have Been Me* to their version of The Temptations' song *I Wish It Would Rain* in 1968. The following year's highlight was the dramatic *Didn't You Know (You'd Have To Cry Sometime)* although their public preferred more uptempo singles as Gladys explained: 'Tunes like *Nitty Gritty* and *Friendship Train* (both 1969) sold better, but we didn't really have anything big again until *If I Were Your Woman* in 1970. That was a gold record and then my cousin William, Bubba, Katherine of The Marvelettes and myself wrote *I Don't Want To Do Wrong*. It was in the can for two years and Johnny Bristol was the only one who saw potential in it. So we started collaborating on a few things and all of a sudden the other producers were approaching us. It's ironic how you have to prove yourself all through life but we're extremely grateful to Johnny for giving us that break.' Now that her writing talent was being taken seriously, Gladys Knight also wrote for Marvin Gaye and Tammi Terrell and Martha Reeves, among others, as well as becoming an established record selling act and major touring attraction with the Pips. Ironically, they never attended Motown's grooming department. 'As a matter of fact,' Bubba quipped 'the lady in charge there came to Gladys to get some hints!'

While the group struggled for American hits during 1971 and 1972, *Help Me Make It Through The Night*, a Gladys Knight solo, reached number eleven in the British charts in November 1972; their fourth top fifty entrant. The romantic mood continued with *The Look Of Love* and *Neither One Of Us (Wants To Be The First To Say Goodbye)* but sadly, from *Daddy Could Swear (I Declare)* in 1973, the calibre of their material declined drastically and the hits stopped.

As one group began the downward trek, others were gaining momentum. Marvin Gaye, for example, took his version of *I Heard It Through The Grapevine* to number one in most countries of the world in 1968/9. He had recorded his version before Gladys Knight and the Pips but his track was canned. Gaye wasn't that keen to release the song because of the Pips' success but he conceded when he heard the finished track. Whitfield worked out a totally new arrangement producing a moody, low-keyed single with a hypnotic rhythm. Gaye: 'I never thought a great deal about the song after recording it. In fact, I wasn't too optimistic about it at all. I had no idea it would be released and sell nearly four million records.'

A few other artists were making waves although not on the same scale. Jimmy Ruffin, brother of David, was one. His single *Don't Feel Sorry For Me* was the first to be released on the Miracle label early in 1961. Three years later he transferred to the Soul label for his second release, *Since I've Lost You* (US release only)

where he stayed until he left Motown twelve years later.

Like his brother, Jimmy was reared on gospel music in Mississippi. His first professional performance was at the Ebony Club in Muskegan, Michigan. It was shortly after this that he auditioned for Berry Gordy. However, it was to be some time before the young singer recorded his own work, as he explained: 'All the time I spent with Motown the nearest I came to making records was helping on other people's sessions. The studio men hired me to snap my fingers, clap my hands and stomp feet, so I used to go along and get a couple of dollars for an hour's work.' Ruffin also worked on Ford's assembly line, where he stayed for three years even though he had recorded for Miracle and Soul. Ruffin: 'Sometimes I had to take leave of absence for a week to play theatres like the Apollo, and to tour with the Revues, with artists who at the time hadn't made it either. None of us had any money.'

It was inevitable that a certain rivalry would develop between the Ruffin brothers. David enjoyed the accolades of early success and Jimmy was referred to as 'David's brother'. Instead of accepting second-best, Jimmy fought to make a name for himself in his own right. He side-stepped the comparison to emerge with his own personality, although he suffered from lack of repertoire. Ruffin: 'It was hard to get good material because all the good stuff went automatically to the top acts.' He persevered and released his third record, a Smokey Robinson song, *As Long As There Is L-O-V-E* in 1965. A year later his fourth, *What Becomes Of The Brokenhearted*, transformed his career. This single was Ruffin's first British release in September 1966.

Ruffin: 'One day when I got home from

Jimmy Ruffin, brother of David, opted for a solo career instead of joining The Temptations. In time his decision paid off and he no longer worked in his brother's shadow.

Prior to the Whitfield/ Strong 'funky' era, The Temptations, pictured here with David Ruffin as lead, were best known for their melodic ballads and smooth dance numbers.

Initially a session musician, Jr Walker's saxophone can be heard on many Motown records during the Sixties. A former Harvey artist, Walker with the All Stars (above right) successfully recorded singles in his own right like Shake And Fingerpop, Road Runner and How Sweet It is (To Be Loved By You).

Fords I went to Motown to try and canvass some material. I heard this tune being sung by the writer James Dean. When I asked him who the song was for he told me The Spinners were going to cut it. But I told him to give it to me instead. He liked my version enough to let me have it.' After its release in June 1966 Ruffin was no longer a second-rate artist. 'This started moving real fast for me, too fast. I wasn't sure what was happening to me. The song had the kind of words one can feel and it was a beautiful, melodic song. At the time my career wasn't going too well and I was getting kicked around quite a bit financially and I really was like a person lost, looking for some kind of hope, needing someone or something to believe in.' More to the point, the record's timely success dispelled anxieties over not joining The Temptations, as the singer explained: 'Everything I'd worked for paid off. All my doubts about turning the group down were dissipated and I was no longer shackled by my brother's success.'

I've Passed This Way Before (1966), Gonna Give Her All The Love I've Got and Don't You Miss Me Just A Little Bit Baby (both 1967), I'll Say Forever My Love, Don't Let Him Take Your Love From Me and Gonna Keep On Trying Till I Win Your Love were all released a year later, yet for some reason Ruffin was more popular in England than America and capitalized on this by touring annually and becoming a big attraction due to regular re-issues of his product.

Recording with him on the Soul label was instrumentalist Jr Walker, who laid the foundation for many a Motown single by providing exciting sax solos. His own Shotgun and Road Runner singles are good examples of his work and he can clearly be identified on other artists recordings. Walker, like Ruffin, enjoyed British success thanks to constant re-releases. His musical interest started by listening to Illinois Jacquet, Earl Bostic and Gene Simmons. Walker: 'They used to play in our town and on Sundays I'd join them. We made a lot of noise, people would complain, but the cops would say "hell, leave 'em be. At least we know where they are, they ain't causing no trouble" and they let us play as loud as we wanted.' Walker, born Autry DeWalt, in Blythesville, Arkansas, claims he was nicknamed 'Walker' because as a child he would walk everywhere. His family moved to South Bend, Indiana, while he was still at school and it was there that the All Stars were formed. During his high school years, Walker was given his first saxophone which he played in his first group The Jumping Jacks, later The Sticks Nix Band. The original line-up of The All Stars appears to be Tony Washington, Victor Thomas, Ray Freeman, Willie Woods and Walker. In 1962 he was asked by Johnny Bristol to join the Harvey outlet, as the saxophonist explained: 'Johnny was singing then and I cut a few hits for Harvy Fuqua who owned the label. Cleo's Mood was the biggest. I also played horn on other singers' records. Then I came back from a tour and found the company wasn't there anymore. It had joined Motown. And he told me to come over too.' Walker recorded two, further singles for Fuqua – *Twist Lackawanna* (US, '62) and *Good Rockin'* (US, '63) which sold reasonably well. The group's debut for the Soul label was *Satan's Blues* in August 1964, followed by his self-penned *Shotgun* (UK, Apr '65). It was his first big seller. Walker: 'I told Berry I had this song. He laughed at me but said "go on then, get yourself into the studio and do it". We cut it and when Berry heard it he said it was a top twenty record.' *Do The Boomerang* (UK, Jul '65), *Shake and Fingerpop* (UK, Sep '65), and a re-issue of *Cleo's Mood* (UK, Feb '66) were all US 1965 releases. A year later the evergreen *Road Runner* was issued and Walker's million seller arrived with a new version of the Marvin Gaye hit *How Sweet It Is (To Be Loved By You)* (US, Jul '66/UK, Aug '66). 'We were fooling around at the start of a session,' the saxophonist recalls. 'Me and the band were playing and there were a lot of people in the studio shouting at us to play. The producer, Lawrence Horn, was in the control room and somebody started telling everybody to keep quiet because we were going to start recording. Then I listened to a tape we'd made and it sounded great, just like a party. So we decided to make the record just like that.' A second single was cut during that session which Walker called *Go-Go-Go-Going*, but it was canned.

Walker's music up to this time consisted of dance instrumentals, with occasional vocals: 'I prefer playing to singing because I can't sing!' When the time came for a change of style, Walker enjoyed his biggest British success to date. The song, an attractive love ballad reluctantly recorded by him, was *What Does It Take To Win Your Love* (US, Apr '69/UK, Oct '69). This was followed by the carbon copy single, *These Eyes* (US, '69/UK, '70). *Walk In The Night*, *Take Me Girl I'm Ready* and *Way Back Home* kept Walker's name in the British charts during 1972 and 1973. As time passed the members of the All Stars changed but their visits to England did not. So loyal were the British to his music that Walker's tours to the UK lasted well into the Eighties.

Singer Shorty Long was so called because of his height (or rather lack of it!) being 5ft 1in (1.3m) tall. Real name Frederick Long, he was born in Birmingham, Alabama, and as a young boy listened to Little Willie John and Johnny Ace, and it was these influences that made him determined to sing as a professional. He sang his way through high school and the Birmingham Baptist Church of which he was a member; he mastered the piano and trained under outstanding musicians like Alvin Robinson. His first professional date came unexpectedly when the regular pianist at The Old Stable, a Birmingham night club, became ill. Long was hired as a replacement and stayed for three years! His ambition to progress led him into radio, where he hosted his own show for two years, and then to join the

Ink Spots group for eighteen months before deciding to work as a solo artist. By this time Long could also play drums, harmonica and trumpet which persuaded Tri Phi to sign him up in 1962. He later moved to Soul, where his and the label's first release was *Devil With The Blue Dress* in March 1964. *Out To Get You* followed in the US in August 1964 with *Function At The Junction* following. All were 'adopted' by England's famous Northern Soul Scene, although it shunned his biggest hit, the tongue-in-cheek *Here Comes The Judge* (US, May '68/UK, Jul '68) when it reached number thirty in the British charts. Long died in a freak accident in Ontario, Canada when a freighter flooded his fishing boat. His funeral was held on 2 July 1969, and when the service ended Stevie Wonder laid his harmonica on the singer's coffin.

These acts and many others played an integral part in building up Berry's company, although many were later neglected when the hits failed. Without these artists though, Gordy wouldn't have had a foundation to work on. Acts like The Supremes, The Temptations, Martha and the Vandellas, the Four Tops and Stevie Wonder kept the national charts occupied, but they were touring extensively and were not always available to record, so other artists were needed to fill the gap. Gordy hoped some of the glitter of his top sellers would rub off on the less well-known acts, and when this didn't happen the acts were dropped and soon left the label. However, one departure that no-one expected was that of Holland, Dozier and Holland in the late Sixties. When their contract was due for renewal the trio was stunned at Gordy's miserly offer and a lengthy battle ensued. During August 1968 Motown filed for damages reputed to be $4 million claiming that H-D-H had not honoured their Jobete publishing contract for at least a year. The company insisted it *had* paid them approximately $2½ million in royalties for a two year period which was yet to expire, and requested the court issue an injunction preventing the trio working elsewhere. H-D-H angrily retaliated by countersuing Motown for an estimated $22 million, citing numerous petitions including, but not limited to, fraudulent and deceitful activities and betrayal of trust. They also asked the court to place Motown's financial business under receivership.

Gordy's contracts were notorious for their meanness, and Gordy's miserliness was legendary. Diana Ross's beloved mother, who signed her daughter's recording contract, was reputed to have said: 'I don't want my Diana signing no contract with no little kid like that,' Yet, when any member of his staff showed loyalty or was responsible for regular hit records, Gordy would reward them. He also gave gifts to his favourite acts and financially supported several charities via the Gordy Foundation Inc. The Negro United College Fund, Martin Luther King Jr's Memorial

Shorty Long is probably best remembered for the 'fun' song, Here Comes The Judge, *in 1968. However, the former Ink Spot was capable of superior tracks like* Devil With The Blue Dress.

Center for Social Change, The Reverend Jesse Jackson's Push Foundation and Sugar Ray Robinson's Youth Foundation were among several organizations which benefited from Gordy's generosity. Gordy also had a facility to assist his artists with loans. Author Peter Benjaminson cites the example when David Ruffin fell behind with his child support payments of $200 a week and Motown bailed him out. However, as artists took advantage of this facility many were stunned when they realized their royalty payments fell accordingly, yet should an act not be successful enough to earn decent royalties, Motown swallowed the expense.

The void left by H-D-H at Motown had to be filled quickly with other writers and producers to ensure a painless transition for the acts. In an attempt to minimize disruption certain artists had already been assigned to new staff: Diana Ross and the Supremes were working with Pam Sawyer, Ashford and Simpson, Frank Wilson, Deke Richards, Hank Cosby and Gordy himself, while the Four Tops turned to

Martha and the Vandellas, like The Supremes, worried about the inferior quality of their recording material when Holland, Dozier and Holland left Motown. However, Martha (left) was determined her group would not suffer.

middle-of-the-road writers like Tim Hardin, Jimmy Webb and, later, Frank Wilson. Levi Stubbs: 'We wanted to do more cabaret, appeal to a broader audience, because we wanted to be known as a more flexible group and wanted to forget the barriers people tried to build up.'

However the Four Tops admit to finding themselves in a vacuum for a time because no other producer could match H-D-H. Duke Fakir: 'We had some good things with Frank Wilson like It's All In The Game, but it was never the same. H-D-H had a magic touch with us and they were the finest friends we've ever met. They worked with us on a person-to-person basis. The reason they were able to write so many good songs for us was that they wrote about us and the things we did. They saw us when we went through love problems, when we went through happy days. They saw us sad, and they wrote about these things. We were constantly in and out of each other's houses and with each other every day of the week. H-D-H were probably, along with The Beatles, the most prolific writers of the era.' Martha Reeves: 'At one time they were our chief producers and although we tried to find others, we went through a lull. We missed H-D-H but then, on reflection, we missed them when they worked with The Supremes. They used to cut our singles, but when The Supremes took off they only did a few B-sides and album tracks for us.'

As Motown and H-D-H were locked in a legal battle, the trio was unable to work publicly. With the little money available to them, H-D-H opened the Invictus and Hot Wax labels, distributed by Capitol and Buddah. Brian Holland and Lamont Dozier wrote material under pseudonyms, like Wayne and Dunbar, for their labels, including Band Of Gold (Freda Payne) and Give Me Just A Little More Time (Chairman of the Board). When Motown and the trio settled the action out of court, and after a string of hits on Invictus and Hot Wax, H-D-H's success story once more turned sour with further court action which led to the trio splitting up. Dozier recorded as a solo artist for ABC, later Warner Brothers, while Holland Brothers worked as freelance producers for . . . Motown!

WHERE DID OUR LOVE GO?

'I talked about this with Smokey and Diana and we were trying to figure out what makes the sound different. . . . We came up with a six word definition "rats, roaches, struggle, talent, guts and love".'
Berry Gordy

'Berry Gordy told me if I went on stage he would throw me off. I didn't go on. I couldn't fight anymore.'
Florence Ballard

Motown was the all American dream come true: Berry Gordy rose from the ranks of small-time businessman into the world of high finance, with a thriving company that he was satisfied would continue to prosper. The 'Motown Sound' acts continued to appeal to the young record buyers, but he needed to inject prestige and credibility into his operation to attack the large middle-of-the-road market. To do this Gordy had to expand his repertoire.

One of the first to be signed to this end in 1965 was the international celebrity Billy Eckstine whose first release was the unexciting *Down To Earth* on the Motown label in the May. The urbane Eckstine did not fit in with the more earthy sound of young America but stayed long enough to release three albums none of which was memorable. The singer/entertainer was born in Pittsburgh, although his family moved to Washington DC where Eckstine finished his education at the Armstrong High School. When he was 17 he won his first amateur show with an impersonation of Cab Calloway. Tommy Miles, a well-known band leader of the time, invited Eckstine to join him but after a while, being a confirmed sports addict, Eckstine left Miles to accept an athletic scholarship to play football at the Lawrenceville's St Paul University. Unfortunately, his sporting career came to an end when he broke his collar bone during a match. The years that followed saw him patching up his singing career with various one-night engagements.

In 1939 band leader Earl Hines recruited Eckstine as a vocalist; he stayed four years. During this time he released his most memorable records like *Jelly's Jell*, *Skylark* and *Somehow I'm Falling In Love* on the Bluebird label, and duetted with Sarah Vaughan, who later joined Hines' band. However the solo urge prompted Eckstine to leave in 1943 to become a top club performer. A year later he fronted his own band and took Vaughan with him. Eckstine's ensemble read like a who's who in jazz and together they became the hottest jazz band on the circuit. National Records released two-million sellers on Eckstine – *Cottage For Sale* and *Prisoner Of Love* – and the band became even more in demand. Touring took its toll and in 1947 the group disbanded. MGM signed Eckstine where he enjoyed further success and for the next five years he broke box office records in both America and Europe.

When Billy Eckstine joined Motown, a young, white Canadian released his first single *Let's Go Somewhere* on V.I.P. in October 1965. R. Dean Taylor, more into country music than R&B, stayed on that label for three singles after which he moved to the newly-formed Rare Earth label in 1970. He was auditioned and signed by H-D-H and became Brian Holland's protégé. It was Taylor's intention to sing but he was pushed into songwriting. Ironically, it was a good move as he was presented with two gold records for his contribution to *Love Child* (Diana Ross and The Supremes) and *All I Need* (The Temptations). By being H-D-H's apprentice Taylor ghost-wrote for them as he explained: 'They were building up an image as a producing team which they succeeded in doing, and they were stingy in letting any of the glory go. They used to pay me cash for whatever I wrote and left my name off. I co-wrote *You Keep Running Away*, *Standing In The Shadows Of Love* and *Seven Rooms Of Gloom*, for the Four Tops, and *Love Is Here And Now You're Gone* for The Supremes, but I didn't get my name mentioned.'

As a youngster Taylor played piano and guitar, later teaching himself to sing. He performed at a country and western show in Toronto when he was 12 which gave him the confidence to start his own group. Once his school days were over his musical interests developed and prompted his visit to Detroit. His second V.I.P. release in 1967 was the classic slice of fright *There's A Ghost In My House* which, when released in England seven years later, reached number three in the national charts. *Gotta See Jane* was next in 1968 (a number 17 UK hit in June 1968) and was the result of him being allowed total freedom in the

With the 'Motown Sound' acts' success, Berry Gordy wanted to expand into middle-of-the-road music. To this end he signed the urbane Billy Eckstine. The ploy failed.

R. Dean Taylor joined Motown as a ghost-writer for Holland, Dozier and Holland. Taylor failed as a singer until he established his own 'white' identity.

(Right) Established gospel singer Blinky stunned audiences with her rip-roaring stage acts, but as a recording artist she failed despite enjoying a British cult following. However, in an attempt to re-capture the magic of the Gaye/Terrell duets, Edwin Starr and Blinky (inset) teamed up to record the Just We Two album.

studio: 'Brian Holland wanted to break me as a white artist with Motown but he kept trying to make me sound black, recording me in the wrong keys and such. That's why I'd never got anywhere.'

Former Ric Tic artist Edwin Starr was moving from strength to strength yet he was more popular in Britain than America due to the former's loyalty to his soul classics like Agent Double O Soul, Back Street, Stop Her On Sight (SOS) and Headline News. Starr's debut Gordy label single was I Want My Baby Back in 1967; I Am The Man For You Baby and Way Over There followed a year later. Starr co-wrote many of his early releases and was one of the few artists to receive both artist's and writer's royalties. Heavy footsteps were an unusual background attraction on his 1969 hit Twenty-five Miles. Motown decided to capitalize on the Gaye/Terrell success, by teaming Starr with a female vocalist, Blinky Williams. According to Starr the move happened because: 'Blinky had a very good single released at the time, I Wouldn't Change The Man He Is. But unfortunately it didn't get off the ground. At the time 25 Miles was big for me and the company suggested we record together because I was a hot name and they hoped that putting us together might draw attention to Blinky'. The duet died although their first single together, Oh How Happy, was one of 1969's classiest soul records. A year later Starr climbed on the political soapbox with War (US, Jun '70/UK, Oct '70). Starr's music followed that of The Temptations, with both acts recording the same songs.

Blinky, born Sandra Williams, in Oakland, California, was raised in Los Angeles. She majored in child psychology and elementary education. As an 11-year-old she sang in her father's church. Her introduction to secular music came when she signed to the Vee Jay label as a member of The Logics. An album was recorded there with future Motown singer/writer Gloria Jones, among others. Williams then moved to Atlantic Records as a solo artist to record Heartaches. She later recorded Hark The Voice for Gospel. To become an all-round entertainer Williams mastered a variety of instruments and built up a loyal, local following. After her debut single I Wouldn't Change The Man He Is on the Motown label in 1968, she participated in the compilation Motortown Revue Live singing a rip-roaring version of I Can't Turn You Loose. (Other acts on this bill were Stevie Wonder, Gladys Knight and the Pips, Bobby Taylor, The Temptations and The Originals.)

Edwin Starr and Blinky recorded one album together, Just We Two, in 1969, an enjoyable but bland release. A further Ashford & Simpson penned single How You Gonna Keep It (After You Get It) by Blinky was scheduled and abandoned. The title was re-listed in 1971, but once again shelved. She also recorded two albums Softly and The Temptations Present which were canned, but her career was not yet over and she was to record for Motown again before leaving to work at Reprise Records with Mickey Stevenson. Meantime Starr and Williams showed promise despite inferior material. However, the in-house competition was stiff as Gaye and Terrell were at their recording peak with Keep On Lovin' Me Honey and Good Lovin' Ain't Easy To Come By. With Williams' failure as a soloist, writers and producers looked desperately for a replacement, but the material and the voices refused to gel. Brenda Holloway and Mary Wells were the exceptions, yet the equally talented Barbara Randolph, Carolyn Crawford and Barbara McNair failed abysmally. A compromise had to be found. The search was fruitless until it was pointed out there was a suitable candidate already working within the company. She was a young, shy, slip of a girl, Rita Wright, later to be known as Syreeta.

Introduced to the company by Brian Holland, she commented in an early 1980s interview: 'I bothered him every day for over a month to see if he had a song for me. One day he actually said he had and that was when I met Valerie Simpson and Nickolas Ashford for the first time. They wrote my first single.' Recorded as Rita Wright and released in 1968, I Can't Give Back The Love I Feel For You although publicly ignored then, became a Motown classic a decade later. Born in Pittsburgh, Syreeta began singing when she was four years old: 'I used to sing "The Lord's Prayer" and my mother would hold her breath until I made the high notes. I always started about eight notes higher than everyone else and I still have that range.' Her father was killed in the Korean War, leaving her mother and

Barbara McNair's You're Gonna Love My Baby was a milestone in black music. She was a middle-of-the-road asset to Motown.

grandmother to raise her. Syreeta was 11 when her family moved to Detroit where she attended private schools. Four years later she moved to South Carolina where she ended her education in a white dominated school. Syreeta: 'I didn't stay too long! I quit to start work and my family were really upset. I originally wanted to be a ballet dancer but my grandparents said it would cost too much so I had to quit that idea. So I decided to write and sing.'

However, Syreeta the charting singer, wasn't going to happen immediately. Working as a secretary in one of Motown's arranging departments, Syreeta was able to look out for suitable material. She was also on hand for session singing and worked behind the scenes for over two years. Brian Holland had promised her a recording career, yet it was Stevie Wonder who gave her a song. He had heard her voice and was told of her composing talent but her first working session with Wonder ended in failure. Wonder's 1970 hit *Signed*, *Sealed*, *Delivered* I'm *Yours* was their first joint effort. Syreeta: 'It was simple for me but I was amazed that lyrics like that could sell over two million copies.' Now confident in her art, she wrote lyrics to Wonder's melodies: 'The music told me what to write about, instead of me trying to get someone to write a tune around my lyrics. Once I had written something I liked, I'd tell Steve. If he didn't like it, I'd go back and work on it again. Or he'd give the song to someone else to work on.' Their working relationship turned into romance and the two eventually married in 1970.

One of the many female performers who failed to make the Motown grade was the versatile Barbara McNair. Signed to the Motown label, her single *You're Gonna Love My Baby* released in 1965 was a milestone in black music. Although she could only be heard on a few singles, all were superior recordings. *Everything Is Good About You*, (also recorded by The Supremes), *Here I Am Baby* (The Marvelettes' song) and the classic *Where Would I Be Without You* are excellent examples. McNair was born in Racine, Wisconsin, and by the time she left high school, her vocal expertise prompted her parents to enrol her at the UCLA for training as a music major. She was invited to play at the Village Vanguard in New York City which led to several Broadway shows including *The Body Beautiful* and *No Strings*. Acting took her into television where she appeared on *Dr Kildare* and *The Eleventh Hour*, and touring took her across America. She was the first black singer to star in the Empire Room at the Shamrock-Hilton in Houston, Texas. McNair, who had the much-sought-after middle-of-the-road appeal, was a great asset to Gordy's company yet her talent was not promoted.

The Supremes had, by now, found a permanent foothold in the charts, and one song in particular, considered by Mary Wilson to be the most ridiculous song in the world, gave them a big boost to superstardom – *Where Did*

Our Love Go (US, Jun '64/UK, Aug '64). When the single (originally written for Mary Wells) was first released The Supremes were touring with Dick Clark's 'Cavalcade Of Stars'. Originally Clark wanted hit-makers Martha and the Vandellas for his tour but Gordy insisted The Supremes be included. Eventually the promoter relented when Gordy negotiated a low weekly salary of $500 for all three, which failed to cover their living expenses. When the song leapt up the charts The Supremes found themselves taking on a different role with their audiences. Diana Ross: 'We started noticing that when we sang the single on stage during the remainder of the tour the kids started screaming and really responding. Previously they hadn't taken too much notice of us.' Needless to say, before the tour ended Clark had re-negotiated a better deal for the trio and had transferred their names from the bottom of the billboard to the top. Being elevated to top recording artists, doors everywhere began opening for them, as Ross remembers: 'We were amazed. We were working constantly and our dreams were coming true. We started lip-synching on television and we were so busy we didn't have time to think about the fact that we were becoming stars.'

When their next single, *Baby Love*, became a simultaneous number one in America and England in 1964, Berry Gordy's empire grossed an overwhelming $10 million. Years later he said this was the outcome of providing music all areas of the public wanted: 'Anything that sells a million records is pop. We had a sound that's a little different from anybody else's. We have that sincere feeling. I talked about this with Smokey and Diana and we were trying to figure out what makes the sound different. We thought back, about the neighbourhoods we were in, the struggles, etc., and we came up with a six word definition "rats, roaches, struggle, talent, guts and love".' While the company boss was totting up his profits, he had to reserve a huge chunk for The Supremes because they, as a unit, had grossed in excess of $300,000 for sales of five million and more. They earned $100,000 during the first six months alone of 1965, and their weekly allowance was raised to $500 each.

Diana Ross put her costume design training to good use by making the group's clothes. They looked resplendent both in their sleek gowns or simple cotton dresses and coiffured wigs (they had over three hundred between them). However, as the gowns were designed to suit Diana Ross's thin build they didn't always show Wilson and Ballard at their best. Although Ross was confidentially in control on stage, she relied heavily on Wilson for moral support. With soaring commitments, The Supremes spent little time in Detroit and it was usual for them to perform for seventy consecutive nights, or thirty-six cities for eleven months a year. The strain was unbear-

able, yet they had to keep touring schedules to cash-in on their record success. A visitor to Ross's Detroit home remarked that the singer had never cooked on the stove, nor sat down in her kitchen.

They all travelled with a full entourage, controlled by one of their early tour managers, Shelley Berger. Part of his job was to collect the group's money which on occasion could top $100,000 half way through a tour. Berger: 'We had so much money I couldn't believe it.' He carried $1,000 bills on his person at all times and when his pockets bulged, he divided it among the musicians and the girls. His nightmare of being mugged prompted him to purchase handguns for himself and certain musicians when one particular tour reached Texas.

In addition to single sales, the trio's albums were also huge money spinners. *Meet The Supremes* (US '63/UK '64) was the first, with *Where Did Our Love Go* (US, UK '64), *A Little Bit Of Liverpool* (US, UK '64) (titled *With Love (From Us To You)* for the British market), *Supremes Sing Country, Western And Pop* (US, UK '65), *We Remember Sam Cooke* (US, UK '65) and *More Hits* (US, UK '65) as follow-ups. By 1966 they had recorded several unreleased projects including *Sing Ballads And Blues*, a live set recorded at the 20 Grand Club in 1964, *There's A Place For Us, A Tribute To The Girls* and *The Supremes Pure Gold*. Many popular artists found success in one particular market and stayed there but not The Supremes. Gordy pushed them into recording other acts' repertoires and middle-of-the-road material, and he even cashed in on the birth of The Beatles and the Liverpool explosion with their third album.

With success came change, not in the group's line-up but in their personalities and image. Ross was the first to notice this: 'We often looked at our early publicity shots and the change there was like the "before" and "after" photos in the magazine. When we first started we didn't wear make-up and we weren't girls any more either, we had become

The Supremes' Baby Love became a simultaneous number one single in America and England in 1964. The trio are seen here shopping in London with Eddie Kendricks and Melvin Franklin (of The Temptations) in the background.

Shelley Berger joined Motown in 1966 and managed many of the early artists. He was also tour manager for The Supremes.

young ladies. We tried to kill the bad image of many girl entertainers. We kept our act clean and off-stage we conducted ourselves in a feminine and lady-like manner. Health was very important on the road, and we had to think of cleanliness and posture and all the other things they taught in school which a lot of kids never thought important.' The Supremes with Ross fronting was Berry Gordy's greatest asset and the unbroken line of number one singles prompted him to comment, 'Wherever Diana Ross goes, so goes Motown.'

As Ross became aware of her privileged position within Motown, so she became more adventurous on stage, earning valid individual praise from the critics. Yet her newly-found 'solo' stardom placed huge responsibilities on her. She wanted the success, but she didn't want the daily strain of it and her nerves became so taut that she bit her fingernails to the quick, wore false ones, and chewed them as well!

The Supremes' first major trip to Europe was during 1964. Diana Ross: 'We had only done the Dick Clark tours and the Motown Revues where we weren't headlining. Going to Europe was the most amazing culture shock. Berry and his sisters went with us and everyone was so excited to see us. It was something we had dreamed of since we were kids. We drove through England and saw all the things that we had read about in school but never

imagined to be real.' Despite the singer's excitement, the tour was marred by disagreement within the group, as she recalled: 'I don't remember how many hit records we had out then but we started having a few problems. Berry was on tour with us and that's when I decided we would have a meeting. I felt that everybody was spreading apart. I remember saying to them "if we don't get it together right now, then there's no sense in us doing this because we're doing this out of happiness and something we love to do. But if it's going to get to be an effort then we don't need to do it".' This was the first of several occasions when the group was in danger of breaking up. Mary Wilson: 'The pressure was enormous by that time. So much was expected of us. We were on stage constantly, never having time to eat or sleep.' During one tour, Diana Ross's weight dropped to seven stone. Gordy was so distressed that he checked her into hospital for three days, leaving Mary and Florence to their own devices.

Naturally it became obvious to Wilson and Ballard that the spotlight was Diana's. That they were being pushed further into the background with every record released did not bother Mary unduly at the time as she was content to be a support vocalist. Florence, on the other hand, took great exception to the move. She was, after all, the founder member of the group and it's original lead singer, and it was being taken away from her. She was also the only trained singer although Ross did take lessons before branching out on her own. In her autobiography Mary Wilson wrote that Motown began engineering appearances to emphasize Diana's role. She gave an example where originally the trio would walk into a room together, followed by Gordy or Shelley Berger. Later it was Ross who walked in first on the arm of a Motown executive, while she and Ballard followed behind: 'It was apparent that neither Diane or Berry gave a damn about what we wanted, and Flo made no bones about feeling betrayed and lied to'. Ballard's solo spot *People* was dropped from their show when she objected to Gordy and Ross's attitude and later she too was dropped mid-way through a tour. Ex-Bluebelle, Cindy Birdsong, was brought in to finish it, and she wore Ballard's stage gown to ensure the audience remained ignorant of the switch. It was reputed Ballard was determined to tarnish the group's image, yet Gordy continued to retain her as a fully paid member of the trio. However now he had Birdsong waiting in the wings, learning the routines and repertoire, which alleviated his immediate problem of a quick replacement for Ballard. It was in his best interests to keep the group together at this time yet it was he who later refused to converse with Ballard, leaving it to Wilson to act as his mouthpiece. Ballard, worried about The Supremes and her future, gained weight and consumed alcohol regularly although not excessively. When her stage work was affected

With success The Supremes were sought after to endorse commodities like white bread and deodorant. Pictured here Diana Ross, Florence Ballard and Mary Wilson add their vocals to a Coca Cola advert against the backing of Baby Love.

The changing faces of The Supremes: the original hit line-up of the group (above) pictured in Manchester Square, London during the Sixties. Florence Ballard, the original lead singer of the group (above centre) and Diana Ross, the world famous lead singer (far left). The last line-up (left) Diana Ross and The Supremes, with Ballard's replacement, Cindy Birdsong.

Wilson covered for her. Sadly, the fun loving, joking Supreme lost her will to fight and became a professional recluse which eventually led to her final dismissal.

Stories of The Supremes' time in the studios were manufactured by Motown's publicity machine. It told of three girls having fun singing together, trying out new ideas and having snacks sent into the studios because they were enjoying themselves so much, or were working throughout the night. The truth is that after 1965 the trio rarely recorded together. When there was a break in their touring schedule the two backing vocalists would take time off to rest while Ross recorded lead vocals. Occasionally, Ballard and Wilson's voices would be added, but invariably session singers were used.

Berry Gordy intended to cash-in on The Supremes' success in any way he could including using them to endorse white products in advertisements. In March 1966 the girls – ignoring the outrage of the black community at their supporting white enterprises – allowed their faces to be wrapped round loaves of bread manufactured by Detroit's Ward Baking Company. A year later they recorded a couple of Coca Cola themes against the backing tracks of *Baby Love* and *When The Lovelight Starts Shining Through His Eyes*, and convinced television viewers that Arrid Extra Dry deodorant would dry any wet spots. However they also endorsed their own brand of make-up which could be obtained outside America.

The Temptations too faced racial problems when they were shunned by the black community for performing in white theatres. Dennis Edwards: 'It was a touchy situation. When you're starting out it's natural that you play for predominantly Negro audiences, such as at the Apollo. But as you become more popular you go where the money is, and that is into the clubs. We like to play white clubs and we like playing the Apollo. We're not deserting anybody, we just play where we're booked. To make it you've got to appeal to everybody. After all everybody likes a little soul food now and again whatever their colour or origin.' Then Diana Ross was attacked for refusing to wear her hair in a permanent Afro style, which prompted media comments like 'the worst thing Diana Ross could ever say was that she wanted to be as popular as Barbra Streisand. She should have said she wanted to be as popular as Billie Holiday or Bessie Smith.' The criticism fell on stoney ground and why not? The Supremes were now guaranteed $10,000 upwards per show, which meant all three could afford expensive homes in Detroit's salubrious Buena Vista Street. However, most of their earnings were put into savings accounts and/or trusts, while they were given living expenses. In time this procedure would become the subject of law suits by both Wilson and Ballard.

In 1966 *You Can't Hurry Love* and *You Keep Me Hangin' On* continued the hit run in both America and Britain which would have delighted any other group. Instead of basking in the world's adoration, the group's discontent at Ross's preferential treatment grew to enormous proportions. Berry Gordy possibly added fuel to the fire when he told *Cosmopolitan* magazine: 'Diana's trying to improve her vocabulary because she knows it will help her. She wants to be somebody and she's going to be somebody. I know she's going to be a great, great star. There's nobody like her in the entire business.' The summer of 1967 saw the release of *The Happening* and Florence Ballard's sacking in the August. She told the *Washington Post* (1975) that she was dismissed at The Flamingo, Las Vegas: 'Berry Gordy told me if I went on stage, he would throw me off. I didn't go on. I couldn't fight anymore.' Upon leaving the group she admitted herself into Detroit's Henry Ford Hospital to recover from stress and exhaustion. Within a year she was penniless. When visiting England several years later, Diana Ross was asked why Ballard left: 'Flo would begin to get lazy, where she wouldn't show up for rehearsals or recording sessions which threw everybody off. We went to a couple of gigs where she just didn't show up and Mary and I had to sing by ourselves. It wasn't Flo's fault, she was just tired.' She also spoke of a letter Ballard had written to her: 'In it she said she was exhausted and was tired and wanted to quit. So she left the group. We had a talk with her and her mother because we wanted to find out if that was really her final decision, but she had made up her mind.' In another interview Ross told the British press Florence wanted to leave so she could look after her family, but she didn't marry until a year after her sacking!

Needless to say, the ex-Supreme was hounded by the press, yet it was to be some time before the truth emerged. She told one American journalist: 'Someone was always talking about exposing me and I never could understand why because I never did anything to expose. Yes, there were some reports that I drank and it took me a long time to realize that there wasn't anything wrong with that. I didn't drink a lot and it never affected my work. I never missed a performance because of something I did personally.' She agreed there were upsets within the group but 'you'll never find three girls working together without little problems happening. Why I left The Supremes, I don't really know. Long before I even began thinking things were getting real bad, someone was being groomed to come in and take my place. People always told me I made a mistake leaving the group. Maybe at the time I thought I had to but I didn't leave on my own. Pressure forced me out. All kinds of things were happening and I was actually forced off stage.' In another interview some time later, she confirmed that the pressure came from Ross and Gordy: 'They were critical of my singing and Berry repeatedly urged me to quit. He'd often say "You're a millionaire at twenty-four, you can leave anytime now".'

The sacking prompted Wilson and Ross to consider their future within the group. Diana Ross: 'Mary wanted to go too. I wanted to pursue my career and wanted to stay in show business. So I told her that if she left me I'd go out on my own. I was now responsible for The Supremes and it was Mary's decision that I should be out front.'

Cindy Birdsong officially replaced Ballard on the *Reflections* single (US, Jul '67/UK, Aug '67) when the label credit read Diana Ross and the Supremes. (Two other major acts too underwent name changes – Martha Reeves and the Vandellas, Smokey Robinson and the Miracles. The Temptations and the Four Tops remained untouched.) Wilson remembers Birdsong joining the group: 'We were trying to figure out who could replace Florence, and it was actually Diane who came up with Cindy. She looks just like Florence. Berry Gordy liked her too so the next thing we knew she was with us. Our first engagement was at the Hollywood Bowl before eighteen thousand people and it was scary. There was a ramp there and we had to walk down it. The audience was so far away that nobody knew it wasn't Florence standing on stage. Anyway, everyone who met Cindy thought she looked a lot like Florence, and even Cindy couldn't even tell on a picture if it was her or Florence. So that was alright for awhile.'

Cindy Birdsong was born on 15 December 1943 in Mount Holly, New Jersey, to Lloyd and Annie Birdsong. She was the eldest in a family of three girls and five boys. At the age of two, her family moved to Camden, New Jersey where she was educated. As a teenager Birdsong worked as a salesgirl in Philadelphia, where she took singing lessons, and later returned to Camden to work as a dentist's receptionist. Birdsong graduated from school before she reached 17 to join the rock/soul group, Patti LaBelle's Bluebelles. While a backing singer with the Bluebelles, Birdsong befriended Florence Ballard when the two groups toured together. Little did she realize she would one day be her friend's replacement.

Although the trio had visited England before, it was their season at the prestigious supper club, Talk Of The Town in London's West End, that won them British acclaim. With Birdsong, they opened a two week run at the venue from 22 January 1968 to standing-room only audiences. Diana Ross and the Supremes flew to London from Cannes, where they appeared at Midem's annual international music conference. Their opening night saw many well-known stars in the audience including Paul McCartney (still with The Beatles), Michael Caine, Cliff Richard, Shirley Bassey, Kenny Lynch, The Tremeloes and Englebert Humperdink. After the show McCartney escorted the girls to The Speakeasy, one of London's 'in' nightclubs, where

they stayed until late. Motown/EMI arranged a press reception for the next day when, according to an NME reporter: 'Diane wore a sexy mustard suit and a sensuous perfume, Joy, and pleasantly rattled off the answers as easily as she makes hit records.' On 28 January the trio appeared with Tom Jones on the television variety show *Sunday Night At The London Palladium*, then joined Eamonn Andrews on his show seven nights later. They also attended a private party thrown by The Duke of Bedford, were presented to the Queen Mother, lunched at the House of Commons and flew to Paris to inspect the year's fashions and be photographed by Lord Snowdon. One latecomer who expected his chat show to be squeezed into the girls' schedule was Simon Dee. His annoyance led to him remarking on air: 'I must say I'm rather upset. I've supported The Supremes for four years. During the opening week of Radio Caroline I played Tamla Motown records before anyone knew what it meant and I helped them for two and a half years on Radio Luxembourg. I actually coined the phrase "Ross Is Boss". Let's face it, they're famous now. They don't need me and I don't need them. But surely there should have been some mutual co-operation.'

When Florence Ballard was sacked as a member of The Supremes in 1967, ex-LaBelle member Cindy Birdsong (left) replaced her. Birdsong's debut on record was Reflections. The label credit read Diana Ross and the Supremes.

Early in 1968 Diana Ross and the Supremes appeared before a capacity audience at London's 'Talk of the Town'. Their performances were later captured on record (left to right: Cindy Birdsong, Mary Wilson, Diana Ross).

The highlights of the Talk Of The Town performances were captured on *Live At London's Talk Of The Town* album (US, Aug '68/UK, Mar '68), their first recorded outside Motown. Meanwhile, the critics wrote glowing reviews. The *Evening Standard*'s Ray Connolly summed up everyone's feelings when he wrote: 'Last night Diana Ross and the Supremes made their debut at Talk of the Town – and they were sensational. In anticipation of an exceptional evening, herds of pop people turned up to welcome the trio and were treated to a lesson in musical showmanship, which, quite honestly, I have never seen bettered. For fifty-five minutes and through thirty songs, Diana Ross in a staggering display of energy and artistry, held the capacity audience in an almost continuous state of applause'. Her backing vocalists remained just that.

In November 1968 the group appeared on The Royal Command Performance, an annual affair attended by the members of The Royal Family. The trio was the first Motown act to be requested to appear before The Queen Mother, Princess Margaret and her husband, Lord Snowdon, Prince Charles and Princess Anne. The girls flew to London from Los Angeles, arriving on the afternoon of the actual performance. While rehearsing they saw for the first time Britain's Black and White Minstrels. Diana Ross took great exception to the white men with blacked-up faces and refused to perform that night if they were allowed to stay on the bill. She was told that the Minstrels were an integral part of the show, so she relented by saying: 'It's so old fashioned and I'm sure the young people of today don't want it. It brings back memories of

sadness for the coloured people . . . although I don't dislike the act itself.'

This was the first of two upsets. The second concerned the group itself. They changed their routine to include Ross' eulogy to Dr Martin Luther King who was assissinated in April 1968 in Memphis. The tribute was curiously omitted from their rehearsals and under normal performance circumstances would not have caused concern. Written by Maurice King it was inserted during the group's version of *Somewhere* from *West Side Story*. As the music faded Ross spoke: 'Yes, there is a place for us, when love is like a passion. Let our efforts be as determined as those of Dr Martin Luther King who had a dream that all God's children – black men, white men, Jews, Gentiles, Protestants and Catholics, could all join hands and sing that spiritual of old. Free at last!' She then led the girls into the closing verse of the song. It received an adverse audience reception and the sequence was cut from the televized version of the show.

A hastily arranged press conference the following morning attempted to rectify the uproar. Ross was spokeswoman: 'It wasn't meant to shock and is it so controversial really? And why shouldn't I have said this in front of the Royal Family? They are human and they must know what's going on in the world as much as anybody. I've said the same things to President Johnson. I didn't say anything bitter; it was more like a prayer. This is very hard for me to explain . . .' She then claimed that black activist Stokely Carmichael should be heard because 'he had a good philosophy and if it wasn't for people like him, things wouldn't be happening today'. The conference was closed when she announced her feelings matched those of James Brown when he declared 'I'm black and I'm proud!' Diana Ross subsequently refrained from mentioning Black Power in European interviews!

Diana Ross and the Supremes weren't the only Motown group to take Britain by storm. The Four Tops beat them by two years in 1966 with two sell-out concerts at the Saville Theatre on 13 November. The Beatles' manager Brian Epstein, who owned the Saville, promoted the visit following a trip to Detroit to see the group. He paid them $32,000 to appear on the Sunday before *Reach Out I'll Be There* topped the British charts. The *On Top* album was released to coincide with the tour. Supporting the Motown quartet were Cliff Bennett and the Rebel Rousers and Bob Miller's Millermen, with compere Tony Hall. Interestingly, *Reach Out I'll Be There* was one of the few songs written for them that they recorded first. For example, H-D-H wrote *This Old Heart Of Mine* for them but it was given to The Isley Brothers before the Four Tops could record it, Smokey Robinson pinched (*Come 'Round Here*) *I'm The One You Need* to release it (in a higher key) by The Miracles, and Kim Weston released *Helpless* as a single while the Four

Tops' version was relegated to an album.

The quartet's 1967 tour, again promoted by Epstein, started on Saturday 28 January with two shows before fourteen thousand people at London's Royal Albert Hall, followed by performances in Liverpool, Leeds, Glasgow, Manchester and Birmingham, among others, with two shows played on each date. Support acts this time were The Merseys, Madeline Bell and The Johnny Watson Band. Once again, Tony Hall compered. *Standing In The Shadows Of Love* was released to coincide with these nine dates. For the first time in music history a special sound system was fitted in the Albert Hall in an endeavour to reproduce the Motown sound on stage. Critics were ecstatic: 'not even in the wildest moments of our wildest dreams could any of us have imagined what happened on Saturday night at the Albert Hall. It was the Saville Theatre twenty times over. It was a spectacle on a scale you wouldn't have expected outside a mammoth film production. It was (like) the fanatical exultation of the Nuremberg Rallies, the incredible enthusiasm of a World Cup football crowd. And it was there for the Four Tops before they even set foot on stage. They didn't have to work for it, but they did work for it. They sang because of it and because this was final proof, if it were needed, of the tremendous love relationship the Four Tops have with their audience, and their audience

with the Four Tops. The Tops ran on to the stage to a cheer which soared to the roof and bounced back off the lights. In the stalls they rushed forward and surged fifteen deep round the base of the stage. Behind stage they stood, swayed and clapped their hands above their heads and cried. . . . The Albert Hall was a swaying, dancing, weeping mass of people, and none of us could really believe what was happening and that we were a part of it.' Four Tops fever had hit Britain. Sadly, Brian Epstein never saw the group repeat this success because he committed suicide in 1967.

Also in 1967 two of Gordy's 'star' groups joined forces, which in time led to two television spectaculars. Diana Ross and the Supremes shared the billing with The Temptations at Anaheim's Melody Theater for a week beginning 26 September for an advance of $95,000. This was the first time the groups had appeared together in Los Angeles; the trio last appeared there at the Coconut Grove during June while The Temptations played at The Whiskey earlier in the year. With the line-up of Eddie Kendricks, David Ruffin, Otis Williams, Melvin Franklin and Paul Williams, The Temptations opened the show with their repertoire including the current single *You're My Everything*. Their version of *Yesterday* prompted one journalist to write: 'It may strike some as over-staged as they cling to microphones, extend their arms heaven-ward

The Four Tops took London by storm in 1967 with their performances at the Royal Albert Hall. One reviewer declared: 'It was the fanatical exultation of the Nuremberg Rallies, the incredible enthusiasm of a World Cup football crowd.'

and perform stilted, with stiff-legged dance routines, but the song showed off the talents of David Ruffin, the dominant leader, and Melvin Franklin, the booming basso. The latter also showed off his flair for gospel music with his rendition of *Ole Man River* and *Swanee'*. After Diana Ross and the Supremes' performance it was, once again, clear from the reviews that Wilson and Birdsong were overlooked. Dressed in skintight silver gowns, they opened their act with a medley of standards, followed by a selection of their biggest singles to date. One reporter wrote: 'Miss Ross prowls the stage with her hand-mike, looking and sounding for all the world like a Thirties torch singer.' The highlight of their performance was *Reflections*, their new single, followed by a medley of show tunes and *West Side Story* classics. The encore was a Sam Cooke tribute. The evening was summed up as this: 'The Supremes aren't nearly as versatile or as turned-on as The Temptations, but the girls have more million sellers to their credit, and they also have Diana Ross who can compensate for anything!'

Reflections was Diana Ross and the Supremes' most unusual single to date. Wilson: 'This was when H-D-H decided to go more mechanical and do weird sounds and things like that, and I believe it came about because of The Beatles era, when writers, producers and artists were influenced by the group.' If that was unusual so was the group's next move. Berry Gordy was anxious to push them into television drama, despite none being coached in serious acting. In October 1967 they played their first major roles as three nuns in an episode of *Tarzan* titled *The Convert* in which Ron Ely played the hero. The trio flew to Las Estacas, Mexico, where the episode was filmed in Chernavaco. Ross played Sister Theresa from the Muganda village, while Birdsong was Sister Ann from Pittsburgh, leaving Mary Wilson to play Sister Martha from Washington. The plot was dreadful, the acting shaky. The sisters were returning to Muganda to build a hospital, but the village chief (played by James Earl Jones) objected to this, and a weak storyline ensured the nuns, assisted by Tarzan, won the day. The show was screened on NBC on 12 January 1968 and was the highest-rated in the series. This episode sealed Gordy's relationship with the television company and led to further collaborations. Diana Ross: 'We'd like to do more television but the problem is they take up at least two weeks work and in that time we could have done fourteen concerts. The money we'd lose isn't worth thinking about.' She turned down a role in the film *Sweet Charity* for this reason.

For the third single of 1968 the trio experimented with new writers (Pam Sawyer, R. Dean Taylor, Frank Wilson, Deke Richards) and controversial lyrics in *Love Child*. Wilson: 'During those days we were doing a lot of different television shows where the producers suffered a lot of censorship. One producer questioned the connotation of a love child and wasn't quite sure whether we should sing it on national television. But, of course, Motown was quite strong and they managed to get it through. I feel it was very pertinent for that time.' To promote the single the girls abandoned their glamorous image to don sweat-shirts and jeans, and replaced their carefully coiffured wigs with short Afros.

Meanwhile, Smokey Robinson and the Miracles were still enjoying their run of 1967 soul-searching ballads with *The Love I Saw In You Was Just A Mirage*, *More Love* and the Grammy-nominated *I Second That Emotion*. The latter song, re-recorded many times over the years, came about by accident as Robinson recalls: 'Songwriting can be a difficult craft but some tunes can happen by accident and that was how Al Cleveland and I wrote that hit. He and I were in a department store and during a conversation with one of the staff, Al meant to say "I second that motion". But the phrase came out wrong and he said "I second that emotion". As we walked out of the store we both realized what a great idea that would be for a song.'

Another good idea was *Jimmy Mack* introduced to the world by Martha Reeves and the Vandellas in 1967. This and the single's flip-side, *Third Finger, Left Hand*, remains one of their most famous releases. Reeves: 'Jimmy Mack was thrilling because originally I wondered just who he was, but he's just a name. The surprising thing was that I met about six Jimmy Macks after we recorded it. All the kids liked it and whenever I'd go anywhere, they'd sing it. And if we left it out of our shows they'd have a fit, so it has to be one of our biggest.' As they were paying tribute to an unidentified male, Stevie Wonder was thinking of his first girlfriend with *I Was Made To Love Her*. Wonder didn't dwell for long on his lost love because it was rumoured he was dating Rita Ross, sister of Diana. In fact, he was courting Rita (Syreeta) Wright. *I Was Made To Love Her* (follow-up to the mediocre *Travelin' Man* in February 1967) reached number two in the American charts, number five in Britain, and requests for tours flooded into the Motown offices. Wonder was no longer a boy, he was 17 years old, his voice had broken, and he was a master on the piano, organ, drums and harmonica. He was gradually realizing his full potential.

Motown talent was continuing to spread across the world and, following Europe, Japan was next to fall for the Motown Sound. Stevie Wonder and Martha Reeves and the Vandellas attracted capacity audiences of over three thousand people at each of the concert dates booked in Tokyo, Osaka and the US Airforce bases. Return dates were requested. The Supremes, had already toured the Far East in

1966, and included appearances at the Kaji-kawa and Yokosuka navel bases and the USS *Coral Sea*. They also visited various hospitals and rice fields, and dressed as geishas for publicity shots.

With the smoke from the Sixties Detroit race riots still stinging his nose, Berry Gordy moved his empire to new premises. After almost nine years of continual growth his company's nerve centre moved from West Grand Boulevard into Detroit's inner city, where he acquired a ten storey block known as the Donovan Building. His operation was run from here until the move to Los Angeles in 1972. Meanwhile in England, writer Tony Macauley was served with a writ from Gordy for infringing the copyright of the Four Tops' track *I'll Turn To Stone*. The sound-alike song recorded by The Foundations was *Build Me Up Buttercup* which sold in excess of one million copies.

The year of 1968 was also one of romance between Diana Ross and Berry Gordy. Rumours of the affair swept across America but nothing was confirmed. The story began one Friday night when a girl claiming to be Ross' secretary contacted a New York radio station saying she had an official announce-ment concerning the recent marriage of Ross and Gordy. As it was the weekend the radio station was unable to confirm the news but the bulletin was circulated nonetheless. Motown, trying to keep the affair a secret, issued an immediate denial although Gordy had publicly said on more than one occasion, 'Diana is easy to love'.

After the Los Angeles stage success of Diana Ross and the Supremes and The Temp-tations, it was decided to present them on record together. The first hit single, *I'm Gonna Make You Love Me* (US, Nov '68/UK, Jan '69), was taken from their debut album *Diana Ross and the Supremes Join The Temptations*. They subse-quently promoted the record on *The Ed Sulli-van Show* where the audience reaction was such that Timex Watches sponsored a televi-sion special, *TCB – Takin' Care Of Business* fea-turing the two groups. The one hour show was screened on NBC in December 1968, and was produced by Motown Productions Inc. in association with George Schlatter/Ed Friendly Productions. It was Gordy's first positive step into small screen entertainment. After its American screening, TCB was offered to the three British networks. It was rejected as unsuitable for a variety show, as the black per-formers would not attract viewers.

Diana Ross was the star of 'TCB' even though she shared the stage with seven other performers. She was portrayed as the enter-tainer, splendidly dressed in a collection of exclusive and expensive designs. The other artists were aggrieved with the Ross spotlight. David Ruffin: 'I asked some executives how the show would be billed. They said "Diana Ross and the Supremes with The Tempta-tions". I said "how in the hell can that happen

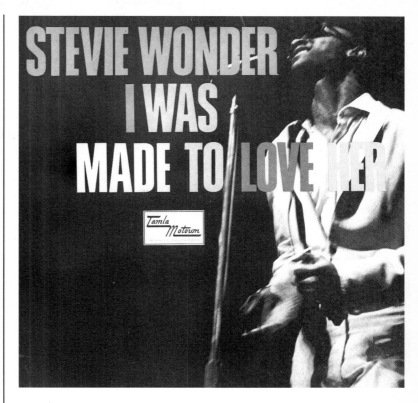

because The Temptations had taught The Supremes everything they knew." To protect my interests and that of the group I suggested that the special be billed "David Ruffin and Diana Ross and The Temptations and The Supremes." A month later I was fired.' The NBC programme and its soundtrack album TCB (US, Dec '68/UK, Jul '69) were a great suc-cess, so a second was immediately prepared titled G.I.T. (*Gettin' It All Together*) on Broadway. Once again an album of featured songs was released in America in November 1969. Again produced by George Schlatter, the two groups presented an hour's colourful and entertain-ing dedication to Broadway classics. Again Diana Ross was pushed into the star's spot-light as she revealed her mimicking expertise with impersonations of Ethel Merman, Julie Andrews and Barbra Streisand, thus fulfilling her fantasies of becoming Broadway's leading lady. Before the *On Broadway* album was re-leased a second studio album *Together* was rushed out in September 1969 (UK, Feb '70). The highlight of this release was the tear-jerking *Why (Must We Fall In Love)* single, which Motown/EMI lifted as a British single in March 1970.

Wilson and Birdsong were powerless to prevent their lead singer becoming exclusive both on and off stage. By now Diana usually travelled separately from them, was referred to as 'Miss Ross' by managers and record company personnel (Mary and Cindy con-tinued to be addressed by their Christian names), and had her own personal secretary. In time the latter was considered to be too much of an extravagance and Diana had to pack her own luggage! Ross was aware that

I Was Made To Love Her was dedicated to Stevie Wonder's first girlfriend. With the release of this hit single Stevie Wonder became much in demand.

Diana Ross and the Supremes and The Temptations joined forces for the television special TCB – Taking Care of Business *screened in 1968. The successful combination led to a further television special and a stream of albums.*

the public thought her aloof and bitchy. When she overheard the comment 'She's from the streets, and for all her glamour this girl will kick your ass all over town if you mess with her' Ross retaliated: 'I know some people want to attack me. It hurts but I deal with that. I never allow myself the luxury of falling apart. If things fail I'm hurt, but I'll scoop me up in my arms and minister to all my hurts and needs. I also have some very good, long-standing friends, people who listen and support when I need both and they accept that I'm a person with feelings.'

During the last week of December 1968 Motown monopolized the US top ten positions with singles from Marvin Gaye, The Temptations and Diana Ross and the Supremes as solo acts or combined, and

Stevie Wonder. The Miracles, too, remained big sellers during the year with *Baby, Baby Don't Cry* written by Robinson, Al Cleveland and Terry Johnson. Wonder also appeared on record as an instrumentalist using the name Eivets Rednow (a name chosen by the marketing division). It was intended to promote the musician as a new artist yet every self-respecting soul fan knew it was Stevie Wonder's name spelt backwards! *Alfie* (US, Aug '68) was lifted from the instrumental album which demonstrated Wonder's talent at playing harmonica, different keyboards, drums and percussion.

Diana, Mary and Cindy once again hit the headlines early in 1969 with *I'm Living in Shame*, the follow-up to *Love Child*, the story line of which dealt with co-habitating. Rumours of

Ross's departure from the group grew and sources speculated possible replacements as Tammi Terrell, Barbara McNair or Rita Wright. Mary Wilson told a British newspaper that the trio was destined to split up but that it would take 'a year or two before it happened'. She confirmed that Ross was taking on more solo spots but she would remain with the group for at least seven months a year. 'It's hard to get good things for three girls and this has a lot to do with Diane branching out on her own. I would love to get married and I think that Mr Gordy and Diane are maybe thinking about that very seriously because they've been going out for three years now.' Birdsong made her own headlines when, in December 1969, she was abducted at knife-point from a bedroom in her Hollywood home late at night. She was held for over an hour by a bare-footed kidnapper before escaping from his speeding car. The Supreme suffered knife slashes and multiple cuts and bruises but following a day's hospitalization she returned home. A caretaker in his late twenties was later arrested and charged.

Stevie Wonder toured Britain again in 1969 and was delighted at the enthusiastic response he received. The Flirtations, a black trio who enjoyed limited recording success, supported him, and received a fair amount of press coverage when member Earnestine Pearce was romantically linked with Wonder. Neither denied the relationship which was probably more of a publicity stunt than the real thing. The tour was an overwhelming triumph and while Wonder was recruiting new fans, Diana Ross and and the Supremes lost some during a performance in New Jersey's Latin Casino. Ross's two pet dogs, Tiffany (a Maltese puppy) and Lil' Bit (a Yorkshire terrier) ate rat poison in her dressing room. Tiffany died in the singer's arms, the other at the vetinerary surgeons. Ross tore up the contract with the Casino and left for Los Angeles with Berry Gordy. The sold-out, two week engagement, worth $55,000 a week, was cancelled. The Philadelphia Office of the American Guild of Variety Artists instructed the girls to reimburse the Casino, and Ross was reputed to have moaned: 'It was murder. I cried my eyelashes off'.

In the recording studio the Motown label boasted two new young singers, Paul Petersen and Chuck Jackson. Jackson was already a known recording artist and Petersen, a white entertainer, had been in the business since childhood. Before signing with Motown in 1967 Petersen had enjoyed a major US hit with My Dad but he failed to repeat that chart success. However, in record collectors' eyes, he did record two classic Motown tracks: the original version of Marvin Gaye's hit Chained and a straight pop song A Little Bit For Sandy, his only British release in 1968.

Despite a glowing association with Wand Records, Chuck Jackson failed to make money for Berry Gordy. Born in Winston Salem, North Carolina, Jackson grew up in South Carolina and Pittsburgh. He showed an interest in music as a child and when he was five made his first radio broadcast. For the next seven years the youngster co-starred in a radio music series. After two years in the Navy, he joined The Del Vikings to record Whispering Bells and Come Go With Me. During one of their performances he was offered a contract with Wand Records, where he released classy soul tunes like Any Day Now and I Don't Want To Cry and duets with the under-rated songstress, Maxine Brown. Once on the Motown label his quality releases included (You Can't Let The Boy Overpower) The Man In You in February 1968; Are You Lonely For Me and Honey Come Back a year later. Also in 1969 he moved to V.I.P. to record four singles – Baby I'll Get It, Let Somebody Love Me, Pet Names and the canned Who You Gonna Run To. Jackson's contract expired in 1972 and wasn't renewed.

Following the release of Jackson's first V.I.P. single, another respected vocalist, New Yorker, Bobby Taylor, was attempting solo success. As lead singer with The Vancouvers (Tommy Chong and Eddie Patterson, guitarists, Robbie King, organist, Wes Henderson, bass, Ted Lewis, drummer) on the Gordy label, he recorded one of the company's finest, yet most controversial tracks, Does You Mama Know About Me, about a white girl dating a black guy (later recorded by Diana Ross and the Supremes for the Love Child album). Unlike other unknown Motown artists Bobby Taylor and the Vancouvers were allowed to tour, and went to Britain as support act to Gladys Knight and the Pips in 1967. Taylor's 1970 V.I.P.

Established soul singer Chuck Jackson signed to Motown where he failed to repeat his previous success. It was a disillusioned artist who left the company in 1972.

debut *Blackmail* was his last until Gordy launched his new label, Mowest, where the singer released *Hey Lordy*.

The Temptations, meanwhile, were undergoing a major change with Dennis Edwards replacing David Ruffin. Otis Williams commented that although the group remained friendly with Ruffin 'we had to let him go because of his "head thing". He would be great on stage and then he'd go off on this ego trip. He'd sit in on our gigs when he'd already left and Dennis felt obliged to ask him up on stage with us.' Dennis Edwards debuted with the group in Los Angeles in 1968, but did not officially join the line-up until 1969. The Temptations lost none of their stage magic despite Ruffin telling the media he felt they were lost without him after his four years and six months stay. Nothing was heard from him for a year and the public presumed he had left the company but this was not so and in 1969 he released *My Whole World Ended (The Moment You Left Me)* (UK, Mar '69) on the Motown label which was an American hit. Ruffin also rehearsed unsuccessfully with a new band, The Fellas, and recorded with his brother Jimmy, to release the *I Am My Brother's Keeper* album which did little to excite record buyers. Two singles were lifted from this album – *Stand By Me* and *When My Love Hand Comes Down* – both were flops. To boost his solo

career, Berry Gordy hired the producer Van McCoy to work with David Ruffin. The collaboration worked perfectly, and the singer's *Who I Am* album (US, Oct '75/UK, Jan '76) was crammed with potential singles. The first, *Walk Away From Love*, was a huge seller and charted in Britain at number ten in 1976. Ruffin was delighted with the McCoy association, saying it was his idea. However Ruffin was unable to maintain this chart success and by 1978 he had left Motown.

By the close of 1969 Berry Gordy's artists had enjoyed or endured another interesting and varied year. Marvin Gaye's million seller *I Heard It Through The Grapevine* encouraged his fellow acts to try harder, and Tammi Terrell's debut album, *Irresistible*, proved to the public she possessed solo potential that begged to be promoted. Jr Walker, Edwin Starr and Marv Johnson toured Britain, where Motown/EMI once again attempted to register Brenda Hollway in the charts by re-issuing her *Just look What You've Done*. A change of musical direction with the white group The Honest Men's *Cherie* drove punters to distraction with its heavy white/pop influence, while Norman Whitfield's computerized psychedelic offerings recorded by The Temptations left their fans wondering when the ballads would return. One of their more controversial songs was *Message From A Black Man* on the *Puzzle*

Vocalist Bobby Taylor recorded with the Vancouvers and as a soloist. The group's finest recording was the controversial Does Your Mama Know About Me.

People album (US, Sep '69/UK, , Feb '70) which, Otis Williams, explained was an experiment: 'We wanted to try something really different which was good. We cut another track, War, which is even more controversial. We had to change our style after Dennis joined because we didn't want David Ruffin part two. We plan to do a couple more singles in the same bag and then move on to something different.' The Beatles' song Hey Jude was also a Puzzle People track. (Diana Ross and the Supremes' version was featured on their Cream Of The Crop (US, Nov '69/UK, Jan '70) album.) Williams: 'The Beatles song came on the radio and I was so knocked out that I knew we had to record it. But at first only Melvin and I liked it. I was a little mad because the end part of the song was exactly the same tune as we used to sing as kids when we were standing on street corners. Then The Beatles came along and made a fortune out of it. That's what I call good business.'

Although Martha Reeves and the Vandellas had suffered the upheavel of Sandra Tilley replacing the sacked Rosalind Ashford in 1968 the group continued their hit run. However, by 1969 the strain began to tell on Reeves, who suffered the first of several nervous breakdowns. During her lengthy illness she was unsure how they would recapture their audiences, but her concern was unwarranted. When they played their comeback show at Detroit's 20 Grand Club their fans rioted. Reeves: 'That first night I didn't have butterflies in my stomach it was more like buffalos. I get nervous as it is when I'm about

to perform but it was rough starting over again. My throat was rough and scratchy although the audience didn't notice.'

The conflict between Martha Reeves and Diana Ross continued. As time passed, Reeves said, it became apparent to all that she stood in Diana Ross's shadow and received inferior treatment. The conflict between the two lead singers was highlighted and exaggerated by the media when Reeves would honestly speak about the Vandellas being given mediocre material and second-hand gowns to wear on stage, or that Diana would ignore her when they walked down the same office corridor. Unlike Ross, Reeves employed her Vandellas and to ensure continued employment, they needed regular chart material. As The Supremes stepped from gold to platinum status, the Vandellas remained on the border of silver and gold, yet their following remained loyal. Despite Reeves' reservations regarding her songs, fans flocked to buy Love Bug Leave My Heart Alone, the Southern drawled, Honey Chile (US, '67/UK, '67 and '68); I Promise To Wait My Love, a low-keyed Vietnam cash-in, and I Can't Dance To That Music You're Playing (US, UK '68). The latter release annoyed Reeves because it was sexist, and in the hope it would be canned she only recorded half the song. The plan backfired as Syreeta finished it and the result was released without Reeves' approval under Martha Reeves and the Vandellas. Also, in a desperate attempt to keep her beloved Vandellas on top, Reeves acquired tapes of songs destined for The Supremes and/or Diana Ross,

The Temptations with Dennis Edwards (left) as a member, pictured during their 'Puzzle People' era. Their costumes hardly reflect the weird, psychedelic sound provided by Norman Whitfield.

After several illnesses Martha Reeves (centre) was unsure how she and the Vandellas would be accepted when they returned to stage work. She need not have worried, her fans were waiting with open arms.

As Motown expanded, Berry Gordy's name was linked to the Mafia. Levi Stubbs commented: 'Whenever anybody attains the degree of success that Berry has you will always find adverse comments by people who simply don't know.'

Like most growing American businesses, Motown was linked to the Mafia in the Sixties. IT (*International Times*) reported that the New York magazine *Rock* had established the connection from FBI files. Motown's initial involvement with the Mafia, it is claimed, began in the mid-Sixties when acts like The Supremes appeared in San Juan and Caribbean venues. These performances coincided with Berry Gordy's gambling which the magazine states included losses of $75,000 nightly in the Puerto Rican casinos controlled by the Mafia. It claimed that the Mafia gained their first real foothold in the company when their man, Michael Roshkind, was brought into Motown as a company executive by Motown lawyer George Schiffer.

Subsequent investigations by suspicious employees showed that Roshkind's credentials were totally false, and Schiffer was the first of many dismissals of long-time employees. Reports later indicated that Roshkind had been empowered to make decisions in Gordy's name, and that Berry was totally unaware of most of them! With the Mafia involvement Motown expanded from a family run company into a recording corporation, and Gordy moved from Detroit to live in Beverly Hills. The FBI and the Detroit Police Department began investigating the Motown/ Mafia situation, but without willing witnesses making indictments against Berry Gordy and/or the Mafia, both departments were powerless to act.

The Four Tops' lead singer, Levi Stubbs, refuted any Mafia connection by saying 'whenever anybody attains the degree of success that Berry has you will always find adverse comments by people who simply don't know. If it makes good copy they'll write it. Mind you, when they print it, if you look closely, they're always careful not to make an accusation. He's an extremely rich man and he doesn't have to do anything like that.'

and recorded them with her own group. The results can be heard on the magnificent *Black Magic*, promoted as their last album, even though it mostly featured Martha and session singers. Released in 1972, it coincided with Reeves' release from Motown.

END OF AN ERA

'The kids didn't have anything to do except go to school and come home. So I had them learn to sing or play some kind of instrument and they worked for four hours every day.'
Joe Jackson

'Motown gave Detroit more prestige and now it's just the motor city, whereas before it was the recording capital of the world.'
Bobby Moore, The Miracles

By the mid-Sixties Motown had grown beyond all expectation and Gordy was richer than even he could have ever anticipated. Between 1968 and 1970 Gordy, as sole shareholder of Motown, made over five million dollars in dividends paid out by the company. Author, Peter Benjaminson, stated: 'Motown declared a $3,100 per share dividend in 1968, a $2,020 dividend in 1969 and a $49 dividend in 1970. Berry Gordy pocketed more than $5 million. The dividends were paid out in 1967-69; the years of 1969 and 1970 were years of cash shortage at Motown. In 1972 and 1974 Gordy increased the number of outstanding Motown shares by 3,955. He gave 236 shares, or approximately $1 million worth, to his sister Esther Edwards, and 235 to Smokey Robinson – both vice-presidents. This distribution of 471 shares left Gordy owning 4,484 of the 4,955 shares of his privately held company. Since Motown was organized under the International Revenue Code as a Sub Chapter S company, Motown's money is Berry Gordy's money. If the company spends money it comes out of his pocket and vice versa.' It also appears that Diana Ross and the Supremes held Motown shares at one point during their career and Gordy invested money for them which in 1960 was worth in the region of $15,000 in stock. Some of that investment was lost when the market fell. The group's money was so tied up that Mary Wilson complained that even in 1974 she still had to acquire Gordy's signature on a cheque before she could buy anything.

Not only did the recording side of Motown generate vast sums of money, but also the management company, Grapevine Advertising, and Jobete, the in-house publishing arm. His writers signed a fee-paying deal whereby Jobete secured rights to all their compositions. With few exceptions, all the early tunes (including all H-D-H's work) are Jobete owned. In later years, when artists wrote their own material, they were encouraged to deal with Jobete, but many opted to open their own companies instead. At one time artists were obliged to include Jobete songs when recording an album to generate further royalties for Gordy. A good example of re-recording is Stevie Wonder's *For Once In My Life* which has been covered more than two hundred times, thus earning enormous royalties for Jobete.

In the late Sixties Gordy purchased one of several luxurious properties for himself. Benjaminson wrote of one in particular: '(It was a) mansion on Detroit's Boston Boulevard. This three storey house, unprepossessing from the street had cost a million dollars to build in 1967. It had a marbled floor, marbled-columned ballroom, a gym, an olympic-sized swimming pool, a luxurious billiard room and two-lane bowling alley, a private theatre linked to the main house by tunnels and an entire authentic pub imported intact from England. Every room in the house was decorated with gold leaf, frescoed ceilings and elaborate chandeliers. Gordy hung oil paintings of his friends and family in the entrance hall.' Despite the trappings of success and operating a multi-million dollar concern, Gordy was reported to be insecure, frightened about what he had and unsure that he could control it. There was no way he could have been prepared for the fortune he amassed which made him the wealthiest black man in America. He was still relatively uneducated on certain levels, and wasn't a good reader, yet he was one of the shrewdest businessmen in the recording industry. It is reported that Gordy fashioned himself on Napoleon, so his sister Esther commissioned a portrait of her brother dressed in the French General's uniform.

During 1970 Motown celebrated its tenth anniversary and introduced to the world its new signing, the Jackson 5. This year also saw Diana Ross leaving The Supremes, Stevie Wonder getting married, the death of Tammi Terrell, the company's move from Detroit to Los Angeles and the closing of the grooming department. If the Sixties were Motown's profitable years, the Seventies would be remembered for expansion, with few of the original acts remaining.

After the release of *Someday We'll Be Together* (late 1969) months of speculation became reality when Diana Ross left the Supremes and embarked on a solo career. As it was intended to keep The Supremes as working artists, her replacement, Jean Terrell (no relation to Tammi, who had signed as a solo artist in June 1969), had already been rehearsed and groomed. *Someday We'll Be Together* was originally recorded by Johnny Bristol (who produced The Supremes' version) with Jackey Beavers. Neither Mary Wilson nor Cindy Birdsong were featured on the Supremes' version although Bristol was. He commented: 'Berry, Diana and myself worked on it. We had been working for hours and Diana was getting tired and a little irritable so I suggested that maybe if we went into another booth and sang with her . . . two people singing back and forth . . . it could take her mind off her tiredness. At least long enough to finish the song. So we did just that and my voice is heard on the final cut because Berry liked it so much.' The single was a world hit, reaching number one in the US and number thirteen in Britain. Wilson: 'The writing was on the wall from the time we became Diana Ross and the Supremes. Jean was rehearsing with us for several months before the news got out. I liked Jean and always did, although she was originally chosen by Berry Gordy.' Wilson was first officially told of the lead singer's pending departure in 1968 when film and television offers flooded Motown's offices for Ross. Motown went to great lengths to deny the move to television and when it was leaked that Diana was working on a solo television show, the press refused to accept the company's protestations. In this case, they were correct for the spectacular *Diana!* was screened within two years.

Diana, Mary and Cindy performed their last concert together at The Frontier Hotel, Las Vegas, on 14 January 1970. The highly-charged emotional performance was recorded and re-

Diana Ross and the Supremes are pictured here following their final emotional performance in Las Vegas during January 1970. Ross's replacement, Jean Terrell, was introduced on stage.

leased as a double album *Farewell* (US, Apr '70/UK, Aug '70). During the show Jean Terrell was introduced to the star-studded audience that included most of Motown's top executives and artists. 'I know I was to blame for the break-up,' Ross told reporters. 'Something had to change. We had stopped communicating and things were different. I had to turn down a lot of opportunities because I didn't want to leave Mary and Cindy with nothing to do. It was a difficult decision to make in some ways, easy in other ways.' Everyone spoke to the media at this time, even Gordy himself: 'Diana's success is almost built-in. She's really not taking a big chance because people are buying her like a stock market. She's up now because everything she's done has been a total success. If she comes out and she's not a smash on the first solo engagement, she'll change things and be a smash.' When Ross began performing she was reputed to be earning between $30,000 and $70,000 a week.

The end of this musical era stunned the public. The reaction of their fans was mixed, some supporting Diana Ross and some The Supremes. Although Jean Terrell replaced Ross, it was left to Mary Wilson to keep The Supremes together. Her first job was to survive the transition period and maintain past popularity without Berry Gordy's help. She accepted her role graciously and diplomatically, with a renewed determination. Jean Terrell did not possess the same extrovert personalities as Wilson and Birdsong therefore she came across as a rather solemn singer who rarely contributed to a press interview. On stage, though, she was a natural performer. Her brother Ernie was a well-known boxer, and she was the youngest in a family of two sisters and seven brothers. They moved to Chicago when she was five, where she was raised in the westside ghetto of Lawndale. Jean's career began when she joined Ernie Terrell's Heavyweights with Vera Ward and K.C. Jones. They played the local club circuit and while performing at the Fountainbleau Hotel in Miami during 1968, Berry Gordy saw Jean perform. She was invited to audition for him but failed. A year later Gordy asked her to replace Diana Ross. Terrell: 'I started singing the day I arrived and that's when I realized what a big position I had stepped into. I knew people would compare me with Diana but I felt I was enough of an individualist to break through. It was tough because I hadn't done much recording. We went straight into the studios and it was difficult feeling part of a team. Mind you, we got on famously as people.' As Ross taught her the group's dance routines, Terrell became anxious about singing the old material because audiences would expect her to sound like Ross. This was to be overcome in time when the new group established its own identity. Meantime, it was inevitable that Ross and The 'new' Supremes would compete against each other, yet,

surprisingly, it was the group who initially succeeded in chart status.

With the three singers dominating Motown's press coverage, other company activities were overlooked, including Berry Gordy buying British. Late in 1969 he took an unprecedented step by signing the white songstress Kiki Dee, an established semi-successful entertainer. She gained recognition as one of Dusty Springfield's session singers and for her solo work for Fontana Records. In an interview in 1970 Dee explained how she signed to Motown: 'I was approached by the company and went over there for eight days to look around. I met the producers, writers and generally got to know what was going on. I signed the contract the day I left, and then returned in the October for two months recording. They taught me about my voice and how to use it. In fact I learnt so much in such a short time I couldn't believe it.' It was planned for her to duet with Marvin Gaye but, for some reason, the project was shelved. During her American stay Dee recorded the *Great Expectations* (US, Jul '70/UK, Aug '70) for the Tamla label and performed 'so that the people who were working with me would have some idea of what I was capable of and to give them a chance to decide what material would suit me best. The idea wasn't for the producers to turn me into a soul singer but rather to record me on material to which I'm most suited.' The album wasn't the hit it should have been, despite the catchy, critically-acclaimed first single, *The Day Will Come Between Sunday And Monday* (US, Jun '70/UK, May '70). After Motown, Dee drifted in and out of the British charts, *Amoureuse* and *I Got The Music In Me* being the most successful, until she enjoyed a US and UK number one single with Elton John in July 1976 titled *Don't Go Breaking My Heart*.

To start Motown's tenth anniversary celebrations, in January 1970, The Temptations performed at London's Talk Of The Town for two weeks and to coincide *I Can't Get Next To You* (taken from their *Cloud Nine* album) was released. Eddie Kendricks missed the opening night; the public excuse was illness. This was not true. Kendricks refused to leave America because he intended to leave the group. However, he relented and arrived in time for the second performance, although within a year he left the group to pursue a solo career. As with all opening nights for Motown acts, the audience was star-packed. The act, shortened by Kendricks' absence, was pop-slanted to appeal to all age groups.

On 27 January 1970 the quintet met Dr Michael Ramsey at Lambeth Palace, London, when they discussed American and British race relations before receiving the Archbishop's blessing. The Temptations told of the work they were doing with various Detroit youth groups, the problems of integration and housing and the effect Dr Martin Luther King's death had on Americans. Although they performed as a group, they told the Arch-

Motown took an unprecedented step by signing UK's talented singer Kiki Dee (pictured here during 1981). She stayed long enough to record the superb Great Expectations *album.*

bishop they acted as individuals in working towards the cause of brotherhood. For example, they were active contributors to the Paul Williams Scholarship, the Chadsey High School Afro-American Club and the Don Bosco Home For Boys. Whatever the reason for this unlikely meeting, the press loved the story.

As part of the tenth anniversary celebrations, Motown/EMI released twelve albums. The highlight was *The Motown Story*, an American five-album boxed set, which featured artist narration between some of the company's best known songs. A limited edition of fifteen thousand was pressed but further public demand required a re-pressing. The British albums fell under the campaign banner 'Gettin' It All Together' between 23 January and 31 March 1970. Special discounts were offered to record shops stocking a certain number of the releases, supported by huge display shop units and extensive press advertising. The Temptations' *Puzzle People*, Diana Ross and the Supremes' last studio album *Cream Of The Crop*, Edwin Starr and Blinky's *Just We Two*, *Motown Chartbusters Volume 3* and the Four Tops' *Soul Spin* were among the featured albums. May 1970 was then declared 'Motown Month' in Britain with imminent tours by Jimmy Ruffin, Marv Johnson, the Four Tops and Martha Reeves and The Vandellas. It was hoped the Jackson 5 would also tour, but they presented problems. The brothers needed special dispensation to enable them to perform on stage and television as English regulations governing television performances of minors were complicated. Basically they restricted the amount of rehearsal time to which a child under 12 could be subjected and anyone under 12 could not appear after eight in the evening. As Michael Jackson was only 10 that ruled out live evening shows. Stage work was assessed on a similar basis and special permission was required for children under 12, therefore it would be some time before the brothers graced the British stage.

Motown's anniversay celebrations were marred by the tragedy of Tammi Terrell's death on 16 March. The 24-year-old singer lost her two-year battle against a brain tumour, despite seven attempts by surgeons to eradicate it. Terrell died at 8.55 pm in Philadelphia's Graduate Hospital. Thousands of rain-soaked mourners joined fellow performers four nights later in a tearful farewell at the Jane Memorial Methodist Church. The Reverend Henry Nichols delivered the final eulogy in praise of the courageous young woman whose death brought a tragic end to a bright and promising career. The choir sang Terrell's favourite hymn, How Great Thou Art, which she

Marvin Gaye's singing partner, 24-year-old Tammi Terrell, died during March 1970. Fans and fellow artists mourned her loss.

once sang with them. Marvin Gaye delivered an emotional dedication to his singing partner, telling of her courage during her prolonged illness and her constant optimism of one day recovering to sing again. Outside the church an estimated three thousand people stood in the pouring rain. Terrell once said of her career: 'I just wouldn't be happy doing anything else. I've lived and loved this business too long not to be part of it.'

Another shadow on the anniversary was also cast in March. The Four Tops, now known as Motown's Ambassadors, embarked on a week of British television dates, and the double topside single I Can't Help Myself/Baby I Need Your Loving was released. British fans were disappointed when public performances weren't included in their schedule but a Motown/EMI spokesman explained: 'It's a problem of getting venues large enough to warrant them coming. They can earn so much more in America. This is always a problem when artists reach the kind of status the Tops have achieved.' The group arrived in London following their appearance at the Grand Gala Du Disque in Holland. In the middle of a press conference at the Mayfair Hotel, Berkeley Square, Scotland Yard drug squad detectives burst into the meeting and arrested Levi Stubbs, lead singer, for possession of cocaine and twelve rounds of ammunition. Stubbs was taken to London's West End Central police station where he was charged and released on £1,000 bail: £500 on his own recognisance and a surety of £500 from Ralph Garcia, the group's manager. The arrest was especially unfortunate as their visit was also to publicize the International Union For Harmony, a movement to promote peace and understanding between people all over the world. In the wake of Stubbs' arrest it was imperative for the group to receive good media exposure, so in an attempt to eclipse the drug incident, the group was pictured visiting the Great Ormond Street Children's Hospital where they entertained the patients.

Why the Four Tops were singled out for a police search remains to be answered, although it is believed it happened after a tip-off. It was also thought the British authorities wanted to make an example of them in the knowledge that the action taken would receive extensive publicity which in turn, the police hoped, would discourage further drug usage. Dope and music had regularly been in the press since the late Sixties when The Beatles openly admitted that their Sgt. Peppers Lonely Hearts Club Band album had been recorded while under the influence of LSD. Other contemporary singers arrested and fined for possession of drugs included Jimi Hendrix and most members of the Rolling Stones. However, Levi Stubbs was acquitted by a jury at the Inner London Sessions for possessing the drug and given a small fine for having the rounds of ammunition in his care. Stubbs explained that in America he often carried a gun for self-protection and he forgot the ammunition was still on his person as the group hurriedly left the United States to fulfil the Dutch commitment.

While the Four Tops' I Can't Help Myself was re-issued in the UK in March 1970 the rest of Europe had Barbara's Boy taken from the Soul Spin album. Prior to their visit to London, the Four Tops had apparently lapsed into semi-retirement for an unexplained rehabilitation process for one of its members, although they denied this to NME: 'The years of touring has taken their toll on us and we just had to get off the road. We were off almost nine months and we've only just got started again. The break also mellowed us professionally and that's made us change our style a little more into the ballad thing.' When the quartet returned to Britain in May 1970 for a full length tour one of those ballads It's All In The Game was issued. Their new 1970 album Still Waters Run Deep, produced by Frank Wilson, was considered to be their best ever. It was a beautifully conceived release dealing with love and peace; the songs were melodic, the lyrics thoughtful, and the gliding orchestra blended delightfully with the mellow voices of the group.

Meantime, Motown staff were grooming five young boys who would monopolize the Seventies in the same way as The Beatles had dominated the Sixties. Never before in the history of Gordy's company would an act make such a huge impact on the world. The Jackson 5 phenomenon was instigated by an ingenious publicity campaign which ensured the boys from Gary, Indiana, gained maximum exposure. Motown told the media that Diana Ross discovered the group and had adopted its members as her protégés. The Jackson brothers – Michael Joe (29 August 1958), Marlon David (12 March 1957), Jermaine Lajuane (11 December 1954), Toriano 'Tito' Adarryll (15 October 1953), and Sigmund 'Jackie' Esco (4 May 1951) – were introduced to three hundred and fifty journalists at a gala party held at The Daisy, one of the 'in' clubs in Beverly Hills, California. Of her so-called discovery Ross glowed: 'I'm very happy to have been able to give a nationally well-deserving group an opportunity to perform because that's how we, The Supremes, got our big chance. Had it not been for Berry Gordy searching for talent in our black community we wouldn't have been discovered.' The ex-Supreme also gave the boys their national television debut on 18 October when she hosted the Hollywood Palace Show; prior to this they had supported The Supremes at The Forum, Los Angeles. Her name was even featured on the group's first album Diana Ross Presents The Jackson 5. The truth didn't emerge that this was all part of a sophisticated marketing campaign until much later in their career when Michael Jackson retorted that if anyone discovered them it was their parents: 'We were in Chicago at a theatre called The Regal, which was a kind of audition place for Motown, and Motown

decided to use Diana Ross's name to introduce us to the public. But she never discovered us. We were an established professional act long before we ever signed to Motown.' However, prior to this performance, both Gladys Knight and Bobby Taylor had tried in vain to persuade Gordy to sign the Jackson brothers.

The Jackson 5's debut single I Want You Back (US, Oct '69/UK, Jan '70) (originally the Freddie Perren song I Want To Be Free) was released on the Motown label mid-way through this flurry of publicity, and it was the first of a succession of million selling singles and albums. Together with the five performing Jacksons, younger brother Randy, sisters Maureen, Latoya, Janet, and their parents would occasionally play on stage.

The children's interest in music came from their father, Joe. In the Fifties he was a guitarist with The Falcons, a Chicago-based blues band. Joe Jackson: 'I was married very young and while my wife was having our nine kids I still wanted to see out my ambition to be a musician. I joined The Falcons and used to rehearse in the kitchen while the kids were crawling around the floor. I could even tell when they liked something they heard. But it takes a lot of money and time to get any group off the ground and I realized that my time was going to have to go one way or another. So I

The young Jackson 5 were destined to monopolize the Seventies in the same way as The Beatles dominated the Sixties.

decided to transfer my interest in music to my family, not that they needed much encouragement. In Gary with all the steel mills the kids didn't have anything to do except go to school and come home. So I had them learn to sing or play some kind of instrument and they worked for four hours every day. My goal was to get them on stage where they could perform with other amateurs at talent shows. It took about a year until I felt they were good enough,' They based their act on The Miracles and The Temptations, from whom they pinched stage routines and songs. Eight-year-old Michael was the lead singer, leaving his brothers to play the instruments and provide backing vocals.

The group's first paying show was at Mr Lucky's where they earned five dollars collected from punters pitching coins on the floor. They began winning talent shows for which their mother designed and made their stage suits, then progressed to the club circuit which they played during the school holidays. The youngsters' local singing reputation spread sufficiently for them to be booked to tour with Gladys Knight and the Pips, and The Temptations. Their first single was I'm A Big Boy Now produced by Gordon Keith in 1968 for Steeltown Records. It was a six month deal and while scouting around for a better, long-term contract, Joe Jackson kept Motown's reputation in mind. When Diana Ross was invited by Gary's mayor, Richard Hatcher, to visit the city, she attended a Jackson 5 concert. She liked what she saw and Motown's publicity hype took over. Before recording, the brothers were groomed for stardom by Suzanne de Passe, her cousin Tony Jones and Berry Gordy, who left nothing to chance. He formed and worked with what he called 'The Corporation' comprising at any one time, Freddie Perren, Fonzie Mizell and Deke Richards, for two reasons. Firstly, he knew the importance and success of a writing/producing team (ie: H-D-H) and secondly he wanted to avoid one writer/producer taking credit for the Jackson 5's rise to fame. Gordy desperately needed the young brothers to succeed because since the Sixties with The Temptations, the Four Tops and The Supremes, Motown had been unable to find a unit to match that success. The Jackson 5 lived up to all expectations, as their young, blue-eyed soul/pop sound lasted for several years, competing against The Osmonds during 1972. On stage, the brothers held their audiences spellbound with their vividly coloured suits, their rhythmic, pulsating music and tight dance routines.

I Want You Back appeared in most international charts, shot to the top of the American charts and reached number two in Britain. ABC (US, Feb '70/UK, May '70) and The Love You Save (US, May '70/UK, Jul '70) followed. With fame and fan hysteria came fortune and the Jackson family became rich enough to move into Diana Ross and Berry

Gordy's neighborhood in Los Angeles. The Jackson's family mansion nicknamed Fort Knox, was a vast twelve-roomed building situated on several acres of land on the San Fernando valley, guarded by heavy electric gates, close circuit television and a selection of guard dogs. Although the mansion was their home, it was their prison too. Michael Jackson once remarked: 'We don't go out much. All we need is right there.' They had a volley ball/basket ball court, large swimming pool, grass court for tennis or badminton, a recreation room housing a pool table and a bubblegum machine always well stocked. A fully equipped recording studio and other rooms held massive collections of records and several types of stereo equipment. The family possessed several cars – Cadillacs, Mercedes, Pantras, etc., and a custom-built road sign reading 'Jackson 5 Street' was nailed to a tree-trunk just inside the front gate.

As the Jackson 5's phenomena flourished, The 'new" Supremes released their debut single Up The Ladder To The Roof (US, Feb '70/UK, Apr '70) with Jean Terrell on lead. Mary Wilson: 'We had a job coming up with a record that would be suitable and live up to our standards, and yet be different. Up The Ladder To The Roof was different enough and yet it was still The Supremes.' It was also a message of racial harmony as was Diana Ross's first, the anti-drug track Reach Out And Touch (Somebody's Hand) (US, Apr '70/UK, Jun '70).

In July 1970 Stevie Wonder was the third Motown act to perform at the Talk Of The Town and Syreeta joined him as a member of his backing vocalists, Wonderlove. It was during this visit that he became aware of public curiosity about his blindness: 'I don't want people to come and see me or buy my records because I'm blind. I want people to dig me for what I've got to offer, for the way I sing and play. If they don't then that's cool but I don't want to be treated differently from any other singer.' This curiosity was fired when critics wrote that he only played various instruments on stage to prove he had overcome his handicap. Wonder was furious: 'If I knew I couldn't play well I wouldn't do it at all. No-one would question the motives if any other performer did the same things on stage. People would credit that as versatility. It's not that I don't like criticism, but I like constructive criticism.' He was also openly condemned for his choice of repertoire which many felt was 'whitewashed' as the songs he sang were all 'commercial' and lacked the gutsy 'black roots' sound. Again he reacted aggressively: 'I don't want to be confined to one bag. People had said My Cherie Amour wasn't really me because it was different from what they expected. That was written in 1966 and was what I was into then, so I don't know how people can say it's not me. However, my new single Signed, Sealed, Delivered I'm Yours is back in the funky groove.'

Of Motown itself, Wonder told Melody Maker

that the small, homely company had grown into a corporation: 'There are more people involved and one has less time to be friends with everyone. In a business like the recording business you can't always have a family relationship with everyone, although you would love to. You have people involved who are just interested in doing their job, making money and getting home.' The singer also recalled Benny Benjamin, Motown drummer extraordinaire, as the two were close friends up to the drummer's death: 'Benny's history goes back a long way in the Motown story. In the beginning there was no Musicians Union as there is today and all the musicians were helping to build something. Nobody expected anything to come out of Detroit – it was a car city. Then all the musicians who lived there began to combine and a totally different approach to music was born. As the idea grew, singers became known and these backing musicians worked hard on their records. They devised backings and Benny was one who devised many beats for a lot of hit singles. Nobody could play like him; nobody had his beat. It gives me a great feeling of loneliness as he has done so much without recognition.'

In its anniversary year, Motown's licensing agreement with EMI Records was successfully re-negotiated for a further three years. EMI was delighted as black/soul music was making healthy inroads on the British charts. Motown led the way, with Stax and Atlantic following. There was a continual demand for well-constructed R&B records and a large market for re-issued material. Brian Hopkins, Motown's product manager, revealed: 'We've found by experience that there is always a big sale for pre-1965 singles and we carefully assess the demand from the letters we receive, together with enquiries from record stores and fan clubs. If a record can sell fifty thousand copies then there is a legitimate reason for its release.' However, a blatant lack of radio needle time still continued, preventing many soul singles from selling sufficient copies to chart. Subsequently, meagre record sales affected the demand for touring artists, as explained by one promoter: 'Only the very big American artists are capable of drawing the crowds, otherwise it's not worthwhile even bothering to present them. Ben E. King, Marv Johnson and Jimmy Ruffin are still capable of doing fantastic business, but then they are good artists. New stars are badly needed.'

Probably the most unexpected Motown hit of 1970 was Smokey Robinson and the Miracles' first British number one *Tears Of A Clown* in August. Once *Tears Of A Clown* reached the top in the UK it was released in America with equal success. An album bearing the single's title naturally followed, and was the

The 'new' Supremes with Jean Terrell as lead (right) debuted in 1970 with Up The Ladder To The Roof. It was a world-wide hit, proving that fans had accepted Terrell.

re-titled American release *Pocket Full Of Miracles*. As well as the inclusion of the title track, the British album featured the re-issue of the number one follow-up. (*Come Round Here*) I'm *The One You Need*, which peaked at number thirteen early in 1971. Smokey Robinson: 'I'm really happy with the success but I can't make out what happened because all the singles we've been having success with are from old albums. It's got me thinking that I should re-service all our old stuff and do nothing new. Seriously though, it's given me a good idea of what people want from us, and the success has certainly shown me what direction we need to take because until now I wasn't sure what to do.' *Tears Of A Clown* was the biggest single in the group's career, selling in excess of 1,800,000 in America alone. Robinson's newly-penned, deliberate soundalike I *Don't Blame You At All* was the American follow-up.

In America, the combination of the Four Tops and The Supremes looked set to repeat the prior success of The Temptations with Ross, Wilson and Birdsong. The first album was the aptly titled *The Magnificent Seven* (US, Sep '70/UK, May '71) from which *River Deep*

Mountain High was released. By 1971 *The Return Of The Magnificent Seven* (with the groups dressed as cowboys and girls on the record sleeve – naturally!) and *Dynamite* had been released. A pot-pourri of writers and producers (including Ashford and Simpson, Clay McMurray, Harvey Fuqua and Johnny Bristol) worked on inferior repertoire for these albums. *The Magnificent Seven* album was by far the best.

As her *Ain't No Mountain High Enough* raced to the top of the American charts in 1970, Diana Ross was actively engaged in rehearsals for her debut concert in the September. Berry Gordy told the *Los Angeles Times* that when an artist made a solo debut in Las Vegas it was essential to have a full house to demonstrate drawing power. For his star's debut he tore $20 bills in half and gave them to people around town promising to give them the other half when they came to the show. The stunt helped fill the room, but caused chaos in the lobby as he and others tried frantically to match up the halves. In desperation he gave the people new $20 bills.

Needless to say, everyone was curious to see what Diana Ross could do alone. With the words 'Good evening ladies and gentlemen, welcome to the lets-see-if-Diana-Ross-can-make-it-alone-show' she opened her three week season at the Waldorf Astoria, New York. On the opening night she worked her way through $60,000 worth of dazzling costumes, various comedy routines and twenty songs. Backed by twenty-five of America's top musicians, support routines from two dancers who were on stage throughout the act, and a three-piece female backing group, The Black-berries (formerly The Andantes), Ross took the theatre by storm. One of the show's high spots featured memories of The Supremes, where Ross sang a medley of their hits while pictures of the group were screened at the back of the stage. Her outrageously expensive wardrobe included eight costume changes on stage ranging from an elegant lady to a 10-year-old child. Meantime, The 'new' Supremes' debuted at the Frontier Hotel, Las Vegas, the venue of Diana Ross and the Supreme's final performance in January 1970.

The first Ross album, *Diana Ross* released in May 1970 (UK, Oct '70) was a big seller. The record's sleeve showed the singer crouched against a sackcloth backdrop dressed as a child: a far cry from the sophisticated woman on stage. Written and produced by Ashford and Simpson, Ross used the latter's demos to [si]ng an album containing both original and [c]over songs. It was a credit to both artist and [c]onceivers. Also in May (UK, Aug '70) The 'new' Supremes debuted with a mediocre *Right On* album credited to Paul Riser, Frank Wilson, Hank Cosby and Jerry Long among others.

One of the highlights of 1970 was Stevie Wonder's marriage to Syreeta on 14 September after a four-month engagement. The cere-mony was held up for forty minutes as the bri-degroom battled with a nose bleed brought on by his nervousness. He was promptly rushed through the gathering crowds and into the side door of Detroit's Burnette Baptist Church where his bride was waiting. Their res-pective parents had arrived earlier for the can-dle lighting that signified the start of the cere-mony officiated by the Reverend Caldwell. Motown employees attended with friends and family: Berry Gordy flew in from Los Angeles joining his parents and his brother, Fuller, and sisters, Gwendolyn and Esther. After the ceremony the couple held a gala reception at Detroit's Mauna Loa Restaurant for the three hundred guests, before honeymooning in Bermuda. Syreeta: 'I used to get very jealous of all the girls constantly hanging around Steve and of the fuss they made of him. But now their attention makes me proud he's mine. I know what a beautiful person he is so I can understand why they admire him.' Won-der's wife also stressed that his blindness was a subject they never discussed, nor did he treat it as a handicap: 'He doesn't like being babied and he likes people to forget he's blind and treat him as any other human being.

When people offer to lead him or help him to a seat he understands their motive, but appreciates doing it himself. He'll show me his grievances but he never shows it if he's angry or depressed in public.' After the honeymoon the couple worked on Wonder's last album, due under his 1960 contract. Titled *Where I'm Coming From* it was a poor seller yet was his first album produced without Motown's creative control.

Motown may have taken the motor city's name, but the company had outgrown its roots. Berry Gordy desperately wanted to expand into television and films, but being unable to do so from Detroit he began transferring the Motown offices to Los Angeles in 1970. His company moved into executive offices on 6255 Sunset Boulevard, where a new television wing, Motown Productions Inc, was opened, alongside a new recording studio. Gordy had opened a West Coast office in 1967 and now had an effective east coast/west coast operation. However, Detroit still played an integral part in the Motown operation for at least three quarters of its records were still cut there and two large studios continued to be used for recording.

Gordy intended to push as many of his artists as he could into films, and while the industry was dwindling in Hollywood, television investment and video cassette softwear was peaking in Los Angeles. Motown's production wing immediately went into action to store up video tapes of artists' performances, particularly those featured on television, plus tapes of acts in the studio, on location and at concerts to build up an extensive library. Motown was expanding into an entertainments complex, but what of the music? The raw rhythms and scratchy vocals of the Detroit sound gave way to a sophisticated, up-market sound. It was white music for the mass market and, on many occasions, lacked the depth and 'feel' of the Detroit sessions. This was a time of change and transition for the Motown sound and it lost many fans as well as gaining new converts.

For the Detroit-based artists the company's move was devastating. By 1972 a few had moved to Los Angeles leaving the remainder to face the same situation they were in during the Sixties – stranded in Detroit looking for a new recording deal. The move, too, was a spiritual blow for the city's black community since Motown symbolized black success. Berry Gordy moved house again to Beverly Hills, and later moved to the expensive Bel Air estate 'Vistas'. Motown was moving up town at, some said, the expense of the artists who had made the company.

Producer/writer Hank Cosby felt Motown lost its whole creative structure when it moved west: 'They had to change the whole thing and their costs zoomed way up. When they were in Detroit they were able to do business at a very moderate rate. In Los Angeles everything sky rocketed and it never came down. In Detroit we had our own village, but what we really had then was a warm feeling and when it became a big corporation that feeling had to go.' The Miracles' Bobby Moore was personally disappointed with the move: 'Motown gave Detroit more prestige and now it's just the motor city, whereas before it was the recording capital of the world. All the producers moved to Los Angeles and we're forced to record in California.'

Martha Reeves was one of the artists to be left behind: 'There were money problems within the Vandellas. We didn't have any records released so our bookings dropped off. We couldn't have continued in that position so it was decided to call it a day and find something else. When the money ran out, I couldn't pay the Vandellas and I lost them. It was as simple as that. (The group's last concert was on 21 December 1971 at Detroit's Cobo Hall.) When Motown moved away it left most of their business behind in a right state, there was no-one for me to speak to. I wasn't asked to go along with them so I felt I owed them nothing. They didn't seem that bothered with the way I felt. I loved being with Motown and they'll always be part of me, but I felt disheartened in the way they treated me toward the end. I did nothing for a year. I just sat around Detroit, lost and dejected. I contemplated taking a nine to fiver but I didn't have the heart to do it. Once a singer, always a singer, especially after all those years. I didn't have any particular direction in mind so I needed someone for guidance and advice and Motown wasn't there anymore.'

A five month legal battle between Reeves and Motown followed to release her from her contract that still had three years to run. She had requested an accounting of her royalties which, apparently, Berry Gordy construed as a criticism of his business integrity. Reeves eventually secured a release, unlike the Four Tops, Gladys Knight and the Pips, and others, who had to sit out their time. The terms of that release were never publicized but it's thought her freedom cost her $200,000 and the loss of the Vandellas' name. The individual Vandellas today are married with regular jobs, with the exception of Sandra Tilley who died in Las Vegas during 1982 from a brain haemorrhage.

Despite Motown's move to Los Angeles, its business was booming. On the Soul label Gladys Knight and the Pips followed their tear-jerking epic *Didn't You Know (You'd Have To Cry Sometime)* (US, Feb '69/UK, Feb '70) with the hard-funker *The Nitty Gritty* (US, Jun '69, UK, Oct '70), then returned to their debut style with *Friendship Train* (US, Oct '69/UK, Oct '70). During 1970 *You Need Love Like I Do (Don't You)* and the powerful ballad *If I Were Your Woman* were American released. Jr Walker and the All Stars enjoyed big success with their new, mellowed style, starting with *What Does It Take (To*

Win Your Love) (US, Apr '69/UK, Oct '69) while David and Jimmy Ruffin searched for that elusive hit. A new name to Motown, Yvonne Fair, tore her heart out with singles no soul fan could ignore. Her career began with the mournful Stay A Little Longer (US, Jul '70) on Soul then she transferred to the Motown label to work with Norman Whitfield on the 1975 album The Bitch Is Black, one of the year's more raunchiest releases, as the title suggests!

Yvonne Fair, a dynamic performer, had been a member of The Chantels known for a series of hit evergreen singles like He's Gone and Maybe. She left to join James Brown's touring revue for five years, before pursuing a solo career. Three years later Fair worked with Chuck Jackson, who introduced her to Motown. Funky Music Sho Nuff Turns Me On (UK, Aug '74) and Walk Out The Door If You Wanna were issued in 1974, and a month prior to The Bitch Is Black (US, May '75/UK, Nov '75) a stunning ballad It's Bad For Me To See You died. Fair's only British hit was a fast-paced version of Gladys Knight and the Pips It Should Have Been Me which peaked at number five in 1976.

Ex-Temptation Eddie Kendricks had released his aptly-titled first album All By Myself (US, Apr '71/UK, Sep '71), while Smokey Robinson had worked with Marvelette Wanda Rogers on a solo album, shrewdly released under The Return Of The Marvelettes (US, Sep '70). The record's sleeve showed a pregnant Rogers with two indistinguishable girls at her side. The Temptations, meanwhile, released the last of their psychedelic Whitfield singles Ungena Za Ulimwengu (Unite The World), and the Tamla label bought the rights to Bob and Marcia's European hit Young, Gifted And Black (US,Jul '70). This release coincided with the so-called Marvelettes' twee Marionette (US, Nov '70) single and Stevie Wonder's plea Heaven Help Us All (US, Sep '70/UK, Oct '70). On the Motown label the Jackson 5 were celebrating more multi-million outings with The Love You Save (US, May '70/UK, July '70) and I'll Be There (US, Aug '70/UK, Nov '70), The Supremes had Stoned Love (US, Oct '70/UK, Jan '71), while the Four Tops knotched up another hit with the moody Still Water (Love) (US, Aug '70/UK, Sep '70) followed by Just Seven Numbers (Can Straighten Out My Life) (US, Dec '70/UK, Apr '71). And the company itself branched out with more labels catering for different musical styles because, for example, a country and western song would not be accepted by the media and public on the Motown or Soul labels. Also, with more labels Motown was guaranteed more airplay and press exposure . . . and that's good business!

(Left) Ex-Chantel Yvonne Fair, brought a unique gutsy soul sound to Motown. Her 1975 album The Bitch Is Black was one of the year's raunchiest albums.

Ex-Temptation Eddie Kendricks debuted as a solo artist with his All By Myself album. It was a collection of thoughtful songs which stood him in good stead for his future career.

The highly talented and
likeable Thelma Houston
was guest of honour at
the Mowest label's
British launch in 1972.
She commanded a
regular and loyal
following and enjoyed a
million seller during her
stay at Motown.

INTO THE SEVENTIES

'We decided that wherever it (the dictionary) came down, we'd blind pick a word on that page. I guess were were lucky really because we could have ended up being the "commodes"!'
William King, Commodores

'You don't mean to tell me that churchgoers don't drink or participate in a little nooky from time to time!'
Spokesperson for Melodyland label

As Motown moved into its second decade songwriters and producers took on an even more vital role within the company's structure, as did the introduction of new labels. It seemed logical that when Berry Gordy moved to Los Angeles a new label should be introduced. Mowest – an abbreviation for Motown/West Coast – was opened to handle records emanating from the LA nerve-centre. Mowest's music was commercial and introduced new acts along with seasoned performers.

I *Want To Be Humble* by The Devastating Affair was Mowest's first listed release in the US in January 1972. Mowest opened in Britain nine months later with a launch at Ronnie Scott's Club, London, where new signing Thelma Houston was guest of honour. The Devastating Affair (Andrew Porter, Harold Johnson, Greg Wright, Karin Patterson, Olivia Foster) joined Motown in 1971 following an audition with Hal Davis. They were under-rated and not promoted yet their sweet harmonies prompted Diana Ross to use them as her backing singers. Following a successful series of concerts in Las Vegas, the group was promoted to support act and toured Europe with her. Their British debut *That's How It Was (Right From The Start)* in September 1973 was issued to coincide with their performance on Diana Ross's British tour (American release on the Motown label was two months later). An album *Devastating Affair Mountain* was recorded but canned, while members of the group went on to write for Ross, notably *You're A Special Part Of Me*, recorded with Marvin Gaye.

Mowest's first American number one was issued a year before I *Want To Be Humble*. Titled *What The World Needs Now Is Love – Abraham, Martin And John* (UK, Feb '72 re-released on Mowest label in Dec '73) it was the brainchild of radio DJ Tom Clay. He was working a three week fill-in at Los Angeles' KGBS station and decided to record a tape which he hoped would 'get across the idea of what we needed was love even though we were up to our armpits in hate, war and killing'. After assembling the material Clay felt the tone was too nega-

tive, so added schoolgirl definitions of hatred, bigotry and segregation at the start and finish of the tape. The Blackberries sang the song's title against the Burt Bacharach orchestra and snatches of speeches by the two late Kennedy brothers and Dr Martin Luther King. A Mowest executive heard it and within a week the finished single was issued. The flipside, *The Victors* was again spoken word, listing the names of men, women and children who had died during the Vietnam war. The single sold over three million copies, but it's follow-up *Whatever Happened To Love* released at the end of 1971 died. Then it was a case of whatever happened to Tom Clay.

Thelma Houston's *No One's Gonna Be A Fool Forever* was Mowest's first British single in October 1972 (American release was in March 1972 as the flipside to *Me And Bobby McGee*). Born on 7 May 1943 in Leland, Mississippi, Houston (real name Thelma Louise Jackson – Houston was her married name) was 10 when her family moved to California. She was one of three daughters and her mother, Gertrude, picked cotton to raise them after their father, Clifton, left. The youngster attempted to escape the harsh reality of southern segregation and poverty by spending afternoons locked away in the local cinema soaking up Hollywood's world of glamour and fantasy. Despite coming from a non-musical family, Houston later sang for seven years with the gospel choir, The Art Reynolds Singers. They recorded an album for Capitol before Houston opted for a solo career. A successful audition at the Purple Benny Club in Norwalk, California, led to regular cabaret work and to her meeting with her first manager, Marc Gordon, whose clients included The 5th Dimension. At Gordon's instigation Houston secured a deal with Dunhill Records where she recorded the *Sunshower* album with producer Jimmy Webb. Prior to this, the singer finished school and married. It ended in divorce following the birth of her two children, forcing Houston to work in health and child care to support them until the music business

The underrated Devastating Affair's I Want To Be Humble was the Mowest label's first listed single in 1972. The group's sweet harmonies prompted Diana Ross to use them as her backing group.

eventually beckoned her to return.

The magnificent *Sunshower* album was praised at every level and when she joined Mowest she encouraged Motown to buy the rights to it. The record was re-released as part of Motown's mid-price 1981 series. Houston: 'I really enjoyed making *Sunshower* and for me it served a great purpose. It was what I wanted to do at the time. I had spent a few months singing everybody else's songs in my night club act and I was hungry to create my own identity and, of course, with Jimmy giving me original material that was exactly what I could do. I know it didn't sell too many copies but most people felt it was before its time.'

Following her debut Mowest album, *Thelma Houston* (US, Jul '72/UK, Jan '73), her recordings were sparse, due, she said, to a lack of suitable material. In 1974 she transferred to the Motown label to release the Grammy nominated *You've Been Doing Wrong For So Long*. During her quiet period Houston recorded four songs for an experimental album *Direct-to-Disc*, which tried to re-create the sound achieved before multi-track recording and was intended for stereo buffs only and not commercial release. The singer then turned to acting, playing bit parts in television films.

Houston's recorded work failed to hit until a third label change to Tamla established her on the disco market with *Don't Leave Me This Way* (Gamble/Huff/Gilbert) during 1976. It topped the American charts, entered most European listings and peaked at 13 in Britain, where it was in direct competition with Harold Melvin and the Blue Notes' version. The latter won the battle with a British number five. Following *Don't Leave Me This Way*, Houston's only hit, she duetted with Jerry Butler. Theoretically the Houston/Butler collaboration was a brilliant idea; unfortunately the repertoire let them down.

One of Mowest's top signings was the Commodores in 1972. The six-manned group debuted in America in March 1972 (UK, Nov '74) with an uninspiring *The Zoo* (*The Human Zoo*), written and produced by Pam Sawyer and Gloria Jones. For their third release a year later the group moved to the Motown label where their selling power began. It was the company's policy for new acts to be assigned to in-house staff for recording purposes, a perfect arrangement for inexperienced bands but not for the Commodores, who felt stifled at not being able to record their own material. Nonetheless they accepted the guidance offered by Sawyer and Jones who pushed their music into an appropriate buying market. Once done, the group (Lionel Richie, William King, Ronald LaPread, Thomas McClary, Clyde 'Walter' Orange, Milan Williams) had studio freedom.

In 1968 the Commodores were freshmen at Tuskegee Institute and prior to becoming the Commodores, Richie, McClary and King sang James Brown material as members of The Mystics, whose lead singer and bassist was

'Railroad'. Their biggest rival at the time was another home-based band, The Jays, of which Milan Williams was a member. When a disagreement split up The Jays the two units merged. To choose a name for the new band they threw a dictionary in the air and 'decided that wherever it came down, we'd blind pick a word on that page', William King told *Blues & Soul*. 'The word was "commodore". It's an old navy ranking from the old days which isn't used anymore. I guess we were lucky really because we could have ended up being the "commodes"! Can you imagine us coming out in paper tissue suits!'

The group members were still college students when their interest in music expanded. King was in business management, Richie economics, Williams and LePread studied engineering, while McClary was in business management and Orange, a business major. King: 'The essence for the group was, and always has been, that we were ready to experiment when it was necessary. We were a black group and we had grown up at the time when The Temptations, Supremes and Miracles were at their peak. What we wanted to know was why The Temptations, as good and as hot as they were, could not put twenty-five thousand people in a stadium on their own. And yet a Beatles or a Led Zeppelin didn't even have to put out a record. All they had to say was that they'd be in town on such and such a day, the tickets would be $20 and it would be a sell-out within twenty-four hours. How come no black group could do it?' The Commodores were determined to change this although the struggle for recognition was to be tougher than anticipated.

During 1969 summer vacation the five left Tuskegee for New York City's 135th Street and 7th Avenue and a club known as Smalls Paradise. While unsuccessfully attempting to secure work with the owner, Pete Smalls, their uniforms and equipment were stolen from outside the club. The group shared one room at the YMCA on 135th Street, where their remaining equipment and money was also stolen. In desperation Milan Williams contacted an acquaintance, Benny Ashburn, who moved them into his home and arranged for Pete Smalls to give them another chance on his Monday audition nights. Unbeknown to the club owner, New York was inundated with Tuskegee students who, following a deluge of phone calls, turned up to support their home group. With such overwhelming enthusiasm the Commodores won the audition; Smalls cancelled his regular group and booked the Commodores for three weeks' work. Following this they performed at the Cheetah Club and when the summer recess was finished they returned to Tuskegee and college.

By 1970 the group recorded an album for Atlantic Records said to be titled *Rise Up* with Jerry Williams (aka Swamp Dog). Information is sketchy but presumably the record comprised instrumentals the group used as demo

tapes on which Richie plays the saxophone. Apparently *Keep On Dancin'* was the only single issued from this unreleased album. When college allowed the Commodores continued to tour their locality, playing the Boston, New York and Carolina circuit, and spending two months in France. Yet still they lacked a solid recording deal and once again turned to Benny Ashburn for help. He arranged a New York showcase for them at Lloyd Price's Turntable Club on Broadway and 50th, inviting record business personnel and the media. The Commodores planned to drive to New York overnight but the journey was riddled with a series of disasters. In Richmond, Virginia, state troopers surrounded their van and searched them suspecting them to be bank robbers. All four of the van's tyres punctured at various intervals and had to be replaced leaving them with no money. After travelling for twenty hours they reached the New Jersey Turnpike only to be turned away because they could not afford the toll fee and then the van ran out of fuel! They jumped the vehicle to the nearest garage and offered their equipment in exchange for petrol. The ploy failed and once more Ashburn came to the rescue on the phone by persuading the garage attendant to fill their tank. The Commodores, hot, tired and hungry, arrived in New York thirty minutes late. However their show convinced Motown's attending A&R executive Suzanne de Passe to secure the group for a forthcoming Jackson 5 tour and a week later forty-two dates from New York to Hawaii were confirmed. The two groups toured together for nearly three years before the Commodores worked with The O'Jays, The Temptations and the Rolling Stones.

In 1972 Motown officially signed the Tuskegeeans and once their education was over they recorded their own material with arranger James Carmichael. The funky, instrumental dancer *Machine Gun* (originally titled *The Ram*) was the result. Milan Williams originally wrote lyrics for the track but Carmichael insisted that as the trend was synthesized instrumentals without lyrics they should jump on the band wagon. *Machine Gun*, released in April 1974, charted in Europe (including Britain), Asia, Africa and the United States, and prompted Ashburn to become their full-time manager. *I Feel Sanctified* (1974, US, '75) and *Slippery When Wet* (1975) were black, funk-based semi-hits, but it took Lionel Richie's romantic ballads like *Just To Be Close to You* and *Easy* to change their silver status into platinum. With record sales came sell-out concerts and international acclaim, and their ambition to become The Black Beatles was in sight. In 1978 the Commodores peaked with a ballad that has been described as the greatest love song of all time, *Three Times A Lady*. It soared to the top of every major chart worldwide and reached double platinum sales in America alone, while in the UK it became Motown's all time top-selling single. Richie wrote the song when his father said that in thirty-five years of marriage he had never told his wife how much she meant to him. Richie was determined that this should not happen with his own wife, Brenda, so wrote the song for her.

Two Commodores' tracks *Zoom* and *Too Hot Ta Trot* became Motown's first British twelve inch single in 1978. This type of record was originally pressed as a promotional tool for club DJ use only because seven inch singles

One of the first publicity shots of the Commodores. Before joining Motown they toured with the Jackson 5 among others. They debuted on Mowest before being switched to the Motown label.

were impractical. The twelve inch was usually far superior in mastering, production and clarity, and pressed to achieve maximum quality over a club's massive sound system. These records also contained full length versions of songs lasting between twelve and twenty minutes, whereas the seven inch was an edited track ideal for radio play. Club promotion has always been imperative in a dance record's life, and usually begins before the official release date of the seven inch single. Sales of both versions now contribute to chart placings and by 1978 twelve inch singles reputedly outsold the seven inch. Prior to the release of the Commodores twelve inch single, other British record companies were beginning to venture into this field encouraged by successful results in America. However, one drawback was that twelve inch singles were manufactured on album presses and as more money could be generated from albums companies were reluctant to commit these facilities to the singles. In time, special presses were allocated to twelve inch singles.

Syreeta's first American Mowest single I *Love Every Little Thing About You* was released in September 1972, three months before Suzee Ikeda's version of the 1968 classic I *Can't Give Back The Love I Feel For You*. Syreeta's single was taken from her self-named album (US, Jun '72/UK, Nov '72) comprising tracks written by her and Stevie Wonder, excluding two *She's Leaving Home* (Lennon/McCartney) and *What Love Has Joined Together* (Smokey Robinson/Robert Rogers). Wonder also produced the album and played most of the instruments. *To Know You Is To Love You* was Syreeta's first British Mowest single in June 1973.

Quite possibly the strangest Mowest signing was Frankie Valli and the Four Seasons. Already 'seasoned' hit-makers, they were encouraged to the label by Gordy and his promise to supervize their recordings. However their stay was short and uneventful when Gordy failed to keep his word due to Diana Ross's filming commitments. A solo Valli debuted on the Mowest label with *Love Isn't Here (Like It Used To Be)* in February 1972, followed by an unreleased group single *The Night* (UK, Oct '72) and a released *Walk On, Don't Look Back* (US, Aug '72/UK, Mar '73). A year later they transferred to Motown but the label change failed to produce hits. In May 1972 the group's *Chameleon* album (UK, May '72) was issued and in September 1975 a solo Valli issued *Inside You* on the Motown label (UK, May '76). Their Mowest stay wasn't totally wasted as they enjoyed a British top ten hit with the re-released *The Night* in April 1975 due to the mass loyalty of the northern soul scene in England.

Prior to reaching their pre-Motown peak The Four Seasons worked through more name changes than group members. As a country and western unit they were known as The Vibrations, said to include Valli, Nick Massi, Tom and Nick DeVito. Valli left to pursue solo stardom but returned after minor success. A name change to The Four Lovers won them a recording contract with RCA, after which they moved to Capitol. They worked as session singers and recorded under various guises like The Village Voices, Billy Dixon and the Tops, and The Romans. Producer Bob Crewe guided them through the Sixties and their future success. By 1960 Nick DeVito left because of ear trouble and was replaced by Bob Gaudio from The Royal Teens. Two years later they became The Four Seasons and moved to Vee Jay before signing with Philips Records, where their second single *Sherry* sold a million. Valli's distinctive falsetto voice became their trademark as the hits became non-stop – *Big Girls Don't Cry*, *Walk Like A Man* and *Ain't That A Shame* (1963), *Rag Doll* (1964), *Let's Hang On* (1965), *Workin' My Way Back To You*, *Opus 17* and *I've Got You Under My Skin* (1966) and *Tell It To The Night* (1967). When the group joined Mowest it was estimated they had already sold eighty million discs.

If Frankie Valli and The Four Seasons were the most unusual signings, then the Sisters Love was the most dynamic. Lillie Fort, Vermettya Boyster, Gwendolyn Berry and Jeannie Long blew the grooves off their singles with an aggressive funk sound, yet they made little impact on the charts. Lead singer Boyster,

from Jacksonville, Florida, was a professional operatic and gospel singer who became a member of the American gospel group, the Clara Ward Singers. Berry, whose first cousins are The Isley Brothers, was one of sixteen children and was encouraged to sing by her grandmother. Long, originally from Waukegan, Illinois, started her career in church and never planned to become a professional singer, while Fort was a housewife. In 1956 the quartet joined The Raelettes, working with the Ray Charles Revue for ten years before signing to a newly-formed company Man-Child to release *I Know You Love Me*. This was followed by a tour of the American Air Force bases in the Far East and a recording deal with A&M Records in 1968. While there, three monster American singles were issued – *Forget It*, *I've Got It*, *The Bigger You Love (The Harder You Fall)* and *Are You Lonely*.

Sisters Love's Mowest debut was *Mr Fix-It Man* (US, Mar '72/UK, Sep '72) following which they supported the Jackson 5 on their first British tour, when they created such a stir on stage that Motown/EMI organized a reception in their honour so that they could perform for the media who were unable to attend the concert. The highlight of the girls' stay with Mowest was the shattering slice of excitement *Learning To Trust My Man* released in Britain in September 1973. An album was recorded but unreleased as the hits failed to follow.

By the end of 1973 Mowest was declared

(Left) Syreeta and Stevie Wonder worked together on Syreeta's self-named album released in 1972. This project was hitless but Syreeta was destined to enjoy success two years later.

Pop hit-makers Frankie Valli and the Four Seasons failed to repeat their past success while signed to Mowest. However, they did score with a British top ten hit The Night during 1975 due to the country's loyal northern soul scene.

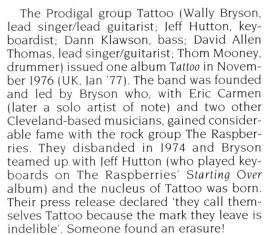

The dynamic Sisters Love perform for the British media at a private reception in London. On stage the group received standing ovations, yet their record sales were minimal.

An early Prodigal label signing, Ronnie McNeir's talent was intended to spearhead Motown's assault on the pop/rock market.

defunct and all the potential hit-makers transferred to Motown. A year later another label, Prodigal, owned by Barney Ales, opened for pop/rock products via acts like Michael Quatro, Dunn and Rubini, Fantacy Hill, ex-Shirelles' member Shirley Alston, Ronnie McNeir, Rare Earth and FoxFire. Prodigal's first American release was Alston's I Hear Those Church Bells Ringing/Chapel Of Love in December 1974, while the British Prodigal label's first single was Dunn & Rubini's Diggin' It in November 1976. Interestingly, Motown's 1982 British chart-topper was the re-issued Charlene's third American Prodigal release I've Never Been To Me in July 1977 (UK, Aug '77).

Ronnie McNeir, an early Prodigal signing, was born on 14 December 1949 in Camden, Alabama. He moved with his family to Pontiac, Michigan where, at the age of fourteen, he was already an accomplished musician/writer. McNeir won a prestigious talent show sponsored by a Detroit R&B radio station which helped secure his first recording contract with La Baron Taylor's Solid Hit-Band Productions. In 1971 the singer headed for Los Angeles where he teamed up with ex-Motowner Kim Weston to produce his first self-named album, co-produced by Clarence Paul and the Four Tops' Obie Benson. In The Summertime was lifted from that release to become a number one in Detroit. Encouraged by this success, McNeir opened his Setting Sun company in Pontiac and wrote Goodness Gracious for Weston. His American Prodigal debut was Wendy Is Gone in March 1975.

A native-Detroiter who was at Prodigal with Ronnie McNeir was Michael Quatro whose early life also revolved around music. His two sisters joined him in the business – Suzi became England's rock queen of the Seventies, while Patti became a guitarist with Fanny, an all-girl group. During 1975 Michael joined United Artists as a solo, prior to which he headed The Mike Quatro Band. His June 1976 Prodigal album Dancers, Romancers, Dreamers And Schemers was a re-issue from United Arists (UK, Oct '76 on Prodigal label).

The Prodigal group Tattoo (Wally Bryson, lead singer/lead guitarist; Jeff Hutton, keyboardist; Dann Klawson, bass; David Allen Thomas, lead singer/guitarist; Thom Mooney, drummer) issued one album Tattoo in November 1976 (UK, Jan '77). The band was founded and led by Bryson who, with Eric Carmen (later a solo artist of note) and two other Cleveland-based musicians, gained considerable fame with the rock group The Raspberries. They disbanded in 1974 and Bryson teamed up with Jeff Hutton (who played keyboards on The Raspberries' Starting Over album) and the nucleus of Tattoo was born. Their press release declared 'they call themselves Tattoo because the mark they leave is indelible'. Someone found an erasure!

Like The Four Seasons on Mowest, another established act Delaney Bramlett failed to repeat prior success on the Prodigal label. Bramlett, born on 1 July 1939 in Mississippi, moved to the West Coast where he joined the famous Shindogs, house band for Jack Good's Shindig television shows. There he met and subsequently married singer Bonnie Lynn. Together they recorded a 1968 Don Nix produced album for Stax, then formed their own band to tour with Blind Faith. Their Accept No Substitute album on Elektra followed. The couple became a popular touring band thanks to their brand of white soul which prompted Eric Clapton to record the On Tour With Eric Clapton set with them. Delaney's Prodigal album, recorded during 1974, included luminaries like Clapton, Ringo Starr, George Harrison and Billy Preston. Entitled Delaney And Friends-Class Reunion, it was released in America in February 1977 (UK, May '77).

In 1976 Fantacy Hill released Minnie Ha Ha US, June '76). The group (Joe Conrad, Doug Golema, Gerson Migiacio, George Durbi, Dan Mullins, Tom Neme) was two years old when it joined the Prodigal label, following radio DJ Johnny Williams becoming their manager and negotiating a deal with Prodigal. The duo Dunn and Rubini's first Prodigal single was Diggin' It (US, Jun '76/UK, Nov '76). Don Dunn was a songwriter/artist, while Michel Rubini was an arranger/producer/session musician of ten years standing. Suzanne de Passe, Prodigal's senior creative executive, signed them as a singing duo. In 1978 the group Fresh issued Just How Does It Feel, their first Prodigal single (US, Mar '78/UK, Mar '78). Fresh, a seven piece line-up of considerable experience (Fred Allen, Bill Pratt, Milo Martin, Paul Marshall, Elaine Mayo, Frank Savino, George England) first joined MCA Records to release the Get Fresh album. During 1977 they toured with top names like Wild Cherry, Brass Construction and the Jackson 5. Prodigal label-mates, Stylus (Peter Cupples, Ashley Henderson, Sam McNally, Peter Roberts, Mark Myer, from Australia, with Ron Peers from Liverpool, England) moved to America to sign with Prodigal. Their debut release, Stylus (US, Oct '78/UK, Jul '79), was released in

Australia as *The Best Kept Secret* which sums up their entire career. All the acts arrived in a flurry of publicity and left quietly.

In November 1976 Motown opened the distributing outfit, Hitsville Distributors, in their former Detroit headquarters. Motown also co-owned Together Distributors in Atlanta, Georgia, with A&M Records and wholly-owned the Motown Of Canada distributing arm. Barney Ales was president of Hitsville Distributors and used the Prodigal label's staff to run the distribution operation.

The group and label that was to push Berry Gordy's company into the heavy rock market in the early Seventies were both called Rare Earth. The white group, who also recorded for Prodigal, broke loose on the Rare Earth label with *Get Ready* (US, Feb '70/UK, Jun '70) and (*I Know*) *I'm Losing You* (US, Jul '70/UK, May '74). *Born To Wander* (US, Nov '70/UK, Apr '72) and *I Just Want To Celebrate*. (US, Jun '71/UK, Sep '71) The group (Peter Hoorelbeke, Gil Bridges, Michael Urso, Ray Monette, Mark Olson, Edward Guzman) worked with Norman Whitfield on the *Ma* album (US, May '73/UK, Sep '73), a most powerful release. Other Rare Earth acts included Rustix, Michael Denton, Sunday Funnies, XIT, the boy/girl duo Stoney and Meatloaf, England's Kiki Dee and the rock unit The Pretty Things whose *Private Sorrow* single was the label's first single in July 1969. The group Rare Earth's first single on the Rare Earth label was *Generation, Light Up The Sky* but they had to wait for the Smokey Robinson composition *Get Ready* to achieve chart status. R. Dean Taylor's debut was the runaway hit *Indiana Wants Me* in April 1970 (UK, Feb '71), followed by the shallow *Ain't It A Sad Thing* (US, Jan '71) which was the first single on the Rare Earth label in Britain during September 1971. The British launch was delayed for two years while Motown/EMI negotiated the necessary clearances, and by the time their first single was released the label was a tremendous American success thanks to Rare Earth's string of hits.

The Sunday Funnies (Richard Fidge, lead vocalist; Ron Aitken, bass/vocals; Richard Mitchell, drums; Richard Kosinski, keyboards), another early Rare Earth signing, were Detroit born and raised, while the six-year-old group XIT (pronounced 'exit') were inter-tribal indians from New Mexico. The members (Michael Martin, lead vocalist/guitarist, a combination of Spaniard and Tigua Indian; Lee Herrere, drums, a mixture of Aztec and Hopi indian; Mac Suazo, bass, a Taos Indian; R. C. Garliss Jr, lead guitarist/piano, part Cherokee Indian) had pledged to devote themselves to the National Cultural Preservation of the American Indian's story before the coming of the white man. XIT fast gained the reputation of being one of the most exciting live bands on the label.

Stoney and Meatloaf's self-named album (US, Sep '71/UK, Oct '72) was delightfully original and was one of the first recordings by future rock superstar Meat Loaf. Stoney spent her first eleven years in Omaha, Nebraska, before moving with her family to Cedar Rapids, Iowa. Her family then moved to Detroit where she joined a local all-girl group, The Lorelies. It was a member of a further band, Mower Pursuit, that she first met Meatloaf, who was appearing on the same Ohio college bill. Meat Loaf's introduction to music came with leading roles in two high school musicals in his hometown of Dallas, Texas. His first professional appearance, however, was a walk-on with The Dallas Civic Opera Company. He then attended the Lubbock Christian College to study radio and television broadcasting. His move to California led to the birth of several groups including Meatloaf Soul, The Popcorn Blizzard and The Floating Circus. While in Los Angeles he met Stoney once again after being asked to audition performers for a *Hair* roadshow. Later they performed as a duo and came to the attention of rock producer Ralph Terrand who signed them to Rare Earth.

Despite a good selection of diverse artists, the rock/pop label was closed by 1977, when it was reported that Rare Earth group had sold in excess of twelve million records.

Jazz was a market untapped by Berry Gordy, although he had distributed records for outlets like CTI. When he secured a distribution deal with Chisa it was his intention to attract the big jazz names and Hugh Masekela and the Jazz Crusaders were the first. Masekela, a pioneer of authentic South African music, formed the Chisa label during 1967 with his associate Stu Levine. His first release under the new arrangement was the *Reconstruction* album in July 1970, the follow-up to his earlier million-selling *Grazin' In The Grass* set. The Jazz Crusaders (Wayne Henderson, Wilton Felder, Joe Sample, Buster Williams, Stix Hooper) already had a loyal following. Their first release for Chisa was the *Old Socks New Shoes, New Socks, Old Shoes* (US, Jul '70/UK, Oct, '71 on Rare Earth label) album. Joining them on this label were Monk Montgomery (electric bassist), Letta Mbula (African songstress), Arthur Adams (singer), Stu Gardner (jazz pianist/organist/composer) and The Five Smooth Stones (a Los Angeles pop group). As with most of Berry Gordy's new labels, Chisa was a failure and was closed in 1971.

Motown's breakthrough into country music came in 1974 with the Melodyland label (not to be confused with the 1962-65 outlet Melody with signed artists of Lamont Dozier, Howard Crockett, The Pirates, Dorsey Burnette and Bruce Channel). Melodyland was launched by Pat Boone's *Candy Lips* in October 1974 and T.G. Sheppard's *Devil In The Bottle* a month later. The latter topped the American country charts encouraging further signings of Jerry Naylor, Ronnie Dove, Kenny Seratt, Barbara Wyrick, Ernie Payne and others. The label was, however, shortlived as a Los Angeles church bearing the same name insisted that material like *Is This All There Is To Honky Tonk?* and *Devil In*

Michael Quatro, brother of England's Seventies rock queen, Suzi, headed his own group and recorded for United Artists before joining the Prodigal label.

Established artist Delaney Bramlett included a host of international artists on his debut Prodigal album Delaney And Friends – Class Reunion, *but it still failed to reach its sales potential.*

The Bottle reflected badly on its image. Apparently, a label spokesperson at the time quipped: 'You don't mean to tell me that churchgoers don't drink or participate in a little nooky from time to time!' Whether that was true or not, Motown was taken to court, lost the action and Melodyland was killed off in 1976. Hitsville took over and a year later MC Records replaced that.

Hitsville debuted in the UK in April 1977 with a specially packaged album *Hitsville – The New Direction In Country Music* featuring ten artists over eighteen tracks. Despite huge promotional campaigns the label was another to die a quick death. In America the label's biggest attraction was Pat Boone, the all-American boy, whose rise to fame was propelled by covering black recordings. His musical introduction came through high school performances and church productions in Nashville, his hometown. Boone became a professional singer after winning the Ted Mack Amateur Hour and the Arthur Godfrey Talent Scout Show. Dot Records released his first single *Two Hearts, Two Kisses* in 1954 followed by *Ain't That A Shame* and *I Almost Lost My Mind*, among others. Two years later he signed a million dollar contract with 20th Century Fox to appear in fifteen films including *Journey To The Centre Of The Earth*. In that same year Boone joined the American Broadcasting Company for his first television series produced by his own production company, Cooga Mooga Inc.

The career of Hitsville signing Jerry Naylor also spans several years. He first gained recognition when he took over the leadership of The Crickets following the death of Buddy Holly. As a teenager Naylor worked with Elvis Presley, Johnny Cash and Johnny Horton, and when his *Is This All There Is To Honky Tonk?* was issued in November 1974 his future career was guaranteed. Ronnie Dove also joined Hitsville as an established artist. His background included thirty pop hits and eight chart albums. Born in Virginia, Dove found popularity with his cabaret-styled act, while fellow-label artist Wendal Adkins was country and western's first sex symbol since Presley. Born in Kentucky and raised in Ohio, Adkins performed with country stars like David Allan Coe and Willie Nelson.

In 1970 Motown entered American politics with its Black Forum label to release spoken word recordings by Dr Martin Luther King and Elaine Brown. King's 1970 *Why I Oppose The War In Vietnam* album, the label's first, won a Grammy Award for artistic excellence rather than for sales. Two further albums were released that year – Stokely Carmichael's *Free Huey* and *Writers Of The Revolution* by Langston Hughes and Margaret Danner. Two years later *Guess Who's Coming Home*, narrated by Wallace Terry, was recorded 'live' by black fighting men in Vietnam, and four albums later the label was defunct! Black Forum's lifespan was greater than Weed which opened and closed

in 1969. With a logo boasting 'all your favourite artists are on weed' only one unpromoted album was released. Titled C.C. *Rides Again* soul fans immediately knew the singer was the V.I.P. artist Chris Clark although she was not identified by name on the sleeve. After this surprising and obscure release, Clark returned to her vice-presidency position in Motown's film division. The last label to be opened in the early Seventies was Natural Resources where a handful of unknown acts (Two Friends, Heart, Corliss, Gotham, Road, Earthquire, Northern Lights) fought for hits. After eight releases the label was used as a re-issue outlet.

In 1970 Berry Gordy bought the worldwide rights to entertainer Sammy Davis Jr's Ecology label, which involved the formation of new publishing companies. Davis, the only artist signed to the label, recorded the *In My Own Lifetime* single in March 1971 and *Something For Everyone* album in May 1970 on the Motown label (UK, Sep '70). Davis and Gordy could not agree on the Ecology label's musical direction and their collaboration ended.

With the opening of these new labels and the increased demand for diverse material in-house writers and producers were pushed to the limit. Many plodded on content with a label credit and royalty, while others recorded their own work or became publicly known from label credits on hit singles. None reached the status of Holland, Dozier and Holland, although Nickolas Ashford and Valerie Simpson came close with their Marvin Gaye/Tammi Terrell, and Diana Ross releases. Michigan-born Ashford was 21, Simpson 17, when they first met in New York City during 1963, where the latter was born and raised. Ashford: 'I went to New York City because everyone said it was the place to make it. I was destitute and was invited to this Baptist Church. I went along to get a good meal and that's where I saw Valerie. She was singing there with three girls, and I thought she looked cute. After the service we talked but I don't think she knew of my situation. We got to know each other socially and talked about writing together. I'd been writing gospel songs all my life and when Valerie's group was invited to perform in this nightclub as a gospel band they didn't have enough material, so they asked me if I would write them some songs.' Through their writing collaboration they landed a contract with Glover Records where their first single *I'll Find You* was released in 1964. Ashford: 'We recorded two songs but nothing happened. It was so rough we decided we'd be better sticking to writing.' From Glover they moved to Scepter Records to write for artists like The Shirelles.

In 1966 Ray Charles recorded their hit song *Let's Go Get Stoned* which got them noticed because of its unconventional lyrics. After Scepter came Motown: 'It was a dream come true. We were just writers and Motown was it. When they called us we didn't hesitate. With a

whole slew of artists there our songs would get the chance to be recorded. It was the best thing that happened to us.' Despite being consistent hit-makers little was known about their talent because of Motown's policy not to publicize its staff. Simpson recalled: 'That's how Motown was. I thought it really strange because they wanted to keep you in the dark. I think Motown was afraid because of our contracts, that outsiders would get to you, talk to you, and perhaps wisen you up.' She called the company's agreements 'slave contracts', although she was quick to stress they learned much during their stay and had no regrets. However, in 1982, when the couple became international performers, Simpson appreciated why Motown was so secretive: 'If you've ever had your words taken and changed around, which journalists are apt to do, then it concerns me a great deal. It bothers me because there are a lot of awful things about Motown, but there were a lot of wonderful things too. I don't mind if two sides get told but if the person just wants to paint a bad picture then they can just take that portion of what you say and use it. I can well see how some people are reluctant to talk because you don't know what's going to be said or written.'

While at Motown Valerie Simpson also wrote and recorded demos used by Tammi Terrell, Diana Ross and others, which they sang in Simpson's style. Simpson felt no animosity when they enjoyed the success based on her singing voice. 'I couldn't have taken Diana's place and couldn't, for example, have sung *Reach Out And Touch*. The public had built an image, with a commercial voice that pleased them. She had that sound whereby she's distinctly Diana and we perceived the type of material we would give her which would be more 'pop' than, say, we would give Gladys Knight and the Pips because we knew her audience was going to be wider and you'd sell more records.' However, before leaving Motown Simpson did record her own songs on the *Exposed* albums (US, '71, UK, '72) which carried Ross's endorsement, *Valerie Simpson* (US, '72, UK, '73) and *Keep It Coming* (US, '77), with an unreleased duo album in between. Simpson: 'We actually had extra material at the time that we didn't need for someone else so we thought we might as well do it on me. Motown didn't quibble about it, but they didn't do much about it either!' When their contracts expired Ashford and Simpson did not re-sign. 'We were considering this thing about being artists and realized that Motown maybe didn't see us in the same way,' Simpson remembered. 'My albums hadn't done very much so they really weren't excited about doing anything on us. So leaving seemed the right thing to do. We got our royalties but we didn't perhaps get what we should have and we ran into trouble with things that were not in our best interests. Motown had the leverage which they did because we signed the contracts, and they took advantage some-

times. But I think we got the best end of the stick when I look back on it, even though they tried to suppress who we were.' The duo signed to WEA Records where success still eluded them until 1978 when they became regular R&B charters with songs like *Don't Cost You Nothing*, *Found A Cure* and *Love Don't Make Me Right*. From WEA they moved to Capitol where *Solid* became a 1985 international hit.

Heading the 'second league' of writers/producers at this time were Gloria Jones and Pam Sawyer. Jones' entry in the business followed the same pattern of many black artists. She was a minister's daughter and studied classical piano for ten years before joining a gospel group to sing in church. Future Motowners Frank Wilson, Blinky Williams and Billy Preston, and Edna Wright (one third of the Honeycone singing group) were also members of this gospel group. Together they worked on Phil Spector's Christmas album and sang back-ups on Bob Dylan's *Gospel Brothers & Sisters Of Los Angeles* set. Gloria Jones then teamed up with Barry White and Gene Page and later with Brenda and Patrice Holloway. Jones: 'While I was with the gospel group we were asked to record some demos and the result was *Heartbeat* which was a successful single for me.' Following this release, Jones worked with the Holloway sisters earning them the nickname 'The Little Hearts of Los

Angeles', and met Pam Sawyer, who asked her to write for Motown. The couple wrote the Grammy nominated *If I Were Your Woman* for Gladys Knight and the Pips, and material for the Commodores, Jimmy and David Ruffin, the Four Tops, Jr Walker, Eddie Kendricks and the Jackson 5. Gloria Jones, who also wrote under the name 'Laverne Ware', commented: 'After working with so many artists I wanted to do an album myself, to prove to myself I could do it. I was fortunate enough to record the *Share My Love* album (US, Sep '73/UK, Jan '74) arranged by Paul Riser, where I wrote most of the tracks myself. However, listening to it later it's not what I'm into but it was an emotional experience for me.' Sawyer and Jones also wrote the splendidly dramatic ballad *It's Bad For Me To See You* for Yvonne Fair's *The Bitch Is Black* album. Jones recalled: 'Because *If I Were Your Woman* turned out so well, Pam and I wrote another eight songs for a concept album. They all stemmed around that one song, like I *Ain't That Easy To Lose* (recorded by Thelma Houston), *It's Bad For Me To See You* and *Is It Really Over*. We actually wrote *It's Bad* for Gladys Knight as the follow-up to *Woman* but she was working with Clay McMurray at the time and when we took the demo to him he couldn't get Gladys into it. If we'd gotten together with Clay and Gladys we'd have had one fantastic album.'

Pam Sawyer, white and British, also partnered Marilyn McLeod, Frank Wilson and Lori Burton. From an early age she had ambitions to compose: 'I was trying to be a lyricist and married a man who wrote melodies. I thought it would be the perfect match but it wasn't. We had a child then split up, and I decided I was going to continue writing lyrics rather than getting caught up being a housewife.' With Burton she wrote *Ain't Gonna Eat Out My Heart Anymore* for The Rascals, and with McLeod wrote *Love Hangover* for Diana Ross.

Leonard Caston and Carolyn Majors, like Ashford and Simpson, recorded their own material on a US 1974 release (UK, Mar '75). Titled *Caston & Majors*, with highlights of *There's Fear* and *Child Of Love*, the album featured both Syreeta and Carolyn on vocals, and was another to suffer from under-promotion. Caston, born on 13 November 1943 in Chicago, was an original member of The Radiants. After a spell in the Armed Forces he joined Chess Records as a writer/producer. When the company's president, Leonard Chess, died the operation moved to New York after being bought out by the GRT Corporation. This prompted Caston to move to Detroit and Motown where he worked with Eddie Kendricks, Stevie Wonder, The Supremes and the Four Tops. Meeting Carolyn Majors was unexpected, as he explained: 'Another producer at Motown was cutting an album on an act but because of contractual reasons it was never finished. The company released the artist and to try to get back some of the money they had laid out, they asked me to see what I could do.

I'd known Carolyn for some time and we had a good working relationship, so we added our voices.'

An album sleeve showing a man massaging a naked lady represented *Musical Massage* (US, Sep '76/UK, Feb '77), Leon Ware's only album. The model, Azeree, a *Playboy* centrefold, had previously modelled for album covers, whereas the masseur was better suited to composing. Leon Ware, another versatile singer/ writer, spent several years with Motown although he had been involved with music for most of his life. Starting in his hometown, Detroit, he formed his first group The Romeos in 1954, with Lamont Dozier and Ty Hunter. When that disbanded Ware worked for ABC Records for four years, before signing with Berry Gordy in 1964. During his first year with the company Ware nibbled at success with The Isley Brothers, then moved to Groovesville Music as an independent producer for two years, followed by a further three at Bell. He refused to succumb to failure and during 1969 worked with the Righteous Brothers, Johnny Nash and Kim Weston. His success there encouraged him to concentrate on writing for other artists. To this end he penned most of the Ike and Tina Turner's *Nuff Said* album and in 1973 teamed up with Quincy Jones at A&M to record the *Body Heat* set. Two years later Ware returned to Motown where he instigated the development of Marvin Gaye's *I Want You* project. Ware: 'Some of the songs had already been recorded on my own solo album but when Marvin heard them he wanted them and I was more than pleased to turn them over to him completely. I had recorded *I Want You* and *All The Way Around* (co-written by T-Boy Ross, brother of Diana) and they were the first ones we did.' *Musical Massage* flopped as did Ware's Motown career.

Many composers have unfortunately been omitted from this book due to lack of success and/or available information. However, no reference to Berry Gordy's hit makers would be

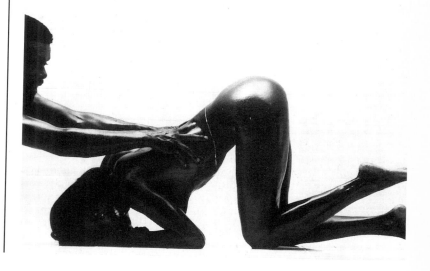

Leon Ware works on a musical massage in 1976. The established and versatile singer/ writer worked with many artists including Ike and Tina Turner and Marvin Gaye before recording his own Motown album.

complete without Johnny Bristol who, like Ashford and Simpson, enjoyed solo success outside Motown. Bristol: 'I was introduced to Berry Gordy through a mutual friend. Berry liked what I was about and heard the compositions I'd written and asked me to sign up with him. Motown was very exclusive in those days. When you worked for him you were not able to work for another record company. So I stayed with Berry for about ten years and I guess I produced just about everyone on the label.' When his contract was due for renewal Bristol moved on. 'I really had no other choice because of the offers they made me. I was one of Motown's top producers and when they came to me, I never talked with Berry, about my contract, they made me a very insulting offer. I felt I couldn't take it.' Once free of Motown Bristol joined Columbia as a producer, later a singer at MGM. *Hang On In There Baby* in 1974 was his first million-selling single, taken from his album of the same name.

As Motown entered its second decade (and four months before her solo television debut) Diana Ross married. Her husband was not Berry Gordy but a younger, white, artists' manager Robert Silberstein (aka Bob Ellis). Ross' fans lived with the assumption that she and Gordy would marry; in fact *Variety* magazine (October 1969) referred to them as man and wife! Gordy admitted that he had twice proposed to Ross, but they had chosen not to marry for several reasons, none of which were publicized.

The romance between Silberstein and Ross reputedly blossomed when they met in a Los Angeles men's store. They subsequently dated for two years before marrying in relative secrecy on 20 January 1971 at the Silver Bells Chapel, Las Vegas, before the Reverend Hutchinson. According to close friends, included in Silberstein's marriage vows was the line 'I will never manage Diana'. Their honeymoon was postponed as Ross had television commitments in Los Angeles. Robert Silberstein's family were garment manufacturers in Elberton, New Jersey. He graduated from West Virginia University to become a teacher but resigned following a dispute with the principal. Prior to becoming an artists' manager he dabbled in real estate and worked as a publicist. Life was not easy for the Silbersteins – or later 'the Rosses' – as Diana's attitude to inter-racial marriages was quite controversial for this time, as she told *Woman's World* magazine: 'People disciminate without even knowing what they are doing. I'm married to a white Jewish man, everyone keeps pointing it out to me and it bugs the hell out of me. Even talking about differences in race or religion becomes a kind of discrimination when it's made a point of all the time. My husband is a wonderful man whose skin happens to be a different color from mine. I suppose my children are going to go through this too, having people ask them what it's like to have a black mother and a white father. I don't want that.' The singer had always pined for a family of her own, and even contemplated adopting a child as a single mother. As she settled down to combining her marriage and career she discovered she was pregnant and was instructed to reduce her workload for fear of medical complications.

The emotional strain took its toll and she left her husband. After five months she returned, a much happier and calmer woman, saying being separated was the best thing to happen to them because it made them realize how much they needed one another. It was later disclosed that Ross had filed for separation one month and four days after her marriage, because she was reputed to be 'fed up with the way my husband treated me, including irrational behaviour in public which I found both demeaning and embarrassing'. Another source revealed 'when they were first married each maintained separate homes, creating the speculation that the marriage had been in name only'.

Seven months after her wedding ceremony Ross enjoyed her first British solo chart-topper with I'm Still Waiting taken from the July 1971 American Surrender LP, which was re-titled after the hit single for British release in October 1971. Prior to this Berry Gordy's first television spectacular for the ex-Supreme was screened. (It was the show her management claimed wasn't being filmed when her leaving The Supremes was leaked to the media.) Titled Diana!, it was televized on Sunday, 18 April 1971 (five months later on BBC2 in Britain). Ross's guest stars were comedians Bill Cosby and Danny Thomas, and the Jackson 5. This was the first presentation from the $15 million budget allocated for various projects within Motown's new television/theatrical division. Producers Bernard Rothman and Jerry McPhie assisted Gordy with director Kip Walton overseeing six scriptwriters. Suzanne de Passe was creative consultant and Gil Askey arranger/conductor while Paul Riser worked on staging the musical numbers. The hour long spectacular showcased Diana's talents as an all-round entertainer – she sang her hits and easily played the role of comedienne. The young Jackson brothers added a fresh vitality by bouncing through their singles, but it was a short number featuring Michael solo, dressed in tuxedo and tails, singing an alternate It Was A Very Good Year, that is best remembered. The most remarkable sequence belonged to Ross and her transformation into Hollywood's greatest – Charlie Chaplin, Harpo Marx and W.C. Fields.

As the ex-Supreme dominated the headlines, Smokey Robinson left The Miracles. It was the end of yet another musical era, Miracle Pete Moore said, 'but as Smokey told us he was leaving a year before he actually left we had plenty of time to work things out. Even so, his leaving was quite psychological and a lot of people just didn't want to recognize the group without him. We weren't so much disappointed as a little hurt when he left because we'd been associated with him for so many years that it was sad.' Although Robinson's departure caused minimal stir in the wake of Ross's tide of publicity, his last performance with the group which covered three dates – 14/15/16 July 1972 at the Carter Barron

Amphitheatre in Washington, DC – was duly recorded and released as an album titled 1957-1972 (Live!). Robinson explained why he left his group: 'The Miracles were a part of my satisfaction on the road. I was with guys I loved so much and got along with perfectly well. The only part I found I hated about the whole thing was the travelling, the hotels, food in restaurants, and so on. It was driving me up the wall. Also I had two very young children and I wanted to be able to be their father rather than a celebrity they saw every now and again. These are the factors that made me decide that I had to stop.' His last group single was I Can't Stand To See You Cry released in November 1972.

Robinson's replacement was William Griffin, who had worked with the group for five months prior to Smokey's departure. Born on 15 August 1950 in Baltimore, Maryland, Bill Griffin came from a gospel singing family. He later graduated to a local group The Last Dynasty. One of his childhood friends was the future Temptation, Damon Harris, and it was through him that Griffin came to the attention of The Miracles. Their first album without their mentor was the low-keyed Renaissance (US, Apr 73/UK, Oct '73). Don't Let It End (Till You Let It Begin) (US, Jun '73/UK, Mar '74) was the first single. Robinson's self-imposed

A musical era ended when Smokey Robinson left The Miracles in 1972. Robinson intended to retire but within a year he launched a solo career with Sweet Harmony.

The Smokey-less Miracles. Smokey's replacement was Billy Griffin (left) whose vocals sounded similar to the group's ex-leader. Their debut album was Renaissance in 1973.

retirement lasted all of a year when his solo American single *Sweet Harmony* was issued . . . two months before The Miracles first single.

In Motown's year of television replacing music, innovative ideas and expanding artist rosters, the world saw the triumphant return of Marvin Gaye. Following the death of his singing partner Tammi Terrell in 1970, Gaye retired from the business to live in self-imposed exile. His marriage to Anna (Gordy) was shaky but they continued to stay together. Gaye's intention was to remove himself from the trappings of show business and the pressure, he claimed, Motown laid on him to work. Much of this pressure stemmed from the singer himself not having a full understanding of the business, and his confinement to conveyor-belt hits which he felt did nothing for his career. He was tired of touring and frustrated at his inability to record his own music, so for three years he shunned the limelight to prepare for his next project which he hoped would satisfy his obsession for artistic creativity. Late in 1970 the singer delivered the finished work, *What's Going On*, to Motown, a project inspired by his younger brother Frankie's return from Vietnam. Motown refused to release the album, whereby Gaye retorted 'if you don't issue it I'll never do another album for you'. Reluctantly the title track (written by Four Tops' Obie Benson, Gaye and Al Cleveland) was released as an American single in January 1971 (UK, May '71). Benson, who also co-wrote *Save The Children* and *Wholy Holy* said writing *What's Going On*

was easy: 'Al and I were just writing and we happened to come up with this tune. It sounded like something Marvin could sing so we presented him with the idea. He produced it and sang it tremendously. I don't think there is another artist who could have got what he got out of it.'

The album (US, May '71/UK, Sep '71), a casual but significant prod at society via Gaye's double-tracking, raced up the American charts, selling two million copies on its way. Motown had been taught a lesson and the original instruction to its sales department to get the album off the market weeks after its release, was hastily rescinded. Two further singles followed, *Mercy Mercy Me (The Ecology)* (US, Jun '71/UK, Feb '72) and *Inner City Blues (Make Me Wanna Holler)* (US, Sep '71/UK, May '72), and both reached gold status, topped the American charts and together sold four million copies. However in Britain the singles died. It was music from the soul for the soul. Gaye: 'I was disillusioned about a lot of things in life and decided to try to do something about it. I had retired from the personal appearance end of the business because I always felt conspicuous on stage. So I spent the three years writing, producing and reflecting. Reflecting on America's injustices, evils and its good.' It came as a shock when the singer, now sporting a beard, realized the implications of the lyrics and sentiments of his work – 'it's true that the album is social commentary but there's nothing extreme on it. I did it not to help humanity but

112

to help me as well, and I think it has. It's given me a certain amount of peace of mind.' The album showed a mature, competent and relaxed Gaye, who had finally discovered his purpose in life. With his newly-found confidence he spoke for the first time about Terrell's death: 'I had such an emotional experience with Tammi and her death that I don't imagine I'll ever work with another girl again. She was a singer who was still developing and her talent was denied her and so many others. I loved her very much.'

Following a small part in the television film *Chrome And Hot Leather* Marvin Gaye, at his parent's request, performed at Washington's John F. Kennedy Centre for the Performing Arts to raise money for the newly-launched self-help organization Pride Inc. Gaye's future concerts were the subject of controversy as more were cancelled than performed, a trait that was to last throughout his life. In defence of his actions he told *The Los Angeles Times*: 'I hate the hassles and restrictions of touring, and I hate getting up on stage in front of people. I know it's an ego thing and I want to be liked but I would hate it if the audience didn't like me. It's a real hang-up for me.' Meanwhile, as Gaye was basking in the glory of *What's Going On*, Motown was getting impatient for his next work.

Fighting for hits with Marvin Gaye was Norman Whitfield's new band The Undisputed Truth with *Save My Love For a Rainy Day* (US, Feb '71/UK, Jun '71). Edwin Starr, meanwhile, was still on his psychedelic kick with yet another version of Whitfield's *Funky Music Sho Nuff Turns Me On* (US, Mar '71/UK, Apr '72) while the Jackson 5 soundalike *Bless You* (US, Sep '71/UK, Nov '71) was released by Martha Reeves and the Vandellas. The Jacksons themselves scored another million seller with *Mama's Pearl* (US, Jan '71/UK, Apr '71) and Diana Ross's *Remember Me* (US, Dec '70/UK, Mar '71) was one of Ashford and Simpson's finest. The solo David Ruffin's *Each Day Is A Lifetime* (US, Feb '71) competed with The Supremes' *Nathan Jones* (US, Apr '71/UK, Aug '71). New signing Bobby Darin issued his first, *Melodie* (US, Apr '71) and Gordon Staples and the Motown Strings' outing of *Strung Out* (US, Mar '71) provided a rare instrumental single.

Whitfield's protégés, The Undisputed Truth, filled The Temptations' vacancy. Billie Rae Calvin and Brenda Joyce Evans (both from Los Angeles) were members of The Delicates, who were introduced to Motown by Bobby Taylor (of the Vancouvers). The girls worked first as session singers on the Four Tops' *Still Waters* project, Ross' *Ain't No Mounting High Enough* and Starr's *War* and *Funky Music Sho Nuff Turns Me On*. In time The Delicates disbanded leaving Calvin and Evans, so Whitfield brought in Detroiter Joe Harris (from the Preps) to form his new group. It was their second single *Smiling Faces Sometimes* (US, May '71/UK, Oct '71) that reached gold and turned them into viable promotion tools.

Whitfield's partner Barrett Strong wasn't involved in the production or material selection for either The Truth or The Temptations (whom he considered to be their 'bread and butter money'): 'Norman always felt he could do a song in so many different ways, but there was certainly never any shortage of material because we were writing new songs all the time.' Unfortunately, The Truth fell short of Whitfield's espectations, as he told *Blues & Soul*: 'They represented a challenge to me. People were saying Motown had become stagnant so I set about making a new group with completely new ideas. In a small way I did the same for The Velvelettes, but my efforts for the Truth were all in vain because the company simply was never into what the group meant. They became pawns in a political situation that had nothing to do even with me. I guess that this was indirectly what led to me leaving Motown. As a company they developed a lack of respect for what people were doing for them, and they lost their creative direction when certain people left.' Two years before he departed, he formed Whitfield Records which he intended Motown to distribute. The negotiations between the two parties failed: 'I guess the way they handled The Truth gave me an insight of the way it would be and I wanted no part of it.' The writer/producer who spent thirteen years in Motown's quality control department before working directly with artists, signed his label to Warner Brothers where he ploughed his talents into Rose Royce.

Another Motown signing was actor/singer Bobby Darin who started with the company in the early Seventies. Darin was notorious for his outspoken beliefs on war, prison injustices, drugs and bigotry. He released the *Bobby Darin* album in 1972 from which various singles were lifted. His first break in show business came in 1956 on CBS-TV's *Jackie Gleason Stage Show* and from there he performed in

Norman Whitfield's new protégés, the innovative Undisputed Truth, promoted his individualistic sound. Their second single Smiling Faces Sometimes went gold. Unfortunately, the trio could not hold on to their success.

most nightclubs across America. Such was
the power of his name that he appeared on
virtually every major television show, sold
over fifteen million singles, three million
albums, won two Grammy Awards and was
nominated for an Oscar.

Born on 14 May 1936 in Harlem, New York,
Darin's real name was Walden Robert Cas-
sotto. Shortly before his birth his father died
and his mother, Paula, and his sister Vanina,
raised him in impoverished conditions. He
was educated in the Bronx and won a scholarship to New York's Hunter College. A year
later he recorded his hit single Splish Splash on
Atco Records. A string of top-sellers followed
in quick succession – Queen Of The Hop, Dream
Lover, the evergreen Mack The Knife, Lazy River,
Multiplication and Things. Following record success he ventured into films and signed a
seven year contract with Paramount and Universal Studios to star in a string of successful
movies. Darin married and divorced Sandra
Dee and died prematurely at the age of 37 following open heart surgery in 1973. Motown released a tribute album to Darin in 1974, Darin
1936-1973 (UK, Aug '82).

Gladys Knight and the Pips were being left

behind in the battle of the charts, not progressing as fast as The Supremes or The Temptations. I *Don't Want To Do Wrong* (1971) helped change their stagnant situation but the slightly inferior material continued to sting. Gladys Knight was worried about the future of the group itself: 'We've had a pretty lean time since I *Heard It Through The Grapevine* which was the biggest seller the company had had. It was hard to come up with a song to top that, or even one that was as good. Maybe we should have chosen a different direction, but it's so difficult to tell what's going to sell and what's not. Thankfully, I *Don't Want To Do Wrong* earned us our third gold disc, but gold discs are just a part of it. Just the beginning of other things. You develop a certain drawing power. The Supremes and Diana Ross can guarantee packed houses wherever they appear and that's what I mean. We haven't got to that stage yet. When we reach the point where we have queues of people stretching blocks just waiting to see us then that's when we've reached the pinnacle of success.' Ironically, her group was forced to leave Motown before they could enjoy the kind of success they rightly deserved.

The Supremes might have been bigger than the Pips at this time, but the group wasn't without problems. With a British tour pending and now minus Diana Ross, it was unknown how Jean Terrell would be accepted by the UK's staunch Supremes' fans. As Ross had been such an integral part of the unit Mary Wilson said it took her a long time to pluck up the courage to agree to the tour but in 1971 they finally began their tour in London. Audiences noticed a marked change in their repertoire as their new-style show included standards and show tunes interlaced with old and new Supremes material. To avoid losing Ross' magic, several songs were taken at a slower pace or emphasis was placed on the backing vocals. By changing their act the trio once more moved further away from black audiences, even though they stressed they had made positive attempts to return to their roots before Diana Ross left. Wilson: 'A lot of people said we've sold out to the white people but what they don't seem to realize is

Even though their record releases were not doing well, Gladys Knight and the Pips continued to thrill audiences with their tightly choreographed shows. Gladys was worried about the group's future and probably realized a change of record company was the only answer.

that we've never been a soul group singing soul music. We've never been a hard, driving soul group, not even with *Baby Love* and things like that. We've always been a very in-between group. When we made it by adding a lot of show tunes and things it might have seemed like we were selling out, but it really isn't true.'

Did the group miss Diana Ross? Jean Terrell: 'I think now that I've joined we're still in the stages of proving ourselves and we're steadily doing that. I really can't understand why we're having such a hard time proving ourselves after all we've had three million sellers. But people are still saying "come on, you've got to show some more", and until we've shown some more they won't properly accept us. The Supremes to me were a status group before I came in and my joining them didn't take away any of the status as far as I'm concerned, but maybe in people's minds it did.' While in England the trio performed with the Four Tops at The Royal Albert Hall on Tuesday 30 November. The joint performance was a secret addition to the Save The Children Charity Gala staged before HRH Princess Margaret and her husband Lord Snowdon.

The Supremes needed all the help they could get to maintain their status without Ross, and when Motown released their album *Touch* to coincide with the tour, Elton John added his weight by writing the sleeve notes. (John had befriended Cindy Birdsong during her Bluebelle days.) The album was sophisticated and melodic, yet it failed to reach previous sales figures. Wilson: 'We were angry with our sales department because we don't think *Touch* (US, May '71/UK, Sep '71) was presented to the public in the right way. We feel it could have been a smash album. So that was a mistake on their part and subsequently we had to suffer. We've always been up there selling millions and that's our aim every time we put something out. Very seldom in the past could I ever listen to our albums, but I think the three we have released since the new Supremes have been excellent. They haven't been presented to the public properly so no-one had any enthusiasm to buy them.' Prior to this release the *New Ways But Love Stays* album (US, Sep '70/UK, Feb '71) was another imaginative release. The record's title was changed from their hit single *Stoned Love* because Cindy Birdsong explained: 'The title was thought to be controversial because people might connect it with drugs. Like being stoned, even though the song was nothing to do with that.' For this reason when the trio appeared on American television *Stoned Love* was omitted from their repertoire. Meanwhile, convinced Motown had abandoned the group Wilson strenuously continued to change the company's attitude. She commented: 'I feel Motown has pulled out on us and just at the time when people were starting to accept our new image and things were looking up for us. I've always believed albums can be sold on sleeves and still do'.

A record that was sold purely on content and not packaging was R. Dean Taylor's *Indiana Wants Me* which raced to number two in the British charts in 1971. This release was conceived from the singer's own experience: 'I'd just arrived in Detroit and was staying in a downtown hotel. I kept waking up at night to the sound of sirens. One night I woke up in my room which faced a store and I could see there was someone in there. I heard this guy with a megaphone yelling "this is the police, give yourself up, you are surrounded". Red lights were flashing all over the place and me, a country boy from Canada, was absolutely terrified.' The single dramatically portrayed the incident in detail and it was this that attracted the British public. Taylor had to wait another three years before his next hit, a fate suffered by many unpromoted artists who eventually succumbed to disillusionment and left the company with little or no prospect of future work. This situation would never befall Diana Ross who, by the end of 1971, had announced her intention to play Billie Holiday in the film *Lady Sings The Blues*.

LADY SINGS THE BLUES

'I tried to find the other side of Billie Holiday that wasn't in the book and that's not on the back of album covers.'
Berry Gordy

'I could never go solo, not with the group being a family thing because it would be like breaking away from my family.'
Michael Jackson

Billie Holiday, born Eleanora Fagan, one of America's greatest blues singers, died in 1959 at the age of 44. Her singing style influenced the majority of contemporary singers and her lifestory has an awesome relevance today – racism, alcoholism, promiscuity and drug abuse, combined with old-fashioned laws, official bureaucracy and the trials of life itself.

Holiday, born on 7 April 1915 in Baltimore, Maryland, stunned the world when she began her autobiography, published in 1956, with 'Mom and Pop were just a couple of kids when they got married. He was eighteen, she was sixteen, and I was three.' Holiday's young life was a series of atrocities – an older cousin assaulted her and her great grandmother, an invalid for many years, died clutching the young girl in her death grasp. Traumatized by these events Holiday spent four weeks in hospital suffering from shock. When she was 10 a man tried to rape her and for that she spent two days in jail. Later, she was confined in a Catholic home with a body of a dead girl as punishment. Holiday was subjected to regular beatings from an aunt who looked after her while her mother sought work in various parts of America. It was inevitable that the abuse and horror of her early years would take their toll, resulting in an emotionally and mentally scarred adult who felt alone, abandoned, vulnerable and inadequate.

In her teens Holiday turned to prostitution and ended up in jail when she refused a black client. In jail she fought off the advances of a lesbian and the fight that followed resulted in her getting an extended sentence. Her escape from the red light district and entry into show business is legendary but throughout her career she suffered untold indignities because of her colour, and turned to drugs in an attempt to block out the ugliness that surrounded her. However her only true escape was singing, and she absorbed the sentiments of a song, singing from her very soul; it's reputed she caused a run of suicides when she sang *Gloomy Sunday*. Holiday met an early death on 7 July 1959 in New York's Metropolitan Hospital, where on her death bed narcotic agents, who had hounded her for most of her life, arrested her. The singer made a fortune for herself and others during her lifetime, yet on that July morning she had $750 strapped to her leg and only seventy cents in the bank. Someone said of her death 'Billie died of everything'.

Billie Holiday was a consummate artist whose problems defeated her at the end. There were intervals in her life that were joyous, highlighted by wealth, love and luxury, earning her the respect of her peers and an international audience. And it was this that Diana Ross intended to bring to life on the screen, although the result was based more on fantasy than fact. Berry Gordy explained at the time that if he had stuck diligently to Holiday's book the film would be a documentary about a singer who suffered one tragedy after another: 'I tried to find the other side of Billie Holiday that wasn't in the book and that's not on the back of album sleeves. I tried to find the person very few people knew about. There were two sides to Billie. There were not all downs, because while she was high and tragic and she got caught up in the whirlwind of dope, she was also a happy person, a funny and loving person.'

When Gordy was approached by producer Jay Weston and director Sydney Furie to finance *Lady Sings The Blues* they suggested Diana Ross should play lead. Gordy was unsure she had the ability to carry it off, but changed his mind when they insisted she would probably be nominated for an Oscar. When Ross was given the script it's said she was, in her naïvity, appalled at the number of scenes she was expected to play in. Subsequently Gordy made a few alternations before submitting it to Paramount after Fox showed little interest. As Paramount were nervous about sinking millions of dollars into an unknown black actress Gordy agreed to share the cost. Other Motown singers joined Diana Ross in the film. Yvonne Fair appeared as a Harlem cabaret singer who collected her customer's cash between her legs as was the Thirties' custom. Blinky Williams, not seen in

Diana Ross adopts Billie Holiday's famous trademark of a gardenia to portray the late blues/jazz singer in Lady Sings the Blues.

the film, sang *T'Ain't Nobody's Biz-ness If I Do*, while during a downtown nightclub sequence Michele Aller performed *Had You Been Around*, and The Lewis Sisters were auditioned for a radio show. Ross's co-stars were Billy Dee Williams, who played her husband Louis McKay, and Richard Pryor.

The film was delayed for a month while Gordy asked Chris Clark, Suzanne de Passe and Terence McCloy to rewrite the script. Once he was satisfied the revised hundred-page script took forty-four days to shoot, with one hundred and sixty-eight different scenes. For the first six days Ross played a teenager and by the fourteenth she appeared old enough to confront a Dixie Klan parade. Ross, working a twelve hour day, appeared in almost every scene. Filming began on 6 December 1971. The original agreement between the film company, Paramount, and Gordy provided that Gordy would pay any costs in excess of $2 million. Eventually he bought out the film company for double that amount following several disagreements. When, after the filming had begun, Ross was unhappy with her wardrobe and insisted she re-design it herself, costs soared. Gordy: 'The producers felt she was a temperamental bitch. So did I in a way but because of what I felt were emotional ties between Diana and

Billie I reluctantly gave in completely to her wishes. We increased the budget for clothes and turned it totally over to her'. The new rags and gowns were designed by Ray Aghayan and Bob Mackie and made up by Elizabeth Courtney. The singer had forty-three costume changes throughout the film ranging from tattered teenagers' sweaters to elaborate stage gowns. Gordy also insisted that the film should run for the full three-and-a-half hours instead of the ninety minutes proposed by Paramount, who could see no reason in filming footage that would be edited out, and he also told Ross to concentrate more on singing and less on drama.

The final selection of the film's repertoire included numbers like *Loverman (Oh, Where Can You Be?)*, *Don't Explain*, *I Cried For You*, *All Of Me*, *Strange Fruit*, *My Man* and *God Bless The Child*. All were re-recorded by Diana under the strict supervision of Gordy and Gil Askey – the film's musical co-ordinator. Several of the musicians including Harry Edison, bassist Red Holloway and guitarist John Collins, heard on the soundtrack, actually backed Holiday's performances. *Lady Sings The Blues* was perhaps Hollywood's most racially integrated film of the time – of the sixty-four speaking parts, thirty-four were played by blacks, while extras included countless

people who knew Holiday during her lifetime or were loyal fans.

Lady Sings The Blues was finished two days ahead of schedule in late 1972, and was premiered on 23 October 1972 in New York City. It was obvious to anyone who saw the film that Ross had studied Holiday and her life thoroughly before attempting such a demanding role. Ross commented: 'I didn't in any way try to sound like her or phrase anything like her. Her music got to me by osmosis. It just came into my body by living with it and playing it constantly. In fact, during that time I don't think I listened to any other music except hers.' Ross's biggest obligation was, she said, not to exploit Holiday's life, but to portray her as a legend; 'I worked very hard with our script and with everybody involved with the film. Through Billie's music you can gain great understanding of what she was all about. In fact, that's how I did most of my research. I felt her in my singing. I also read between the lines to understand the things that were happening to her in her songs. I felt that she expressed her total being in her songs, what she felt about life and death at that time.' Two famous Holiday classics distressed Ross: 'The first was *Strange Fruit*. I'd never seen men hanging from a tree with a rope around their necks and I found one pic-

ture in the research that helped me understand the song. Seeing that photo was very emotional because it was like something you don't really believe. The other was *God Bless The Child* which is a philosophy that people had to make it and work to do things they wanted to do in this life. A philosophy they could live with. Them's that got shall get, and them that's not shall lose. You've got lots of friends hanging around your door when you've got it, when it's gone, they don't come round no more. I found that Billie was aware of all the problems and she subsequently showed them in her songs.'

During her media tour prior to the premiere, Ross faced an onslaught of criticism concerning her lack of qualifications to play the Holiday role. Ross retaliated in *The New York Times*: 'People felt I couldn't play the tragedies. They think I was born with a silver spoon in my mouth. I was surprised how good I was. The first time I heard a Billie Holiday record I thought *what's so great about her*? I didn't really care about her until I did research on her, until I began hearing snatches of people's memories of her. That's how it all started. She brought sophistication and class into music. She was a beautiful lady up on stage, and she became a legend because of her craft and talent. I felt that if I got an acting offer that was

Although *Lady Sings The Blues* was Diana Ross's first leading role as a serious actress, she won critical acclaim on a worldwide scale. She was Billie Holiday and her performance kept the late singer's legend alive.

119

good it'd be a challenge for me to get involved in dramatics or stage plays.' She also felt there was a public feeling that, unlike Holiday's, her own life had been uncomplicated and easy: 'I'm not saying that the problems that Billie faced are the same as any that I've had but I can relate to problems and tragedies also. In many ways I'm glad that the film has shown people that I've a brain too. To begin with there was such a total "no" about the whole idea of me playing Billie, especially since there were so many others in line for the part. I was so upset by it that I phoned Berry and asked if we were too late to stop it before we'd actually started. Naturally he said we were too committed so I just gritted my teeth and got down to it. I'm happy that I did my best for the film'.

Most of the film's critics agreed Diana Ross excelled in this her first dramatic role but were angered at the film's betrayal of Holiday's life. The British weekly music paper *Melody Maker* printed: 'In many ways this is a pointedly anti-white film. Billie is first turned on to junk by one of the white musicians in the band with whom she is touring. Miss Ross bears no resemblance to Billie Holiday, either facially or vocally, and this movie is true to the great singer's life only in skeletal detail. It's tone, like its colour, is glossy; the actual pock-marks are filled in. It's Diana Ross acting out something altogether different. Once or twice she'll tug at your heart in a way The Supremes never did. Wherever the eye of the film makers might be, the heart of its star is in the right place'.

Disc's critic wrote: 'In the film she is seen to have one lover, while in her life Billie had two husbands and more than a few relationships. One of them was with tenor saxophone giant, Lester Young, who, according to the film, never existed. Also according to the film, John Hammond, who produced her records and brought her to the white audience, never existed. It was in fact Billie's first husband who introduced her to heroin, while in the film, since her first husband didn't exist, it is the white band leader who does the deed. Another fault is the film's ending which tries to compress the sorded events of Billie's last year into superimposed headlines during her performance at Carnegie Hall in an effort to close the film on a note of triumph and joy. There was triumph but very little joy in Lady Day's life. But, and this is a very big but indeed, Diana Ross's performance carries the film so convincingly that she will certainly be a big contender for the Best Actress Academy award next spring.'

A double soundtrack album was released in December 1972 (UK, Mar '73) and became Motown's fastest-selling album, at the rate of 300,000 in its first selling week. It shot to the top of the American charts and stayed in the listings for a year.

Despite some media criticism both Diana Ross and the film were showered with awards, including three NAACP Image Awards: Actress of the Year, Motown Picture of the Year and Actor of the Year (Billy Dee Williams). Ross also received the Golden Globe Best New Star Award, *Cue Magazine*'s coveted Entertainer of the Year, and she was nominated for an Oscar for Best Actress, while Clark, de Passe and McCloy were nominated for the screenplay, Michel Legrand for the music score and Gil Askey for the orchestration. At the 45th Annual Academy Awards ceremony on 27 March 1973, Diana Ross lost to Liza Minnelli for her performance in *Cabaret*. After the ceremony she moaned: 'I really worked hard on that god-damned film and I really felt that I deserved that Oscar. But just because I didn't get it doesn't mean to say I won't try again.' Gordy too thought Ross should have won and prior to the Awards ceremony saturated the press to encourage Academy votes. It had the opposite effect. However her nomination led to thirty film offers which she refused, being signed to Paramount for at least one other movie. In its first week of release *Lady Sings The Blues* grossed in excess of $6 million. The next step was Europe. . . .

Motown/EMI had already geared its promotion towards the film's premiere, working with Paramount Pictures to embark on one of the biggest campaigns seen in Britain for both film and soundtrack. A wide slection of incentives were distributed, and the company pressed two hundred and fifty records containing selected tracks which were played in cinemas two weeks prior to the film's screening. A fifteen-minute film extract was also prepared for the university circuit. The British premiere was at midnight on 4 April in Shaftesbury Avenue's ABC-1 cinema in London. Ross attended and stayed in the country long enough to include two television appearances on BBC 2's *Film '73* and ITV's *David Frost Programme*. It was intended to use this premiere as the start of her first solo tour but as she was required to attend further European premieres the tour was postponed until August.

Berry Gordy decided the most appropriate launching pad for *Lady Sings The Blues* was the forthcoming Cannes Film Festival in France, where he intended to make such an impression that nobody would forget his film and star. Upon their arrival (Gordy travelled with her) Ross was transported to the Carlton Hotel in a 1923 Rolls Royce with a twelve motorcycle police escort. The hotel's front was covered with twenty thousand flowers spelling out 'Welcome Diana Ross', the eighty-piece Nice Symphony Orchestra sat on the terrace playing songs from the film, and the Garde Republican, especially imported from Paris, lined the Croisette from the Carlton Hotel right up to the doors of the flood-lit Palais, forming a human corridor along the longest red carpet known to French history. The Palais, one of France's most historic structures, held the Film Festival's activities, where Gordy decided to feature both Ross and film on the closing night. Prior to the screening Ross performed before two thousand international show business representatives and thousands more outside listened to the show through strategically placed loud speakers. *Lady Sings The Blues* and its leading lady were instant hits at Cannes, and Berry Gordy was now ensconced in the film business. However, he was wise enough to realize one hit would not guarantee a prosperous future, and began considering a follow-up movie to suit his new actress.

A year after the release of the *Lady Sings The Blues* soundtrack, Diana Ross released her best album to date *Touch Me In The Morning* (US, Jun '73/UK, Aug '73). Ross was pregnant during the recording sessions which may, she said, have had something to do with the album having a baby theme. Two tracks, John Lennon's *Imagine* and Marvin Gaye's *Save The Children*, were the singer's first attempts at producing, but it was the album's title track, written by Ron Miller and Michael Masser, that outshone the others. It was released as a single eighteen months after it was recorded (US, May '73/UK, Jul '73) and after a sluggish start was nominated for a Grammy (in the Best Pop Vocal Performance – Female section) and deservedly became an American number one. British buyers were less enamoured as the single only reached number nine. A further track *Young Mothers* (produced and co-written by Tom Baird) was also recorded for the album, but was edged out and canned. It was later included in her 1983

Anthology album, where a second unreleased track *Baby I Love Your Way* (written by Peter Frampton and produced by Richard Perry) was also included.

The *Touch Me In The Morning* single was followed by *Last Time I Saw Him* in December 1973 in America, whereas Motown/EMI released *All Of My Life* in November 1973 which also peaked at number nine. *Last Time I Saw Him*, taken from the album of the same name (US, Dec '73/UK, Feb '74) was eventually issued in April 1974 and peaked at thirty-five. *Sleepin'* was the next single to be lifted in America during April 1974 and was Ross's biggest failure since her early days as a Supreme. Motown/EMI released *Love Me* to secure a British top forty hit.

For his second film Gordy chose a story that was lightweight and glossy, a total contrast to the dramatic *Lady Sings The Blues*. The new film also demanded less of Ross as its principal actress. Instead of developing this second film under the structure of the first, where he became executive producer, Gordy moved into the director's chair. The film was *Mahogany* and Ross was slotted to play Tracy Chambers, a poor girl with ambitions of becoming a top fashion designer. John Byrum wrote the screenplay from a story by Toni Amber. Rob Cohen and Jack Ballard produced, and later Cohen was hired to head Motown's film division where he was responsible for its third film *The Bingo Long And The Travelling All-Stars And Motor Kings*, adapted from William Brashler's book on black baseball leagues.

Michael Masser, familiar to Motown but not soundtracks, was asked to write the score.

For her second feature film, Diana Ross played Tracy Chambers in Mahogany. She is seen here with co-star Anthony Perkins who played the part of a disturbed photographer. Ross's second co-star was Billy Dee Williams, who played the dedicated politician Brian Walker.

He studied in Illinois Law School where he proved he had a promising career in music, yet he left to move to New York City to work at menial jobs to help keep his parents. Masser then studied classical composers and played piano with various musicians but as his family were dependent on him he once again abandoned music to become a Wall Street financial adviser. When he was 30 he moved to California to write and it was here that Motown asked him to work with Diana Ross. His first was the hit single *Touch Me In The Morning*, which he co-wrote and produced, whereupon he became a company writer. In 1975 he was asked to write the score and title song for *Mahogany*, and used a song he had previously written with Gerry Goffin and recorded with Thelma Houston titled *Do You Know Where You're Going To* as the film's title. Houston: 'We did the basic background work but it was never finished off properly and I guess it was just hidden away. Then the movie was in the pipeline and Masser resurrected the song and as Diana was the star of the film it was only natural that she should sing it.' Houston realized the potential of the song but felt no resentment towards Ross re-recording it: 'Let's put it this way, if I was the star of a movie I wouldn't expect someone else to sing the credit. I'd want to do it myself.' All but one tune (Eddie Kendricks' *Let's Go Back To Day One* written by Patrice Holloway and Gloria Jones) on the soundtrack were original compositions. Masser was credited with the composition and production of the album although he was actually responsible for seven tracks: *Feeling Again*, *You Don't Ever Have To Be Alone*, *Can You Hear It In My Music*, *Christian's Theme*, *After You*, *My Hero Is A Gun* and *Mahogany Suite*. The remainder were *Cat Fight*, *Sweets (And Other Things)* and *Tracy*, written, arranged and produced by Gil Askey; *Erucu* and *She's The Ideal Girl* were written and produced by Jermaine Jackson and Don Daniels, with Askey as arranger.

The soundtrack was released in October

When *Mahogany* was premiered, Diana Ross's version of the film title track shot to the top of the US charts. American critics slated the film, while British reviewers tolerated it.

1975 (UK, Nov '75). Prior to this the title track *Theme From Mahogany (Do You Know Where You're Going To)* (US, Sep '75) (the only song performed by Ross in the film) was issued as the follow-up to *Sorry Doesn't Always Make It Right* (US, Feb '75/UK, Feb '75). In the UK the film's title was also released in the October 1975 whereupon the media treated it as a mediocre Diana Ross ballad. However, when the film was premiered the single shot to number five in the UK in April 1976 and raced to number one in the States!

The film grossed $7 million during the first two weeks of its release yet was not nominated for a 1976 Oscar. Gordy was furious because although the film had been panned by American critics, it was a box office success. The Academy was embarrassed by Motown's protestations and agreed to submit *Theme From Mahogany (Do You Know Where You're Going To)* in the Best Original Score and Song category. Diana Ross was midway through a Continental tour when the Awards ceremony was screened so she was seen singing the song in the freezing cold via a satellite link from an Amsterdam street at 4.30 am. Alas it still didn't win!

Even though American critics slated the film, British reviewers were kinder: 'Love conquers all, and I have to say that Ms Ross conquers all and very nearly makes you – or me at any rate – overlook the plots, improbabilities and other shortcomings. She is in the most positive fashion stunning, spell-binding, appealing and blessed with superstar juices' (*Melody Maker*). 'The film is a traditional money spinner, an anodyne romantic epic, featuring a rags to riches heroine who makes good as a model and then as a designer. Americans have been flocking in their thousands to see this unflattering insight into some of the more hypocritical aspects of showbusiness/political life' (*Ms London*).

After *The Bingo Long And The Travelling All Stars And Motor Kings* film, Billy Dee Williams starred as the ragtime pianist Scott Joplin in Motown's next film which flopped. Two years on, in 1978, Motown co-produced *Thank God It's Friday* with Columbia and Casablanca Records and Film Works. Based around a nightclub's activities, starring Donna Summer and the Commodores, the film was another poor box office attraction. Likewise *Almost Summer* featuring Tim Matheson and Didi Conn. Gordy was undeterred – there was still Broadway which was a wise and profitable move for his company. In 1972 he invested $140,000 in *Pippin* which ran for six years, earning Motown millions of dollars profit. The company released the soundtrack (US, Dec '72/UK, Nov '73) which featured *I Guess I'll Miss The Man* (US, Sep '72/UK, Jan '74) (recorded by The Supremes), *Corner Of The Sky* (US, Oct '72) (the Jackson 5) and *No Time At All* (US, Feb '73) by Irene 'Granny' Ryan (the oldest singer to be signed to Motown), who starred in the comedy television series *The Beverly Hillbillies*.

Encouraged by this success Motown became involved in other stage shows including *The Baker's Wife* (a joint venture with David Merrick) and a black version of *Guys And Dolls*. Both were failures. However, in the Eighties, Motown Productions released four films of note – *The Last Song* starring 'Wonderwoman' Lynda Carter (she also performed the title song); *Callie And Son* featuring the 'Bionic Woman', Lindsay Wagner, and *A Small Killing* and *Happy Endings*.

Away from the fantasy of the film world, the reality of Jackson 5 mania had peaked by 1973. The hysteria of The Beatles success had returned with a vengeance as concerts were sold out before the tickets could be printed, merchandizing became a booming business, and mayhem followed their every move. Motown's film and television department was quick to exploit the brothers and hotly followed *Diana* with their own *Goin' Back To Indiana* television special. The hour-long programme was based around their triumphant return to their hometown and featured Diana Ross, Bobby Darin, Tommy Smothers and Bill Cosby in a variety of sketches until the finale at Indianapolis Arena where the brothers performed. The show's soundtrack was US released in September 1971. The programme was also offered to the British television stations but rejected as unsuitable although the Jacksons' animated series was seen on British television.

The media attempted to stir an air of competition between the Jackson 5 and the equally popular Mormon brother group, The Osmonds. It's suspected Michael Jackson's move into solo recordings was prompted by Donny Osmond's success in the same field. Jackson hotly denied this, telling reporters: 'I just wanted to try recording alone. People seem to think that because The Osmonds

Michael Jackson followed Donny Osmond's lead by embarking on a solo career in 1971, while remaining a member of the family group. As a soloist young Michael enjoyed a string of top sellers.

became big with records that sounded something like ours we should have something against them. But it's not like that. I think they're a good group and I certainly have nothing against them.' He also denied he was leaving his brothers: 'I could never go solo, not with the group being a family thing because it would be like breaking away from my family. Anyway, the other guys are doing some solo things too and we're still recording as a group.' His first solo single *Got To Be There* in October 1971 (UK, Jan '72), bore the same title as his debut album, and was the first in a run of million sellers. *Rockin' Robin, I Wanna Be Where You Are* (the flipside to the British single *Ain't No Sunshine* in Jul '72) and *Ben*, a youngster's hymn to his killer rat and theme from a mediocre horror film were all released the following year. Michael's success was punctuated by solo releases from brother Jermaine whose debut album *Jermaine* was released in July 1972 (UK, Jan '73). *That's How Love Goes* was taken as a single a month later (UK. Dec '72) although another track *Daddy's Home* (US, Nov '72/UK, Apr '73) gave him his first American hit. As a group *Sugar Daddy, Little Bitty Pretty One* and *Lookin' Through The Windows* kept their fans at fever pitch.

By 1972 all the brothers were legally old enough to tour Britain, so they flew to London following concerts in Paris, Amsterdam and Frankfurt. Their first performance (with the Sisters Love as support act) was at the Birmingham Odeon on 9 November, followed by

(Left) Diana Ross helps the Jackson's make-up prior to a television appearance. The brothers, at the height of their Motown career, were featured in their own television special Goin' Back to Indiana.

Manchester's Belle Vue, two concerts at Liver-pool's Empire and one show at London's Wembley Arena. Nine-year-old Randy joined his brothers for this tour that was highlighted by hordes of screaming, clothes-tearing fans who not only caused riots at concerts but also outside The Churchill Hotel where the group stayed. Prior to their London debut the Jack-son 5 performed at The Talk Of The Town be-fore a specially invited audience, then appeared at the HMV record shop in Oxford Street where the police cut the stay short due to uncontrollable crowds of youngsters. Before the brothers returned to America they became the second Motown group to perform on the prestigious Royal Variety Show, while Gladys Knight and the Pips performed at the London Palladium on 5 November. Their short tour pushed Help Me Make It Through The Night (US, Mar '72/UK, Oct '72) to a British number eleven single, prior to which the re-issue of Just Walk In My Shoes (UK, Jun '72) reached thirty-five. The success of Help prompted a specially compiled album 20 Golden Greats/Help Me Make It Through The Night which also contained their next UK hit The Look Of Love (UK, Feb '73). The Neither One Of Us (Wants To Be The First To Say Goodbye) (US, Dec '72/UK, May '73) single was the group's last hit before leaving Motown for Buddah in March 1973, the same month Gladys Knight and her husband, James Newman, were divorced. Two years later the group sued Motown Records, Multi-Media Management and Jobete for $1 million in damages, and demanded owner-ship of their compositions recorded while signed with them, and royalties from label sales of the four albums released after their recording contract had expired. They also sought to prevent Motown releasing further material which would clash with their Buddah recordings.

On 13 May 1971 Stevie Wonder had his 21st

birthday and his contract with Motown expired. He spent the next year reflecting on his past career and experimenting with new music. Wonder: 'I decided to not sign with anybody for a while and just cool it. I was thinking of looking at other companies and talked to just about every company there was.' He knew his career was stagnating – 'I just kept repeating The Stevie Wonder Sound and I didn't express how I felt about what was hap-pening in the world'. With a few half-written songs and the $1 million held in trust for him by Motown, Wonder went to New York to the Electric Lady Studios, among others, to work on his own music without any Motown interference.

In January 1973 Motown pooled its music publishing, recording and television depart-ments under a parent company, Motown Industries Inc. Berry Gordy surrendered his Motown Records presidency to become head of this parent operation and chairman of the board. Ewart Abner, who replaced Gordy as president of Motown Records, had been aware of Stevie Wonder's frustration for two years yet was powerless to stop him searching for a new deal. While isolated in New York Wonder met Johannen Vigoda, a music busi-ness lawyer whom he hired to negotiate his next recording contract where the synthesized Music Of My Mind album was to be the first product. Wonder, reluctant to leave Motown when his contract expired, allowed Vigado to conclude a deal that would allow him total creative freedom (where Motown had to accept whatever he delivered) as well as con-trol of his compositions via his own Black Bull Publishing Company, and a higher royalty rate. Wonder also formed his own production outfit, Taurus Productions, so called after his birth sign. He was happy to give Music Of My Mind to Motown 'partly because of my new contract and partly from a verbal understanding. And partly because they don't understand what I'm doing, so they just let me get on with it.' Motown's A&R people were unhappy because the album contained no single material, an unheard of move under his last contract. Nonetheless the album was extensively marketed in March 1972 (UK, May '72) and *Superwoman* (*Where Were You When I Needed You*) (US, Apr '72/UK, Sep '72) was lifted as its first single. Commercially the releases failed, but Stevie Wonder hadn't.

Early in 1972 Wonder began a tour of Britain and it was an excited singer who told the press that by using his Moog and ARP together he had created a new dimension in sound on *Music Of My Mind*: 'I first heard the Moog in 1971 and became interested in its possibilities. Now I'm working with a VS04 and used it on the album because that's exactly what it is, music in my mind, because a synthesizer has allowed me to do a lot of things I've wanted to do for a long time but which were not possible until it came along. It's added a whole new dimension to music. After programming the sound you're able to write or process the melody line immediately and in as many different manners as you want.' On this tour Wonder introduced yet another instrument, the Bag (a strange tube-like device which fits into the mouth) – 'you don't actually make the sound with your voice, you just mouth the shape of the words and the air pressure acts on a resonator to produce the sound'. He then toured with The Rolling Stones for fifty days from Vancouver to New York. The last time Wonder played with them in 1964 he had top billing!

Blues artist, Luther Allison, was signed to Motown in 1972. Born in 1939 in Forest Hill, Arkansas, Alison had been playing the blues since 1954 when he joined his brother's band. After a three year stay with the group, Allison performed with the Four Jivers, until he worked with Muddy Waters, Little Richard and Chuck Berry. In 1961 Allison settled into his own band and moved to the West Coast where he was eventually signed by Berry Gordy. His first album *Bad News Is Coming* was released in the US in December 1972 but due to lack of marketing support this and his two follow-up albums died.

With the lack of regular hit material, the Four Tops' career was also in a nosedive. As their sales potential dropped Motown became increasingly uninterested in them leaving the quartet with no option but to look elsewhere for a recording deal. It was with reluctance that the Four Tops left their beloved organization in 1972 to sign with ABC Records. At first they enjoyed success with singles like *Keeper Of The Castle* and *Ain't No Woman* (*Like The One I've Got*) a year later, indicating the move was a wise one. However, by 1975, their product was inferior and their sell-

ing power once again negligible. It took six years before they charted again via a deal with Casablanca Records when the *When She Was My Girl* and *Don't Walk Away* singles were released.

The Supremes, too, were struggling with their new line-up following a pregnant Cindy Birdsong's retirement in 1972. Lynda Lawrence, from Wonder's Wonderlove backing group and one-time stand-in for Jean Terrell, replaced her. From Philadelphia, Lawrence began singing at the age of 4 when she joined her gospel singing father's band. By 15 she had formed her own outfit with her brother on organ. At this time, The Supremes' releases were erratic and diverse. The *Floy Joy* album (partly written and wholly produced by Smokey Robinson and the follow-up to *Touch*, it took a year to release after their *Promises Kept* album was abandoned) featured both Birdsong and Lawrence on vocals. Singles like the catchy but sugary *Automatically Sunshine* (US, Apr '72/UK, Jun '72) and *Your Wonderful Sweet Sweet Love* (US, Jul '72/UK, Nov '72) failed to meet their prior high standards. Something was definitely wrong, particularly when Robinson's Midas touch failed. However, before the trio reached rock bottom, Stevie Wonder stepped in and wrote *Bad Weather* (US, Mar '73/UK, Mar '73) for them. Wonder: 'I'd been listening to Jean Terrell for a long while and felt the way she'd been handled wasn't right. She got into certain riffs which have sounded

The Supremes lost a pregnant Cindy Birdsong in 1972 following her marriage to Charles David Hewlett late in 1970 at San Francisco's Fairmont Hall. Birdsong's replacement was the shortlived Lynda Lawrence (right).

great but she hadn't been given the material on which to develop them.' He intended to cut an album with them and recorded certain backing tracks, but didn't progress his plans in case Bad Weather flopped. Terrell told Disc magazine at this time that the group's recording problems were due to their heavy touring schedules which left little time to discuss suitable repertoire with writers and producers who, she felt, were too out of touch with what the public wanted: 'There's so much we wanted to do for a long while but there was no-one at Motown except Stevie who could interpret things the right way. Bad Weather goes chugga-chugga-chugga instead of ticka-ticka-ticka, the sound we've been doing before. We've all had things going around our heads for so long now we're ready to make the change. For so long there's been that typical Motown thing – the double-time drums and that very strong bass sound – but Bad Weather gets away from that. Stevie was the only person we knew who was able to get into what we wanted ourselves.' As the single's backing track featured shrill whistling, The Supremes threw plastic whistles into their audiences at the close of their shows!

With the record's British release the trio undertook a three week tour in the spring of 1972 with the line-up of Terrell, Wilson and Lawrence. Their The Supremes Produced And Arranged By Jimmy Webb (US, Oct '72/UK, Mar '73) album was also available. Beautiful in lyrical content and mood, it was their worst seller! In the same Disc interview Terrell expressed her disappointment: 'I really felt it was one of our best and I liked every song. Working with Jim Webb was a fantastic experience for us, and of course, it was a great change for us to work with a person of his calibre and someone from outside Motown.' Mary Wilson: 'I think if we had been successful at the time the album would have sold. I guess it was a shot in the dark because we were looking for a new identity at the time.' While in Britain Wilson was romantically linked with television personality David Frost, who a month earlier was spurned by Diahann Carroll (a later Motown recording artist and an Eighties soap opera star in Dynasty).

When Berry Gordy lost interest in The Supremes after Wilson refused to replace Terrell with Syreeta, the singers felt betrayed and unsettled although their public was ignorant of the troubles. Wilson: 'We came close to leaving Motown more than once. Every group has problems, but we've always known we'd continue somehow. I'm a fighter, I have the faith and right now we're fighting for our freedom. I've worked hard since 1964 and now that all these recent problems have come on top of our professional commitments, it's taken a toll on me. We work every day and that gives us little personal life, but it's got to be like that otherwise we wouldn't be here now.'

A year later in August 1973 Jean Terrell appeared on television with the group for the last time. She left the group because she was tired of her working lifestyle and the way Motown failed to support her: 'I also felt I was losing a lot of time, valuable time, being on the road, when there was another life for me. My first instinct is to be a woman and I've always wanted a child so my husband and I decided to have one. I'm twenty-seven years old and not getting any younger. I was dissatisfied and I was unhappy about how they treated me and the group. I took it personally when my career's at stake and I figured why should I stay and take this.'

Ex-Glasshouse member Scherrie Payne replaced the departing Supreme, making her television debut in January 1974. Detroit-born Payne, like her elder sister Freda and friends Holland, Dozier and Holland, attended Detroit's Central High School. Freda had already embarked on a professional singing career when Scherrie enrolled at the Michigan State University in East Lansing, where she received a Bachelor of Science Degree in Medical Technology. However, she abandoned medicine to work for a teaching certificate at Wayne State University and spent two years teaching maladjusted senior high school boys, before joining Glasshouse. The group was signed to H-D-H's Invictus label when Scherrie was approached to audition for The Supremes.

In the New Year (1973) Stevie Wonder flew to London to record two numbers on a Burt Bacharach television special including the Bacharach composition Alfie which Stevie recorded under the name Eivets Rednow. Superstition from his Talking Book album (US, Oct '72/UK, Jan '73) was released in Oct '72. This was his first hard funk record and he wrote it originally for Jeff Beck (who was once signed to Motown but didn't release a product). Wonder: 'I did a show with Jeff in Detroit and he told me he'd like to record something funky (referring to Superstition) so I said I'd cut it too and maybe include it on my next album. He said he didn't want my track to sound like his and I assured him it wouldn't. I played on his session, then finished off my own version and put it on the album. But Jeff's version didn't come out. Then Motown told me they wanted to lift my version as a single. In fact, they really insisted because I hadn't put out a single to coincide with my last album. I understand Jeff got upset about it but it wasn't my fault. So I tried to call him but he wouldn't take my calls. I even offered to write another song for him but he never got back to me.' Wonder's version topped the American charts and reached number eleven in the UK in February 1973.

Marvin Gaye wasn't so lucky with songs, as he divulged ten years later: 'I don't think Motown ever gave me the respect which I felt was my due. There were disputes over financial matters, over promotion, over a whole heap of things. Also my marriage to Anna was over. I didn't know what I was going to do. I knew what I wasn't going to do and that was to come back with something pretty much like what I'd done already. To me, that was a job finished and I was off to new adventures.' That adventure instigated another concept album *Let's Get It On*, co-produced and written by Ed Townsend. This album's title song was released in June 1973 (UK, Aug '73), two months before the album (UK, Sep '73), which one journalist referred to as 'the most incredible collection of screwing music available', topped the American charts. When Gaye's father heard the single he told his son 'don't go any further – you're supposed to be a minister's son'. In defence of his work the singer explained he wanted to record an album that looked at physical love in a much more open and honest way than he was able to do with other producers and writers: 'I think sex is great! And I'm a fantasy person. I think there's a point where you can live out your fantasies and not go over in perversity. I also think society makes people creep and crawl about and it only accentuates perversity. I suppose that makes it more fun for the pervert though.' While recording this huge-selling work, 30-year-old Gaye met his second wife, Janis Hunter.

Let's Get It On was brilliantly conceived with blatant sexual lyrics, heavy breathing and simulated orgasms against moody music which made tracks like *Just To Keep You Satisfied*, *Come Get To This* and *You Sure Love To Ball* more erotic. Gaye, the 'love' man, pictured wearing a woolly hat (his future trademark) on the record's sleeve, bragged to NME magazine: 'I was talking directly to the girls out there, but I hoped it would be an aid for men as well. Maybe it'll have some aphrodisiac power. I had a lot of fun doing it.' Once again Motown's marketing division shuddered at the album's content which media censors would edit heavily. Happily, most of the songs were played uncensored and the album went gold in America.

By this time Marvin Gaye had a steady drug habit and had been arrested for carrying dope. Motown bailed him out. Gaye: 'It's well known that certain drugs will open up one's creative facilities and perception banks. Color and sound centres can become more apparent by the use of drugs. So, in some cases they can play a part in creativity but certainly one can reach those levels without the aid of such drugs. On the other hand, the abuse of stimulants can be very detrimental and harmful. It's all a question of balance and maintaining control.' He might have been able to sustain a balance at this time, but by the late Seventies the scales had tipped against him.

Shortly after *Let's Get It On* hit the shops in August 1973, Stevie Wonder released *Innervisions*, his first album written without outside help. Interestingly, the artist had stockpiled at least one thousand songs by now which were catalogued for future use. *Innervisions* was a personal statement of social issues with

New signing Willie Hutch's debut album The Mack *was the soundtrack of the movie of the same name.*

tracks like the single *Living For The City* (US, Oct '73/UK, Nov '73) which portrayed anger, *Too High* dealing with drug abuse, and the ballad *All In Love Is Fair* justifying the breakdown of his marriage to Syreeta. Wonder scooped five Grammy Awards for this album, and a year later a further five for *Fulfillingness' First Finale*, which prompted 1975 winner Paul Simon at the Awards Ceremony to quip – 'Thank you Stevie for not releasing an album this year!'

Three days before *Innervisions* was simultaneously released in America and Britain, Wonder was nearly killed in a car accident. His cousin, John Harris, was driving him from Greenville, South Carolina after a concert, to Durham, North Carolina. Wonder's manager, Keith Harris, declared that nobody was really sure what happened, but it appeared that Stevie was asleep in the back of the vehicle when the driver attempted to overtake a lumber truck which was swaying across the road. The truck stopped suddenly sending logs crashing on to Wonder's car. The singer was rushed to the Rowan Memorial Hospital in Salisbury and later moved to the intensive care unit of the North Carolina Baptist Hospital on 6 August, where a bruise on the brain and possible broken skull were diagnosed. Although no surgery was immediately contemplated, first reports suggested Wonder was dying as he was comatose for over a week. Ira Tucker, his mentor, stayed at his bedside all the time, singing softly into Wonder's ear the words to *Higher Ground*. When he regained consciousness, Wonder had temporarily lost his sense of taste and smell. Wonder: 'I wrote *Higher Ground* before the accident but something must have been telling me that something was going to happen, to make me aware of a lot of things and to get myself together. This is like my second chance for life; to do something more, and to value the fact that I'm alive. And if I felt that not living would be better, to conclude it.' Although he made a complete physical recovery, doctors were unable to measure the side effects of his brain injury but were convinced there was no permanent neurological damage. While convalescing he met Yolanda Simmons, the future mother of his children, and appeared on stage at the Madison Square Gardens singing *Honky Tonk Woman* with Elton John, although full length tours were banned for six months. Stevie still bears the facial scars, but as he said – 'what's a few marks here and there, I've got my life!'

In April 1973 (UK, Aug '73) new signing, songwriter/singer Willie Hutch released his debut album *The Mack*, the soundtrack to the film of the same name. The film, telling a rags-to-riches pimp story featuring Richard Roundtree in one of his first roles, flopped, but the soundtrack spawned two R&B hits, *Brother's Gonna Work It Out* (US, Feb '73/UK, Aug '73) and *Slick* (US, Jun '73), for Hutch. Before joining Motown Hutch wrote for the 5th Dimension, Al Wilson and Johnny Rivers.

Eddie Kendricks enjoyed the biggest hit of his solo career with Keep On Truckin': *the single was inspired by the currency of the catchphrase.*

During the summer of 1973 Motown/EMI took the unprecedented step of establishing a division to sign and record British acts in an attempt to increase the company's activities outside the States. Headed by ex-Motown label manager, John Marshall and former Rolling Stones label manager, Trevor Churchill, and with Phil Cordell and Hetherington among the first signings, this outlet failed abysmally and was shortlived but thankfully, a handful of Motown artists kept the flag flying in England. For example, ex-Temptation Eddie Kendricks enjoyed a number eighteen British hit and American number one with *Keep On Truckin'*, probably because of the currency of the catch phrase. A year later, *Boogie Down* was his second and last solo British hit.

In September 1973, after the Jackson 5 had returned to America from yet another sell-out Japanese tour, Jermaine began promoting his *Come Into My Life* album (US, May '73/UK, Sep '73), about which he said: 'There are a lot of songs on it which I hoped would be included. There are slow ones, since I do ballads better, although maybe people who like to dance will be unhappy about that. But on the whole the album sounds really good.' He also confirmed he was dating Berry Gordy's daughter, Hazel, although he stressed they had no plans to marry.

Before the close of the year Diana Ross kept her word and confirmed concert dates for her first solo tour of Britain, slotted in as part of her European itinerary. The first date was at Birmingham's Odeon on 15 September, followed by three nights at London's Royal Albert Hall and dates in Manchester, Liverpool, Glasgow and Newcastle. Ross was backed on stage by a twenty-five-piece orchestra, her own rhythm section and The Devastating Affair, while her personal staff included her seamstress, secretary, husband and their two daughters, Rhonda Suzanne (born 14 August 1971) and Tracee Joy (born 29 October 1972). The dates were instantly sold-out as curious fans and critics flocked to see Motown's biggest star. The reviews were glowing: 'She appeared, walking down the side-steps to the stage, giving a perfect rendering of her latest hit *Touch Me In The Morning* and going from strength to strength. From the moment she appeared on stage, her magic held the audience in the palm of her hands. *The Lady Is A Tramp*, followed by *Reach Out And Touch Somebody's Hand* had the entire audience holding hands and waving them in the air. She sang with the perfection she always strives for. *I'm Still Waiting* met with thunderous applause, as did the old Supremes' numbers. The concert wouldn't have been complete without songs from her enormous film debut *Lady Sings The Blues*. Diana donned a Billie Holiday gardenia for *Good Morning Heartache*, *God Bless The Child* and *T'Ain't Nobody's Bizness*, all performed with as much feeling and expertize as in the film. Her smash hit *Ain't No*

Mountain High Enough was another enormous success with musical and vocal backing harmonizing perfectly. She could do no wrong. She was brought back again and again for encores of *Ain't No Mountain High Enough*, which met with standing ovation. Diana Ross is certainly a true superstar' (*Record Mirror*).

Minor controversy, however, was generated in some newspapers by Ross's choice of watermelon motif on one of her costumes which the writer claimed was not a symbol loved by progressive blacks: 'It has uncomfortable associations with the starvation diet of the plantation slave trade, and Miss Ross is not easily identified with those days with the shadow of hunger and privation. Her choice of sartorial decoration therefore has a flippant touch of Uncle Tom about it'.

In October 1973 (UK, Dec '73), four weeks after her British stage debut, Ross's album with Marvin Gaye was released, despite his vow when Tammi Terrell died that he would never record with another partner. Ross: 'I've wanted to do something with Marvin for so long. It's like everybody wants to get one of The Beatles on their records because they're the best sessions players.' Eighteen tracks were recorded, ten were released in November 1973. *You're A Special Part Of Me* was the first single to be lifted (US, Sep '73, UK, Nov '73). Hal Davis, one of the album's producers, told J. Randy Taraborrelli: 'It was an album that had to happen. These were two of Motown's biggest superstars and (I) was laying down something that'll go down in history because they'll probably never get together again.' Davis played the diplomat in the studios – 'I would get my artistic points of view across without hurting either one. Of course we had some touching moments in there, but you're bound to have that when you've got two major stars working together like that. They had their individual opinions and I had to be the mediator.' Berry Gordy was executive producer with contributions from his best like Ashford and Simpson, and it is interesting to note that Gaye allowed his name to feature second in the credits. For his previous duets it had been the reverse. Gaye: 'Diana and I have known each other since the outset of Motown. This is a good duet album and I like to think we could do it better than most people. I'm hoping the album will be a classic one day.' The collaboration was a commercial success and sales from both album and spin-off singles ran into millions. Gaye was delighted by the way the work was accepted, although he stressed it was an experience he'd rather not repeat: 'It's always enjoyable to work with someone. It's something new, a new excitement in my life. But I don't like to follow my footsteps and my shadow. Singers are afraid to branch out and try something new, but I wasn't.'

American taste in popular music diversified during the early Seventies. The British were making their presence felt with Elton John and solo Beatles George Harrison, Paul McCartney and Ringo Starr, who competed against Helen Reddy, Roberta Flack, Carly Simon and Cher. Nonetheless, Motown secured five number one singles – *Superstition* and *You Are The Sunshine Of My Life* (Stevie Wonder), *Touch Me In The Morning* (Diana Ross), *Let's Get It On* (Marvin Gaye) and *Keep On Truckin'* (Eddie Kendricks) during 1973. However, it was generally felt that Gordy's music had lost direction due to his move to Los Angeles. No longer could a Motown single be recognized from the song's opening bars or chorus. Smokey Robinson probably discovered part of the problem when he said Motown had lost Detroit's support when the company moved to Los Angeles: 'For a long time after we left it was hard for us to get our records played in Detroit. I think it felt let down by us. The newscaster on the television the day we actually closed the building made it sound like an obituary. It was a big let down for the people there, and it was our roots so we were sad too. We'd put Detroit on the map for something other than automobiles.' Although several big name acts were still able to deliver number one hits, newly-signed artists were difficult to establish.

On 7 May 1974 Mary Wilson married Pedro Ferrer in The Candle Light Chapel, Las Vegas. Her sister Catherine was bridesmaid and her adopted son, Willie, best man. The wedding march was *I Hear A Symphony* played by the trio's rhythm section. The couple honeymooned in Las Vegas, later living in Wilson's Hollywood home. It was also in 1974 that Ewart Abner drew up an agreement whereby Wilson would own fifty percent of The Supremes name, with Motown retaining all rights to exploit the name whether or not she was a member of the group. Her percentage enabled her to receive half the profits made should Motown opt to sell off the name 'The Supremes'. Wilson could not use the name

Despite vowing never to duet again, Marvin Gaye teamed up with Diana Ross for the one-off Diana and Marvin *album released in 1973.*

The Miracles finally enjoyed a hit without Smokey with Love Machine *lifted from their* City Of Angels *album – a tribute to Los Angeles.*

gether.' Two of the singles lifted, *Spinnin' And Spinnin'* (UK, Aug '74) and *Your Kiss Is Sweet* (UK, Jan '75) were her first British hits (number 49 and 12 respectively). She flew to London in January 1975 to promote the latter hit, her first visit since backing her ex-husband at The Talk of the Town as a member of Wonderlove. The hit came as no surprise to her: 'The British people are more involved in mainstream music and have often been ahead of the States when it comes to musical taste. For instance, they even picked up on my first single I *Can't Give Back The Love I Feel For You*, whereas America had never heard of it.' *Harmour Love* (US, May '75/UK, June '75) became her last solo British hit in July 1975.

While Syreeta was enjoying her first taste of success, Marvin Gaye released the *Live* album (US, Jun '74/UK, Jul '74) recorded at the Oakland Alameada County Coliseum (his first stage performance in three years) as a fill-in until his next studio album, I *Want You*, was completed. This concert led to a full sell-out American tour although Gaye's heart wasn't in it. He needed the money and touring was the quickest way of securing large sums. Performing before an audience terrified him because he felt inadequate on stage: 'I used to watch acts like Jackie Wilson, those highly visual acts, possessing a great co-ordination and dancing ability such as James Brown, and I used to get uptight about that because I was never much of a dancer. I always had to go on feeling.'

The second British Jackson 5 tour was cancelled when a young fan died at a David Cassidy concert prior to their arrival. Lack of security was blamed and the group was concerned for their fans' safety. On the brighter side, and despite earlier reservations, Jermaine Jackson married Hazel Gordy with brother Marlon as best man. Jermaine was the second brother to marry – Tito wed Dolores Martes in June 1972 – and the wedding ceremony was broadcast over closed-circuit television and cost Berry Gordy $200,000. Among the many attractive decorations were two hundred doves in white cages, artificial snow-covered pine trees and seven thousand white camellias. Smokey Robinson sang a song he wrote for the wedding, *From This Time And Place*, and to celebrate the marriage Gordy also footed the bill for one thousand Christmas dinners for underprivileged black families.

New signings of the sister/brother group The Allens (Mitzi, Larry, Gary, Ronny, Tony) scheduled *High Tide* on the Motown label in 1974, although their debut *A Bird In The Hand* was released a year later, with Motown insisting they would become the next Osmonds. It wasn't to be. Continued success also eluded The Dynamic Superiors (Tony and Maurice Washington, George Spann, George Wesley Peterbank Jr, Michael McCalpin), a group formed from the ranks of two Washington DC bands. Ewart Abner signed them to work with Ashford and Simpson. Their 1975 debut

itself to record elsewhere, although when the group finally disbanded she used it for touring purposes.

In June 1974 (UK, Jul '74) the *Stevie Wonder Presents Syreeta* album was issued which Wonder said reflected the failure of his marriage. Syreeta commented on the project: 'The track *Cause We've Ended Now As Lovers*, well, I won't say he wrote that for me, but I was there when he wrote it. What I can't make people understand is a relationship just doesn't end with a piece of paper being signed. The love and feelings don't end. It's just that that particular phase is dissolved. We were divorced then, yet the whole idea of the song was to make people understand why two people split up. When I wrote *Blame It On The Sun* people reckoned it must have reflected Steve and I having gone through a bad time, but we never had bad times and I actually wrote that song when we were first married. People thought I'm *Going Left* was a love song, but it's about politics. The whole album is very special to me because every song holds a story. Steve and I will carry on creating and fantasizing through music because we work well to-album *The Dynamic Superiors* spawned two American hits *Shoe Shoe Shine* (US, Aug '74/UK, Jan '75) and *Leave It Alone* (US, Feb '75) likewise their second *Pure Pleasure* (US, Jul '75/UK, Feb '76) with *Nobody's Gonna Change Me* (US, Jul '75) and *Deception* (US, Sep '75/UK, Nov '75).

The Miracles eventually struggled from their Smokey-less doldrums in September 1975 (UK, Nov '75) with their *City Of Angels* album, a tribute to the critique of Los Angeles. Produced by the group's Pete Moore and Bill Griffin, the album concentrated on a young man following his gold-digging girl-friend to Los Angeles, and his subsequent rise to stardom. The project was conceived when the producers were in Hollywood. – 'and it occurred to us that nobody had really paid a musical tribute to the city. It took us eighteen months to work out the concept and write the songs because we felt it was very important to include all aspects of life in the city.' One track, *Ain't Nobody Straight In LA*, ran into some criticism from the Californian gay community, leaving Motown wary of the whole project. Griffin told *Blues & Soul* magazine: 'They didn't want to put their money behind something like this and then we even had problems at the musical level. People tried to tell us that the lyrics didn't fit the melodies, the whole musical direction. But we had to believe in what we were doing and we're pleased at the acceptance the album has received in spite of all the scepticism we encountered. The acceptance indicates to us that people are ready to deal with reality, and we felt it was time for us to talk about what was really happening. We wanted to do something more meaningful than the usual love lyric theme. For too long people have seen The Miracles in one particular vein and it was time for us to let them know we are more than capable of doing other things. One of the secrets of being able to have a successful album with something which is new and different is to put on there something that people can take from the album, which at the same time can stand on its own, like *Love Machine Part I*.' That title, re-written four times as a six-minute track, used machine parts to describe a person and was produced by Freddie Perren. *Love Machine Part I* (US, Sep '75/UK, Nov '75), with Bobby Roger's growl as an introducition, became their biggest hit since Robinson's departure. With success came demand and by design their stage act became more flexible. Bobby Moore told *Echoes* newspaper: 'It's something we didn't get a chance to do when we worked with Smokey. In the old days we'd change songs from one city to another, trying to anticipate the differences in our audiences. Now we feel very strongly that we have a broad enough stage act to appeal to whoever we play to. Our audiences will take us for what we are.' The hit formula of *City Of Angels* wasn't repeated which led to the group looking for another recording deal.

At this time the Jackson 5 were also on the move, leaving Motown in 1975. Their father, Joe Jackson, was unwilling to sign his sons' publishing rights to Jobete, so negotiated a multi-million dollar deal with CBS/Epic. Motown continued to own the name 'Jackson 5', so The Jacksons were born. Jermaine Jackson remained with Berry Gordy's company, a move that remained unpublicized until CBS announced its new signing. Jermaine commented: 'I had to think of my own career and after weighing everything up it seemed obvious to me I'd be better off all round sticking with Motown because I believe in the company and it's always been good to me.' His bitterness showed when he said: 'Usually when you hear of a group moving companies, at least you'll all sit down and have a discussion about it. But I was camping with Barry White and his wife, and when I returned my father told me to come over to the house without Hazel, so I knew something was wrong. I went to his room and on the bed were all the contracts from CBS/Epic already signed by my brothers. I just said I wasn't going. I made my decision and I knew I had to live by it. I believe that if it was meant for me it would have happened in a nicer way. My father wasn't able to adjust quickly and he was initially upset but I have given my word. A lot of people told me I had betrayed my family and that I wasn't going to be successful. All this was on my mind and I became a different person for a while because I felt the whole world was mad at me. My brothers were hurt by it but they

Freddie Perren masterminded the six minute version of The Miracles' Love Machine; the lyrics used machine parts to describe a person.

Jermaine Jackson married Berry Gordy's daughter Hazel in a lavish ceremony. Smokey Robinson sang From This Time And Place, a song he wrote for the occasion.

didn't show any anger towards me, although they couldn't understand how we'd been raised together and I could go one way and they the other.' The first album to be issued under his solo contract was *My Name Is Jermaine* in August 1976 (UK, Oct '76), amidst a great flurry of publicity, while younger brother Randy replaced him in the group.

The exact details of The Supremes founder, Florence Ballard's legal battles with Motown were for several years not publicly known. She was forbidden to tell the media at the time and Motown kept tight-lipped. Rumours were persistant but the truth was never told. With information now made available from various sources, including American author Randall Wilson's 1987 thesis titled *Forever Faithful!*, the details appear to be as follows. When Ballard signed her group release in July 1967 she also gave up all rights and claims to all and any future income from the group. Ballard, without taking legal advice, signed the release which offered her $15,000 over a six year period and forbade her to publicly use the name The Supremes. Two months later, she realized her error and hired a lawyer and business manager Leonard Baun from Baun, Okrent and Vulpe, and he secured approximately $76,000 from Ballard's joint Bank of the Commonwealth account with Motown in September 1967. This, however, was not a settlement figure, but money that was rightly hers. Now funded, Baun persuaded Ballard to open Talent Management with him as treasurer of the company, whereupon author Randall Wilson reported 'Baun issued himself $5,000 of her money for Talent Management stock for himself. The proceeding against Motown continued through the fall and on 5 December Motown released stock possessions in Florence's name to Baun. At this time and using his home address Baun applied for credit cards in the name of Florence Ballard, Thomas Chapman (her husband) and himself. $10,003.39 of the trust fund was used to buy 341 shares of diversified growth stock and 343 shares of Dreyfus funds in Florence's name. In 1968 Baun paid himself $43,050.24 in attorney fees.'

Between 1967 and 1968 Baun negotiated Ballard's claim for unpaid monies from The Supremes with Motown's lawyer Ralph Seltzer and negotiator George Schiffer. As Motown never issued The Supremes with touring documentation, Randall Wilson reported: 'Florence and Baun tried to reconstruct her performance schedule from her passport. From the reconstructed history, Baun and Florence deducted that The Supremes grossed $1.6 million in 1967 out of which hotels, expenses on the road and in the studio were paid. International Talent Management Inc, the Motown subsidiary, received 15%.' As Motown continued to be uncooperative with Baun, Ballard's personal finances were getting low, and when Motown agreed she could audit their books at her expense,

Ballard could not afford to do this. Instead, she reluctantly requested an out of court settlement.

Meanwhile, ABC Records wanted to sign Ballard to a two year recording contract, but the deal could not be finalized until she had an approved separation from Motown. When Baun was able to prove that the July 1967 release signed by Ballard without legal advice was nul and void, Ballard's release contract was finalized in 1968. Randall Wilson said that Motown agreed to pay the ex-Supreme the lump sum of $160,000 (Supremes Vocal Group – $20,195.06, Diana Ross and the Supremes – $5,000, Motown Record Corporation – $134,809.40). The money, taken from trust, was paid to Leonard Baun.

While Baun's legal negotiations were taking place, not only could Ballard not sign the ABC Records contract, but booking agents were reluctant to work with her for fear of retaliation from Motown. Baun said that it was obvious that Motown did have a lot of influence, that many booking agencies had contracts with Motown, and that certain agencies would not 'touch Florence because she was hot. They received no threats and no-one ever told me that, nor did anyone ever say that Motown had gone out of its way to try to impede Miss Ballard's ability to perform as an individual. (It) was in the back of our minds that (Motown) might try.' Baun asked Motown for their reaction to this and a company spokesperson laughed: 'We wouldn't do anything to harm Florence. She is our friend!'

During March 1968 Florence Ballard signed with ABC Records. In the spring of that year she travelled to New York to record her first single *It Doesn't Matter How I Say It (It Is What I Say That Matters)*. It was duly promoted without any reference to The Supremes. Ex-Motown producer Robert Bateman, who knew Ballard, was hired to work with her on four songs and *Love Ain't Love*, written by Van McCoy, was chosen by ABC as her second single. Both releases flopped reputedly due to ABC's indifferent treatment regarding promotion. With the release of these singles Ballard returned to live performances albeit on a small scale. Ballard: 'Things looked good when I first started out as a single. I had signed with a new company and was pleased with the initial releases and even had a few engagements lined up. Then all of a sudden it seemed as if I was black-balled. My records weren't played and there were no bookings.'

After performing at President Nixon's January 1969 inaugural celebrations, the ex-Supreme's career nose-dived when after the release of *Love Ain't Love* ABC terminated her recording contract and shelved her tentatively titled album *You Don't Have To*. Also, Leonard Baun told her she was practically fundless.

In a frantic attempt to continue the investigations into Motown's settlement and Baun's suspected embezzlement of her money, Ballard hired lawyer Gerald Dent from Patmon,

Young & Kirk in 1969. When Dent died halfway through the case, David Tate took over and took Motown, Berry Gordy and Diana Ross to court in 1970. The $8.5 million suit claiming they had conspired for her to leave under fraudulent settlement was dismissed by the Michigan Supreme Court, who ruled that Ballard's release agreement remained binding unless she returned the $160,000 to Motown. This, of course, was impossible because of the way Baun had handled her finances.

Ballard was at her lowest. She gained weight, was mugged and robbed twice, then hospitalized for nervous strain and exhaustion. Talent Management folded and her husband found work as a road manager. The bank foreclosed on her West Buena Vista home in Detroit, despite the desperate singer pawning her valuables. Then her husband left her, forcing her and their three children (twins, Michelle and Nicole, and Lisa) to live with her mother and sister Pat. Ballard told local newscaster Dave Diles: 'I kept saying to myself, at least couldn't I have just kept my home if nothing else? For my children's sake, couldn't that at least have been paid for.' With no income Ballard's family was supported by AFD (Aid To Families With Dependents) with monthly payments of $135. A friend was so incensed at the way Ballard had been treated by Motown that she told *The Washington Post*. The story was syndicated, resulting in offers of work which included her 1975 Detroit appearance at a benefit concert for The Joan Little Defence League where she sang Helen Reddy's *I Am Woman* and The Supremes' *Come See About Me* to a thunderous response. Also in 1975 Ballard won her lawsuit against Leonard Baun and received a settlement of $50,000 which enabled her to purchase a new home for her family.

But it was all too late. In February 1976 Florence Ballard was found by her sister, Maxine, lying paralyzed on the floor in her home. She was rushed to Detroit's Mount Carmel Hospital where, on the 22nd, the 32-year-old ex-Supreme died following a cardiac arrest. The police report stated 'she ingested an unknown amount of pills and consumed alcohol'. The pills were for her overweight and high blood pressure which she took to prepare herself for her new and much longed for career.

The funeral, which Motown paid for, was held at the New Bethnal Baptist Church where the Reverend Franklin conducted the service. In tribute a nearby record store blasted *Where Did Our Love Go* as thousands lined the streets to see celebrities arrive including the Four Tops, Mary Wilson, Stevie Wonder and Diana Ross (who was booed by the crowds). Following the eulogy before Ballard's body – dressed in a blue choir robe laid in a silver and blue coffin – five thousand mourners outside the church rushed to read the floral tributes like a heart-shaped carnation arrangement from Ross saying 'I love you Blondie' (Blondie was

Florence Ballard in happier times, pictured here with her husband Thomas Chapman. Florence died in 1976, and her husband died during the Eighties.

Ballard's childhood nickname), and Berry Gordy's 'Goodbye Flo'. Ballard was buried in Detroit's Memorial Park after which Diana Ross opened a trust for the late singer's three daughters with an unspecified sum matched by Gordy. Ross told *Sounds*: 'You can't help people, some people are victims until they realize they're victims and get out of that. People tried to help Florence, oh, they did everything. Florence called me . . . and finally she got it, the point that nobody's doing it to you, you're doing it to yourself. She finally got that and then what happened I have no idea.' Ballard, shortly before her death, told friends 'I want to get back to work and get into everything – records, television, clubs, films. I want to go around the circuit by myself for the first year. I need to do this to bolster confidence, then I plan to get together a package show. By then I will have an idea of what I want, what kind of deal will best suit my style and personality.'

Ewart Abner had controlled Motown Records for three years but during 1976 Berry Gordy reclaimed the company and Abner was given a consultancy position. Stevie Wonder's contract was once more due for renewal and after negotiations were finalized the singer was guaranteed approximately $13 million over seven years, a sum more than equal to

Florence Ballard, generally regarded as the world's favourite Supreme.

(Right) Stevie Wonder's Songs in The Key Of Life had advanced orders of one million in America. When it was released in England it carried Motown's new label logo.

recent deals of Elton John and Neil Diamond combined. A delighted Wonder said money had not been the most important factor: 'I'm staying with Motown because it's the only viable surviving black-owned company in the record industry. Motown represents hope and opportunity for new as well as established black performers and producers. If it wasn't for Motown many of us just wouldn't have had the shot we've had at success and fulfilment. In the record industry we've all seen many cases where the big companies eat up the little ones and I don't want this to happen to Motown. I feel young black children should have something to look up to. It is vital that people in our business, particularly the black creative community, make sure that Motown stays emotionally stable, spiritually strong and economically healthy.'

Berry Gordy felt the deal was a bargain: 'I knew what (Stevie) could do, what he was as a human being, and I know how he spends his money and time on making records. In other words it's impossible for Stevie to put out a bad record because of his fortitude, his insight. It doesn't matter what it costs, I felt I could not get hurt with Stevie. With some of the other artists who are motivated by money, or who had not grown as much as a human being as Stevie, I would be very skeptical of doing something like that.'

Prior to his re-signing Wonder visited Africa and became so obsessed with its culture that when Yolanda gave birth to their first daughter on 7 April 1975 he named her Aisha Zakia (meaning strength and intelligence). Then before the year ended he met up with Bob Marley and the Wailers in Jamaica and

became interested in the roots of reggae music, which would influence some of his future work. However, all was not as rosy as the public believed because trouble lurked within the singer's organization. His brothers Calvin and Milton were employed to protect him from outside influences, insulating him from the daily running of his companies and thus allowing him to concentrate on his art. And it was probably the inability to reach Wonder that the source of his musical inspiration, Malcolm Cecil and Robert Margoulett, quit, leaving his music catalogue in disarray. Stevie's first album under his new Motown deal was Songs In The Key Of Life which, without Cecil and Margoulett's help, was reputed to have been compiled in confusion. The double album package, with a single insert and a twenty-four lyric booklet, was eventually delivered after a two year wait. At one stage, with the singer's assurance the completed work would be available on a specific date, Motown arranged a media preview. Wonder withdrew the work at the last minute for further remixing. Instead of publicly moaning at the delay, Motown cashed in on the ever increasing wait by distributing 'Stevie's Almost Finished' tee-shirts!

Songs In The Key Of Life was eventually issued in America and Britain in September 1976 and set a precedent for his 'inability' to deliver the product on time. In future Motown's licensees and public alike added at least six to twelve months to the announced release date of an album. Wonder shrugged off his 1976 delay by saying: 'It's all about pleasing myself, not everybody and anybody, but myself. I'm the hardest person for me to please, and when I finally please myself I know I have made something good. I also know that people expect great music from me, that doesn't bother me, but they don't understand that you can't make good music overnight. I do the best I can no matter how long it takes.' Songs In The Key Of Life went platinum in America with over one million advanced orders. A Motown spokesperson said: 'The anticipation of this album has been phenomenal. It is the hottest album we've ever had. Every account has reordered and it was our biggest initial order and volume ever.' The British release marked the introduction of the new label logo – a large 'M' placed against a pale-blue background, encircled in a dark-blue edge.

The double album's content, Wonder explained, related to experiences of people all over the world as well as being significant to his life: 'It involves taking a look at the problems we experience in life and giving them the kind of constructive criticism and assistance that will make life better. It's for those who believe in a positive idea of tomorrow and is an album we hope everyone can enjoy because we gave a good deal in it,' The project was also dedicated to Yolanda and their daughter, for whom Wonder wrote Isn't She Lovely with the instruction that it should never be released as a single. David Parton covered it and enjoyed a British number four hit in January 1977. Motown/EMI were furious because they knew the original version (garnering most radio play as an album track) would have topped the charts. However, I *Wish* was the first single release in November 1976 (UK, Dec '76), followed by *Sir Duke* (US, Mar '77/UK, Mar '77), *Another Star* (US, Aug '77/UK, Aug '77) both American number ones, and *As* (US, Oct '77/UK, Nov '77).

Motown was now an extremely powerful and successful record and film company but with this expansion and development came personal and professional upheavals. The Supremes, for example, would never enjoy the same success as they did when Diana Ross was lead singer, but through the determination of Mary Wilson, the group's career was secure for several years. Motown, too suffered with the departure of the Jackson 5 and the Four Tops, yet publicly the losses seemed to make little difference to the company's financial situation. Established names like Diana Ross, Stevie Wonder and Marvin Gaye, moved Motown into diverse areas (films, political and social commentary readings), and had more control over their professional lives than ever before. All these changes meant the beloved 'Motown Sound' created by musicians and artists to launch Motown in the Sixties was merely a memory. Motown's new policy was dollars, sophistication, supply and demand, a policy that was to overtake the quality of the music itself.

When Stevie Wonder's album Songs In The Key Of Life was further delayed he and Suzanne de Passe advertized the fact with specially made T-shirts.

Two of Motown's brightest stars, Tata Vega and Michael Lovesmith, led the company's new roster of artists into the Eighties.

STANDING IN THE SHADOWS

'She's been a Supreme for half her life, so it's time for her to show the world what she's capable of . . . It's fair to say that without her who knows where The Supremes would have gone.'
Susaye Green on Mary Wilson

'Without sounding petulant, I don't think I'm treated properly.'
Marvin Gaye

With the Eighties looming, Motown continued its search for new artists to become future stars. They signed many acts that were as diverse as they were unusual, including The Boons, Jerry Butler and Albert Finney. Signed acts were still making their presence felt: Diana Ross, for example, enjoyed her twelfth number-one single (with The Supremes and as a solo act) on *Billboard's* charts with *Theme From Mahogany (Do You Know Where You're Going To)* in 1976, beating Elvis Presley whose total was seven. In the spring The Supremes released *I'm Gonna Let My Heart Do The Walking* (US/UK, May '76) which was adopted by the American Heart Association to launch a promotional campaign urging the public to 'let your body do more walking for your heart's sake'. The single, which was far superior to their recent recordings, was lifted from their Brian and Eddie Holland-produced album *High Energy* which featured both Cindy Birdsong and her replacement Susaye Green. Mary Wilson's husband, Pedro Ferrer, took over as the group's manager when Berry Gordy dropped them to manage Diana Ross. Ferrer had edged Birdsong from the group and hired Green thus introducing a different vocal sound. Wilson was pleased with *High Energy*: 'Being back with Brian and Eddie was itself a step in the right direction because they knew better than anyone what we needed to be successful. We left it to them to pick the songs and I was pleased with every one they chose'.

The Supremes needed the good publicity offered by the Heart Association to counteract the effects of a disastrous autumn '75 tour of South Africa which the group had agreed to despite grave misgivings by all involved. With Birdsong still a member, twenty-four dates were arranged for them before integrated audiences. The group discovered, to their disgust, that they were treated as honorary whites and that 'racial permits' were required for each show. When Scherrie Payne discovered that their show advertisements failed to notify blacks that

tickets were available to them, she bought these permits and gave them away to black people in the streets. The trio told a Durban newspaper at the time, 'We are allowed to do things here that people who are born and live here can't do. We feel it is an insult that we can stay in a hotel that a black African is not allowed in.' Following this and other contentious interviews, on the completion of their tour the South African government gave the group four hours to leave the country. Payne: 'We were glad to leave. It's a beautiful country but it's run by a bunch of bigots.'

Prior to being a Supreme, Susaye Green worked as a backing singer for Stevie Wonder and Ray Charles: 'I actually started out with Harry Belafonte but the time I spent with Ray was the first period of learning for me. Without that experience and the time that I later spent with Stevie I don't think I could have been ready for this period in my career. Being a Supreme is very important to me and since I believe that show business is a question of steps and sections, I attach equal importance to every era I undertake.' She was less discreet when she told journalists that she was pleased to be singing old Supremes' repertoire 'because in a way I feel as though I was involved with them already because as a teenager I fanticized to those songs!'.

In March 1976, Smokey Robinson signed an exclusive long term artist/producer/writer contract with Motown. Barney Ales: 'He structured the foundation on which Motown was built, and all of us in the family are happy to have him remain an important part.' Robinson: 'If it had not been for Motown so many of us would not have enjoyed the world-wide acclaim that comes with success in the entertainment industry. Aside from my immediate family there is no other family that means more to me than the Motown family.' The aptly titled *Smokey's Family Robinson* (US, Feb '76/UK, Apr '76) was the first album to be issued under his new contract with Motown.

On a less magnanimous note, Motown added $15 million to their lawsuit against the departed Jackson 5. The original suit dated December 1975 claimed $5 million in damages. The higher figure was claimed when Jermaine Jackson's picture (a Motown signed artist) appeared in an advertisement for his brothers' CBS-TV summer series. Motown claimed financial and credibility loss on behalf of their artist.

In June of 1976 Diana Ross, who had given birth to her third daughter Chudney Lane (a name she made up) in November 1975, filed for a divorce from Robert Silberstein on the grounds of irreconcilable differences. The divorce wasn't leaked to the press until two weeks later when Ross was granted custody of her three daughters, while her petition stated that property and financial settlements had been reached between herself and her husband. Following the divorce, granted a year after her petition, the singer sold her Beverly Hills home and moved her family to New York, away from friends, personal staff and Motown, to start a new life. Silberstein: 'My wife belongs to Motown. She's totally dominated by a man who has never read a book in his life. I just can't stand it anymore to hear them calling Stevie Wonder a genius. Whatever happened to Freud?' Diana Ross told *Rolling Stone* magazine: 'Robert and I are divorced but still good friends. It's very difficult in a marriage to have a career and we agreed we needed time to part. We had five good years of marriage and then one difficult year.' She told British reporters: 'Being a successful woman is hard enough because in our society, women are not supposed to be successful, that's a man's province. Men feel small when their wives are big. We've all grown up with the notion of what roles we should play. I'm a good wife and my husband a good husband, it's just getting the two together that's the problem. A long time ago I realized I'm just a shell of me without my work. I can't give it up and just stay at home and be bored, just because a long time ago someone, probably a man, wrote that a good wife should be at home with her family. I have learned that what you give your children has less to do with the quantity than the quality. And I don't have to prove anything to them because they know I love them.'

Prior to filing for her divorce in March 1976, Ross embarked on a European tour under the title *An Evening With Diana Ross* The British leg opened in Birmingham on 14 March and ended at London's New Victoria Theatre on 20 April. On stage the star was joined by mime dancers, backing vocalists (including The Jones Girls) and more than thirty musicians, including her own eight-piece rhythm section selected by Richard Perry who was working on Ross' next album due to be recorded at the end of the tour. *An Evening With Diana Ross* was

a brand new, ninety-minute, $½ million production conceived and directed by Joe Clayton, whose most recent success was with the Bette Midler Show on Broadway. Bob Mackie and Ray Agyahan designed the singer's wardrobe, while Tom John designed the sets. It was Las Vegas razzmatazz at its best. Adam White reviewed the performance in *Music Week*: 'Midway through performing *Love Hangover*, Diana Ross left the stage. At the same time, the orchestra ceased playing, and its members – while remaining in full view of the audience – took to reading newspapers, passing round drinks, and talking amongst themselves. But the music did not stop. Without a discernible break, the theatre's sound system began to relay the recorded version of *Love Hangover*. A couple of minutes later Miss Ross returned to the spotlight and to her in-person performance of the song, once more aided by the orchestra. Ten years ago or even less, Diana Ross and the Supremes would never have dared such a device on stage . . . It was difficult not to conclude that the singer's music has lost some of its fire, the passion and emotion it once contained. Hollywood may be part of the trouble. Pursuing a career in movies seems to have diluted her vocal commitment, for so little of the London concert had to do with singing. It was an eye-dazzling show, with countless costume changes and attractive-enough musical cameos of Billie Holiday, Ethel Waters, Josephine Baker, Bessie Smith. Her children were constantly invoked in an ambitious but over-long rendition of Nilsson's *The Point* complete with mime troupe. Obligatory Broadway outweighed obligatory Motown, even several of the latter songs were not performed in full. As for The Supremes days, they were dismissed by a fairly skimpy medley. The speed with which Diana Ross charged through these seemed to emphasise the lack of vocal commitment. It's risky to desert one's prime asset unless there's a strong enough replacement. Showbiz sparkle and stunning dresses will never be a substitute for the voice that launched a thousand hits. Only once during the New Victoria concert did Diana hint at that glorious ability, when she sang (in the true sense of the word) *Do You Know Where You're Going To*. It was marvellous, made all the more so by its isolation in a sea of musical blandness. But does she really know where she's going to? Or perhaps more to the point, has she forgotten where she's been?' An album of Ross' performances was released in January 1977 (UK, Feb 77) and the show was screened on NBC-TV during March – her second television spectacular.

Her show-stopper *Love Hangover* was actually hidden away on her current album *Diana Ross*. Another track, a sultry ballad *I Thought It Took A Little Time (But Today I Fell In Love)* was released to coincide with the British tour. Meanwhile, the American vocal group,

Diana Ross' $¼ million production An Evening with Diana Ross *was sheer Las Vegas razzmatazz and disappointed many British fans who preferred to see Ross without the showbiz trappings.*

138

The 5th Dimension, re-recorded *Love Hangover* and hastily issued it. Barney Ales returned to America to kill The 5th Dimension's hit by rush-releasing Diana's original and losing *I Thought It Took A Little Time (But Today I Fell In Love)*. Lamonte McLemore, member of The 5th Dimension told *Blues & Soul*: 'Our manager had checked out the song on Diana's album. At the time Motown had released another cut on her to follow *Do You Know Where You're Going To*, so we decided to cut *Love Hangover*. However, as soon as ours was released it caused a good deal of controversy at Motown. They rushed out Diana's version, something we were hoping they wouldn't do. We realized that if they hadn't done so we could have had a million seller on ourselves. Still, it did us good because we got a good deal of publicity behind it because whenever people talked about Diana Ross' version they talked about ours.' It may also have resulted in them being signed to Motown within two years!

Love Hangover followed *Do You Know Where You're Going To* to the top of the American charts, while reaching number ten in Britain. Following her European tour, Ross took her show to New York's prestigious Palace Theater, for her Broadway debut. She broke house records there: in the first two weeks she grossed $427,901.50, the highest figure in the sixty-three years of the theatre's history. The previous house record was set by Shirley McLaine with a gross of $297,680.70 for her April engagement. Due to ticket demand Ross extended her New York stay by a further week and was hailed by critics as 'the only glamorous woman to come out of the Sixties'. As well as being a first for the singer, it was a coup for promoter Danny O'Donovan who was the first British impressario to present a major American attraction on Broadway.

William Goldstein, born during the Second World War in Newark, New Jersey, pushed Motown into the Seventies' disco explosion. He studied at the Manhattan School of Music as a teenager, and under Lehman Engel's direction participated in the BMI Musical Theater Workshop for two years. By 1964 Goldstein had *A Bullet For Billy The Kid* screened on CBS-TV, two years later the Smithsonian Theater produced his *The Peddler* and during 1967 his *The Waters Of Babylon* was performed at the Washington Theater Club. He later became a staff composer at Screen Gems Columbia Music where he became famous for his television scores and commercials. Berry Gordy was impressed with his work and signed him to a long term composer/producer/arranger/artist agreement. Goldstein wrote the score for *The Bingo Long And The Travelling All Stars And Motor Kings* movie before cashing in on the universal disco boom with compilation albums like the *Discotech* album

Established singer Jerry Butler brought his special brand of 'iceman soul' to Motown. The ice melted as his solo and duet work (with Thelma Houston) failed.

series in 1975. Motown/EMI also released a series of disco albums during 1976 and 1977, inspired by Goldstein's American releases which ended in 1976.

Rose Banks (sister of Sly Stone), who, at the age of five sang at the All Nations Church of God in Christ in Vallejo, California, was another Seventies signing. Banks joined Sly's band, The Family Stone, as a keyboardist, but the urge for solo recognition prompted her to leave. Her husband, Hamp 'Bubba' Banks recorded a selection of songs with her and arranged for a Motown executive to hear them. Banks: 'The company couldn't wait to issue it as an album but said they'd prefer it if I included some repertoire from their publishing company, Jobete. I really didn't want this as my husband writes for me, but I gave in because it was Motown's policy.' The singer's initial enthusiasm with her signing was soon dampened: 'When I first arrived I felt part of the family but it seemed they weren't pushing my album as much as I'd have liked. Basically I wanted Rose Banks to have had the support of Diana Ross. I mean, who knew her when she first arrived. It seems I'll always be known as Sly Stone's sister, but I wanted to establish memories of my own.' The mentioned album *Rose* was her only one released in May 1976 (UK July '76), and the sleeve carried a caricature of her. Banks: 'I wasn't fond of that picture. There weren't any good photos of me at the time. My dress was low cut and it looked as if it was too big for me, and parts of me were exposed that shouldn't have been.' Despite failing on vinyl, Banks garnered support from touring with Marvin Gaye on his first European tour.

Berry Gordy's biggest signing of the Seventies was established soul singer Jerry Butler, a consistent hit-maker since 1958, and responsible for promoting Philadelphians Kenneth Gamble and Leon Huff. Butler was born on 8 December 1939 in Sunflower, Mississippi, but his family moved to Chicago in 1942. There he sang with the Olivette Institute and the Mount Sinai Baptist Church choirs before joining the Northern Jubilee Gospel Singers. While singing with the Travelling Soul Spiritualistic Church he met Curtis Mayfield, and together they joined the soulful doo-wop group, The Impressions. Butler: 'The group was formed by Richard and Arthur Brooks and Sam Gooden. And with Fred Cash they had a group called The Roosters. They asked me to sing with them and I persuaded Curtis Mayfield to join as well. Ewart Abner, who was then working at Vee Jay and who also brought me to Motown years later, really liked a song we'd written called *For Your Precious Love*, but they didn't like the name The Roosters so we changed it to The Impressions. The company chose to release the single as "Jerry Butler and The Impressions" which put me out in front and was something I wasn't ready for. It caused some bad feeling in the group, particularly when the record took off and the limelight fell increasingly on me'.

Butler left the band for a solo career and Mayfield became his writing partner for most of his solo Vee Jay releases, including duets with Betty Everett. The money they made from these helped them create the Curtom Publishing Company. In 1966 Butler joined Mercury Records where he enjoyed further success with singles like *Mr Dream Maker*. His association with Gamble and Huff resulted in two classic albums *The Iceman Cometh* and *Ice On Ice*, yet the trio split up. Butler: 'We were already well into our third album when Gamble and Huff decided to re-negotiate their Mercury deal, but the company wouldn't hear of it. So they left.' The singer, now left to his own devices, decided to invest in a Songwriters Workshop, which later groomed his brother Billy and Chuck Jackson into recording artists. Butler: 'When I left Mercury I seriously thought about signing with Philadelphia International to join Gamble and Huff, but in the end I settled on Motown. Motown has the flexibility to deal more personally with artists and I got complete control'. Butler's *Love's On The Menu* album came first in June 1976 on the Motown label (UK, July), hotly followed seven months later by *Suite For The Single Girl* in January 1977 (UK March). Butler: 'All the songs on the second album are relevant to a girl's world, unmarried girls who are making it on their own and who are involved with different kinds of guys. It's about some of the girls I know, and their problems and pleasures. The album takes on a mature, yet youthful sound, but the two aren't conflicting with each other.' Despite both being stunning albums neither was particularly successful, so Berry Gordy suggested

Sister of Sly Stone, Rose Banks signed to Motown to establish recording memories of her own but her only success was as support act to Marvin Gaye.

Butler record with Thelma Houston. Butler: 'Because my duet work with Betty Everett and Brenda Lee Eager was especially good for us it seemed logical to work with Thelma. Of course, this happened before Thelma's hit *Don't Leave Me This Way*. Actually we started work on our first album together before *Suite For The Single Girl* was even thought of. The project with Thelma was something I dearly enjoyed because she is such a professional and the whole thing seemed to fit into place as it went along and that's always a good sign.' Butler's instincts let him down because both the *Thelma And Jerry* (US, May '77/UK, Jul '77) and *Two To One* (US Jun '78/UK Sep '78) albums flopped. His last Motown release was his solo *It All Comes Out In My Song* album in 1977. By the end of 1978 Jerry Butler had left Motown to be reunited with Gamble and Huff.

The most successful of Motown's new signings at this time was the loveable, overweight-talent of Tàta Vega. Born Carmen Rose Vega on 7 October 1951 in Queens, Long Island, New York, she travelled the world as a youngster with her airman father. As a 17-year-old Vega joined the Los Angeles cast of *Hair* where she befriended another struggling entertainer, Dobie Gray, who later left the company to form his own group, Pollution. In time Vega joined him but after a two-year stay retired from the business a disillusioned and frustrated singer. She was then persuaded to join a second band, Earthquire. Vega: 'I was supposed to be a backing vocalist but when we went into the studio to record an album, the other singers couldn't cut it. So I did the lead singing and was subsequently sued by the other two singers! I was totally disgusted, there was a lot of bad feeling in the group and I just had to get away.' Their eponymous album was released in January 1973 on Motown's Natural Resources label.

Vega's second retirement was once again shortlived when Iris Gordy, impressed with her lead vocal work, urged her to record as a solo artist. Vega: 'I was reluctant to go back into the record business because the situation was too political. The people were concerned more about politics than they were about me. I wanted to sing because I've never really known anything else but I couldn't work with people like that.' Her confidence grew when she joined Motown and her debut album, *Full Speed Ahead*, was released in August 1976, (UK Oct '76). After hearing this release which included tracks written by Ashford and Simpson, Stevie Wonder and the singer herself, critics compared her with Chaka Kahn, Minnie Riperton and Janis Joplin. Within a year Vega's second album *Totally Tàta* was issued (US/UK, '77) on which the track *Come In Heaven (Earth Is Calling)* was the highlight.

There was a two year gap before her single *I Just Keep Thinking About You Baby* in April 1979, lifted from her best album to date *Try My Love*

(US, Feb '79/UK, Apr '79) Vega: 'I like to put into my songs a feeling that gets people spirited inside, but I don't know if you can categorize that as rock, R&B or middle-of-the-road. I like to think of it as just good music that reaches people. When I put emotion across, whether it's pain or joy, it's because I try to express honest feelings.' I *Just Keep Thinking About You Baby* and *Get It Up For Love* were released as a double A-sided single in Britain, because although the latter was the better song, it wouldn't gain radio airplay due to its risqué title. However, the single sold on that title thanks to disco plays which pushed it to number fifty-two in the charts, whereupon Vega undertook a promotional tour of the UK.

Vega's fourth and last album *Givin' All My Love* was released in Britain, where she had become a popular artist, during March 1981. America passed on the album due to lack of interest. Her electronic version of The Supremes' *You Keep Me Hangin' On* was lifted from that album as a single, but despite extensive marketing and promotion it died. Vega was subsequently dropped from Motown's roster, in spite of protests from Motown/EMI. At one point a new contract was discussed but that failed to materialize and today Vega's name can be seen on gospel recordings and as a featured vocalist on instrumental albums.

Motown's established singers had an easier and more successful time on the recording front. David Ruffin was flushed with the chart success of *Walk Away From Love* (US, Oct, '75/UK, Dec '75) a mournful ballad that would have better suited his former group, The Temptations. Ruffin commented on his and the group's material: 'It's not that I always record sad songs, it simply depends on how that person accepts my songs. If a person just listened to my songs, they'd probably think I'd had the saddest love affairs in the world. However, The Temptations' I *Wish It Would Rain* was a true story for the guy who wrote it. As a matter of fact he cried throughout the entire recording session. That record was released

The Supremes disbanded. The trio are pictured here at their farewell party held in London's Mounkberry Club.

on New Year's Eve. We were in Cherry Hill, New Jersey, and it rained there for three days and nights. It was strange but the rains came about an hour before the writer of the song took his own life.'

Unbeknown to their public, The Temptations were going through a number of upheavals behind the scenes. Their producer/mentor Norman Whitfield left Motown to set up his own label with Rose Royce and The Undisputed Truth as his first acts, and their line-up changed yet again. David Ruffin's replacement, Dennis Edwards, left because, among other things, he felt he had never gained recognition and acceptance within the group. His last performance with the group was in October 1976 (seven months after he married for the second time, his bride was Joy Hamilton) and he hoped to build up a successful solo career with Motown. Instead he found himself in a miserable and somewhat hopeless situation. He recapped his career as follows: 'When Eddie (Kendricks) left I thought he was one of the most stabilizing factors of the group. And when Paul (Williams) left I was tempted to leave also. When I got into the group I told them the most important man there was Eddie, but a lot of the guys didn't want to give him credit. I never will forget when Eddie left because I had to sing his parts. At one time I really had pride because I thought they (The Temptations) were the baddest group in the world. I think everyone who is a replacement is reminded of that in the group. The original members run the group because it's their group. We had a democracy thing though and I had one vote, so it was very fair. But if you're with a democracy and everything's fair and you're still not getting your say, what can you do?'

Also, according to Edwards, Damon Harris was too outspoken although he meant no harm: 'Sometimes you cannot bring up stuff when you're dealing with old guys who are set in their ways. I like Melvin (Franklin) as a brother, but I cannot go along with him on some of his ways (like) The Temptations' supremacy thing. All that was great but I don't feel that way now. When we were number one I was very cocky and I told everybody about it. But when we started to slip, I was the first one to say something ain't right.' Edwards' feelings were not publicized previously because interviews were, he said, conducted by the group's original members, Williams and Franklin. There were also problems regarding recording and the number of songs Edwards would sing on. On their *A Song For You* album (US Jan '75/UK Jan '75) he had a lot of lead vocals – 'and it was after that that we got to the point where the members were unhappy because I was doing a lot of leads. So we started having all types of little confusions.' The *Wings Of Love* album (US Mar '76/UK Apr '76) featured his voice and only two of The Temptations: 'Some songs only have me singing lead with no backings, and on others the background voices don't belong to The Temptations. And while we were squabbling over who was going to lead what, the album was released!'

As a solo artist Edwards intended to release an album once the inevitable pitfalls were overcome: 'I asked for something and I found out that in this business you can't ask for nothing if you're a nobody. I'm finding out that after ten years I'm a nobody!' He also defended himself against the public's belief that he was arrogant and egotistical by saying people did not know him because of his inability to conduct interviews: 'I hated the fact that people felt like that about me. I've never been on a star thing. I've just always been trying to make a living. I've been in the streets, been a hustler all my life, so I'm going through a little hurt now. After all these years and I'm put on the shelf.' His last years with the group made him little money, he added, and lawyers negotiating with Motown bit heavily into his savings.

For some reason, Edwards' departure from the group was kept a secret and Motown's press statement offered no insight into the move – 'The Temptations and Dennis Edwards have mutually agreed to terminate their association in order for Edwards to pursue a solo career. A replacement will be announced in the near future.' What that release failed to reveal was that The Temptations, with Edwards' replacement Louis Price, were planning to leave the company. Berry Gordy reputedly interfered with their negotiations with CBS Records when he insisted they owed his company money and that he owned The Temptations' name. The group retaliated by claiming Gordy owed them a huge sum in unpaid royalties and filed an appropriate law-suit. Eventually the group was given back its name to sign with Atlantic Records and Motown publicly confirmed the group's move when Atlantic scheduled its debut album!

Replacement Temptation Louis Price was introduced to Melvin Franklin by The Impressions, who had rejected him as a member of their group. At junior high school Price formed his own band, The L.K.'s (said to be similar to The Temptations), and while still at high school his talent was spotted by Gloria Lewis, choir leader and sister of Ramsey. Price was chosen to represent his school on a Chicago-based television show and won a scholarship to Autora College where his interest in music expanded. In August 1974 Price was granted a teaching credential from the Chicago Board of Education to lead two choirs, before joining The Temptations. He never recorded with the group at Motown but is featured on their Atlantic albums *Bareback* and *Here To Tempt You*, and left, in 1979, when Dennis Edwards returned.

The shock of The Temptations' defection was followed by another musical tragedy – The Supremes disbanded. Their *Mary, Scherrie & Susaye* album in October 1976 (UK, Dec '76) was their last studio album. After this release, the trio performed their farewell show at London's Drury Lane Theatre in June 1977, when the audience was treated to a visit down memory lane. The performance, featuring a pregnant Mary Wilson, showcased the individual talents of Payne and Green, but was marred by the Las Vegas touch of Wilson's young daughter, Turkessa (born in April 1975), being introduced on stage during her mother's solo spot. (The group's last visit to Britain was in September 1975 when promoter Danny O'Donovan scheduled an across-country itinerary. On 5 September the IRA bombed The Hilton Hotel in London where the group was staying. Two people were killed and thirty injured. The trio was shocked but unharmed.) Following their farewell tour, Wilson's husband and group's manager, Pedro Ferrer, arranged a further tour which Green and Payne declined to honour. Cindy Birdsong and new girl Debbie Sharpe joined Wilson on the road.

Mary Wilson had been considering a solo career for five years but felt the timing was never right: 'I wanted to see The Supremes through to its natural conclusion. I made my final decision about what I should do and agreed with Motown that, rather than replace me, we should disband the group and that Scherrie and Susaye continue with whatever they felt they wanted to do. It would have been quite easy for me to leave the group after Diana Ross left, but I just felt we had to go on because there was so much more to do and I think we made some great records after she left, comparable to some of the real great ones we had with the original line-up. I don't think all of those records got the acknowledgement they should have. We certainly maintained a level of consistency that I'm proud of. My being with The Supremes were the happiest times of my life. Yes, I am leaving after so many beautiful years but I'll continue to sing and entertain. I think it's time for me to find out who Mary Wilson really is.'

Mary Wilson (middle) leads Scherrie and Susaye through one of their last performances together as The Supremes.

143

Susaye Green: 'Mary has always been the group's backbone and she has never received the credit that was due to her. That goes back to the Diana Ross era. The truth is, Mary is a very talented lady and it's time for her to show the world what she's capable of. She's been a Supreme for half her life, so it's fair to say that without her who knows where The Supremes would have gone. She feels she has done as much as she could ever do within the group.'

Actually, Motown intended to replace Wilson with Karen Knox, but Berry Gordy eventually decided the group must die. Green and Payne did go on to record together, and Wilson pursued a solo career. Pedro Ferrer, who rarely enjoyed a good rapport with Motown and who had caused a lot of friction within the group, was also blamed for the demise of the trio. Ferrer admitted at the time: 'I suppose I pushed Mary into leaving because I thought it was best for her future. And now I will be selling my share in The Supremes back to Motown. I wasn't happy with their last album *Mary, Scherrie & Susaye* and that's when I decided it was best for Mary to leave the act.'

The Temptations and The Supremes weren't Berry Gordy's only problem: a warrant

Marvin Gaye proved to British audiences that his legend was real when he opened at the Royal Albert Hall in 1976, his first major UK visit in ten years.

was issued for the arrest of Marvin Gaye by a Los Angeles court for non-payment of $6,000 in alimony and child support. As the artist had little, or no money available, Motown paid his debts and suggested he should tour. A European schedule was hastily arranged with promoter Jeffrey Kruger, which included Gaye's first major visit to Britain in ten years. His opening night was at London's Royal Albert Hall on 27 September 1976, with support act Rose Banks. Gaye arrived at Heathrow, London, on the day he opened the tour. Motown/EMI released *The Best Of Marvin Gaye*, roughly assembled from the American *Greatest Hits* album released in the August, to coincide with the tour. Needless to say Gaye's dates were instantly sold out as his British fans had waited for so long to see their hero on stage, and the opening night was an emotional event. Gaye strode confidently on to the Royal Albert Hall stage to sing *Let's Get It On*. Off came his green jacket, yellow tie and waistcoat, as he gave his best to his appreciative British audience. Two dancers entertained while he re-dressed to play *Trouble Man* at the piano. His famous knitted hat, which he had worn publicly since his *What's Going On* project appeared as he sang a somewhat jumbled and distorted medley of his solo hits like *Ain't That Peculiar, You're A Wonderful One, Little Darlin'* and *I Heard It Through The Grapevine*. The dancers re-appeared and this time Gaye joined them for some casual foot-tapping. The mood then quietened as he introduced his *What's Going On* medley, and a further medley of duets with Florence Lyles, who represented the late Tammi Terrell, on *Ain't Nothing Like The Real Thing, Ain't No Mountain High Enough* and *You're All I Need To Get By*. His show was short but was long enough for Marvin Gaye to prove his legend was real.

Prior to his opening night, a lavish press reception was held in Gaye's honour at London's Carlton Towers Hotel. Gaye was overwhelmed with the attention he received from the British: 'I'm so happy to see the response because in my early years I wasn't much of a visual performer. I was struggling in the States and didn't feel that audience reaction. Now it seems to be at the level that I can appreciate it as an artist. I got something more than I ever expected, or dared dream of, to get from English fans.' One of the reasons he was so astounded at the reception was that he had been told that his record sales in Britain were negligible: 'I didn't get paid a lot of money in American royalties for English record sales. The fact that I'm sold out on most of my British performances has obviously nothing to do with the fact that I don't sell records. Low sales signified to me that there was no point in touring Europe, as much as I wanted to. Actually, when I arrived in England to find out I'd not only sold out the tour but that an extra show had been added, it made me wonder what the hell was going on.' It's unlikely that his overseas sales would be omitted from his royalty statements although his payment schedules could have differed from Berry Gordy's other artists. However, Gaye claimed that even if he had enquired about his non-American royalties, all he would be told was '"yeh, you're probably right, you have sold some records", then they'll go on not paying me my English royalties and I'll be happy like we dumb artists are supposed to be!'

The singer conducted interviews from his hotel room. He told reporters he had already written his best work but that Motown would never see it, because 'I don't think they would handle this work correctly so I don't think they deserve it. Without sounding petulant, I don't think I'm treated properly'. The British media, until now, were unaware of his personal and professional traumas, and headlined his more inflammatory remarks like 'I've had some really classic fights with Berry, mostly because he is so control-conscious and power-orientated, and I feel I am an artist and not meant to be treated as a marionette!' Research has revealed that it wasn't Motown as a company Gaye felt strongly about, but Gordy himself, for a variety of personal reasons. It also became obvious that if Gaye was unable to have his own way with the company, he took his feelings out on Gordy who, for the most part, turned a blind eye to much of the singer's antics. However, when Gordy did take a stand against Gaye, the singer aired his discontent in public, which wasn't always a wise move.

The singer's performance at the London Palladium was recorded and released in the US as a double album package in March 1977 (UK, Apr '77). Three sides of Live! At The London Palladium accurately captured the magic and atmosphere of those stunning performances, while the fourth side contained the eleven-minute studio track Got To Give It Up recorded in Los Angeles and written by Gaye. His brother Frankie and common-law wife Janis Hunter sang back-up vocals. The track was edited for single release in March 1977 when it raced to the top of the American charts, and a month later in Britain, when it didn't.

At the beginning of 1977, Syreeta, now married to Curtis Robertson and mother of their first son, Jamal, released her One To One album in January (UK, March). It was a totally different and more intense album than her work with her ex-husband Stevie Wonder, and was influenced by a three-month course studying transcendental meditation in Ethiopia, following her divorce from Wonder. Syreeta: 'The meditation really brought my head together when the hard times came. The courses gave me calmness and I returned with the ability of seeing me in a different way. It rids the body of

In an attempt to cash in on the Marvin Gaye/Tammi Terrell success, Syreeta duetted with G.C. Cameron. Their only album was Rich Love, Poor Love in 1977 which fell short of its potential.

stress but it's basically up to the individual how to use particular methods. For myself, I usually take two lots of twenty minutes out of each day to meditate.' To complement her spiritual needs Syreeta practised yoga and changed her outlook on several activities including sex: 'It's even more critical now to think about having children with the problems two parents face, or parents who can't handle the responsibility of children. Making love isn't a game anymore, it should be taken seriously as an expression of genuine affection. Sex is great as long as the people involved know what they're doing and my philosophy is that anyone can do what they want as long as it's natural to them.' In August 1977 (UK, Nov) Syreeta teamed up with G.C. Cameron to release the Rich Love, Poor Love album. The intention was to repeat the Gaye and Terrell/Ross duets, and boost both Syreeta and Cameron's careers. However the album had the opposite effect, although Syreeta would in time duet successfully with another partner.

March 1977 saw the Commodores embark on their first British tour which began at Birmingham's Odeon Theatre. Their support act was Muscles, a respected band of the time.

Motown/EMI released the Fancy Dancer single in January 1977 to promote the tour then rushed out a three-track single featuring Easy, Machine Gun and I Feel Sanctified in May. By this time the group had released five albums (Machine Gun – 1974; Caught In The Act and Movin' On – 1975; Hot On The Tracks – 1976; Commodores – March 1977) and to cash in on the tour Motown/EMI re-titled their last American album as Zoom for British release. Performing with the Commodores on this sell-out tour were a guitarist, trumpeter and saxophonist, who also provided additional vocals. The visual excitement of the dense dry ice, flashing lights and cannon-fired confetti, almost obliterated the excellent sound system and superb repertoire which ranged from the funky *Machine Gun*, *I Feel Sanctified* and *Slippery When Wet* to the ballads of *Just To Be Close To You* and *Sweet Love*. They were fun-packed and highly-charged performances – the Commodores had conquered Britain!

The group's music had developed and was no longer confined to one particular sound. Lionel Richie: 'We bore so quickly that if we made an album that sounded the same it would be a disaster, simply because we would tire of it long before it got completed. And the vast variety of musical tastes within the group is another reason, and you've got six musicians, six arrangers and six producers, so that's why we span so many musical styles. If everyone was the same and had the same loves, we'd never have got where we are. So far we've been accepted by the disco fans, the funk ones, pop and ballad fans. I think our next step could be onto double albums. As there are six of us we each come up with say, forty songs for an album and then we cut down the two hundred and forty to nine!'

One consumer complaint that bugged the group had been the absence of any group identity on album sleeves. Invariably, the record cover would carry a painting of the record's title track, and possibly a group photo would be hidden away on the back of the sleeve. Richie was aware of this: 'If we had our own way every sleeve would be different, but then we can't do everything and we have to rely on other people to take care of some things. In some cases we didn't even see the sleeve concept before the record was released and then it's far too late to do anything about it. It has been a gradual process throughout the four years with Motown but we have now taken on the responsibility for our own career and that includes record sleeves. We now have our own logo which will remain on our album jackets in one form or another.'

Motown's weirdest new Seventies' performer was Mandre, the Masked Marauder, a space-funk creature who wore evening dress, with a 'groove gun' slung over his shoulder and a space helmet made from 'impenetrable getdownium' for his publicity photographs. Motown's marketing and publicity departments built up a nonsensical press campaign for the release of the debut *Mandre* album during April 1977 (UK, July). They claimed Mandre came from another universe 'where the stars cluster closest together and where there exists a tear in the very fabric of space and time, and his mission was to 'correct the errors of mankind with a message of love'. Due to this superhero's vow of silence, his interviews were conducted by Andre Lewis, who told *Blues & Soul*: 'I am just thankful that I've been chosen to work with Mandre because I have learned so much about electronics, physics and the aesthetic part of producing from him, and they are things that I

could otherwise never have come to learn. Immediately after the release of *Mandre 2* (US, Mar 1978/UK, Jun) he disappeared into the universe so we have no way of contacting him.'

Back down to earth, Stevie Wonder became a father for the second time in April 1977, when Yolanda gave birth to a boy Kieta Sawandi (meaning 'worshipper' and 'founder', a combination of South and West African words) in New York. Wonder: 'My daughter and son changed my life for the better. They're the one thing that I have needed in my life and my music for so long. The significance of my $13 million contract with Motown was not to have money and abuse it but for my family to be secure and to use it where they really needed it.' Prior to his son's birth Wonder flew to Nigeria to perform in the 1977 African cultural festival, FESTAC '77. While there he was due to be linked by satellite to the Grammy Awards ceremony. When the transmission failed, host Andy Williams stupidly asked 'Stevie, can you see us?' Wonder collected five Grammy awards for *Songs In The Key Of Life*. To advertize this exceptional and emotionally based album, a four storey billboard – the largest in the world – was erected in New York City! In October 1976 *Songs In The Key Of Life* shot to number one in the American charts. Three months before this accomplishment Marlon Jackson married 18-year-old Carol Parker in Las Vegas. He was the fourth brother to marry. (Jackie married Enid Arden in 1976. Nine months later they filed for divorce, reconciled, and remained married until the mid-Eighties.)

Son of a bookmaker, Albert Finney, one of Motown's more surprising signings, was born in Salford, Lancashire. He worked his way through the Royal Academy of Dramatic Art (RADA) to win the Emile Little Award for a consistently high standard of achievement. He stayed at the Birmingham Repertory Company for two years when he joined the Royal Shakespeare Company at Stratford in 1959. Finney's film debut was in *The Entertainer* starring Laurence Oliver, but it was Karel Reisz's *Saturday Night And Sunday Morning* which turned him into an overnight star. In 1962, Finney appeared in his next blockbster *Tom Jones*, and further years saw him working on stage and in films, until his next major role in 1974 in *Murder On The Orient Express* where he worked with several top international actors. A year later he sang his way through the musicals *The Lily White Boys* and *Scrooge*. Essex Music's David Plat, impressed with the way Finney handled the two musicals, suggested Finney write his own material. Finney did this and, with Dennis King, recorded *Albert Finney's Album* which was released by Motown in June 1977 (UK, Sep '77).

Actor Albert Finney recorded one album for Motown amidst a flurry of publicity. When his singing career failed Finney returned to what he does best – acting!

High Inergy – Motown's new Supremes. After initial chart success the trio struggled for recognition.

With the death of the old The Supremes, the new 'young Supremes' were signed – the talented High Inergy (Linda Howard, Michelle Martin, Barbara and Vernessa Mitchell). The group was born in April 1976 after the quartet had been accepted into Pasadena's Bicentennial Performing Arts Programme. The Mitchell sisters were singers, while Howard and Martin were dancers. Calling themselves High Energy, they combined their talents for a one-hour show which they performed five hundred times during the eight months of the federally-funded Programme. In October 1974 they came to the attention of Motown's Gwen Gordy-Lupper, who groomed them for her brother's company and changed the spelling of their name to 'Inergy' because she said 'they have so much energy coming within God's energy that we felt the name was appropriate'.

Turnin' On was their debut album release (US, Sep '77/UK, Dec) which spawned one of the year's classiest singles *You Can't Turn Me Off (In The Middle Of Turning Me On)*. High Inergy's first professional performance at Motown was at an invitation-only celebrity extravaganza hosted by Dinah Shore at the Century Plaza Hotel. *Turnin' On* hit gold status in America and the single reached the top ten, so it looked as if Berry Gordy had indeed found a new generation of Supremes. This displeased Mary Wilson but confirmed her belief that Motown intended, once and for all, to bury the world famous trio. High Inergy's second album was *Steppin' Out* (US, Jun '78/UK Aug '78) followed by *Shoulda Gone Dancin'* and *Frenzy* during 1979, when the group was reduced to a trio when Vernessa Mitchell left because she felt the music she was singing went against her religious beliefs.

In the autumn 1977 *Billboard*, the American music trade magazine, reported that Mary Wilson-Ferrer had filed a petition against Motown which stated that Motown had acted illicitly on her behalf and violated state rules governing their activities. Part of the petition was that the name of The Supremes revert solely to her. She claimed she had full rights to the name and not a half share as Motown claimed. Wilson further asked that Motown should not be allowed to release material by Diana Ross and the Supremes, or The Supremes, if Mary was not featured on the songs. The petition, filed before the Labor Commissioner of the State of California by her lawyer, also alleged that Wilson would need permission from Gordy if she wanted to purchase personal and real property, including but not limited to the Petitioner's automobile and house in Los Angeles. It was also maintained that Motown extended their discipline over her earnings for a large amount of her career with The Supremes, giving her a weekly allowance which was reputed to be $200-$300 a week and required her to obtain the signature of Berry Gordy to make any sort of withdrawal from her savings account. Her lawyer also contended that Motown actually used other singers to back Diana Ross on *Love Child* and *Someday We'll Be Together*: 'If this turns out to be true, then it is a direct violation of a clause in Mary's contract that states Motown cannot replace her in The Supremes except in cases of her "death, mental or physical incapacity, or if she should refuse to perform or live up to her contract".' It was also contended that Motown and its management company had operated as one company which was illegal under Californian law, and that when Wilson and her mother signed her contract with the company and Berry Gordy Enterprises, her mother was illiterate. Upon signing that contract Motown owned all and every rights concerning The Supremes, even though Wilson insisted the name was chosen by the group. Her recording contract also prohibited her and the other group members from using the name should she, for a variety of reasons, not be a member of the group. Wilson claimed this restriction was unjust. She further claimed Motown intended to re-form The Supremes without her and towards this end had pursuaded Susaye Green and Scherrie Payne to leave her.

Wilson then filed a reputed $30 million lawsuit against Motown Records which was settled out of court, whereupon she was contracted to the company to record one album, Mary Wilson, in August 1979 (UK Oct 1979) before being dropped from the roster. In March 1978 Scherrie Payne filed a $1.5 million lawsuit in the Los Angeles Superior Court against The Supremes Inc, Mary Wilson and Pedro Ferrer. Payne demanded an accounting of the group's earnings, previously denied her, and alleged fraudulant activities and breach of contract. The outcome wasn't publicized.

An original Supreme, Diana Ross, released her Baby It's Me album (US, Sept 77/UK, Oct) produced by Richard Perry. While Ross was recording this she was also recording a further album with Hal Davis because Motown wanted sufficient canned material to cover the time the singer would spend on her third movie The Wiz. It was intended Ross would record with Perry during the day, leaving the nights free for Davis. Ross: 'It's usually hard for me to do two songs in one night. The Perry album is a love album. We wanted to make a record that people could make love to, the other album is for dancing.' Baby It's Me, showing the singer in a glitzy showbiz pose, included Gettin' Ready For Love, Top Of The World, Too Shy To Say and Come In From The Rain with Ray Parker Jnr, Lee Ritenour, Tom Scott and James Newton Howard in the musicians' credits. Despite Ross' romantic intentions the project flopped.

When Ross and her three children moved to New York, following her divorce, she rented a Long Island house and during the week stayed at the St. Pierre Hotel while rehearsing for The Wiz, a Universal Pictures and Motown Productions venture. Prior to this production there were two other successful versions – The Wizard Of Oz movie released in 1939 starring the immortal Judy Garland in the role of Dorothy, and the Broadway musical The Wiz which opened in 1975 and starred Stephanie Mills.

During 1970 Ken Harper (a former employee of New York City's WPIX Radio) conceived The Wiz – an all-black, contemporary version of The Wizard Of Oz. The musical was premiered during October 1974 in Baltimore, before opening on Broadway in January 1975. After a shaky start, the musical went on to win seven Tony Awards during that same year. More significantly, however, was the fact that The Wiz was written, created and acted by blacks. Newcomer to the stage Stephanie Mills earned both critical and public acclaim for her role as Dorothy. A native of New York, this was the teenager's third stage part, her second on Broadway. At the age of 9, Mills sang in New York talent shows before securing her first role in Maggie Flyn during 1968. Five years later the 14-year-old recorded her first album Movin' In The Right Direction for Paramount Records, where she stayed for six months. In 1974 Mills secured the role of Dorothy in The Wiz which she subsequently played for two years. During one of her performances she was spotted by Jermaine and Hazel Jackson who invited her to visit Berry Gordy in Los Angeles. Mills later recorded one album for Motown entitled For The First Time, produced by Burt Bacharach and Hal David (US, Nov '75/UK, Mar '76) It was a disaster. Mills said years later: 'I really enjoyed working with them and I was naturally very excited at the time. But I now know that it was too sophisticated as a debut, even down to the album sleeve. It was definitely into the Dionne Warwick/Bacharach sound and although I learnt a great deal from doing it, it may have been a mistake as a first effort.' The film and publishing rights of The Wiz were owned by 20th Century Fox who optioned them to Ken Harper, the original Broadway producer. He, in turn, negotiated a deal with Universal Pictures and Motown Productions in 1976. As Stephanie Mills was such an outstanding stage success (and a Motown recording artist to boot) it was assumed she would play Dorothy in the pending movie. However this was not to be because Diana Ross wanted the role – an added blow for Mills as Ross was her idol.

American freelance writer, Joseph Bell, wrote that Ross became interested in The Wiz following a conversation with Ted Ross, who played in the Broadway version. She was aware that Motown had an interest in the project and told Bell she had seen the show: 'After I saw Ted Ross I couldn't sleep and I laid there for a long while thinking about the play and the old Judy Garland film. We had a videotape of that movie and at 2am I went downstairs and watched it through.' Ross then telephoned Berry Gordy telling him she wanted to play Dorothy, But would not pursue the desire if he felt the part was unsuitable for her. Ross: 'I just didn't want to wait until after the film was released and say "I wanted to do that but never told anybody".' Gordy was against the

Young Stephanie Mills was the star of the stage show The Wiz. *Despite recording for Motown, she did not appear in the company's film version of the show.*

idea but by the following morning had changed his mind and for the second time in her short movie career Diana Ross caused controversy over a leading role. When John Badham, the director of the movie, was informed she was to play Dorothy, he resigned, claiming the story was based around a young girl: 'I wouldn't know how to make the film with a mature lady as much as I respect Diana's talents. I didn't want to quit but I didn't understand what concept they had in mind.' Ross' interpretation of the Baum book was different, as she told *Rolling Stone* magazine: 'I started doing a lot of reading and found out that (Baum) never described who Dorothy should be, her age, or anything about her. If you were to read the book and not have the pictures to go along with it, you would never know that it was supposed to be a young girl. It was just a girl. And I read a book that explained why he never described Dorothy because everybody, all women, all men, have a Dorothy, a youthful something inside them that's searching for who they are. So, to me, when she meets The Scarecrow and he's looking to have some brains, everything she's talking about is herself – she's looking for her own brains and her own heart . . . and a lot of us, even today, are looking for that one person who's gonna give us all the answers (like) The Wizard, The Wiz.'

Sydney Lumet replaced John Badham as director and Rob Cohen was hired as producer: both supported Ross. Quincy Jones was musical supervisor; British born Oswald Morris in charge of photography; Louis Johnson, head of choreography; Joel Schumacher, screenplay writer; Tony Walton, in charge of production design and costumes, and Charlie Smalls responsible for music and lyrics.

At the recommendation of Diana Ross, Michael Jackson also appeared in *The Wiz*

movie playing the Scarecrow, alongside Mabel King (Evilene) and Ted Ross (Lion) both from the Broadway show, Lena Horne (Glinda), Richard Pryor (The Wiz) and hundreds of extras. Quincy Jones, who had never worked on a musical before, was head of the movie's music team which comprised nine singing principals, one hundred and twenty dancers, six sound technicians, three conductors, three hundred musicians, one hundred and five singers (including Whitney Houston's mother, Cissy, Roberta Flack and Rhetta Hughes), nine orchestrators, six copyists and five music editors. And it was this mammoth group that supported Diana Ross as she played a 24-year-old school teacher from Harlem, who, with her pet miniature Schnauzer 'Toto', is whisked away by a snowstorm to the land of Oz. In her attempt to return home she sets off along the yellow brick road to meet the Scarecrow as he tends a corn patch in Harlem. They journey together until joined by the Tin Man, and while passing by a library, one of its stone lions bursts into life to join them. The quartet reach the Emerald City where The Wiz agrees to help them if they first kill The Wicked Witch, Evilene who runs a sweat shop. She hears of the pending fate and recruits the Flying Monkeys – half-monkeys, half-motor bikes – to capture the quartet. The Good Witch, Glinda, rescues them and helps Dorothy home.

An estimated fifty-two sequences were plotted, with thirty-two on outside locations and twenty inside the Astoria Studios. And one of the most staggering props was the twenty miles of yellow vinyl used for the yellow brick road which cost in the region of $237,000 to make. In her desire for authenticity Diana Ross undertook her own stunts, and in doing so endured a leg injury when clipped by a Flying Monkey. Her fingernails

'Smokey Robinson is, along with the moon landings and the motorcar, one of the wonders of the age.' (Melody Maker)

sion seldom encountered since the good ol' days of the movies . . . to see *The Wiz* is like experiencing a ride on a magic carpet that is an "open sesame" into an extravagantly beautiful world of fantasy, sentiment and melody.' Whereas *Variety's* reviewer commented: 'Director Sidney Lumet has created what amounts to a love letter to the city of New York; the real-life sequences melt easily into the splendidly designed production numbers, as the dialogue equally blends smoothly with the numerous tunes . . . a big, rousing, juicy hit.'

Diana Ross once again embarked on an exhausting promotion tour, although she was absent from the movie's British premiere held at The Dominion, Tottenham Court Road, London, on 5 April 1979. The British critics were unimpressed with the celluloid extravaganza. The *Sun* newspaper reported: '. . . Making Dorothy a neurotic twenty-four-year-old school teacher who looks forty and is forever squeaking "Toto, Toto, Toto" is hard to swallow. She is so wet that you could wash the yellow brick road with her. The songs are good, the dancing ditto and the spectacle spectacular. But it does not work.' The *Daily Mirror* carried the headline 'Wiz That Never Woz', while The *Financial Times* glared 'The Wiz In Blunderland'. The movie was so poorly received that it was hard-pushed to make London's West End. MCA Records released the soundtrack from which *Ease On Down The Road* by Diana Ross and Michael Jackson was lifted as a single.

Since leaving The Miracles, Smokey Robinson's solo career had so far failed in Britain. His sophisticated, subtle (and often uncommercial) singles were ignored by record buyers although his work was ideally suited to British radio. In 1977 Robinson attempted to rectify the situation by undertaking a tour of the UK in October. Meanwhile the singer had expanded his talents by writing the film score for *Big Time*, (US, Jun '77/UK, Sep '77) an area he had planned to become involved in for some time. Robinson: 'The film is my project so that's why I did the soundtrack. Christopher Jay, Leon Isaacs and myself adapted a short story and then directed the movie between us. That meant I actually became involved with the daily shooting, down to the cutting and post production as editor. I've got close to half a million dollars invested in it, although I feel confident that I'll make that back because it is a quality movie. Much of the filming was done in friends' homes and in the streets of Los Angeles, so we all feel we got off cheaply. The basic story is about a black guy whose father has a stroke and he suddenly has the job of supporting his family and paying the hospital bills. So he borrows money from a friend who is involved with the syndicate. Then when it comes to payback time, he can't raise the money and so starts to arrange phoney accidents so that he can

were broken to the quick and she suffered temporary blindness from gazing into the eyes of The Wiz when laser-like spotlights shone from his enormous silver head. It was reputed Ross received $1 million for playing Dorothy, and the movie's original budget was approximately $35 million, extended by a further $10 million before completion. The movie had to recoup at least $60 million to become a success.

The Wiz was premiered on Broadway on 24 October 1978, followed by a spectactlar party held at the 'Windows Of The World' restaurant at the World Trade Center. American critics praised the movie. The *Hollywood Reporter* printed: 'It signals the return of mind-boggling entertainment of a quality and dimen-

claim from the insurance companies. The whole thing is a comedy and ends up quite uproarously'. The movie flopped and Robinson lost his money.

Robinson's British tour delighted audiences with its laid back, no-nonsense presentation. Critics hailed him as a living legend. *Melody Maker* printed: 'Smokey Robinson is, along with the moon landings and the motorcar, one of the wonders of the age.' Another reviewer wrote: 'Smokey was in a class of his own. A living legend whose voice effortlessly turned half the audience into emotional lumps. I got more shivers up my spine per song than I've ever had before.'

Robinson continued as Motown's vice-president and remained involved in the signing of new acts, although his office had expanded to more than fifteen members of staff to cater for the increasing A&R demand: 'So I'm free to do my own thing unless someone asks me to become involved in a certain project. Or, if I see something going down that I'd like to become involved in, then I'll do it.' Despite leaving The Miracles because the touring aspect of their career tired him, Robinson resumed touring once his solo career took off. He commented that he actually began missing his audience: 'I decided live dates were a very intricate part of me, and when it came down to it I really loved doing them. I've been doing |solo| dates in the States since 1975 but not of course at the pace that I used to with The Miracles. I'm freer to do them at my own pace because there's no-one else involved.' His act varied from show to show because – 'I believe in pleasing people who come to see me. So the first four or five numbers are formated – just to get started – then we sing whatever the people want to hear. Whatever they yell out, we sing it, because that's why they came to see us.'

Robinson also intended to record an album with his wife, Claudette, and towards this end had completed four tunes, although he had doubts about working with Claudette: 'It's very difficult on some nights to work, if you see what I'm saying! And in the studios I might criticize her with something, as I would do any artist, when maybe she doesn't wanna hear it. So, I think that in order to complete this particular project we're gonna have to get another producer!' The album was never finalized and Robinson underwent musical changes of his own with the release of his *Deep In My Soul* album, none of the tracks of which were written by him. Robinson: 'I got comments like "you've petered out" or "you don't know how to write songs anymore". But that album was a lifesaver for me because it should let young writers and producers know that Motown is very open-minded about good material. They can come anytime and record an album on me, somebody who has been doing his own stuff for several years. However, because of *Big Time* I couldn't have possibly done a quality studio album at the time. I've actually got a thousand songs that simply have never been finished. Now that I have a little more time I want to concentrate more on writing, and once the creativity starts to flow again, I'll be writing my own stuff again.'

Unexpected visitors to Robinson's London concert were Stevie Wonder and Yolanda who flew to London from Paris as part of their European holiday on 1 November. Motown/EMI were unaware of their arrival until they appeared in the offices. They met Robinson in their company's headquarters, where they sang an impromptu 'Happy Birthday' to secretary Noreen Allen before presenting her with a bouquet of flowers. As well as attending a Robinson concert, Wonder appeared on stage with Elton John at Wembley Arena, to play keyboards for the British star's finale.

Before the close of 1977 Motown Industries was the top black-owned company in America for the fifth year running. Record sales rose from $43.5 million in 1975 to $50 million in 1976, putting Motown $2.4 million ahead of its closest competitor, Johnson Publishing.

At the start of 1978, while ex-Temptation Eddie Kendricks joined Clive Davis' Arista Records as a solo artist and Lenny Williams joined ABC Records, Motown signed a slew of new acts. The first to release an album was 21st Creation in January (US). Titled *Break Thru* (UK, March), it followed the release of their *Tailgate* single in 1977. 21st Creation (Fred Williams, Alphonso Smith, Tyrone Moores, Pierre Johnson, Alonzo Martin) hailed from Chicago's west side, attended the same

Stevie Wonder and Yolanda paid a surprise visit to London. During their stay Wonder appeared at Wembley Arena with Elton John.

schools, grew up in the same neighbourhood and began singing together in the early Seventies as 21st Century. Reggie Sykes signed them to his Gold Tone Productions Inc to record *Remember The Rain?* which sold twenty thousand copies in two weeks. When RCA Records secured them the single went on to sell six hundred thousand copies. Motown's Hal Davis subsequently approached Sykes with a deal offer and the group were signed. Although they had a loyal following, they never produced a hit.

Switch (Greg Williams, Bobby and Tommy DeBarge, Eddie Fluellen, Jody Sims, Phillip Ingram) was born from the nucleus of the 1975 band White Heat who, with singer/composer Barry White as their mentor, recorded an album with RCA. When White Heat disbanded through lack of success, Ingram financed the reformed outfit renamed First Class to cut an album in Ohio. Sims and Williams took their demo tape to Motown where they met Jermaine and Hazel Jackson in the elevator. The Jackson brother took their tape, and a day later telephoned them with a proposal. They met to finalize their agreement in the hospital where Hazel Jackson was giving birth to their son, Jermaine Jr. In May 1977 the group officially joined the company and changed their name to Switch. Jermaine controlled the young band and produced their first album *Switch* (US, Jul '78/UK, Oct '78) from which the platinum single *There'll Never Be* was lifted. A year later another hit followed with *Best Beat In Town* from their *Switch II* album (US, Apr '79/UK, Jul '79). Jermaine Jackson: 'Switch remind me of Earth, Wind And Fire, a group I love. Sometimes it's not good to sign a group that sounds totally different because they might not fit into our system. But Switch had the looks, the charisma, everything.' Jackson's

enthusiasm for his group was accepted by the American market only.

The 5th Dimension, who suffered in the battle with Diana Ross and *Love Hangover*, released their first Motown album *Star Dancing* on the Motown label (US, Jan '78/UK, Mar '78). *You Are The Reason (I Feel Like Dancing)* was lifted as a single. The group's line-up when it was signed was Florence Le Rue Gordon (wife of Marc Gordon, their manager), Lamonte McLemore, Danny Miller Beard, Terri Bryant and Michel Bell. Two original members, Billy Davis and Marilyn McCoo, left to form a duo. The group had been together for over fifteen years prior to joining Motown and had received in excess of fourteen gold records for million selling singles like their first *Up, Up And Away, One Less Bell To Answer, Wedding Bell Blues, Stoned Soul Picnic* and *Aquarius/Let The Sunshine In.* Lamonte McLemore: 'We were innovators of a sort because we were the first black group to accomplish a number of things. We opened the doors for a lot of other people and unfortunately those achievements are glossed over. Places like Vegas, where we became a "main room" attraction from the beginning, and rooms like The American in New York. They'd never really used black acts until we came along.' The group's Motown stay was non-productive despite Florence La Rue Gordon being adamant the relationship would work: 'We felt it would be the best marriage. We could really make music history – a top record company and an established group like us.' After the release of their second American album *High On Sunshine* a year later, the marriage ended in divorce.

When The Main Ingredient lost Cuba Gooding as their lead singer in 1976, his future solo recordings were eagerly awaited. He had begun negotiations with RCA, Lambert and Potter's Haven label and Warner Brothers, when Motown offered a deal that attracted him more. Gooding had joined The Main Ingredient after Donald McPherson died, and the group enjoyed success with hits like *Just Don't Want To Be Lonely.* When Gooding, a New Yorker, signed with Berry Gordy's company,

(Right) *After losing the 'Love Hangover' battle with Diana Ross, The 5th Dimension recorded their own songs with Motown. The established group felt signing to Motown was a good marriage. Unfortunately, it ended in a hitless divorce!*

Jermaine Jackson introduced Switch to Motown because they reminded him of Earth, Wind & Fire, but even with Jackson's guidance Switch failed to reach expectations.

he moved to the West Coast to be nearer Motown, where he recorded as a solo artist and produced in-house acts. *The First Cuba Gooding Album* was issued in February 1978 (UK, May), with the second *Love Dancer* a year later. Gooding was destined to become another new signing who failed.

New signing Platinum Hook, on the other hand, were more fortunate in that they had the guidance of the Commodores' manager, Benny Ashburn, even though it failed to turn them into stars. Ashburn spotted the group performing in a New York club, but as he was involved with the Commodores they had a two year wait before being signed up with the Commodores own company, the Commodores Entertainment Corporation. Platinum Hook (Robin David Corley, Stephen Daniels, Tina Renee Stanford, Robert Douglas, Elisha 'Skip' Ingram, Victor Jones, Glenn Wallace) wrote most of their own material and it was this and their ability to versify that attracted Ashburn. Their first album *Platinum Hook*, (US, Mar '78/UK, Jun '78) was well received but sold poorly. Within two years their Motown career was over.

Another Commodores Entertainment Corporation signing were three young Detroit girls (a familiar ring!) known as 3 Ounces Of Love. The Alexander sisters (Elaine, Ann, Regina) had worked their way through church choirs, talent contests and session work before joining Motown. Once signed they supported the Commodores on their American and European tours. 3 *Ounces Of Love* was their only album (US, Apr '78/UK, Aug '78) and the dance track *Star Love* was taken as single a month prior to the album's release followed by *Give Me Some Feeling* in July. The girls' aim was to make a name for themselves: 'The Supremes did it, and well. We hope to do just as well, but in our own way.' Unfortunately, the Alexanders set themselves too big a task.

Major Lance, a Soul label signing born on the northside of Chicago, was one of twelve children. After an unsuccessful boxing stint, Lance turned to singing and formed his own gospel group, The Five Harmonaires. It later disbanded in 1959. Lance became a dancer on the American television show *Bandstand Matinee* before recording *The Monkey Time* for the Okeh label. *Hey Little Girl* and his biggest seller *Um-Um-Um-Um-Um-Um* followed; the latter was a number forty British hit in February 1964 and when re-recorded by the British group, Wayne Fontana and the Mindbenders, reached number five in Britain in October 1964.

When Lance's American hits stopped, he recorded and worked in England, where his keyboardist was Reg Dwight, aka Elton John. Lance's debut album for Motown, aptly titled *Now Arriving* (US, Jul '78/UK, Oct '78) was produced by the singer Lance, Otis Leavill and Kent Washburn and was the last album on the Soul label.

After cutting their 1977 British tour short due to the death of Ronald La Pread's wife Kathy, the Commodores returned for a Spring 1978 tour, with the 3 Ounces Of Love as support act. The tour included April and May dates in Bristol, Brighton, Birmingham, Newcastle, Edinburgh, Glasgow, Manchester and three dates in London. The group at this stage of their career were still attempting to expand their music outside the black buying market, despite the restrictions of American radio stations. Milan Williams: 'Certain stations considered our music too black for listeners. *Just To Be Close To You* was one. But if that tune was too black to be played on a pop station, then how the hell did it get to number seven in the national charts!' Thomas McClary: 'Statements about music being too black are hindering the people that are listening to the music and they are also hindering the artist. Whatever we create should be accepted and rejected by people as a whole. Why should we have to sell eight hundred thousand copies at number one in the R&B chart before we get accepted as pop? When people make those kinds of statements it's because of the fact that they are usually afraid to make a step.' Lionel Richie: 'What we're dealing with is that age old problem of people's hang ups. In the music business you'll find that musicians are universal people. We can go to Japan, Colombia, South Carolina, and I can meet someone I've never seen before in my life and immediately we have something we can identify with and that's music. The problem is musicians are very open minded people dealing with a very closely-minded society!'

The problem was to resolve itself in June 1978 (UK, July) when the emotional love ballad *Three Times A Lady* was released. It became a worldwide number one and when news-

A British cover version robbed Major Lance of a top ten hit prior to his joining Motown to record his debut album Now Arriving, in 1978.

After experimenting with musical styles, the Commodores got it right with the Lionel Richie ballad Three Times A Lady, which topped most of the world's charts.

paper headlines heralded the Commodores as 'The Black Beatles', their ambitions had been realized. The song also won most of 1978's prestigious awards and honours. Lionel Richie wrote the song as a track for their Natural High album released simultaneously in Britain and America during May 1978. However, the track was not immediately lifted as a single in the UK, even though it was the best on the album and radio play on it was extensive, because – as far as Motown/EMI were concerned – the song would garner additional album sales, thus generating more money. Richie explained how the song was conceived: 'I attended my parent's wedding anniversary and my father made a speech about how much he loved my mother and appreciated the way she had stood by him for thirty-five years. It was beautiful, but started me thinking about my own life and how my wife, Brenda, stands by me, and how she does so many things without being asked or thanked. So I wrote Three Times A Lady for her. I think my next door neighbor summed it up when she said that if any man wanted to buy her a gift, all he need do was buy her this record and he wouldn't have to say anything else. But, personally speaking, the song has given me so much personal satisfaction, and I think it's a songwriter's dream to be totally accepted. From the masses of awards that song has won, it seemed the whole world really does love it, and it's a great feeling.'

The Commodores were touring America when Three Times A Lady broke. Richie: 'It started out as a sixty-eight day tour and we had to extend it by another forty days. We found more and more dates coming in, and in places that groups like us don't usually play. That was primarily because the single got into every possible market, including country and western. Now the trick is to hold on to all of those newly found fans.' The group stayed on top for eighteen months but never repeated the success of Three Times A Lady.

Motown's new signing, Rick James, was destined to become the company's most outrageous and outspoken artist of the decade, and a major recording force who introduced his own distinctive brand of punk music to the world. James, real name James Johnson, was born and raised in Buffalo, New York. As a teenager he played with local R&B groups before joining the Navy Reserve when he was 15. When the Forces called him up, James decided against joining and absconded to Toronto, Canada. James: 'I called myself Ricky James Matthews and joined a group called The Mynah Birds that included Neil Young, Goldie McJohn and Bruce Palmer, who later became Buffalo Springfield, Crosby, Stills, Nash and Young, and Steppenwolf. Then I actually joined the Navy and went absent without leave. I had joined under-age and it took a year to resolve. After that I went to London for a year and a half, and that's where

I went back to studying. There were so many starving bands trying to make it there, that I realized I'd have to be extra great. Believe me, when you starve in London you really starve!' As a child James had ambitions to join Motown as a performer following his admiration of Stevie Wonder and The Temptations. However, when his lawyers began negotiating for a recording deal Motown was not an automatic choice because the singer was worried about the company's dealings with its artists. James: 'I later found out the rumors to be completely untrue, like how they ripped everybody off. The only way these groups get ripped off is by not looking after their own interests properly and by not having the right lawyers and accountants. Because of Motown's musical tradition I was scared they would lose my first album but the deal was so great that I didn't care if the first album flopped; in fact I expected it. But I had a guarantee for the second one. As it turned out I was lucky because the first album Come Get It came out at the time when negroids and whiteroids were doing some serious dancing. There were negroids, whiteroids, jewroids, then there were a******* and hemorrhoids. Anyway, all the "roids" were really dancing and listening at the time, although the disco situation helped break the record once the R&B market got it off and going.'

Come Get It, released on the Gordy label in April 1978 (UK, Jul '78) was the album from which James' first single You And I (UK, May '78) was lifted a month earlier, followed by Mary Jane (US, Sep '78/UK, Oct '78). James: 'I wrote You And I about my ex-old lady. She was the main woman in my life for many years and it's crazy because as we broke up the song became a hit. Mary Jane is one of several titles for marijuana which is the greatest thing since ice cream and I'm not afraid to admit it. I wanted to treat it like a girl because I like to look at it like it's a girl.'

His public views on drug abuse brought violent criticism from the media who claimed he should not influence his younger followers. James disagreed: 'Kids are no longer kids. They are able to decipher and decide what they want. You can't sit down and tell a thirteen year old anything about anything because they pretty well know what's going on. Their brothers and sisters were junkies and/or prostitutes, they've been through the marijuana trip, and they may even smoke it. I don't propogate anything. I don't say "everyone smoke grass". I say "I love Mary Jane". It makes me feel good, it hasn't lowered my IQ, nor has it been deterimental in any way. There is nothing wrong with marijuana, scientifically, or any other way. Another thing I'd like to know is, why didn't people ever put down Bob Marley for his use of marijuana? He used it as his whole religion.'

Bonnie Pointer and her sisters (Ruth, Anita, June) were born to Reverend and Mrs Elton

Pointer, and raised in Oakland, California. They sang in their father's church choir before embarking on a professional singing career. They recruited a manager who sent them on dates that didn't exist but did inadvertantly lead them to session work with acts like Cold Blood and The Elvin Bishop Group, with whom the sisters later toured. The Pointer Sisters' first headlining appearance was at The Troubadour, Los Angeles, where they enthralled their audience with their flashy revival of the Forties' scat-jazz singing. In time, the sisters played international concert dates, won prestigious awards, and in 1973 joined the ABC/Blue Thumb Records label to record two gold albums, *The Pointer Sisters* and *That's A Plenty*.

They were the first popular act to appear at San Francisco's War Memorial Opera House, which led to the release of a double album *Live At The Opera House*. Their most adventurous change of music came with the country and western song *Fairytale*, which topped the American country charts, won a 1975 Grammy Award and led to a string of concerts at The Grand Ole Opry venue.

In 1977 the Pointer Sisters left ABC to join Elektra/Asylum Records and Bonnie Pointer left her sisters to join Motown. Leaving the highly successful Pointer Sisters was a risky, perhaps unwise move for Bonnie, especially as since her departure her sisters have gone from strength to strength to become international million sellers and standing-room-only attractions. Pointer realized the potential danger of her move: 'I knew I had to split so that I could grow and learn more about myself so we came to a decision that I should do so. I missed being with them and the contact and dependency that comes from being part of a group, especially with it being a sisters' group situation. It took me a little time to realize that if I wanted something done I had to do it all myself.'

Jeffrey Bowan produced Bonnie Pointer's self-named debut album, released in October 1978 (UK Jan, '79). A month prior to the American release of the album, Pointer's first single *Free Me From My Freedom* was issued (UK, Oct '78). It's lyrics told of bondage and caused considerable controversy. Pointer: 'We didn't plan it as a controversial tune. People with strange minds might think it means something else but the storyline is about a lady who leaves her man figuring that making it alone is easier until she finds she misses him and wants him back. People will just think what they want anyway.'

Pointer's second album *Bonnie Pointer/2* (US, Nov '79/UK Feb '80) comprised vintage Motown classics including the March 1979 release of The Elgins' song *Heaven Must Have Sent You* as a single, which flopped. Motown/EMI released a new version of the track during July but that too died. Pointer explained her motive behind the second album: 'As a child I

Bonnie Pointer left her sister group to embark on a solo career with Motown. After releasing two albums she ended up in a legal battle with Berry Gordy.

idolized those old songs and the artists who sang them. It's amazing how these songs are actually new to most of today's buyers. For me, it's a nostalgic trip and I think a lot of people in their twenties and thirties will feel that way.'

One original song did, however, creep into the album, the sweeping, poignant ballad

The contrasting moods of Bonnie Pointer! This picture was used in Europe to promote her poignant ballad Deep Inside My Soul.

(Right) Florence Lyles joined Marvin Gaye on stage to add her distinctive vocals to the duets made famous by Gaye and Terrell

Deep Inside My Soul which was eventually lifted as a single in March 1980 (UK, Apr '80) as the follow-up to I *Can't Help Myself* (*Sugar Pie Honey Bunch*) (US, Nov '79/UK, Jan '80). Despite Pointer's recording enthusiasm and Motown's good intentions, something went drastically wrong. In 1981 Berry Gordy filed a complaint in a Los Angeles Court after Pointer and Jeffrey Bowan (whom Pointer had married) had threatened him and had libelled Motown claiming defraudment of their royalties. Pointer later retrieved her recording career to enjoy brief success with CBS/Epic, while her sisters reached superstardom.

On 21 November 1978 Berry Gordy's 90-year-old father 'Pops' Gordy died. According to author J. Randy Taraborrelli he was survived by seven children, twenty grandchildren, fifteen great grandchildren, a sister and two brothers. Throughout his life Gordy had been a constant support to his son and when Motown was properly formed he became a vital figurehead in the organization. Loved by every artist for his consideration and kindness, four of Berry's finest paid tribute to him on record. Diana Ross, Marvin Gaye, Smokey Robinson and Stevie Wonder recorded the Sawyer/McLeod song *Pops, We Love You*, originally written as a birthday gift for Gordy's father. The single was released in the US in December 1978 (UK, Feb '79) and later became the American 'Father's Day Song Of

The Year', when a limited edition was pressed in red heart-shaped vinyl. In April 1979 the *Pops, We Love You* album was issued (UK, Jun '79) featuring tracks by the mentioned artists and others.

During December 1978 Marvin Gaye released his first studio album since I *Want You* in 1976, titled *Here, My Dear*. This was his personal statement on the breakdown of his marriage to Anna Gordy following his secret marriage to Janis Hunter in October 1977. Prior to the release of *Here, My Dear* Gaye faced bankruptcy. He filed two voluntary bankruptcy petitions – a personal one and one for his Righton Productions. The Righton petition consisted of an estimated $1.8 million in liabilities and assets of $1.27 million. Gaye agreed on a monthly repayment scheme less the administrative fee for disbursement. His personal petition concerned legal fees, estimated at $1.6 million and confirmed he owed roughly £523,000 in unpaid taxes for the years 1974/75 with unsecured debts estimated at $7 million (*Billboard* 1978). Some of these problems arose when the singer, through Righton Productions, delivered finished masters of his work to Motown instead of recording them direct. The California State Board of Equalization was also demanding tax arrears and to help out with this, Motown reputedly advanced Gaye a large sum of money in January 1978, which showed up as a liability in the petition. The Court trustee estimated Gaye had earned in excess of $1 million in the previous six years, and personal monthly expenditure was estimated at $35,000. Gaye also borrowed approximately $154,000 to buy property. In September 1978 he renewed his recording contract with Motown for a further seven years, the company paying him

$600,000 for each of his first two albums and $1 million each thereafter. Within two years the singer would break that contract.

Gaye spoke to British journalists about these bankruptcy charges and was annoyed at the conflicting reports: 'I heard I owe six million dollars although the press say it's around three million. It's more like two million which I owe my manager. I got into that state because I prefer to handle my own life and affairs and I guess I'm not the smartest in business. There's a lot of people saying I owe them money. I don't know why I'm involved in the lawsuits either. I always thought I was such a decent person, but I am involved in them because of my unswerving faith in human nature. I never learn. I wish I could stop believing in people. I'm an easy mark, and now I'm not sure I've even got the best legal counsel in the world. I'm not, though, what the authorities call a poor bankruptcy, there's just a lot of buzzards around.'

Eighty per cent of the royalties from *Here, My Dear* would be paid to his ex-wife Anna Gaye: 'The album took at least three months to record properly, although it had been on master tape for at least a year. The work was unfinished because I was involved in political fighting with Motown, and then the Federal Court felt the album was part of my estate for bankruptcy. I had to write and record the album specifically as part of a very unusual divorce deal that was a decision handed down by the judge. At first I thought I'd put out a lot of garbage for the album because all I had to give was one album. There was no stipulation that it had to be a good one, so Anna was taking chances here. Then I thought of my fans and started recording. The more I cut, the more I got involved. After a certain point I forgot I was mad and angry, and did some decent work. The result was, I think, pretty fair. I listened to it for over a year and I felt poor when I realized I wasn't going to make any money from it.' The project was a self-conscious, haunting, bitter and somewhat morbid collection of songs. *When Did You Stop Loving Me, When Did I Stop Loving You, Is That Enough, You Can Leave, But It's Gonna Cost You* were produced and arranged by Gaye and he wrote all the tracks with the exception of *Anger* (co-written with Delta Ashby and Ed Townsend). The album sleeve showed two views of Rodin's 'The Kiss' with the artist wearing a toga. The back sleeve showed Gaye surrounded by a decaying city, with the words 'Pain And Divorce' edged on a wall to the left of an embracing couple. Inside the gatefold sleeve a board game entitled 'Judgement' was shown; on the right of the game a woman's hand hovers over a pile of $500 bills, a house and a limousine, with dice, insects and coins lying alongside a dress ring. On the left of the picture a man's hand clutches a record, under which is a Revox tape machine, a piece of recording equipment and a single dollar bill. A red rose, a burning chair and a skull can be seen in the foreground, and the board game squares consist of playing cards, hearts and daggers. The design was Gaye's own, illustrated by Michael Bryan, and attracted as much attention as the music. Gaye: 'I would not like to suggest this album would hurt Anna because I'd love to see some happiness in her life. I like the institution of marriage although this album makes it look as if I don't. There is a terrible imbalance with the whole divorce thing and I don't like it. It doesn't matter who's right or wrong, the man must pay the wife everything. Pay for the divorce and give over to her the custody of the children, yet the man can still take care of his child because a father can be a mother too. American law cannot see that and it's horrible.'

Marketing *Here, My Dear* presented Motown with problems with its controversy and lack of potential singles except A *Funky Space Reincarnation Parts* 1 & 2 released in January 1979 (UK, Feb '79). There were no musicians credits on the album sleeve which caused friction with the American Musicians Union. Gaye: 'I cut all the sessions under the table so to speak. I have enough union problems without listing the musicians as well!'

LOVIN', LIVIN' AND GIVIN'

'Smokey was the revolving door, as we called him, because he helped us leave Motown and then he helped us come back.'
Otis Williams of The Temptations

'I think things are going to be a whole lot better for me now, anyway, because my head is in a different place and I understand more about the business.'
Jimmy Ruffin

With the loss of The Temptations, the Jackson 5 and The Supremes, Motown concentrated on pushing the new signings. Many failed to develop into major stars because, they claimed, the company was too involved in promoting Diana Ross, Stevie Wonder, the Commodores and Marvin Gaye. However, the established artists were not a continuous threat to the newcomers as they insisted on quality releases rather than on quantity; but it is true to say that when a 'star' product was released it was afforded massive marketing campaigns to ensure top sales to keep Motown financially stable.

With the expanding roster of new acts and diverse types of music, there was now no 'special' Motown Sound to attract new and loyal followers. Motown had become just another record company fighting for hits in an industry that had by now reached saturation point. Through the mid-price Natural Resources label, Motown was able to pad out their release schedules with re-issues and 'Greatest Hits' compilations, but with a new decade looming, priority had to be given to new faces if the company was to remain successful.

Of the new names signed in 1979, the group Bloodstone from Kansas City, Missouri, was the most successful thanks to their pre-Motown hit *Natural High*. Bloodstone (Eddie Summers, Willie Draffen Jr, Charles Love, Charles McCormick, Roger Durham, Harry Williams) were known as The Sinceres when they played club and hotel dates in Los Angeles. While in California they met George Braunstein and Ronald Hamady, who arranged for them (now known as Bloodstone) to record and tour in Britain. Upon their return to America *Natural High* on London Records became an international hit. Further releases like *Never Let You Go, Outside Woman* and *That's Not How It Goes* kept up the momentum. In 1976 Bloodstone produced their own avant-garde musical comedy *Train Ride To Hollywood* and the group was reduced to a quartet (Love, Draffen Jr, McCormick,

Williams). It was this line-up that signed with Motown where their debut Motown album *Don't Stop* was issued (US, Jan '79/UK, Apr '79). Tàta Vega's manager, Winston Monseque and her duettist, Al Johnson, produced the album.

Also on the Motown label Diana Ross' brother, Arthur 'T-Boy' Ross, released his *Changes* album in February 1979. Ross, an ex-law student, first came to public notice with Marvin Gaye's *I Want You* project. Ross: 'It was supposed to have been mine but Berry Gordy explained to me it would be better if I gave the project to Marvin because it would build up my reputation better that way. And I understood how hard it would be to break a brand new artist at the time so I went along with it. Marvin was such a fine, versatile performer that I was proud to hear him doing my songs, although he didn't sing them exactly the way I wanted which is why I included *I Want You* on my album.' T-Boy Ross was influenced by his sister and her rise to stardom, as he explained: 'I have sat back and watched Diana since I was a little boy, and just watching her and Motown grow has been a lesson in itself, and I'm proud to be a part of Motown now. Diana influenced me a great deal.' Prior to singing, T-Boy Ross was a writer of ten years standing: 'Everybody kept telling me I couldn't sing, so I had to build up my confidence to the stage where I felt I could. I started doing demos of my songs, and that gave me confidence. I don't think Motown was sold on me as a singer until I proved it to them. They then gave me total control so if there were any mistakes made they were my own. I knew I had to get it right because I had given so many good songs away.'

One of the most exciting songstresses to be signed by Berry Gordy during the late Seventies was Teena Marie, a white blonde Californian who grew into an immensely talented writer/singer/producer. Marie nèe Mary Christine Brockert fronted her own band as a 13-year-old, and mastered the guitar and piano. Marie: 'I used to listen to all the early Tamla things like Stevie and Marvin. I was

During a 1976 press reception in London Marvin Gaye showed off his drumming expertise to an appreciative audience.

Diana Ross' brother, Arthur, gave one of his best songs to Marvin Gaye before embarking on a singing career.

introduced to Howard Davis who got me an audition with Berry Gordy. Berry wanted me for a movie he was planning at the time. Anyway, the project got shelved but he still wanted me on the label.' After being signed for three years and following several unsatisfactory recording attempts, Teena Marie was pursuaded by her manager, Winnie Martin, to work with Rick James. Marie: 'I didn't know who he was, and I was really fed up all the way around. Why should Rick be able to work with me after everyone else had failed? I didn't like the idea of working with him. However, that was before I got to know him. I've worked with other producers and none of them got into the way I felt about music the way Rick did.' James produced her first highly acclaimed album *Wild And Peaceful* (US, Mar '79/UK, Jun '79) on the Gordy label. The singer was not featured on the album sleeve because Motown didn't want the public to know she was white; the disco hit *I'm A Sucker For Your Love* was lifted as her first single (US, Apr '79/UK Jun '79). She failed to keep up the momentum by releasing the unimaginative *Don't Look Back* as its follow-up, Marie: 'Rick knew there were feelings in my heart and songs upon my lips. He didn't say "this is a white girl, I can't produce her" because he doesn't think in those terms. Our relationship grew into something really beautiful. Rick told me once that I was the only other person that he loved besides his mother and sisters. There is so much understanding and respect between us and I think it shows in our work together.' Rick James: 'Teena is a very sensitive, soft, intelligent and emotional human being.

We're both bachelors and we both care for each other.'

Marie's second album *Lady T* (US, Feb '80/UK, Mar '80) was co-written and produced by her and the late Minnie Riperton's husband, Richard Rudolph. Marie was fond of Riperton's work and asked Rudolph to work with her. Marie: 'All the songs on *Lady T* are personal to me and reflect what goes on inside, though I may use my imagination and write about things I haven't experienced.' *Lady T* spawned *Behind The Groove*, her biggest ever single, and as it climbed the British charts, the singer undertook a week's promotional tour of the country from 6 August 1979. It was one of the toughest itineraries drawn up by Motown/EMI which involved continuous interviews during the day and a series of club appearances at night. Marie was a willing worker, although she was prone to moodiness and was interested in little other than her work.

Irons In The Fire (dedicated to her late father, Thomas Leslie Brockert who died in 1976) and *It Must Be Magic* albums followed in 1980 and 1981 respectively. The singer wrote and produced both albums which were stunningly exciting, particularly the epic tune *Portuguese Love* with Rick James' ad-libs on the latter album. Although it is an asset for a singer to be entirely responsible for an album, Marie gradually fell into the trap of self over-indulgence in her productions, which eventually suffocated the rawness and simplicity of her earlier work. Motown reputedly promised Marie a gold album for *Irons In The Fire* if she re-signed with them for a further period. According to an American trade publication, when the album reached gold status, Marie failed to keep her side of the agreement and signed with CBS Records, where she has failed to repeat her Motown success.

Prior to Rick James working on Marie's *Wild And Peaceful* album, he released his second *Bustin' Out Of L Seven* (US, Jan '79/UK, Mar '79). *High On Your Love Suite*, *Bustin' Out* and *Fool On The Street* were issued as singles throughout the 1979 before his next *Fire It Up* album in the autumn. This was a further expression of his 'back street' upbringing. James compared *Fire It Up* to his others by saying: '*Come Get It* was an experiment in simplicity for me. I hadn't made it then and everything was simple. *Bustin' Out* was a step further in concept. In some ways that was too experimental, but it was a better album than *Come Get It* although it didn't come over sound frequency wise as much. On *Fire It Up* I knew what I wanted and went after it'. Although most of James' singles were up-tempo, semi-commercial hard punk funk releases, as demanded by the disco market, his preference was for writing and singing ballads: 'But I don't know if I'm ready to do what Lionel Richie and the Commodores have done and that is stun my audiences with an over-abundance of sensitivity.'

Berry Gordy's most prestigious signing at this time was Billy Preston, an established performer yet struggling vinyl artist. Preston, born in Houston, Texas, spent his childhood in Los Angeles. His elder sister, Rodena, began playing the piano when she was two and taught Preston as he sat on her lap. By the age of seven Preston played his local church's organ and directed the choir that included singers several times his own age. By ten, he had appeared with a symphony orchestra and in the Mahalia Jackson Show, recorded with the Reverend Alex Bradford, and made his film debut as the young W.C. Handy in St. Louis Blues.

During 1962 Preston joined Little Richard's band. Preston: 'We met in church and he was getting ready to go to England to do a gospel tour. Or so we thought. We got over there and it turned out to be a rock and roll tour. That was the first time that I ever played rock and roll because until then I had been strictly gospel. I learned a great deal but the thing I remember most was Little Richard leaving me in London stranded. He was going through some enormous mental changes at the time. He had given up rock and roll for gospel and now he was being forced back.' Co-starring on that tour were Sam Cooke, Gerry and the Pacemakers and the Beatles; the latter was Preston's favourite group whom he befriended – 'One night they even asked me to join them on stage but I had to say "no" because Richard would get mad.'

Preston's keyboard expertise impressed Sam Cooke enough for him to sign Preston to his own SAR label where Preston's first album, Sixteen Year Old Soul, was released. When the label folded Preston moved to Vee Jay and later to Capitol Records. While a session musician on Jack Good's American television series Shindig, Preston met Ray Charles, and subsequently worked with him on stage and record for three years. Preston: 'On stage Ray's band and the Raelettes and I would perform the first half with me sitting in Ray's place. He was very gracious to me and would introduce me to the audience by saying that he was counting on me to carry on for him after he's gone.'

On leaving Ray Charles, Preston re-met George Harrison in Europe when the Beatles asked him to record for their newly-formed Apple label. Preston's biggest hit there was That's The Way (God Planned It) in 1969 and with his involvement in the group's Let It Be movie and album, he was known as the fifth Beatle. However, as a solo artist Preston's career declined. Apple's tangle of legal problems eventually led to its downfall so Preston asked Harrison to release him from his contract. The artist moved to A&M Records to release, among others, the I Wrote A Simple Song, Music Is My Life and Everybody Likes Some Kind Of Music albums, and enjoyed a number one American pop single with Outa-Space in 1972

and the R&B hits Will It Go Round In Circles and Space Race.

Preston left A&M Records after a period of inactivity to be introduced to Motown by the management team of Suzanne de Passe Le Mat (temporary name change due to her marriage to actor Paul Le Mat in 1978) and Tony Jones. His first project was to work with Syreeta on the soundtrack album for the basketball movie Fast Break (US, Mar '79/UK, May '79). The score had already been completed and the couples' vocals were added in two days. Go For It was released as the movie's first single, pressed in brown vinyl and packaged in a cardboard baseball. The project made little public impact but Preston and Syreeta became friends and this led to her contributing to Preston's solo album Late At Night (US Jul '79/UK, Sep '79). Preston: 'The whole thing about this album was that I had some outside help and support, whereas before it was all down to me to do everything. This time I had writers to help and the fact that it was a team effort makes me feel very satisfied. Dave Blumberg did the arrangements and he's very good. I am an ideas man, so an arranger was very important to me because it all has to be put down on paper. And he put together some great musicians. In the past most of my albums were done with my own band but this time we used James Gadsen, Ollie Brown and a lot of guys that I had always wanted to work with.' Ex-Motown writer/producer/singer Gloria Jones and her brother Richard wrote the track You, while former Supreme Scherrie Payne, and gospel legend Jesse Kirkland joined others as backing singers for the song.

Billy Preston and Syreeta's With You I'm Born Again, featured on both Fast Break and Late At Night, was released as a British single in August 1979 while America opted to issue It

Billy Preston and Syreeta became Motown's favourite duo in 1979 when their With You I'm Born Again became a huge British hit single.

Will Come In Time, which died. Meanwhile, the British single, released because Motown/EMI felt it had hit potential, had a sluggish start. It slept for two months but the company's record promotor, Chris Marshall, continued to promote it until it reached number two in the national charts and earned the duo a silver disc. The single was subsequently hastily released in America. Preston and Syreeta flew to London on 21 December 1979 for a three day press and television promotion tour which included opening the city's new nightclub 'Heaven' in Charing Cross. Syreeta: 'I didn't expect *With You I'm Born Again* stood a chance of success because everyone is into disco and not love songs. The people in England worked super hard to break it and we owe our success in America to that British breakthrough. It's been a funny song all the way through because in Los Angeles my managers always believed in it and it's one of the songs that I liked best myself. And now it's ended up being my biggest success so far and I certainly don't mind sharing it with Billy because he's such a nice guy to work with.' The couple was not contractually tied as a duo, as was originally thought, as Syreeta explained: 'We were both swept into the *Fast Break* venture and up to that point we had no pre-conceived ideas about working with each other, although we were familiar with each other's work. With the success we've achieved it's likely we'll do further projects together. But we do have our separate paths to travel. This single provided us with a good stepping stone.'

The couple returned to London in January 1980 to tape a performance for the *Search For A Star* television spectacular due for Easter screening. Although they never undertook a national tour, they did perform in selected American airbases. *With You I'm Born Again* was their only success, and after an uninspiring *Pressin' On* album in 1982, Billy Preston left Motown to sign to the Hi-NRG label Megatone, based in San Francisco. Six years later

Preston returned to Motown to release one single *Since I Held You Close*.

Also among the new signings was Patrick Gammon. Born on 15 January 1956 in Seattle, Washington, Gammon discovered music through his church-singing mother. Gammon learnt to play the piano when he was five, while his brother, Robert, formed his own band which included a young guitarist named Jimi Hendrix. When Gammon was ten he took trumpet and organ lessons. In 1973 he joined a local Seattle group Family Affair which gave him the confidence to work with Ike and Tina Turner for two years, before the urge to pursue a solo career took him to Munich, Germany. There he met Gerhard Augustin, his future manager and co-producer, and became a session singer and demo recorder. In 1976 Gammon released *Party Hardy* on the Galaxy label before securing a deal with Chrysalis Records in America. That relationship failed when the company tried to market him as 'the black Elton John'.

During 1978 the German Metronome label released Gammon's *Satisfaction* single which sold sufficiently for Gammon and Augustin to finance a demo tape featuring their combined work which they called 'black rock'. Augustin took it to Iris Gordy, then head of Motown's A&R division. Augustin: 'Although Patrick and I felt quite happy with the project we weren't quite sure as to how other people would react. Iris listened carefully to the tapes, several times I might add, and eventually remarked "it's weird, but I love it."' On Gammon's debut album *Don't Touch Me* (US, May '79/UK, Sep '79) the 23-year-old displayed his versatility by co-writing, co-producing and singing all the material. Gammon said upon the album's release: 'It represents my frustration and a lot of effort. It's my thing, no-one elses. Maybe I could have been the world's best carpenter, or an Olympic gold medal winner, but I chose music and naturally I want to climb as high as possible in my chosen career. However I'm not in any wild rush to get there. I'm planning a careful, but steady course and aim to be arround for a long time.' Gammon visited London for promotional activities at the time of his album's release. He was eager to work with Motown/EMI and, impressed at the way his career was being handled there, purchased gifts for each staff member in appreciation. He left Motown without a hit.

On the Tamla label, Shadee (pronounced 'shah-dee') debuted in June 1979 with his *I Just Need More Money Parts 1 and 2* single. Born in Mississippi and raised in Detroit, Shadee was a composer. He moved to Hollywood to join Jobete where he wrote for Diana Ross, Stevie Wonder and the Jackson 5 under the guidance of Anna Gordy Gaye. Together they worked on Shadee's debut album *I Just Need More Money*, released in July 1979, from which the single was lifted.

Actress Mira Waters' Motown input was

short, rather bland and disappointing. Born in Philadelphia, Pa, her debut single was *You Have Inspired Me* on the Gordy label in June 1979 (UK, August) followed by *Rock And Roll Me* a year later in the US only. As a youngster Waters intended to become a doctor but after attending a Harry Belafonte concert decided her future life was in entertainment. She studied at New York's Academy of Dramatic Arts before securing a part in a Broadway play, later co-starring in Gordon Park's acclaimed 1969 movie *The Learning Tree*. While studying piano at Detroit's Conservatory of Music Waters became involved in lyric writing with her late sister. When confident of her art, she sang her compositions and joined Motown. A close friend of Berry Gordy's, Waters later abandoned her recording career and took an administrative position within Motown.

In July 1979, the Commodores' *Midnight Magic* album was released on both sides of the Atlantic, and during August and September they undertook a world tour which included England, Holland, West Germany and Belgium. Commodore William King: 'The musical content of this album comes from all angles. We went as far as putting a steel guitar on one track and that's pure country and western. We have a tune on it called *Still* which a lot of people are going to take as the follow-up to *Three Times A Lady*. Then there's *You're Something Special* that has a Calypso beat to it and Walter Orange wrote the R&B flavoured *Gittin' It*. The title cut is a disco track, and as we're not a heavy disco group we had to write it especially'. Also at this time the Commodores re-signed to Motown for a further seven years which obligated them to record an album every nine months, instead of one per year. The group was now guaranteed standing room only audiences at their concerts, thanks to their spate of million selling records. King: 'In the last two years we've done more money in attendances than any black group has ever done. Our plan has always been to surpass the Beatles. I feel they are the epitome of pop music, the strongest entity to ever exist in the entertainment world. They changed the world and we want to surpass them. But they missed out on a couple of things purely by timing. For example, the R&B crowd would never touch the Beatles – even if they liked them – because they came during the conflict between black and white. You don't see Beatles' records all over the floor of the average black home, like you do today to a small extent with the Bee Gees. Times have changed because now it doesn't matter a helluva lot what color you are.' He illustrated his point by citing the Commodores' recent American mid-west tour where eighty per cent of the audience was white, and their performance in Seattle, Washington, where ninety-nine per cent was

white. King: 'The world is getting better. It may not always look like it but it is improving.'

Away from Motown both The Temptations (Franklin, Street, Leonard, Price, Williams) and The Miracles (Moore, Rogers, White, Griffin and his brother Donald) were going through sticky patches. At Atlantic The Temptations' second album *Bare Back* re-united them with Brian and Eddie Holland. The last time they worked together was in 1966 but that previous magic failed to materialize again. Otis Williams: 'Atlantic felt we didn't need to be pushed and these days it doesn't matter who you are, you have to have money spent on you. Although maybe our first album *Hear To Tempt You* wasn't as strong as it should have been, the response to our current one has been far more encouraging. It really hasn't been as difficult for us to adjust as we expected because the company has given us so much latitude. We just didn't get that kind of freedom with Motown. We always got the feeling that they didn't want us to learn that much.' After producing *The Temptations Do The Temptations* album (1976) while at Motown, they were eager to progress in this area, as Williams explained: 'We always felt that the (Motown) album never got the sales it should have got. It was a political thing because the company knew we were unsettled and thinking about moving and so they didn't promote it in their normal way. I guess they were trying to teach us a lesson because they didn't want us getting into writing and producing. At the time I remember Stevie Wonder telling us that he had gone through exactly the same problems when he first wanted to produce himself.'

Although they were signed to different record companies David Ruffin and The Temptations were considering recording one more album together. Ruffin: 'Eddie (Kendricks) and I are in favor of it, and Otis (Williams) and Melvin (Franklin) like the idea. We would bring in Dennis (Edwards), who's all for it, so it could actually happen.' He intended to use a variety of producers before offering the completed project to an enthusiastic record company. Ruffin: 'Otis and Melvin are with Atlantic and I'm with Warners, so that's family. Eddie is with Arista, so he'd need permission, and Dennis isn't with anyone.' The idea was to reach fruition but not in the way Ruffin originally intended.

The Miracles at Columbia/CBS released their *Love Crazy* album which died. The first three years after leaving Gordy's company were hard, they said: 'There was always a skeleton of Smokey Robinson in the closet and I think it took that time to finally put that behind us. We'd say that *Love Machine* and the *City Of Angels* albums were the only things that did it for us. When Smokey left we had made up our minds to continue and to try to progress, and stay positive in our thinking. After all, entertaining and recording is our whole

Mira Waters opted for a singing career after attending a Harry Belafonte concert. After releasing two unsuccessful singles, she abandoned her music career for a nine-to-fiver.

Dr Strut spearheaded Motown's new jazz division in the late Seventies. Despite a massive promotional campaign Motown's further attempt to crack the jazz market was unsuccessful.

life and it's our means of earning a living too.' The group was still friendly with Robinson but wanted the public to know that during their Motown years, they had taken care of their own business and careers and that Robinson had not influenced them from the day he left. Billy Griffin said the group's Motown stay without Robinson was similar to a marriage that had gone sour: 'We realized we needed a new "loved one" with more enthusiasm, more willingness to work with us and to a degree, more money to put behind The Miracles. Motown ceased to be a family the day they moved from Detroit to California. It's a business now, just big business. And a lot of acts at Motown feel that too much effort is being put behind Diana Ross. While she may be deserving of that effort and while she may even need it, there are a lot of acts that are being bypassed over there. To our way of thinking it must be possible to concentrate a company's efforts on more than one act.' Little more was heard of The Miracles after *Love Crazy* although they continued to tour on the American circuit. In time, Pete Moore and lead singer Billy Griffin left the ailing group; the latter recorded the 1982 hit *Hold Me Tighter In The Rain.* Bobby Rogers and Ronnie White recruited two new members until the group split up during the Eighties.

In yet another attempt to crack the jazz market Motown opened a new jazz division (not a label) which was spearheaded by Dr Strut. The group (Dave Woodford – reeds; Everett Bryson – percussion; Peter Freiberger – bass; (Englishman) Kevin Bassington – keyboards; Tim Weston – guitar; Claude Pepper – drums) released their eponymous album in May 1979 (UK, Oct '79) from which its most attractive track *Struttin'* was lifted a year later as a single. The group's low-key, late night music appealed to the connoisseur but failed to attract the mainstream record buyer despite Motown's enthusiasm for the new outlet.

The year 1979 was an active one for the former members of The Supremes. Diana Ross worked with Ashford and Simpson on her magnificent May album (UK, Jun '79) *The Boss,* her sixteenth solo release. The first

single was also *The Boss* (US, May '79/UK, Jun '79) followed by *It's My House.* In Britain *No-One Gets The Prize* in September was the second release hotly followed by *It's My House* when the British group Storm re-recorded it to enjoy a number thirty-six hit. Ross' version struggled to number thirty-two. Ross had recently completed a six week American tour which was her most expensive to date. She was backed on stage by a fifty-piece orchestra, nine dancers and thirteen singers, and flanked by a screen which featured a special laser light show. On the other hand, Mary Wilson was struggling for success following the release of her self-named album during August 1979 (UK, Oct '79) which spawned the James Brown rip-off single *Red Hot.* Hal Davis produced the album. Wilson: 'We wanted Marvin Gaye to produce it but he was committed to his own project and it would have taken time before he got to me.' Wilson needed to finish the album before she toured Britain, so approached Davis because she was impressed with his work with Diana Ross and the Jackson 5. Wilson: 'I don't mind if it's not a million seller because I know I did my best at the time. But I feel that what we've come up with is just right as a debut album. I did quite a lot of background on the album too, I guess I just couldn't stay away from it. I'd regarded myself basically as a ballad singer because I knew I could do that, so I had my doubts about how I'd approach the up-tempo material. I knew we had to do some because of the way the whole disco thing was happening. I feel that disco music has given the music business a lot of excitement but I'd have to say that a lot of R&B acts may have suffered a little in the process.'

(Right) Mary Wilson signs a solo recording contract with Motown. The Supreme is pictured here with Michael Roshkind, then vice-chairman and chief operating officer for Motown Industries.

Mary Wilson recruited two backing singers Karen Jackson and Kaaren Ragland to tour England with her. Advertizements read 'The Supremes featuring Mary Wilson' because she was unable to use Mary Wilson and The Supremes. As a result of the Wilson v. Motown court case over ownership of the name The Supremes, Wilson was reputedly given 50 percent of the name and was able to use advertizing reading 'The Supremes' Mary Wilson'. Wilson: 'When I started to perform solo I told my audience "here are some of my greatest hits". Then I sang just the backing parts, all the "oohs" without any lead vocals. When those who weren't laughing cheered, I told them "so you listen to the backgrounds too!"'
(Scherrie Payne and Susaye Green followed in Wilson's footsteps by producing a sadly inferior album *Partners* in October 1979. The album was not issued in Britain through lack of interest.)

Another artist having problems with Motown was Grover Washington Jr. 'I signed a mutual agreement with CTI and Kudu and then a separate contract with Motown', he told journalists in 1979. 'That meant I have to supply Motown with two completely new albums, and they also acquired the back catalogue of Kudu which gives them the right to package a "Best Of" album. It broke my heart that they got the old material because I tried to buy it myself. I did ask Motown and they simply said "no" and there was no negotiating on the subject.' This situation was confusing for record buyers as Washington's releases were available throughout Europe on different labels, and Motown's licences were unsure what albums belonged to them. However, *Reed Seed* was his first official album in September 1978 (UK, November) which was, once again, an ideal vehicle to break Motown into the jazz market. Washington: 'They won't get a better chance to prove themselves in that market. *Reed Seed* is, in my opinion, my best album to date, and I want to thank the people at Motown for giving me total creative freedom. They gave me the opportunity to present my product in the form I believed was best.' His *Skylarkin* album followed about two years later.

Motown/USA and Motown/EMI worked closely together to achieve the much-publicized simultaneous release of *Stevie Wonder's Journey Through The Secret Life Of Plants* in October 1979, three years after he had started working on it. His twenty-fourth album, it was the soundtrack to a Paramount movie. The release was planned to coincide with the opening of the movie but Paramount Pictures decided to temporarily shelve the project. This prompted Wonder to return to the studios to re-mix his work and add three more titles so that the album could stand up without the movie.

American author Peter Tompkins and biologist Christopher Bird wrote the book on which the movie was based. It was an investigation of all the documented information available concerning plants and their sense and feelings, an exercise which involved researching hundreds of documents written by scientists all over the world during the last century. Michael Braun, who worked on the screenplay of the movie, approached Wonder to pen the soundtrack after seeing him perform at London's Rainbow Theatre in 1974. The idea appealed to the singer who stressed the project would have to be shelved until he completed his *Songs In The Key Of Life* album. Braun was also instrumental in assisting Wonder by explaining the contents of each movie sequence in meticulous detail and how much music was needed for each sequence.

The ninety-eight minute documentary dwelt on the looks rather than the thoughts of flora. *Variety* magazine carried the following review for *The Secret Life Of Plants*: 'The use of microscopic lenses and time lapse photography is extensively employed, and on a certain level there's not much difference between this pic and numerous "National Geographic" tv specials except the Dolby sound . . . There are several scenes, both historical and current, of experiments proving plants say their own equivalent of "ouch" when pinched, but nary a word from the opposition, in this case the majority of scientists. Not helping the matter is the BBC-like pretentious narration by author Tompkins, Elizabeth Vreeland and Ruby Crystal who pounce on phrases like "the touchstone to the universal consciousness". And the spectre of "comrade" plants in the USSR or a Japanese woman talking to her cactus, may inspire ridicule rather than converts. *The Secret Life Of Plants* may find its greatest audience ironically from those who don't converse with plants, but smoke them. The extraordinary imagery and excellent score by Stevie Wonder should bring the same audience that turned another

Jazz supremo Grover Washington Jr was the ideal artist to push Motown into the jazz market. His music appealed to the specialists but was largely ignored by mainstream buyers.

sleeper *Up The Smoke* into a box office smash.'

The double album was criticized by many of Wonder's fans. It was basically an instrumental release, beautifully written and arranged. Wonder defended his work by saying: 'It is about the emotional, physical and mental relationship between plants and between men and plants. It is a musical way to help people understand and appreciate the film, even though I cannot see it. I achieved what I wanted to do. I appreciate it may throw some people because it's not what they expect from me. When people are basically hearing the kind of music they expect, they can tolerate a few songs that are out of the ordinary. But the songs on this album are in an unusual context for me and I think my fans will accept it . . . but I'm not totally sure.'

The double album (digitally recorded on the Sony PCM 1600 process perfected during the time it was recorded) featured Syreeta and Tàta Vega's vocals and the former's lyrics. Syreeta: 'Steve couldn't come up with a lyric for *Come Back As A Flower*, so he gave me a tape of the music but at first I couldn't come up with anything either. One day I was daydreaming and I got all these mental images of gardens, flowers, dawn and dusk and the lyrics just came. I did a demo and Steve liked it so much that he kept it the way I did it, even though I begged him to let me do it over again. I think the music is valid but the movie didn't really hold up. I feel this is Steve's most creative piece of music yet and if the film had been more up to par, it would have done better.'

To announce that Stevie Wonder (who had recently purchased a Los Angeles radio station KJLH for $2 million through his company Taxi Productions) had finished *Journey Through The Secret Life Of Plants*, Motown distributed copies of the paperback which inspired the movie, and packets of sunflower seeds to record retailers with the message that the album would be delivered when the seeds had sprouted – however fully grown flowers actually graced record stores by the time the record arrived! A scent was created by an American chemist intended to perfume the record's packaging and a phial of the perfume was flown to Motown/EMI for analysis by EMI's technical department, where they discovered that one of the scent's ingredients attacked the vinyl, causing surface damage. It was EMI's practice to test any unusual or unfamiliar chemicals planned for inclusion on record sleeves by heating both sleeves and vinyl in ovens to test reactions in different climatic conditions. The packaging remained scent-free upon release!

For the first time on a Wonder sleeve the artwork carried a message in braille: 'Inside the embossed square is the outline of a flower with veined leaves. Stevie Wonder, Journey Through The Secret Life Of Plants'. The singer threw a 'listening' party in the backyard of his

To promote Stevie Wonder's Journey Through The Secret Life of Plants *record retailers were supplied with packets of sunflower seeds. Fully grown flowers graced record shops before the album was released.*

Malibu home in November to which he invited five hundred guests. In keeping with the 'journey' aspect of the album, his guests were ushered through six giant tents to hear different sides of the records. In the last tent, Indian, African, Oriental, American and Middle Eastern food was served. On 2 December, Wonder premiered the work in New York's Metropolitan Opera House, where he devoted the first hour to the new album accompanied by the National Afro-American Philharmonic Orchestra with scenes from the movie projected above the stage. After the interval Wonder was joined on stage by Wonderlove for a selection of past repertoire, plus his first hit single *Fingertips*. In all, the performance contained forty songs and lasted three hours.

Send One Your Love, *Black Orchid* and *Outside My Window* were lifted from the soundtrack as singles in 1979 and 1980. Only *Send One Your Love* became a top five hit, reaching number four in the American charts but all the tracks became British top one hundred hits. Compared to previous Wonder albums, this work was considered a commercial failure. A Motown/EMI staff member quipped: 'The album shipped silver and returned platinum!' Yet the work's true beauty was appreciated years later when Motown released the compact disc version.

During 1978/79 Wonder had a number of other commitments in his life. For example, as part of his devotion to the memory of the late Dr Martin Luther King, Wonder performed in a special benefit concert in Atlanta to commemorate King's fiftieth birthday (his first concert in four years) where the proceeds were donated to the Martin Luther King Center For Social Change. (In less than two years the singer was to lobby the American government to make King's birthday a public holiday.) Wonder also became involved in other charitable functions, like those for sickle cell anemia, underpriviledged children and so on. Wonder: 'It's good to do something for sickle cell anemia or for the Black Panther Party if they want to give clothes to kids or food to the community. If it's really a sincere move on one's behalf to do something for people and I can contribute my services I will do so.'

On the recording side, Wonder appeared on Smokey's *Where There's Smoke* album (US, May '79/UK, Aug '79) which also featured Robinson's wife, Claudette, and Jerry Butler. One track *Cruisin'* was lifted as a single in August (a month later in Britain) to become his biggest solo American hit. Despite being re-promoted in Britain, *Cruisin'* died, although it was a popular radio record. Robinson told *Blues & Soul: Cruisin'* is a formula song because Marv Tarplin wrote the music and his music has inspired me to write a lot of songs. We actually started on that song about a year and a half before I moved to Los Angeles. I've changed it twice completely. It was originally called *Easy Rider* written for a girl group that I was going to record at the time. Then I canned it. And every time a new session came up I'd start on it again but it never seemed quite right to me. On the *Where There's Smoke* album we did some other things to it and it came out right. I never usually have a favourite song on my albums but *Cruisin'* happens to be mine on this one.' When Robinson previewed *Where's There's Smoke* to Berry Gordy and his staff, the unanimous decision was to release *Get Ready* to cash in on the disco market. However, radio stations refused to play it as unsuitable. Robinson: 'I then did a charity show for under-privileged children at the WVON radio station in Chicago. I was asked not to sing *Get Ready* on the show because they wanted *Cruisin'* and sure enough that's where it took off and snow-balled from there. It made me really happy because it took me away from discos!'

Robinson, now celebrating his twenty second year in the music business, agreed to introduce further members of his family on record. This time it was his nephews Keith and Darrell who, when 12 years old, begged their uncle to record them. He promised to do this if they won high school diplomas. Upon their graduation, Robinson kept his promise and, unlike his previous work with his wife Claudette, his nephews' was finished. Their *Feel The Fever* single was issued in America in October 1979.

Motown/EMI had a long standing agreement with Motown/USA which allowed the annual release of the *Motown Chartbusters* album. Each year's hits were featured on these compilations and 1979 marked volume ten of this successful series being issued. Motown/USA also permits specially compiled albums (usually comprising catalogue items) to be issued on a regular basis throughout the world, as long as these albums do not interfere with new and current releases. In 1979, to cash-in on the British Mod revival, *20 Mod Classics* was issued backed by an extensive marketing campaign. The album featured

tracks by The Marvelettes, Mary Wells, The Supremes and The Temptations, among others. It was a good seller, unlike some which appealed to a very specialist market. *20 Mod Classics Volume 2* followed in April 1980. In time, these British compilations (usually the brain-child of Motown/EMI's Gordon Frewin) were over-ridden by those emanating from Motown/USA, who preferred their albums to be released world-wide.

In November 1979 details of Marvin Gaye's album *Love Man* were circulated to Motown's licensees. Tracks included *Ego Tripping Out, Life's Just A Game Of Give And Take, Life Is Now In Session, I Offer You Nothing But Love, Just Because You're So Pretty, Dance 'n' Be Happy, Funk Me, Funk Me, Funk Me, Lover's Plea* and the album's title. The record's artwork was duly shipped to licensees and the product was scheduled. Gaye reported that *Love Man* was controversial, best described in two words 'sensually social'. Gaye: 'Some of the songs may be changed around a bit but the material itself has been settled and most of it completed. The tracks are all up-tempo or mid-tempo.'

Love Man never materialized although *Ego Tripping Out* had been released as a single during September 1979 (UK, Nov '79). *Love Man* was rejected by Berry Gordy as inferior and returned to Gaye for re-recording. Motown had already printed 450,000 sleeves and if Gaye wanted to change the album's track listing he would have to foot the bill himself. The artist was angry at Gordy's decision. Gaye: 'I took the tapes of *What's Going On* to Motown and they didn't like it and said it wouldn't sell. I took them the tapes of *Live! At The London Palladium* and they said it was no good, and it wouldn't sell because it didn't have any new material on it. If I do something that's revolutionary or innovative, or just

Marvin Gaye and his son Bubby arrive at London's Heathrow Airport in 1980. During his visit Gaye managed to snub royalty, kidnap his son and confuse concert promoters.

hasn't been done before, then everyone starts to panic. They can panic if they want to because I've got it, and they're afraid to admit it. I need a record company who knows what they have, who knows that I'm different and I may have a miss or two, but what the f***.' Several of the tracks from *Love Man* eventually appeared on Gaye's last album for Motown titled *In Our Lifetime* in 1981 which was also sub-standard and packaged in a different sleeve!

Meanwhile Gaye's second marriage to Janis Hunter was on the decline and the singer once again needed finances. Prior to Christmas 1979 promoter Jeffrey Kruger announced details of Gaye's New Year tour, part of a European itinerary to include Holland, Switzerland and France. The British leg would open at 'The Biggest Disco In The World' to be staged at Birmingham's National Exhibition Centre (NEC) on 19 January 1980, followed by dates at Edinburgh's Usher Hall (21); Liverpool's Royal Philharmonic Hall (23); London's Royal Albert Hall (25); Brighton's Centre on 2 February and Manchester's Apollo Theatre on the 3rd. Edwin Starr was booked as support act, and all performances were sold out within days of the tickets being available.

Gaye at this time was living in Hawaii, where he had performed several concerts. He had been forced to retreat to the island to escape heavy tax demands and Janis' affair with his best friend, soul singer Teddy Pendergrass. After his Hawaiian dates and in between periods of deep depression and sickness, Gaye toured Japan. His wife attempted to patch up their marriage by visiting her husband with their children after his return from the Far East, but the reconciliation attempt failed and she returned home with their youngest, Nona, leaving Bubby with his father. Early in 1980 Janis tried a second reconciliation; once again she failed. Gaye: 'I may have had successes in the entertainment

business but in the marriage stakes I'm a two time loser. That's not to say that I've not had my fair share of good times. I have, it's just that I don't seem to be too well equipped mentally and emotionally to handle a long term relationship. I must have been difficult to live with but I don't regret any of it. Marriage is a very personal thing between two people and it's their business, nobody else's.'

Of his financial situation Gaye admitted he was unable to return to his home state and the authorities had taken every asset he owned. Gaye 'I've lost my home and my studio. I've never really given a s*** about where my money went and I don't think I'm going to change now so I'll probably be in trouble again. I don't know how to hold on to cash for Uncle Sam. If someone needs money I'll give it to them and always forget I have a tax bill coming in at the end of the year. As for my creditors, well, most of them are just pure extortionists. Still, at times like this, you learn who your real friends are. There are a lot of people around me who I lent money to years ago and never asked for it back, but when I got into trouble they didn't rush to help me. On the other hand, Harvey Fuqua, who I hadn't heard from in years, sent me some dollars to help me out as soon as he heard the trouble I was in. He was one of the few people to seek me out and offer help.'

One disaster was followed by another. In January 1980 'The Biggest Disco In The World' was cancelled through a breakdown in negotiations between the promoter and the NEC. By the end of the month Gaye's whole tour had been postponed. Jeffrey Kruger's press statement blamed this on the artist's personal problems which, coupled with extreme physical and mental exhaustion, had left him unable to travel. The statement also stated that Janis Hunter had left her husband for good to live with Teddy Pendergrass. Kruger then flew to Hawaii to pursuade Gaye to honour his touring commitments: 'He was packed and ready to leave when I arrived, but his doctor said he was in no way well enough to travel. He was in a pathetic state. He was emaciated because he had just been eating bread, and looked like death. He just couldn't hold himself together.' Gaye's drug intake had become excessive and he had tried to commit suicide by overdosing on cocaine. A weakened and confused Gaye spent his recuperation period with his mother, Alberta and son, Bubby, on Maui, Hawaii, where he lived in a milk truck. Gaye: 'It wasn't that I couldn't afford a conventional home, I just wanted to be free to float around and that's exactly what I did. It was a wonderful therapy because I like being close to nature and Maui is a beautiful place although very expensive.' He admitted he was lonely: 'I just wished I had someone to love me for myself, someone who didn't care about my moods and my entertainer's nature. I'm a ram and a fire sign, I might singe, but I'm full of love and sensitivity. Bubby keeps me balanced now but it's been a problem trying to see he's properly looked after. Fortunately, I've had strong support from my family.'

Jeffrey Kruger re-arranged Gaye's British tour for June. To ensure he honoured the commitment Kruger allowed Mrs Jewel Price (a longstanding friend of Gaye's), Gordon Banks (his musical director), an aunt and Gaye's mother to accompany him to England. Bubby also travelled with his father when Janis failed to collect him at an appointed time.

Interestingly, an April tour of Britain by Teddy Pendergrass, promoted by Kruger, was cancelled via a terse telegram from the singer's management. Gaye's revised itinerary included the venues already booked with an additional performance at London's Venue on 4 July to celebrate American Independence Day. Gaye was also booked to perform at a Royal Gala charity event to be staged at The Lakeside Country Club, Camberley, on 8 July before HRH Princess Margaret. A close friend of the Princess had approached Kruger to recommend a suitable artist for the evening. Kruger: 'When I suggested Marvin Lady Patricia Neatrour was thrilled to bits and asked if I thought he would agree to stay on for it. It seemed the Princess is a great fan of Marvin's records. Marvin would be the star of the show and afterwards he and his mother were invited to dine with the Princess which was a tremendous offer for them.'

'We finally made it, we've had a few problems and what can I tell you? We like to keep you guessing!' laughed Marvin Gaye on his opening night at London's Royal Albert Hall, by way of explaining his five month postponement. *Blues & Soul's* Jeff Tarry summed up Gaye's performance: 'There was certainly a good measure of joy to be gleaned from merely being present on such an auspicious occasion. Good vibes filled the Hall as Gaye's staunch followers had a field day identifying each song from the merest hint of an introduction. But sadly, Marvin's rather intimate projection failed to reach parts of the audience, and seemed better suited to a far smaller venue. However, it was a belated qualified success with a degree of audience satisfaction depending on where you happened to be sitting. Edwin Starr opened the show with a performance which on most bills would have served as a worthy headliner.'

The evening of the 8 July at The Lakeside Country Club was a total disaster and did untold harm to Gaye's reputation. Tickets for the Gala had sold out and the proceeds were to go to the Dockland Settlement of which HRH Princess Margaret was President. Shortly before midnight the Club's management received a message saying Gaye had cancelled his performance through mental exhaustion. Shortly after this message was received, another followed saying Gaye had left his London hotel and was travelling to Camberley. This prompted Surrey's chief constable (who was among the Club's guests) to arrange for a police car to escort the singer's vehicle along the motorway. Gaye eventually arrived at the venue to perform at 1.40 a.m. Princess Margaret had already left and Jeffrey Kruger was forced to face the attending journalists. Kruger: 'Marvin knew about the Gala three months in advance and had even brought members of his family to England to meet the Princess, then he waited until they were all dressed up in their finery and broke their hearts. He disgraced the American people, his own black people, his profession, and will lose the admiration of hundreds of fans when they read about this. I am absolutely disgusted by his behaviour and words cannot express what I feel about this. It is a snub for the Royal Family and he has absolutely no excuse for his behaviour.'

Gaye's decision to appear at The Lakeside Club followed a telephone conversation with Berry Gordy who was alerted to the situation

By 1979 Marvin Gaye's second marriage to Janis Hunter was on the rocks. The couple are pictured here during a British visit in 1976.

by Motown/EMI. Gordy is known for his fondness of the British monarchy and therefore refused to allow his artist to insult Princess Margaret. Unfortunately, the damage was already done.

The Kruger Organization later released an official press statement that included the following: 'We fully realize that Marvin is going through enormous personal and business difficulties but we have bent over backwards in an attempt to resolve these problems for him and to make the tour as pleasant and free from strain as possible. That is why we fell in with his wishes and didn't set up a heavy press and radio interview schedule. Marvin did some great shows but sadly he still has not got his head together and consequently there were considerable problems involved in trying to fit in with his somewhat erratic approach to everything.'

Gaye told *Melody Maker's* Paolo Hewitt that he had good reason for his behaviour: 'I am controlled by my emotions and feelings, and if my emotions or feelings say I shouldn't do something because of a very strong principled position that I must take, then in spite of the consequences, in spite of all that is facing me from a detrimental point of view, then I have to remain true to my artistic nature. That was a decision I had to make involving my pride and my dignity, and it had nothing to do with the Royal Family. I'm dreadfully sorry I had to make such a decision. The fact is that nobody was snubbed despite it being written I snubbed Royalty. Because of the pressures put upon me I couldn't go out there and sing. I refused to do it until certain people, who were social-climbing, were removed. So, when I got there Princess Margaret had gone, but if she'd stayed a further fifteen minutes, she would have seen my show.'

Meanwhile, Motown/EMI had further problems. Despite being told Gaye had recorded in Hawaii there were insufficient tracks for an album, and because of his bad relationship with Motown/USA Gaye refused to co-operate with its British office. In time he agreed to embark upon promotional activities which were invariably conducted in a non-professional manner. For example NME's Chris Salewicz told author David Ritz: 'Marvin snorted quantities (of cocaine) during the interview . . . it had an adverse effect on him . . . he began to feel ill and explained this was due to the dodgy substance the cocaine had been cut with . . . he attempted to clean out all the impurities from the cocaine . . . snorted the purified powder to blast the rubbish from his system.' Salewicz's interview was the first of several Gaye conducted to announce he was leaving Motown, but that he had no quarrel with Motown/EMI, it was the American operation he was rebelling against.

Jermaine Jackson, the only remaining brother at Motown, had his first taste of major success with his biggest selling hit ever *Let's*

Get Serious (US, Feb '80/UK, Apr '80) taken from the album of the same name (US, Mar '80/UK, Apr '80). The single was written by Stevie Wonder and Lee Garrett for Wonder to record but Berry Gordy heard it and insisted his son-in-law record it. Jackson: 'As well as Stevie writing and producing the three songs for the album he also involved himself in the songs I did for myself. So much so he wanted his songs to fit my concept. He said that my songs inspired him to write two completely new songs *Let's Get Serious* and *Where Are You Now* (with Renee Hardaway) and the third *You're Supposed To Keep Your Love For Me* which I recorded years ago with the Jackson 5, and sang lead on.' Jackson's *Let's Get Serious* album was dance-orientated much against his wishes; he felt disco music had damaged the industry, with record companies saturating the market with a basic four/four beat at the expense of other types of music. However, Jackson conceded when he realized this could be his most successful album to date despite his two year absence from the recording studio. Jackson: 'I decided to stop what I was doing and go over my past to make sure *Let's Get Serious* was the best. I'm the first to admit that my previous albums I did on my own didn't do as well as I hoped, but they did give me valuable experience and I learned from those. The lack of my success forced me into searching for the right ingredients and I believe that's what has made this new album so acceptable.'

The *Let's Get Serious* single was a typical Stevie Wonder composition: he even sang the middle chorus – therefore when Jackson (with his wife Hazel) flew to London in May 1980 to promote it on British television Jackson was forbidden by Wonder to sing the song 'live'. However, television exposure was later possible via a Continental video featuring Jackson singing Wonder's part, unbeknown to the song's writer. Jackson's British promotional tour was a tight schedule of daytime media interviews and night-time personal appearances. At The Empire Ballroom in London's Leicester Square, the singer was mobbed by hundreds of enthusiastic fans, losing his shirt and jacket as he and his wife fled for safety. Once again Jackson mania hit Britain, but this time fans flocked to see the shy, deep-thinking brother with the nervous stutter.

The follow-up to *Let's Get Serious*, which was nominated for a Grammy in the best R&B Male Vocalist section, was *You're Supposed To Keep Your Love For Me* in June, while Motown/EMI issued another dance track *Burnin' Hot* (originally titled *I'd Rather Dance, Disco Fever*) in July, with the American follow-up in the September. Jackson: 'Berry Gordy said the song was a smash hit but we weren't singing about anything. He changed the title because by the time the album came out, disco was finally burnt out. So we changed it to *Burnin' Hot*, added a little sex appeal and so forth.' The single, although a good seller, failed to repeat its predecessor's success. This was to be Jackson's only period of continued success while at Motown, even though his future releases maintained a high standard. He was a regular visitor to Britain where he invariably acted as his father-in-law's spokesman. In fact, Gordy sent Jackson to London in December 1980 to host Motown/EMI's Twentieth Anniversary champagne party held at the EMI Records' headquarters in Manchester Square.

The Stone City Band (Tom McDermott, Oscar Alston, Erskine Williams, Lanise Hughes, Levi Ruffin Jr) recorded for Motown after working with Rick James, who wanted to build up his own company of musicians. James already had the Punk Funk Horns (Cliff and John Ervin, Danny LeMelle, and vocalists Lisa Sarna and JoJo McDuffie). The genesis of the Stone City Band was formed in 1978 following James' return from a European tour. With Levi Ruffin Jr's help, the singer assembled the group to support him on his platinum-selling album *Come Get It* and the two units joined forces on stage throughout 1979 and 1980. Ruffin: 'We don't want to be known simply as a funk band or a rock 'n' roll band. Our primary objective is to be Stone City – a band that people will respect. Our music is different but there's nothing complicated about it. Basically the dream of the whole band is to build up a corporation. We have the Stone City family, Rick and us, and we want to produce and record ourselves, and also produce some musicians back home in Buffalo.' The Band's first album *Rick James Presents The Stone City Band: In 'n' Out* was released in the US only in February 1980 and could easily have been classed as one of their mentor's albums. Ruffin disagreed: 'As a producer Rick is very demanding. He can draw out the best in you, and as an arranger he's fantastic. But we do our material in our own way, we're not a carbon copy.' The Band's second album *The Boys Are Back* (also British released) a year later, was more adventurous, yet after a handful of single releases it was apparent they would gain more success as James' backing group.

Thanks to the success of her duet with Billy Preston on *With You I'm Born Again*, Syreeta's career picked up again. During April 1980 (UK, June) her *Syreeta* album was released. Syreeta was excited about this album because she was more involved in this than any of her others: 'Things got so congested towards the end that I was working on some of the

Rick James' backing group, the Stone City Band, released their own album in 1980. Although the music was heavily influenced by their mentor, it failed to sell in the same quantities.

arrangements and in selecting the material like *Signed, Sealed And Delivered* which Steve and I wrote, and *Blame It On The Sun* which I was able to do my own way. I only wrote one song this time but have included two duets with Billy – *Please Stay* and *One More Time For Love*.' Backing tracks originally produced by Richard Perry in 1977 for his proposed second album with Diana Ross were used on *Syreeta* – *Let Me Be The One, Love Fire, He's Gone* and *You Bring Out The Love In Me*. Richard Perry coached Syreeta in the studios to ensure the best was brought out in the unfinished tracks. The result was a delightful album. Prior to this release Syreeta's recording contract was due to be re-negotiated, and she was unsure of what step to take: '. . . then came *With You I'm Born Again* and things started to happen. Motown wanted a new album, so I re-signed.'

During 1980 Motown celebrated its twentieth anniversary (even though the celebration was a year short) and records and merchandizing carried a specially-designed logo to celebrate the fact. More artists visited Britain during this year than ever before and due to the high quality of music the company enjoyed its best year since the Sixties.

Like its parent company, Jobete was also celebrating its twentieth anniversary. The European branch of the publishing company is controlled by Motown's International Department's offices based in London which, in turn, is part of the American Division based in Los Angeles. Peter Prince became vice-president of Motown International when Ken East left in 1979. Prince, a music veteran of nearly thirty years, worked as a Motown promoter in the early stages of the label's existence in Europe. In 1980 Prince was responsible for Motown being licensed in thirty four countries using eighteen different companies. Each licensee is reviewed every three years, whereupon Motown is free to seek another.

Motown's anniversary also coincided with the surprise return of The Temptations (Edwards, Williams, Franklin, Street, Leonard). While the group was signed to Atlantic Records, Dennis Edwards had to support himself so worked for his uncle's construction company where one of his jobs was to lay driveways in Cleveland. Edwards: 'I really wanted to go out there and see what a nine to fiver does and how his life is. I learned a great lesson behind that and I'm a better man for it. By doing this I found out that I was a special person and that this type of work wasn't for me. Also I had crowds gathering around where I was working and I'd almost have to do a show when they confirmed that I used to be a Temptation.'

The Temptations' return to Motown was instigated by Smokey Robinson. Otis Williams: 'Smokey was the revolving door, as we called him because he helped us leave Motown and then he helped us come back. At

this point in time – December 1979 – Dennis had re-joined the group and we were in a state of limbo.' The group had been offered proposals by Norman Whitfield and Gamble and Huff, when Robinson stepped in. Williams: 'So, I decided that if we're going to talk to Smokey at all, we'd better be open-minded enough if he says he wants us to come back to Motown. True enough, that's exactly what he wanted. The wheels were put into motion to reunite the two recording institutions. We just aired our differences, knowing that if we're going to get back together, we'd better make sure the sheets were clean. Motown is like a father who really wants to do right. Motown did a lot of things for us that we felt we wanted to do ourselves. It took us a while to find out that the things they were doing for us were great, and you realize that the people you talked bad about were the ones thinking of your career. I don't feel that any record company can produce or sell The Temptations like Motown can. We're five individuals that yield into one, and we're hard to get along with.'

Williams also admitted that initially Motown was in fact the last company they considered approaching, although they were curious to see if Robinson could negotiate a deal on their behalf: 'Berry Gordy had (co-) written a song called *Power* and he felt it was perfect for us. At the time we were still contracted to Atlantic, but we had stayed in touch because we were too good friends not to do so. Berry felt the song would be good for us, so he decided that rather than give it to somebody else, he'd wait. We met Berry at an impromptu meeting in Smokey's office and before we knew where we were, we were gathered around a piano rehearsing *Power*. It all seemed to fall into place and we ended up recording the song before the legalities were completed.'

The *Power* single and album were released in April 1980 (single: UK, May; album: UK, Jun '80). Produced by Berry Gordy and Angelo Bond, The Temptations wrote three tracks for the album – *Isn't The Night Fantastic, Can't You See Sweet Thing* and the suitable *I'm Coming Home* – and were pictured on the record's inner bag, suitcases in hand, walking into the 'Hitsville USA' building, 2648 West Grand Boulevard, Detroit, Motown's original home. In spite of an unprecedented marketing and promotion campaign the group's return was treated with indifference by the public. The situation turned sour because the single was highly political. Williams: 'We got caught up in the riots in Miami and the jocks were saying "oh no, five black guys talking about the masses and moving mountains". They just didn't want to go back to the Sixties stuff. They didn't trust it. In the Sixties everybody was marching and protesting and the jocks couldn't hold back on what people wanted to hear. It's not that way now.'

New signings Ozone released their debut

album *Walk On* during April 1980. The group (Jimmy Stewart, Charles Glenn, Benny Wallace, Thomas Bumpass, Ray Woodward, William White, Greg Hargrove, Paul Hines) can be traced back to Nashville, Tennessee and a group called The Endeavors. The founder members Stewart, Wallace and Glenn, travelled to Hollywood to work and later performed at a birthday party held for 'Pops' Gordy. In June 1977 the group changed its name to Ozone to work as a backing unit for Motown acts like Billy Preston and Syreeta before recording their first album. Two further albums *Jump On It* and *Send It* were issued a year later, the latter being the last on the old-styled Motown label listing. A talented group Ozone's success was confined to America.

During May 1980 (UK, April) six re-mixed Supremes' tracks were sequed (run on with a break between tracks) to make a ten minute dance record. The songs used were *Stop! In The Name Of Love*, *Back In My Arms Again*, *Come See About Me*, *Love Is Like An Itching In My Heart*, *Where Did Our Love Go* and *Baby Love*. The original medley was conceived by sound designer Bill Motley and DJ Trip Ringwood for New York's Disconet Music Subscription Services in Los Angeles. The 'bootleg' attracted immediate radio exposure in New York whereupon Motown identically re-recorded it to release an official version. For the single's British release, the old black and silver Tamla Motown label was used. It was the first twelve inch single to be released carrying this label. The American seven inch single flipside contained Diana Ross' *Where Did We Go Wrong*, whereas the twelve inch single contained Ross' *No-One Gets The Prize/The Boss*. The British seven inch contained *The Medley Part 2* and the British twelve inch a seven minute version of *Love Hangover*. Meanwhile, Mary Wilson recorded four demo songs including *You Dance My Heart Around The Stars* and *Green River* which Motown considered for release but later rejected.

Also in May 1980 the $20 million lawsuit filed against the Jackson brothers by Motown was settled. The original lawsuit was filed by the company in 1975 when the brothers signed with CBS because it was claimed they were still contracted to Gordy. Motown appealed and won the case whereupon the Jacksons paid Gordy approximately $600,000. Gordy also continued to own the name the Jackson 5. The settlement also provided full usage by Motown of all Michael Jackson and Jackson 5 records recorded while they were signed to Motown.

Black Russian, the first Soviet rock band to sign with an American record company, released their first eponymous album in the US in May 1980 (UK, Sep '80). While Serge, Natasha and Vladimir were resident in the USSR they were successful contemporary musicians, writing and producing hits and maintaining hectic concert schedules as they received no record profits. The band members were fairly typical in their knowledge of Western music. Natasha: 'Even though Western music was condemned in Russia, we knew what was happening in the world. We listened to the Voice of America broadcasts, the major European radio stations and got records from our Western friends or bought records on the black market. I can still remember the day Jimi Hendrix died because there were black arm bands all over Moscow.' Towards the end of their Russian career, the trio was permitted to perform one quarter of its material in English although it was confined to middle-of-the-road repertoire. Natasha: 'Serge was also in demand as the "black Russian" who could be called upon by a daring record producer who wanted to add a little "soul" to a track, but both had to be extremely wary. We were at the top of our careers – well paid, well known but not satisfied.' During May 1976 Black Russian and their families landed in New York City with no money or friends, and took regular jobs. Following several attempts to secure a recording deal they met Guy Costa (head of Motown's Studio Operations) who introduced them to Berry Gordy. Black Russian naturally attracted extensive publicity both in America and Britain but their record sales were few.

Rick James began promoting his fourth album *Garden Of Love* (US, Jun '80/UK, Sep '80) following a spell in hospital (one of several confinements). It marked a change in musical style for the punk funk master, with flowery titles like *Gettin' It On In The Summertime*, *Summer Love* and *Mary-Go-Round*. James was forced to re-think his musical direction when his last album *Fire It Up* failed to reach its sales potential. The new album worked, and it spawned the hit single *Big Time* (US, Jun '80) which following its release in England in August became his second top fifty single (*You And I* reached number forty-six in July 1978). James' hospitalization was a result, he said, of his high-speed lifestyle: 'I wound up being over-

tired and my liver was in bad shape. It has meant that I have had to cut out a lot of things. No drugs, no alcohol although I still smoke my Mary Jane. It was a case of live or die and I realized that I had been taking in too much alcohol and coke. The funny thing is that my creativity seems to have heightened since I quit those things. And my sex life is much better.'

Diana Ross, too, needed outside help to revive her flagging recording career. At the time the top selling dance outfit was Chic, who were guided from one success to another by members Nile Rodgers and Bernard Edwards. For the first time in her career, Ross handed over her next album *Diana* to this talented couple, who wrote, arranged, and produced all the tracks. Unfortunately, the result sounded too similar to their own releases; it was difficult to distinguish Ross from one of Chic's own vocalists. Berry Gordy and Ross were unhappy with the finished tapes, although Ross thought the album would be a big seller anyway because of Chic's reputation. However, Ross returned to the studios to re-mix the album with producer Russ Terrana. Ross said at the time: 'When I first listened to the tapes they sounded pretty much like Chic or Sister Sledge. In fact, they were a bit too disco and that's not what's happening today. You have to remember that both Nile and Bernard have only been in the industry for two or three years and in re-mixing the album I felt that I may be able to put a little of Diana Ross into the product. In many cases all I've done is change some of the musical interludes.' Rodgers and Edwards were furious that their work had been tampered with because it bore little or no relation to the tapes they had given her. They demanded that a public disclaimer be given as they disassociated themselves from the project. Bernard Edwards told *Blues & Soul* in 1980: 'We're definitely not happy with the

Manager Keith Harris guides Stevie Wonder from London's Abbey Road Studios following a playback reception for Stevie's Hotter Than July *album*.

album. When we finished it and turned it in, Diana wasn't happy with her vocals. So, she almost went for a re-mix, and still felt her voice was too thin. So we gave her the tapes to do what she felt she wanted and despite the fact that it shouldn't have been done contractually, another re-mix was done. The album was on the streets before we had even heard it. We started to take some kind of legal action to have the album stopped but we decided against it. Apparently, Diana loves it so we thought we would just sit back and see what happens. If we made a mistake, it was in giving the tapes away so that changes could be made, but you live and learn, and we've definitely learned.'

Interestingly, all the tracks were written with Diana Ross in mind, and working with her Edwards admitted, was a 'learning experience' for them. The songs he liked were *Give It Up* and *Tenderness*: '*Upside Down* is OK, though we don't exactly love it. The mix is what spoils that one for us. But they really lost *Now That You're Gone*. It was a beautiful ballad when we finished with it and they re-mixed it and used a practice bass line that is completely out of tune. Now that's embarrassing for us and it has shocked a lot of people in the business that we could have allowed it to happen. But it's too late to change it now.'

The album was packaged in a black-and-white gatefold sleeve which showed Ross dressed in tattered jeans and T-shirt, with a full colour inner sleeve showing the singer in more elegant attire with her 'Friend to Friend' signature, indicating the album's probable original title. Choosing the first single caused problems between the artist and record company. Initially *Have Fun Again* was voted the more popular choice, but was replaced by *I'm Coming Out* at the last moment, released in August 1980. Motown/EMI, on the other hand, lifted *Upside Down* for its first single a month earlier, which became a number two hit and earned Ross a silver disc for British sales in excess of 400,000. The album *Diana* went on to sell one million units in Britain alone following its June 1980 release (US, May '80).

Prior to this album's release, Diana Ross had flown to London to tape an episode of The Muppets Show due for screening on Good Friday and had sung *He's A Jolly Good Fellow* with The Muppets to Berry Gordy when he received the 1980 Whitney M. Young Award at an American reception. Ross turned down Motown/EMI's request to publicly accept her silver disc for *Upside Down* and other awards held by the company on her behalf. This was a blow to the mammoth marketing campaign which was underway, which included three hundred giant-sized posters displayed at major underground stations and life-sized 3-D cut outs of Ross for in-store display. Motown/EMI were aware that Ross' contract was due for renewal and wanted to use this marketing strategy as a means of good faith.

Upside Down was the album's second single to be released in America in June 1980 – and the last due to lack of public interest. However, in Britain, Ross' new sound was being devoured by her fans. *My Old Piano* was issued in September to become a number five hit, followed by *I'm Coming Out* in November which reached number thirteen. Ross was delighted with her British success and during a private holiday in London with her boyfriend, Gene Simmons (a member of the wild rock group Kiss) she agreed to host a press reception at the Inn on the Park hotel. During the reception she was presented with the numerous awards for British record sales held by Motown/EMI, following which she consented to film a promotional video for *My Old Piano*. The result was rather banal, featuring the singer prancing around a white piano. It was filmed at very short notice with few takes, and was reputedly against the Musicians Union's regulations, therefore Motown/EMI had to convince the authorities it was filmed during a lightening visit to Geneva so that it could be screened on television.

Perhaps inspired by Motown's twenty-year success story, Berry Gordy emerged from his reclusive lifestyle to grant an interview with *Record World* magazine and spoke about Motown's achievements and future at length. Gordy: 'We have had twenty years of understanding where mistakes were made, and I'd rather look at our mistakes than our successes because success will happen by itself. That's not hard to deal with. We have talented people here, and that's why we are at the tip of the iceberg and we can go into any area. There's a lot of planning and programming, thinking and managing that we have to do. It's an impossibility to say specifically what we'll be doing (in the future) because we don't know. And if war breaks out everything changes. It can certainly be important to say we want to be a hundred million dollar company, or whatever you want to say, but there are many ways you can do that that would be destroying you as a human being. The key to life, the way I feel, is happiness. So I take that into consideration in every calculation I make – happiness not only for me but for the people who surround me.' Of his reclusive lifestyle Gordy said: 'I enjoy my privacy because it's hard to be happy after success. But I don't consider myself to be over-private. I'm just not interested in building myself up, or doing anything but the simple things I enjoy. I'm very happy with what I'm doing and I hope to continue doing exactly that. And I'm not going to change it for anything in the world.'

Gordy also recalled his company's early days, how he chose his artists and the staff who worked with him: 'Most of the writers and producers had no formal knowledge, but they had the freedom and the ability to think, create and get some self-confidence, self-awareness, and be able to communicate.

Many of our artists came to us by word of mouth or through The Miracles who were our first group. Stevie Wonder came in for an audition one day when he was just a little kid, nine years or so, and he had a very baby voice. He had some good ideas though and was very enthusiastic, so we started working with him. Diana Ross and the Supremes lived down the street from Smokey Robinson and The Temptations, who at the time were The Primes, and the boys used to sing on their street corners. Marvin Gaye I noticed at a party we were having at Motown. He was sitting there playing the piano.'

Motown/EMI's second anniversary tribute was released on 6 September 1980 by way of a twenty-one single box set which included a metallic twentieth anniversary badge with the company's logo featured in gold against a maroon background. Record stores had to order this box set between July and September 1980 because it was deleted upon its release date. Twenty of the singles were forty original Tamla Motown British hits; thirty five reached the top twenty, with the remainder entering the top forty when first released. All forty songs had been unavailable commercially for some time. The twenty-first single was exclusive to this box set and was not available separately. The two A-sides, recorded during 1965, were canned tracks from Kim Weston and The Marvelettes titled *Do Like I Do* and *Finders Keepers, Losers Weepers*, respectively.

While Diana Ross was in London, promoters Marshall Arts secured Stevie Wonder for dates at Wembley Arena – his first European concerts for six years. The show, 'Stevie Wonder's Hotter Than July Music Picnic' was spread from the 1-7 (excluding the 4th) September 1980, and featured old repertoire and tracks from his new album *Hotter Than July*. Motown/EMI scheduled *Masterblaster (Jammin')*, a track from the pending album to coincide with the tour. It was hoped the album would also be available but it did not materialize. However, its tapes did arrive from

Marvin Gaye and Diana Ross join Stevie Wonder on the Wembley Arena stage. It was a spectacle the British audience will never forget.

The two sides of Diana Ross as portrayed on her Chic album Diana which sold in excess of one million copies in Britain alone.

(Right) An unusual combination – Diana Ross and Muppet Fozzie Bear. The singer flew to London to tape an episode for an Easter screening.

America in time for a playback reception attended by Wonder at Studio No 2 at EMI's famous Abbey Road Studios on 2 September.

Needless to say, all the Wembley dates were instantly sold out, and the critics glowed with enthusiasm. Melody Maker's Geoff Brown wrote: 'Material came from as far back as 1963, when he was hailed as the twelve-year-old-genius, and from as recently as his next album. Many black American artists do scant justice to their past hits, preferring to plug new and usually inferior songs and dismissing old times in a flippant medley. Wonder's catalogue is far too rich, and he too mindful of its rare quality for it to be so treated. He did full justice to the old hits played, and in fact took them to greater heights by frequently adding vamps and allowing himself and his excellent band, Wonderlove, to stretch out. After a particularly memorable and torrid Higher Ground, I recall, he was moved to laugh "Phew, we really got carried away on that one". And they do. He started with For Once In My Life and never let up for the next hour and a quarter. It was one of the best played sets I've ever heard. A warm romantic My Cherie Amour, an exuberant Signed Sealed, Delivered, a lovely If You Really Love Me, and truly beautiful Superwoman (although much of the deft guitar work was sadly inaudible) into a grand piano backing for You And I, Too Shy To Say and, re-joined by the rhythm section, All In Love Is Fair. After Lately, he gradually increased the pace through Don't Worry 'Bout A Thing which kicked along powerfully into the burbling funk of the exciting Higher Ground and built to a thrilling climax with Golden Lady. Boogie On Reggae Woman, during which he danced lasciviously with each of his four background singers, led into a steaming version of Let's Get Serious, and a mightily tough Living For The City finished the first half.

'Thirty minutes later one of the sax players introduced, with a moderate bellow, "Little

Stevie Wonder". Dressed now in an old style blue tuxedo jacket, white shirt and bow tie, Little Stevie did homage to his very first hit Fingertips. Honest, amusing, nostalgic fun. Wonderlove took a solo spot while the boss changed togs and returned for a thumping Sir Duke, a rolling, tumbling I Wish, a rich You Are The Sunshine Of My Life, and a thrilling Superstition. The final half of his second set led him deeper into the philosophical areas which much of his Seventies work has predominantly inhabited. The beauty of his melodies is such that the messages don't suffer from the sanctimonious air that often infests other artists' attempts at cosmic thoughts. Even when Wonder plays no music and just speaks from his heart, there is such an obviously unrehearsed feeling in his thoughts that he wins full attention. Finally, two new songs Masterblaster and Did I Hear You Say You Loved Me, more communal singing, then his band left the stage one by one until the drummer was left to thunderously bring this wholly memorable event to a close. It was marvellous, thoroughly involving entertainment. I shall play nothing but nothing but Stevie Wonder records for the next fortnight in an all too vain effort to recapture the night's magic.'

On Wonder's free day (4 September) he allowed a promotion video to be filmed of him singing Masterblaster (Jammin') at Wembley Arena, provided it was completed in two takes. On the last night of his Wembley concerts Wonder was joined on stage by Diana Ross and Marvin Gaye (who was still exiled in London) to sing Gaye's What's Going On. This was the first and last time a British audience was treated to three of Motown's superstars on stage simultaneously. Needless to say, it was a spectacular sight, which neither the audience nor the promoters had expected.

On Monday, 8 September Wonder performed a charity show at London's Hammersmith Odeon. He announced this additional date during his last Wembley show, whereupon Marshall Arts' personnel worked through the night to transfer stage equipment to the new venue because Kiss were due to follow Wonder at Wembley. After the performance Marshall Arts hosted a party at Mayfair's

Gullivers Club for Wonder, his musicians, crew, Motown/EMI and all personnel involved in the tour. Wonder left the nightclub at 5 a.m. after DJ Graham Canter had played every record he possessed twice!

Although Wonder's tour bore the name of his new album *Hotter Than July*, the actual record was not released until October 1980. It was written, produced and arranged by Wonder and recorded and mixed at his Los Angeles Wonderland Studios. Tracks included his reggae flavoured single *Masterblaster (Jammin')*, the sensitive ballad *Lately*, his dedication to the late Dr Martin Luther King *Happy Birthday*, his political statement *Cash In Your Face*, *All I Do* (with Michael Jackson and Betty Wright on backing vocals), *As If You Read My Mind* (with Syreeta on backups) and *Did I Hear You Say You Love Me* (featuring ex-Supreme Susaye Green-Brown on backing vocals).

Once again Motown/EMI embarked on an expensive marketing campaign as the album was Wonder's first contribution to the Eighties. To enhance the advertizing programme, approximately 600 display pieces and 3,500 full colour posters were made available for in-store displays. *Hotter Than July* shipped gold with advanced orders in excess of 100,000 Motown/USA's promotional activities were equally as impressive, as were the initial album sales.

Upon his return to America following the tour, Wonder announced his intention to 'respectfully demand' Congress to declare Dr Martin Luther King's birthday, 15 January, an American national public holiday. This highlighted the work the artist had undertaken in King's memory. Wonder: 'Like no other American, Martin Luther King stood for, fought for and died for American Democratic principles. The holiday would be the first commemorating the enormous contributions of black people in the United States.' The artist added that he intended to head a rally in Washington DC in 1981.

One of Motown Productions more impressive projects was the $2 million CBS movie *The Last Song*, which candidly exposed the perils of uncontrolled pollution and starred ex-Wonderwoman, Lynda Carter. The Kenny Rogers' produced single (written by Ron Miller and Kenny Hirsch) was released in England in September 1980 to coincide with Carter's pending tour. When the single flopped, it was not released in America and Motown declined to take up the option on Carter's recording contract.

Born in Phoenix, Carter was the youngest of three children and considered the 'ugly duckling' of the family as she towered above her school friends and wore size ten shoes. At four years old Carter debuted on a local television talent show as a performer, and upon leaving high school joined a travelling musical group. After winning a Miss World-USA contest, Carter successfully auditioned for the proposed

television series *Wonderwoman* in November 1975, which was an immediate hit.

After three successful series Carter became a household name worldwide, and left her star-spangled Wonderwoman outfit to concentrate on a singing career. During July 1978 Carter debuted at Caesar's Palace, Las Vegas, with a $50,000 wardrobe, laser effects, a troupe of dancers and a twenty-six piece orchestra and a film sequence to entertain her standing room only audience. Two years later she hosted her own CBS showcase 'Lynda Carter's Special' which was one of several shows. During her short stay with Motown Carter showed herself to be a true professional without losing any of her naturalness and warmth. Certainly Motown/EMI considered her to be one of the friendliest of their performers.

By mid-1980 Marvin Gaye had consented to work with Motown/EMI to assist the promotion of his music during his confinement in London, although several activities were marred by his irrational behaviour. One incident concerned the company's head of promotion, Les Spaine, who had arranged to escort the singer to Manchester for a television date. On arriving at Heathrow Airport, Gaye visited the men's room and, unbeknown to Spaine, climbed out of the window to return to his London hotel! Gaye: 'I did it because I didn't feel like going to Manchester, and to admit such a thing would be unheard of for other artists. I'm sure they'd cover it up. I was reacting to a negative action from somebody else, and I don't f*** around. Sometimes I give my word to do something in a general way, just to see whether people are b*******. If I find out they are b******, then I feel I don't have to keep my word.'

Gaye's son Bubby lived with him in a variety of hotels and apartments, where his father's nights were spent in the company of London's glitterati including Lady Edith Foxwell (ex-wife of film producer Ivan Foxwell) and Princess Margaret's son Viscount Linley. During October Gaye arrived unannounced at the Four Tops concert at the London Palladium where he performed on stage with them. Meanwhile, Gaye's estranged wife, Janis, threatened to snatch Bubby back, claiming the singer was an unfit parent. Certainly her son was subjected to a most erratic lifestyle. Gaye: 'You might say I've kidnapped my own son, but I love him and he loves me, and he's happy. I don't have custody of him. My wife lives in Los Angeles and I don't suppose she's too thrilled about it.'

During the autumn of 1980 ex-Motowner Jimmy Ruffin enjoyed his biggest selling British single since leaving Motown. Titled *Hold On To My Love* released on the RSO label, it was the brainchild of Bee Gee Robin Gibb and reached number seven in the charts. (The same position as Ruffin's *I'll Say Forever My Love* ten years earlier.) Since leaving Berry

Lyinda Carter abandons her Wonderwoman outfit to become a serious singer and actress.

In 1980 Jimmy Ruffin enjoyed his first hit single since leaving Motown. Titled Hold On To My Love, it was the brainchild of the Bee Gee Robin Gibb.

Lionel Richie left the Commodores to work with country and western singer Kenny Rogers. The result was the Lady single which sold in excess of 16 million copies.

Jazz pianist Ahmad Jamal released some of his best work at Motown but it failed to push him into superstardom.

Gordy's company Ruffin had recorded for a variety of labels with little success, but felt no animosity towards Motown for severing their deal: 'I feel philosophical about it all now. Fortunately things are happening for me now so I have no reason to complain. I think things are going to be a whole lot better for me now anyway because my head is in a different place and I understand more about the business.' Irrespective of his confidence, it was to be another five years, 1985, before Ruffin enjoyed a further British hit with *There Will Never Be Another You* on the EMI label.

During 1980 Lionel Richie branched out from the Commodores to work with Kenny Rogers. Richie gave the country and western singer one of his best ballads *Lady* which eventually sold in excess of sixteen million copies and earned Richie $1 million and part share in a cosmetics range of the same name. The collaboration became possible when one of the Commodores was injured in a motorbike accident, forcing the group to cancel the remainder of their 1980 American tour. Richie: 'Apparently Kenny was impressed with *Three Times A Lady* and said he would like me to write a song for him. Of course I was thrilled but I had to say "no" because there was no way I could break from the tour and do the song with him. Exactly a week later, Clyde fell off his motorcycle and so, after fourteen years of constantly working with the Commodores, I had three weeks off while we waited for Clyde to recover. I immediately called Kenny and asked if he was still interested. That same night I was in Vegas playing him *Lady*.'

Richie found it difficult to give Rogers a song he'd planned to record with the Commodores, who were in need of a hit single at this time, but the challenge was one he needed. It also afforded Richie the opportunity to become involved with Kenny Rogers' *Share Your Love* album. Richie's wife, Brenda Harvey, was also acknowledged as the album's co-ordinator although she was actually the production assistant. Richie: 'Brenda had been peeping over my shoulder and watching people like Suzee Ikeda, Suzanne de Passe and James Carmichael for the last seven years or so. I thought she was playing about when she'd come into the studio with us. When she said she wanted to be my production assistant, I really didn't take her seriously. But I agreed to try her out on Kenny's album and she was so organized and so much on top of everything that it scared me. Not only did she do what a production assistant should do, but she organized my entire day ... and my meals!' With Richie's solo work, rumblings of him leaving the Commodores were rife. Even though all rumours were strenuously denied at this time, it was a move he would make within a year.

Three new signings on the Motown label released debut albums between August and October 1980. The first was Michal Urbaniak, a jazz violinist who released his *Serenade For The City* album in the US in August and *Nanava* single in Britain in November 1980. Polish-born Urbaniak absorbed jazz from The Voices Of America radio broadcasts, which in turn prompted him to become a saxophonist. He later returned to the violin to form The Michal Urbaniak Constellation, a popular jazz outfit on the Continent, before moving to America to pursue his musical interests more fully.

Jazz pianist Ahmad Jamal's *Night Song* album was issued in October 1980 (UK, Dec '80). It featured the *Theme From M*A*S*H* (Jamal was one of the originators of the tune used in the movie) Isaac Hayes' *Deja Vu* and *When You Wish Upon A Star* from *Pinnochio*.

Born on 2 July 1930 in Pittsburg, Jamal began playing the piano at the age of three. He later studied under noted concert singer and teacher, Mary Caldwell Dawson, and while at Westinghouse High School made his debut as a pianist. On leaving school at the age of eighteen Jamal worked with the George Hudson Band, before joining The Four Strings. When they broke up Jamal toured briefly as an accompanist for the then popular song/dance team The Caldwells. A year later Jamal formed his own trio, and changed his name from Fritz Jones to Ahmad Jamal after adopting the Islamic faith. The trio recorded their debut album *But Not For Me* for Argo in 1958. It was recorded 'live' at Chicago's Pershing Hotel and became one of the year's biggest selling albums by staying in the top ten for one hundred and eight consecutive weeks. The album spawned the hit single *Poinciana*, later re-issued on Chess' offshoot, Cadet, with whom Jamal signed in 1965. Prior to this he recorded for numerous labels including Okeh, Parrot and Epic.

After recording approximately twenty-one Cadet albums, Jamal left in 1968 to sign with Impulse and ABC, before joining 20th Century in 1974 to record the *Jamaica* album. Jamal described his music as 'contemporary American music' and abhors the word 'jazz': 'I've never called my music jazz, neither have most of my contemporaries. We are musicians. I never accepted the word "jazz" because it can mean anything, and it's a comedown to people who have devoted their lives to something called jazz. Our music was called jazz deliberately to suppress it, but it's the only art form that was developed in the United States. It has built this billion dollar industry called music. It's the base of the industry and I challenge anyone to disapprove it. Like Duke Ellington said "there are only two kinds of music, good and bad" and I always strive for the best I can possibly offer.' Unfortunately, Jamal's best was just not good enough at Motown.

The most enterprising of 1980's signings

was The Dazz Band, although their hits were not immediate. Rob Harris, founder member of the group, worked with others under the name Bell Telefunk in 1971. Three years later Michael Calhoun, Kenny Pettus and Ike and Mike Wiley joined. Together they became a regular attraction at the Kinsman Grill in East Cleveland, owned by Sonny Jones. Jones became involved in the group's career and insisted on a name change to Kinsman Dazz. Under this name the group signed to 20th Century in 1977.

The horn and keyboard sections of the outfit changed regularly until trombonist Ed Meyers, trumpeters Skip Martin and Pierre De Mudd, guitarist Eric Fearman and keyboardist Kevin Kendrick joined. After a relatively successful stay at 20th Century, the group joined Motown during 1980 where their debut album *Invitation To Love* was released in October 1980 (UK, Dec '80).

Before the close of 1980 Stevie Wonder released I *Ain't Gonna Stand For It* as the follow-up to *Masterblaster* (*Jammin'*), which had reached number five in the American pop charts and number two in Britain and its packaging featured photographs of the solo Wonder and Wonder, Ross and Gaye; both shots taken at Wembley Arena. The hitless trio High Inergy released their fifth album *Hold On*, produced and arranged by Narada Michael Walden, who had recently enjoyed success with his own releases and production work for Stacy Lattisaw. Billy Preston and Syreeta issued *Please Stay* taken from her solo 1980 album, and Teena Marie issued I *Need Your Lovin'* from her third album *Irons In The Fire*.

The Commodores tried for chart success with *Jesus Is Love*, the third track to be taken from their tenth album *Heroes*. The gospel flavoured song, ideal for the Christmas season, featured Yvonne Fair, Venetta Fields, Merry Clayton, Clydie King and Sherlie Matthews on backing vocals. Of their ten albums released, all passed gold status in America; two albums reached platinum, one album double platinum and two albums triple platinum. The slump in sales of *Heroes* was worrying, yet it did not affect the Commodores' standing-room-only touring schedules. Lionel Richie: 'When we left the ballad off *Heroes* we knew we were getting a little risqué. But to finish the circle off we knew we had to do a gospel song and the only way to do that was make it the main feature. So we decided we'd take the gamble and do it that way, realizing that we were going to sacrifice the commercial airplay. There's an old saying that Elvis Presley wasn't Elvis Presley until he started singing gospel tunes. All of a sudden our fan mail concerned religion and that is forever because that crowd will never leave you. It isn't all about a hit record anymore, all of a sudden it's about personalities that people can hang something on. That's where the Commodores are trying to go now. Hit records are one thing

but they are year by year thing. Personalities are forever. We have to develop personalities so that when we write and sing a specific song people will say "I know why they wrote that".'

Behind-the-scenes technology was advancing to keep in line with the growing artist roster. In America Motown announced the development of 'an unprecedented and super secret identification process to be applied immediately on all Motown records and tapes which will revolutionize the industry's continuing fight against bootleggers and pirates'. Michael Roshkind, vice-president of Motown Industries, gloated: 'The system is absolutely foolproof and is so clever that I could invite a counterfeiter to our meetings when we discuss the whole idea, and there would be nothing he could do about it.' The elaborate system, conceived by OPREC (Owner Protection Company), involved computer use which would automatically reject any unauthorized duplication. Roshkind: 'No one person, or combination of people, either at Motown or OPREC will know the entire code so there is no way human frailty can break down the system.'

Towards the end of their anniversary year, in December 1980, Motown/EMI announced the year's sales as the best ever. The company sold three million singles – including one million for Diana Ross sales – and approximately one-and-a-half million albums. Artists who contributed to the figures included Jermaine Jackson, Teena Marie, Stevie Wonder and Billy Preston and Syreeta. The magnitude of the success was surprising but obviously gratifying in a climate that was dominated by spiralling costs within the record industry. It also gave a boost of confidence to Motown and its staff, who were determined this anniversary year would be remembered for its hits. Motown had weathered twenty years and there was no reason to suspect the success and acclaim would not continue. However, it was not to be . . .

The Commodores' album Heroes *was a poor seller but their live performance attendances were unaffected. Lionel Richie: 'Hit records are one thing but they are a year by year thing. Personalities are forever.'*

DO YOU KNOW WHERE YOU'RE GOING TO?

'I will always love her but I will always be disappointed with her too.'
Berry Gordy on Diana Ross

'I can't imagine I'll ever record another album with Motown unless a miracle happens.'
Marvin Gaye

'The record business can be very cruel . . . It's a business full of broken promises and I was often fooled by them.'
Charlene

On 15 January 1981 Stevie Wonder led a rally in Washington to celebrate the birthday of the late Dr Martin Luther King. Between 150,000 and 200,000 people shrugged off the thirty-degree weather to participate. Crowds arrived in over two hundred and fifty buses from over thirty cities nationwide, including sixteen vehicles hired by the Philadelphian chapter of People United To Save Humanity, and twenty hired by Johnson Publication's radio station, Chicago's WJPU, which carried most of its entire staff. Numerous record company executives (Kenny Gamble, Curtis Mayfield, George Clinton, Le Baron Taylor) and recording artists (Johnny Taylor, Teddy Pendergrass, Bootsy Collins, Stacy Lattisaw, The BarKays, among others) lent their support. Most black-owned radio stations generously devoted their airwaves in support. For example, New York's inner city broadcasting's FM outlet, WBLS, cancelled all advertizing for the 15th to play Dr King's speeches. Wonder's own station in Los Angeles chartered a plane to transport two hundred passengers to Washington, as well as carrying 'live' transmission from Washington in conjunction with a Washington-based station. Churches held special services or took personal holidays in support and record companies loyal to the cause closed for the day.

The march began at 10 a.m. from the Capitol steps, down Constitution Avenue to the Washington Monument grounds where the two hour programme started at noon. Wonder told the crowd: 'Martin Luther King Jr is a man America can be proud of and . . . the words he spoke spring from the vast and eternal ocean of true principles – a message of peace, love, human dignity and freedom.' The singer then performed *Happy Birthday* followed by the civil

rights anthem *We Shall Overcome*. A year later Wonder told *Blues & Soul* editor Bob Killbourn: 'It was a very moving day for us all, and the people who came to join in with us in the celebration gave me a lot of satisfaction in confirming what I believe to be a just and rightful cause in honoring such a man. I am personally honored, as should all black people be, that Dr King was part of black culture, but I am honored, simply as an American, that a fellow countryman was able to make such a great contribution. His life was one which should inspire us all. He did so much in so short a period that I believe the very least that the American peoples can do is to officially acknowledge and celebrate the birthdate of such a humane and caring person.'

With the opening of the Broadway musical *Dreamgirls*, loosely based round the rise and fall of The Supremes, Mary Wilson once again attempted to reform the trio. The story revolved around three girls, The Dreamettes, who later became The Dreams, then Deena Jones and The Dreams, who found success via their ambitious manager, Curtis Taylor Jr. The trio enjoy the trappings of their success until the fattest group member is asked to leave. The manager falls in love with the lead singer as the stout member is replaced, and unlike The Supremes' story, she re-joins the group for a reunion performance. The original Dreamgirls featured Sheryl Lee Ralph as lead singer, Jennifer Holliday as the 'fat' member, Loretta Devine and Deborah Burrell. Holliday later left the show to become a successful soloist following the release of her showstopper and Grammy award-winning *And I Am Telling You I'm Not Going*. Managed by Motown's Suzanne de Passe and Tony Jones, Holliday's debut album *Feel My Soul* was released on

(Left) During 1981 Stevie Wonder led a Washington rally to celebrate the late Dr Martin Luther King's birthday. Wonder addressed the 200,000 crowd before singing Happy Birthday.

Geffen Records, after signing with the company in 1979. Holliday: 'I'm glad I didn't join Motown because I don't want my management and my record company to be too close.'

After seeing *Dreamgirls* Wilson was convinced it was The Supremes' story because it was an accurate portrayal: 'I was surprised they had portrayed Florence's character so prominently in the play instead of the obvious Diane angle which would have been effective. There was so much truth in it and now people can see what really happened.' Diana Ross, on the other hand, retorted: 'This is my life. This is not a f.....story!' and refused to allow her children to see the show.

Mary Wilson told *Soul* magazine that the resurgence of interest in The Supremes was staggering: 'There are thirty-five-year-old people who've formed clubs for teenagers to compare records and photographs of The Supremes. Before I left Motown in 1979 I told them everything was going back to the beginning, musically. The Fifties and Sixties seem to be coming back and that era has inspired many people to reach for the past. Because I was in Europe so much I had no idea that the energy about The Supremes was so strong in the States.' The singer also felt the trio was cheated of historical achievements because Motown was not at the time recognized by the RIAA (The Record Industry Association of America). Wilson: 'We were also cheated in Diane's emergence as a star. What they did for her was wonderful but what Motown did to us, wasn't. I want to rectify history and make sure The Supremes have their rightful place in history books as far as black equality in entertainment is concerned. Like the Beatles, The Supremes should be recognized as being historical. As it stands now all the credit goes to Diane and it shouldn't be that way.' Cindy Birdsong was the only Supreme Wilson was prepared to work with because, she stressed, none of the others appreciated the significance of the group. However her plan never materialized.

In January 1981 Motown/EMI released two movie title tunes. The first was Diana Ross' *It's My Turn* from the film of the same name (*Sleepin'* was on the flipside, the song's first British outing) and the second was The Temptations' *Take Me Away* from the film *Loving Couples* (American releases were September and October 1980, respectively). Smokey Robinson, meantime, released the *Being With You* single (US, Jan '81/UK, Feb '81) the title track from his thirty-third album due in February (UK, April). The album was produced and arranged by George Tobin, and of the nine tracks only four were penned by Robinson. The result was his most commercial work to date. Also in February Robinson appeared at an anti-angel dust rally in Los Angeles, where he spoke at length about the horrors of the drug PCP and offered his status in support of the campaign, while confirming he had

forbidden drug taking during his concerts. *Being With You* became an American number one. It also became Motown's eighty-eighth chart-topper in the American R&B charts and Robinson's sixth number one, four of which were recorded with The Miracles (*Shop Around* – 1960; *You've Really Got A Hold On Me* – 1962; *I Second That Emotion* – 1967; *Tears Of A Clown* – 1970; and a solo release *Baby That's Backatcha* – 1975).

Motown/EMI were subjected to immense American pressure to repeat the success of *Being With You* in Britain. It was an ideal radio record but sales were, initially, sluggish. After an industry push the single became Robinson's first British solo number one. In 1981 Motown celebrated Robinson's silver anniversary year by booking Sunset Boulevard billboards in his honour, in-depth artist profiles for both radio and television (including a ninety-minute programme *Salute To Smokey Robinson*) and the exploitation of his back catalogue. Robinson, too, offered support by embarking on an extensive American tour, with plans to visit Britain to celebrate his chart-topper. This trip failed to materialize, much to the disappointment of Motown/EMI, due to his American commitments. If the British trip had occurred at this time, it would have boosted Robinson's career in Europe and perhaps have ensured regular future success. However, to support *Being With You* Robinson did feature in a promotional video filmed at Berry Gordy's beach house which, when shown on Britain's chart show *Top of the Pops*, was partly obliterated by the programme's closing credits, reinforcing the public and industry's feeling of the BBC's somewhat negative attitude towards black acts.

In America Motown's celebrations were highlighted by a concert held in Smokey Robinson's honour at the Los Angeles' Shrine Auditorium. Performers included Stevie Wonder, Natalie Cole, Teena Marie and Aretha Franklin. Robinson: 'It was a very special occasion for me and one that I will never forget. It was a magnificent gesture by everyone who came and I have to confess that I was totally choked-up inside by their show of affection.' Although Robinson was used to success, it was not something he expected to enjoy automatically: 'As long as I am in show business, I'm going to have to pay my dues. I have never reached a point where I feel that I had it made. I know that I've been pretty lucky up to now, but I still have plenty of ambitions left. There's an awful lot of talented competition out there, and I continually strive to compete. When that drive stops, then I'll retire.'

Motown's first 1981 signings, Nolen and Crossley, released their eponymous album in January. Curtis Nolen and Ray Crossley met at a Los Angeles high school and over the years developed into prolific songwriters after studying with Stevie Wonder for a year. With a

During 1981 Smokey Robinson celebrated his silver anniversary in the music business by enjoying his sixth American number one single, Being With You. This record also became his first solo British chart-topper.

catalogue of two hundred and fifty songs, Nolen and Crossley were introduced to Motown's writer/producer Hal Davis. Crossley: 'We met Hal when we placed a song on Thelma Houston's *Ready To Roll* album called *Am I Expecting Too Much*. Hal told us he also needed a song for Diana Ross and Billy Preston. We played a few choice songs we had. He told us to record the tunes ourselves and he would produce them for us. He even put his own money up for the first few tunes.' Their second *Ambience* was transferred to the new 6000 Series for February 1982 release when the Gordy label became defunct.

Marvin Gaye, still exiled in London, ended twelve months of frustration to release his *In Our Lifetime* album (US, Jan '81/UK, Feb '81), his first studio album since *Here, My Dear* in 1978. It largely comprised songs he had written for the aborted *Love Man* project and was finally completed in November 1980. Motown/USA issued Gaye with an ultimatum to finish the work within a specified period otherwise the work would not be released at all, as it was now becoming a financial burden for Motown, reputedly estimated at $1 million, which included Gaye's living expenses. This figure Motown either had to recoup or write-off, and the longer Gaye spent in the studios the bigger the financial commitment became.

The material had been recorded in the Seawest Recording Studios, Honolulu, the singer's own studio, and finished in London's Odyssey and Air Studios. Gaye said at the time of the album's release: '*Love Man* is *In Our Lifetime* because I'm asking the same question'. Although the songs were old compositions, he did not consider them to be dated: 'They're all changed. If I were an artist who painted pictures I have just erased half of the image I put on canvas and replaced it with something else. I finished off the album in London because the energy is something incredible. When I recorded my "live" album at the London Palladium I recognized a different energy than I had in the States, and it's like a lift for me at this point.'

The *Love Man* title represented the conceptual aspect of the album, and a warning to imitators and competitors as Gaye explained: 'At the time we were trying to combat the disconcerting tide of young black males, supposed sex symbols and pretenders to my throne.' Due to his sex orientated recordings Gaye encouraged the media to nickname him the 'love man', the ultimate symbol of sex, and although he laughed off the title, it was one that meant a great deal to him. It placed him above his contemporaries and allowed him to expand and exaggerate his exploits and lyrics: Marvin Gaye was one of a kind.

A British artist was commissioned to design the *In Our Lifetime* sleeve. Gaye was delighted with the result, which was a somewhat complicated, intense picture of life fighting death. The morbid, thought-provoking

design was submitted to Berry Gordy for approval. He failed to share his artist's enthusiasm but passed it, probably to avoid any further conflict. The album's title, however, was incorrect. It should have read *In Our Lifetime?* but the question mark was omitted from the final artwork, despite being included on the draft, which annoyed Gaye. The project was doomed from the start so it came as no surprise when he publicly disowned the work upon its release: 'The album was taken from my hands and taken back to Los Angeles and done with it what Motown saw fit to do with it. They (Motown) have the control, they have the album, and they'll do what they jolly well please. I'll probably not receive any royalties from it either, as they know this is my last work for them, which is okay. I just want out.'

The re-mixed and edited track *Praise* was lifted from the album in February 1981 (British release a month later) because it was considered the most, if not the only, commercial track. *In Our Lifetime* did not sell well and Gaye knew he had to face his critics and, more importantly, his fans. In typical fashion he had his explanation prepared: 'What I wanted to do conceptually was to show the contrast between two very powerful forces that are very important here on earth. These two forces are good and evil, positive and negative, light and dark, however you want to put it. I wanted to show with music and the illustration on the cover that this is an area we should be concerned with most. But I didn't get the chance to clearly illustrate that with this work because I was stopped about three quarters of the way through, conceptually speaking. Motown simply confiscated the masters before I finished and they released it in that unfinished form. They released it to make money. So at the end of the day I can't really claim this piece of work as my production because the liberties taken by Motown were appalling. In fact I disavow publicly this being my work.'

Despite experiencing Gaye's private and public wrath, Berry Gordy continued to support his artist and encouraged him to work. Gaye was, of course, contractually tied to Motown and Gordy intended he should honour the deal. The singer summed up his feelings to *Melody Maker*: 'There is a horrible

conflict between Motown and myself. If one's artistic nature is true, then he or she is more likely to run into tremendous difficulties with those who are concerned with deadlines and commerciality and control and all those nasty little things which make us very ill. I can't imagine I'll ever record another album with Motown unless a miracle happens. I'm not bitter. It's expedience and it's a step upwards for me actually. I feel that if I can find another record company that's more interested in me as an entity, a complete entity of artist, producer, arranger, musician, and who recognizes those qualities in me, and who feels that these qualities are eventually good and that I should be respected, and that one should be treated special if one is special, then that is the company I'll sign for.'

Stevie Wonder's ballad Lately was the most played track from the Hotter Than July album in Britain. The singer was reluctant to give permission for this track to be released as a single, but when a cover version of the song was rush released by Ensign artist, Rudy Grant, Wonder conceeded. Lately was released in February 1981 in Britain (a month later in America) and was available in both vinyl and cassette form, the latter being fashionable in the UK at this time. The cassette sold in excess of fifteen thousand copies which boosted the single to number three in the charts.

During February Stevie Wonder, with his girlfriend Stephanie, flew to Monserrat, a tiny volcanic island off the West Indies, to record Ebony And Ivory with Paul McCartney, a track for the ex-Beatle's forthcoming Tug Of War album. The song was a plea for racial harmony disguised in a strong, commercial melody. The duet shot to number one in Britain in April 1982, Wonder's first, with sales helped by one of the most expensive videos ever made. Wonder's part was filmed in America and superimposed on the final copy to show the two artists singing together. Wonder: 'Even though I did not write the song, I am in total agreement with what the lyric was saying and because of that I felt it would be right for Paul and me to do the song together. I felt that for whatever significance we both have in a multi-racial society, we're all many different colours and cultures, it would be good for us to sing something like that. And so when I was approached to do it, I said it would be really good to do it. It was my pleasure, outside of being a fan of his, the fact that we had mutual respect for each other throughout the years. It was a good time and a good song to get that message across about ebony and ivory.'

Early in 1981 two Motown stories were widely reported by the media both of which shook the music industry. Since its formation Jobete, Motown's publishing arm, boosted Berry Gordy's finances and was considered to be his most important asset bringing in a regular income. Thus it was a surprise when New York's Wall Street Journal reported that Entertainment Corporation had acquired Jobete for an estimated $30 million. It was reputed Gordy had cash flow problems and wanted to invest in future movie projects. Selling Jobete would solve that problem, and for Gordy to sacrifice his company's heritage emphasized the seriousness of his financial dilemma. The sale was aborted within a year when Jobete signed a worldwide sub-publishing three year deal with the Columbia publishing subsidary, CBS Music. Jobete would continue to administer its own business in North America and in Japan via its sub-publishing agreement with Taiyo Music. The new deal with CBS Music would facilitate worldwide royalty payments in dollars via CBS Songs.

The second story reported a suit being filed in Los Angeles' Superior Court by the Motown Record Corporation against former vice-chairman of Motown Industries, Michael Roshkind. The suit alleged that Roshkind had caused Motown to lose approximately $7 million over a two year period that began when Roshkind became Motown's chief operating officer in 1978. Roshkind's wife, Dorothy, was also named in the suit which sought punitive damages amounting to $2 million. In 1968 Roshkind was convicted of one count of income tax evasion and was sentenced in September of that year to eighteen months imprisonment, to be served under two separate work furlough programmes. Jay Lasker, one of the music industry's most experienced figures, replaced Roshkind as President and Chief Operating Officer of Motown Records.

At the same time, Berry Gordy, now chairman of the board of Motown Industries, announced that Motown Productions would be budgeted to produce movies as well as television specials and would have a music department specializing in soundtracks using Motown and non-Motown products, and that Suzanne de Passe would be President of Motown Productions. De Passe had been with Motown since 1968 after meeting Gordy a year earlier after a Diana Ross and the Supremes rehearsal in Manhattan. Gordy's limousine was not available following the rehearsal so Cindy Birdsong offered him a lift in her friend, de Passe's, car. Gordy recalled the incident in an American magazine: 'I was surprised. Something was strange. There was this young kid sitting there with this big limousine. I didn't know what to think.' The 20-year-old de Passe worked as a talent co-ordinator for a New York nightclub and, on late nights, rented a limousine to take her home because cab drivers would not transport blacks after a certain time. In 1968 de Passe worked for a booking agency when she met Gordy again, to complain of his company's inefficiency regarding booking artists for dates. Impressed with her outspoken yet professional attitude, Gordy offered her the position of his creative assistant. From that post de Passe became involved in various projects. She filmed the Jackson 5's Motown audition tape and later choreographed their stage routines; she persuaded Gordy to sign the Commodores and in 1970 she co-wrote Diana Ross' debut television spectacular and wrote the Jackson 5's special. Two years later she received an Academy Award nomination for her work on *Lady Sings The Blues*.

Berry Gordy guided de Passe through her career while allowing her total freedom to run Motown Productions. Gordy: 'In fact she's helped my own career, so you have to look at who shaped who. Sometimes the shaper becomes the shapee.' With the two working so closely together rumours circulated that de Passe was Gordy's lover. De Passe: 'Everyone in Detroit thought I was his girlfriend, but I would never have had to work so hard if I had been his old lady.'

As Motown continued to deny Diana Ross' pending departure, it released the album *To Love Again* (US, Feb '81/UK, Mar '81) produced and co-written by Michael Masser and marketed as a tribute to Masser who had worked with Ross since 1973. The canned and old tracks included *Stay With Me, Cryin' My Heart Out For You*, and *One More Chance* which was taken as the first single in February 1981 (a month later in the UK). The old tracks included *Touch Me In The Morning, I Thought It Took A Little Time (But Today I Fell In Love)* and *Theme From Mahogany*.

Unbeknown to the public at this time Diana Ross was dissatisfied with Motown's royalty accountings of her recent releases and took the unprecedented step of overseeing her business affairs. The singer felt let down by the company and began scrutinizing recording offers from other companies. Neil Bogart of Broadwalk Records reportedly offered $15 million for Ross' signature on a recording contract. Geffen Records were likewise interested in securing her. Neil Bogart had also offered Mary Wilson a recording deal but meanwhile Berry Gordy was planning to reform The Supremes with Wilson as lead singer. Wilson refused Gordy's offer in favour of a solo career. Unfortunately, Neil Bogart died and Wilson's deal died with him.

Diana Ross publicly contributed to the departure rumours when 'A Diana Ross Production' ran in the closing credits of a television spectacular *Diana* screened on American television during March. The show featured Quincy Jones, The Joffrey Ballet, Dallas' J.R. Ewing, Larry Hagman and her protégé Michael Jackson, where their familiarity on stage fuelled further rumours of their 'romance'. The spectacular featured 'live' footage at Los Angeles' Forum before twenty thousand people, and interior shots taken in the singer's dressing room. It was a magnificant, Las Vegas-styled performance with Ross including most of her hit repertoire both

as a soloist and as a Supreme. Before *Diana* could be screened in Britain the singer left Motown to sign a seven-year contract with RCA Records in March 1981, reputedly worth $20 million, for North America and Canada. Capitol Records, a subsidiary of EMI Records, signed Ross for the rest of the world. Berry Gordy was devastated by Ross' decision to leave. It was suggested that he had refused to agree to the substantial financial advance demanded by the singer, and further implied his proposed sale of Jobete was instigated to raise the financies required to keep Ross with Motown. However, in terms of record sales Ross was not a big seller in America. The bulk of her sales emanated from Europe, particularly Britain. Ross' departure therefore did not leave a big a gap in Motown's market percentage and would not, as the industry envisaged, damage future overall sales figures.

Berry Gordy recalled his feelings at this time to *The Sunday Times Magazine*: 'I felt personally insulted and very hurt. And to leave as she did strictly for money. I would think that if any person leaves for that reason then they should not be with Motown. If they don't understand what we did for them, understand about the care and love and all the other stuff they had, and rate everything in dollars, that to me is not very bright. But with Diana I felt even worse, because I had spent a tremendous amount of time with her. I felt like a failure. I will always love her, but I will always be disappointed in her too.' Of Ross' future Gordy said: 'I feel that with Diana, big as she is, and she's certainly the biggest artist we ever had, if she doesn't have the right team behind her she will have trouble. And she doesn't have that team.'

Diana Ross' new contracts reputedly required her to deliver one album per year and allowed her leave to participate in further movies. Bhaskar Menon, on behalf of Capitol Records, told the media: 'All of us at Capitol and EMI are absolutely thrilled at our new association with Diana Ross. EMI music companies in most countries have already represented Diana's product over many years throughout our former licensing agreements with Motown, but it is very exciting to be able to work with her direct now.' Smokey Robinson told *Blues & Soul*: 'Diana was always regarded as family within Motown and it's always hard to lose a member of one's family. Motown is a university of music, we always prepare and groom our artists from stage presence to hygiene. I believe that Diana was a showcase for that special preparation we have at Motown but, in the end, it was her decision to leave. Nobody could ever replace her, she was and is a very special and unique talent. However, we do have one or two other acts still at Motown!' Ross told J. Randy Taraborrelli: 'All of a sudden I felt like here I was thirty seven years old with three children and through a divorce, but yet not able to take full

Diana Ross' last Motown album was To Love Again. *It featured old and canned material and was promoted as a tribute to Michael Masser.*

responsibility for my own decisions. I don't want to pick up the phone and call Berry Gordy, Motown or anyone if I want to buy a car. I want to know where my bank accounts are.'

The singer's quest for personal and business control was encouraged by an accountant with New York's Price Waterhouse company. Glenn S. Kanery handled Ross' business and was found guilty of swindling her out of approximately $200,000 and using the money for his own means. Ross: 'I got the hell screwed out of me and began realizing I was very vulnerable to people taking advantage of me.' To prevent this happening again Ross established the RTC Management Corporation (named after her three daughters) as the management headquarters of her new companies. This included Diana Ross Productions, the parent company for her recording activities under which the singer would produce her own albums; two music publishing outlets to cater for her new deals with RCA and Capitol, Rosstown Music dealt with the American arm and Rossville Music dealt with EMI; Chondee Inc was responsible for her touring schedules, while Anaid Film Enterprises (Diana spelt backwards) concentrated on developing and producing television specials, record promotion videos and feature films. The first project to fall under this company was said to be the Josephine Baker biography *Naked At The Feast*, which to date has not materialized. JFF Enterprises Ltd was established to research and develop fashion and cosmetic projects, and Diana Ross Enterprises oversaw all creative and business aspects of her entertainment companies. The artist formed these companies to control her career and finances and to protect her expanding business interests. Ultimately, Ross controlled every detail of her professional life. Ross' first RCA/Capitol single was a version of the Frankie Lymon original track *Why Do Fools Fall In Love* which was an international hit, taken from her debut album of the same name which she also produced. Motown responded by releasing an *All The Great Hits* compilation album.

Flushed with the success of Smokey Robinson's *Being With You* becoming its fastest selling single since the Commodores' *Three Times A Lady* reached the top spot, Motown/EMI celebrated a second number one in 1981. A 1975 Michael Jackson track *One Day In Your Life* was re-released in March (a month later in Britain on the old Tamla Motown label) and replaced *Being With You* at the top. Originally a track on Jackson's *Forever Michael* album, Motown/EMI's then product manager, John Marshall, lifted it for British release in April 1975. The single died, so Motown/USA didn't pass it for release. During 1981 a re-mixed version of the song was released in America and it was this mix that became the UK number one.

Robinson's *Being With You* was certified a gold single on 12 June 1981, the same day as *One Day In Your Life* was certified silver. This was the first time in Motown/EMI's history that one artist followed another to the top! Robinson: 'It doesn't matter how many hit records you may have had before, it's a great feeling. In fact, the older you get, the more appreciative you become. From the moment I heard the completed tape I knew it was a winner. I was pretty sure of the mechanics of the record beforehand, but you never quite know whether it will have the certain "touch" until it's finished. Fortunately, this one did. It was very satisfying too, as a few people at Motown were not too sure of the record.'

The DeBarges, a family group, released their self-named debut album on the Gordy label during April 1981. Bobby and Thomas DeBarge were the first of the family of ten children born to Etterlene and Robert to become professional entertainers as members of Jermaine Jackson's outfit Switch. When that disbanded, sister Bunny and brothers Eldra, Mark and Randy joined them to form the DeBarges.

The family was born in Grand Rapids, Michigan, where the eldest Bunny said they were raised on music: 'When we were little our mother's brother was the choir director at the church we attended. He bought out of us as children what was in us, and kept us around professional musicians. Not "professional" like in a recording company but people that hadn't had a break. He was a big help to us in our music, along with another uncle who was a pastor. And when we weren't being trained by our two uncles, we were being herded into a radio station by mom so we could sing for the people there. All of which helped add up to a rather well-rounded musical education.' Through Bobby and Thomas, the new group was auditioned and signed to Motown to replace its other family group, the Jackson 5. When the DeBarges' second album *All This Love* was released a year after the first, brother James had joined the group and they were known simply as DeBarge. *All This Love* (US, Jul '82/UK, Jul '83) sold a million copies in America, as did their next *In A Special Way* in 1983 (UK, Mar '84).

Hot on the heels of the Stone City Band's *The Boys Are Back* album, Rick James released his most imaginative and spectacular album to date, *Street Songs* (US, Apr '81/UK, May '81) featuring Teena Marie, The Temptations and Stevie Wonder, alongside his house groups the Stone City Band and the Mary Jane Band. The single *Give It To Me Baby* had previously been released during March (British release a month later) to test the market potential for the album. Both records raced into the American charts with the album passing platinum status. James: 'I have gotten a lot of things off my chest with this album. I think that some of the songs and lyrics are among

Rick James' Street Songs album was one of the decade's biggest, with sales in excess of 6 million. He became one of Motown's most successful acts.

the best. *Super Freak* is a personal experience, just as *Fire And Desire* relates to me. That's the track that is really selling the hell out of the album.' Indeed that song, featuring Teena Marie, was a magnificent piece of epic drama and was possibly the album's highlight. *Street Songs* pushed James into the megastar position and he undertook a sold-out fifty-eight city American tour thanks to the album's success. With Teena Marie as his support act, James conquered his audiences with his stylish, fast moving, glitzy performances. In the Midsouth Coliseum, Memphis, his audience figures matched those of Elvis Presley and broke the attendance record held by Elton John at the Long Beach Arena. In Baton Rouge, Louisiana, forty thousand people were turned away from the concert, a line of cars extended for six miles outside the arena and a woman gave birth to twins during his concert. Rick James had taken America by storm. However the success at Memphis led to James receiving serious death threats. James: 'The police took them seriously, after all Martin Luther King was killed there. So when a whole bunch of rednecks start making that kind of threat it soon loses its joke appeal. It was interesting in Memphis too. Elvis Presley was so big there that the people simply refuse to let his memory die and the thought of a black guy coming in, breaking the record and kissing white girls was just too much for them to take. Especially when they knew I'd end up smoking grass on their stage too.'

Indeed, the flamboyant artist was now a powerful musical figure. However, one wonders how much his rebellious nature and total disregard for authority contributed to his success. According to NARM (National Association Of Record Merchandisers) *Street Songs* was one of this decade's biggest selling albums with sales in excess of six million. It was named as the top crossover album of 1981, was nominated for two Grammy Awards and won the best soul album category in the American Music Awards. James: 'The biggest effects have been financial. I earn a lot more money now for doing just the same thing as I've always done. The other satisfying thing is that I'm getting to a wider audience.' As James' public appeal grew to alarming proportions he became one of Motown's most successful acts ever. The company was thrilled with him even though his lyrics, attitudes and behaviour continued to defy its clean image.

During May Stevie Wonder embarked on a fifteen-city European concert tour as part of his world tour, said to be his last. The tour, overseen by promoters Marshall Arts, began in Rotterdam and closed in Paris during June. Before starting his European trek Wonder appeared briefly on London's Apollo Theatre stage during one of Teddy Pendergrass' performances. This prompted rumours of Wonder adding British dates to the end of his

itinerary. However, he declined requests from Marshall Arts and Motown/EMI by saying further dates would follow his Wembley Arena performances too closely. Interestingly, Wonder would not give permission for any of his European shows to be filmed for television or video uses, claiming his public would not attend future shows if they could be seen elsewhere.

Following his last Paris concert Wonder conceded to Motown/EMI's pressure to return to London for a private holiday and to re-mix *Happy Birthday*, his dedication to the late Dr Martin Luther King, for British release in July 1981. The single featured a digital version of the song on the topside and a singalong version on the flipside. Wonder was originally reluctant to release this track because: 'I do not want the meaning of the record to be overshadowed by any commercial consideration. This song means a lot to me and I had to be sure the intention to release it was right.'

Berry Gordy made a surprise public appearance during one of Stevie Wonder's Paris performances which marked the close of the singer's European tour.

Following the release of his *Praise* single Marvin Gaye contemplated touring again. The singer and his son Bubby were living in Ostend, where promoter/manager Freddy Cousaert supported them financially. It was Cousaert who persuaded Gaye to return to the recording studios to experiment on future projects. Meanwhile, NEMS Enterprises announced a string of British dates for Gaye following the completion of his European tour. Prior to his leaving England, Jeffrey Kruger oversaw Gaye's activities and said the singer's biggest problem was his inability to rid himself of unsavoury colleagues 'who not only bled him dry financially but in addition used Marvin's generous nature to sustain their own nefarious drug habits, and instead of building up Marvin's confidence, encouraged him to drink and take uppers and worse when he was down in spirits. They would give him downers when he couldn't sleep, so his system was riddled (with drugs) which, in turn, clouded his judgement and left him in a permanent state of lethargy.' Kruger also stressed that Gaye could be rational when lucid: 'He was able to understand that he had no problems that couldn't be solved relatively easy. But then as the day wore on he went back to the clutches of his own mob. They undid all the good previously drummed into Marvin by his friends, like Berry Gordy, Mike Roshkind and Lee Young Jr, all of Motown and who were always in Marvin's corner, if only he was prepared to take the guidance and advice offered to him.'

Later, in May 1981 promoters Outlaw/Kiltorch/IMCP announced a second tour of England. For this Gaye planned to use a regular American rhythm section with British backing singers and horn section. A Motown International executive advised Motown/EMI that the singer was now rational and rid of the people who had been responsible for his previous problems, and that the promoters had safeguarded themselves against cancellation. Safeguard or not, the tour was cancelled within a week of the tickets going on sale, with the excuse that Gaye's American musicians were unrehearsed and therefore unable to perform within the time limit. Jeffrey Kruger: 'The tour was cancelled because I threatened to take legal action to prevent it from taking place. I am perfectly agreeable for Marvin to work in Britain, he is too big a talent to lay dormant. However, a contract is a contract and must be honoured. As far as I'm concerned Marvin has two alternatives, to tour with my company or with another company but with my prior agreement as to terms and conditions. I do have Marvin's best interests at heart, and believe that he is not always completely aware of what is involved in certain contracts presented to him.'

Kruger's statement, prompted by Gaye touring with another company while under exclusive contract to him, led to Marvin Gaye returning to London for a series of business meetings which culminated in a third promoter announcing British dates in June. Concorde Management negotiated an acceptable deal with Kruger and Gaye's manager, Freddy Cousaert. Kruger: 'Following several weeks of intense negotiations to settle outstanding contractual obligations, a mutually agreeable settlement has been reached by Freddy Cousaert, who has promoted the previous two Gaye European tours. Under the terms of the settlement Marvin Gaye has paid an undisclosed sum to (my company) in consideration of which Marvin is now free of any former contractual options with the Kruger Concert Organization.' Kruger had had the option of the singer's European services until 1983 but by this settlement Gaye would self-promote his own tours in future. The June tour was therefore confirmed, and Motown/EMI released a second single from his In My Lifetime album titled Heavy Love Affair (US Apr '81/UK, May '81). This single faired no better than Praise.

Titled A Happy Love Affair Tour 1981 Marvin Gaye's support act was the established but hit-less band, UK Players. Part of the merchandising supplied for this tour by Peter Harding's Harpo Publicity were controversial tee shirts showing various poses of couples making love. The shirts were made to Gaye's own design and due to the nature of the artwork Motown/EMI refused to allow its logo to be used within the design!

Mid-way through Gaye's Apollo Theatre performance on 17 June, Stevie Wonder made an unscheduled guest appearance. Together Gaye and Wonder sang I Heard It Through The Grapevine. Reviews of the show were favourable: 'The Apollo performance was low key. Marvin was relaxed during this informal show. It wasn't a night for new material, instead it was one hour and a half of old favourites, where the highlights were Distant Lover, What's Going On and Inner City Blues. It is still a thrill to attend a Marvin Gaye concert because he really is that bit special.'

Following his concert tour Gaye's determination to leave Motown was achieved when Berry Gordy relented and freed him from his recording contract. Losing Gaye in the wake of Diana Ross' departure was a blow to Motown's public image, yet the company survived. Gaye: 'I've had my differences with Berry Gordy, but one thing I or anyone else cannot take away from him is the very simple fact that it was him who made the dream come true for a lot of people including me. Berry Gordy has survived in one of the toughest businesses around and to do that takes a lot of balls, a lot of work, and a lot of risks. Believe me, he's given out a lot of s*** in his time but he's had to take a whole lot himself. Nobody, particularly a cocky black guy fresh from the assembly lines in Detroit, gets to make it that big without making a few enemies and taking a few cuts. Deep down in my guts, I admire the man immensely. He'll be remembered a damn sight longer than any Motown artist.'

Columbia/CBS Records in America expressed an interest in signing Marvin Gaye. Larkin Arnold, trained as a lawyer, was vice-president of the company and negotiated Gaye's contract. Arnold, who had first met Gaye in 1972, spent much time in Belgium with the singer. Arnold: 'Marvin was having extreme difficulties not so much with Motown but with his internal revenue problems. They filed against his future earnings, so that meant any money he generated would go to them. We spent many hours talking about his life and shared tales on many things. In fact, there's not too much to do in Belgium except talk, especially where Marvin was.' Before Gaye could secure a deal with Columbia/CBS, Motown had to be compensated. Arnold: 'Berry Gordy was great and totally respected Marvin's wishes. They finalized things between them and subsequently there was no problem between CBS and Motown. We reached a very amicable relationship.'

It was reported that Motown would receive a small percentage from Gaye's future record sales to off-set Motown's shortfall on his recordings. Further, Motown was unable to market Gaye's unreleased product for a specified number of years. Gaye: 'I'm sure they have a tremendous back catalogue of unreleased material, but I don't think any of it is any good.'

Larkin Arnold was aware of Gaye's past working attitude and the risk he took in securing him as an artist: 'There were a few negative thoughts about signing him. Marvin hadn't had a hit in seven years. People said he was old, music had passed him by and he wasn't mentally stable. It's true to say a lot of people were surprised at my signing him and I don't know if anyone else would have taken a chance on him. I respect Marvin so much, and he means so much to black people and so much to the music business generally, and his genius is still there. But I was told, if you're willing to take the risk, a two and a half million dollar risk, well, I put my career on the line.'

Gaye asked Arnold to recruit Harvey Fuqua to assist with the recording of his first CBS album. Titled *Midnight Love* the project, recorded at Studio Katy in Chaine, Belgium and ARCO Studios, Munich, was totally his own work, and was dedicated to his three children, Marvin Jr, Nona, Frankie, and to Judge Mednick who assisted in Gaye's bankruptcy case. Prior to the album's release late in 1982 the first single in America and Britain was *Sexual Healing* in October 1982. Gaye: 'I started praying to God that it would become a hit. Coming from one record company to another, to have it come out and bomb would have been really bad for me. It would have been the kiss of death for me in the record industry. Luckily, it went to number one in many places, and I know there would have been a time when that fact would have made me overjoyed from an egotistical point of view. But that's not enough any more. I'm overjoyed because I see the single and the album as a means to an end. It's a means of getting proper exposure and with the proper exposure I can deliver my proper message.'

Shortly before Diana Ross left Motown she recorded a duet with Lionel Richie, and during June 1981 (UK September) the result was released. Titled *Endless Love*, it was the title song from the movie of the same name, directed by Franco Zeffirelli and starring Brooke Shields. Richie: 'Polygram called me and asked did I have a song for their new movie. I didn't have, so I went to see the movie although I really didn't want anything else to do at that time. Then Polygram said all they wanted was an instrumental, and that I could do on a weekend – no problem. Next thing I know, Polygram want lyrics and wanted me to sing them. So I agreed because it was still only a weekend thing. Then I'm told Polygram have got Diana Ross to sing it with me - now I had a problem! It was turning into a bigger project by the minute but it turned out to be a wonderful weekend. Diana was in Atlantic City doing some concerts and I was in New York, and neither of us had the time to visit each other. So we met in Nevada. She finished her concert at one in the morning and drove down, while I flew in. Diana was a real professional, she kills a song. We thought about recording a follow-up as well but decided *Endless Love* couldn't be followed. It was a great duet but these aren't recordings that come by easily. Just think of all the wonderful duets there have been before, like Marvin and Tammi, or Diana and Marvin, so it was pointless trying to out do *Endless Love*. It has to be a project you can come back to every now and again.'

Endless Love became an American number one for nine consecutive weeks, reached number seven in Britain (where it became the last single to be released under Motown's licensing deal with EMI) and was nominated for a Grammy Award. By the end of 1981 Lionel Richie was represented in the American top hundred with six singles – *Endless Love*, the Commodores' *Oh No* (which he wrote and co-produced) and *Lady (You Bring Me Up)* (co-produced by him), Kenny Rogers' *I Don't Need You* and follow-up *Share Your Love*, and *Still* re-recorded by John Schneider.

The Commodores released their *In The Pocket* album in June 1981 (a month later in Britain). For this release Lionel Richie hired a public relations company to handle his public image, once again fuelling rumours of his imminent departure from the group. Richie told *Blues & Soul* that *In The Pocket* gave Clyde Orange the unique opportunity to express his

The Commodores advertized their group logo on a range of jeans to promote their album In The Pocket. Unfortunately, the album's marketing did not include free jeans for the media!

Lamont Dozier, one third of Holland-Dozier-Holland, released his debut Columbia album Working On You *in 1981. This deal followed unsuccessful relationships with ABC Records and Warner Brothers.*

talent: 'Before the Commodores made it in terms of records, Clyde was the lead vocalist. I was the horn holder and the shoo-shoop guy. For the past few years because I wrote the songs I came to the front as being the lead singer. On this album he's now coming to light as the great performer he is. The direction, in terms of overall recording quality, is excellent. We tried recording in Atlanta for the first time and it was super. What we're trying to do is bring the group into another area. We started out in disco, went into funk and then ballads. What we were actually doing was writing a musical résumé, showing people that we are about more than one usual avenue. We have six arrangers, six producers, six writers and six performers. The problem was that when we just started out at Motown we wanted to revolutionize the music business. Norman Whitfield gave us the best advice in the world when he told us that before we go out and revolutionize the music world, we should take four steps back and develop a following first. We developed a vocal sound that took over from our instrumental sound. So, as the time goes on, we're going to take that circle all over again.'

By highlighting the individual Commodores Richie was ensuring that when he left the group, it would survive without him as lead singer, and by the group contributing more tracks to their albums, the absence of his compositions would not be so apparent. However, at the time of *In The Pocket*'s release, Lionel Richie continued to deny his pending departure.

One of Motown's biggest marketing campaigns took place during mid-1981 with the re-release of sixty albums in America. Under the marketing banner *The Artists and The Music That Started It All* the mid-priced albums were packaged in their original jackets, and represented the largest exploitation of the company's back catalogue to date. The sixty albums included material by Gladys Knight and the Pips, The Isley Brothers, Michael Jackson, Stevie Wonder, Martha and the Vandellas, David Ruffin, Mary Wells, The Marvelettes, Marvin Gaye, the Jackson 5, Diana Ross with and without The Supremes, Eddie Kendricks and The Temptations. To coincide with this mammoth release an extensive search was made for former Motown acts to become involved in media interviews via specially compiled open-ended interview albums. Motown/EMI chose thirty of the American titles for release and marketed them under *Motown Superstars Series – The Legendary Sound Of Motown*. The series was released on 10 August 1981 and heralded one of the most extensive campaigns in the British history of the company. Included in Motown/EMI's campaign were *Diana & Marvin* (when issued in 1973 it sold in excess of 300,000 copies), *Reach Out* (Four Tops) (which became Motown's first big selling British album in 1967), Thelma Houston's classic *Sunshower*

album (available for the first time via Motown), Smokey Robinson's first solo album *Smokey* and Stevie Wonder's *Down to Earth*, *Uptight*, *My Cherie Amour* and *Signed, Sealed & Delivered* albums.

Also in August 1981, former Sixties recording artist Chris Clark was appointed as Motown Production's vice-president, in charge of its internal creative department. This move to work with Suzanne de Passe signified once and for all the end of Clark's recording career, much to the disappointment of her fans who had hoped she would return to the recording studios. As Clark turned her back on performing, Jermaine Jackson felt his career slipping. Despite the success of his *Let's Get Serious* project, Jermaine Jackson (who had recently re-signed to Motown with an exclusive production and artist contract that enabled him, via his own production company, to develop talent for the company) faced career problems. He attempted to retrieve his past success with his *I Like Your Style* album (US, Aug '81/UK, Oct '81) where the packaging showed him wearing clothes bought from Harrods during his last British visit. *I Like Your Style* featured Jackson's own work, except for Stevie Wonder's *Signed, Sealed & Delivered*. Jackson was aware of his professional dilemma: 'Obviously there are areas where there's a lot more room for me to grow, but that's something that the public may not understand or be able to see, but I know it's there. However, it would be so nice to be a star again, but I guess I can wait.'

Jackson had also become involved with his second group, Lovesmith: 'I'm very excited about them. Lovesmith are four brothers from St. Louis. They used to record as the Smith Connection on the Holland, Dozier and Holland Music Merchant label. They got a lot of experience with Brian and Eddie, and just as it took me four to five years to come into my own, so it is with Lovesmith. They've devoted so much time and effort to what they're doing that I think their time is here now.' Lovesmith's self-named album, released in the US only during August 1981, pleased Jackson although he stressed: 'With them being a new act and with the way the business and economy are now, it's hard for a new act to get the chances that used to be available. We took a lot of time and effort in presenting them properly, and it took six hours to shoot the album cover right. We wanted to build a concept behind it, because that's the way I started with Switch.' Jackson's efforts were doomed to failure.

Lamont Dozier, one third of the history-making composer/producer trio, Holland, Dozier and Holland, released his debut album for Columbia Records entitled *Working On You* in the late summer 1981. Following the demise of the Hot Wax and Invictus labels (where Dozier's biggest hit on the latter was *Why Can't We Be Lovers*) Dozier signed to ABC Records to enjoy two further hits, *Fish Ain't Bitin'* and *Let Me Start Tonite*, before joining Warner Brothers. After producing three albums there Dozier left during 1978: 'It was fine but the marriage wasn't working. I just decided it wasn't the place for me to be. When I signed with the company, disco was what was happening and I wasn't a disco artist. Some of the music I made got lost and I felt there was some material in there that was real good. Fortunately, other artists have always tended to listen to my records to find good songs like Odyssey recording *Going Back To My Roots* which I was happy about.' Ironically, this hit cover version launched Dozier's career as a performer!

Dozier confessed astonishment that Holland, Dozier and Holland's fifteen-year-old back catalogue at Motown was still being recorded: 'It's a real acknowledgement and it's one of the things that keeps me motivated to just keep writing.' To date, Dozier estimated he had at least three hundred and fifty compositions completed and canned, ready for his own or other acts' use. Of the mountain of compositions written by Holland, Dozier and Holland many originated from personal experiences. For example, the Four Tops' *Bernadette* was born from Dozier's teenage love for a girl; The Supremes *Stop! In The Name Of Love* was an expression used by another girlfriend, and Martha and the Vandellas' *Jimmy Mack* was about a young boy. Dozier: 'He was a kid who wrote a song that was very popular. I met his folks at the BMI dinner in 1966 and was quite moved by his tragic story. He had gotten killed and his mother was there to pick up a top ten award. So when a melody came about that name seemed to spring up and fit well with the music we were writing at the time.'

Another ex-Motowner, Thelma Houston, released her second RCA album *Never Gonna Be Another One* (which spawned her hit single *If You Feel It*) produced by George Tobin who was responsible for Smokey Robinson's *Being With You* album. Houston: 'We nearly worked together when I was at Motown, so when we were looking for a new producer for this album, George had been calling the office and was so persistent that I decided to meet him and see if our ideas gelled. I immediately liked him and his ideas, he seemed to know what I needed and his material seemed to be the kind of commercial thing that I knew I had to have.' *Never Gonna Be Another One* was a splendid album, a credit to both artist and producer. To date, though, Houston's Motown single *Don't Leave Me This Way* was her biggest hit. Houston: 'It was the best thing that has ever happened to me. Even today you'll still hear the record on the radio and people are still dancing to it. It's one of those records that people seem to always remember and that has kept me working and kept my name out there. I'm only sorry that I was never able to follow it up at Motown properly. *I'm Here Again* was too similar and when *Saturday Night*

and Sunday Morning came along I was getting to leave the company.'

Houston felt no bitterness towards Motown regarding her lack of hit material as she considered that merely being associated with Berry Gordy was a success of its own: 'It was a new experience for me and I have been fortunate to have hit records, but the key is to be able to establish a foundation that can be built upon no matter what happens and that you don't allow yourself to just fade away.' A year later Houston left RCA to sign with MCA Records and married actor/musician/songwriter Cliff Frazier.

Ex-Temptation Eddie Kendricks debuted on Atlantic Records during 1981 with his *Love Keys* album, after an unsuccessful two album stay at Arista. *Love Keys* was recorded in Birmingham and represented his first time in the studio working with white producers and musicians. Meantime, Barrett Strong released his *Love Is You* album on the Michigan-based label, Cherie Records.

Although these ex-Motowners failed to reach their Motown hit standards, these current (and past) releases did prove that leaving Motown was not necessarily the kiss of death, unlike the situation which faced departing acts during the Sixties.

In October 1981, after an eighteen-year association with EMI Records, Motown signed a new licensing deal with RCA Records in London. (In 1987 RCA changed its name to BMG Records and will be referred to by that name from now on.) Motown's move resulted in five of the enthusiastic and loyal EMI working team being made redundant despite the intervention of EMI's managing director, Cliff Busby, who wanted the successful team to continue, as did the media and Motown fans. Motown International's vice-president, Peter Prince, based in London, told journalists: 'We are looking forward to a new partnership with BMG, who have impressed us by the way they have become a major force in today's record market. For the past eighteen years we have enjoyed a highly successful relationship with EMI who have helped Motown maintain their position as one of the leading independent record companies in the world.' BMG's managing director, Don Ellis: 'We are very pleased to have the opportunity to join forces with the world's premiere black music company and look forward to a period of mutual success.'

The change of licensors was confusing for record stores. When dealers completed their 5 per cent returns for the quarter ending 30 September 1981, Motown product from EMI could not be returned to that company and BMG refused to accept them. EMI agreed to accept faulty Motown records for a limited period, when BMG would then accept them provided record sleeves were overstickered indicating BMG had marketed the record following the acquisition of EMI's Motown stock. When the

The soulful troubadour José Feliciano joined Motown where he became a top seller in the Latin American market.

The talent of Bettye Lavette (pictured in an early Sixties pose) was secured by Motown to release the splendid Tell Me A Lie album. Lavette: 'I felt I could get lucky with Motown as an overnight success that took twenty years.'

new trading arrangements settled down, record releases resumed at a regular pace.

A blind kid from Spanish Harlem, who found fame as a soulful troubadour, joined Motown to release his first album *José Feliciano* (US, Oct '81/UK, Nov '81). Feliciano taught himself to play the guitar at an early age and when 16-years-old played the New York club circuit where he was spotted by an RCA Records' executive. Feliciano recorded several Spanish language albums for the company, establishing him as a top-selling artist in Latin America. During 1968 Feliciano recorded the now classic single *Light My Fire* which transformed him into an international figure. This multi-million seller was followed by others like *Rain, Destiny*, his own composition *Affirmation* and *Feliz Navidad*. The artist also scored the soundtrack for the Columbia Pictures movie *Aaron Loves Angela*, and in October 1980 debuted with his guitar concerto *Concerto de Paulhino* with The Detroit Symphony Orchestra. Feliciano later expanded his talents by appearing in television shows like *Kung Fu, McMillan and Wife* and *Chico And The Man*. It was estimated that prior to joining Motown Feliciano had received thirty-two gold albums, two Grammy Awards and had received numerous guitar acclaims. His popularity in the Latin market continued via his Motown albums like *Escenas De Amor (Love Scenes)* in 1982.

Following the release of her new album *Set My Love In Motion* (US, Oct '81/UK, Dec '81), Mrs Curtis Robertson aka Syreeta became the first artist to visit London early in 1982. The mother of two (Jamal and Hódari) used this promotion trip to guest at a belated Motown/ BMG celebration in Soho's Le Beat Route club. Syreeta was adamant her new family would not be exposed to her professional life

and went to great pains to keep the two separate. Syreeta: 'I'm usually up at seven to fix the kids and my husband their breakfast, then I'm in the office for nine. I try to be back home early afternoon so that the family can spend some quality time together. I want to be Syreeta Robertson, mother and wife, and I want my kids to feel they have a normal mother like everyone else.' The singer felt her new album was her best yet. Berry Gordy acted as executive producer. Syreeta: 'He was also involved in selecting the songs, and once we got into the studio, Berry wanted the album in three weeks from start to finish. He helped with some of the vocal dubbing on *Move It, Do It* and *There's Nothing Like A Woman In Love*. He's great in the studio because he has a way of making you feel relaxed and then pulling the best out of you. I've always had the greatest respect for the way he created Motown as a company and made it such a major force in the music world but that respect deepened through working on the album with him.'

Syreeta wrote the *Wish Upon A Star* track with the late Minnie Riperton in mind. *Out Of The Box* was initially recorded as an instrumental: 'so I wrote some lyrics in the studio during one of the breaks. *Out Of The Box* is jive talk which means "it's ridiculous" and the song is just that. The little kid's voice on the front of the song is mine.' The track *I Love You* Syreeta dedicated to John Merrick, The Elephant Man: 'I was so moved by how one person cared so much for him and by how this terribly lonely man found joy in that blessing, that it started me thinking about all the people who have cared for me.'

New signing Bettye Lavette's debut album, *Tell Me A Lie*, was issued during January 1982 (UK release April). *Right In The Middle (Of Falling In Love)/You Seen One You Seen 'Em All* had been lifted as a single in December 1981, and the flipside was released as the A-side in Britain during March.

Born in a Michigan suburb, this superb R&B songstress was one of two daughters. In 1962 the teenager recorded for Atlantic before moving to Lu Pine, and later Calla to record her classic single *Let Me Down Easy*. Lavette toured with Don Gardner's band and recorded with other labels before returning to Atlantic Records in the early Seventies to enjoy R&B hits with *Heart Of Gold* and *Your Turn To Cry*. An album, *Child Of The Seventies*, was also recorded but canned. After recording briefly for the Epic label, Lavette moved to the New York based West End label to release her disco hit *Doing The Best That I Can*. Lavette: 'At that time I was doing *Bubbling Brown Sugar* which I did for three years, and that record was kind of a way to break back into the record business.' When Lavette refused to record further dance tracks because, being a soul singer, that market was of little interest to her, West End terminated her contract. She then signed to Motown: 'I didn't choose them. I'm from Detroit but Motown was the furthest thing from my mind. My producer, Steve Buckingham, did *Tell Me A Lie* for another company while I got married. He then phoned me to say Diana Ross was leaving Motown and that it made sense for me to be there. Motown was interested in me because they wanted to work with an established female artist. I thought it was a wonderful idea because I'd grown up with The Temptations and The Supremes. Motown was basically known for their own type of R&B. I know all the intricacies and techniques of R&B and thought until now that I'd suffer there. Then I felt I could get lucky with Motown as an overnight success that took twenty years!' *Tell Me A Lie* was devoured by R&B fans, grateful for a new release by this very talented singer. However sales were not sufficient to persuade Motown to release another record.

José Feliciano was the second Motown artist to visit London in 1982 when he performed a one-off concert at The Dominion Theatre on 16 January. Motown/BMG released his version of the Michael Jackson hit *I Wanna Be Where You Are* to coincide. In America, Motown celebrated its ninety-second number one R&B single with the release of The Dazz Band's *Let It Whip* in February 1982 (UK June). The single was the first chart-topper for the Cleveland-based group, won them a 1982 Grammy in the Best R&B Vocal Duo or Group category, and a nomination for Reggie Andrews and Leon 'Ndugu' Chancler in the Best R&B Song category. *Let It Whip* was one of nine Motown nominations for 1982.

High Inergy, meantime, were still searching for a hit. Their *So Right* album in April 1982 (UK August) was sufficiently weighted with contributors like Ollie Brown, George Tobin, Hal Davis and Berry Gordy, to ensure success, yet it flopped. High Inergy's Michelle Martin admitted that they were still experimenting and with the introduction of different producers hoped to find their musical niche at last: 'Perhaps using these different ideas causes the album to be unbalanced and the concept lost because each producer sees things differently, but until a particular market is found for us, this is the only answer.' High Inergy's lack of recorded success continued to worry them. Martin: 'After our initial success it's been a downhill climb. We are trying with every release to repeat that success, everyone who works with us is trying. I think that the timing isn't right yet. We haven't given up and we don't intend to.' For their next album *Groove Patrol* (produced by George Tobin) a year later, Smokey Robinson was an added attraction, duetting with Barbara Mitchell on two tracks *Blame It On Love* and *Just A Touch Away*. But still no success.

A month after the release of High Inergy's *So Right* album in April, ex-Supreme Susaye Green-Brown filed a lawsuit against Motown

The Dazz Band's Let It Whip won them a 1982 Grammy Award and became Motown's 92nd number one R&B single.

Records, Stone Diamond Music, Black Bull Music and Jobete Music, seeking $1 million in damages and lack of financial accounting. Part of Green's action arose from unpaid royalties for sales of *I Can't Help It*, a track she wrote with Stevie Wonder for Michael Jackson's *Off The Wall* album. Meantime, another ex-Supreme, Diana Ross, was given a star on Hollywood Boulevard's Walk Of Fame.

Before releasing his next album *Throwin' Down*, Rick James hooked up with The Temptations (who had sung background vocals on his *Street Songs* album) to write, produce and record with them the *Standing On The Top Parts 1 and 2* single (US, Apr '82/UK, May '82). This hard, funky track, recorded in the distinctive Rick James style, gave The Temptations a much-needed hit. James: 'I didn't write the song with the group in mind, but when I heard their album I felt it needed a hit single. I played *Standing On The Top* to them and they loved it.' Ex-Temptations Eddie Kendricks and David Ruffin had by this time temporarily re-signed with Motown and joined the rest of the group (Otis Williams, Melvin Franklin, Dennis Edwards, Richard Street and Glenn Leonard) to record the appropriately titled *Reunion* album (US, Apr '82/UK, Jun '82) from which *Standing On The Top* was taken. *Reunion* was a musical disappointment lacking, as it did, direction and containing little of the group's past magic. Rick James: 'It was strange producing them. I grew up listening to them and felt it was an honor to work with them. I didn't feel self-conscious, only a little strange in the beginning. But I tried to fit in because it was business and that's part of what I do. The outcome of it I knew would be so strong that that took away all the strangeness and emotions. The Temptations are probably the most important vocal group in the history of black music. I care for them more than any other vocal group that ever lived.'

After The Temptations contributed to James' *Super Freak* track, interest in the group was re-kindled in America with tour promoters keen to book them to satisfy public demand to see the historical line-up. The Temptations subsequently embarked on a fifty-city American tour during May 1982 to support the *Reunion* album. *Black Echoes'* journalist, Clifton Miller, reported that their show was divided into sections, featuring the full seven man line-up, the five man line-up, four group members with David Ruffin, and solo performances by Eddie Kendricks and Ruffin. Miller: 'This wasn't as stiff or as staged as it sounds because the music was virtually non-stop and because every one of the group made stage entrances and exits with just enough wit and panache. When Ruffin began singing *My Whole World Ended*, for example, he looked around in mock horror as the other members of the group ran into the wings. What also served the show well was The Temptations' willingness to perform in full most of the Sixties hits that the crowd was expecting to hear. Eddie Kendricks was in excellent form, David somewhat frayed but the harmony parts were close to perfection. Dennis, of course, was his ever-energetic self, verging on gospel intensity on a couple of occasions. The choreography was obviously more informal than it was fifteen, sixteen years ago, but appreciably received.' David being 'frayed' was understandable. In November 1982 he was sentenced to six months imprisonment after pleading guilty at Detroit's District Court for fiddling his tax returns filed in 1976, and was also fined $4,500.

Although the *Reunion* tour was an historical occasion and one that delighted the group's followers, away from the public eye the tour was a nightmare, as the two founder members explained. Melvin Franklin: 'It should have been great but the only time it came off was when everyone was on stage. And that wasn't for every show sadly. There was a beautiful and positive side to it for the fans and Otis and I regret that it didn't work out better. I guess there was just too much of a lapse of time between the old days and 1982. Once guys go solo and start doing things their way, it's tough to discipline yourself and think about other people around you. But if you don't have the right frame of mind, it'll never work out. This is a business and you have to accept it and deal with it as such.' Otis Williams: 'It was fine right up until we played Baltimore. On stage there was all of the old electricity and you could see the egos being reborn. From then on, it was all downhill to destruction. All the old internal jealousy. In fact, it was even worse because we had new problems stemming from the lead vocalist situation because not only did we have David and Eddie back, we also kept the new lead singers in the group and Glenn Leonard started kicking up because he wanted to know why he wasn't singing lead anymore. I could not understand where he was coming from over that because if there had never been an Eddie Kendricks (in the group) there would never have been a Glenn Leonard. The hurtful

thing about the whole project is that it should have been beautiful and it could have worked. In fact it became an experiment in terror.'

Originally released during 1977, Charlene's *I've Never Been To Me* single was re-released to top the British charts in May 1982; Motown's first under its new deal with BMG. The single subsequently climbed the American charts and convinced the company to re-sign her. Charlene (Duncan) was actually living in England at this time, having become disillusioned with the music business, and had settled in Ilford where she was working in a confectionary shop and caring for handicapped people in her spare time. Now a born again Christian, Charlene returned to California to re-start her career with Motown and promote her *I've Never Been To Me* album issued in March 1982 (UK June). The singer told *Music Week* why her 1977 single was re-promoted: 'There was a DJ, Scott Shannon, in Tampa, Florida, and he began playing the song on his show. This station was swamped with calls enquiring about it. Jay Lasker became aware of its potential, tracked me down and re-signed me to the company.' When the single was first released, Charlene was mid-way through divorce proceedings: 'I got married at sixteen and had a baby daughter soon afterwards. Not surprisingly the marriage flopped because we were much too young. So I was left with the baby and a broken heart. On top of that I got involved with drugs and that messed me up even further. The guy I was married to got me into singing and eventually some of my songs were played to Berry Gordy and I was signed to Motown. The record business can be very cruel, especially when you're not prepared for it, and I wasn't. It's a business full of broken promises and I was often fooled by them. I fought for ten long years to make it

(Right) A surprise British chart-topper in 1982 was Charlene's 1977 single I've Never Been To Me. *It was her only hit but Motown re-signed her for further recordings.*

as a singing star then finally gave up.'

Charlene's new found solo success was shortlived as the chart-topper's follow-up It Ain't Easy Comin' Down, another old track, died after its release in June 1982 (UK, July). However, the singer boosted her career by recording a Spanish version of I've Never Been To Me (Nunce He Ido A Mi) on Berry Gordy's Latino label. This Latin subsidiary later featured other artists including the obvious José Feliciano. Charlene also duetted with Stevie Wonder on the stunning Used To Be single (US, Oct' 82/UK Nov '82). The controversial lyrics written by Ron Miller, bitterly condemned the atrocities and uncaring attitudes of modern life. Despite being an American hit, the single failed miserably in Britain, probably due to its content. With the lyrics in mind, an edited single was pressed for radio play while the American version was commercially available. Charlene subsequently released an album titled after the single in October (two months later in Britain) but the decline in her British career had already begun.

Interestingly, to date Rick James has never performed in the UK, although British television viewers saw his performance at the Rockpalast, Essen, West Germany during 1982 on The Old Grey Whistle Test television programme. James did not visit London following this concert, using the excuse that he had no new material to promote. So, British journalists were ferried to West Germany to interview him. Since Street Songs had escalated James into a position where he felt superior to other Motown acts, the singer claimed that artists who were hitless only had themselves to blame and cited Smokey Robinson and the Commodores as being out of touch with what the public wanted. He also opined that Motown's new signings failed to grasp the public's needs because they clung to the company's heritage in the hope that some of its prior success would rub off on them. James told NME's Lloyd Bradley: 'Much as what Motown means to me I can sit back and say that a lot of those cats want to come down out of those f****** hills and get their a**** back on the street. For me it's about the green. For the people who are buying the records, it's about the music. They put you up there, so give them the best you can. But as fast as you come up, you can go down, so prepare yourself for the future.'

James' own relationship with Motown was entirely honest, particularly where money was involved, as he explained: 'If they ever f***** up over a royalty cheque or if ever an audit came back not correct, then Motown can kiss my a**. I make millions of dollars for Motown and I do not need a record company j****** me off. I love Motown but I didn't grow up with Motown. I'm not the cat who came up with Berry Gordy and Berry says "hey, remember when I helped you out and loaned you a hundred dollars in Detroit" and all that s***

like he does with a lot of people. If Motown ever f**** me around then I want the f****** money and I'm out. It's like those agents that book me on these tours. They're making a pile of money off me, but when I had an album that didn't sell, I couldn't find the m******. Where were they then? After Street Songs I can go back to them. But I'm a fair guy, so I tell them OK, you f***** me before but now we're going to do some serious f******.'

The outspoken singer's stay at the top was further secured with the release of the Street Songs follow-up, the gold album Throwin' Down (US, May '82/UK, Jun '82). James was under pressure from Berry Gordy to quickly release a follow-up album but he was working on a Stone City Band project at the time. That was abandoned when James argued with Levi Ruffin Jr, the group's leader, so the prepared songs of Money Talks, Throwin' Down, Dance With Me and Happy were used for James' new album. Once again a bevy of artists including The Temptations, Roy Ayers, Teena Marie, Narada Michael Walden, Grace Slick and Jean Carn, assisted on the project. The album sleeve featured James wearing a loin cloth and posing with ex-Playboy playmate Anne Marie Fox in a compromising position.

To promote Throwin' Down James toured America. On 12 August 1982, after completing forty-five minutes of his performance at the Reunion Arena, Dallas, before a capacity audience of nineteen thousand, James collapsed after complaining of lower abdomen pains prior to the show. The singer was admitted to hospital, suffering from exhaustion. The strain and rigours of the past three years had taken their toll.

With his contract due to expire, Stevie Wonder decided to compile an album of his best known material. Titled Stevie Wonder's Musiquarium Volume 1 it was a collection of his post 1972 repertoire including Isn't She Lovely and Superstition plus four new compositions, Do I Do (with Dizzy Gillespie on trumpet), Ribbon In The Sky, That Girl and Frontline. All were single releases during 1982 and 1983. The double album package was originally scheduled to cash-in on the 1981 Christmas period but it was delayed when Motown rejected three sides of the proposed release as being technically unuseable. It was eventually released simultaneously in England and America during May 1982.

Once Musiquaraium was released Wonder re-signed to Motown for an undisclosed figure (the singer signs his contracts with his thumb print), and told journalist Paulo Hewitt why he chose to release a compilation instead of a new album: 'There are many songs that I write, many songs that could have gone on, say, Innervsions or Talking Book which are in the can, and I had to make a decision about those songs. An example of that is You Are The Sunshine Of My Life which was supposed to be on Music Of My Mind, but it was better for me to put it on *Talking Book*. I've never done an album consisting of all the songs I've done over the last two years, a kind of review, so I decided it was best to do that now.' The artist also announced the forming of his own label, Wondirection, where signed acts included Grease, Wonderlove, Little Willie John's sons, Kevin and Keith, and Boots Rising.

At his signing reception, Wonder told reporters that it was important for him to have continuing happiness with Motown: 'Only when I'm happy can I give the best I have to give. I don't think there's anywhere else in the world where I could get the kind of creative control I have with Motown.' Berry Gordy, also at the reception, stated money was not the most important factor of the deal: 'Most people don't understand that there are also relationships. Honesty, loyalty and a lot of things that make up one's life. Stevie is not only a genius in his music but also as a human being. I am extremely grateful that a man of his calibre, who has been a legend for many years now, realizes at a time when we are in a recession, that money is only part of the value.'

To launch *Musiquarium* in Britain, a media reception was held in London's Regent Park Zoo, where a pre-planned telephone link with the singer in New York was to be the highlight. The link never materialized and 'modern technology' was blamed.

A month prior to the release of his compilation, Wonder was one of the few entertainers to be invited to the funeral of the Egyptian leader, Anwar Sadat. The singer intended to pay tribute to Sadat, John Lennon (who had been killed by Mark Chapman outside his Manhattan apartment building on 8 December 1980) and Dr Martin Luther King by recording *The Day World Peace Began*. The title has yet to be released.

Wonder then teamed up with the reggae group, Third World, to record two songs including the hit single *Try Jah Love*. They first met in 1969 in Kingston, Jamaica, before performing together in the 1982 Sunsplash Festival. Third World member, Stephen 'Cat' Moore: 'Then he (Wonder) suggested we go into the studio together. He wanted to get into reggae and from there our relationship grew into a strong friendship. He wrote the single and *You're Playing Us Too Close* practically on the spot in the studio. We offered suggestions and it eventually turned out to be a two-way thing. The songs are kicking hard against certain people and informing people as to what "Jah Love" is, and to look towards certain directions. The song is also meaningful because it is the first time a black American has written a song that really involves the Rastafarian movement as such. We got the feeling that when Stevie wrote those songs, he had listened to what we'd done before and just brought an extension of concept.' Working with Wonder was a 'natural' experience,

although the Motown star insisted on strict working conditions. Moore: 'He was very tight although relaxing, but we all felt extremely confident. It took us three days to lay down the rhythm track on the two songs he wrote, then another five weeks for us to do the whole album.'

Bobby Womack was born in March 1944 in Cleveland, Ohio. One of five sons, Womack's childhood centred around church activities. The Womack Brothers, as they became known, were discovered by Sam Cooke, and toured with him when he was a member of the gospel group The Soul Stirrers. During the late Fifties when Cooke crossed over from gospel to popular music he persuaded the Womacks to do the same and signed them to his SAR label. Changing their name to The Valentinos, the brothers transformed the gospel song *Couldn't Hear Nobody Play* into their first hit *Looking For A Love*. *It's All Over Now* was the follow-up, and later became an international hit when The Rolling Stones re-recorded it.

Cooke's ambitions for The Valentinos ended tragically when he was shot dead in a motel by a call-girl in 1964. Bobby Womack married and divorced his widow, Barbara, and Womack's brother Cecil (following his divorce from Motown singer Mary Wells) married Cooke's daughter Linda. Curtis Womack then married Mary Wells. Guitarist Bobby was the most talented of the Womack family and following Cooke's death worked with Aretha Franklin and Wilson Pickett. During 1968, as a solo artist he recorded his first hit *Fly Me To The Moon*, followed by the powerful *Womack Live* album. In the Seventies Womack enjoyed a string of hits on United Artists like *That's The Way I Feel About Cha*, *Woman's Gotta Have It*, *Harry Hippie* and *Lookin' For A Love*. Womack's writing expertize also earned him million sellers for artists like George Benson and the J Geils Band.

However drug abuse gave Bobby Womack the reputation of being volatile and difficult to work with and his recording career nose-dived. In 1979 Womack had reached rock bottom: 'I felt it was the end of the line. When you're doing drugs and you're depressed some voice in your mind tells you you'd be better off ending it all. My mind did that a few times. I lost my creativity through losing a son, losing my brother and my dad. There was just too much happening.' In an attempt to save his career Womack signed with Otis Smith's Beverly Glen, a new small independent label which was willing to take a chance on him. Womack's first album *The Poet* in 1982 sold a staggering one-and-a-half million copies, but numerous business conflicts between Otis Smith and Womack resulted in *Poet II* not being released until 1984. After *The Poet* had spent six months in the American soul

Motown licensed Bobby Womack's two Poet albums from Beverly Glen for the world outside America and Canada. Both albums were exceptionally good sellers.

charts, including six weeks at the top, Motown secured a licensing deal for the rest of the world outside America and Canada for the two albums and their singles. *The Poet* was released in the UK in May 1982. *So Many Sides Of You* was lifted as a single in June 1982, followed by *Secrets* in September 1982. *Poet* II was released in April 1984, from which *Tell Me Why* and *Surprise, Surprise* were lifted as singles during the year. By 1987 Motown had lost the rights to the product.

Like Bettye Lavette, new signing Jean Carn released only one album *Trust Me* (US, May '82/UK, Aug '82) which was a showcase for her immense R&B talent. Born Sara Jean Parkins in Columbus, Georgia, Carn sang in her local church choir from the age of 4. She majored in college, then married jazz musician Doug Carn and joined his band. In time the couple befriended Earth, Wind and Fire, and Carn featured on two of their Warner Brothers' albums *Earth, Wind And Fire* and *The Need Of Love*. The Carns moved to New York where she worked with Duke Ellington and musician Norman Conners, for whom she participated on two albums and the hit single *Valentine Love* with Michael Henderson. Carn later teamed up with Kenny Gamble to join the Philadelphia organization. While there the singer recorded four albums on the Philadelphia International label between 1976 and 1980, before joining Motown.

Trust Me spawned one hit *If You Don't Know Me By Now*, (US, Jun '82/UK, July '82). Originally recorded by Harold Melvin and the Blue Notes, Carn's cover version featured The Temptations and is now regarded as one of the decade's classic recordings. Carn decided not to record a second album with Motown because she had no creative control and she felt *Trust Me* was badly promoted. She had to wait a year before signing with another record company because of her Motown contract restrictions.

While Billy Preston and Syreeta were touring Europe, including a performance at London's The Fair Deal Theatre in Brixton on 28 May 1982, Martha Reeves was searching for a further recording deal, following the breakdown of three (Fantasy, Arista, MCA) since leaving Motown. The absence of a new release did not, however, affect her touring bookings as Martha Reeves and the Vandellas in America or Britain. In fact, such was Reeves' pulling power in the UK that she headlined regular annual visits. Touring was her only means of income as she told *Black Echoes*: 'I gave up my royalties with Motown to be freed. It's the same thing with Fantasy, Arista and MCA, the deals weren't firm. I guess it was my time to be educated. I know my records have sold well because I've seen them in tape form and I know records aren't made into this form unless they've reached a certain number of sales. I think they were all solid records and have sold, and I've signed enough contracts to

know that I'm not dreaming. As far as record companies are concerned, I've got little response and no royalties whatsoever. I've spent quite a long time now looking for a proper deal, but I've had four major contracts and I'm still looking for the right one!'

Reeves' Motown hits, sung in a lower key, are naturally an integral part of her stage shows, because her audiences demand to hear them: 'I will give my audiences what they want although it does become repetitive, even mundane but that depends on me. I do try to incorporate more recent material because I'm not a walking, talking, singing yesterday!' The singer's experience as a Motown act did, inadvertantly, prepare her for a future solo career, although she confessed she could have fallen into the drug trap that is synonomous with the music business: 'I've certainly had my fair share of drug problems. I was started off on tranquilizers but I didn't get started on the street drugs because we were chaperoned. We were also working with men like The Temptations and The Miracles and they wouldn't let anyone near us. We were trained and taught how to be ladies and programmed what to do to keep from being destroyed.'

Motown's researchers maintained a close watch on Diana Ross' BMG/Capitol releases and finally decided to release a single, produced by Eddie and Brian Holland, from a 1973 recording session. Titled *We Can Never Light That Old Flame Again/Old Funky Rolls* and released in the US in June 1982, it was a flop commercially. As her third single on BMG/Capitol, *It's Never Too Late* (written by Dan Hartman) from her platinum *Why Do Fools Fall In Love* album, was released as the follow-up to the energetic *Work That Body*, Motown/BMG released *Old Funky Rolls* as the topside to *The Boss* in the UK in September. That too died.

During August 1982 Motown/BMG re-promoted Smokey Robinson's former American number one *Cruisin'* released in August 1979 in America (UK, Sep '79). The single, which marked Robinson's comeback as a number one artist after four years, did not sell well in the UK. In the wake of his British success with *Being With You* and its follow-up *Your Are Forever* the re-issue was inevitable. Once again it died. Tragedy struck the Commodores on 16 August 1982 when their manager Benny Ashburn died at his home in Englewood, New Jersey, following a heart attack. He was 54-years-old and was survived by his sister Miriam Walker and his four-year-old daughter Benyvette. The Commodores were stunned, and admitted that without Ashburn's guidance they would not have become the stars they had. Lionel Richie: 'We came through this thing together. After all the hard and terrible days of struggling to make a living we wanted to enjoy our success together and for Benny to share it all with us. For the five years we were on a big scale, the group didn't live next

Following months of denial Lionel Richie left the Commodores to embark on a solo career and set a precedent for his future success with Truly, which raced up the world's charts.

door to each other. We couldn't call each other daily, so we'd all phone Benny and he told us what was going on and where to meet up. He was the middleman, who kept us all together. He was also like a father to us.' In the same interview Richie explained that he now felt responsible for the Commodores: 'Even with my work outside the group, I am more concerned that I don't disrupt their organization. It must remain intact. I've always been a Commodore and we must keep our heritage alive above all else. Former ABC Television executive, Charles Smiley, replaced Benny Ashburn as the Commodores' manager.

Released in August 1982, following Billy Preston's solo album *Pressin' On* (British release November), *Second To Nunn* was the debut album from Bobby Nunn, marketed as a Rick James' soundalike. Nunn stressed that he and his band had heavily contributed to James' first album *Come Get It* and that James had in fact pinched his ideas. Nunn: 'When Rick and I first worked together I was still learning the music business and I wasn't ready to record myself. I don't even think I could have been as popular as he is right now because I didn't know how to handle the situation should it have arisen.'

Bobby Nunn, like Rick James, lived in Buffalo, and as a teenager decided on music as a career. While performing on the local club circuit Nunn recorded in his own 4-track studio and sold his records in Buffalo. Upon moving to Los Angeles, the artist signed to Columbia Records as a member of the band who played on the James' session. Under the collective name Splendor, they recorded a Phillip Bailey produced album there, before their contract expired. Nunn returned to demo recordings, which Iris Gordy like sufficiently to sign him. The funk dance track *She's Just A Groupie* from his self-penned *Second To Nunn* album was his first single in August, and was pressed as a promotion single only in the UK. However, Nunn's second album *Private Party* was British released in January 1984, following its American outing in September 1983.

Private Party pushed Nunn further into the Prince and/or Eddie Kendricks' vocal style, while his use of computers made musicians obsolete in the studios. Many of Motown's new signings, like Nunn, also controlled their own recordings (writing, producing, arranging) although invariably an in-house producer, even Berry Gordy himself, would oversee a recording session although generally this was unnecessary. The unique Motown sound no longer existed and breaking these new artists was difficult for a company known for a particular sound which was now not sufficiently different from competitors. Even acts whose music was different enjoyed only shortlived success. Motown now kept up with the changing musical trends instead of setting them. Bobby Nunn fell into this category,

Bobby Nunn worked with Rick James prior to releasing his own material. Inevitably, Nunn was originally marketed as a James soundalike which was not strictly true.

although *Private Party* (featuring Tata Vega's Spanish rap on *Hangin' Out At The Mall*, and the album's highlight, a mid-tempoed *Do You Look That Good In The Morning*) was the best during his Motown career. Nunn's product was afforded reasonable marketing and promotion but, possibly due to his Rick James' connection (however loose), Nunn's career ended when his *Fresh* album was scheduled during 1984 but not released. Yet another talent was lost.

With the release of his first solo single, the powerful ballad *Truly* and his self-named album both released in September 1982 (British release for both in November) Lionel Richie confirmed his intention to leave the Commodores. Richie undertook an American media promotional tour, while conducting international interviews on the telephone during rest periods. It was a vast and gruelling itinerary, but imperative to his future solo career. Both album and single raced up the world's charts (US No.1, UK No.6), and were to lay the foundation for one of the most successful careers known in the music business. Richie confirmed that it was a strange feeling recording alone after working with the Commodores. Richie: 'When I thought about cutting something on me, I realized I'd have to have nine to ten songs ready. Over the years I've written eighty to a hundred songs and I still had those so I had to decide which ones were best. It was such a hard task that I asked James Carmichael to help me. He's one of the Commodores really, as writer and producer, so I felt he was the right person, and he really wanted to give it a go.'

Richie insisted on using studio musicians and not the Commodores on his album because he wanted to avoid the selfcontained group situation. Interestingly, the piano

Richie played on the tracks was the same one Carole King used on her *Tapestry* album. Richie: 'I wanted to begin the album with a straight-to-the-gut approach, so I chose *It Serves You Right*. For me R&B lyrics and country lyrics are the most direct in the world. They go straight from one person's mouth to another's ears. *Wandering Stranger* is a song that sums up my inner feelings. It deals with my search and I think the search of a lot of people right now who are wandering around the streets without a clue as to what's going on.' *You Are* was co-written by Richie's wife, Brenda Harvey (who also acted as production assistant); *You Mean More To Me* and *My Love* featured Kenny Rogers on second lead and backing vocals; *Tell Me* featured tennis player Jimmy Conners on vocals. *Truly* was inspired by demand. Richie: 'I was performing in either Philadelphia or New York and there was a little girl in the audience who kept saying *Endless Love* was her favorite song. She came backstage after the show with her mother, father and grandmother. They all said *Endless Love* was their favorite song. The little girl asked me to write a song for her, which resulted in *Truly*.'

With the Commodores' career declining, Richie was naturally criticized for not recording those songs planned for his debut solo album with them. Richie explained: 'Everyone in the group writes songs and a lot of them are used on our albums. If I was lucky I got two of my compositions on an album. There's six guys with a song each, so there wasn't too much room for me anymore. I was never the writer for the Commodores, it was just that some of my songs became singles and were hits, and everyone assumed the role was mine. A lot of the Commodores' non-success is lack of communication and co-ordination. There's also a lot of competition, and getting six guys in a studio wasn't easy when we were all doing different projects.'

You Are was released as the follow-up to *Truly* (US, Dec '82/UK, Jan '83) while *Lionel Richie* was certified platinum and was the first album from a black act to pass the one million sales figure in 1982.

Rick James once more was associated with another of Motown's new signings. This time he persuaded Motown to release musician Bobby Militello's one and only album *Blow. . .Rick James Presents Bobby M* (US, Oct '82/UK, Dec '82). The album is best remembered for the hit single *Let's Stay Together* (US, Nov '82/UK, Jan '83) with Jean Carn on vocal. Militello: 'Once the track was recorded we felt in order to give it the full potential it shouldn't stay an instrumental but should have a vocal. Not a male vocal because that would have been too much like Al Green's version. So we decided to go female to give the song a whole different spectrum. I wanted Jean Carn and as she was signed to Motown everything came together quickly.'

Militello, a versatile horn player, was another native from Buffalo, New York, who graduated from high school to spend three years studying classical and jazz alto saxophone with John Sedaol. After playing with the show group, the Al Fiorello Quartet, and The Showcasemen, Militello formed the fusion band, Moxie, before joining a jazz quintet New Wave featuring Barbara Rankin. In 1975 Militello played baritone saxophone, alto and soprano flutes and piccolo with the Maynard Ferguson Orchestra, and presented jazz clinics in high school and colleges throughout the United States and Canada.

Rick James first met Militello after his performance with his band RPM (the musician's initials) in Buffalo. James: 'He was blowing everybody's minds with his playing, winning at the same time many industry awards. Motown had lost Grover (Washington Jr) so I said to Berry Gordy "how about giving the man a chance?"' Militello: 'Rick stuck his neck out for me, invested a lot of money in me and basically put his reputation at stake.'

Although Militello's album reads *Rick James Presents*, Elektra Records artist Lenny White produced it. Militello: 'I wasn't that sure of myself as it was, after all, my first solo project and I wanted to get it right. Sure I had the ideas and input but I took Lenny's lead. As a performer I had nowhere near the knowledge he had so I took a back seat.'

Let's Stay Together and *Blow. . .Rick James Presents Bobby* M were the first single and album to be released on the Gordy label, introduced in Britain during January 1983. This Gordy subsidiary was launched in America in March 1962 but never previously used in the UK. The British logo carried a hyphen on the yellow and purple label due to copyright problems, and all Gord-y's releases were incorporated into the existing record numbering system.

After numerous attempts to tempt Rick James to visit Britain, Motown/BMG finally succeeded in November 1982. It was a long overdue, five-day promotional trip which turned into a nightmare. As no new James' product was available *Super Freak* was re-promoted as a single, and was the only mistake the company made during his stay. Motown/BMG compiled a comprehensive schedule for James which would have brought him maximum publicity. However, more than half of the media interviews and nightclub appearances were cancelled as James cried off through illness. Those radio interviews James honoured were drastically edited before being broadcast. A media reception held in his honour in Piccadilly's Xenon nightclub was also attended by most of the city's luminaries – Wham!, Mike Nolen (Bucks Fizz), Garth Crooks, Haysi Fantayse – and visiting American artists Shalamar and Sylvester. Rick James appeared before his guests astride a Harley Davidson as the climax to a spectacular light and smoke presentation. Following this James snorted cocaine taken from his cod

Jean Carn's vocals on the Al Green classic Let's Stay Together, recorded by horn player Bobby Militello, turned it into a hit. The single was the first to be released on the British Gord-y label.

Willie Hutch's recording career took off again with In And Out, a song he took to Motown for The Temptations to record.

piece before allowing Sylvester to introduce him on stage. Sylvester: 'What Rick doesn't realize is that despite being a big star in the States, he means nothing in this country. So, OK, he doesn't want to perform in the clubs. But I did it and it worked. Subsequently I got several hit singles. If Rick doesn't do it, he won't make it. It's as simple as that.' James: 'I get paid $75,000 to sing in the States, and if anyone wants me to sing here, they'll have to pay me.'

The last night of James' stay in London was the most crucial regarding personal appearances. Being a Saturday night, potential record buyers filled night clubs. Despite this James cried off his obligations through illness, and yet was photographed partying at Stringfellows in London's West End just hours after his appearances had been cancelled. Blues & Soul reported: 'On meeting Rick, we would underline there was nothing Motown or the independent promotion company, Eyes & Ears (who co-ordinated the personal appearances) could have done to help the situation. Rick doesn't want this market badly enough to put himself out, and for that reason, we'd be very surprised if he ever cracks it. It'll take a massive change in personality and of course a couple of good records!'

Defending his attitude in England, James later complained he was very tired after visiting eight countries in under two weeks: 'London was the last stop and they had me going to clubs all night partying, filling me with drink and throwing women at me all the time. Then, at eight in the morning, there'd be a knock on my hotel room door and they'd expect me to be ready for interviews. The truth is I just couldn't physically handle it.' What the artist failed to realize was that Motown/BMG's staff worked exactly the same hours as he did but declined the offers of alcohol!

Also during November 1982 Motown attempted to cash in on the careers of Thelma Houston and Stephanie Mills. The albums Reachin' All Around and Love Has Lifted Me both failed to dent either singer's current sales.

This year also saw the return on record of Willie Hutch, whose recording career was reactivated with his one-off hit In And Out (US, Aug '82/UK, Nov '82). Prior to this single Hutch worked for Whitfield Records: 'Norman Whitfield is a great producer but I think he made the mistake that a lot of people make – he started wearing too many hats. By that I mean, you have to surround yourself with efficient, talented people, and his problem was he didn't have the right kind of support to help him through. In my case, I was happy with the music we made, but the business thing didn't work out and I couldn't stay any longer'.

Hutch's return to Motown was an accidental move after he had visited Ray Single-

One of Motown's better unknown signings, Gene Van Buren failed to enjoy success with his highly acclaimed What's Your Pleasure album.

ton, then head of the A&R department, with material for The Temptations. Singleton wanted Hutch to record the single In And Out himself, but as Motown were not negotiating big album deals because of the unstable economic situation, Hutch agreed to accept a singles deal. Hutch said at the time of signing: 'In the old days there was always a Marvin Gaye or Diana Ross record out to battle with for maximum exposure but now there aren't that many acts on the roster. And the fact that all of my success had been with Motown contributed a lot towards me going back, and now I'm back I feel good about it.' As In And Out climbed the British charts Hutch was signed to a five year contract, and an album titled after the single, comprising tracks from 1973 and 1977, was prepared for British release in February 1983. Hutch had many further releases but never enjoyed another hit.

Another new signing, Gene Van Buren's single You've Got Me Where I Want You was taken from his debut album What's Your Pleasure, both released during December 1982 in America. Van Buren sang in church choirs before joining the US military for five years. While in the service he decided to become an entertainer. Van Buren: 'I was a green kid looking for a fantasy, hoping that a dream would come true. I became very tired of being a starving artist, experiencing the disappointment of being turned down after an audition, and then having to return to a motel room and call it home dictated a new reality for me.' The singer's determination eventually led to a recording deal when Anna Gordy Gaye was impressed with his work. What's Your Pleasure, although not a top selling album, was an interesting and enjoyable piece of work and was well received by the media. This prompted Motown to record further with Van Buren.

Also in December 1982 ex-Genesis drummer Phil Collins took his version of The Supremes' hit You Can't Hurry Love to the top of the British charts, while Lionel Richie's self-named debut album fought for that spot in America. Billboard magazine's chart registered Men At Work at number one for the sixth consecutive week, The Stray Cats at number two and Lionel Richie at three. Incensed that Richie's record should hold the top spot, Motown bought a full page advertizement in Billboard stating 'Despite what you read in this magazine the Lionel Richie album is now, and has been, the number one best-selling pop album in this country.' It is astonishing that the magazine accepted this advertizement at all, bearing in mind their research department costs approximately $2 million annually to operate. However even if the Billboard chart was not an accurate reflection of the success of Richie's album, this did not prevent Motown and Richie celebrating ending the year at the very top.

THE ECSTASY AND THE AGONY

'Today is twenty-five years of climbing and building and opening doors and breaking old rules. Today is also love songs and guy-and-girl songs, and songs of protest and anger, songs of gentleness and songs of wounds left unattended for far too long . . . Today is the birthplace of forever.'

Marvin Gaye

In 1983 Motown celebrated its 25th Anniversary and throughout the year the company released a deluge of new and compilation albums and held a gala show during March. Smokey Robinson's *Touch The Sky* and the Dazz Band's *On The One* were the first new albums released in January 1983 (UK, Mar '83). Robinson's was a predictable classy collection of self-produced songs, whereas the Dazz Band on their Reggie Andrews' produced album concentrated on hard dance tracks. The exceptions were the doo-wop version of Robinson's *Bad Girl* and the haunting *A Love Song* written by the group in tribute to their fans.

During February 1983 Marshall Arts promoted two British concerts by the Commodores (minus Lionel Richie) at London's Hammersmith Odeon and Motown released the single *Reach High* taken from the group's *All The Great Hits* album. *Record Mirror*'s Paul Sexton reviewed the Commodores show: 'They have a new challenge, that of smoothing over the crack left by Lionel Richie's departure. The hits still have to be played of course, and although Clyde Orange is now officially lead singer, they share it around and even introduce a new voice, Kevin Smith. Smith sounds their best hope for the future, because none of the others are really singers and Orange was painfully hoarse on this second London night. It meant on *Three Times A Lady* and *Still* there was much bottling out of tricky notes, and much tension in the audience to see if he'd actually make it through the song. Most of the Richie songs sounded pretty pale, but new material, *Painted Picture* and *Reach High*, was quite spirited and well received. Perhaps there will be Life After Richie.'

The Commodores, however, confidently predicted that Richie's departure would affect them personally more than professionally. William King: 'He was family and to us he's still a Commodore, and maybe down the line we'll get back and do something, or maybe not. Richie and I were room mates for ten years, we were probably the closest in the group, and I miss him.' Lionel Richie: 'I never wanted to leave the Commodores in the first place. It was stifling in the group, particularly when it got to the point where all of us wanted to write and produce. It was very, very competitive. I'd been a member of that group for fifteen years or so, and to leave wasn't the easiest of things for me to do. I do miss the Commodores but we knew it wasn't going to work, particularly when the friction started.'

Although the group's biggest hits were Richie ballads, King stressed he was not the group's prime writer: 'We felt like we had got in a rut with ballads. We'd had four in a row, and we like to change up. We've never released anything by the rest of the group, ballad-wise, because we've always felt that they had other things to contribute. The songs Clyde sang many people think Richie sang. When you start a ball rolling, you sometimes can't stop it. Many interviewers have assumed that Richie sang all the lead vocals. Clyde sang *Brick House*, *Too Hot Ta Trot* and many uptempo things. We even put out press releases to try and clarify who was singing what.'

Inspired by the success of Phil Collins' cover version of *You Can't Hurry Love*, Motown/BMG released a series of golden oldies under the banner *Motown Gold-The Classic Hit Series*. The twenty titles included The Supremes' original of the Collins' hit, *Three Times A Lady* (the Commodores), *One Day In Your Life* (Michael Jackson), and titles from Marvin Gaye, the Isley Brothers, Four Tops and Mary Wells among others. Jobete/UK was also enjoying success with reggae cover versions of its songs. To this end the company cited recent examples of *Just My Imagination* by Al Campbell (Exclusive Records) and *The Tracks Of My Tears* by Honey Boy and The Blackstones (Empire).

Following the release of the *On The One* album in January, the Dazz Band wound up their European tour with two nights at London's The Venue on 25 and 26 March. NME's Paolo Hewitt wrote: 'Saturday night in their ridiculous Travolta white suits, their outdated Motown dance routines and suffocating funk music, it was impossible to take them seriously. Their main problem is that any interesting riffs, rhythms or melodies they somehow came up with they totally drown in a sea of synthesizers, percussion and guitar, destroying all the subtlety they displayed on *Let It Whip*. That they were nothing more than a routine, mediocre funk band with one great song and an armful of dross to hand out didn't seem to bother most people, let alone the Dazz Band.'

To cash in on Valentine's Day Motown/BMG released the two-year-old track *A New Way To Say I Love You* by Billy Preston and Syreeta, taken from the duo's first album recorded together, *Billy Preston & Syreeta*, released in July 1981 (UK, Sep '81).

To break the monopoly of established Motown acts now pouring out new and old releases, Rick James launched his protegees, the Mary Jane Girls with their debut single *Candy Man* (US, Feb '83/UK, Apr '83). It was a startling release and the accompanying video was full of sexual suggestions and exaggerated sexual movements, and doubtless went a long way in helping the single's sales! *Candy Man* was also afforded extensive advertising which portrayed four scantily-clad, raunchy looking ladies who were an extension of Rick James' own personality and would record repertoire unsuitable for his own use. James knew exactly what the public needed and shrewdly planned the launch of his girls to ensure their successful future career. The Mary Jane Girls (Jo Jo McDuffie, Kimberly 'Maxi' Wuletich, Cheri Wells, Candice 'Candy' Ghant) were chosen by James from two hundred hopeful applicants. McDuffie, the group' lead singer and former James' backing vocalist, was a native of Buffalo, James' hometown. Wuletich lived in Pittsburgh before moving to Los Angeles to audition for the group. Wells, a native of New Jersey, studied dance, drama and voice in New York prior to becoming a Mary Jane Girl, and Ghant, born in Detroit, was a session singer for Smokey Robinson and Johnny Bristol, and composed with Junior Walker and Marilyn McLeod.

Once chosen the girls started to rehearse. Ghant: 'It was weird because Rick took us up to meet Jo Jo, the authentic Mary Jane Girl. I guess she thought we were just some girls who maybe Rick brought up to do some work in the studios. She had no idea we were going to be put together as a unit.' It was James' intention to mould each girl to represent a sexual fantasy by individually outfitting them as a street queen, a tom girl with a whip, a valley girl and a vamp. His plan worked as Motown's publicity machine capitalized on the quartet's good looks and image to lay the foundation for their debut album *Mary Jane Girls* (US, Apr '83/UK, May '83). Written and produced by Rick James it was a musical landmark, a superb release crammed with excitement although, vocals apart, it could easily have been their creator's own album. The girls were compared to Vanity 6, a female group formed by James' musical rival, Prince, and

In 1983 Rick James introduced his Mary Jane Girls to the world. The quartet were an extension of his own personality and were chosen from 200 applicants.

although unwarranted this comparison enraged James who claimed Prince had stolen his Mary Jane concept. James: 'That just fueled my enthusiasm for the Mary Jane Girls' album.'

Although *Candy Man* was well received by the media and public, the *Mary Jane Girls* album was still to offer its best - the monster hit *All Night Long* (US, Jun '83/UK, Jun '83). As the single climbed the British charts, the quartet visited London and delighted the public with their outrageous stage act and warm off-stage manner. Their career had all the indications of international success for as long as Rick James could keep his fantasies alive.

The highlight of this 25th Anniversary year was the five hour spectacular *Motown 25: Yesterday, Today, Forever* staged at Los Angeles' Pasadena Civic Auditorium on 25 March 1983, with the proceeds from this gala event donated to the National Association of Sickle Cell Disease. Suzanne de Passe co-ordinated the evening's spectacular entertainment, Gil Askey was the musical director and Lester Wilson the choreographer. Past and present Motown acts flocked to honour Berry Gordy's achievement, and as Smokey Robinson announced early on in the show 'Once a Motowner, always a Motowner'. Robinson also shared the master of ceremonies duties with comedian Richard Pryor, as well as performing and reminiscing over Motown's musical history. Yes indeed, the artists returned with style, irrespective of hit record status, to re-live Motown's memories, even though many were allocated only a few minutes stage time to do so.

The Gala's highlights were released on video and included the opening moment which featured a film of the front of 'Hitsville USA' and glimpsed The Miracles and The Supremes in the studio before Robinson was reunited with three of the Miracles - Pete Moore, Bobby Rogers and his wife Claudette – on stage to perform (Ronnie White was absent from the line-up). Dick Clark then appeared on stage to demonstrate, with visuals, Motown's musical revolution and how its music influenced white artists and their successes. Stevie Wonder followed with his *I Wish* before an emotional tribute 'to all of you who have made it possible for a man from a black culture to have a dream fulfilled. The moments of magic that I've experienced because of you, the artists, management and staff of Motown, encouraged me to create music.' Wonder closed his performance with *My Cherie Amour* and *You Are The Sunshine Of My Life* to a thunderous reception. Robinson returned to show further Sixties film clips of The Temptations, Martha and the Vandellas, The Miracles, The Marvelettes and the Four Tops performing their classic dance routines that made them and other Motown acts visually exciting. Robinson then welcomed the Four Tops and The Temptations (minus Eddie Kendricks but including Glenn Leonard) on stage to trade hits during a performance that saw the groups battling with vocals and dance routines. (A single of their medley performance was released in June 1983 (UK, Oct '83) when even the novelty aspect of the release failed to chart it.)

In contrast Marvin Gaye was sophisticated, cool and reflective, sitting alone at the piano to recall the roots of black music. Gaye: 'Maybe today is the result of yesterday spent in wooden churches, singing the praises of our Maker in joyous harmony and love. Part of it has to be the songs we sang, working under the blazing sun, to help pass the hard times. Yesterday was also Bessie Smith, New Orleans and gospel choirs, folk songs, Bojangles. Yesterday was the birthplace of today. Today is twenty-five years of climbing and building, and opening doors and breaking old rules. Today is also love songs, and guy and-girl songs, and songs of protest and anger, songs of gentleness and songs of wounds left unattended for far too long, songs to march to, to fly to, to make love to. It's music pure and simple and soulful, and if you insist, full of promise and determination, unity and humanity, today is the birthplace of forever.' This moving oration climaxed with *What's Going On*.

The Gala returned to its glitzy showbusiness theme with guest DJs who introduced at high speed hits by Martha Reeves (*Heatwave*), Mary Wells (*My Guy*) and Junior Walker (*Shotgun*) via thirty second cameo appearances by all three acts. A DJ then welcomed the Commodores who, minus Richie, performed a thirty second version of *Brick House*. Lionel Richie was in Japan so was seen on film in a recording studio singing *You Mean More To Me* to little six-year-old Lanette Butler (who was featured in the sickle cell advertising campaign).

Then it was time for The Jacksons – Michael, Jermaine, Randy, Tito, Jackie and Marlon! Their entrance was heralded by a sequence of videos which included an excerpt from their Motown audition tape in 1968 and the audience response was deafening. The Jacksons performed shortened versions of *I Want You Back*, *The Love You Save* and *I'll Be There*, all highly-charged, emotional and exciting. Jermaine Jackson said after the show: 'I would have performed on the show with or without them, and when I asked could I join them they thought it was a great idea to do a show together. We had a couple of short rehearsals but the idea was to keep the performance very free and spontaneous. I loved it because it was very emotional for me, the whole evening was emotional for us all. It really felt like being home again.' Michael's electrifying solo of *Billie Jean* was the only song of the Gala to be lip-synced and was possibly the evening's highpoint. After Jackson's performance Fred

Astaire told him he enjoyed the performance so much that he had taped it for further viewing.

Berry Gordy's younger generation of current acts were represented by DeBarge singing *All This Love* and High Inergy's *He's A Pretender*. Both acts exuded vitality and a youthful energy, as they confidently impressed the audience with a fastpaced performance. Richard Pryor returned to lightheartedly narrate the making of Motown from Berry Gordy's boxing and car assembly line experiences to company boss. The inclusion of Britain's Adam Ant and his version of The Supremes' *Where Did Our Love Go* was embarrassing by comparison. Ant, now an established artist in America, was added as a white attraction for the pending television screening of the Gala. Half-way through his song Ant was visibly shocked when Diana Ross, for no apparent reason, appeared on stage for an unrehearsed dance routine, which did nothing to salvage Ant's contribution. Ant: 'Being on the show was like Hollywood with people like Jack Nicholson in the front row. I thought I was doing all right when suddenly everybody cheered. I thought, great, I've cracked it. I turned round and ten yards away was Diana Ross dancing. I didn't know she was coming on. I go over to her, dance a bit and as I turn round, she's gone. What can you do to follow that?'

Following this, film clips of The Supremes led the way for Ross to return to the stage to sing a moderate version of *Ain't No Mountain High Enough*. Once that finished, she called for Mary Wilson and Cindy Birdsong to join her on stage. It took Wilson at least sixty seconds to respond to the request; she either missed her cue or failed to hear the onstage instruction. Wilson reported in her autobiography that when she and Birdsong arrived on stage, Ross stopped singing. Wilson presumed she had forgotten the lyrics and took over lead. Ross responded by introducing the two once again and moved away from them to the front of the stage. When Wilson and Birdsong followed her, Ross pushed Wilson away. The trio paid the shortest of tributes to The Supremes' memory with two verses of *Someday We'll Be Together*. It was a shambles. Robinson hastily returned to the stage to retrieve the Gala's finale featuring all the participating acts singing *Reach Out And Touch (Somebody's Hand)* although the original ending for the Gala was The Supremes performing three songs. However, Robinson was powerless to interfere with Ross' lead. During the finale Mary Wilson extended an invitation to Berry Gordy to leave the audience to join them on stage. This seemed to aggravate Diana Ross, who snatched Wilson's microphone to proffer the invitation herself, saying 'Berry has always felt he's never been appreciated. But it's not about the people who leave Motown, it's about the people who come back. And tonight

we all came back.' In spite of the slip-ups the Gala was a rare treat, and certainly represented the true magic of Motown's twenty-five years of music:

After the show, Diana Ross glowed: 'It was amazing. There were some people there I hadn't seen in thirteen years. Berry Gordy is like a daddy to everybody who was there, and it was just real warm thoughts there. Like Michael and Stevie, they were all backstage with me, and seeing Billy Dee Williams after I hadn't seen him for a long time. . . and even Suzanne de Passe was crying backstage. It was just wonderful. I know that the people in the audience saw a glorious special but they didn't really see everything.' Berry Gordy too was delighted with the Gala: 'It means a great deal, the culmination of twenty-five years of success that has been even greater than we realized. You don't realize all these accomplishments because you are so busy moving forward. It's mind-boggling all that happened. We've developed and discovered every artist we've had. We never bought an artist who was already at the top. We took the kids off the street. If they were good enough we'd advance them the money and work with them.'

The Gala's more unsavoury incidents were edited out before its American television transmission in May 1983 and to ensure the show's running time was under two hours several artists were omitted, like Ashford & Simpson, Syreeta, Charlene and other artist duets. The televized show was watched by fifty million Americans and was nominated for nine Emmy Awards, but was awarded only one for Outstanding Variety Music Show. One section which was edited out included a tri-

bute to Motown's songwriters and staff. The composers, including Harvey Fuqua, Mickey Stevenson, Ron Miller, Lamont Dozier and Norman Whitfield, were filmed sitting around a piano singing and reminiscing. As the film closed, they walked onstage to a thunderous welcome. Motown's staff tribute saw secretaries and executives singing the Smokey Robinson-penned company song, publicly printed for the very first time:

'Oh, we have a very swinging company working hard from day to day,
Nowhere will you find more unity than at Hitsville USA.
Our main purpose is to please the world with songs the DJs are glad to play
Our employees are all the best here at Hitsville USA.
Our employees must be neat and clean and really have something on the ball
Honesty is our only policy, we're all for one and one for all.
We have a very swinging company working hard from day to day,
Nowhere will you find more unity than at Hitsville USA, I said Hitsville, than at Hitsville USA.'

The song has never been recorded and its Gala exposure was probably the only time it has been heard outside Motown's offices.

After two years of lengthy negotiations with the participating non-Motown artists a video of the televized Gala was made commercially available in 1985.

After the Gala, The Temptations and the Four Tops toured together. Known as the T'n'T shows, the tour took the acts to Australia, New Zealand, Hawaii and across America, including sell-out dates on Broadway. The idea for the T'n'T tour was actually born prior to the Gala, as Four Tops' Duke Fakir explained: 'A year before we did the 25th show, we had talked with several Motown acts about taking a show on the road. A lot of them sounded excited, but never came back to us so the idea got shelved until we got together for the anniversary show, and that's what prompted The Temptations and us to get together and do it for ourselves. And it's been so successful and rewarding.'

In April 1983 *Music Week* reported that Motown had added to the problems confronting independent distributors by defecting from the Pickwick organization in California: 'Motown is setting up its own distribution branch in Los Angeles, and MS Distributors of Chicago has taken over Motown for the Atlanta/South-Eastern territory from Pickwick. According to Motown president Jay Lasker, the decision to leave Pickwick stems from the latter's change in discount policy which has cut the number of days a retailer has in which to pay his bills. Previously, a 5 per cent discount was allowed for bills paid within sixty days, but that period has been halved by Pickwick which, Lasker says, has limited orders of Motown product in Pickwick-covered locations as a consequence.' Within three months of this announcement, Motown closed down its Los Angeles branch to become the last major label to be independently distributed in America, and switched to MCA branch distribution. *Music Week* further reported: 'The announcement comes on the heels of the intended consolidation of Warner and Polygram, and removes yet another level of competition – the indie (independent) network – from significant participation in the industry. Given the US Justice Department's attention to the recent Arista switch to RCA distribution, it is likely that both the Warner and the MCA/Motown deals will undergo close scrutiny before gaining approval. With the recent removal of Arista from the independent ranks, the major indie operator Pickwick shuttered its distribution division. Like several other majors, Pickwick is shifting more toward home video and home computer and game product lines.'

With MCA distributing Motown's product, Motown's cashflow would improve. Instead of the possible irregular payment system used by other independents, Motown could guarantee MCA prompt payments. With an improved cashflow system Motown would have more money to invest either in artists or films. The latter was still an important area for Berry Gordy, and one he wanted to develop further, in view of his past successes, including the *Lady Sings The Blues* film and the *Motown 25* television special. MCA's distribution would also be more efficient and effective in the market place, thus more sales could be generated with new releases and catalogue items. Motown's association with MCA fuelled rumours of a record company take over, although such a move was strenuously denied at the time.

In this 25th Anniversary year Berry Gordy reminisced over the early years of his company: 'We had a lot of rules and regulations which you could never have today. Some people would accuse us of being authoritarian. That's not true, but when you've got people in your care, especially when they're coming in under age, it is your responsibility to develop them as human beings, because there's nothing worse than having a person become a star and not grow mentally. The first they're going to do is get into all sorts of problems, drugs and so on. Sometimes you can't stop that, but you can do what your conscience and morality tells you, you should do.' In 1983 Gordy oversaw much of his company's activities from his Bel Air mansion. He was, however, constantly aware of Motown's daily running, new artists signed and studio uses. He also approved his company's musical changes while retaining personal responsibility for his newer acts. Gordy: 'When we get an artist young I still take an authoritarian approach, because their mothers and fathers are handing them over and I take a parent's responsibility. I won't let them do songs I think are degrading, songs that are filth, or drug songs. When they become stars and over twenty-one, I have less control. I let them express themselves even if it costs us a little more sometimes.'

Berry Gordy must have been delighted with his protégé Michael Jackson, who was the first artist in the Eighties to have two singles (lifted from his *Thriller* album) in the top five of the American national charts simultaneously. Jackson achieved this feat with the number one single *Billie Jean* and *Beat It* which entered the top five. Interestingly, the last artist to have enjoyed two singles in the American top five was Donna Summer during 1979 with *Hot Stuff* and *Bad Girls* in July, and *Dim All The Lights* and *No More Tears* in November. By the end of 1983 Jackson would break other industry sales records and receive many accolades for his album *Thriller*.

In March 1983 Motown/BMG marketed 'Flip Hits', a series of ten maxi-singles available only in double-play cassettes. Featured artists on these British four-track tapes included Stevie Wonder, Diana Ross, the Four Tops and Martha Reeves and the Vandellas. A month later (UK, May 1983) Syreeta released *The Spell* album, produced by Jermaine Jackson. A proportion of the tracks were three years old as Syreeta had abandoned composing due to the non-appreciation of her work by the company. *The Spell* represented a new musical identity, enhanced by Jackson's input. It took four months to finish the eight

When the Motown 25 Gala *was screened on television and released on video, Ashford & Simpson were among several artists whose performances were edited out.*

Jermaine Jackson attempted to push Syreeta back into the limelight by producing her The Spell *album. The collaboration resulted in a new musical identity for Syreeta which was not supported by the mainstream record buyers.*

Although their album was not British released Kagney & the Dirty Rats *created a buzz on the imports charts. Their eponymous album featured Junior Walker, The Temptations and Smokey Robinson among others.*

Finis Henderson worked with Richard Pryor before signing to Motown to release his debut album Finis *in 1983.*

tracks, highlights of which were the classy ballad *The Other Me*, *To Know*, written by The Corporation, and her duet with Jackson, *Once Love Touches Your Life*.

New signings Kagny & the Dirty Rats (Steven St James, lead vocals; Cliff Liles, bass/vocals; Mark Torien, guitars/vocals; Jerry Blaze, drums) recruited The Temptations, Smokey Robinson, Norman Whitfield, Merry Clayton and Junior Walker for their only self-named album in March 1983. *At 15* was the first single from that album released the same month (there was no British release for either). In 1984 a solo Kagny album *Mind Control* was scheduled but canned.

Following the March 1983 (UK, April '83) release of Lionel Richie's *My Love* single, the first 30,000 of which were British released in a wrap-around colour poster and the third single to be taken from his debut album *Lionel Richie*, he won a grand prize at the Tokyo Music Festival which he shared with Joe Cocker and Jennifer Warnes for their single *Up Where We Belong*. On this first solo tour of Japan, he told the Festival's audience that his share of the award would go towards establishing a Japanese music scholarship fund: 'I feel proud to be able to put this money back into the young talent of Japan. If I hadn't had the help and the breaks early in my career I would never be in a position to do this.'

One of 1983's better signings, Finis Henderson, released his debut album *Finis* (US, Apr '83/UK, Jul '83) featuring the ballads *Crush on You* and *Skip To My Lou* the first single in April (UK, Jul '83). Born in Chicago, Finis Henderson was raised in show business: his father was a song-and-dance man and later became vice-president of Sammy Davis Enterprises. As a teenager Henderson joined The Dynamic 4 group and worked with the Chicago Community Music Foundation before teaming up with Weapons Of Peace in 1970 for eight years. After two small hits on Playboy Records the group disbanded, and Henderson moved to California to become a comedian. He was working at Hollywood's Comedy Store when he was spotted by Richard Pryor, then preparing material for his *Live On Sunset* movie. This led to Henderson supporting Pryor on tour, and during one of the performances Henderson was spotted by Suzanne de Passe. At the time he was working with Al McKay on Prophesy, a group project, but when a recording deal failed to materialize, Henderson joined Motown as a soloist. Henderson: 'I had better offers than the one I accepted at Motown, but then which other company has a movie division. I want to progress further than just being a recording artist.' Unfortunately, neither his recording nor acting career reached reality at Motown.

Junior Walker returned to Motown in May 1983 after guesting on the *Kagny & the Dirty Rats* album. Walker had left Motown because he felt his career could progress no further

and that signing with a new company would be beneficial. Walker: 'It didn't quite work out that way, and although I was always very busy on the road, the records I cut for Whitfield Records never really got to first base. The break helped me put things into perspective.' The saxophonist's new Motown liaison was shortlived as only one album *Blow The House Down* was released (US, Aug '83/UK, Oct '83). Happily, the album represented Walker's old style. *Sex Pot* was a cross between *Road Runner* and *Shotgun*, while *Closer Than Close* was in the *What Does It Take (To Win Your Love)* mould. The album failed as did its first single, *Blow The House Down* (US, Jul '83/UK, Oct '83). Junior's group, the All Stars, were now listed as Autry De Walt Jr (Walker's son), R.C. Ratcliff, Delby Littlejohn and Darly Buchanon.

The next newcomer of 1983 was more successful albeit in Britain. Michael Lovesmith, already an established and accomplished writer/producer had all the potential to become a top league artist with his debut album *I Can Make It Happen* released in June 1983 (UK, Sept '83). His 'workaholic' career began as a musician in the late Sixties with the Isley Brothers. From this association Lovesmith moved to Stax Records before moving to Holland, Dozier and Holland's Invictus Records in the Seventies. Lovesmith: 'I signed a recording deal with them with my brothers. We were known as The Smith Connection. I also produced with the Hollands for groups like The Honeycone. I was part of the production team of Holland, Dozier and Holland Productions which was a collective name for many. As part of this team I was trained to do many things, but when Invictus took a dive they lost a lot of their acts.'

H-D-H planned to leave Detroit to work in California with other companies, including Motown. Lamont Dozier had, by this time, left the company so Lovesmith was asked to replace him. The first group the trio worked with was the Jackson 5. Lovesmith: 'Michael and Jermaine were obsessed with music, whereas the others were hip but not all consuming.' This was the start of Lovesmith's ten year association with Motown as a writer/producer/singer. His time was spent in the studios turning other acts into stars. Lovesmith: 'I was committed to my career in music and dreamt of knowing everyone who was famous and now I was in the position of fulfilling that dream with Diana Ross, The Temptations and of course the Jackson 5. Others like me had the opportunity but not the commitment. I worked day and night to the point of exhaustion to make my mark.'

While working in the studios with Michael Jackson, Lovesmith made that mark when Berry Gordy and Suzanne de Passe met him for the first time: 'They had no idea that I was this teenager who was conducting an orchestra, writing the music, tutoring the engineer and so on. So Berry Gordy came to the studio and stood in the corner. I was getting irritated by him and the other people there, and was about to ask them to leave when Berry said how fantastic I was. However, I owe my signing to Suzanne de Passe and Jermaine Jackson.' The latter befriended him and together they worked on the *My Name Is Jermaine* album, before Jackson urged him to go solo.

When computers replaced musicians in the studio, Lovesmith, like many contemporary artists, became an operator and was able to programme all the aspects of a song. Lovesmith: 'Writing takes one thousandth of the time it used to because I write straight on to the computer and everything is played back to me. I programme the drum machine for instance, and all the other instruments are added on the way. The song is finished in an hour.' *Baby I Will* was his first single lifted from the *I Can Make It Happen* album (US, Jun '83/UK, Aug '83). Lovesmith sounded remarkably like Marvin Gaye so he returned to the studio to change the sound, not wanting to be trapped in the soundalike market.

During mid-1983 Stevie Wonder turned comedian and appeared on American television in *Saturday Night Live*, the comedy programme that had pushed Eddie Murphy and Dan Akroyd, among others, into stardom. Wonder, complete with British accent, portrayed Rodney Rhythm, a rock music critic, and assisted by Murphy and other show regulars, skitted through a burlesque imitation of television commercials, the sordid side of music business management and revealed his pleasure in artists who had abandoned songs of social comment to concentrate on sex (i.e. Marvin Gaye). Wonder's sharp wit, however, offended some viewers, but as he told author John Swenson: 'My feeling was that the whole show is such an obvious joke in the first place, that if you're going to participate, you have to be that. And it was fun, I'd like to do it again.'

Eddie Murphy, too, upset viewers during a *Saturday Night Live* appearance with his impersonation of Wonder! In reply to the complaints Murphy included in his act the following: 'Stevie 'n I are in the car and I just say "shut the f*** up, Stevie. You're a genius 'n all that s*** 'n we hang out 'n it's nice 'n all that

s*** but I don't appreciate all the flak. Personally, you know how I feel about the piano 'n the singing. I ain't that impressed. You wanna impress me? Take the wheel for a while!"' (*Time Out*)

The first single to be released on Stevie Wonder's Wondirection label was Gary Byrd & The GB Experience's rap *(You Wear) The Crown* in June 1983 on twelve inch (UK, Jul '83 on twelve inch). The 10 minute 56 second track, marketed and distributed by Motown, was also available in Britain on chrome cassette (aptly called 'the chrome dioxide blaster'). Teena Marie, Syreeta and gospel singer Andre Crouch were featured backing vocalists while Wonder played piano, drums, synthesizers, tambourines and wood blocks.

A native of Buffalo, Byrd, born in March 1949, real name Gary De Witt, describes himself as a 'communicator' and not an 'entertainer', who as a youngster became a public speaker at high school.

At 16 years old, in 1966, he began a three year spell on Buffalo's local radio stations. A year later he had his own show on WUFO Radio and was exposed to rapping DJs who compiled poems to a record's musical beat. As there were no Buffalo rappers Byrd collected tapes of Baltimore's Maurice 'Hotrod' Hulbert and New York's Jocko Henderson to formulate his own style while playing funk, soul and gospel music. With practice Byrd became a successful rapper and moved to New York to join WWRL, a black orientated station where his style of introducing miniraps over record introductions became immensely popular with listeners. In time he expanded his spoken repertoire with social and political verse. Byrd: 'I first met up with Stevie Wonder in Buffalo. I know he made an impression on me and I guess I made some kind of impression on him because the friendship lasted.'

The master of rap Gary Byrd worked with Stevie Wonder to record (You Wear) The Crown which became England's second top selling 12-inch single.

Stevie Wonder put his music second to host the American TV comedy programme Saturday Night Live. His sharp wit inadvertently offended some viewers as did Eddie Murphy's follow-up sketch!

During 1971 Byrd recorded his first rap record *Every Brother Ain't A Brother* on the Real Thing label, before recording the *Presenting Gary Byrd Experience* album for RCA. In 1974 he released *Soul Travellin'*, the same year as he wrote Millie Jackson's *I Cry* track for her *Hurt So Bad* album. Three years later Byrd re-met Wonder to write the lyrics for two songs *Village Ghetto Land* and *Black Man* for his pending *Songs In The Key Of Life* album. Byrd: 'Stevie had always taken an interest in my work and had kept in touch since that first meeting. He phoned me one day and told me about this new project he was working on and asked if I was interested in writing some lyrics. He played me *Ghetto Land* and explained what he wanted. He like what I did and the same thing happened with *Black Man*.'

Byrd began writing *(You Wear) The Crown* in 1979 and in 1981 Wonder heard his completed lyrics and insisted he write the music. Byrd: 'I played it to Stevie over the phone and he told me to fly to Los Angeles to record it with him. Stevie laid down the backing track quickly and I did the vocals and the company were excited about releasing it. I couldn't believe Stevie was so satisfied because all his songs go through a long, evolutionary process.' Byrd's rapping lyrics ran through two successive dimensions: his interest in African history and knowledge gained from motivational literature. Byrd: 'My main mission is to expand people's consciousness because what I dislike most is the world's ignorance. Not ignorant people necessarily, but what ignorance does to people. So, if there's a way through art to help eliminate that, then that's what I intend to do.'

(You Wear) The Crown took Britain by storm and raced to number six in the charts in July 1983: an incredible achievement for a twelve inch single. Despite plans to record a follow-up, this was Byrd's only Wondirection release, however as a DJ he has gone from strength to strength.

Motown International, headed by vice-president Peter Prince and based in London, was eight years old in 1983. This division is responsible for record markets outside North America, Europe being Motown's second biggest market and one that is monitored constantly. Prince: 'Motown is still the biggest independent in the United States. In addition to being our springboard to the world, the UK charts are equally important to international territories as a launching pad for breaking our records. For the past eight years the policy has worked well for Motown and we have a unique operation that is of benefit to our licencees and of course to Motown itself.'

During August 1983 Motown attempted to terminate agreements with three of its American distributors, Associated Distributors, Big State and Schwartz Brothers, to switch to MCA. Schwartz charged Motown with fraudulent conduct and conspiracy and breach of oral contract and reputedly demanded $5 million in damages. Their suit claimed 'Motown was induced by MCA to cut off its distributors without reasonable advance notice'. Motown and Schwartz settled out of court for an undisclosed payment. A Phoenix judge ruled against Associated Distributors, while Big State awaited formal filings from Motown and MCA. Motown also bought the rights to the Hi Records catalogue, which included Al Green's product, for the regions North America and Canada only.

After months in the recording studio Lionel Richie released a taster from his second album *Can't Slow Down* (originally titled *Positive Space*) with the single *All Night Long (All Night)*. Released in August 1983 (UK, Sep '83) it was a different song from the Mary Jane Girls' *All Night Long* and shot to the top of the American charts. Indeed that success was repeated in eighteen countries except Britain where it peaked at number two. The single also raced into the British dance chart at number four. Record stores in Britain tried unsuccessfully to order the twelve inch version of the single because Motown/BMG abided by Motown/USA's instruction not to release an extended version as copies would flood the American market disrupting the progress of the American seven inch single. When the single topped the British dance charts copies of the American twelve inch became available in specialist shops. The American twelve inch differed from the late arrival of its British equivalent in that it featured the re-mixed album version of the song, with the instrumental on the B-side, whereas the British single featured the seven inch version. Had the British twelve inch single been available earlier, Richie could well have enjoyed a UK number one.

Richie, recently nicknamed the black Barry Manilow because of his ballads, broke away from the middle-of-the-road market with this funky, calypso-flavoured single. Part of the song's verse included the phrase 'Tom bo li de say de moi ya, yeah, jambo jumbo' which Richie identified as one of reggae star Bob Marley's chants, which had no real meaning. The single's credits include Dr Lloyd Byron Greig as dialect coach. Richie: 'He's really a gynaecologist from Los Angeles. He would come by and visit us and I started listening to his accent. We got talking a lot, and when I was in the studios working on the single, I kept phoning him up, saying talk to me because I wanted to imitate him.'

All Night Long (All Night) was supported by a powerful dance video produced by Mike Nesmith, former member of The Monkees, and directed by Bob Rafelson who was also connected with the Sixties quartet. Richie was frightened by the single's success, as he explained: 'It's one thing to have a hit in America and Britain but for the record to take off all over the world, well, that's something very hard for me to believe. I suppose you consider it as competing against *Three Times A Lady* and that was frightening enough for us as it was.'

When *All Night Long (All Night)* topped the American charts Richie had secured six number one singles in six years. His first was *Three Times A Lady* with the Commodores during 1978, and *Still* a year later. In 1980 Kenny Rogers' *Lady* reached the top, while Richie's duet with Diana Ross, *Endless Love* (1981), and his solo single *Truly* followed (1982). Interestingly, only John Lennon, Paul McCartney and Barry Gibb have matched this achievement.

Can't Slow Down, produced by Richie and James Anthony Carmichael (US/UK, Oct '83), spawned further hit singles, one being *Running With The Night* (1983), which was supported by a promotional video directed by Bob Giraldi, responsible for Michael Jackson's *Beat It* video, among others. Richie wrote the song with Cynthia Weil, whose work with her husband, Barry Mann, includes *Walking In The Rain*, *We've Gotta Get Out Of This Place*, *Looking Through The Eyes Of Love* and *You've Lost That Loving Feeling* with Phil Spector. Richie's following singles, *Hello*, *Stuck On You* and *Penny Lover* followed in 1984. Producer/writer Norman Whitfield could be seen as a nightclub bouncer on the video for *Penny Lover*. All three songs were typical Richie ballads, although the finest was *Hello* which became an American, British and European number one. *Can't Slow Down* was conceived to appeal to both black music buyers and, via the ballads, to the middle-of-the-road audience. The album sold in excess of four million copies during the first ten weeks of its release. His first album took six months to accumulate the same total. *Can't Slow Down* went on to sell in excess of ten million copies in America alone, 15 million worldwide, tying with Bruce Springsteen's *Born In The USA* which is one of the strongest selling albums in the history of the charts.

Richie admitted he faced a musical dilemma with *Can't Slow Down* because as much as he yearned to break free from the ballads, he knew to do so would lose him at least four million fans. Richie: 'And if *All Night Long* hadn't been a hit and I dedicated the whole album to that sound I'm in trouble because that's it until the next time I go into the studios. Recording up-tempo tracks is my way of lightening up things now and again. I don't want to fall into the trap of giving people what they expect, or have come to expect from me. I was also afraid of falling into the middle-of-the-road market with slow songs because that's not what I want to do right now.' All the tracks were written specifically for the project and not, as previously suggested in the media, from his vast back catalogue: 'I was looking for more up-tempo songs this time that wouldn't sound like everybody else's. Michael Jackson seems to have that market

sewn up for the next few years or so, and I wanted to create my own unique sound. I prefer to write new songs for new projects, although I'm sure I must have some good songs in store by now that I've forgotten about.'

Richie followed Michael Jackson's precedent by simultaneously securing the number one position in the American pop and black album and singles charts with the album *Can't Slow Down* and the single *All Night Long (All Night)*. Jackson's achievement was with the *Thriller* album and the *Billie Jean* single.

Following the album's release Richie embarked upon an American tour. In spite of his vinyl success and having The Pointer Sisters as support act, the dates were not sold out. During his performance Richie sang *Endless Love*, his duet with Diana Ross. Richie: 'Diana comes out of the darkness and you'd think it was the Oscar ceremony all over again. For a minute the audience really think she's there.' Ross actually appears life-size on a video screen and the stage lighting gives a three dimensional illusion. At the song's close Richie, much to his audiences' amazement, holds Ross' hand! (Diana Ross was not available for the tour because it was said she considered the ticket prices too low ($7.50) for her appearance. Whether this was true or not is conjecture; a more likely reason for her absence was due to her own touring commitments.) Richie was surprised to see a change in his audiences: 'It's amazing. There's eight year olds, their mums and dads, grandmas, granddads, there's kids with red hair and orange hair, guys dressed in leather and chains, Rastafarians, all colours. It's more like

Lionel Richie, nicknamed the black Barry Manilow, released his second solo album Can't Slow Down which sold in excess of four million copies during the first ten weeks of its release.

the United Nations than the United States, but I like it that way. I never know who's going to sing the songs – me or them. I never get to finish a song. People are crying, some are fainting, screaming and shouting. It's like I'm just the cheer leader. When we sing *All Night Long*, the stage is crowded because everyone gets up there with me.'

Michael Jackson attended Richie's Los Angeles performance. To avoid being recognized he wore an afro wig and an oversized baseball jacket, and laughed as he watched Richie doing a *Billie Jean* rap before telling his audience how he had taught Jackson to dance! Richie donated the proceeds from his New York show to various local arts projects, including $10,000 to a junior high school where pupils were stunned when he delivered the cheque personally prior to singing a selection of his material on the school piano. In November 1983 Richie narrowly escaped death when the plane in which he was travelling crashed in Arizona. Richie and his entourage were travelling to Tucson for a concert date when the plane's wheels collapsed, the tail section was damaged and the runway was so chewed up that it was closed for two hours. Initial media reports claimed Richie had died in the crash. Later, the relieved ex-Commodore quipped that he was 'ten times more famous since being assumed dead!'

The Motor City Crew, under the guidance of writer/producer Benny Medina, attempted to push Motown into the rap 'n' scratch market with *Let's Break* in August 1983 (UK, Nov '83, where the B-side of the US twelve-inch, *Scratch Break* (*Glove Style*), was the UK A-side. Released on twelve inch only). Medina decided to form the studio ensemble after scouting Los Angeles nightspots to discover punters' musical preferences.

He then walked the streets to watch the growing numbers of break dancers and became obsessed with the dance movement. The single found a niche in the specialist market, which gradually became more popular due to acts like the Sugarhill Gang.

In August 1983 Smokey Robinson's *Blame It On Love & All The Great Hits* was released (UK, Oct '83), containing four new songs, *Blame It On Love*, his duet with High Inergy's Barbara Mitchell, *Just A Touch Away*, *Don't Play Another Love Song* and *Just Like You*, and six tested tracks. Rick James released *Cold Blooded* (UK, Sept '83), an exceptional album containing a duet with Robinson, *Ebony Eyes*. This was later released as a single in November (UK, Jan '84) credited to Rick James and Friend. Two other outstanding album tracks were P.I.M.P. The S.K.I.M.P., based on a true story of a prostitute friend who died on a trick, and 1-2-3, *You, Her and Me*, a composition about a love triangle. James promoted the new work with The Cold Blooded Unity American tour with the Mary Jane Girls and the Stone City Band. The album's title track, influenced by Prince, was

lifted as a single in July 1983 (UK, Aug '83). Both album and single topped the American soul charts but no matter what James released in Britain, nothing worked. Nightclubs unreservedly supported his material but that support did not turn floor fillers into national chart positions. James' instantly recognizable style was of a high commercial standard, yet without valuable British radio exposure his work might as well have remained unreleased. There seemed to be no answer, but Motown/BMG continued to release his product to ward off American import sales and to satisfy his cult British following. This situation contributed to James' decision not to tour Britain despite serious requests from promoters who were convinced the colourful singer would attract full houses.

Michael Jackson topped the forty-five million mark for overall CBS/Epic record sales while brother Jermaine left Motown in August 1983 to sign with Arista Records. The deal, which covered all world territories, marked the departure from Motown of the last Jackson brother. This move crushed rumours of The Jacksons returning to Gordy's company, but Jermaine's departure was said to have had the approval of his family. Jackson decided to leave his father-in-law's company because he had reached the stage where he wanted to be on his own. Jackson discussed his plans with Gordy before making his final decision, which resulted in Gordy releasing him from his recording contract which still required him to record at least two more albums. Jackson was unhappy with someone in Motown's operation, so he turned to his long-standing friend Clive Davis, who owned Arista Records. Jackson: 'Arista is the place where I can communicate with a person directly, rather than having to go through a committee. Also, being with Clive, who's a record person, makes a lot of difference. We can talk together about the structure of songs, lyrics and the recording of good, commercial material.' Jackson's first Arista single *Sweetest Sweetest* was backed by his duet with brother Michael *Tell Me I'm Not Dreaming* lifted from Jermaine's *Dynamite* album. Michael consented to the duet on the understanding the song would never be released as an A-sided single. A further album track *Escape From The Planet Of The Ant Men* featured all the Jackson brothers.

The Commodores, celebrating their 15th anniversary in the music business, visited Britain again in September 1983 as part of another European tour. Gary Byrd was support act and showed clips from *Motown 25* accompanied by two robotic dancers. Motown/BMG released the Commodores 13 album, their first without Lionel Richie, to coincide with the visit. Unlike the group's previous releases, producer James Anthony Carmichael was not involved. He had been working on Richie's second solo album. Richie: 'The Commodores made the decision that they wanted to produce themselves. There's five producers in the group, so it wasn't James' decision. I reckoned that if you find something that's worked for eight or more years on hit records, why change it. So James works with me now. I don't know why the group made the decision they did. It seems so strange. I like 13 but they need an identity, a focal point, they need a face. When I was with them, I was the lead singer and mine was the face of the group, like Mick Jagger and the Stones, or Michael Jackson and the Jacksons. I think Clyde should be that face for them. He's a prominent singer and seems to be the strongest. The album as a whole is, I think, geared towards the US. It's not a set for outside, although I do think it's a very good beginning for them.'

Motown also released two film soundtracks at this time. *Get Crazy* was the first in August 1983 (UK, Oct '83) but it was the second, *The Big Chill*, that attracted more attention (US, Sep '83/UK, Feb '84). Written and directed by Lawrence Kasdan and starring American stage actors Kevin Kline, William Hurt and Jo Beth Williams, it was a reunion story of burying the Sixties. A thoughtful, tragic comedy with soundtrack songs from Marvin Gaye, Smokey Robinson, The Temptations and Aretha Franklin, among others. However, even *The Big Chill* was overshadowed when *Christine* was released, the John Carpenter film based on Stephen King's horror novel. Although a box office disappointment it was a very popular television and video item. The Motown soundtrack for *Christine* released in November 1983 (UK, Feb '84) included Little Richard, Buddy Holly and Danny and The Juniors.

Two months after Diana Ross' triumphant shows in New York's Central Park in July at the start of her 'For One And For All' American tour, Mary Wilson made a cameo appearance in *Tiger Town*. This was the first feature film made for the Disney Channel. The cable television film, shot in Detroit in September, saw Wilson singing the National Anthem *a cappella* before the final Detroit Players play-off game which formed the film's climax. Although constantly touring, Wilson was still without a recording deal.

Stevie Wonder embarked upon his 1983 American tour taking in dates in Atlantic City, New Jersey, Boston, New York and San Carlos, California. At the Radio City in New York, Wonder performed two new songs, *Overjoyed* and *Go Home*, from his forthcoming album tentatively titled *People Move Human Plays*. He also paid tribute to Lionel Richie by singing a snippet from *All Night Long (All Night)*, claiming it was his favourite record at the time. At the same New York concert Eddie Murphy, who recently sang *Super Freak* with Rick James at his Madison Square concert, joined Wonder on stage to do his Stevie Wonder impersonation during *Ebony & Ivory*.'

Before Wonder could finish his American

tour his dream came true when Congress passed a bill, seventy-eight votes to twenty-two, to make Dr Martin Luther King's birthday a national public holiday, despite opposition from North Carolina's republican Jessie Helms and Ronald Reagan's comments concerning King's suitability as an American hero. The holiday would start in 1986. It was a relieved and overwhelmed Wonder who said: 'It is believed that for a man to lay down his life for the love of others is the supreme sacrifice. Jesus Christ by his own example showed us that there is no greater love. For nearly two thousand years now we have been striving to have the strength to follow that example. Martin Luther King was a man who had that strength. He showed us, non-violently, a better way of life, a way of mutual respect, helping us to avoid much bitter confrontation and inevitable bloodshed. We still have a long road to travel until we reach the world that was his dream.' Motown/USA released Wonder's *Happy Birthday* in celebration in the US in November 1983. The twelve inch single's flipside contained extracts from four speeches by King (I *Have A Dream*, *Drum Major Instinct Sermon*, *Dr King's Desired Eulogy*, *I've Been To The Mountain Top*). Despite *Happy Birthday* being British released in 1981 to become a number two hit, Wonder refused permission for its American release until agreement was reached on King's public holiday. Motown/BMG had no choice but to re-issue the single to counteract American imports flooding the market. Unfortunately, the *Happy Birthday* used for the A-side was the original album track as opposed to the extended re-mix which was first released. In other words, the British single was the version promoted three years previously, before the re-mix was available!

During October 1983 Motown/BMG once again rifled through its catalogue to cash in on the anniversary year by releasing a series of cassette superpacks designed for in-car and 'Ghetto Blaster' use. *Studio Tape One* was divided into four categories *Cruisin'*, *Drivin'*,

After years of campaigning by Stevie Wonder, Congress passed a bill to make Dr. Martin Luther King's birthday on 15 January a public holiday.

The Commodores toured England in 1983 with Gary Byrd as the support act. To coincide with the tour the group's 13 album, their first without Richie, was released.

Edwin Starr was among the artists featured in Motown/BMG's 1983 cassette superpacks for in-car and 'Ghetto Blaster' use.

Motown Blaster and Motown Instrumental Blaster. Cruisin' included tracks by The Contours and Diana Ross; Drivin, Martha Reeves and the Vandellas and Edwin Starr; Motown Blaster, Mary Jane Girls and DeBarge; Motown Instrumental Blaster, High Inergy and Rick James. Studio Tape Two was likewise divided into four – Smoochin', Funkin', Motown Blaster 1 and Motown Blaster 2 featuring tracks from Eddie Kendricks, Smokey Robinson and the Miracles, Finis Henderson and the Commodores.

Specially compiled anniversary albums were also released during 1983 like 25 Years Of Motown Classics-The Grammy Award Winners and The Artists And Songs That Inspired The Motown 25th Anniversary TV Special. The latter album's title was as long as its track listing as it featured medleys from The Temptations and the Four Tops, Martha Reeves and the Vandellas, Gladys Knight and the Pips, Four Tops, Diana Ross and the Supremes, and the Jackson 5. Others included 25 US No 1 Hits From 25 Years and The Motown Story, an updated, five-record set (three-cassette package) narrated by Smokey Robinson and Lionel Richie and featuring fifty-one hits; Motown Superstars Sing Motown Superstars contained canned cover versions of hit records.

Motown's policy at one time was that once a certain song was a hit, other acts and producers were encouraged to re-record it with the theory that the song could be an even bigger hit the second time around. For example, Bonnie Pointer's Heaven Must Have Sent You (original version recorded by The Elgins) and Diana Ross' Ain't No Mountain High Enough (originally recorded by Marvin Gaye and Tammi Terrell). The only restriction with this type of re-recording was that should a song be a hit for a female group, Motown would re-cut it on a solo performer or male group, thereby giving the song a different interpretation. The system was not always successful, but the company usually got an album track or small hit by using this method.

The tracks on Motown Superstars Sing Motown Superstars were shelved, not because they were inferior versions, but because the acts had better material on sale at the time. The album included Shop Around by The Spinners with lead vocalist G.C. Cameron and Reach Out I'll Be There by Thelma Houston. This track was recorded three years prior to her Don't Leave Me This Way. Beauty Is Only Skin Deep by Jimy Ruffin and produced by Norman Whitfield, was recorded at the same time as The Temptations' original. The Tracks Of My Tears by Martha and the Vandellas was recorded during 1966 and produced by Frank Wilson. Forever Came Today by the Commodores, recorded in 1974, was produced by James Anthony Carmichael and the group.

For Once In My Life by Diana Ross was produced by Hal Davis in 1977. This was one of over two hundred versions of the song. And Love Hangover by Junior Walker, recorded during 1970, three months after Diana Ross' chart-topper, was also produced by Walker.

While Motown were reactivating old songs, one of its ex-artists, Michael Jackson, was breaking records on his own. In 1980 he became the first solo artist to lift four top ten American hits from one album. Titled Off The Wall, the singles were She's Out Of My Life, Don't Stop 'Til You Get Enough, Rock With You and the album's title track. Jackson's second solo album Thriller became the first album in music's history (excluding compilation albums) to produce five top ten American singles: Billie Jean, Beat It, Wanna Be Startin' Something, Thriller and Human Nature. Thus Jackson enjoyed nine consecutive top ten hits on Epic Records. Only five other acts in popular music's history have achieved longer consecutive runs – Elvis Presely with 30, the Beatles with 24, Pat Boone with 14 and Brenda Lee and Rick Nelson each with 10. The Supremes and Aretha Franklin are the only black acts to match Jackson's achievement of nine.

The total sales from the Thriller album's singles reached a staggering twelve million in 1983, with five million originating in America. Thriller itself sold more than fourteen million copies worldwide and became CBS/Epic's best selling album ever to become the world's top selling album of all time with sales in excess of 25 million.

Smokey Robinson, whose plaque was laid along Hollywood's Walk Of Fame between Fanny Brice and Joan Caulfield, returned to Britain for a series of dates in October 1983 beginning at Croydon's Fairfield Halls. It was Robinson's first tour since 1978 and was intended to be a major contribution towards Motown/BMG's anniversary celebrations. Quiet Storm backed him and his line-up included vocalists Pat Henley and Ivory Davis, Motown sessioner Sonny Burke and his musical partner Marv Tarplin. Black Echoes reported: 'To begin with the show ponderously waded through Smokey's vast catalogue of recorded works, with the emphasis on his more recent material. Then Smokey threw the show over to his audience and challenged them to suggest any oldie of their choice, and at this point the real memories began to pour back as the band rushed through the really early stuff. Most people had come to hear that voice. Nobody really cared about the lack of stage show and sound balance, and in the end, when you've got a repertoire as rich as that, and there was so much left out! – you don't really have to prepare much more.'

Junior Walker and the All Stars followed Robinson to Britain by performing in a string of low-key clubs and US Airforce bases. 'Junior is not so junior anymore, but he sure can deliver the goods,' NME's Lindsay Shapero wrote. 'We listen ecstatically to Road Runner; I

purse my lips for *Pucker Up Buttercup*; you wave a lot and play *Party Time*. And then the ultimate love song *How Sweet It Is (To Be Loved By You)*, and dutifully we sing and clap along – such bliss. His voice is like a defunked James Brown – rounded at the edges, yet retaining that bite. He makes it look so easy: perfect timing and notes that fairly trip off his instrument into *Sex Pot* from the new album and oldie *Come See About Me*. Junior plays tirelessly, occasionally disappearing for a wipedown. Culminating with *Green Onions*, he was just so slick, so good, it was like music to my ears.' Walker: 'I've always just been into putting a band together, getting on the road and making some money. And I don't get tired of playing because I love music. I always have just played. I never tried to make a style, it just came together automatically.'

Ron Tyson, from North Carolina, who first performed as a Temptation on Motown's 25th Anniversary Gala, became a fullyfledged member for the group's *Back To Basics* album (US, Oct '83/UK, Nov '83). The album also reunited them with the man who had immortalized them, Norman Whitfield, and was a musical continuation of their jointly produced glory era of *Papa Was A Rolling Stone*, *Masterpiece* and *Just My Imagination*. The Temptations' duet with the Four Tops on *The Battle Song*, produced and written by Willie Hutch, was the album's highlight, whereas *Miss Busy Body* and *Stop The World Right Here* were the more commercial tracks. *Back To Basics* was released at the same time as *Back Where I Belong* from the Four Tops (UK, Nov '83). Following their participation on *Motown 25* the group, not surprisingly, re-joined Motown after their deal with Polygram ended. While rehearsing for the Gala, Berry Gordy asked if they would experiment with some material for him. Duke Fakir: 'Berry told us how proud he was of us and that he was glad we had survived and then he asked us if we'd like to come back. It took us all of three seconds to say yes.' Berry Gordy: 'I would not ask anybody back for sentimental reasons. If an artist was good enough

to be with us twenty years ago, they're still good enough.' The result was *Back Where I Belong* with tracks like *Hang* with The Temptations and *What Have We Got To Lose* with Aretha Franklin. Fakir: 'That came about when we did a song with Aretha on her album and she asked us what kind of deal did we want. So instead of going for a royalty, we suggested we do a trade-off and she could do a song with us on our next album. But what it has done is show us what could be done if we were ever to do an album together.' One side of *Back Where I Belong* was produced by Holland, Dozier and Holland, while Willie Hutch, Berry Gordy and Gil Askey, among others, produced the second side. Levi Stubbs: 'Unfortunately we got caught in the crossfire when there were some disagreements between Berry and Eddie Holland and Lamont Dozier. The result was the album didn't do very well.'

During December the Four Tops toured Britain to support the album's release. The tour began on 12 December with a twenty-four show run at Blazers in Windsor, and closed with a five-night season at Birmingham's Nite Out from 9-14 January 1984. The group's wives and families flew to England for a holiday during Christmas and the New Year. By now, the Four Tops' stage act was more suited to a cabaret environment than a pop venue. Their sound was easy to listen to although many of the hits were confined to medleys and the act, while slick, was occasionally dull.

While CBS were waiting for Marvin Gaye's new release, Motown/BMG leased selected tracks to Telstar to release his *Greatest Hits* album. Motown/BMG, meanwhile, released a three track single in November 1983 with the A-side *What's Going On*. *I Heard It Through The Grapevine* and Gaye's original of Paul Young's cover-version *Wherever I Lay My Hat (That's My Home)* were on the flipside. The latter track was the original B-side of Gaye's 1969 hit *Too Busy Thinking About My Baby*, when it was a

Monalisa Young, born into a musical family, attempted to make a name for herself as a solo artist by recording cover versions of the Jackson 5 hits.

Lovely Scherrie Payne was never without work after The Supremes disbanded. Her projects included performing in the Dream Street musical and providing backing vocals for James Ingram.

revived archive song, originating from an 1963 album. *What's Going On* received more attention this time around (it was previously released in 1971) but still failed to become a British best seller. The *Greatest Hits* album, with a painting of the artist on the front sleeve, faired much better, racing into the top ten.

New signing Monalisa Young's *Knife* album was released in the US in November 1983. It was a rather disappointing release featuring cover versions of The Marvelettes' *Don't Mess With Bill*, Stevie Wonder's *Superstition* and three Jackson 5 songs: *Dancing Machine*, *I'll Be There* and *Never Can Say Goodbye*. *Dancing Machine* was lifted as a single in February 1983 (UK, Apr '83). Young was born into a musical environment in Los Angeles. Her father was a composer, her mother a singer. Young: 'Music was always around our household. I'd tag along with my mother to her vocal lessons. Some people can remember when music entered their lives, but I can't, it was always there.' At school Young became involved with various groups until 1975 when she secured her first professional engagement as a member of the Del Vikings. She later joined St Tropez who scored with *French Fatale*, before becoming lead singer with Arpeggio and session singer for Neil Diamond, Joe Cocker, Jermaine Jackson and Tina Turner. In 1981 Young was nominated as Best Background Vocalist by NARAS (National Academy of Recording Arts And Sciences). Hal Davis produced *Knife* after working with Young for almost ten years. Young: 'This album is special to me because I'm not working behind any group names or bands that exist simply in the studio. Now I get the chance to show what I can do.' Unfortunately, her talent was not appreciated by the public.

Ex-Motowner Mary Wells returned to the music business briefly when Allegiance Records released her *The Old, The New & Best Of* album. It contained re-recordings of her Motown hits and did nothing to progress her possible new recording career. Her re-working of *My Guy* was lifted as a single, as she told a British newspaper how Berry Gordy ignored her: 'I don't think Berry has really forgiven me for leaving the company. It has been a long time but he hasn't forgotten. I have tried to speak to him but he will not speak to me. I think I can make it without being on the Motown label. After all Diana Ross and Michael Jackson have managed it.' To date, Wells has not been able to achieve this. Lamont Dozier also hit the news before the close of 1983 when he signed a licensing deal with Demon Records, an independent British label. The deal secured Dozier's artistic, writing and producing talents and the first release was his *Bigger Than Life* album, which spawned *Scarlett O'Hara* as a single. This was later followed by *The Motor City Scene*, his personal tribute to Motown. Lasting over eighteen

minutes, the twelve inch single featured thirteen classics in medley form.

As Motown scheduled a Teena Marie album titled *You Got The Love* in late 1983 (it was later canned), CBS/Epic released her *Robbery* album despite Marie still being locked in a legal battle with Motown. Marie was unable to speak out publicly about the action but admitted 'I had one year left of my contract and I was suing Motown. I couldn't record. What it has done is make me stronger and in future I'll be watching people far more closely. I won't be as vulnerable as I've been in the past.'

The New Year of 1984 started with celebrations when a star-studded line-up including Ray Charles, Lena Horne, Joan Baez and Irene Cara performed at Washington's Kennedy Center on 8 January in a Gala commemorating the memory of Dr Martin Luther King. Alex 'Roots' Hailey was responsible for the show's script which traced King's career. The two hour performance was filmed for American screening on 15 January, the birthday of the civil rights leader. Stevie Wonder celebrated by performing at Washington's Capitol Center on King's birthday. Billed as the 'people's concert' Wonder insisted that admission be pegged considerably lower than his usual ticket prices.

Also during January 1984, in Britain BMG signed a new multimillion dollar contract with Motown. The new deal extended BMG's sales and distribution in the UK for a further three years, and included additional European territories like Germany, Switzerland, France and Scandinavia to BMG's already held licences in Portugal and Spain.

In America Suzanne de Passe contracted ex-Supreme Cindy Birdsong to work with her in Motown Productions in Los Angeles. Prior to this position and after leaving The Supremes, Birdsong lived under her married name (Hewlett) in Culver City and worked at the UCLA Medical Center. Her neighbours were unaware of her former singing career. Another ex-Supreme, Scherrie Payne, performed in the musical *Dream Street* and sang backing vocals with former Supreme Susaye Green on *Animal Party*, a track on James Ingram's *It's Your Night* album. The Supremes would have celebrated their twentieth anniversary in 1984, calculated from their first hit record. Mary Wilson: 'The years have been special, and the ladies I've worked with over the years are all special to me. They are all talented in their own right and it was a pleasure working with them. I've had a fantastic career and life.' Susaye Green: 'Being a member of The Supremes will always be a special memory for me. I met so many lovely friends and I will always feel blessed to have worked with such special ladies.' Scherrie Payne: 'Those Supreme years were some of the most exciting in my lifetime. I never dreamed I would one day travel so extensively and meet so many people. Cindy Birdsong: 'The real essence of The Supremes was the closeness we had when we worked together. We were one unit in three parts. When we toured together it was us against the rest of the world. It was a definite feeling, very strong, almost as strong as a passion. When I look back it is always with fondness and love, for it was a fairytale, a dream come true.'

While American radio stations were being offered the ten hour *Motown 25th Anniversary Radio Special*, Britain's BBC Radio 1 began broadcasting *Hitsville USA* in January 1984. The series was presented and produced by Stuart Grundy, who was the first radio presenter to interview Berry Gordy during all the years of Motown's existence. Gordy granted the interview because the BBC Transcription Service intended to make the series available to radio stations in the Caribbean and Africa – for a price!

Lionel Richie took a break from his recording commitments to host the eleventh American Music Awards ceremony in January 1984 where he also received the Favourite Soul Single Award for *All Night Long (All Night)*. He smoothly co-ordinated the ceremony with his warm personality and was an integral part of the show's success. Dick Clark, executive producer of the ABC-TV annual broadcast, asked Richie if he would be the solo host for the next Awards Ceremony in 1985. When Richie agreed he became the first artist to achieve this role two years running. The 1984 Ceremony was dominated by Michael Jackson when he won eight Awards (Best Pop Album and Best Soul Album – *Thriller*, Best Pop Single – *Billie Jean*, Favourite Pop and Soul Male Vocalist, Best Pop and Best Soul Video – *Beat It*) and a Merit Award presented to him by Diana Ross who described Jackson as a dream in motion.

Michael Jackson had also been nominated for a staggering twelve Grammy Awards, eleven for his *Thriller* project and one for his narration of the MCA Records E.T. album in the Best Recording for Children category. Lionel Richie fell behind Jackson with five Grammy nominations. Also, early in 1984, *Billboard* reported that *Thriller* had spent twenty-five consecutive weeks at the top of the American national pop charts, second only to Fleetwood Mac's *Rumours* which stayed at the top for thirty-one weeks during 1977 and 1978.

Early in 1984 Pepsi Cola announced their intention to sponsor The Jacksons' (including Jermaine) American *Victory* tour. Part of the arrangement with the soft drink company necessitated the brothers endorsing the product via television advertising. During the filming of one commercial Michael Jackson suffered second degree burns on his scalp after an accident involving the special effects smoke bomb. The young Jackson was hospitalized and continued to receive daily treatment upon his discharge.

Michael Jackson's voice could be heard on *Somebody's Watching Me* (US, Dec '83/UK, Jan '84) the debut single by Motown's new signing, Rockwell. The single was taken from the synthesized album of the same name released in January 1984 (UK, Feb '84). Rockwell's signing was unusual. His initial publicity refused to reveal his true identity and Jackson's involvement because Rockwell intended the single should stand up on its own. *Somebody's Watching Me* was a worldwide pop and soul hit, and while it was climbing the charts it was revealed that the unknown new signing was in fact Kennedy Gordy, Berry's teenage son. Rockwell: 'I had told my father that I had a good writing ability and that I could sing but he didn't believe me. He felt I should become a comedian. He didn't even know I was signed to Motown until the record came out.' Rockwell auditioned for the company like any other act, even though certain personnel knew who he was. Rockwell: 'I asked them to keep my true identity a secret because I realized that once it was generally known, rumours would spread that my father was responsible for any success I might have.'

After high school, where he formed the Rock band, Rockwell (so named after his school group) left the Gordy household and lived with an aunt to prove to his father he could succeed in a career. He worked a nine-to-five job and composed songs in the evenings. Rockwell: 'When I played my father my songs and asked him for advice he would reply "why should I work with you when I'm working with Diana Ross. Come back and let me hear your music when you're as good as she is". Gordy was a strict father who had no intention of spoiling his children. Rockwell: 'He told us that he had worked hard and we

Great secrecy surrounded Rockwell's debut single Somebody's Watching Me featuring Michael Jackson. When the record was a hit it was revealed Rockwell was Berry Gordy's son, Kennedy.

DeBarge continued to go from strength to strength in America. In 1984 they supported Luther Vandross and stunned their audiences. However, it was becoming apparent that lead singer Eldra was preparing for a solo career.

should do the same. He's the type of person who says "if you want something you'll have to go out and get it because when I was your age I had to do that, so why shouldn't you. Do anything you want but don't expect me to give you any special favours". That was always his line, and that's the way he's always been. When I was growing up I really resented this because I thought he could give us anything and I was upset when he didn't. However, now I appreciate the way he acted.' Rockwell's devotion to writing songs paid off when Motown's A&R division signed him as a staff writer. Encouraged that his work was appreciated, Rockwell wanted to take his career one step further by recording his own work. Columbia Records offered him a contract but Rockwell decided to join Motown because the company had played such an important part in his life. Rockwell wrote *Somebody's Watching Me* after noticing a neighbour spying on him regularly until he got so annoyed that writing the song was the only way to rid him of his fury.

Michael Jackson and Rockwell had been good friends since being youngsters. Rockwell: 'He heard I was working on some music and wanted to hear what I was doing. So I played him a tape and the single stuck out in his mind, and he asked if he and Jermaine could do the background vocals. Michael really wanted to do the song because he identifies so much with its message – he often feels like a fish in a bowl, always being watched by people wanting a piece of him.' Although the media and public believed they were hearing Jackson's distinctive voice on *Somebody's Watching Me*, this fact was not confirmed until the single started selling. Once his identity was revealed, it undoubtedly pushed Rockwell's sales. The record sold over 250,000 copies in Britain alone and Rockwell was presented with a silver disc during a short

trip to London. In America both album and single passed gold status, a unique achievement for a newcomer's first project. Main Line, an American Master Mix signing, recorded a cover version of *Somebody's Watching Me* which also included sections from *Thriller*.

For the British release of the *Somebody's Watching Me* album in February 1984, the new ZL prefix was used to fall in with the European numbering system used by BMG. The famous STML series, loved by Motown collectors, ceased to exist. The album comprised Rockwell's self-penned songs except *Taxman* written by ex-Beatle George Harrison. The album was recorded after the single began selling, probably hastily, to capitalize on the success. *(Obscene) Phone Caller* was the second single to be lifted in April 1984 (UK, Mar '84). Rockwell: 'I had been getting dirty phone calls about my body and what I should do with it. I got so mad that I changed my phone number and wrote a song about it. The calls stopped as soon as the record came out.' Unfortunately, this catchy song failed to repeat its predecessor's success, but Rockwell continued to record.

DeBarge (Mark, Randy, Bunny, Eldra, James) supported Luther Vandross on a four month American tour. In February 1984 Vandross sold out four nights at the Radio City Music Hall in New York. Journalist David Nathan wrote: 'Motown's family group have created a growing audience with silken soul-filled love songs. The hit *All This Love* drew the expected response, and when performed on stage lacked none of the impact of the recorded version. I *Like It* the group's big 1983 hit proved a winner and the only disappointment was that we were not treated to a full version of their current winner *In A Special Way*. The group is energetic and playful and sing with enthusiasm and sincerity. With obvious teen appeal, the group is able to get across to adult audiences too, so they're on the right track if they intend to pursue their career together with longevity.' Eldra DeBarge: 'Luther Vandross was very supportive of us, but there has always been a level of understanding we had about gospel and secular music. It's business and we understand that. Everything was a surprise to us. But I always say that with success comes a great responsibility and you have to discipline yourself.' Bunny DeBarge: 'I think our image is dignified, not a slummy down-in-the-gutter image, and that's why we have no problem with what we're doing. DeBarge is a clean and wholesome group. Kids like us and parents don't mind their kids becoming fans of ours.'

As lead singer and pin-up of the group, Eldra DeBarge obviously attracted more attention than the others but he was criticized for basing his act on Michael Jackson, whom he also resembled. In response to this Eldra said: 'I've been trying to hold back so those things wouldn't be said. But I might as well let go now, then I can really show some stuff. No matter what I do it's going to be there and if I can be compared to a superstar like Michael, I'm definitely on the right track.'

The group's *Love Me In A Special Way* single was on release to coincide with the Vandross tour, as the follow-up to *Time Will Reveal* in September 1983. In an attempt to repeat DeBarge's astounding American success, Motown/BMG released a four-track twelve inch single in March 1984 featuring *Time Will Reveal* (from the *In A Special Way* album released US, Sep '83/UK, Mar '84), *I Like It, All This Love* and *I'll Never Fall In Love Again* from the 1982/83 *All This Love* album. Once again British buyers declined to support the clean-cut pop group.

James DeBarge hit the headlines in September 1984 when he married Michael Jackson's sister Janet. The wedding ceremony was held privately and against their parents' wishes. The marriage didn't last because Jackson filed for divorce proceedings in May 1985.

Motown's new pop/rock label, Morocco Records, was launched at Hollywood's Dar Maghred Restaurant on Sunset Boulevard in February 1984. The label's signings like Paul Sabu, Tiggi Clay and The Coyote Sisters attended the launch with two hundred others, including Berry Gordy, Jay Lasker, Howard Rosen (Motown's director of pop promotion) and Stevie Wonder. Morocco's new acts were each contractually guaranteed video promotion. Phil Caston, the label's international manager, told *Billboard* in May 1984: 'We still believe radio airplay is what makes a record but video contributes more and more. If you're looking at a total artist budget, you'll find there's less tour subsidy and more video investment.' However Tiggi Clay's video for *Flashes* failed to be shown on MTV (America's music video channel) because the group was considered to be 'too black', but it was seen on local stations. Duke Jupiter, on the other hand, a white group, had no problem getting wide screenings of their *Little Lady* video. It was suggested that as Morocco was a Motown subsidiary it was difficult to break the racial barriers to gain mainstream radio and television exposure. Phil Caston: 'If we were worried about a racial trip we wouldn't have been in the business for twenty years. I was turned down by MTV in the beginning because my videos were "too black". By opening our mouths and screaming about it, we've been able to change the face of MTV. There is still a bias but we haven't experienced the problem with Morocco. It's the advertizers who are causing these narrow casting ideas to change. Pepsi Cola won't deal with MTV unless they reach a broad demographic. They've had to expand.'

Flashes, the first single by Tiggi Clay (Romeo 'Breath' McCall – keyboards, Fizzy Quick – vocals, Billy Peaches – bass) was released in January 1984 and was taken from their self-named album. For the group's British debut another album track, *The Winner Gets The Heart*, was released in April 1984. This was to be their second American release. Due to its European sound, Motown/BMG had high hopes of a crossover hit. It wasn't.

Paul Sabu, born in Burbank, California, was raised in San Francisco Valley. He was the son of the late actor Sabu who starred in films like *The Elephant Boy, The Thief Of Baghdad* and *Jungle Book* during the late Thirties and early Forties. Sabu learned to play the guitar following his admiration of Jimi Hendrix and The Beatles, and as a proficient guitarist he formed several local groups before touring with the James Gang, Guess Who and The Undisputed Truth. In 1979 Sabu signed a deal with Arista Records where his band recorded the top five European hit *Loose Lucy* before joining MCA Records in 1980. While working with the group Sabu wrote and produced albums for Debbie Jacobs and Ann-Margret on MCA, after which he engineered Handshake Records' releases by Johnny Bristol and Amii Stewart. From there he worked with Linda Clifford and The Jones Girls, and composed songs for films like *Vice Squad, Deadly Force* and *Spring Fever*. Sabu's debut album was released under the name Kidd Glove and titled *Killer Instinct* (US, Feb '84/UK, Apr '84), from which *Good Clean Fun* was the first single in March 1984 (UK, Apr '84). Neither was successful.

Ex-Temptation Dennis Edwards released his *Don't Look Any Further* album at this time (UK, Apr '84). Produced by Dennis Lambert, the album's title track was a duet with Siedah Garrett and was released as a single in January 1984 (UK, Mar '84). It was a relaxed, mid-paced, deep soul song turned into a Motown classic by Edwards' gravelly voice and Garrett's sweet harmonies. Edwards originally wanted Chaka Khan to be his duettist but as the song was recorded over the Christmas period Khan was unavailable. However, Garrett had already demoed the song which persuaded Edwards to use her and subsequently credit her on the record label.

Garrett began singing in 1976 with DJ Rogers before forming her own group Plush in 1980 and singing jingles and demo recordings. Garrett told journalist Mark Webster: 'I spent quite a time with Sergio Mendes and then I went for an audition with Quincy Jones

Paul Sabu, Morocco label signing, released his first album Killer Instinct *under the name Kidd Glove.*

Ex-Temptation Dennis Edwards teamed up with Siedah Garrett to record Don't Look Any Further *taken from the album of the same name.*

Tiggi Clay released the first single, Flashes, *on Motown's new pop/rock label Morocco, launched in 1984.*

to be in a band he was forming called Deco.' The group failed but it did give Garrett the urge to write and it was this talent that attracted Jones who signed her to his Qwest label. When Jones and Michael Jackson began working on the 1987 *Bad* project they decided to use Garrett to duet with Jackson on the first single lifted from the album *I Just Can't Stop Loving You* (an international number one record) and to include her composition written with Glen Ballad *Man In The Mirror* which became a 1988 single.

Dennis Edwards attempted to record his *Don't Look Any Further* album while performing with The Temptations on the T'n'T tour. An exhausting experience, he said, but he left the group for creative reasons, no other. 'I've been wanting to do this kind of thing for sometime. When I was with The Temptations it was like a democracy, and you had to do things everybody wanted to do. But now I'm on my own, I've finally got a chance to express my own feelings in this business. I left because by staying with the group I'd have had to keep up the same image we'd established. No break up is like peaches and cream, but I can't hate the guys. The Temptations' career was profitable.' Edwards, now divorced from June Pointer ('We had real problems because either I was on the road or she was, so we never got to see each other') played his last date as a Temptation in Albuquerque during August 1983. Jermaine Jackson intended to record *Don't Look Any Further* with Whitney Houston for his debut Arista album *Dynamite*. When Edwards recorded it first Jackson opted to use *Take Good Care Of My Heart* instead.

Bobby King, born in South Carolina, was the son of a preacher and one of a family of thirteen children. At the age of five King sang in church and idolized Sam Cooke, and in order to pursue his interest in popular music he left South Carolina in 1968 to live in Los Angeles. King's brother, Billy, moved with him and together they performed as The Relations for five years. King: 'I made a few contacts which culminated in my first break. In 1971 I was offered the preacher's role in the gospel musical *Don't Bother Me I Can't Cope*. The production lasted for three years and it led to my deal with Warner Brothers.' Under the 1973 Warners' contract King released two singles, one being Bobby Womack's *Looking For A Love* which probably would have been a hit if Womack hadn't rush released his own version. During this period King also became an established session vocalist by working with Billy Preston, Boz Scaggs and George Harrison. He also worked with Ry Cooder on a world tour. King chose background work because he did not want to become a part of the late-Seventies disco boom. He told journalist Ralph Tee: 'The market was contracting for good singers and songwriters. Those who were already well established hung in there, but if you were unknown it was very difficult.

That cheap disco stuff became very fashionable and as a vocal artist there was no point in jumping on the bandwagon.'

During 1981 King once again recorded for Warner Brothers with producer Steve Barri to release the *Bobby King* album. It was lost because of poor record company promotion. With the emergence of independent labels at this time, King decided to finance his own recordings to self-produce demo recordings. When Barri joined Motown's A&R division, he signed Bobby King. King's first album was the well balanced, soulful *Love In The Fire* (US, Mar '84/UK, Apr '84) which contained seven tracks co-written and co-produced by Englishman Brian Potter, who had been writing songs for Motown for some time. The funky *Lovequake* was lifted from the album in March 1984 (UK, Apr '84). Initially, the first single was to be *Midnight Shine* with *Lovequake* on the flipside, but this was later admitted to be a printing error on the record label and *Lovequake* became the topside. The album's highlights included the future single *Close To Me*, King's sweet ballad with Alfie Silas, released in June 1984 (UK, Aug '84), *Ain't Never Met A Woman Like You* and *Fall In Love*.

When Lionel Richie's single *Hello* was British released in March 1984, a month after its American outing where it was Motown's first official picture disc, his *Can't Slow Down* album had sold over 600,000 copies to become one of Britain's top three best selling albums alongside Michael Jackson's *Thriller* and George Benson's *In Your Eyes*. *Hello* became a worldwide number one record, and became Motown's 302nd British hit (including reissues) since 1964 when Mary Wells' Stateside single *My Guy* reached number five. Richie's British sales were helped by the twelve inch version which contained extended instrumental versions of *All Night Long (All Night)* and *Running With The Night* on the flipside. When *Hello* and *Can't Slow Down* became British chart-toppers simultaneously, Richie was holidaying in Hawaii prior to returning to Los Angeles to start work on his next album. *Hello* spent six weeks at the top of the British charts, beating the Commodores' *Three Times A Lady* as the longest running number one with five weeks followed by Diana Ross' *I'm Still Waiting*, four weeks, Marvin Gaye's *I Heard It Through The Grapevine* and the Four Tops' *Reach Out I'll Be There*, three weeks each; Michael Jackson's *One Day In Your Life*, Smokey Robinson's *Being With You* and The Supremes' *Baby Love*, two weeks each; Charlene's *I've Never Been To Me* and Smokey Robinson and the Miracles' *Tears Of A Clown*, one week each.

To promote *Hello* Richie starred in a promotional video, directed by Bob Giraldi, with 25-year-old Laura Carrington playing a blind girl. Richie's wife, Brenda, was seen in the opening shots of the video although this was not disclosed at the time of its release. It was

The under-rated Bobby King worked with Billy Preston and George Harrison, among others, before recording for Motown.

an emotional love story, which certain quarters of the media criticized as being in bad taste. *Melody Marker*'s Dessa Fox wrote: 'The leading lady has been given a white stick, told to flutter her eyes, look "enigmatic" and in general behave like a sugar-fed Bambi. What she is not doing is acting human like the rest of us. The sleaziest section of *Hello* comes at the end of the bed sequence. The telephone rings and – in an insult to blind people everywhere, who know exactly where familiar noise sources are – this "actress" attempts to squeeze tears from us sentimental record buyers by groping around for the telephone.'

Richie, in fact, played a drama teacher, coaching a class of students in scenes which could have been swiped from *Fame* and falls in love with a blind student. The video shows Richie 'haunting' her which, some journalists suggested, could be interpreted as a trailer for a John Carpenter horror/thriller film. One scene was actually edited from the video. Laura Carrington: 'I did a naked shower scene, where the camera panned up my legs and back as I got out of the shower and groped for a towel. But neither Lionel nor Bob Giraldi thought it was suitable because they wanted the video to be wholesome.' Playing a blind girl was a challenge for the young actress: 'It took enormous concentration to block out everything that passed in front of me. But playing opposite Lionel was one of the biggest breaks an actress could wish for.'

Hello became Motown/BMG's biggest-selling single so far with sales in excess of 800,000. When *Hello* topped the American charts, 1984 became the seventh consecutive year that a Lionel Richie composition occupied this position. Irving Berlin is the only sole composer in music's history to beat this with nine. Richie tied with Cole Porter, also with seven. Paul McCartney is third with six. However, as the single's sales peaked, an allegation of plagiarism from a New York housewife, Marjorie White, was made, claiming she had written the song under its original title *I'm Not Ready To Go*.

Also during March 1984 Lionel Richie signed a major deal with the soft drinks company Pepsi Cola in what was described as the largest and most comprehensive agreement between a corporation and a recording artist. The two year contract ensured that Pepsi Cola would sponsor Richie's 1984/1985 concerts and fund a television spectacular and/or film. Richie, on the other hand, would endorse Pepsi Cola via a series of commercials and compose a certain number of songs for the company's advertising campaigns. Pepsi Cola felt Richie's public image was suited to their marketing strategies and paid an estimated $8 million for the privilege. The drinks company was determined not to repeat a twenty-year-old mistake when it turned down the Beatles for a similar venture!

Richie's agreement with Pepsi Cola

followed hotly on the heels of a similar deal the drinks company made with The Jacksons - it would sponsor the group's *Victory* tour in return for television advertizing endorsements. It cost Pepsi a cool $5.5 million to conclude The Jacksons' agreement. When the first Pepsi commercials featuring the group were shown on American television, after being premiered at the Grammy Awards broadcast, they were shown free of charge because the television station considered them to be news stories! This saved Pepsi $3 million in airtime costs. Not to be beaten, Pepsi's biggest competitor, Coca-Cola, announced a three year, $7 million contract with Spanish heart-throb Julio Iglesias.

Tour sponsorship was big business during the Eighties. Sponsorship meant the sponsors' product would be advertized extensively throughout the tour (tickets, posters, merchandise, etc) although the artist was not necessarily required to mention the sponsor from the stage. However, when Germany's Adidas (the sports equipment company) sponsored Rod Stewart's European tour, he was required to kick their footballs into the audience.

Touring costs soared drastically, particularly for international stars like Lionel Richie and The Jacksons, who both insisted on elaborate and expensive stage sets and lighting. For example, promoter Charles Sullivan paid approximately $45 million ($12 million in cash in advance) for the rights to promote The Jackson's American *Victory* tour, which was expected to generate $100 million. Prior to this the biggest gross figure generated by an American tour was $34 million by The Rolling Stones in 1983. The Jacksons also gave underprivileged children in excess of $1 million worth of tickets, while Pepsi Cola gave away a further 24,000 tickets via a drinks campaign. Journalist John Abbey further reported that a tour rider was added to The Jacksons' touring contract that (incredibly) included stage barricades, a five-story sound mixing tower, portable toilet, seventeen experienced spotlight operators, twelve carpenters, ten wardrobe attendants, eight stage roof assemblers, four forklifts with operators, two pyrotechnic technicians, generators for extra power, twenty-four fire extinguishers, indoor parking for twelve forty-eight foot tractor trailers and eight limousines, and outdoor parking for a similar number of tractor trailers, two thousand foot of clear plastic sheeting, four hundred foot of rubber matting to cover lighting and sound cables, and a minimum of two thousand pounds of dry ice. The Jacksons also demanded twenty-four hour security, three security guards for every one thousand people during performances, fourteen plain clothes guards for stage areas and two armed guards to accompany their touring vehicles. Their three dressing rooms, each with showers, were to be furnished with rugs, sofa,

Meat Loaf, who recorded an album with Stoney for Motown, later recorded Marshall James Styler's composition Don't You Look At Me Like That. Styler later became a member of Duke Jupiter.

coffee-tables and maintained at a seventy degree temperature, and new, pre-washed terrycloth bath towels and a large bars of soap for the group, and sixty towels and fourteen bars of soap for the backing group and production crew! These requirements aren't cheap!

Before Lionel Richie could step foot on stage he was condemned by The Promoters Association (which represents prominent black promoters in America) for not involving local black promoters in the tour. The Association charged that of the tour's forty-one dates black promoters were responsible for four. Jesse Boseman, founder of the Association, told Billboard: 'Richie's situation is gross. Blacks helped make Richie when he was with the Commodores. He had a black manager and a black base. Now he has a booking agent, Howard Rose, who has stopped adequate black participation.' Richie's then manager, Ken Kragen, retaliated by saying the Association was attempting to turn a business arrangement into a civil rights issue: 'Lionel doesn't hire on a basis of colour, he's only interested in who can do the best job. Lionel's attitude is not to buckle one inch to this kind of approach. He doesn't want to bow to unreasonable and unfair charges and pressure.' However, Kragen did admit that Richie no longer had a strong black following. On the singer's last tour black attendance was as low as two per cent, but stressed that for the forthcoming tour black radio stations would be used substantially to advertize the shows. And added that with Richie's deal with Pepsi Cola much of the sponsorship money would be funnelled into black communities.

The Jacksons too were similarly criticized but, unlike Stevie Wonder who insisted on black personnel working for him during his European Hotter Than July tour, neither acts were known to hire whites in preference to blacks. Richie subsequently met the Reverend Sharpton who was to lead the demonstrations at his concerts. Sharpton agreed to abandon his plans when Richie agreed that six black promoters would co-promote thirteen to seventeen concerts.

In the UK, Gary 'The Crown' Byrd hosted the first hour long programme on 11 March 1984 of his new Radio 1 series Sweet Inspirations. The 'disc journalist' intended to play a wide selection of popular gospel without taking a particular theological direction. Byrd: 'We're going to present the music so that someone can actually see the roots of the music. People have heard for so long that artists like Aretha Franklin have the church in their origins but they've never heard the music which represents that.'

In March 1984 Bob Dylan and Stevie Wonder were joint announcers for the Best Song category at the Grammy Awards ceremony. Dylan opened the envelope and handed the brailled card to Wonder to read, whereupon Wonder quipped; 'Bob, you've given it to me upside-down!'

Morocco signing Duke Jupiter (Marshall James Styler – keyboards/lead vocals, Greg Walker – guitars/vocals, Rickey Ellis – bass/base/vocals, David Corcoran – drums/percussion/vocals) released their debut album White Knuckle Ride in April 1984 (UK, Oct '84) with Little Lady their first single released the same month (UK, June '84). Duke Jupiter began as an instrumental group in 1973, playing the club circuit in their native Rochester, New York. The line-up then was Styler, Walker, George Barajas and Earl Jetty and they took their name from a saxophone player they knew. During 1975 Jupiter released the instrumental single Days Between Us on their own label which caused local interest. As a vocal group Jupiter signed with Mercury Records during 1977 to record three albums. Three years of line-up changes, no success and the untimely deaths of two group members (Barajas died after a long illness related to a brain tumour, Jetty from delayed stress syndrome incurred while serving in Vietnam) Duke Jupiter was on the verge of abandoning the music business. However, they decided to give it one more try and during 1980 recorded a four track EP Begin Again on their own Powerglide label which led to a contract with CBS's Coast-to-Coast label a year later. Rickey Ellis joined the group at this time to enjoy the hit single I'll Drink To You and the hit video I'm Available. Jupiter toured with big-name groups including Foreigner and REO Speedwagon, but with no continued success Styler composed for other acts, including Don't You Look At Me Like That for Meat Loaf, while Ellis acted in the film Joey before recording a demo tape with the group. This was heard by a Motown executive during 1984 and their recording contract was signed within thirty-six hours. Following the release of the White Knuckle Ride album, produced by Glen Kolotkin, the group embarked upon a three month tour with Stevie Ray Vaughan and Huey Lewis. Duke Jupiter's second album The Line Of Your Fire was released in September 1985. Steve Scharf and Glen Kolotkin shared the production credits, and for the first time in their career Duke Jupiter collaborated on the material.

In a quiet part of Los Angeles, just before noon on Sunday, 1 April 1984, Marvin Gaye was shot dead by his father. The sequence of events leading to the murder have been reconstructed from police evidence and press interviews as follows. Gaye's mother, Alberta, was talking to her son in an upstairs bedroom. Gaye's father, a retired pentecostal minister, was downstairs searching for insurance documents and called up to his wife for assistance. When she failed to respond he joined her and Marvin, who was still dressed in his maroon dressing gown, upstairs. Gaye told his father that he resented the tone he had used to ask for his mother's assistance and an argument between the two men ensued concerning the unfound insurance papers and plans for a party the following day to celebrate Marvin's 45th birthday. Eventually the argument subsided and Marvin demanded his father return downstairs. His father refused and a pushing match began whereupon Alberta Gay tried desperately to calm them down. She eventually succeeded in parting them and her husband marched off downstairs in a temper. Within minutes the Reverend returned upstairs, still in a temper, carrying a .38 calibre handgun. In front of his wife, he aimed the pistol from a distance of about six feet and fired a single shot at Marvin which hit him near his heart. A second shot followed, fired at point blank range, which hit Marvin's left shoulder. The Reverend walked out of the bedroom and downstairs into the garden where he threw the gun away. Upstairs Marvin lay dying in his mother's arms until she raced downstairs into the garden screaming for help.

When the police arrived the Reverend was sitting on the outside porch waiting for them. Marvin was immediately rushed to the California Hospital Medical Center where, after several attempts to revive him failed, he was pronounced dead. The time was just after one o'clock on a warm, sunny afternoon.

Marvin Gaye's 70-year-old father was arrested and taken into custody accused of manslaughter. Later he was charged with murder, at the recommendation of the Deputy District Attorney, who said: 'The killing was committed with malice and premeditation, which constitutes murder rather than a heat and passion manslaughter.' When he was arrested Marvin's father pleaded 'not guilty' explaining he shot his son in self-defence: 'Marvin had struck me and his eyes are glazing. He was like a man possessed. I managed to get free of him and grab a gun I kept in case of burglars. I had no choice but to shoot him.'

Gaye's father stood before a Los Angeles court on 4 April, and a police spokesperson stated that the self-defence motive had been rejected: 'There was only one witness to the shooting and that was the Reverend Gay's wife. She has given a different account to that of her husband. We don't believe this was a shooting in self-defense. Also at this time there is no evidence to support Mr Gay's claim that Marvin had been high on drugs.' The autopsy report stated the cause of death was gunshot wounds to the chest while results from toxicological tests for drugs and other substances indicated evidence of cocaine.

Gaye's body was then moved to lay in state for private viewing only at the Forest Lawn Memorial Park in the Hollywood Hills. However, before the star could be buried more than thirty thousand fans filed past his open coffin on the evening of 4 April, with some waiting for up to twelve hours to pay their respects. A further twenty thousand mourners were turned away. It was reported that not since the funerals of Clark Gable in 1960 and Jeanette MacDonald five years later had so many people flocked to the cemetery's Church of the Hills.

The Reverend Gay, meanwhile, made another court appearance where he was remanded for three weeks in the custody of the county health department for mental tests. From his prison cell Gay told journalists: 'I didn't mean to do it. I do know I did fire the gun. I was just trying to keep him off me. I want the world to know it wasn't presumptious on my part. Marvin grabbed me and he slung me to the floor and he started beating me, kicking me. He kicked me everywhere he could kick me. He knocked me on the bed and when I fell my hand happened to feel the little gun under the pillow. I finally got to my feet and he lets me have one right in the side. I laid there and tried to get my poor self together, and he stomped out of my room into the hallway. Ma was crying, trying to tell him to stop.' Gay also insisted more than once that his son had been approximately twenty feet away when he turned on him again, threatening 'oh, you want some more do you?' Gay: 'I pulled the trigger. The first one didn't seem to bother him. He put his hand up to his face like he'd been hit with a blank. And then I fired again. I was backing up toward my room. I was going to go in there and lock the door. This time I heard him say "oh," and I saw him go down. I didn't know whether the injury was real or put on or what. Ma comes in, she says "Marvin's bleeding". I went down the hall and looked. "Babe" I said "call the paramedics". Now I am wondering what was in the gun, and the paramedics came and took him away. I still didn't know how bad it was.'

When told by detectives that his son was dead Gay said he did not believe it. During these interviews from his prison cell, the Reverend stressed time and again that his son had been taking cocaine heavily: 'I heard him sniffing all the time. He turned into something like a beast-like person.' Lieutenant Bob Martin, from the Los Angeles Police Department, who was in charge of the case admitted: 'Gay had some bruises on his shoulders and legs and had apparently been injured by somebody. We can only assume it was his son.' When asked by police if he loved Marvin, Gay replied: 'Let's put it this way, I didn't dislike him.'

Marvin Gaye's funeral was held on 5 April. His body, wearing a military styled white uniform, lay in a silver coffin. This was the outfit Gaye had worn on his last American tour, with the jacket decorated in white braid and a collar of white ermine. Wreaths from friends and fellow artists, including Diana Ross, were placed at the foot of the coffin, the lid of which

was closed. The service, which began with a tape of Gaye singing the American national anthem, was conducted by Bishop Rawlins, a long-standing friend of the Reverend Gay. Five hundred people attended, including Marvin's immediate family – his first wife, Anna, and their son Marvin Jnr, his second wife, Janis, and their children Bubby and Nona, his brother Frankie and half-brother Michael, and sisters Zeola and Jeanne. Industry figures included Harvey Fuqua, Berry Gordy, Norman Whitfield, Brian and Eddie Holland, Larkin Arnold, Quincy Jones, Stevie Wonder and Smokey Robinson. Several of the mourners gave tributes including Wonder who sang a song inspired by Marvin's death *Lighting Up The Candle*. At the end of the service Gaye's body was cremated, and a thirty-five piece band played *What's Going On* while the mourners filed out of church. The next day his three children and Anna scattered his ashes at sea.

The Reverend Gay did not attend the funeral because he was still being held at the Los Angeles County Men's prison. His next date in court was on 25 April, pending the results of the medical reports. When these reports were made public they revealed that Gay was suffering from a brain tumour which had gone undetected until now. However, the court-appointed psychiatrist said Gay was competent to stand trial: 'He is fully-orientated, alert, aware of the nature of the proceedings and open to suggestion and direction.' NME reported that the Presiding Superior Court Judge, Michael Pirosh, had delayed his final ruling on Gay's competency until 16 May after the attorney for the defence had insisted that further investigation of the tumour was required, alleging 'It may have caused the behaviour leading to the shooting'. The size and nature, benign or malignant, were undetermined but, the defence attorney claimed 'It was necessary that the tumour be removed lest it render Gay blind – or perhaps even kill him – within months'.

NME further reported on Marvin Gaye's last months at his parents' home: 'Numerous contacts have told the US press of the extremity of the singer's cocaine use, his increasing paranoia and depression (which, it is alleged, led Gaye to surround himself with both guns and unsavoury associates ever since his '82 comeback) and to the long standing nature of his estrangement from his strict father. What has been established is that prior to the events of 1 April, the forty-four year old singer and his parents had lived for some time in a residence where drug pushers and hangers-on of every description could ring the door bell at any hour or wander in from any of the house's many entrances.'

Marvin Gaye had left huge amounts of unpaid alimony and tax bills unpaid, and Gaye's manager, Marilyn Freeman, Harvey Fuqua and promoter Ron Russom contended they were owed money. Gaye did not leave a will, so his estate, in the region of $1 million, was to be handled by his eldest son. Meanwhile, on 16 May, two neurosurgeons operated on Marvin's father in the Los Angeles County University of California Medical Centre and removed a tumour the size of a walnut from his pituitary gland. Eight months after Marvin's death, the Reverend Gay walked away from prison; he was given five years probation. The sentence was agreed after Gay's attorney succeeded in proving the self-defence plea. Before he was freed, Alberta Gay issued divorce proceedings.

It is probably true to say that most people accepted that Marvin Gaye would not see old age because of his drug intake and that when death did arrive, it would be by his own hand. Gaye was not afraid to die and treated it in much the same way as he did most things in life, with caution, respect and courage. However whatever he did throughout his life, it was his music that will be remembered. The sensitive, caring lyrics, the sensual rhythms, the statements and suggestions. Gaye gave more to music than he took out. The impression he made with his music will never be repeated, nor matched, and through his art he will never be forgotten.

Gaye's brother Frankie suffered a double-fold grief, as he told *Blues & Soul*: 'When Marvin died the pressures on me were enormous. The whole incident was a shattering experience, for the father I loved so deeply had shot the brother who had done so much for me. It was hard to come to terms with such a tragedy.'

Jeffrey Kruger, Gaye's one-time European promoter and representative, said he had lost a friend, a worthy opponent and master of his art: 'For all his personal troubles, Marvin will be remembered for the countless years of pleasure via his outstanding ability to combine a lyric and melody and write the great songs he did. He'll be sadly missed.' Valerie Simpson who, with Nickolas Ashford, wrote the Gaye and Terrell hits, and who now always include a medley of those songs in their stage act, said: 'Marvin has always had part of us through music. I always felt his career was exceptional early on and he became even more brilliant when he went into *What's Going On*. Marvin and Tammi were such a powerful magnum and now they've both gone. And quite honestly, the fact that both of them have gone is something I still can't believe; it just doesn't seem fair.' Harvey Fuqua, who regularly worked with Gaye through his career: 'In my opinion Marvin was the most well-rounded singer I have ever known, from R&B to gospel to classical. He was awesome. I am grateful for having had the opportunity to have worked with him.' And Smokey Robinson who first worked with Gaye in 1964: 'One of my greatest pleasures was to work in the studio with Marvin, singing one of my songs. He was a producer's and songwriter's dream. You simply had to show him the song once or twice, and he proceeded to "Marvin Gaye-ize" it, which turned out great.'

Numerous artists paid tribute to Marvin Gaye on record, but neither Motown nor CBS immediately cashed in on his death with memorial albums. Such was the respect that Gaye demanded from the industry and public alike.

In May 1984 Wolf & Wolf debuted with their self-named album on the Morocco label (UK, Aug '84). Peter Wolf, a native of Vienna, Austria, studied classical piano for ten years. At the age of 11 Wolf developed an interest in American jazz, and five years later left his classical roots to join The Art Farmer Quartet in Europe. In 1976 he moved to South California to record with Frank Zappa's Band, later playing with Survivor and Grace Slick, among others. Prior to his Morocco debut, Wolf recorded five European instrumental jazz albums. Ina (pronounced 'eena') Ganahl was born in Western Austria and sang and studied folk music with her parents from an early age. Upon leaving high school, she moved to Vienna to study opera for five years at the Academy of Performing Arts. During these studies, Ganahl recorded two solos albums under the name Christina. She met Peter Wolf in Vienna during 1975 and the two married four years later.

Their first public performance was as opening act for The Rolling Stones in Vienna, and when the Morocco label was opened Wolf & Wolf's brand of 'bohemian pop' was considered suitable for the subsidiary's image. Record buyers thought otherwise and the project including their first single *Don't Take The Candy* (US, Apr '84/UK, Jul '84) flopped.

At the request of England's northern soul scene, Motown's vintage singer Richard 'Popcorn' Wylie performed to standing room only

audiences in Hinkley and Darlington during May 1984. While at Motown Wylie appeared on the Motown Revues as well as becoming a mid-selling recording artist. He left the company when Berry Gordy failed to support him over a Musicians Union problem. Undeterred Wylie worked for a number of other independent labels like Karen and Carla, and wrote and produced classic singles including I *Spy For The* FBI. Wylie's biggest hit was *With This Ring* recorded by The Platters. Performing before a loyal British audience, Wylie was staggered when they demanded he sing songs long forgotten. Wylie told Neil Rushton: 'Some of the records these guys seem to live for were just throwaway B-sides. I'm shocked but very grateful!'

In America Johnson Publishing Co Inc (publishers of *Jet* and *Ebony* magazines and owner of WJPC, a Chicago based radio station) became America's top black business with gross sales of $118 million in May 1984, pushing Motown Industries which grossed $108.2 million into second place for the first time in twelve years. *Billboard* reported: 'Motown slipped to second place, though it grossed $4 million more in 1983 than 1982, the first year of its distribution deal with MCA. In addition, Motown's operating costs were lower than those of Johnson Publishing. Johnson employs 1,690 to Motown's 231.' The listing of the American top one hundred black businesses is published by *Black Enterprises* magazine annually. *Billboard* further reported that overall black communications companies represented 7.6% ($176.4 million) and black entertainment companies 6.8% ($158.5 million) of the top one hundred's combined $2.3 billion in 1983. Automobile dealerships accounted for the largest share of companies on the Black Enterprises list, generating sales of 23% ($548.3 million).

Koko Pop from Columbus, Ohio, was formed by Chris Powell, an ex-member of Rick James' Punk Funk Horn section. Powell went in search of writers and players to assist him in one of his own recording projects and chose bassist/lead singer, Recco Philmore, keyboardist, Eric O'Neal, and guitarist, Keith Alexander, while he played saxophone and sang lead vocals. They produced a demo tape which impressed Motown's A&R department sufficiently to sign them. *Baby Sister* was their debut single in the US in May 1984 taken from their self-titled album also issued in May. I'm *In Love With You* was the follow-up single (US, Aug '84/UK, Dec '84) which became a semi-hit.

Motown's vaults were raided to resurrect forty unreleased songs by Michael Jackson to release the nine track *Farewell My Summer Love* album during May 1984 (UK, May '84). This album spearheaded an extensive re-promotion of the Jacksons' catalogue, presumably to cash in on their new Epic/CBS album *Victory* and the American tour of the same name. However, Motown claimed the forty songs

Jazz artist Peter Wolf married singer Ina Ganahl and brought their brand of 'bohemian pop' to Motown. The music flopped with record buyers.

223

Chris Powell from Rick James' Punk Funk Horn section formed Koko Pop to record their self-titled album for Motown.

had been missing for some time which prompted an Epic spokesperson to state: 'We're intrigued that Motown waited until now to cash in on the success we have had with Michael!' Motown also packaged a replica of Michael Jackson's white glove (he always wore one on stage) with a picture disc of 14 *Greatest Hits Of Michael Jackson and the Jackson 5*, and with a cassette containing sixteen greatest hits. Motown singer Michael Lovesmith, Steve Barri and Tony Peluso overdubbed and re-mixed the 1973 tracks for *Farewell My Summer Love*. Lovesmith: 'The album was a reproduction of a lot of music not put out by Michael. The job I had was to get him at his best. It's not the quantity that counts, but quality.' The album's title song was the first single, released a month prior to the album's release (UK, May '84) to become a UK hit. Other album tracks by the 14-year-old Michael included The Miracles' *You've Really Got A Hold On Me*, *Call On Me*, and a version of Al Green's *Here I Am (Come And Take Me)*.

Also during May 1984 Detroit instigated a *Do It In Detroit* campaign spearheaded by the Four Tops and Sammy Davis Jr. The Four Tops still lived in Detroit and recorded *Be A Part Of The Heart Of Detroit* which was used to initiate the campaign. Local radio stations and nightclubs played this song – reminiscent of The Supremes' *You Can't Hurry Love* – as part of their public broadcasting service. Berry Gordy and Willie Hutch wrote *Hello Detroit* for Sammy Davis Jr (US, May '84/UK, Sep '84) while other Detroiters, like Aretha Franklin, became involved in promoting Detroit's image.

Smokey Robinson's name was omitted from the first pressings of his *Essar* album (US, May '84/UK Aug '84) for the simple reason that *Essar* equals SR, his initials. However, further pressings did carry his name. *Essar* was another sophisticated and commercial release containing *Train Of Thought*, *Gone Forever* (the theme from the *Cry Of The City* film) and *Close Encounters Of The First Kind*. The first single *And I Don't Love You* was issued prior to the album in April 1984 (UK, Jun '84). A dedication to *Emgee* (Marvin Gaye) was printed on the album sleeve; the first of several tributes made by Motown acts to their lost friend. At this time Stevie Wonder was angry at the negative stories circulating the industry about Gaye's last days, and told *Rolling Stone*

magazine: 'All those things people are saying about Marvin after he died are just incredible. When I die, I'm going to have my people gagged.' Wonder, by now, had decided to drop a lot of his early material from his concerts. He performed four shows in Detroit which earned him $1 million and were filmed for a cable television special titled *Stevie Wonder Comes Home*. All the shows were dedicated to Marvin Gaye. In June 1984 Wonder took his show to Britain. This time Harvey Goldsmith promoted the performances which were Wonder's first since his Marshall Arts tour in 1980. The British dates at Birmingham, Brighton and London were part of Wonder's European trek.

Meanwhile, five new signings released records in America. The first were three white girls, The Coyote Sisters (Renee Armand, Marty Gwinn, Leah Kunkel) so named because according to American Indian legend, coyotes are special animals in harmony with the world around them. Renee Armand worked with John Denver: 'I was getting crazy after spending five years on the road with thirty men. The only women I ever saw were airline stewardesses and I was getting desperate to sing with other female voices.' As a soloist Armand recorded two albums *The Rain Book* and *In Time*, and as a, composer enjoyed an American top ten country and western hit with *Boney Fingers* by Hoyt Axton, and an international hit with Michael Jackson's *One Day In Your Life*.

Actress Marty Gwinn originally studied at the East Coast Repertory Theatre and appeared in productions at the Yale Repertory Theatre, Joe Papp's Public Theatre and Cafe La Mama. Gwinn also appeared in a Robert Altman production, *Keeping It Off The Streets*, before writing and singing on film soundtracks. Before settling in Massachusetts with her child, Walker Gwinn Townsend, Gwinn recorded with Jackie De Shannon, John Mayall and Johnny Rivers. Leah Kunkel, an established soloist and backing singer, performed with Graham Nash, Art Garfunkel and Jimmy Webb among others. Also a prolific songwriter with Cass Elliott and others recording her work, Kunkel recorded with James Taylor and Jackson Browne. Like Gwinn, Kunkel was a single parent and lived in Massachusetts.

The Coyote Sisters was formed by accident. Gwinn: 'I had met Terry Kirkman of The Association, and he suggested I should think about a female trio. About three days later I got a call from Leah. Her car had broken down near my house and she needed help. I didn't know her very well because we'd only done one Dirt Band session together, but she remembered my number. So I picked her up and we went out for breakfast.' Over the meal the two decided to form a group and asked Armand to join them. After working on their act, the trio contacted an old friend composer/arranger Tony Berg to work with them. Together they joined Motown, where their first single *Straight From The Heart (Into Your Life)* was released in June 1984 (UK, Jul '84) lifted from their first album *The Coyote Sisters* (US, Jul '84/UK, Oct '84).

Jakata (pronounced 'jer-carter) was the second new signing. The group (Jimmy Felber, keyboards/composer, Steve Kragen, lead vocals/horns, Chuck Coffey, bass/vocals, Chris Myers, drums/percussion/guitar) was formed in Long Beach, California, in Felber's studio home. The group then spent 1983 preparing demo recordings with British producer and ex-Jobete employee Patrick Sherlock (who had married Motown/USA's international coordinator Karen Spencer). The individual members of Jakata had a collective professional experience of over thirty years.

Jimmy Felber, the son of a navy officer, studied classical piano and organ as a child, and at the age of 18 wrote songs for and played with Ike and Tina Turner. As a songwriter Felber wrote the Jermaine Jackson *Burning' Hot* track on his *Let's Get Serious* album. Steve Kragen, also from a naval family, grew up in San Diego, California. By the age of six he studied the alto saxophone and jazz musicians like John Coltrane, Charlie Parker and Cannonball Adderley. In his later life Kragen became interested in mainstream music. Chuck Coffey, born in Atlanta, Georgia, spent his early life travelling with his musician father. By the age of 16 he was proficient enough to work in the recording studios and perform alone. During the late Seventies Coffey performed the Paul McCartney role in the soundtrack to *The Birth Of The Beatles* film. Although Coffey did not appear in the film, all vocals and bass parts were his. Chris Myers, the son of an immigration officer and born in Miami, Florida, was raised in Southern California. A drummer from an early age, Myers toured with the Quicksilver Messenger Service in the mid-Seventies before recording and touring with The Sanford Townsend Band.

Jakata (an amalgam of sound to convey a feeling) released their first single *Hell Is On The Run* (US, Aug '84/UK, Oct '84) which was taken from their debut album *Light The Night* released in the same month (UK, Oct '84). A further single *Golden Girl* was released in March 1985 (UK, Apr '85). The releases were potentially hit material but when Jakata's second album *Designs Of The Heart* was scheduled for 1986 release, it remained permanently canned.

Sam Harris, another talented and experienced performer, was the next new signing, from whom Motown expected instant hits. He was raised in Oklahoma, where his father, a former band leader, encouraged his interest in music. Harris left school at the age of 15 and worked for two years in summer theme parks in Nashville and St Louis. In 1979

he moved to Los Angeles and enrolled at the ULCA as a student in Theatre and Musical Comedy programmes. Two years later Harris won a 'Frank Sinatra Pop Vocal Competition' and met Jerry Blatt, director/writer for Bette Midler. Harris: 'He gave me the confidence to be different to do whatever I wanted to do and let it be right. Until I met him, whenever I tried to figure out and do what other people wanted from me, it wouldn't work. Jerry taught me how to trust my own judgement.'

For the next two years Harris performed on the club circuit with his one-man show, wearing big, sloppy clothes and mixing class and schlepp. Following one of his performances at The Horn in Santa Monica, Harris auditioned for the television talent series *Star Search* and won the entire series as best male vocalist. Motown snapped up Harris for a recording deal as the television series ended and sank hefty finances into transforming this versatile singer/performer into a star. Harris' self-named debut album was a musical gem. Released in August 1984 (UK, Oct '84) it was produced by Steve Barri and Tony Peluso, and showcased Harris' diverse talents. *Sugar Don't Bite* was the first single (US, Aug '84/UK, Nov '84), but his version of Patti LaBelle's *Over The Rainbow* was the album's highlight, and his third single in America. Harris: 'I think this album may confuse some people because it's such a departure from what they know of me. But the music is a part of me too. One of my goals is to be able to do all kinds of music. Call it old-fashioned but what I really want to be is an all-round entertainer.'

Harris was certainly a coup for Motown, and his good looks, cheeky personality and versatile talent, made him an instant favourite in mainstream music. Unfortunately, the momentum could not be maintained and by 1987 Harris had been dropped by Motown.

Ain't No Turnin' Back was the debut signing from the fourth new signing Phyllis St James. Released in August 1984 (UK, Nov '84) it was an exciting release from this young talent. St James, born and raised in Oakland, California, intended to become an actress and to this

After winning the TV talent series Star Search *as best male vocalist, Sam Harris was quickly signed up by Motown. This versatile artist was an American hit, but elsewhere his talent went undiscovered.*

Renee, Marty and Leah, chose the name The Coyote Sisters because according to American Indian legend, Coyotes are special animals in harmony with the world around them. The legend, however, did not guarantee hit records.

Phyllis St. James' sweet vocals were an asset to Motown. Her Ain't No Turnin' Back album was a musical pot pourri of her talent. Sadly, it was her only album.

end earned a BA in Dramatic Arts at Berkeley's University of California. After singing with her gospel colleagues, Andre Crouch and the Hawkins Family, St James made her first mainstream performance in 1976 with Boz Scaggs, who was enjoying success with his *Silk Degrees* album at the time. Now established, St James worked with Tina Turner, Ray Charles and the Commodores, and did TV commercials. St James teamed up with producer Velton Ray Bunch and together they approached Motown's A&R executives Kerry Ashby and Benny Medina. The four were responsible for *Ain't No Turnin' Back* for which she wrote six of the nine songs, including the first single *Candlelight Afternoon* (US, Aug '84/UK, Sep '84), the funky *Phonemate* and the passionate *Livin' On The Border*. St James: 'To me the album is a reflection of most of my experiences as an artist. Who's to say if it's my best work because this is only the beginning. But I'm very proud of what we accomplished. It can only get better from here.' Andre Crouch and Alfie Silas were among the backing vocalists on the album, for which St James also arranged the vocals and played percussion. It was a superb presentation and an encouraging start to her Motown career which, sadly, was not shared by record buyers outside the black market. The album's title track, *Ain't No Turning Back*, was scheduled to be St James' second single, but it was canned and no further material was forthcoming.

When Rick James had vehemently condemned Prince's Vanity 6, claiming the raunchy, scantily-clad female group was identical to his own Mary Jane Girls, he could not have envisaged that a member of Vanity 6 would later sign with Motown. Vanity left Prince and abandoned her chance to star in his autobiographical *Purple Rain* movie to pursue a solo career. Vanity: 'I figured if I didn't get out there when I did I would still be with the Prince thing. I would have been in *Purple Rain* and still in Vanity 6 and I'd have been a national name. However, I would be known as Vanity 6 and I wanted to be known as Vanity. Eventually I had to go because I don't want to share with two other girls. It was always my dream to be a solo artist. I always wanted to be the lady in front. For example, I've always wanted to be Diana Ross, not a Supreme.'

Vanity was born of a German mother and black father in Niagra Falls, Ontario. When her parents divorced Vanity was raised by her father and stepmother. Even as a youngster Vanity wore colourful and outrageous clothes that attracted too much attention. When Vanity's father died, she lived with her natural mother. Vanity: 'My mother gave me the choice between going to modeling school or learning karate. I loved both but chose modeling. I was told I'd never be a model which made me determined to succeed. At sixteen, I got my first apartment. I lived above a restaurant and worked as a waitress. I couldn't

afford to go to school and live on my own, so I had to leave even though I loved art, reading and writing.' A year older, Vanity moved to Toronto in search of modelling work, and was finally hired by the Pearl Drops Tooth Polish company. Vanity: 'I found out about Prince there because I liked his music so much. I flew to New York to see one of his concerts and it was there I met the people who managed him. I gave one of his managers a tape of some lyrics I'd written and surprisingly he came back to me and asked me to go to Minneapolis.'

Vanity became a member of Vanity 6 with Brenda and Susan. Under Prince's guidance, and with flimsy camisoles as their trademark, the group recorded one album *Vanity 6* which sold in excess of 470,000 copies, whereupon they delighted their audiences with their risqué and sensual stage performances.

Vanity's first Motown album was *Wild Animal* (US, Aug '84/UK, Oct '84) for which she co-wrote the tracks with producer Bill Wolfer combining rock and roll, funk and classical music. *Pretty Mess* was released as the first single in August 1984 (UK, Oct '84). With such a beautiful and desirable artist to market, Motown had little trouble in securing media coverage, but persuading the public to buy her records was a problem. Promotion aids for *Wild Animal* included a kit entitled 'My Private Parts', with pink fact sheets covered in black lace and photographs more appropriate for a soft-porn magazine. Motown also embarked on a 'Miss Audio/Visual 1984' campaign, where posters of a scantily-dressed Vanity were the highlight. Vanity: 'I love sex. So that's what I sing about. I just wish I had more time for it.' A second album track *Mechanical Emotion* was issued as a single in November 1984 (UK, Jan '85), but the product, although successful in the black charts, wasn't as widely accepted as the accompanying promotion material.

Stevie Wonder released his American and European number one single *I Just Called To Say I Love You* during August 1984. The single entered the British charts at number three, the highest position a Motown single had gone into the charts on both sides of the Atlantic. During the first week of the ballad's British release it sold over 130,000 copies, becoming Motown/BMG's fastest selling single. It was Wonder's first solo British number one, and his first American chart-topper since 1977 (*I Wish* and *Sir Duke*). In Canada *I Just Called To Say I Love You* sold in excess of 300,000 copies, earning Wonder a triple-platinum single, the first ever awarded.

The single was lifted from Wonder's self-penned and produced soundtrack album *The Woman In Red* (US, Aug '84/UK, Sep '84). As well as singing four tracks – *Don't Drive Drunk*, *Love Light In Flight*, *The Woman In Red* and *I Just Called To Say I Love You* – Wonder duetted with Dionne Warwick on *It's You* and *Weakness*. The album's background vocalists included Susaye Green, Gene Van Buren and Finis Henderson. The Woman In Red film, a romantic farce, starred Gene Wilder, Charles Grodin and Judith Ivey and was based on the screenplay Un Elephant Ca Trompe Enormement. The soundtrack was an exceptionally strong Stevie Wonder album and passed platinum status in America at the same time as Diana Ross' RCA/Capitol album Swept Away earned a gold disc.

I Just Called To Say I Love You won an American Academy Award for Best Original Song, and was nominated for both a Grammy and Oscar, but the latter's eligibility was jeopardized because the song was written in 1977 and only compositions written during the year prior to the Oscar ceremony are eligible. Wonder told the Awards Board that although the song was partly composed seven years ago, he had written it especially for The Woman In Red movie. His explanation was accepted, but the song did not win a Grammy. It did, however, win an Oscar.

A year later in 1985, at the United Nations, Wonder dedicated his Oscar to the imprisoned black leader Nelson Mandela. Wonder told the United Nations audience of his feelings regarding the new South African working policies: 'If it is so important to have black laborers living near the industrial centers, why must they be separated from their wives and children while living in a shack? If the black people of South Africa really do want to live together all in one place, then why have so many given their lives and others protested to avoid these great new resettlement camps? The resettlement camps are wrong. If they're so great, why don't the whites want to live there?' As a result of this speech, Wonder's records were banned by the South African government for a time.

In the meantime, Wonder was being sued by Lee Garrett and musician Lloyd Chiate for $10 million claiming I Just Called To Say I Love You was their composition and not Wonder's. Garrett and Chiate claimed that they wrote the song in 1978 while staying with Wonder at Hollywood's Regency Hotel. Wonder heard the duo rehearsing and was given a demo tape of the track. In reply to the claim Wonder said: 'My music and integrity speaks for itself.'

Love Light In Flight was the second single to be lifted from The Woman In Red album (US, Nov '84/UK, Nov '84). This single failed to repeat its predecessor's success, as did the third track Don't Drive Drunk released in America on twelve inch single only in December 1984 (UK, Dec '84 in seven and twelve inch versions). Wonder wrote this song before agreeing to work on The Woman In Red soundtrack after seeing television commercials on the horrors of car accidents. Don't Drive Drunk was featured in a video commissioned by RCA in Spain, and was a joint effort between the American Department of Trade and the Chrysler Corporation. The Spanish government flew a film crew to America to shoot the thirty second commercial for television use. The single's marketing in England coincided with the British government's Christmas campaign to ban drinkers driving, although it did not officially form part of the campaign.

By August 1984, and after Motown had finally abandoned hopes of succeeding with the female trio billed as the new Supremes, High Inergy, the group's former lead singer Barbara Mitchell released her debut album Get Me Through The Night on Capitol Records. Produced by George Tobin, the album contained a version of Martha and the Vandellas' I'm Ready For Love.

At the Olympic Games, held in Los Angeles in 1984, Lionel Richie fulfilled an ambition. At the request of the organizer, David Wolper, Richie sang a specially-written version of All Night Long (All Night) at the closing ceremony of the Games. Within four months of Richie's appearance, his Can't Slow Down album logged fifty-two consecutive weeks in the American top ten national charts. It was only the third album in pop history to complete a full year in the top ten and to produce four top ten singles. The only other albums to have achieved this were Fleetwood Mac's Rumours and Michael Jackson's Thriller.

During September 1984 (UK, Nov '84) the Dazz Band released their Jukebox album as the follow-up to Joystick, released a year earlier. Also released in September 1984 was their biggest hit Let It All Blow (UK, Oct '84, where it became their only British hit peaking at number twelve). Jukebox was the first album the group recorded in Los Angeles and was a marked improvement on their previous releases, as it had more of a rock element to it. Group member Bobby Harris said their recorded work was the result of feedback from their concerts: 'Live work is a good barometer and when an audience yells out a certain tune it's a good indication of what tracks we should be doing.' Harris also admitted that there had been differences of opinion between Motown and the group, but now with four American top ten records, both parties were happy to exist with a 'comfortable cushion between them'.

While Motown was compiling the The Greatest Songs Written by Ashford & Simpson compact disc, as part of their future 'The Composer Series', the duo were enjoying their third and most successful album for Capitol Records in October 1984. Titled Solid, the first single lifted was the album's title track which became an international top seller, and their first top three single in Britain.

The release of The Temptations' Truly For You album (US, Oct '84/UK, Nov '84) saw Ali-Ollie Woodson join Otis Williams, Melvin Franklin, Richard Street and Ron Tyson to enjoy a huge European hit with the relaxing Treat Her Like A Lady, lifted as a single in October 1984 (UK, Nov '84). Woodson, a native Detroiter, had been a member of The

Ex-member of Prince's Vanity 6, Vanity released her debut album Wild Animal in 1984. The accompanying promotional aids for the album included a My Private Parts kit.

Treat Her Like A Lady gave The Temptations a much needed European hit in 1984. Melvin Franklin said the polite lyrics contributed to its success.

(Far right) Diana Ross expanded her business interests by launching her own range of pantihose and designing dress patterns.

Thomas McClary left the Commodores to release his solo self-named album in 1985. The project failed miserably and marked the end of his singing career.

Temptations since their *Back To Basics* album in 1983. Following his audition in 1977 which he failed in favour of Louis Price, Woodson regularly kept in contact with Melvin Franklin, until he was offered a place in the group. *Treat Her Like A Lady* was the group's first British hit (number twelve) since 1982's *Standing On The Top (Part 1)* peaked at fifty-three. *Treat Her Like A Lady* was not as popular in America. Franklin said the polite lyrics contributed towards the European success. The *Truly For You* album, produced by Al McKay and Ralph Johnson, was the group's strongest since returning to Motown, as it blended the Sixties and Eighties sounds. Remarkably *Treat Her Like A Lady* was the only hit from the album. The Temptations, meanwhile, continued to tour America both as a solo group and as part of the T 'n' T package, and Franklin credited their success to his and Otis Williams' group leadership, strong management, dedicated group replacements and supportive record company policy.

In the Autumn of 1984, ex-Motowner Diana Ross branched out from her recording career to sign a two-and-a-half year deal with Nantucket Hosiery Mills to launch a pantihose line. The deal, showed her photo and signature on the pantyhose packaging. A limited edition of two foot high Diana Ross dolls, made by Marilyn Houchen, were also available. And Ross' venture into dress designing saw seven of her original dress patterns on sale by Simplicity Patterns. Ross: 'The clothes I design are like the songs I sing. They run the gamut from just-for-fun, funky pieces that can really move to elegantly dramatic ones that are sultry and sexy. I hope the broad range of my designs will widen the choice of clothes a woman feels she can wear, and will inspire her to explore new areas of her personal life.'

Despite great hopes following *The Wiz*, Ross had not starred in a movie since she walked down the yellow brick road. The reason, she said, was unsuitable scripts. Ross: 'I finally got tired of waiting for the perfect script and that's how my film company was born. My goal for Anaid is to run off productions from feature films to television mini series to variety specials. It's the fastest growing of all my companies, with offices in New York, Los Angeles and the United Kingdom.' The company had already produced a television presentation of one of her 'For One And For All' concerts, four music videos and bought the rights to several books for film and television projects, including the life story of Josephine Baker, in which Ross intended to star.

However, as Diana Ross continued her megastar recording and touring career, sadness entered her life when her much beloved mother, Ernestine Ross Jordan, died of cancer at the age of 68. She was buried in Detroit's Woodland Cemetery. Mrs Jordan was born in Allensville, Alabama, the youngest of twelve children born to the Reverend and Mrs William Moten. When she was 21 years old, Mrs Jordan moved to Detroit where she married Fred Earl Ross in 1972. When they later divorced she married John Jordan in 1977.

By November 1984, Thomas McClary had left the Commodores, to release his first solo, self-produced eponymous album (UK, Feb '85). The first single lifted from the release was *Thin Walls* (US, Nov '84/UK, Jan '85) featuring another ex-group member, Lionel Richie. *Man In The Middle* was the follow-up in the US in February 1985. McClary claimed his departure from the group was due to the increasing difficulties in satisfying his own creative needs: 'I had fifteen great years with the Commodores and I think we accomplished all the goals we set out to do and we'll certainly go down in history for what we achieved. However, there has always been this dream inside of me to grow and to attain new goals. Things that couldn't be implemented from inside the group. And they require time to devote to them and being part of a group such as the Commodores made it impossible.'

McClary, who had already worked with Klique on their American hit *Doggin' Around*, said the disappointing sales of the Commodores' 13 album had no bearing on his decision to leave: 'I have been working on this move for quite some time. However, the lack of success did affect us. Having an album that didn't go gold disturbed us.' To show there were no hard feelings about leaving McClary offered to contribute towards the Commodores' new album. The group declined the offer, preferring to make a clean break. McClary's debut album was a one-off for Motown.

A month after the release of *Thin Walls*, the Commodores released their first and only hit since the departure of Lionel Richie. Titled *Nightshift* (US, Dec '84/UK, Jan '85), it was a beautiful and poignant dedication to the late Jackie Wilson and Marvin Gaye, and boosted the Commodores' flagging career by winning a Grammy in the Best R&B Vocal, Duo or Group category. The *Nightshift* album followed in January 1985 (UK, Feb '85) and was a disappointing release, falling into the rock and contemporary pop category. However, apart from the title track, *Janet* and *The Woman In My Life* were outstanding highlights. The group, with James D. Nicholas replacing Richie, were happy with the result. William 'Wak' King: 'Basically I'd say the new album is a team effort between the group and Dennis Lambert (the producer). We have always listened to outside material but we always felt we could come up with better songs ourselves, but this album is different in that respect too, because three of the songs on it were written by people outside the group. They felt so good that we just had to cut them. Working with Dennis was really great, it was like having (James Anthony) Carmichael back with us again.'

A second album track *Animal Instinct* followed in April 1985. It's British release in May 1985 marked Motown/BMG's changing to the European numbering system ZB (seven inch) and ZT (twelve inch) used for mainstream BMG releases. This replaced the TMG and TMGT system used since the Tamla Motown label was introduced in 1965.

With no further hits the Commodores' strained relationship with Motown ended with the group signing to Polygram. Their debut single *Goin' To The Bank*, a track from their pending *United* album, was released autumn 1986 (US/UK). The group left Motown because they needed a fresh start as Milan Williams explained: 'Leaving was something like a divorce but it had to happen. Even though *Nightshift* was a big record for us, I think the move was on the cards back then. We always did our best for Motown and we've left some dear friends behind. But it was time to move on. Time to get out of Richie's shadow.' Williams also admitted that since 1982 the group suffered the most traumatic period in their twenty year career: 'Now we have a fresh start. There are no personality conflicts within the group and no ego problems. We realized we had to let go of the Richie sound, we left that behind at Motown.' Ronald LePread also left the group to pursue other interests when they signed to Polygram, and the Commodores remained a quartet.

YESTERDAY'S DREAMS

'People are losing their jobs. People are starving. They can't wait for some brave new world that's going to happen tomorrow. Some of them are about to lose everything today.'
Lionel Richie

'The whole Supremes thing is taking off again in a big way. Everyone is getting into oldies again which for me is just great.'
Cindy Birdsong

Following the television coverage of horrendous scenes of the starving and dying people in Ethiopia, the Boomtown Rats' lead singer Bob Geldof was moved to approach the cream of the British recording artists, including Boy George, George Michael, Sting, Paul Weller, Phil Collins, Simon Le Bon, Marilyn, Martin Kemp, Tony Hadley, Bono, Rick Parfitt, Francis Rossi, Siobhan and Sarah (Bananarama), to record a single about the tragedy and dedicate all the royalties to Ethiopia. The single, *Do They Know It's Christmas?* written by Geldof and Midge Ure, was recorded at London's Sarm Studios and released by Mercury/Phonogram under the collective name of Band Aid. The British public flocked to buy the single which became a 1984 Christmas number one and an international million seller.

The British project prompted singer Harry Belafonte to organize a similar recording session in America. Michael Jackson and Lionel Richie wrote *We Are The World* for the project, and Quincy Jones conducted and produced the session held at A&M Records' studio in Los Angeles during 1985. Following the British lead, over forty-five major artists contributed their time to take part in the recording, including Diana Ross, Tina Turner, Hall & Oates, Smokey Robinson, Bruce Springsteen, Ray Charles, Stevie Wonder, The Jacksons, Dionne Warwick, Bette Midler, Al Jarreau, Lionel Richie and Michael Jackson. After the recording session Wonder lightened up the seriousness of the occasion by laughing: 'It gave me a chance to see Ray Charles again. We just sort of bumped into each other!' And when the session started to run overtime, he quipped that if the song wasn't completed on the last take he or Ray Charles would drive everyone home! *We Are The World* by USA For Africa was released by CBS in April 1985 and repeated the British single's success. Diana Ross was the only ex-Supreme to take part in the recording sessions, and when *We Are The World* was released two former group members attracted media attention. Scherrie Payne and Ronnie Phillips became parents of

a baby girl named Shoshana, and Mary Wilson flew to London to perform at a private party at Burkes Club.

Lionel Richie said that after the single's release he was inundated with letters from Americans in need: 'People told me about losing their farms, people who are losing their way and can't quite figure out what to do about their lives, and people losing everything their families were built on.' Richie, like Stevie Wonder, was deeply concerned at the state of the world, particularly his home country: 'I look at a desperate world we're creating. We're wiping out the people who are the foundation of what America is about. The guys who don't have an IQ of 150, who never wanted to be anything but a shoemaker and now have no work. All you have to do is say "America's in trouble" and they're the first ones who will fight your wars for you. But don't use them and abuse them. These are the people who lost their two sons in Vietnam. These are the people who, when there's a tax increase, will be hit by it. I don't mind growth and progress but in this thing called change we are losing the most important thing there is – people. Awareness is what I'm concerned about now. Your responsibility to yourself and the world, your contribution. I'm at the point and at the world's point where there's no more time for dreaming about pie in the sky. People are losing their jobs. People are starving. They can't wait for some brave new world that's going to happen tomorrow. Some of them are about to lose everything today.'

On 13 July 1985 Bob Geldof and concert promoter Harvey Goldsmith staged Live Aid at Wembley Stadium. It was the world's largest music festival, and following the British spectacular during the day, the American contribution lasted during the night and was transmitted live by satellite for worldwide viewing. In Britain the Live Aid marathon was televized live by the BBC. Acts in Britain included Queen, Sade, Sting, Phil Collins, Dire Straits, David Bowie, Status Quo, Elton John, Kiki Dee, Boomtown Rats, Spandau Ballet and

Bryan Ferry, while the American gala included Tina Turner, Mick Jagger, Patti LaBelle, Madonna, Bob Dylan, Bryan Adams, Kool and the Gang, Hall & Oates, David Ruffin and Eddie Kendricks, Rick Springfield and Lionel Richie. During the marathon, countries including Australia, Tokyo, Norway, Russia, Austria and Yugoslavia presented their own acts. The British leg of the Wembley marathon was criticized for being white dominated, and prior to the trans-Atlantic link up, certain black acts complained to the American promoter that black music was not sufficiently represented.

Prior to the music marathon, Mick Jagger and David Bowie teamed up to record and video in secret Martha and the Vandellas' *Dancing In The Street*. The single became an international chart-topper and all the royalties went to the Ethiopian Fund. Various other Live Aid fund raising activities took place in the ensuing months on both sides of the Atlantic, including the running marathon Sports Aid, and the club DJ sponsored Disco Aid, organized by Steve Walsh and Theo Loyla.

Early in 1985 ex-Motowner Gary Byrd formed WGBE Productions, a radio production company, where the first project was Dance Music International, a syndicated show broadcast during January. Byrd was still employed by New York's WLIB station and the BBC as host of the popular gospel show *Sweet Inspirations* for Radio One. Jimmy Ruffin, meanwhile, returned to the recording studios to release *There Will Never Be Another You* in Britain on the EMI label, and joined Paul Weller's Council Collective project to record the single *Soul Deep (Part 1)* in support of the miner's strike.

DeBarge were among the first Motown acts to release a record in 1985. In January (UK, Mar '85) they issued their next American hit and first British hit, *Rhythm Of The Night* which was an ideal record for the young market and peaked at number four in Britain. Motown/BMG were thrilled that, after years of struggling, DeBarge had crossed over into the national charts. The single was the title track from an album released in February 1985 (UK, May '85) produced by Jay Gordon and the group. *Rhythm Of The Night* also appeared on the soundtrack album of *Berry Gordy's The Last Dragon*, while another album track, the ballad *Single Heart* was featured in the *D.C. Cab* movie. *Who's Holding Donna Now* was another highlight and was lifted as a single in May 1985 (UK, Jun '85). With this release, DeBarge continued in their role as one of Motown's biggest American acts, and the breakthrough in the UK was expected to secure an equally successful career there. However, following the release of *You Wear It Well* (US, Aug '85/UK, Sep '85; credited to El DeBarge with DeBarge) which became a number fifty-four British hit, the group's career came to a sudden halt. *The Heart Is Not So Smart* followed before the close of 1985 which marked the end of the DeBarge's recording career altogether, although the group was credited on the B-sides of the first solo singles by Eldra (shortened to El) and Bunny in 1986.

Flushed with the success of the *Somebody's Watching Me* album and single in 1984, Rockwell plunged into the world of rock/pop to release his second album *Captured* in January 1985 (UK, Jun '85). Unlike his debut album, there were no outside influences on this one, except Stevie Wonder's backing vocals on the track *He's A Cobra*, which was the first single lifted in December 1984 (UK, Mar '85). Rockwell: 'We were in the studios doing a rough mix of the song when Stevie was walking down the corridor, and he came in with the backing singers. Originally I said "no" to his involvement because I thought people would say I couldn't make a record without a top star on it. I really didn't think I needed Stevie but in the end I was delighted when he joined in. Who wouldn't be?' *Peeping Tom* was the second single released in February 1985 (UK May '85). Rockwell was unable to repeat his earlier success, although he persevered with *The Genie* album a year later from which *Carmé Part 1* was lifted as the first single.

A month after the release of the film soundtrack to *The Flamingo Kid* (US, Jan '85/UK, Oct '85), featuring Barrett Strong, Maureen Steele, The Impressions, Dion and Little Richard, the Mary Jane Girls released their second dynamic album *Only Four You* (UK, Apr '85). *In My House* was the first single (US, Jan '85/UK, Feb '85). The group's Jo Jo McDuffie told journalist John Abbey: 'It's a good dance number, the lyric is good and easy to identify with and it has a freshness that makes it appealing to more than one audience.' McDuffie was quick to recognize that Britain had broken them with *All Night Long*, and provided the foundation needed for American success. Ironically, *In My House* flopped in Britain, yet was an American and European hit! McDuffie put its British failure down to R&B marketing and not pop. The group's tremendous success, she

Recording artists in America and England rushed to support Bob Geldof's plea to help the people of Ethiopia. The British contingent (Band Aid) released Do They Know It's Christmas?, *while the Americans (USA for Africa) released* We Are The World. *The picture shows the contributing American artists.*

added, was attributable to the open-mindedness of the Eighties society which would not have been the case a decade ago; 'Most of the groups at that time were normal and society could deal with them. If we'd been cutesy and girlie, maybe we'd have made it too. That was a time when it was taboo for a woman to be bold. We feature a lot of sexual overtones in our act and in our music, so that makes us more than a little risqué. In fact, we're even a little different for 1985.'

With the release of *Only Four You*, R&B singer Patti Brook's daughter, Yvette Martin replaced Cheri Wells. Like the remaining girls Martin was given a character name, 'Corvette'. Martin: 'Rick is a close friend of my mothers and was an uncle figure to me. When he was forming the Mary Jane Girls the first time around I begged him to let me be in the group. He said I was too young, but promised one day. When I learned Cheri was leaving I phoned Rick, he auditioned me and kept his word.' *Only Four You*, produced in the classic Rick James style, contained seven up-tempo tracks and the powerful ballad *Shadow Lover*. It was a superb album, depicting the fresh and vital sound of James' new generation of music. Even though the Mary Jane Girls were less than two years old, their eponymous debut album reached gold status in America and their stage act showed four ladies each dressed in character costumes, created from Rick James' wild fantasies. He gave them no-nonsense lyrics, and bold sexual personalities without being obscene. They were now a legitimate female funk and rock band and were an integral part of James' American tours. He was happy with the group's progress since he felt there had not been a strong female group since the Sixties: 'I knew it was time for us to have a group of women that combined today's reality and sexuality.'

The soundtrack to Motown's first ever feature film *Berry Gordy's The Last Dragon* was released in February 1985 (UK, May '85). The album included DeBarge, Charlene, Vanity and Rockwell. When compared to Motown's other soundtracks this was surprisingly boring, although healthy sales were generated when the film went on general release. *Berry Gordy's The Last Dragon*, a kung fu and dance film, starred karate expert Taimak, Vanity and Julius Carry III. Directed by Michael Schultz, the film dealt with morality where good finally defeats evil and the hero ends up with the girl. A witty and enjoyable film, which grossed in excess of £25 million from July 1985. It opened in Britain to mixed reviews.

At the 1985 Grammy Awards ceremony held during March Lionel Richie won the Album of the Year category with *Can't Slow Down*, and Producer Of The Year with James Anthony Carmichael. Michael Jackson, who won eight awards in 1984, won one Grammy for his *Making Michael Jackson's Thriller* video, while Tina Turner collected three. After Diana Ross

had made the presentation to Turner, Ross sang *I Just Called To Say I Love You*.

Meanwhile, Motown left the industry trade group RIAA (Recording Industry Association Of America). Jay Lasker explained why: 'We do not feel the organization, as it is presently constituted, represents the interests of an independent record company such as Motown. The fact that the board consists of a group of the rich and famous is certainly not a reflection of its good efforts.' However, when Motown teamed up with MCA for distribution, they took membership with the RIAA. Motown also consented to licence its logo and name to a New York merchandizing company whose clients included the Harley-Davidson Motor Company and Coca Cola.

As the Dazz Band returned to Britain for a March 1985 tour and Motown/BMG released *Heartbeat*, the follow-up to *Let It All Blow*, and the second single to be lifted from the *Jukebox* album, The Emotions released their first album *If I Only Knew* (UK, Jun '85). The female trio, Sheila Hutchinson, Adrianna Harris and Wanda Vaughn, became an established act via their Seventies' hits like *Best Of My Love* and *I Don't Wanna Lose Your Love*, and tours with Earth, Wind & Fire, with whom they recorded the 1979 hit *Boogie Wonderland*. Prior to this the sisters (Harris replaced Jeanette Hutchinson) spent seven years with Stax Records where they worked with Isaac Hayes, Homer Banks, Al Bell and many others. The girls' notable R&B releases were their debut hit *So I Can Love You*, *Show Me How*, *Put A Little Love Away* and *My Honey And Me*. When The Emotions' Stax contract expired in 1975, Earth, Wind & Fire's leader Maurice White, who remembered them from their gospel days, produced their *Flowers* album. The group's popularity declined when they joined Motown and the company could not retrieve it. *If I Only Knew* spawned their debut single *Miss Your Love* (US, Mar '85/UK, May '85) with *If I Only Knew Then (What I Know Now)* the follow-up in May 1985. The product was welcomed by the group's diehard followers but not mainstream record buyers.

Rick James, however, returned like a thunderbolt with his best album since *Street Songs*. Titled *Glow* (US, Apr '85/UK, May '85), the album reflected a cleaner, fresher and more relaxed artist, with a positive musical flow rather than the complex sound that tended to dominate his recordings. *Can't Stop* was released as a taster from the album in March 1985 (UK, Apr '85), followed by the album's title track *Glow* in May 1985 (UK, Jun '85) and *Spend The Night With Me* (American released only) before the end of 1985. The promotional video for the *Glow* single was startling. It was autobiographical and was filmed at the Beverly Theater in Los Angeles, and at Leo Carillo State Beach in Malibu. It also featured his future protégé Val Young and the Stone City Band. The *Glow* album's new sound stemmed from James' recent drug and alcohol rehabilitation programme. James: 'I finally came face to face with the fact that I had been spending nearly $15,000 a week on cocaine and when I wasn't using that I was drinking or smoking marijuana. Things had gotten so bad ... I'd disappear for two or three days at a time. I'd lock myself up just to get high and stay high. I started to break down physically, mentally, emotionally and spiritually. My self-esteem was at its lowest and my sex life had gone out of the window. I could barely function without drugs or drink.' James stopped taking drugs by working with black comedian Eddie Murphy, prior to recording his *Glow* album. James: 'I found out that I actually did have a disease, that this addiction was just that. Since I came out of the programme, I've had the chance to go talk with some adolescent addicts and I can tell them just what I've been through.' James now banned his musicians from taking drugs and refused to keep company with anyone who did.

At this point in his career the Punk Funk master felt the music industry had not given him any recognition for his musical input via his own recordings and his work with Teena Marie, Smokey Robinson, Mary Jane Girls, Stone City Band, Process & the Doo Rags, and The Temptations, having given the latter a career-saving single. However, his attitude made him more determined to explore other entertainment areas, and he prepared for his first film *The Spice Of Life*, an autobiographical exposé which James had nurtured for several years. When Prince beat him to the big screen with his own autobiographical movie *Purple Rain*, James temporarily abandoned his plans.

New signing Maureen Steele, born in Massachusetts, had no intention of getting involved in the music business. Steele: 'My brothers, sister and father were all musicians and played together in a group and they kept bugging me to sing with them just for fun. And as I wanted to keep peace with the family I did it.' The fun turned into serious business when Steele dropped out of college in 1977 to join her brother Bobby in the showband, The Second Chance. After an extensive American tour, Steele and Bobby decided to stay in Los Angeles where Steele found regular employ-

ment for two years. Steele: 'I told myself if all I wanted to do was sell clothes and be a secretary I might as well have been back home with my parents. So I figured I'd better start singing again.' For a further two years she performed with various groups until her brother became Paul Sabu's keyboardist. Through Bobby's position Steele was eventually auditioned by Motown's Steve Barri and Eddie Lambert, and subsequently signed to the company in September 1984. Steele: 'It all happened so fast for me that I feel guilty. I'm not one of those people who's been singing since the age of two. I was actually a psych major who didn't sing professionally until I was nineteen. But what the hell, if it was meant to happen this way, so be it!' *Nature Of The Beast*, Steele's debut album, was recorded between September 1984 and February 1985, and released in April 1985 (UK, Jul '85). Co-produced by her brother Bobby and Steve Barri, it contained tracks like *Bad Girls Do It Better*, *My Shy Lover* and *Sidetracked*. *Save The Night For Me/Boys Will Be Boys* was the first single also released in April. In August *Boys Will Be Boys* was issued as the topside. Steele's debut British single was also *Save The Night For Me/Rock My Heart* in June 1985, and *Boys Will Be Boys/Rock My Heart* followed in September. It seems that neither Motown company could make up its mind what to release, but this didn't matter because Steele failed to enjoy solo success. However, as a session singer she did better. For example, she can be heard on Michael Lovesmith's *Rhymes Of Passion* album released in June 1985 (UK, Aug '85).

In order to boost its back catalogue Motown/BMG re-released forty deleted classic songs in a series of twenty double A-sided singles including *For Once In My Life/I Was Made To Love Her*, *Do I Do/I Ain't Gonna Stand For It*, *He's Misstra Know-It-All/Boogie On Reggae Woman*, *I Wish/Sir Duke* (Stevie Wonder), *Got To Be There/Rockin' Robin* (Michael Jackson), *My Old Piano/I'm Coming Out*, *Love Hangover/Remember Me* (Diana Ross), and tracks from the Four Tops, Thelma Houston and Jimmy Ruffin. A month later ten mid-priced albums were issued from acts like Jermaine Jackson, Smokey Robinson, the Commodores, and the compilation *All The Great Motown Love Song Duets*. Motown's re-issues and re-promoted items were always popular in Britain, the country of nostalga lovers, and although only the more outstanding became hits they were regular catalogue sellers after their initial release.

In America, Harlem's Apollo in New York was the home for black performers from 1935 until 1976, when it closed, another victim of Harlem urban decline. In its heyday the Apollo (which carries a similar musical heritage to England's London Palladium situated in the city's West End) was the stronghold for black music. Inner City Broadcasting, NBC and Motown Productions brought the Apollo

Maureen Steele had the potential to become a top seller following her one-off Nature Of The Beast *album. When it flopped, Steele sang back-up vocals for Michael Lovesmith.*

Mary Wilson is pictured here with the late Florence Ballard's daughter, Lisa, during an exhibition held in Florence's memory in Los Angeles. The exhibition was organized by the late singer's fan club.

(Far right) Marvin Gaye as his fans remember him.

back to life again following a $10 million rehabilitation project, with a gala concert which coincided with the theatre's 50th anniversary. The concert was screened on NBC during May 1985, and the proceeds went to the Ethiopian Relief Fund. The stage spectacular included Thelma Houston, Mary Wilson, Jennifer Holliday, Martha Reeves, the Four Tops, Stevie Wonder, Billy Preston (who paid tribute to Otis Redding with Try A Little Tenderness), Luther Vandross (who remembered Marvin Gaye with How Sweet It Is), Patti LaBelle who joined forces with the New Jersey Mass Choir for You'll Never Walk Alone, George Michael sang with Smokey Robinson on Careless Whisper and with Stevie Wonder on The World Is In Need Of Love Today. Wonder then sang with Boy George. Diana Ross flew to the concert by helicopter in time for the finale I Want To Know What Love Is with the Mass Choir. A member of the audience told an American magazine: 'In the middle of so much despair in Harlem, the Apollo revival comes as a hope for us all'. Stevie Wonder, who performed Fingertips at the theatre when he was a mere 11-year-old, told People magazine: 'The Apollo was like my home after school and I would study backstage between shows.' The dynamic Patti LaBelle who, according to most of the concert's critics, stole the show, recalled: 'I miss the card games between shows and the way people used to sell hot furs and jewellery backstage. And we used to have hot dogs for dinner there. We put them on light bulbs to heat them up and ate them after the show.' Motown Returns To The Apollo won a Emmy Award for Best Variety Programme.

Willie Hutch, whose own album Making A Game Out Of Love featuring The Glow with Syreeta and Inside You with The Temptations was released in June 1985 (UK, Jul '85), wrote and produced three tracks on the Four Tops album Magic (US, May '85/UK, Jul '85). Reggie Lucas and Johnny Bristol produced the remainder. Magic, for some reason, included two inferior cover versions of I'm Ready For Love (Martha and the Vandellas) and Remember Me

(Diana Ross), while Phyllis Hyman was featured on Maybe Tomorrow. The album showed how the quartet had mellowed, yet despite containing slick and sophisticated presentations, the hit ingredient was missing. The group, however, were pleased with the response the album received, although it was minimal compared to their earlier work.

During June 1985 CBS Records released Marvin Gaye's Dream Of A Lifetime album with all the tracks taken from two sources: Gaye's mother, who was given the songs by Gaye for safe keeping, and the remainder from the album Gaye had started for Motown but had abandoned. The three Motown songs were Symphony (co-written by Smokey Robinson), It's Madness and Dream Of A Lifetime. The latter track was originally titled My Wonderful Life which Gaye began recording with Sammy Davis Jr in the early Seventies for his Ecology label licensed to Motown. CBS's Larkin Arnold compiled Dream Of A Lifetime, which carried a warning on the cover that two tracks Savage In The Sack and Masochistic Beauty were sexually explicit and could be considered offensive to some listeners. The highlight of this release was, however, Life Symphony describing how Gaye's conflict between his religious upbringing clashed with his lifestyle. Sanctified Lady (originally Sanctified P****) and It's Madness were lifted from the album as singles. The last CBS Marvin Gaye album was Romantically Yours in December 1985, the content of which was exactly what the title suggested.

Lionel Richie, meanwhile, was in the studios recording his third solo album, but before he finished the project he once again joined the list of Motown artists to be sued. In June 1985 songwriter Gene Thompson alleged Richie had copied extracts from his composition Somebody's Got To Love Her in Stuck On You and Hello. Motown, James Anthony Carmichael and Brookman Music were also defendants in the case filed in Los Angeles' Federal District Court. Thompson alleged he gave Richie's agent a copy of the song in June 1980, followed by a second copy a month later.

Ex-Temptation Dennis Edwards once again stunned his fans with his second solo album Coolin' Out (US, Jun '85/UK, Aug '85). Edwards: 'I wanted this album to be better than the first one. I think the public will like it and it will be successful. I want to see it go all the way from gold to multi-platinum. With the first album, we really weren't sure what direction we were taking Dennis Edwards, solo artist. With Coolin' Out I think we're right on target'. This splendid album included Edwards' duet with Thelma Houston, Why Do People Fall In Love, and a version of Otis Redding's Try A Little Tenderness and The Temptations' composition Coolin' Out. Siedah Garrett, Phillip Ingram and the album's producer Dennis Lambert, among others, provided backing vocals.

In Britain, Motown International in

The dynamic Val Young was another of Rick James' protégés. Young only released one album Seduction in 1985 but could be seen supporting James on tour.

London, signed singer Jake Jacas. Born in Clapham, South London, and raised in Essex, Jacas spent nine years in the care of Dr Barnardo's (a home for orphans) before joining the British Army, where he received his initial training as a bandsman before leaving at the age of 21. Jacas joined the British soul group, Gonzales, to enjoy a UK top twenty hit with I *Haven't Stopped Dancing Yet.* Jacas' first single was *Hold Me* in June 1985 which flopped, and unfortunately this exceptionally talented singer was not given a second chance with Motown.

The Dazz Band introduced their new guitarist Marlon McClain on their July released *Hot Spot* album (UK, Sep '85). Dazz Band leader Bobby Harris: 'We did everything differently on this album. It's totally different from the *Let It Whip* days. We wanted to go in a new direction and try to update the Dazz Band's sound. We spent some time in Europe this year and the influence of that is felt on the album.' The new-sounding album was a poor seller when compared to their previous releases and before 1985 was out, the group left Motown to sign with Geffen Records. Their first single *Wild And Free*, the title track from their forthcoming album, was released mid-1986. Motown cashed in by releasing a *Best Of* album.

With the Mary Jane Girls' single *In My House* and his own *Glow* album in the American charts, Rick James launched his next protégé, the vivacious Val Young. Prior to the release of her suitably titled *Seduction* album (US, Jul '85/UK, Mar '86). Young released the single *Mind Games* in the US in June 1985. *Seduction*, which featured both Rick James (as writer, co-producer and vocalist) and the Stone City Band, was a powerfully compiled release, with tracks that amply suited Young's distinguished voice. Once again, James' discovery attracted considerable media interest as Young was marketed as the 'black Marilyn Monroe'. Young: 'My blonde hair was Rick's idea. He convinced me that blondes have more fun and more funds! I'm the same person inside, but I do like it. When I look in the mirror, I like what I see. Sure, people do stop and look at me but I don't mind that. Mostly I get compliments and the only one or two negatives have come from people who don't know me.'

Val Young was raised in Detroit, Michigan, where, at the age of eleven she sang in church and school. She intended to finish her education to ensure she had a profession to fall back on should a singing career fail. In 1978 Young got her first professional break as a 'Bride Of Funkenstein' with George Clinton's Parliament Funkadelic. She stayed with Clinton for a year before working with the Gap Band and recording one of their many hits *Ooops Inside Your Head* and being featured on five subsequent albums. While touring, Young approached Rick James: 'I just walked

up to him, told him I loved him and wanted to sing with him. Getting to work with him has been the most exciting thing that has ever happened to me.' *Seduction*, although not a huge money spinner, represented an aggressive unique talent and with the right marketing and promotion could have turned Young into Motown's number one songstress. A single of the album's title track (British release on twelve inch only, Nov '85) and *If You Should Ever Be Lonely* (UK, Feb '86) were released before the end of 1985, and although all were nightclub hits, none crossed over into the national charts. A Christian and mother, and later wife of Process and the Doo Rags' member Dennis Andrews, Young was careful with the lyrical content of her material, despite calling her album *Seduction*, which she interpreted as meaning 'Sexy and showing everything you've got, but you can only admire it, you can't have it. In my case, my eyes are my seducers, they do my talking for me. I think my album is seductive but it's also tasteful.' Rick James introduced Young to American audiences via a five month tour with the Mary Jane Girls and Process and the Doo Rags. The latter was a further Rick James' project whom he intended to sign to Motown, but the negotiations broke down even though an album was scheduled, and the group joined CBS Records instead.

Before Val Young could release a second album with Motown, Rick James and his unequalled stable of artists became the subject of dispute with the company. Scheduled product was temporarily shelved as the wrangle continued and careers came to an unexpected halt.

Even though Marvin Gaye was dead, his turbulant lifestyle continued to command attention in court. During August 1985, Motown bought the film rights to David Ritz's controversial book *Divided Soul*, based on the life of Gaye, for a reputed $100 million, following an auction in a Los Angeles Superior Court. The auction was ordered when three people, including Harvey Fuqua, claimed Motown's original deal with Ritz for an estimated $70 million was too low. When Gaye was shot it was said he had left a debt of $10 million, and that Motown had bought the book's rights to prevent any other company purchasing it. Yet, Motown did intend to produce a film of Gaye's life and Jermaine Jackson confirmed he had been asked to play the late singer. However, to date the movie has not materialised. Jermaine Jackson's brother, Michael, was also in the news in August 1985. Following a legal battle between Paul McCartney and the late John Lennon's wife, Yoko Ono, Jackson bought the rights to ATV Music for approximately $5 million which owned nearly three hundred Lennon and McCartney compositions from 1964 to 1970.

In August 1985, a 1970 Mercedes Benz '600' Pullman limousine was included in a Sothebys auction of Rock and Roll Memorabilia in London. This car was built for the late John Lennon, who later sold it to fellow Beatle George Harrison. In 1975 the vehicle was purchased by Mary Wilson and her husband Pedro Ferrer, in whose name the vehicle was bought. During May 1980 the Mercedes was subsequently placed with The Supreme Vehicle Body Repair Specialists, a garage in Basingstoke, Hampshire then jointly owned by Thomas Lubbock-Smith and Kenneth Trodd, for a complete re-spray and a repair estimate for the non-running engine. The garage began working on the Mercedes but stopped when the bill due for previous work carried out on a Mercedes Benz Saloon (owned by Ferrer) was not paid. When Ferrer paid his bill the work re-commenced on the Mercedes Benz '600'. When a second bill was not paid the Mercedes Benz '600' was sold to another Basingstoke garage to cover the cost of the repair work. From there the Mercedes had several owners before being sold to a used car salesman from St Louis, Missouri. When Mary Wilson was informed that the Mercedes Benz '600' was to be auctioned, she instructed her lawyers to stop it being included in the Sothebys sale. Wilson now had to prove her ownership of the vehicle in a British court in the spring 1988 where the defendants were The Supreme Vehicle Body Repair Specialists, who, she alleged, sold the Mercedes unlawfully.

Meanwhile ex-Supreme Jean Terrell abandoned her singing career to work in her brother, Jimmie's, hair salon in Los Angeles. Jean had studied hairstyling for six months and told *Shoptalk* magazine: 'I gained a lot of experience working with Anglo, Spanish and Oriental hair, but I wanted more experience working with black people's hair. I do everything, nails, hairstyling, haircutting, whatever my clients want. There's also a lot of security in working in a family enterprise, and with people you love.' Prior to this, Terrell had toured briefly with Lynda Lawrence as backing vocalist performing Supremes' material. Terrell's solo association with A&M Records ended following the 1978 release of her *I Had To Fall In Love* album and when she reputedly disagreed with the company's plans for her because they clashed with her Jehovah's Witness beliefs.

Following strong British response to his *Break The Ice* track, Motown/BMG released Michael Lovesmith's *Rhymes Of Passion* album in August 1985, following its American June release. To promote the single Lovesmith flew to London for a promotional visit. Lovesmith: 'I love the British culture and have been intrigued by the accent for some time. Europe is an entirely different world. You can travel from state to state in America and everything is more or less the same. In Europe everything is different and attitudes are remarkable.' Lovesmith's home was now in the San Fer-

nando Valley: 'I live middle-class, executive class. I have had a pretty successful and lucrative career outside of singing, so I've made quite a bit of money'. Lovesmith was an instant hit with the British media and nightclub punters, but it was not reflected in record sales and by 1988 he had left Motown.

In America, Smokey Robinson became television host in August 1985. He spearheaded a series titled *The Motown Revue*, a Motown Productions project, where his guests included Mary Wells and Diana Ross. Despite having the right ingredients for a variety show, the series failed to attract viewers.

Before the end of 1985 Stevie Wonder, one of Motown's three remaining megastars, released his *In Square Circle* album. Although criticized by the media, the US/UK September release did win Wonder a 1986 Grammy in the Best R&B Vocal, Male, category. *In Square Circle*, a straightforward collection of pop/love songs, was his first 'proper' album for five years since *Hotter Than July*, and featured Syreeta, Deniece Williams and Luther Vandross. Wonder said the album's delay was due to his other commitments: 'I'd been working a lot on making Martin Luther King's birthday a national holiday and was also working on *The Woman In Red* soundtrack, and it just took me a long time to get the songs I wanted together. The album represents who I am in this decade, and it also represents what I'm seeing in a lot of situations with a lot of people.' The album's theme was intended to represent life's beauty but, Wonder said: 'People have to work at making things happen at the time.'

Ex-Supremes' lead singer Jean Terrell abandoned singing to become a hairdresser in her brother's Los Angeles salon.

The original line-up of the Mary Jane Girls (left to right: Candi, Cheri, Maxi and Jo Jo, with the release of their second album Only Four You. Yvette Martin joined the group to replace Cheri Wells.

A month prior to the album's release, the brisk, catchy *Part-Time Lover* was issued (UK, Sep '85). Wonder needed another *I Just Called To Say I Love You* following two near-misses with *Love Light In Flight* and *Don't Drive Drunk*, so as an added sales attraction the single was re-mixed by Wonder and extended to eight minutes playing time. The twelve inch version, with Luther Vandross on the introduction, was also issued on cassette. This marketing ploy worked and *Part-Time Lover* became Wonder's twenty-sixth top ten single on Billboard's charts, and peaked at number three in Britain. Other *In Square Circle* album tracks lifted as mid-selling singles were *Go Home* in 1985, the ballad *Overjoyed* and *Land Of La La* in 1986. Wonder wrote the music to *Overjoyed* five years prior to adding the lyrics: 'I usually come up with the music first and then come up with an idea about the song. I sing out loud and change it right away if it sounds like there's too many words.' Many of his ideas originate from news broadcasts, everyday life, and the world's injustices. Wonder: 'Unfortunately, some of the things that are negative in the news keep happening. Man never seems to learn.' His views on apartheid were once more strongly aired on the album's two-year-old track *It's Wrong (Apartheid)* which he recorded to encourage people towards taking positive action: 'You know it's wrong, like slavery was wrong, like the Holocaust was wrong.' At the time of the album's release Wonder was the only American artist to have reached the number one spot with a debut album, and to have had seventeen American number one singles in the pop and R&B charts. He also had more records on catalogue than any other Motown artist, and every one of his albums released since 1973 had reached the top ten in the American pop charts. Wonder now lived in Beverly Hills, while his children Kieta and Aisha, lived with their mother in New York. Shortly after the album's release, Wonder led a host of international names like Dionne Warwick and Ashford & Simpson to record tracks for the album of the British musical *Time*, the brainchild of Dave Clark (the drummer with the Sixties group Dave Clark Five). The first single lifted from the album was Cliff Richard singing Wonder's song *She's So Beautiful*.

Lushus Daim, like Vanity, was a signing whose beautiful looks attracted more attention than her voice, a fact fully exploited by Motown who announced her as mysterious, passionate, strong and cunning and the seventh child of the seventh son, born in the seventh month. Daim's debut album *More Than You Can Handle* was released in September 1985 under the name Lushus Daim and the Pretty Vain, and was the first Conceited Records album to be distributed by Motown. The album's title track and *The One You Love* were lifted as singles in 1985, but the project failed. *More Than You Can Handle* was released

in Europe but not Britain.

Born in Los Angeles, Daim spent her early life in Germany before travelling with her parents and three brothers and three sisters around the world's US military bases. While travelling on board a plane, Daim asked two music executives to listen to her taped songs. That meeting resulted in Daim moving to Los Angeles permanently and signing with managers Ron Perry and Louis Williams, who in turn introduced her to Leon Sylvers. Sylvers produced the *More Than You Can Handle* album, a combination of rock and R&B, which should have been an ideal foundation for a future singing career but was virtually ignored by the record buying public.

However, the public *did* come out in force to attend Diana Ross' British dates in September 1985, her first visit since 1982. Ross had recently enjoyed a huge American hit with *Missing You*, yet despite several re-promotions the single died in Britain. The poignant ballad was dedicated to the late Marvin Gaye. Ross: 'It actually came out of a conversation that Smokey Robinson and I had one evening about how we were missing Marvin, and what he meant to us, as well as to music. Then Lionel (Richie) and I got to talking about how we need to tell people that we love them while they're still alive. Lionel used all this to write that beautiful and special song.' The emotional sentiment behind the song was best realized through Ross' promotional video which featured footage of Gaye, interspliced with Ross performing the song. Still shots of the late ex-Supreme Florence Ballard, ex-Temptation Paul Williams, and Ross' mother were also briefly shown in one of 1985's best videos. *Missing You* was lifted from Diana Ross' fourth Capitol album *Swept Away*. Lionel Richie and James Anthony Carmichael produced the single and Ross produced six of the album's ten tracks.

In October 1985, Lionel Richie came into his own once again by releasing the *Say You, Say Me* single (UK, Nov '85). The song was the main title from Taylor Hackford's *White Nights* movie, based on two dancers trying to escape from the Soviet Union. Motown was forced to release *Say You, Say Me* prematurely (it was intended to hold it until Richie had completed his album) when Columbia Pictures, who distributed the film, sent the taped song to American radio stations to promote the movie. In December 1985 the single became Richie's ninth American chart-topper and his ninth solo British hit, reaching number eight. It also won an American Academy Award for Best Song and the Golden Globe Award for Best Song in 1986. Richie: 'You think I'm talking about a boy and girl (in the song) but there's something else whispering at you under the surface. It could be about a romance, but it's about the awakening of the inner person to stand and be strong. It's about the *White Nights* movie but if you never see the

Diana Ross recorded her personal tribute to the late Marvin Gaye with the Lionel Richie composition Missing You.

movie, it'll still apply to the barriers that you run into in a love affair.'

Stevie Wonder was also active at this time, taking part in possibly the largest live phone call in history. During an Al Jarreau concert in Portland, Oregan, Jarreau's two thousand strong audience called Wonder up on the phone. The two way conversation of songs and poetry lasted thirty minutes and was carried on the sound system at the Portland Meadows outdoor amphitheatre. Prior to this Wonder wrote and produced *Everything's Coming Up Roses* for Eddie Murphy's *How Could It Be* album, while Rick James wrote and produced *Party All The Time*. During November 1985 Wonder, Gladys Knight, Dionne Warwick and Elton John topped the pop and black singles charts with *That's What Friends Are For*. The profits from the single went to the American Foundation for AIDS Research, headed by the actress Elizabeth Taylor.

In October Motown/BMG released an eight album box set in the UK titled *150 Hits Of Gold*. These albums featured 150 titles in chronological order beginning with Mary Wells' *My Guy* and ending with DeBarge's *Rhythm Of The Night*. Every track was a British hit. A ninth bonus album, *Motown – Today And Forever*, was also included in the box set featuring Motown's current releases. The eight albums

could also be purchased separately.

Following their performance with Hall and Oates on the Live Aid spectacular, David Ruffin and Eddie Kendrick (now minus the 's' on his surname) were featured on the RCA duo's *Live At The Apollo* album. The two ex-Temptations joined Hall and Oates in the medley *Get Ready, Ain't Too Proud To Beg, The Way You Do The Things You Do* and *My Girl*. The latter two tracks were lifted as a single. The two acts decided to join forces on stage and record after performing together at the United Negro College Fund charity night. Following their Hall and Oates sessions, Kendrick and Ruffin went on to record as a duo.

Before 1985 ended Martha Reeves toured Britain once again. Her deal with the American company Airwave had ended recordless when the owner tragically died, but since her appearance on *Motown* 25 her touring commitments had soared. Reeves: 'I now have three agents in the States and they've had me working constantly since that show. I'm turning down dates now because they can't be fitted in.' Reeves' performances still included many of her Motown hits but she longed to perform the canned songs that the company still held. Reeves: 'There must be at least three hundred songs somewhere in Motown that the Vandellas and I recorded. I could fill the gap in my career between 1970 and 1980 with these songs. However. I still make a good living, don't get me wrong, and I thank God for that, and also that London and Europe still care for me.'

The Temptations, whose *Touch Me* album was issued in November 1985 (UK, Dec '85), were also touring but in America. They occasionally teamed up with The Four Tops onstage, but the majority of their dates were solo gigs. The continual rigours of touring had taken its toll on Otis Williams who underwent foot surgery for a complaint common with dancers. Williams: 'Our choreography is still part of our show and still comes easily. I don't remember all the early routines we used to do, but I remember enough. We're not chickens any more, maybe seasoned chickens, so as long as we rest up every now and again we can manage to keep the pace.' In between recording and touring The Temptations were featured in Lee Major's television programme *The Fall Guy* and planned to appear in Peter Faulkner's *Happy New Year* movie, although they had to shelve an appearance in *Rocky 4* due to recording commitments.

At the close of 1985 Carl Bean's *I Was Born This Way* was re-issued in the UK on 10 Records. The song was originally released on the Motown label, in March 1978 (UK, May '78). Once again the gay communities adopted the song as their national anthem, particularly in the face of the AIDS epidemic being blamed on them. This may have been the reason the single was re-released, because it gave gays the solidarity needed to

Ex-Temptations David Ruffin and Eddie Kendrick joined forces with Hall and Oates on record and stage before signing their own deal with RCA/BMG.

(Left) Martha Reeves toured Britain in 1985 and said that since her appearance on Motown 25 she was turning down concerts due to her heavy touring schedule.

Carl Bean's I Was Born This Way single, originally released by Motown, was re-issued in Britain ten years later. Once again it was adopted by the gay community.

Warp 9 only had one opportunity to record at Motown. Their Fade In, Fade Out *album, released in 1986, was a musical showcase.*

overcome heavy public condemnation.

During 1986 rumours continued to run rife in the industry that MCA intended to buy Motown for an estimated $75 million. How such a takeover would affect Motown could not be ascertained, although the prospect of Berry Gordy losing control of his company, and possibly losing his creative input, could only drastically change the company's reputation. Although Motown of the Eighties had lost the magic of the Sixties, and was considered to be just another record company, it was still held in high esteem by the public. To have Motown run by a conglomeration was unthinkable, although from a business point-of-view it probably made good sense. However, Motown's quest to break new talent never wavered, nor did the financial investment in acts.

The first new signing of 1986 was the duo Warp 9, Chuck Wansley and Katherine Joyce, with their debut album *Fade In, Fade Out* (US, Jan '86/UK, Mar '86) which contained *Skips A Beat* their single release in December 1985 (UK, Feb '86). Born in New York, Joyce began playing the piano when she was seven years old. Her ambition was to become an actress so she attended the New York Performing Arts High School. In time it became apparent to her that there were more singing jobs than acting parts, so she chose the former and worked on the Manhattan club circuit. Joyce then joined the group Electrified Action to tour American military bases in Europe before joining Sparque to enjoy the dance hit *Let's Go Dancin'*. From there she joined The Shades Of Love to record the *Keep In Touch (Body To Body)* single. Joyce's acting ambitions were fulfilled with theatre bit parts, a role in an off-Broadway Shakespearian musical *Where The Wild Thyme Blows* and performances with Richard Pryor.

Chuck Wansley was born into a musical family and learned to play drums at school. In his junior high school, Wansley's drumming expertise got him into adult bands. Prior to graduating from the University of Hartford,

(Right) After spending most of her time as a backing vocalist and duettist, Alfie Silas recorded her own That Look *album in 1986.*

Wansley toured the world with the Up With People group. This tour included performing before the Pope in the Vatican Theatre in Rome, and President Kenyatta in Kenya. When he returned to America, Wansley returned to college to learn musical techniques before working with Mary Wells, Martha Reeves and Phyllis Hyman. Wansley and Joyce first met in Motown's recording studios where Warp 9 was formed, however, after their exciting debut project, no further recordings were released.

Also in January 1986 Alfie Silas debuted with her *That Look* album, produced by Michael Durio (her husband), Norman Whitfield and Willie Hutch. Silas, an expressive and soulful singer, had previously released her contribution to the *Berry Gordy's The Last Dragon* soundtrack album. Titled *Star*, the single was released in 1985. Silas was born and raised in Los Angeles, the youngest of five children, in a musical environment. As a church choir member she was promoted to lead vocalist in her first, contemporary gospel group Geary Lanier & We. Her professional career began in the mid-Seventies when she toured Canada with Martha Reeves prior to making television appearances on *Gimme A Break* and *The Jeffersons*. As well as singing, Silas was a prolific songwriter and keyboardist. As she grew up with the Motown Sound it was natural her ambition would be to join the company. Unfortunately *That Look* was her only album and it wasn't released in Britain.

For his album *Smoke Signals* (US, Jan '86/UK, Mar '86) Smokey Robinson gave total creative control to Tony Peluso and Steve Barri. Robinson: 'They said they wanted to do this album in a manner where I just shut up. I didn't have any opinions. I just went into the studios and sang. They wanted to put me into what they feel is the mainstream, the musical sound that is happening now. It was much easier than any album I've ever done.' However, Robinson did contribute more than his vocals as he co-wrote five tracks: *Hold On To Your Love*

(co-written with Stevie Wonder), *Hanging On By A Thread*, *Be Kind To The Growing Mind* (featuring The Temptations on backing vocals), *Because Of You* (*It's The Best It's Ever Been*) and the Spanish track *Te Quiero Como Si No Hubiera Un Manana* (*I'm Gonna Love You Like There's No Tomorrow*) featuring Herb Alpert on horn. Robinson: 'Usually whenever we play there's a large Chicano following. So I thought with *Aqui Contigo/Being With You* being so popular in person, why not record it? I think I'll probably include a Spanish or bilingual tune on all my albums from now on.' Robinson also considered *Be Kind To The Growing Mind* the most important on the album because he was pleading with artists to bear in mind the influence they have over young fans: 'The point I'm making in the song is that we have a lot of young minds out there. Morals are a joke, but I don't think it should be that way. I think that by fellow artists hearing this from me, it will be more effective than all the wives, committees, parents and stuff like that in the world.'

A month after *Smoke Signals*, Vanity released her second album *Skin On Skin* (UK, May 1986). Produced by Skip Drinkwater and Tommy Faragher, Vanity's vocals outweighed her sexy image this time. However, Motown's marketing included the album sleeve showing her as a 1930's diva and the advertizing for the first single *Under The Influence*, in February 1986 (UK, Apr '86), featured her in half-naked poses. Despite being a better album than her debut, sales were not sufficient for crossover success.

On 1 February 1986 Diana Ross married for a second time. Her husband was Arne Naess Jr, a 47-year-old Norwegian shipping magnate

and Everest climber with three children Leona, Katinka and Christoffer. The wedding was held at the Abbey of Romain Motier, Switzerland, before two hundred and forty attending friends and relatives, including Stevie Wonder and Gregory Peck, flown in for the marriage. Ross wore a pearl-embroidered satin dress, with a white veil of antique Norwegian lace. During the ceremony the forty-five member Norwegian Silver Boys Choir sang, while Pastors John Pierre Tuscher and Graham Ferguson-Lacey conducted the event. And Stevie Wonder sang I *Just Called To Say I Love You*: 'I have known and loved Diana for twenty years, singing at the wedding was the best present I could have given.' The ceremony cost over one million pounds, including the choir's airfares and hotel costs, security staff and chauffeurs, friends' and relatives' airfares, etc, white blooms flown in from London for the Abbey's decoration. Mr and Mrs Naess honeymooned on Tiano (re-named Diana), Naess' private Tahitian island.

Diana Ross had met Arne Naess in May 1984 while holidaying in the Bahamas. They kept in touch with each other and when Naess was to be knighted in Oslo, he invited Ross to be his guest. After the ceremony he asked her to marry him. Ross told US magazine: 'We came from completely different worlds. He doesn't know about the show-business world, which is refreshing really. Our conversations aren't about the gossip of show business or Hollywood. I've never had the adventure that he brings into my life. I've been to Norway, and I met his family and I find them all extraordinary. It's like something else came alive, something new. He is able to blend into my life with all this chaos very easily, somehow. We get involved with things I wouldn't normally get involved with: dedicating this museum in Norway, or going to Africa on a safari. I expected to feel a oneness with the tribes there, and they found me very strange. I think you go to see your heritage, (but) black Americans are really just completely different. You can't send us back to Africa, because we don't belong there either. But you do see faces that remind you of your history. Mostly, it was about the animals for me. I've never seen animals free like that.' Prior to their fairy-tale wedding in Switzerland, Ross and Naess were married in a civil ceremony in New York City in October 1985.

Motown's most exciting new signing of 1986 was Pal (Rhett and Sinden Cellier, Rebekha Sweet). The female trio never released a record in America but they enjoyed some success in Europe with their first single *Talk We Don't* released in March 1986 and taken from their April album *Truth For The Moment*. The trio was formed after the Cellier sisters had toured America as a duo while solo Sweet learned to programme computerized instruments. Sweet: 'We were later spread out all over the industry, one of us even worked for a

Diana Ross married for the second time in 1986. Her husband Arne Naess was a Norwegian shipping magnate. The couple had a civil marriage in New York, followed by a church ceremony in Switzerland where this photo was taken.

Rick James (top left) in his famous Street Songs pose. Val Young (top right) was marketed as the 'black Marilyn Monroe'. Their hard freaky sound was miles away from the European pop sound of Pal (below left) and the classic style of Sam Harris (below right). These artists represent the varying hit sounds of Motown during the Eighties.

The Mary Jane Girls (far right) were Motown's legitimate female freak and rock group: 'We feature a lot of sexual overtones in our act and in our music, so that makes us more than a little risqué.'

lawyer, where Motown was a client. We really worked to finance our demos and because we wanted to produce high quality ones, that took a lot of money.' Pal circulated those demos around record companies with no results. Motown actually turned them down six times! A&R executive Steve Buckley received Pal's demos while employed by Capitol Records and intended to sign them. Before he could, he left to join Motown so took Pal with him. The trio's tapes were subsequently sent to Peter Prince, Motown's vice-president based in London, who was sufficiently impressed to arrange for them to tour Europe. Prince: 'We tried with them but unfortunately they didn't happen. Motown signed them for the world and because of my enthusiasm for the act, and their European sound, Motown thought it would be a good idea to break them in Europe first. We have had success in this way before with, say, Billy Preston and Syreeta and *With You I'm Born Again* which happened in the UK and Europe before being released in America.' The trio's young, vibrant, pop sound was ideal for the Continent, and their colourful, flamboyant performances attracted a young audience. During their lengthy European stay a *Talk We Don't* video was filmed in a warehouse in London's Battersea, which was extensively used in nightclubs. Why Pal failed in Europe remains a mystery.

Welsh superstar Tom Jones was Troy Johnson's first biggest influence before embarking on a musical career. By the time he was 13 years old Johnson played piano, saxophone and bass guitar, and had played with numerous local groups by the age of 16 years. His first break in music business came when he sang *I Must Be Doing Something Right*, the theme song from the 1983 film *Blame It On Rio* starring Michael Caine. Three years later Johnson met a representative of producer/writer Leon Sylvers, a Kallista label's A&R executive, in his hometown of San Bernadino, California. This meeting led to Johnson recording his *Getting A Grip On Love* album for that label, whereupon Motown distributed it during March 1986 (UK, Jun '86). It's *You* was lifted as its first single a month earlier in the US only. Johnson, nicknamed Kallista's toy boy, wrote or co-wrote five of the album's tracks and co-produced it with Leon Sylvers. The result was an attractive pop/R&B release which failed to create much excitement among record buyers.

Guinn (brothers Skip, Earl, Randy, Michael; sisters, Margie, Bonnie and honorary member Loni Thorton) had sung together since 1970. The Guinn sisters were the first to perform before an audience and they encouraged the boys to join them. Skip Guinn told journalist Mark Webster in 1986; 'We have been singing around Philadelphia for a while now as a band, although at one point we did split up to do our own things. But we missed each other.

It feels much more natural singing together.' Guinn came to Motown's attention when they appeared with other acts on a showcase in Philadelphia. Their performance secured a recording contract. Guinn's eponymous debut album (US, Mar '86/UK, Apr '86) was a classy collection of songs which portrayed their tight, smooth vocal harmonies. It was an excellent release and deserved more public support than it received. The single *Dreamin'* was released prior to the album in January 1986 under the name 'The Guinn Family'. This was followed in June 1986 by *Open Your Door*, released in Britain a month earlier. This family group's Motown stay was ill-fated and to date they have not recorded a further record.

While CBS attempted to recoup the advances paid to the late Marvin Gaye via their *Midnight Love* and two posthumous albums, *Dream Of A Lifetime* and *Romantically Yours*, Motown released their memorial album *Motown Remembers Marvin Gaye* (US, Mar '86/UK, May '86). The twelve-tracked American release featured unreleased songs recorded during the Sixties and early Seventies, with musical overdubs by Hal Davis. One duet was included by Gaye and Kim Weston titled *Baby (Don't You Leave Me)* from 1965, produced by Clarence Paul. Other tracks included the album's first American single issued in May 1986 *The World Is Rated X*, originally produced by Hal Davis in 1971, who said: 'I remember how elated Marvin was the night he recorded (this). He got in the car with me to share his enthusiasm, excitement and joy that we were working together again. Marvin to me was comical, articulate and very rhythmic, with an unusual way of phrasing lyrics and writing songs which would coincide with the present and future times of man's existance.' *No Greater Love* (circa 1965), produced by Harvey Fuqua was gospel based and included Monalisa Young, Oma Drake and Terry Young on backing vocals. *Loving And Affection* (1963) and *I'm In Love With You* (1967) were also co-written and produced by Paul, while Berry Gordy wrote and produced the 1964 song *I Gotta Have Your Lovin'*, and Ashford & Simpson wrote and produced the 1969 track *Dark Side Of The World*.

The British release of *Motown Remembers Marvin Gaye* included the additional track *I Heard It Through The Grapevine* which was released as a single in Britain in April 1986. This re-issue became a top ten single after Levi's used the song in its television advertizing for 501 jeans. *The World Is Rated X* was its follow-up in June 1986. Other Motown songs to be used in television advertizing at this time included *Reach Out I'll Be There*, *ABC* and *Heatwave*. Through Levi's nostalgia pitch in selling their original 501 jeans, other artists enjoyed renewed success with old records such as Sam Cooke's *Wonderful World* which became a British top ten hit. And when Levi's launched their new campaign, the company once again used soul classics – Percy Sledge's *When A*

Kallista's Troy Johnson secured a recording deal with Motown for his Getting A Grip On Love *album. Unfortunately, his good looks did not attract record buyers.*

Man Loves A Woman and Ben E King's *Stand By Me* which was also the title song from the film of the same name. The single became a British number one in 1987.

To celebrate the 25th anniversaries of both The Temptations and Diana Ross and the Supremes, Motown released two special albums in 1986. Instead of being just straight re-issues, the albums contained previously unreleased material as a buying incentive. The Temptations' exclusives included A *Tear From A Woman's Eye* (featuring Eddie Kendricks), *Wherever I Lay My Hat (That's My Home)* (featuring the late Paul Williams), *Truly Yours* (with David Ruffin's lead on this Spinners' hit), *Soulmate* (a leftover track from A *Song For You* album) and two of their earliest recordings *So Much Joy* and *It Don't Have To Be This Way*. Diana Ross and the Supremes' release contained tracks like *The Blue Room* and *Manhattan* (originally recorded for *The Supremes Sing Rodgers & Hart* when it was intended to be a double album release), *When You Wish Upon A Star*, *Heigh Ho* and *Someday My Prince Will Come* (from a proposed 1967 album *The Supremes Sing Disney Classics*), *Surfer Boy* (from a cameo appearance the group made in the *Beach Ball* film) and the much in demand Coca Cola Commercial (circa 1965 using *Baby Love* as the backing track).

Also in April Motown/BMG lifted *You Keep Me Hangin' On* from Diana Ross and the Supremes' anniversary album. However, the single's packaging featured Mary Wilson, Diana Ross and Cindy Birdsong, when in fact Florence Ballard should have been seen instead of Birdsong. Both Wilson and Birdsong were upset at Ballard's absence, although it was too late to rectify the error. Meanwhile, Diana Ross had enjoyed her first British number one single, *Chain Reaction*, since leaving Motown. Cindy Birdsong: 'The whole Supremes thing is taking off again in a big way. It's amazing because it's not only in England but in the States also. Everyone is getting into oldies again which for me is just great.'

The Temptations took their anniversary celebrations one step further by touring Britain in April 1986 and Motown/BMG released the *I'm Fascinated* single to coincide. The group's performance at London's Hammersmith Odeon was received with a rousing welcome from the audience. The Temptations launched straight into *Superstar*, a brilliant (I Know) *I'm Losing You* and *I'm Gonna Make You Love Me*. After a pause for introductions further hits rolled by – *Get Ready*, *The Way You Do The Things You Do* and *Ain't Too Proud To Beg*. The Temptations, although older in years, still produced a fast-paced show, although the more highly choreographed routines were less intricate. Motown/BMG later released *My Girl* as a single because they considered it to be the concert's highlight.

In May 1986 (UK, Jul '86) El DeBarge re-

leased his first solo album, and unlike the DeBarge albums, none of the songs was composed by him. Titled *El DeBarge* the album mixed soul sounds with crossover commercial tracks like *Who's Johnny*, the theme song from the *Short Circuit* film, which was also the first single in April 1986 (UK, May '86), and *Love Always* the second single in July 1986 (UK, Aug '86). Motown invested heavily in the solo DeBarge, who, as a member of the group, attracted the most fan attention. The intention to promote him as the second Michael Jackson seemed imperative to Motown's marketing division. It worked for a time, and with his recorded success and to broaden his public appeal, El appeared in an episode of *Miami Vice* as well as performing on numerous television shows. Leaving the security of the group was a risk, but DeBarge said: 'The group needed the break as much as I did. They need the space and opportunity to express their talents, and there'll be more opportunity for them now.' *El DeBarge* featured some of the industry's top writers and producers like Michael McDonald, Burt Bacharach and Carole Bayer Sager and Vanity. DeBarge: 'We tried to come up with a well-balanced album that offers a little of everything. I feel they are great songs although I'm probably my own worst critic when it comes to my work.' To promote his solo debut, DeBarge toured America as support act to The Pointer Sisters. His album was a big American seller, as was *Who's Johnny* which became a top five hit.

El's brother Chico followed hotly with his solo debut *Talk To Me* in August 1986 (UK, Oct '86), a track from his self-named album issued in September 1986 (UK, Nov '86). Chico was not a member of DeBarge, although he wrote for them; he had opted for a solo career because he felt his music was different from his family's style. Whereas DeBarge was smoothly soulful, Chico's was hard funk/rock, influenced by Phil Collins and Tears For Fears. DeBarge: 'I'm different whether for good or bad so it wouldn't have been compatible to work as part of DeBarge.' Chico enjoyed some American acclaim but in Britain, despite a promotional visit in 1987, his releases went unnoticed. Within a year, El DeBarge too was a forgotten name.

Stevie Wonder wrote *I Think It's Love* with Jermaine Jackson, a track lifted as a single from the latter's new Arista album *Precious Moments*. This was their first musical liaison since *Let's Get Serious* in 1980. Jackson supported the release of the single by performing at the DJ Convention at London's Hippodrome, his first live British date for six years. Jackson also announced the opening of his WORK label (Worldwide Organized Record Kompany) which would be controlled by his wife Hazel. They opened WORK to sign international artists and intended to open a European branch in London. Meanwhile, Jermaine's younger brother Michael had more of his

As was expected El DeBarge left his family group to embark on a solo career. His first self-named album was afforded heavy investment by Motown.

Following in his brother's footsteps Chico DeBarge released his first solo album in 1986. Chris was not a member of the DeBarge group but had written for them.

Motown catalogue resurrected to release the *Looking Back To Yesterday/Never-Before-Released-Masters* album in February 1986 (UK, May '86). It contained twelve tracks recorded by Jackson and the Jackson 5 between 1969 and 1975.

The year 1985 was Rick James' worst as far as record sales were concerned, but his Stone City Band Music, the publishing subsidiary of his company Mary Jane Productions, earned in excess of $500,000 in 1985, generated from material by Val Young, Eddie Murphy and the Mary Jane Girls. The recording situation was one that James intended to change with the release of his *The Flag* album (US, May '86/UK, Jul '86). A new look, short-haired singer delivered an extremely powerful, imaginative and thoughtful album, the highlights being *Funk In America/Silly Little Man* and *Sweet And Sexy Thing*, the first single lifted in April 1986 (UK, Jul '86). James: 'The flag on my album is the Freak Flag. A free flag for the people, not just a country. My flag is green, red and black. The green represents Mother Earth, the planet which we are destroying and which we must save. The red stands for passion and/or love and also for blood, which must not be shed. The black is alpha-omega, ying-yang, the beginning and the end. We have to rally around the green, red and black.' Prior to the album's release James appeared in two American television programmes, the soap opera *One Life To Live* and *The 'A' Team*. Meanwhile his first protégée, Teena Marie, released her third Epic/CBS album *Emerald City*. It was a diverse release incorporating rock and roll, calypso, ballads and dance music, and was an impassioned work from an intense Marie. Her fans were split in their support.

In May 1986, Motown/BMG re-released the 1965 album *We Remember Sam Cooke*. The record's packaging was identical to the original release, deleted eighteen years ago, except Diana Ross' name was added before the Supremes on the sleeve. This was the practice with re-issues from acts like The Supremes, Martha and the Vandellas and The Miracles, whose lead singers were given full name billing. Motown/BMG re-released this album due to the resurgent interest in the late Sam Cooke's music kindled by the Levi's 501 Jeans television advertizements.

Ex-Supreme Cindy Birdsong returned to the British stage in May 1986, performing at London's Hippodrome. Diana Ross and her husband Arne Naess were in the audience and visited Birdsong backstage where, in an unprecedented move, Ross agreed to pose for press photographers. Within two months a Diana Ross lookalike, Diana Keen, posed for promotional photographs when *Ain't No Mountain High Enough* was re-released by Motown/BMG after the song was featured in the British DHL couriers' television advert.

In America, Rockwell released his *The Genie* album in May 1986 (UK, Jul '86). It was a strong release that failed. However, Rockwell con-

tinued to push home his opinions via tracks like *Carmè (Part 1)*, the first single in May 1986 (UK, Jul '86). Rockwell: 'Carme is a love song that symbolizes the perfect girl out there who I have yet to find. *Baby On The Corner* is about social diseases. I'm not a religious fanatic but I do believe in God and I try to live with good moral values and standards. *Man From Mars* is where I tried to communicate what I was feeling about what's happening today (the speeded up track featured a covoderized rap representing a higher form of life). *That's Nasty*, well, America is already oversexed as it is. You look at it on television, you see it on billboards, do we have to listen to it on the radio as well. There are ways to say things without being so liberal.'

June 1986 saw Stevie Wonder back on the road, at the start of a sixty-date American tour. At his opening night in Seattle he stunned his audience when he sang twenty-five songs during a two-and-a-half-hour show. The Temptations left their touring stint long enough to record their *To Be Continued* album (US, Jun '86/UK, Sep '86), produced by Peter Bunetta and Rick Chudacoff. And new signing, Nick Jameson released his debut album *A Crowd Of One* in July 1986. Like so many of these one-off signings, no information was available and the release passed almost unnoticed in America.

In the summer of 1986 Motown/BMG announced what it called the greatest British catalogue competition of all time. Up to 30 August 1986 twenty of Motown's best-selling albums contained an entry form containing four Motown-related questions and a tie-breaker poser. The first prize was a seven day trip for two to Los Angeles as guests of Motown. Follow-up prizes were Lionel Richie videos and the 150 *Motown Hits Of Gold* box sets. A specially compiled album *Motown '86* could be obtained free by collecting stickers on the twenty albums.

Lionel Richie delivered his third solo album *Dancing On The Ceiling* (US/UK, Aug '86) following its title track being issued as a single in June 1986 (UK, Jul '86). The album was the follow-up to his fourteen million seller *Can't Slow Down*. Richie was inspired to write the *Dancing On The Ceiling* track following a late night drive down Sunset Boulevard: 'I pulled up after hearing a load of noise coming from people inside a club. Sitting in the car listening to them, I heard a voice say "what's been going on in there?". The reply was "man, we've been dancing on the ceiling". I wrote the title down and drove home. The excitement that could be generated from that one line was incredible.' The single's promotional video was directed by Stanley Donen who had previously worked with Fred Astaire and Gene Kelly. The idea for Richie's video came from the 1951 film *The Royal Wedding* (British title *Wedding Bells*) where Astaire danced floor to ceiling and upside down, and Richie and his dancers repeated this routine. The Astaire sequence took six weeks to perfect, whereas Richie learned his routines in seven days.

Other tracks on *Dancing On The Ceiling* included *Ballerina Girl* which Richie wrote for his adopted daughter Nicole: 'There are people out there who want to hear me doing a love ballad and I wanted to make sure I didn't let those people down. This time I related those feelings to a child by portraying a child's innocence.' *Deep River Woman* began its life as a ballad before Richie decided he wanted to record a country and western tune: 'And I wanted to use Alabama. I was told they don't duet or do backing vocals for anyone, but when I phoned them they said they'd love to do it. I ran all the way to Nashville and took a day and half to cut the song. We ate southern style food for breakfast, lunch and supper.' *Sela* was an expression his wife's grandmother used which meant 'listen', and *Love Will Conquer All* represented emotional power. Richie: 'The power of the Olympics where I performed and the 2.6 billion people watching that, then to do the *We Are The World* single followed by the Live Aid concert watched by something like 1.8 billion people. All those people turning on their tv sets and the whole world singing that song, well, I can't say I wasn't affected in some way. This track is where my insides come out, and I just had to write it down, to get all these feelings out of me. Cynthia Weil helped me with the lyrics, and the other female singers like Marva King just brought it all out.' Richie said his third album showed his growth and revealed for the first time his inner thoughts. Richie: 'A lot of feelings have opened up here. When it comes down to the cross section of songs, let's say I pulled out my musical resumé.' The album was pop-orientated and his soul fans refused to buy. Richie had, after dabbling with pop on two albums, crossed over into mainstream music.

Love Will Conquer All was the follow-up single to *Dancing On The Ceiling* (US/UK, Sep '86) and *Deep River Woman/Ballerina Girl* was next in the US in November 1986. Motown/BMG in Britain made *Ballerina Girl* the 'A'-side on its release in December 1986, whereupon America followed suit when *Deep River Woman* failed nationally. To help push the struggling single Motown released a promotional twelve inch single titled *A Special Service To Country Radio* featuring *Deep River Woman*, *Stuck On You* and *Sail On* (with the Commodores). The commercial twelve inch single of *Ballerina Girl* featured a previously unavailable instrumental version of *Dancing On The Ceiling* on the flipside. Neither single repeated the success of *Dancing On The Ceiling*, although they were both hits.

To promote the new album Richie embarked upon an American tour titled 'Lionel Richie's Outrageous Tour.' Richie, known for his charitable activities, arranged with the American promoters for special dis-

Lionel Richie's third solo album Dancing On The Ceiling *was treated as a pop release by the media and his fans. Richie toured America to support its release.*

pensations to be given to inner city children in the areas he was booked to appear. Those children who had maintained a B-average or higher at school, and who had avoided disciplinary action over a specified period of time, would be eligible to win free concert tickets, tour jackets, and have the opportunity to meet Richie himself. Richie: 'Education is real important to me, and it's even more important to the future of this country. I grew up on a college campus. Most kids don't have that privilege. I loved school so much that I still hang on to my college apartment. I'd like to help kids feel a little of the fun of being a good student.' His student campaign supported by school superintendents in forty cities, was given a tremendous boost when Pepsi Cola donated 100,000 Lionel Richie Superstudent T-shirts and 10,000 tour jackets, and who, with Richie, donated two college scholarships to the grand prizewinners.

The Outrageous Tour, with Sheila E as support act, sold in excess of 400,000 tickets a month after tour got underway during September 1986 in Phoenix, Arizona. The ninety-minute, fifteen-song performance opened with *Hello* and continued with Richie concentrating on his hits like *Say You, Say Me, Dancing On The Ceiling* and *Deep River Woman*, when the country group Alabama was featured on video. The tour included October performances at New York's Madison Square Gardens (where he was joined onstage by his wife Brenda while he sang *Lady* to her before 20,000 people to celebrate their eleventh wedding anniversary) and December dates at Los Angeles' Forum. By the close of the tour Richie had played before an estimated 1.5 million people. The staging for this tour was designed to keep the special effects from upstaging the performers. There was no stage, instead the musicians and instruments stood on ten foot high modular hydraulic units that moved around during the show. Hanging immediately above these mobile islands were twenty tons of equipment, including one hundred and fifty computerized, swivelling lights and six hundred stationary lights. As the final touch, Richie's nine foot long Yamaha grand piano was motorized. Richie intended to take the tour to Britain in 1986 but due to the continuing terrorist threats between America and Libya, he, and countless other American performers, cancelled or postponed British tours at this time.

However, Richie did take his 'Outrageous Tour' to Australia where he opened at Melbourne's Entertainment Centre. His audience included a slew of tennis stars like Martina Navratilova, Pam Shriver, Ivan Lendl and Yannick Noah, and visiting British star Elton John. Back in America Richie became one of the few black artists to appear in the country top thirty charts with *Deep River Woman*.

In Britain, Diahann Carroll, better known to television viewers as Dominique Devereaux in the soap opera *Dynasty*, had her eponymous album released in August 1986. The ten track album was originally released in 1974 and was re-released on Motown/BMG's budget series to cash-in on her soap character's popularity. Born in New York, Carroll began her career by singing in church choirs before enrolling in New York's High School of Music And Art. When she broke into mainstream entertainment, Carroll became successful as an actress on television and stage. She became the first entertainer to win the talent show *Chance Of A Lifetime* three times consecutively, and the first black actress to secure her own television series, *Julia*, which was nominated for an Emmy Award. It was Carroll's television success that prompted Berry Gordy to record her album in 1974. Carroll's breakthrough was what Gordy intended for Diana Ross, and by signing Carroll Gordy hoped the industry might recognize Motown as a complete entertainment outlet and not simply a record company. Carroll's most startling film role was possibly her portrayal of Claudine in the 1974 film of the same name, where she played a ghetto mother who, with her family, lived on welfare. The events of their everyday life and the traumas of raising a young family won Carroll on Oscar nomination.

Motown's new signing, General Kane group, was the brainchild of Mitch McDowell, who attracted a great deal of media attention with their first single *Crack Killed Applejack* in the US in August 1986. The single was taken from the forthcoming *In Full Chill* album (US, Oct '86/UK, Feb '87). Crack, a highly potent form of cocaine, is America's biggest drug killer, and the single was possibly Motown's first hard-core street statement on vinyl. It was originally titled *Death Lives In A Rock House* (rock being the West Coast word for 'crack'). Mitch McDowell: 'Crack is something that knows no prejudice, it destroys the lives of housewives, lawyers and the kids on the street. I wanted to paint not only an ugly picture but the most horrible, which might prevent someone experimenting with the drug in the first place. Somebody has got to stop it.' McDowell was inspired to write the song when Len Bias, a basketball player, died from taking crack: 'I was watching television when the Celtics drafted him to the tune of several million dollars. Everyone was happy, then two days later Len was dead. It was the most depressing and senseless thing. I've seen what crack can do to people. You've got a guy. He's gone crazy, with no sense of values. He's lost his car, his house and his wife. All he's got left is smoking crack. That stuff means death.'

Mitch McDowell, one of six children, was born in San Bernadino, California. His family planned a football career for him, but he chose music. As a teenager McDowell attended Military School because 'it was a happening and not a punishment'. While there he met an unconventional officer nicknamed General Kane who taught McDowell to play the drums. Upon leaving Military School McDowell joined other struggling musicians and writers until he led the Booty People, which included future members of War, who recorded for Tabu Records. Then Steve Buckley signed McDowell to Motown. McDowell: 'I must have played at least three hundred songs for him. Some were different versions of the same song. I think there's eleven different versions of *Applejack* before we were ready to record it properly.' *Hairdooz*, a comedy rap about different hairstyles, was the follow-up single released in November 1986 (UK, Jan '87, with *Crack Killed Applejack* on the flipside). However, success was minimal because the group's music was too Americanized for European taste. In June 1987 (UK, Jul '87) *Girl Pulled The Dog* was the first single lifted from General Kane's second album *Wide Open* issued in July 1987 in the US only. Other album tracks included the George Clinton/Parliament standard *Flashlight*, a Herb Alpert soundalike, *Woppity Wop*, and the only ballad, a cover version of Peaches and Herb's hit *Close Your Eyes*, on which group members Danny Macon and Cheryl McDowell took lead.

Chico DeBarge, said to be Motown's strongest new artist at this time, released his eponymous album in September 1986 (UK, Nov '86). The first single *Talk To Me* (US, Aug '86/UK, Oct '86) was an American hit but flopped in Britain. The 20-year-old DeBarge, who was never a member of the family group, said his solo work was very different from that recorded by DeBarge. He told *Blues & Soul*: 'If you listen to my album then you'll appreciate that I don't sing like they do, nor do I have the same musical direction. I'm different whether for good or bad so it wouldn't have been compatible to work as part of them. As a solo album I wanted the freedom that this album has given me. I wrote and co-wrote some of the tracks and had the choice of other producers.'

Stacy Lattisaw was a Jay Lasker signing in 1986. Her debut album *Take Me All The Way* was a stunning collection of songs. Lattisaw was no newcomer to the business as she had been signed to Cotillion Records where her first album *Young And In Love* was produced by the late Van McCoy in June 1979. Two more albums followed *Let Me Be Your Angel* and *With You*, both produced by Narada Michael Walden. Lattisaw also enjoyed single success with *Jump To The Beat*, *Dynamite* and *Love On A Two Way Street*. With vinyl success Lattisaw was in demand to perform and in 1981 she toured America with The Jacksons for thirteen weeks. Lattisaw: 'The best part about it was meeting Michael. I watched The Jacksons' show from the wings every night and every night I learned something new.' This led to her signing with Motown. Lattisaw: 'We negotiated with different companies before deciding on Motown, and they didn't have a female singer like myself.' Her signing was seen as an attempt by Motown to fill the gap left by Teena Marie, and certainly the company desperately needed a young, vivacious songstress to captivate the younger audience. Lattisaw's first Motown album *Take Me All The Way* (US, Sep '86/UK, Nov '86) was produced by Kashif, Leon Sylvers, Jellybean, Narada Michael Walden and Steve Barri. Lattisaw: 'It was Motown's choice to work with different producers because we wanted to produce an album of variety to show what I could do.' The dance track *Nail It To The Wall* was the first hit single in August 1986 (UK, Oct '86) followed by *Jump Into My Life* in December 1986 (UK, Feb '87). Lattisaw's second album *Personal Attention* took two years to be released in 1988.

After much re-scheduling the Four Tops' *Hot Nights* album looked set to be issued in the autumn of 1986. Tracks included *Red Hot Love*, *This Is Love* and *Indestructable* with Smokey Robinson. The album's producers included David Wolfert, Steve Barri and Tony Peluso. Wolfert was the group's producer for their last major hit *When She Was My Girl* for Polygram. *Hot Nights* was placed on permanent hold when, surprisingly, the Four Tops left Motown

for a second time to sign with Arista Records.

After joining in the American race to press albums on compact discs, Jay Lasker, president of Motown Records, spearheaded the company's intention to revolutionize the selling of CDs by using back catalogue items in 1986. The $1.5 million '2 on 1' marketing campaign featured eighty-four of Motown's most popular Sixties and Seventies albums, with two albums on one CD selling for the price of one. With this campaign Motown became the first American company to exploit this form of CD marketing. Lasker: 'Some of the big record companies are so tied up with other things that they don't really look ahead on something until it hits them in the face. But I think they'll soon be following along. Within a year, everyone will have these packages.' Lasker was adamant that these CD re-issues would not affect Motown's sales generally: 'The CD audience is older and they are in effect replacing their record collection with CDs. Not every album, but their favourite ones. Once they buy a CD player that album is like an old hat thing. The music sounds terrible by comparison. We are in an especially strong position because that yuppie audience grew up on Motown music.' Lasker further explained that the cost of making the CD and the artists' royalties were the same as on vinyl releases but the songwriting royalties were double. The '2 on 1' campaign was expected to recoup $10 million in sales.

In October Motown/BMG released ten of the '2 on 1' CDs, with plans to release more throughout Europe. The initial British releases included Stevie Wonders' *My Cherie Amour/Signed, Sealed And Delivered* and *For Once In My Life/Uptight*, the Commodores' *Natural High/Midnight Magic*, The Temptations' *Cloud Nine/Puzzle People* and the Four Tops' *Reach Out/Still Waters*. When Jay Lasker left Motown in late 1987, the '2 on 1' series was replaced by a new mid-priced series.

As ex-Supreme Scherrie Payne signed to Superstar International Records in Los Angeles, and the Four Tops appeared, dressed in bear outfits, in a television commercial for Sun County wine coolers, Martha Reeves

The young, versatile Stacy Lattisaw joined Motown to release a stunning first album Take Me All The Way. *Her signing was seen as Motown's attempt to fill the gap left by Teena Marie.*

Confusion surrounded the non-release of The Four Tops' Hot Nights *album until Arista Records announced it had signed them. This was the second time the quartet had left Motown.*

headlined a British tour featuring the Mamas and Papas, Lou Christie, Scott McKenzie and Gary 'US' Bonds, in November 1986. The tour was riddled with ego problems, arguments and drug useage but Reeves, in her totally professional manner, held the show together so that the public were unaware of the backstage traumas.

During 1986 the brown-and-yellow Tamla Motown label celebrated its 21st anniversary in England. The first single on the label was The Supremes' *Stop! In The Name Of Love* in March 1965. Although there was a label change to the big blue 'M' in the Seventies, the Tamla Motown label continued to appear on mid-priced and certain re-issued records. At this time Jay Lasker told *Blues & Soul* how European sales contributed towards Motown's overall sales figures: 'Outside America, including Canada, the sales run established is generally about the same. We can sell one million albums in America, and one million in the rest of the world, which is a fair assumption. Certain acts achieve hit records outside the States and are more popular overseas than at home. For example, Diana Ross always sold great outside America, and there's more loyalty to our artists overseas. We have a much more fickle market. So an artist's longevity is that much bigger outside than inside America and for that we're delighted.'

During the autumn of 1986 another milestone was achieved when Supreme Mary Wilson published her autobiography *Dreamgirl: My Life As A Supreme*. The story, based on diaries kept since she was 17-years-old and research carried out by American and British fans and Motown artist interviews, was an insight into the personal lives of the world-famous trio, including Florence Ballard's tragedies and Diana Ross' ambitions. The book gave The Supremes' fans the chance to glimpse behind the success and partake in Wilson's own personal life. What Wilson could not have envisaged was the split her ghost-written book would cause between her fans and those of Diana Ross.

When *Dreamgirl* was published in Britain in the spring of 1987, it had sold in excess of 250,000 hardback copies in America, with an estimated one million sales expected on the paperback version. Mary Wilson undertook a lengthy American promotion trip, including radio and television spots and bookstore signings. The in-store advertizing for the book included enlarged newspaper quotes, as reported by journalist Keith Russell: 'Diana Ross can never seem the same to you after you've read this book'. With advertizing like this and Wilson's own written and spoken comments, it was widely considered her book defamed Diana Ross, without whom The Supremes would not have reached international status.

Diana Ross, who warmly welcomed Wilson

Mary Wilson's much publicized autobiography contained controversial references to Diana Ross. The book was compiled from Wilson's diaries and interviews and research by her American and British fans.

at the American Music Awards ceremony after the book's publication, did not publicly comment on Wilson's book until journalist Christopher Connelly was granted an interview for US magazine. Even then Ross remained the totally professional public figure that had transformed her from a group member into an international megastar. When Connelly asked if she wanted to respond to Wilson's unflattering portrayal of her, Ross replied: 'It's mostly confusing. Mary and I were best friends, growing up. I just feel like each of us is able to have our own opinions, and if that is really the way she saw the time, it's completely different than how I saw it. There have been other books that have been written and, yeah, it hurts. But I remember that if I could keep my eyes on the bigger picture, then it's better for me . . . I had a notion that there was some survival involved there. People don't remember. I've been away from The Supremes longer than I've been with The Supremes. I don't know what's going on really in her life. I just wish her the best. I'm the godmother to one of her children (Turkessa). I don't see the girl very much anymore, because if your heart is broken, I find it really hard to be close. But I really don't bear ill will.'

After Diana Ross left The Supremes, she and Mary Wilson remained close friends, and Ross always proved to be a kind and helpful ally to Wilson. Should Wilson want to see Ross perform in, say, Las Vegas, Ross would always ensure a table was reserved for Wilson and her entourage at no cost to them. Ross, however, rarely saw Wilson perform on stage, although during a private visit to London Ross, with her husband, attended a Cindy Birdsong performance. Wilson also knew that for personal and financial dilemmas she could always turn to Ross who, it was said, rarely let her friend down.

Ex-Supreme Cindy Birdsong said Wilson's viewpoint in the book was different from hers in a lot of areas: 'But it's only natural it would be. We have had the same experiences but our perception is different. Mary perceived things as she saw them. If I was to write about the same situations I would not write them that way. Probably Diana would come along with a whole different perception too. The only way to get the real story is for each of us to write books as we saw our life, and then put all three sides together.'

Birdsong did not feel the book harmed The Supremes' memory: 'People are going to think what they want to think. Mary has been quite controversial which, I believe, caused some people to think harshly about Diana. And, sure, Mary got criticized for that. I don't feel she's done any real damage to the reputation of the group because it can stand on its own.' Birdsong also felt that Wilson was entitled to write exactly what she wanted although 'I am not saying I saw Diana Ross as Mary saw her. Regardless of what Mary said I no longer see Diana as that same person of the Sixties. She's totally different, like day and night. We have all seasoned through experience, marriage and so on. I don't think it was Mary's intention to attack Diana, she wanted to write the truth as she saw it, nor was it her intention to cause controversy. She wanted to do this from way back when we were young women. Our only goal in life then was to be successful, but Mary was the one who kept notes and kept on writing.'

Ex-Motowner, Martha Reeves, was also mentioned in *Dreamgirl*. She felt the book was good although didn't appreciate being referred to as a fighter. Reeves: 'I have never put my hands on them (The Supremes) and we have had fights too. But Mary should have referred to them as debates. Mind you, I know other girls who have fought with them. I think also, Mary damaged The Supremes' mystique, but she didn't know enough about my private life to bring me down. All I can say is that no-one snatched a microphone from my hands.' Reeves was also involved in writing her own book on her life and Motown career which, she laughed, '. . . will give me the chance to strike back as a journalist!'

At the close of 1986 Diana Ross hit the headlines, this time due to rumours circulating the industry that she intended to return to Motown. Ross had been performing now for twenty-five years and fuelled the rumours by telling E*bony* magazine: 'I would re-sign if it were something that turned out to be interesting. I'm in love with Berry and I'm in love with the power there. I'm crazy about Suzanne de Passe (president of Motown Productions) and her entire staff. I don't know if I'll ever go back into that situation again, but I respect their talent. In fact, going out on my own has made me really value how good Motown was to me. It's made me see that they did a whole lot that I'm doing for myself now. But it's so much better to control your own life.'

The third member of the DeBarge family, Bunny (married with three children), followed in her brothers' footsteps by releasing her first solo album *In Love* in January 1987 (UK, Apr '87). The album was as colourful as the sweater she wore on the record sleeve. A *Woman In Love* and *Never Let Die* were strong, melodic ballads while *Save The Best For Me* was lifted as the first single prior to the album's release in December 1986 in the US only. Although Bunny's vocals lacked strength, they had a distinctive edge that promised a successful career. However, Motown thought otherwise because after her fine debut she was dropped from the roster. With El, Chico and Bunny pursuing solo careers the remainder of DeBarge (James, Mark, Randy and new recruit and ex-Switch member/brother Bobby) left Motown to sign with former Motown executive Barney Ales' Striped Horse label. Their first single was *Dance All Night* from the debut album *Bad Boys*, written and produced by the group.

Before joining Motown, Bruce 'Bruno' Willis rose to fame with his loud-mouthed character, David Addison, in the popular television series *Moonlighting*, in which his co-star, Cybill Shepherd (Maddie Hayes), tolerated his off-beat and extremely irritating antics. Both are unlikely detectives who solve a variety of far-fetched crimes, while arguing and bickering with each other. Willis: 'One of the greatest compliments I get on the show is when people say "it looks like you're making everything up". It takes a lot of hard work to get your work to look effortless, and the more relaxed you are on camera, the better the comedy sells.' Interestingly, due to the fast dialogue, *Moonlighting* scripts are twice as long as an average television programme and thus cost more to make.

Before Motown released *The Return Of Bruno album* (US, Jan '87/UK, Apr '87), a unique marketing ploy was devised to promote Willis. As it was considered imperative to portray him not as an actor crossing over into music but a singer first and foremost, the character 'Bruno Radolini' was invented with a fictitious musical biography to match, an entertaining ploy. Signing to Motown itself seemed a strange move for Bruce Willis, and the man responsible was Jay Lasker who said: 'I just saw a personality on television, and I knew he could sell a lot of records. This is only the second time I've done this. The first time was with Alan Alda on M*A*S*H and we found out he couldn't sing at all.' When the two met, Willis told Lasker how much he loved the Motown sound which was encouraging. However, Lasker merely intended Bruce to record a couple of tracks for him: 'But, he says to me

Bunny was the third member of the DeBarge family to embark upon a solo career. Unfortunately, her career began and ended with the superb In Love album.

Moonlighting *star Bruce Willis persuaded Motown to let him record an album. The Return of Bruno was released amidst a huge marketing campaign whereupon his first single* Respect Yourself *became Motown's highest ever American chart entry by a white artist.*

Georgio, a semi-established and ambitious singer, brought his youthful sound to Motown via his Sexappeal album.

''Jay, let me go, let me make an album. I can give you a hit''. I don't know if I'd had a couple of drinks too many, but his enthusiasm was so overwhelming that I said he'd got a deal!'

When Willis was in the studios recording his first album, Jay Lasker did not like the tracks, so Willis encouraged him to hire The Heaters, a band he had heard in a Sherman Oaks bar. Lasker agreed and the album was finished to his satisfaction. Bruce Willis rewarded Lasker's faith in him when his first single – a re-recording of The Staple Singers' *Respect Yourself* (US, Dec '86/UK, Feb '87) became Motown's highest ever American chart entry by a white artist. To add a little soul credibility in the accompanying video June Pointer (of The Pointer Sisters) performed with Willis. Bruce's live debut was at The Ritz, in New York's East Village and was a resounding success. He was joined on stage by Ben E King and Billy Joel before a star studded audience.

Bruce Willis's debut album *The Return Of Bruno* went on to spawn further singles like *Young Blood* in the US in March 1987 (UK, April '88) and another hit *Under The Boardwalk* (US, May '87/UK, May '87). This was a re-recording of The Drifters' classic and Willis' version featured The Temptations. Without Willis' singles Motown/BMG would not have enjoyed any British top ten hits during 1987. The three singles were the most commercial on the album, yet Motown released two more: *Secret Agent Man/James Bond Is Back* in the UK only during September 1987 and *Comin' Right Up* early in 1988.

Apart from hitting the headlines with his music, the tv series *Moonlighting* and the film *Blind Date*, the singer's personal life regularly made the papers and kept the Los Angeles police department busy. Bruce's neighbours regularly complained about his late night parties, and on one particular occasion, when a squad car arrived at his home, Willis hurled abuse at the police and allegedly punched one, knocking him to the ground. He subsequently spent three hours in jail. His hell-raising antics on screen were gradually becoming a reality, which, Willis said, stemmed from his inability to cope with the stardom, attention and money he now had.

Bruce Willis was born in Germany on 19 March 1955, where his father was stationed in the US Army. He had met his German-born wife there and two years later they moved to New Jersey. His father worked at the Camden Shipyard while Willis attended the Penns Grove High School in 1969. Willis told *Rolling Stone* magazine: 'In the four years I was there we had full-scale race riots. By senior year it had really escalated. Now I wonder whether it was actually racial tension or just seventeen-year-old guys looking to beat on somebody. Because I'll go back and see these guys now and we laugh about it.' He was also president of the student council although conceeds he was a bad pupil: 'It was a real ugly time. A lot of teachers came forward and invented things they said they saw me doing. So my father had to hire a lawyer to go before the school board, and this lawyer was like Perry Mason.' Bruce was found not guilty, was reinstated, and graduated with honours.

His first job was working at the Du Pont plant, driving trucks, but following an explosion he decided it wasn't the job for him: 'It happened in this giant autoclave, a drum the size of a room they mixed chemicals in. They knew the explosion was coming two minutes before, but they couldn't stop this one guy who was driving a truck right by the building. they found parts of him all over the place. I wasn't so shocked by it, but I saw how the older guys took it. They were gone, just white. So I quit about a week later.' Willis joined a local band, Loose Goose, as a harmonica player and worked as a night security guard at a nuclear generating station in Delaware to pay his bills. To curb boredom during his shifts, he played his harmonica over the station's loud speaker system, then developed 'walking pneumonia' and was switched to a desk job. This he loathed, so decided to study acting.

In January 1977, after studying for eighteen months, Willis appeared in a play called *Heaven And Earth*. His next move was to New York. 'I got most of my experience from working onstage and off-Broadway, for no money, just working in front of a house.' Four years later he performed in *Railroad Bill*, a play being shown at the Labor Theatre, while playing harmonica in between performances. Then he won the leading role of a construction worker with an unhappy marriage in *Bayside Boys* for which he earned good notices. Willis' television break came when he was featured in the Levis' 501 Jeans advertizements which led to further theatre roles and the part of a reporter in the movie *The Verdict* and bit appearances on several television shows. When *Desperately Seeking Susan* was being cast, Madonna was looking for a suitable co-star to play opposite her as her boyfriend. Willis went to Los Angeles to audition but the part went to Robert Jay. While there his agent suggested he should try *Moonlighting*, a proposed television series. As it was the last day of the auditions, Bruce had no time to prepare so: 'I just went in and said "Hi, how are you. I'm Bruce Willis, let's do it". I knew I could do this man's material because I recognized an off-beat character, who's horsing around out there where the air is real thin. I just did this thing, this rocking scene that's in the pilot, and said "Thanks, see ya' and walked out".'

Cybill Shepherd had already been cast as Maddie Hayes and the show's producers felt Bruce fitted the bill of her 'real man' co-star. Shepherd: 'The first time Bruce and I were in a room together there was a reaction. Sparks flew. He's attractive and funny which not too many people have had. People misunderstand the chemistry thing. The chemistry's not between Maddie and David, it's between Cybill and Bruce. And that is what we use. That sexual attraction can't be faked or acted. It's there or it's not.'

Another Bruce Willis album is proposed as and when film and television commitments allow.

Motown's Anthology series was streamlined, updated and revised for a series of two-CD packages. *The Motown Story* was the highlight of this new series and was featured on three CDs, where the first 10,000 were individually stamped and numbered with 'Limited First Edition No. . .'. A total of sixty-one songs covered the three CDs, which varied from its vinyl and tape equivalents.

The rumours surrounding Rick James' legal wrangle with Motown continued, and when it was announced in early 1987 that Val Young had been dropped from the artist roster, and the Mary Jane Girls' album *Conversation* was permanently shelved, fans knew the time was nearing when James himself would leave the company. After months of silence he eventually left Motown in autumn 1987 to sign with Warner Brothers, presumably taking his stable of artists with him. Meanwhile, Jo Jo McDuffie bored with not working, left the Mary Jane Girls to pursue a solo career.

New signing, Blake & Hines, released their debut single *Sherry* in January 1987 from their self-named album issued in March 1987. Detroiters, Cory Blake and Andra Hines were discovered by veteran scout Forest Hamilton, who founded the Cameo outfit, managed Isaac Hayes and worked with the Taste Of Honey. A second single *Road Dog* followed in April 1987, but none was British released.

Motown's new signing Georgio was another direct stab at the younger record buyers. Already semi-established, this ambitious 21-year-old from San Francisco was a self-taught DJ who promoted his own dances. Georgio: 'I'd rent a hall, give a party, charge at the door and mix the music.' He later bought various instruments, taught himself to play them, and migrated south to Los Angeles. Georgio: 'I met them all there. Big record artists, record executives, but no-one talked about really helping me.' Undeterred he wrote, produced and financed the sassy *Sexappeal* which became a top ten single for two top radio stations in Los Angeles. The single was released on Georgio's own label, Picture Perfect, and when he could not meet the public's demand for it, Motown stepped in with a deal. Georgio: 'They were interested in allowing me the chance to do my own thing without looking over my shoulder. That's really all an artist can ask for.' *Sexappeal*, released in February 1987, was a hit in the States but flopped in Britain when released there in March. The *Sexappeal* album was issued in the US in March 1987. It's British release in December 1987 differed from the American album as it contained three twelve inch re-mixes on *Sexappeal*, *Tina Cherry* and *Lover's Lane*. The *Tina Cherry* single topped the American Dance Charts following its release in May 1987 (UK, Oct '87) and *Lover's Lane* (US, Aug '87/UK, Feb '88) became Georgio's first British hit. Georgio's music reflected his many moods – sensual, aggressive, moody and funky: 'If Motown promotes me in the way CBS promoted Michael Jackson, I'll be great. I have everything he has – and more!'

Further new signings FGO (For Girls Only) (Mike Harris, lead singer, Scott Weatherspoon, backing vocalist/keyboardist, Raphael Merriweathers, backing vocalist/percussionist/drummer, Mike Banks, bass keyboardist/guitar) are still waiting for a record to be released. The group met at school although they were members of rival bands. Eventually the future members of FGO left their respective groups to form Mike and the Mechanics and became a popular touring attraction. No further information was made available by Motown. Their debut single *Nice Girls* was scheduled for February 1987 release but cancelled, likewise their second single *I'll Be Around* and their *Give Her What She Wants* album were cancelled.

Smokey Robinson returned with one of his most commercial albums of the Eighties. Titled *One Heartbeat* (original title *Keep Me*) (US, Feb '87/UK, Apr '87), it spawned *Just To See Her*, his first hit in some time, in February 1987 (UK, Mar '87). The album marked Robinson's first collaboration with Rick Chudacoff and Peter Bunetta who, among others, worked on The Temptations' *To Be Continued* album. Robinson told reporter David Nathan: 'It's a powerpacked (album). I love the overall

As Motown shelved the Mary Jane Girls' album Conversation, *original group member Jo Jo McDuffie left the quartet to pursue a solo career.*

sound, the tightness of the production, the vocal performance. What I really loved about these guys was that they weren't afraid to get in there and give me input.' Berry Gordy was executive producer of the album which, Robinson said, brought back memories of them working together during Motown's early days. From the fourteen songs recorded Gordy made the final selection.

Album tracks included *Why Do Happy Memories Hurt So Bad* written by Robinson and his guitarist Marv Tarplin. Robinson: 'Marv had the music down for it about two years ago and just last year I finally came up with a lyric. But that's not unusual – I probably have ideas for hundreds of songs that I've started and haven't yet gone back to.' It's *Time To Stop Shoppin' Around*, the 'answer' song to his *Shop Around* in 1960: 'A friend of mine, Marsha Gold, was complaining that all the guys she knew had followed the advice in *Shop Around* and she had a problem because she wanted to get married. That's how we came up with the new song and I figured that since it was an "answer" song I'd throw in some references to *The Duke Of Earl*, *Jimmy Mack* and *Back In My Arms Again* and some other oldies-but-goodies that people may remember from those *Shop Around* days.' Robinson was recently added to the Rock & Roll Hall of Fame for his contribution to music: 'How many people actually get to achieve something like that during their lifetime? I felt especially blessed and it was real special to be there with so many of my peers. So many people I love and respect – Ashford and Simpson, Bruce Springsteen – a lot of great folks.'

During March 1987, and while still signed to Motown, the Four Tops' lead singer Levi Stubbs received good reviews as the voice of the people-eating plant Audrey II in the film *Little Shop Of Horrors*. When he was first approached by film producer David Geffen to do this Stubbs was sceptical about adopting his voice to represent a pod that grew sixty feet high! Also during this month Lionel Richie, with promoters Marshall Arts, took his 'Outrageous Tour' to Paris, West Germany, Sweden and Norway, after dates in Britain's National Exhibition Centre (NEC) in Birmingham during March 1987. His London dates at Wembley Arena were to follow in May because Richie said: 'I wanted to crank up the show so that by the time we get to London it will be ready, be ablaze.' The Birmingham shows were sold out in three hours. The British Telecom Computer logged 90,000 calls an hour into the NEC Box Office where fifty emergency lines were hastily installed with extra staff hired to man the calls and cater for the lengthy queues wanting tickets. These were Richie's first solo performances in Britain. Richie then added an extra date to his Wembley Arena performances on 6 May. It was a charity event in aid of the Prince's Trust, was attended by the Prince and Princess of

Wales, and all proceeds from the performance were donated to the Trust.

Motown/BMG released a souvenir double package featuring Richie's new single *Se La* with photos from his current world tour on the sleeve. Each package also contained a competition form, with the first prize being two tickets to see Richie at Wembley. *Se La* was remixed by Steve Thompson and Michael Barbiero for single release and Richie filmed the promotional video for it in New York.

When Lionel Richie performed at Wembley Arena he took London by storm. Prior to appearing on stage to sing *Hello*, his computerized piano played the song's opening bars. Once on stage Richie saw the audience rise as one to welcome him. *All Night Long* and *Running With The Night* followed where he and his band simultaneously danced together against a backdrop of exploding fireworks and a stage light display. The pace then slowed down for *Truly*, *Three Times A Lady* and *Sail On*. The response was deafening. The piano rose off the stage for *Say You, Say Me*, then disappeared through the stage at the song's close. Richie then left the stage, his exit well disguised by dry ice. Upon his return Richie duetted with Vickie Randle on *Love Will Conquer All* and *Endless Love*. His time with the Commodores was further remembered with *Brick House* and *Still*, whereupon *Lady*, the song he wrote for Kenny Rogers, brought screams of delight by the thousand. A second exit and return saw Richie funk to *Don't Stop*, the band once again joining in the dance routines. Each group member played an integral part in the show and a more professional outfit could not be found for this type of show. Halfway through *Dancing On The Ceiling* several band members were suspended high in the air above the stage while Richie remained with both feet firmly on the stage. When the stage rose to meet the 'dancing' musicians, the audience as one went hysterical. British critics were varied in their reviews. The die-hard soul fans hated the hi-tech and showbiz flavour that American audiences love, while mainstream critics praised the entire performance as the best in popular music.

Performing still scared Richie but, he said, his audiences helped him overcome his nervousness, particularly his European fans. Richie: 'European audiences have always come forward to tell me their feelings and of course they have always played my music. It's only ironic that the tragedy of terrorism has marred so much travelling around for so many artists. It's a strange thing, but no matter how great you are in America, you never get the respect you get in England. You're only as big as your last hit single, yet in England artists who have been ice-cold in the States for years are always welcome. People like Chuck Berry and all those wonderful blues and soul performers come any time because England treats them as legendary. And that's a

After months of speculation Lionel Richie eventually brought his Outrageous Tour to the UK as part of a European tour. He amazed his British audiences with his polished, hi-tech shows.

254

wonderful feeling I can tell you.' Being an international figure, Richie was a target for personal attack. Yet even with the senseless killing of John Lennon continually on his mind, he refused to be intimidated by possible threats: 'I could never get into the situation of not flying or not walking in the streets. Unfortunately, this problem is the nature of the world we live in. We have all been brought up with the idea that the bomb will go off at any time. There's only one safe bet in this world and that is that death will always come as a surprise. Yes, I'm always recognizable, but I do hang out with a lot of people and that is extremely important to me. I can't walk down the street anymore and I miss that. Although there are certain times I can go out, usually night time is the best time. During the day you won't see me for longer than a block. So that's some of the rough points.'

Ironically, Richie spent his earlier life praying to be famous. Now that he was, he said, it was like being in a capsule that isolated him from being a normal human being: 'You are offered the world with everything you could want, but you're separated from normal people by bodyguards and limousines. So you have to struggle to get back to real human life. Every person is judged according to his own merit, not the title. You judge a man because of what he offers in his work. That is what I was taught. And that is how I live my life, basically that's the foundation of what I'm about. However, there is one thing that I'll never let happen. I will not be locked away behind walls, or be shut out of this world entirely.'

Richie had been invited to perform in Russia after his 'Outrageous Tour' was finished in Europe. It was something he wanted to do despite the country's governmental restrictions. Richie: 'If you take away the governments of the world, people are people, and fans are fans. In isolated places of the world people are oppressed, but people get around any obstacle. Like they listen to their records – R&B, rock and so on – and they go to discos or something similar on weekends, just like everybody else. It's the ideas of the older generation that are making this oppression, but they're dying off now, leaving the newer generation to bring in what they want. I believe certain morals are good and I'm sure the governments are going to change and that Russia, in particular, already has a brand new breed in there. They will get back into the race, into the competitive world. I mean, look at all the technology that exists now . . . that is a positive progression in itself. Music is bringing people together. Music is a medium and a strong force that has cut through areas where politicians, for example, can't. Attitudes and situations get changed with the least resistance. The key civil rights movement succeeded with non-violence and I'm convinced you can get through to anyone with music.' (In June 1987, Richie was sued

once again for copyright infringement. This time Michael Frenchick alleged that Dancing On The Ceiling was partly his composition.)

Meanwhile, the Marvin Gaye and Tammi Terrell memory lived on via footage on the promotional video for George Michael's duet with Aretha Franklin titled I Knew You Were Waiting (For Me). The single became a British number one in March 1987 and a Grammy R&B single winner in 1988. It was a most unusual musical combination, although Franklin did team up with Annie Lennox of the Eurythmics in 1985 to record Sisters Are Doin' It For Themselves. This single held more credibility as Lennox's talent was acknowledged by black music followers.

New signing Carrie McDowell's debut single Casual Sex Part 1, written by Willie Hutch, was later renamed Uh Uh, No No Casual Sex (US, Jun '87/UK, Sep '87). The track was lifted from her eponymous album due in July 1987 (UK, Nov '87). Uh Uh, No No Casual Sex pushed home the point of safe sex as a direct response to George Michael's single I Want Your Sex. Other artists like Janet Jackson (Let's Wait Awhile), Smokey Robinson (It's Time To Stop Shoppin' Around) and Jermaine Stewart (We Don't Have To Take Our Clothes Off (To Have A Good Time), also supported safe sex in their records. Hutch said the single was his intention to make people think before acting: 'I have a teenage daughter and I really felt it was time to make a statement that would hit it right on the head – if you're not thinking, start thinking.' The song was originally titled Mr Promiscuity but Berry Gordy felt the title should be changed. Gordy: 'Casual sex is out. Willie impressed me when he said this was the most important song he'd written. I can't cure AIDS but Willie could try to create a hit song to make people conscious of it. So as I like to help people achieve their goals, we went with it.'

The 24-year-old Carrie McDowell from Des Moines, Iowa, was no newcomer to the entertainment business. At the age of 10 McDowell had appeared three times on Johnny Carson's Tonight show and had been the opening act on tour for Liberace, Rowan and Martin, Danny Thomas and George Burns. At the age of 14 McDowell left the business to return to school. McDowell: 'I couldn't relate to the kids. Other girls were worrying about getting a date for the football game, while I was worrying about learning a new song.' When she left high school, McDowell moved to New York and pursued acting. She was featured in the Showtime cable production The Me Nobody Knows and worked as a model and starred in commercials. She was the original Jordache jeans girl. McDowell then formed her own group Uptown Function, which prompted her to move to California to embark upon a recording career. McDowell's neighbour, who was a Motown backing vocalist, heard her sing and urged her to approach Motown for an

audition. Willie Hutch was impressed with the young singer and decided to work with her. McDowell told *Cashbox*: 'Willie and I started working together for about four or five months to really get to know each other. So he could really get to know my voice and me and what I sound good on. It took us about a year to do the album. Willie Hutch will work you until you feel like you can't even lift a finger anymore. He really opened me up and taught me to do so much more and go over what I could do. It's all paying off right now.'

McDowell's self-named album was a strong commercial, yet soulful release, the white singer's voice capably handling tracks like *It's The Power Of Your Love* (*Growing On Me*), *Just Dance*, *Up The Down Side Of Love*, *Fly* (*White Bird Fly*) and her second single *When A Woman Loves A Man* (US, Sep '87/UK, Nov '87), the 'answer' record to Percy Sledge's *When A Man Loves A Woman*. Following the release of the album, McDowell toured America with Smokey Robinson. McDowell: 'It was scarey, but Smokey was so nice!'

In March 1987 (UK, Jul '87) a further soundtrack album was released. This time it was the album to *Police Academy* IV and included *Rescue Me* (Family Dream), *Rock The House* (Darryl Duncan), *I Like My Body* (Chico DeBarge), *It's Time To Move* (SOS Band), *Winning Streak* (Gary Glenn) and *Let's Go To Heaven In My Car* (Brian Wilson). The first three *Police Academy* films grossed $185 million and this new film reunited the complete original cast. The Chico DeBarge, Darryl Duncan and Family

Dream's tracks were issued as singles. Meanwhile, The Miracles' *Tracks Of My Tears* was featured in the Grammy Award winning film *Platoon* and as part of a television advertizing campaign for Budweiser beer.

Diana Ross, pregnant with her fourth child, switched from Capitol Records to EMI Records in Britain, with the release of her *Dirty Looks* single, taken from her pending *Red Hot Rhythm & Blues* album. Ross, meantime starred in her own American television spectacular named after the album, which was a musical reflection of her life and traced the history of black music. Ross then embarked on an American tour. Journalist Keith Russell reviewed her Las Vegas show: 'Caesars Palace is really a magical place. An intimate showroom of around one thousand seats each offering an unrestricted view of the stage. Diana plays two one-hour shows every night during her two week engagement. The acoustics and excellent sound system provided the best sound I've heard. Ross has used an British sound crew, Tuscan Sound, ever since her last European tour in September 1985. During the ballads you really get to appreciate the special qualities of her voice, usually only fully captivated on record. Although billed as the 'Red Hot Rhythm & Blues Tour' Ross has yet to include material from her new album. According to an insider the band has rehearsed four new songs but not perfected them enough for Diana to feel happy about including them in her show. But all the hits were there – *I'm Coming Out*, *Upside Down*, *Chain Reaction*, *Touch Me In The Morning*, *Missing You* – with sixteen songs in the sixty-minute show. Diana's voice has never been in better shape. Obviously pregnant, she still demonstrates a high level of energy although, I was told, she does tire easily. Seasoned Vegas visitors agreed that she has never looked better.'

At the first annual Soul Train Music Awards held during April 1987, Stevie Wonder received a Special Heritage Award from NAACP's Dr Benjamin Hooks. Among the numerous stars present at this ceremony was Mary Wilson who told David Nathan that she had not spoken to Diana Ross since her *Dreamgirl: My Life As A Supreme* book was published: 'But, we don't have any kind of feud going on. The media has made up so much about our relationship.'

Also in April 1987 new signing Kim O'Leary released her first single *Put The Pieces Back* in the US only, taken from her as yet unreleased self-named album. Born in Melbourne, Australia, O'Leary's parents were both singers. She began singing children's radio commercials at the age of 12, and two years later studied drama with the Melbourne Theatre Company where she stayed for three years performing on stage and television. From 1974 to 1978 O'Leary joined numerous rock/blues groups to play at small clubs around Australia, as well as becoming a session

One of the Eighties new signings, Kim O'Leary showed a huge potential with her first single Put The Pieces Back. *She was one of Motown's new generation acts who brought their own musical style to the company.*

singer. In 1977 Geoff Bridgford (ex-Bee Gees drummer) and O'Leary formed the One Foundation group. A year later they moved to America to base themselves in Los Angeles and play local clubs and record demos. O'Leary met and worked with Nick Jameson and pursued a solo career while the remaining band members returned to Australia in 1981. During 1984 Jameson and O'Leary produced a three song demo tape which was sufficient for Johanan Vigoda to secure a recording deal with Motown.

On 31 May 1987, during a tour of England, Mary Wilson's coach was broken into while parked outside a Manchester theatre. The thieves gained access through the coach's skylight and stole two suitcases containing stage gowns for the group. Wilson wore street clothes and her two vocalists wore the musicians' tuxedos on stage that night. The thieves were never caught but Wilson had suffered from fans stealing her gowns prior to this in Sheffield, England, and Melbourne, Australia. Ironically, it was six years to the very day in 1981 that Gill Trodd was held at gun point during their Irish leg of a British tour. Trodd, who managed the tour with Wilson's adopted son, Willie Pitchford, as stage manager, was carrying the group's earnings in a suitcase when she was robbed by a masked gunman near the village of Birdhill, County Tipperary *en route* for Dublin. The trio had travelled ahead in their coach and were una-

ware of the robbery. Originally, the group's promoters did not want the tour to go ahead because the incarcerated political activist Bobby Sands, who had been on a hunger strike, died the day the trio arrived in Ireland and rioting was predicted. It was later discovered that the trio's Irish promoter had instigated Trodd's hold up and was subsequently jailed.

Back in America, a young new talent released her first single L-O-V-E (*Love*) in May 1987 in the US only. Fourteen-year-old Angela Cole (originally Coleman) issued this single as a taster from her as yet unreleased *Turn Up The Beat* album, produced by Hal Davis, who had been searching for a new artist to work with. Cole began singing when she was three years old, and by the time she was six was singing gospel professionally in the Los Angeles area. Cole never studied music formally but had the ability to reduce her audiences to tears when singing gospel songs. By the age of 10 she had appeared with Barry White, Stevie Wonder, Count Basie, Sarah Vaughan and Andy Gibb, and had entertained stars like Muhammed Ali and Cab Calloway. This extraordinarily young talent, mature beyond her years, wanted to record secular music for Motown, and the debut album, which included her versions of The Temptations' *Get Ready* and Jermaine Jackson's *Let's Get Serious*, was a good foundation for her future career.

Also during May 1987 Stevie Wonder, Quincy Jones and Nile Rodgers participated in a unique audio/visual demonstration linking two studios, 3,000 miles apart, to record Wonder's anti-cocaine song *Stop, Don't Pass Go*. During the demonstration, a two way audio/visual satellite link through Teleport Communications' regional fibre optic network connected Rodgers at the MSA Studios in New York, and Jones and Wonder in the latter's Los Angeles Wonderland Studios. This technological breakthrough underscored the capability for multi-city, digital audio recording, removing geographical barriers as a logistical concern in arranging artistic collaborations. The demonstration was sponsored by several organizers including Sony Professional Audio. Wonder: 'In the beginning of communications, it instinctively happened that the message, the rhythm and the spirit was carried through the drums of Africa, and now in the 20th century, it must be said that man's desire to spread the same message, rhythm and spirit must be accommodated. At best, in this being the first bi-coastal simultaneous recording in history, it is appropriate in our civilization's most powerful and significant ways, that we communicate energies of positiveness to the young. Need I say, that it is far greater than just an honour to have two great architects, Quincy and Nile, involved with the creation of this great future technological foundation.'

New signing The Superiors (Dana Sequeira, Dwight Burgess, Keith Jones, Lee Dias, Parris Phillips) began singing together in 1981 and appeared in numerous clubs and schools in the Boston area. The young group was auditioned by Travis L. Gresham (then manager of the successful New Edition) and Brook Payne who signed them to their entertainment company. Under this deal The Superiors recorded *Be My Girl* for the Boston based label Critique Records. The group then worked on a song titled *Picture Perfect* which interested producer Maurice Starr who proposed them for the Hollywood of Talent Contest, a show that gave Boston groups the opportunity to win a recording contract. Starr then wrote and produced *Step By Step* for them which Motown picked up to release in June 1987 in the US only.

Smokey Robinson made a rare trip to Britain for a promotional tour in June 1987 following a trip to Belgium, and Martha Reeves and the Vandellas, Marv Johnson and The Velvelettes toured Britain's clubs under the banner 'The Sounds Of Motown'. The tour, promoted by Henry Sellers, was a tremendous nostalgic success. During their time in England, Marv Johnson and The Velvelettes recorded for Ian Levine's Nightmare label. Prior to this former Motown soloist and Marvin Gaye duettist Kim Weston flew to London to record for Nightmare. The first Weston single was *Signal Your Attention*, released in the autumn 1987. Weston: 'I first met Ian Levine when he was fourteen and I knew he was interested in what I was doing then because he asked such a lot of questions. All these years later, Henry Sellers contacts me about recording for Ian's label. It's a small world.' Before the Levine sessions, Weston's singing career had been confined to church and educating young people. She founded a Detroit Summer Youth Programme for financially disadvantaged youngsters with talent, who received professional tutoring in their particular area. Weston opened this programme with fifty youngsters and by 1983 five hundred had enrolled for the summer sessions. Weston's work for the black community was recognized by US Congressman John Conyers Jr at a reception on Capitol Hill. In Detroit she hosted her own programme *The Good Citizens Award* on WCHB where food was distributed free on a weekly basis to people in need, and created a further programme *Rap With The Mayor's Office* which enabled the community to phone various city officials about community problems. Weston: 'I didn't really want to retire from the music business entirely, but when I took my leave of absence in 1972, people insisted I get involved in so many things that my break ran into years!'

The Velvelettes (Millie Gill-Arbour, Norma Barbee-Fairhurst, Carolyn Gill, Bertha Barbee-McNeal) recorded a new version of their Motown classic *Needle In A Haystack* for Nightmare Records, their first single for twenty years. The group decided to reform during the Eighties when Barbee-Fairhurst received a telephone call: 'It was from a DJ in the Washington area. He was a lover of The Velvelettes and asked over his radio show did anyone know me. He wanted me to reform the group. So I phoned the girls and we got together for the first time in twenty years.' Now reformed, The Velvelettes played at special functions including a Motown Revue with Junior Walker, Martha Reeves and others. Barbee-Fairhurst: 'We opened the show in front of 6,000 people. It was fantastic because we had not seen the other acts in years. People even sent us notes saying we should stay together.' When Henry Sellers booked them for his 'Sounds Of Motown' tour, The Velvelettes were astonished at the warm reception they received. Barbee-Fairhurst: 'We were shocked that British people remembered us. We thought The Velvelettes were long forgotten. We never knew we were known in England. In fact, Motown never told us we had released singles there.' Upon the release of *Needle In A Haystack*, the group said it made them the only group with the same line-up to re-record their own Motown single outside the company.

The 'Wicked Pickett', Wilson Pickett, was born in Prattville, Alabama, before his family moved to Detroit. He began recording with the Detroit-based group The Falcons during 1960 and spent most of his formative years in Detroit before embarking upon a solo career. Pickett told David Nathan that he used to look

Fourteen-year-old Angela Cole appeared with Barry White, Stevie Wonder and Sarah Vaughan before joining Motown. This young talent worked with Hal Davis to produce the Turn Up The Beat album.

The Velvelettes joined Martha Reeves and the Vandellas and Marv Johnson to tour England. The quartet then re-recorded Needle In A Haystack for Ian Levine's Nightmare label.

after Berry Gordy's children when Gordy was married to his first wife, Thelma. Pickett's rasping, gritty vocals were subsequently heard on a slew of hit singles during the Sixties for Atlantic Records including In The Midnight Hour (1965), Don't Fight It (1965), 634-5789 (1966), Ninety-Nine-And-A-Half (1966), Funky Broadway (1967), I'm A Midnight Mover (1968), A Man And A Half (1968), Hey Jude (1969), Mini-Skirt Minnie (1969) and You Keep Me Hanging On (1969).

Wilson Pickett left Atlantic during 1973 to record for various labels prior to joining Motown. He originally intended to sign with Elektra Records and to this end had recorded three songs. Berry Gordy heard the material and offered Pickett a better deal. Pickett: 'It was the best thing that ever happened. I figured if Gordy wanted them, there must be something going on. He doesn't let too many fishes get away.' His first single was the ballad Don't Turn Away released in the US in June 1987, taken from the American Soul Man album (US, Aug '87/UK, Oct '87), which was one of Pickett's few to be recorded outside Muscle Shoals studio in Alabama. Pickett: 'I got a whole lot of songs from writers that were new to me. I was very careful about what I picked. I was looking for hits but the songs had to have a worthwhile story because that's what I'm about.' When asked by Nathan how he had survived for so long in the music business, Pickett answered: 'Some (artists) got strung out on dope, some weren't as strong as others and some had problems with their husbands and wives and whatever. But right now, I'm

doing what I'm doing for the money, not for the love of it. I loved it a long time ago.'

American Soul Man, produced by Robert Margouleff, included tracks like A Thing Called Love, When Your Heart Speaks, A Man Of Value and Can't Stop Now. Pickett: 'The most interesting thing about the record is that I've never cut like this. My hits were made under different circumstances. Down in Muscle Shoals, we'd record a lot of the stuff together, the band there and me singing. But this album was recorded using synthesizers, computers, and in the beginning I didn't see how it could be all done and keep my sound. But Robert Margouleff and Robert Martin, who played a lot of the instruments and did some arrangements, brought it all home. I'm proud to say this is one of the best albums I've ever done.'

Pickett's second single was another album track, his re-working of In The Midnight Hour in October 1987 and his first British release a month later. A strange choice when his original version was considered to be one of black music's classics. Pickett: 'Since I wrote it, it makes sense to do it because it's the kind of song I can make money on to feed my kids with. The song has been good for me and, after all, no-one wants me to get away from it.'

During 1987 Pickett was originally booked to perform with Tina Turner on her 'Break Every Rule' world tour and video. The tour began in Germany during March and included sixty-four concerts in thirteen European countries during the spring and summer. The tour, promoted by Marshall Arts and sponsored by Pepsi Cola, reached the UK during June 1987, where for the first time on a British stage Diamond Vision screens were installed at the venues to ensure all members of the audience could see the performances clearly. However, Pickett was hastily replaced by celebrated blues guitarist Robert Cray when, following a disagreement and reputed illness during the filming of the video project in London's Camden Palace, he was taken off the set and returned to America. Needless to say, Pickett lost a golden opportunity by not touring with Turner and Robert Cray's career was boosted almost overnight.

During July 1987 in the absence of a new Stevie Wonder record, Motown/BMG released the mid-priced British compilation The Essential Stevie Wonder as a double album package. The albums contained thirty-nine tracks ranging from 1962 to 1971. The compact disc version of this release was the first British CD compilation and the first mid-priced CD. Tracks included a seven-minute version of Uptight (Everything's Alright), Wonder's original version of Aretha Franklin's 1974 hit Until You Come Back To Me, Blowin' In The Wind, A Place In The Sun, I Was Made To Love Her, For Once In My Life and If You Really Love Me. Two months later in August 1987 The Temptations' back catalogue was rifled when Motown/BMG released the 1972 Grammy Award winning hit Papa Was

A *Rolling Stone*. It was not a straight re-issue as this 1987 single had been heavily re-mixed by Freddy Bastone to become a huge British hit. The re-mix was not American released.

New signing Garry Glenn's debut single was *Do You Have To Go* in the US in July 1987, lifted from his *Feels Good To Feel Good* album released during June 1987 (UK, Oct '87). Glenn's falsetto voice complemented this superb collection of songs, the most outstanding tracks being his duet with Sheila Hutchinson (of The Emotions) on *Feels Good To Feel Good*, *Torch For You* and the first single. All the songs gelled perfectly as album tracks which made single selection difficult, in much the same way as Marvin Gaye's *What's Going On* album did in 1971. Glenn: 'It has been a dream of mine to record this type of material, soulful, sophisticated stuff that calls for real singing and playing, and it's always been a fantasy of mine to record for Motown.' Glenn, known as the 'writer's writer' due to his immense experience and ability to compose powerful, melodic songs, was quite possibly Motown's top signing of 1987, although Jobete did not own his publishing rights.

Born in Detroit, Glenn was one of seven children: 'I grew up in a religious family where everyone played, sang and wrote. My earliest experiences of working in music were with my older sister Beverly, who made gospel records. When she toured I travelled with her, playing and singing.' Upon leaving school Glenn turned to secular music and when The Dramatics recorded his composition *Sing And Dance Your Troubles Away* during 1977, and Phyllis Hyman recorded *Be Careful*, his professional career began. Following this, Glenn produced the Detroit group, Al Hudson and The Soul Partners' album *Spread Love* for ABC Records, before submitting songs to Maurice White's Kalimba Productions, where Glenn was hired as a backing vocalist for The Pockets until White used one of his songs on The Emotions 1980 album *Come Into Our World*.

By now, Glenn's songs were widely used by acts like Earth, Wind And Fire, Philip Bailey and Anita Baker who recorded his co-written *Caught Up In The Rapture*, originally intended for the Isley Brothers. Glenn: 'Anita hired me to play keyboards and do background vocals which kept me solvent during 1984 and 1985.' He then toured with Billy Ocean before returning to compose two American top forty songs – Jean Carne's *Flame Of Love* and the group R.J.'s Latest Arrival's *Heaven In Your Arms* – and writing and being guest vocalist on *Pieces Of A Dream*. After producing *I Can't Let You Go* in 1986 for Freddie Jackson, Glenn recorded *Winning Streak* for Motown's *Police Academy* IV soundtrack album, whereupon the company signed him.

Another new signing Ada Dyer issued her debut single *I Bet Ya, I'll Let Ya* in the US only in August 1987, from her album *Meant To Be* (US, Apr '88). The single and album were produced by James Anthony Carmichael who, since the Seventies, had confined his production work to the Commodores, Lionel Richie and Atlantic Starr.

History was made during August 1987 when Motown's original Detroit 'Hitsville Studios' at 2648 West Grand Boulevard, were officially opened as a museum as part of Michigan's 150th birthday celebrations. David Nathan reported: 'Just entering the reception area of 2648, an immediate sense of history becomes apparent as you glance at all the gold records, the picture sleeves for obscure 45s and two awards for the legendary Supremes from 16 *Magazine* from the year 1966. But true awe will take a hold of your very soul as Doris (Holland) leads you into Studio A. The board in the studio looks ancient, like it may have been the first one ever invented, and it takes a great deal of imagination to get to the fact that virtually all the Motown classics that you've ever listened to were actually recorded on this machine. You'll see faded sheet music, reminders that David Ruffin stood at the mike, that Martha and her Vandellas swooned *Honey*

Writer/producer/singer Garry Glenn introduced a sophisticated, sweet soul sound to Motown. Prior to this, he wrote for countless other artists like Anita Baker, Earth, Wind and Fire and Jean Carne.

Chile, that Diana, Flo and Mary were there some time before you got out of short trousers singing a Supremes medley. The sleeve of a San Remo Golden Strings album touches a respondent chord, (and) full size photographs adorn the walls: The Miracles, The Temptations, a relatively Little Stevie.

'But it isn't the sheet music or the album sleeve or the photos that will stop you in your tracks. No, it's taking a moment to sit at the now out-of-tune Steinway piano and reflect that maybe one of the famous Holland, Dozier, Holland team may have sat in this very seat, going over *Reach Out I'll Be There* with Levi Stubbs of the Four Tops. Step across the room to the drum booth where Benny Benjamin, the renowned session drummer, would lay down a crisp beat behind The Velvelettes as they chirped *He Was Really Sayin' Something*. Marvel that, here behind the microphones, Kim Weston stood as maybe James Jamerson thumped on the bass and Earl Van Dyke pounded on the piano while she wailed *Helpless*.'

On the second floor you '... pass the souvenir shop, selling T-shirts, record labels made into mats for cups, and fan club buttons, and enter into the world of photographs and album sleeves, reminders of the many artists whose careers have been affected by this one building. Turning the corner into the next room, more photos and some copies of the monthly magazine published by the Tamla Motown Appreciation Society, created by (English) soul veteran Dave Godin back in 1963. The adjoining room (is) dedicated for the most part to Jobete Music. On display is a catalogue of songs from 1959 to 1963 and although Jobete copyrights have been recorded by a variety of artists through the years, back then many of the songs had not been cut.' (More photographs and concert posters followed). 'I look over at sequined outfits used by The Temptations, now secured in a closet and smile as Doris Holland tells me that, yes, many of the artists do come back to 2648 just to stop and re-live their lives for a few minutes – Diana Ross, Stevie Wonder, Smokey Robinson walking around, reflecting on days long gone. Even Berry Gordy made the trip back in 1984 and after sitting down at the piano in Studio A for a long time, he was moved to tears, realizing the work that his sister Esther had put into preserving the history of a musical phenomenon. No visit to the USA is complete without at least an hour at 'Hitsville'. As Martha and the Vandellas once said so aptly, come and get these memories . . .'

Various members of The Supremes were active during the summer of 1987. Cindy Birdsong and Scherrie Payne, with Jayne Edwards, were backing vocalists on John Kydd's hi-energy version of *Up The Ladder To The Roof*. Jean Terrell, Scherrie Payne and Lynda Lawrence performed as The Flos (The Former Ladies of Supremes) at Los Angeles' Wilshire Ebell

Theater in August 1987 and recorded the *We're Back* single for the Superstar International label. Unfortunately, the label reputedly closed before the single could be released. Meanwhile, solo Scherrie Payne released *Chasing Me Into Somebody Else's Arms* and Mary Wilson recorded her first single since 1979 *Don't Get Mad, Get Even*. Both were released on the Nightmare label to become hi-energy/gay hits.

In September 1987 CBS/Epic released Michael Jackson's long-awaited *Bad* album. His duet with Siedah Garrett *I Just Can't Stop Loving You* became an international number one single prior to the album's release. Naturally, *Bad* was afforded a tremendous marketing campaign by the record company as it became a worldwide number one album. To date *Bad*, *The Way You Make Me Feel* and *Man In The Mirror* have been lifted as singles, although the album's highlights were *Liberian Girl* and the Stevie Wonder duet *Just Good Friends*. Although Jackson had been absent from the recording business he still attracted regular media attention with his cosmetic surgery. Upon the release of his *Bad* album Jackson embarked upon a world tour. His opening dates were in Japan in September 1987, where a raunchy, sexual star, dressed in a black-leather, bondage cat suit debuted before 40,000 fans in Tokyo. His sexy act, he stroked his thighs and crotch constantly, angered Japanese parents in the audience while their offspring squealed in delight. During his performance, Jackson announced he had grown into a man and that his appearance demonstrated that change. At a private function before his opening night he told guests: 'For different people, growing up can occur at a different age and now I'm showing the world that I'm the man I always wanted to be.'

At the same time as the *Bad* album was released, Jackson's 30-year-old brother Marlon released his first solo album *Baby Tonight* on Capitol Records. Marlon Jackson told *Blues & Soul*: 'I was always signed to Epic Records as a solo artist even though all my records came out as part of The Jacksons. After we did the *Victory* tour in 1984 I went to the company and told them I wanted to do a solo album, they said they wanted a group album first, that maybe I could do a solo project after we did that, so that's when I decided I should officially leave the group. It had been in the back of my head for some time to actually begin working on a solo album and that kinda clinched it.'

The Temptations, now twenty-seven years in the business and still working ten months in every year, released their *Together Again* album in September 1987 (UK, Nov '87). This album reunited Dennis Edwards with the group but it was thought he would also pursue a solo career. Edwards replaced Ali-Ollie Woodson, who sang lead on *Treat Her Like A*

Michael Jackson released Bad as his follow-up album to the world-beater Thriller. Following the release of Bad Jackson began his world tour in Japan where his raunchy stage act upset Japanese parents but thrilled the kids!

Lady, and who intended to pursue solo activities. *Together Again* included *I Wonder Who She's Seeing Now*, the first single issued prior to the album in August 1987 (UK, Nov '87) and its follow-up *Look What You Started* in December 1987 (UK, Jan '88). Ron Tyson: 'We're trying to maintain the roots of the group. Singing harmony, rather than trying to venture out into other areas where all these people are experimenting with computers. The Temptations are trendsetters, so it's not necessary that they follow the trend.'

The album's producers Peter Bunetta and Rick Chudacoff wanted to use Dennis Edwards on all the lead vocals. This caused disagreement between them and the group. The matter was resolved when it was agreed that Ron Tyson and Richard Street would take certain significant lead parts, with the remainder sharing the leads. Dennis Edwards actually re-joined the group at the beginning of 1987, as Melvin Franklin told *Blues & Soul*: 'Ron Tyson was visiting his family and Dennis expressed the feeling that his solo career really wasn't working out and that he missed the camaraderie of being with a group. We sat down and talked and worked everything out so he's back with us now.' It was an easy transition for Edwards and the group, although he had to perfect their choreography routines once again. Franklin: 'After ironing out some rough spots, particularly on some of our more recent material, he fitted right back in.' Despite the numerous line-up changes The Temptations' career was one envied by their contemporaries. Even with the absence of regular hit singles the group was assured packed theatres. Franklin admitted that 'having a hit puts the spit-shine on your career and I'll be honest we'd love to have the same kind of adulation that Tina Turner began to get a few years ago. Apart from that, hit records represent another step-up. We can work bigger venues and maybe spend six months instead of ten on the road while still maintaining our income level. Hits add to your self-esteem and I'd love to pick up the trade publications every week and see our names in there and know that we'll be invited to the Grammy Awards as presenters. That's the kind of stuff that hit records bring.'

Ex-Supreme Cindy Birdsong returned to the recording studios in England to record the *Dancing Room* single for the Hi Hat label during autumn 1987. Birdsong: 'When I was working around Motown after I left The Supremes, I always wanted to sing again. I used to think about it constantly. It was like a physical thing, like a pressure building up in my chest. I would never have forgiven myself if I didn't do it now. The new music of today was a great incentive because clearly the opportunity is there to really experiment.' Returning to the studios was, she said, a new experience: 'It's all more hi-tech and computerized now, and the studio was huge. I felt I lost the personal

side in such a big place because I felt like a speck of sand in the desert. It was strange being by myself, it's not the same as singing in a small booth with the others.' To promote *Dancing Room* Birdsong undertook an extensive British promotional tour during September 1987 before returning there for further activities in February 1988.

During her interviews Birdsong was able to speak openly about The Supremes and, more importantly, dispel any rumours that she was involved in forcing Florence Ballard out of the group. Birdsong: 'When I first went to Detroit I was told they (Berry Gordy) wanted to meet me, but I didn't know who I was going to replace. When I arrived in Detroit I was met at the airport by Motown executives and driven to Berry Gordy's home where the group was having a meeting with him. I had no idea what was going on in the other room. I was still a member of LaBelle at the time and didn't even tell Patti I was going to Detroit because I planned to return. The door to the room swung open and Florence came out in tears. Her mother came out with her. Florence was so upset, so shaken, she didn't see me. Florence and I were the best of friends since the Patti LaBelle days. Florence was very open and warm, and we had this thing that people always said we looked alike.'

When Birdsong first joined The Supremes, she said there was a lot of tension within the group: 'When Florence left Mary Wilson didn't feel good about it because they were so close. There were a lot of different working arrangements like separate dressing rooms and we were, I suppose, the backing group to Diana Ross in a sense. Mary felt it more than I because I was new to the group. There were

In 1987 Cindy Birdsong recorded Dancing Room on the Hi Hat label.

times when there were clashes of personality, which is bound to happen with three women. With the name change (to Diana Ross and the Supremes), the way of recording changed. We knew we would separate and that's when the confusion and feelings came in.'

Birdsong blamed her divorce from Charles Hewlett on her demanding Supremes career: 'Our schedule was so hectic, working ten months out of a year, with a day off here and there. It was hard to keep a good relationship going. I had my son David then and I had to leave him at home to be raised by his father and our housekeeper. I asked them to come on the road with me, but my husband had a full time business to run, so he couldn't come. That started our relationship to decline. You can't leave a handsome man behind. We divorced when our son was two years old and his father lives five minutes away from us now.'

Prior to the release of *Skeletons* in September 1987 (UK, Oct '87), the first single from his *Characters* album due for American and British release in November 1987, Stevie Wonder performed at a benefit concert in Los Angeles for retinitis pigmentosa, a degenerative eye disease that has so far affected 400,000 Americans. Wonder agreed to perform because his private tutor from his school days suffered from the disease. The proceeds from the concert went towards establishing a Los Angeles research and care facility, Wonderland. For his performance, Wonder programmed his music on to a computer instead of using musicians on stage. Julio Iglesias joined Wonder on stage to sing *My Love* with him. Wonder wrote the song, and subsequently recorded a duet with Iglesias.

To coincide with the release of *Skeletons* Wonder completed his British tour, postponed from May 1987, and once again his shows were sold out. Before Wonder appeared on the Wembley Arena stage, four large, suspended screens showed white-gloved hands clapping against a black background, thus encouraging the audience to do the same. Throughout the performance Wonder surprisingly hit several low points, but it was his older material (*My Cherie Amour, Uptight, Fingertips*) that saved the show. New York ghetto footage was shown during *Living For The City* to ensure nobody missed Wonder's message. But once again, it was the hits that got the audience to fever pitch – *Lately, You Are The Sunshine Of My Life, Supersitition, I Just Called To Say I Love You* and *Part-Time Lover*. The computer-programmed *Skeletons* was the last song, which, bearing in mind the single's failure, was not a good choice for a finale. Wonder's music throughout the show relied heavily on technical input and many fans fear that much of his live visual excitement will be lost because of his insistence in using computers in the studio and on stage. Following the British tour, Stevie Wonder underwent

neurological surgery to remove a neuroma on his index finger. After a brief convalescence, he toured Australia and New Zealand before Christmas 1987.

When the *Characters* album was released, it faced stern reviews. Only his die-hard fans supported the work because of the failure of *Skeletons*. Wonder: 'The album is about many characters, characters in politics, the character of people in relationships, the different moods of people, bringing out their character. The album comes in two parts. Twelve songs now and more in a few months time. Some of the songs are about ten years old, but most of them are recent. When you listen (to it) you'll find out things about me and things about yourself.' The album was full of intense messages dealing with romance, loneliness, religion and apartheid, including Gary Byrd's *Dark 'n' Lovely* and Wonder's duet with Michael Jackson *Get It* (almost Jackson's *Beat It* part two). Wonder did not have the song ready in time for Jackson to add his vocals in America, prior to the start of Jackson's world tour so, when Wonder was in London performing he asked for a member of his Wembley audience to act as courier to take the tape to Los Angeles to give it to Jackson. The offer was taken up by Barry Betts who made the free trip and delivered the tape under the glare of the world's press. Jackson's voice was recorded over Wonder's track in Japan, where his tour opened. On the *One Of A Kind* track, British singer Junior Giscombe was a backing vocalist, and blues guitarist B. B. King was featured in a solo spot on *Come Let Me Make Your Love Come Down*. The ballad *You Will Know*, the

'The album is about many characters, characters in politics, the characters of people in relationships, the different moods of people, bringing out their character.' Stevie Wonder.

second single to be lifted from the album in December 1987 (UK, Jan '88) was also available on compact disc. It flopped.

Characters was a disappointing project. Wonder's regurgitated political and religious statements were predictable and the music was saturated in technological programming. Television personality and journalist, Jonathan King wrote: '*Characters* is his biggest flop in sixteen years. His single *Skeletons* did virtually nothing. I think the reason for his popular collapse is simple. He is enormously talented. But his real gift – pure, exuberant soul, so magnificent on *Fingertips* – has been replaced by cold, calculated technology. Rather like Paul McCartney, he is now totally professional and writes, sings and plays from his head instead of his heart. He won't even do an interview without his electronic instruments spread out in front of him. Computers, synthesizers and amplified buzzes have replaced raw guts. He has become a master of slick, emotionless pop.'

Following the release of Chris Rea's album *Dancing With Strangers* which Motown picked up for American release only, Chico DeBarge issued his second album *Kiss Serious* in the US only in September 1987. The 21-year-old DeBarge co-wrote only one song *Shame Shame* with Claude Allen and Brownmark (former bass player for Prince's defunct Revolution and new signing to Motown). DeBarge: 'I had originally written some tunes for this album but I wanted to be free to concentrate on my performance. I wanted to be careful because last time I ended up wearing too many hats (*Chico DeBarge* album) and I wanted this album to be different and special. I had a desire to establish myself as an individual performer.' The first single lifted was *I've Been Watching You*, issued prior to the album's release, in August 1987. Meanwhile, Chico's brother El's second album *Real Love* scheduled for 1987 release, was canned. El wrote and produced six of the nine tracks with his younger brother, Darly. The album included *Turn The Page*, *Broken Hearts*, *After You*, *Love Life* and *Real Love*. The non-release of this album could have been due to El DeBarge becoming bankrupt in late 1987.

During Wilson Pickett's tour of Germany during October 1987, he was involved in a bloody fight with his musicians, which resulted in him being hospitalized. A clash of egos and alcohol were blamed. Meanwhile, Smokey Robinson's Pittsburgh performance, as part of another American tour, passed more smoothly, as reviewer Terry Hazlett reported: 'In concert, he has the luxury of performing for hardcore fans, black and white, prepared to listen to anything Robinson chooses to sing. Smokey performs his hits, but they have little in common with his records. Briefly, he even pokes fun at the doo-wah harmonies on *Bad Girl*, and the choreographed on stage delivery of all Motown acts.

Then he performs his 'have to' song, *Ooo Baby Baby* and has the audience so spellbound, it almost forgets to applaud. After the silence, there is a standing ovation. It is not the last of the night.

'It's all the more impressive in that this is not a teenaged crowd of idol worshippers. These are primarily "over-the-hill" adults who, nonetheless, cannot quite believe what they have just heard. The singer is unaffected by the empty seats in the balcony. Like a youngster with his first top forty single, the forty-eight-year-old Robinson waits anxiously in the wings as the orchestra wraps up its overture, before bursting on stage. He warms up the audience with *More Love* and *Shop Around*, then defuses the cat-callers – the irritating fans who keep requesting songs – by immediately opening the floor to requests. The highlight, unquestionably, comes when he joins guitarist Marv Tarplin, his collaborator on hundreds of songs. Together they play and sing parts of a dozen of them. Without the nuisance of the dance beat, the lyrics and music come together with entirely superior results. The concert is not all serious stuff. Robinson tells Motown tidbits, jokes with his back up singers and band, and divides the audience for a singing contest. It is a gimmick he does not need. At the concert's end, a female fan, visibly moved by what she had heard, sat riveted in her seat, then said, to no-one in particular, "It was worth every penny". And then some.'

Golf addict, Robinson had recently divorced from his wife of twenty-seven years, Claudette Rogers. Robinson: 'That was difficult, still is. But I can't think of anything I would change.' They had two children from that marriage, a daughter Tamla and a son, Berry. Also at this time, Robinson revealed the origin on his nickname 'Smokey'. It was given to him by his uncle Claude, because, he told the *Florida Sentinel Bulletin*, when I was born I was white. I had blonde hair, blue eyes. In Detroit then, they had segregated nurseries. A nurse put me in the "Whites Only" nursery. Nobody could find me, not my parents or the doctors. I was lost for a whole day!'

During October 1987 another ex-Motowner returned to the recording studios. This time Brenda Holloway, Motown's first West Coast signing during the Sixties, flew to London to record for Nightmare Records. Holloway: 'When Ian Levine (Nightmare's owner) asked me to come over I thought I'd give it a go. I did a day of praying about it because it was a crazy situation to be in. I didn't know where it was going to lead me. I was going to a country I'd never been to before, to meet a man I didn't know. But somehow it all felt comfortable to me.' Now a wife and mother of four children, Holloway, prior to flying to London, worked as a hotel receptionist. Early in 1988 Nightmare released her *Give Me A Little Inspiration* which became a Hi-NRG hit.

With Michael Jackson's *Bad* album rapidly becoming another multi-million seller for CBS/Epic, Motown capitalized on the success by releasing *The Original Soul Of Michael Jackson* (US, Nov '87/UK, Feb '88). This album spearheaded the re-promotion of other catalogue items by Michael solo and as a member of the Jackson 5. The first single lifted from the album was Michael's cover-version of Edwin Starr's *Twenty Five Miles*, released before the album in October 1987. Motown/BMG opted to release a Christmas extended play single featuring the evergreen tracks *I Saw Mommy Kissing Santa Claus, Frosty The Snowman, Santa Claus Is Coming To Town/Up On The Housetop*. Iris Gordy, Motown's A&R vice-president: 'We put this out (the album) to remind people how well Michael sang, even as a child. Very few people were aware, even here, that Michael had done some of these tunes.' *The Original Soul Of Michael Jackson* was re-mixed, Gordy said, 'to sound as good musically as possible. This is the best possible collection we could put together at the time.' The album comprised the Michael Jackson solos *Melodie, Ain't No Sunshine, Got To Be There, Doggin' Around, Rockin' Robin, You've Got A Friend* and *Twenty Five Miles* and with the Jackson 5 *Dancing Machine, It's Too Late To Change The Time, If I Don't Love You This Way* and *Forever Came Today*. All the tracks, except *Twenty Five Miles*, were previously released. Michael Jackson's last Motown album *Farewell My Summer Love*, containing unreleased material and issued in 1984, sold in excess of 250,000 copies, proving there was still a huge market for his Motown recordings.

Before the close of 1987 Holland, Dozier and Holland were given long overdue lifetime achievement awards by the American National Academy of Songwriters. The Academy hinted the trio were 'under-recognized publicly' for their contribution to black music. While at Motown, Holland, Dozier and Holland remained in the background, to allow the acts recording their songs to take the limelight, unlike Smokey Robinson, Stevie Wonder and others, who also performed.

On New Year's Eve 1987 *The Motown Story* was screened on British television. The programme, introduced by Paul Gambaccini, was produced and directed by Rod Taylor. Reputed to be at least two years in the making, the programme featured archive film footage and featured Motown artists like Martha Reeves and Mary Wilson. The programme was welcomed by Motown fans, although many were disappointed at the sketchy way in which the company's history was re-told and the lack of original filmed material. Indeed, when compared to the film collections of many British Motown fans, which can include material from all over the world, this programme fell short of its potential. These personal collections, often taking years to compile, would probably put Motown Productions' collection to shame.

The deeply soulful Mistress of Emotion, Brenda Holloway, flew to London to record for Nightmare Records. As well as recording as a soloist, she duetted with Jimmy Ruffin.

Motown Records suffered an extremely lean year in 1987. It slipped to eighth position on *Billboard*'s annual listing of top labels in black music and earned only two gold albums during the year. British business was likewise dismal. Established acts like Lionel Richie, The Temptations and Stevie Wonder failed to repeat past achievements, and once again Smokey Robinson's success was confined to America. Motown relied on these artists to produce hits, to offset the risks involved when breaking in new acts. The company always attracted a great deal of attention from competitors because of its uniqueness and its musical history, and was always looked upon as the company to follow. However, Motown's past success with artists continued to attract new signings who wanted to be a part of its historical heritage. Yet, when its superstar acts failed, the battle to break fresh talent was doubled. Although it is too early to judge career longevity, the recent batch of new artists are so far hitless on the national charts.

Generally speaking, the standard of their music was to blame, although there were some exceptions, like Garry Glenn, Carrie McDowell and General Kane. Musical trends in the marketplace were continually changing and Motown failed to keep abreast of this. Also, the company's music was too varied, and any hint of a positive musical direction was lost in promotion. The struggle was not confined to Motown. Its competitors, to a certain extent, faced the same battle, but if Motown failed, the fall was harder because of its heritage and past successes, which had continued while others had failed. Motown was very much aware of its decline over the past few years and decided to take positive action. It was decided many of the problems stemmed from its marketing and promotion teams, and these were areas destined for change early in 1988 with the appointment of veteran industry figure, Al Bell, ex-vice-president of Stax Records from 1965 until 1976. Bell was appointed in the newly created position of president of Motown's Creative Division

following the demise of the pop publicity and promotion departments. This move prompted *Billboard* to speculate that Motown was moving its emphasis and financial resources from pop to R&B promotion. Staff reductions were apparent in the pop areas as Motown increased its profile of several national black promoters while hiring extra black regional representatives.

Al Bell, whose most recent venture was forming the Los Angeles-based Edge Records with partner Rick Frio, joined Motown's top management team with Group President Lee Young Jr and label president, Skip Miller. Bell told the *Los Angeles Times*: 'We are taking the necessary steps to insure the roots of this tree are well planted. We want to be sure we have a solid foundation in so-called R&B music, since this is how the company was founded and built.' Capitol Records' Shep Johnson welcomed Bell's appointment: 'Over the past few years Motown has not been the Motown that it used to be. That's obvious – the whole industry knows that. But they're trying to regenerate that old spirit and make Motown stand for what it used to stand for back in the Sixties.' The effect of Bell's appointment is

The General Kane group was the brainchild of Mitch McDowell (standing third from right). Their debut single was the strongly worded anti-drug song Crack Killed Applejack. *McDowell: 'I wanted to paint not only an ugly picture, but the most horrible, which might prevent someone experimenting with the drug in the first place.'*

too early to judge at the time of writing, but he summed up the industry's feelings by saying: 'Berry Gordy was, and is, my role model. Berry Gordy and Motown were the lighthouse and direction-setter for me in building Stax.'

To start its thirtieth anniversary two new young artists injected fresh blood into Motown. The first was Brownmark with his *Just Like That* album in February 1988 (UK, March '88). His *Next Time* single had been released two months prior to the album. The second was Darryl Duncan's *Heaven* album from which *James Brown* (Part 1), a tribute to the great entertainer, was also lifted as a single in December 1987.

Brownmark was the second, after Vanity, from Prince's musical camp to join Motown. Also a native of Minneapolis, Brownmark became interested in music at high school at the age of 16, when he played bass in a local band, Fantasy. While playing at the First Avenue club in Minneapolis during 1980, Prince asked him to play bass guitar for his band. Brownmark told David Nathan: 'Those six years (from 1980-1986) had good and bad moments and I'd have to say honestly that there wasn't a great deal of freedom involved to express oneself musically.' Brownmark played on Prince's albums *Controversy, 1999, Purple Rain, Around The World In A Day, Parade* and on one track (*It's Gonna Be A Beautiful Night*) on his *Sign Of The Times*. Prior to working on his Motown debut album, Brownmark produced tracks for Stacy Lattisaw, Chico DeBarge, Lakeside, Mirage and Mazarati. Brownmark then met Berry Gordy, when, he told Nathan: 'We spent about two or three hours together and, in his own words, he said that I was the kind of artist he'd been looking for. I signed with the company because I can tell that they will represent me as an artist but will also take care of me as a person. I feel that they're a

company who will take pride in my work and not use it as a write-off.' *Just Like That*, written and produced by Brownmark, except for *Why Can't We Be Alone*, which he co-wrote with Chris Boone, included the tracks *Want You Back, Contagious, Stakeout* and *I Used To Be In Love*.

Darryl Duncan, born in Chicago, took an interest in music while at grammer school, after his parents bought an organ for him. At high school Duncan wanted to be an architect but formed the group Cashmere instead, prior to working in five other bands in Chicago clubs. Duncan's first break came in 1982 when he wrote the *Simply Beautiful* track on Jerry Butler's *Ice And Hot* album. Two years later he met horn arranger Tom Tom, with whom he worked for a year before writing with Maurice White of Earth, Wind And Fire and Chaka Khan. During 1986 Duncan composed *Rock The House* for the soundtrack album *Police Academy IV*, moved to Los Angeles and joined Almo/Irving Publishing, a subsidary of A&M Records. Duncan then produced the group Foxy for Hush Productions. *Heaven*, which Duncan wrote and produced, included the jazzy *One Touch*, the ballad *My Dream* and the fast moving *Boomerang*.

The third 1988 album was the second from Stacy Lattisaw titled *Personal Attention* (US, Feb '88/UK Mar '88). *Every Drop Of Your Love* was released as a taster from the album in the US only on December 1987 and flopped. How-

Brownmark was another artist from Princes' camp to join Motown. Brownmark: 'I feel that (Motown) is a company who will take pride in my work and not use it as a write-off.'

Darryl Duncan wrote a track for Motown's Police Academy IV soundtrack prior to recording his own Heaven album which he also wrote and produced.

ever, *Personal Attention* was a superb showcase of the maturer Lattisaw, now working with producers like Ron (*Have Mercy*) Kersey, Brownmark (whose production work was a little excessive) and Vincent Brantley on tracks that included *He's Got A Hold On Me* and *Changes* (which Lattisaw wrote with Brownmark), *Find Another Lover*, and the album's title. Lattisaw: 'This record is more me. I enjoyed singing these songs. It was as if some of them were written especially for me. As I get older, I have to really feel what I'm singing and my executive producer, Debbie Sandridge, was understanding of that. It made recording just that much smoother.'

As Motown entered its 30th year, the company seemed to complete its musical circle by reverting to its original idea of concentrating on a small roster of new artists and engaging a marketing team to promote the product at street level – a formula which stood the company in good stead thirty years earlier. Smokey Robinson told *Rolling Stone* magazine – '(In those days) Berry had an idea about making records. He wanted to make records that would have no race and no barriers, and that's what we set out to do, to make music for people of all races and nationalities.'

Robinson added that it was Gordy's intention to create the sound of young America, not the sound of black America, and that sound was the Motown Sound: 'When people talk to me about the Motown Sound, it's something audible, something you hear when you hear a Motown record, especially an old Motown record. To anyone who was not part of it, that's what you consider the Motown Sound. Now to me the Motown Sound is the people who made it. We're the Motown Sound.'

In January 1988 the third annual Rock & Roll Hall Of Fame induction dinner was held at the Waldorf-Astoria Hotel in New York City. Over one thousand people paid $300 to watch numerous artists being inducted into the Hall Of Fame, including The Supremes, The Beatles, The Drifters and The Beach Boys. Mary Wilson and the late Florence Ballard's daughter, Lisa Chapman, collected The Supremes' award. Diana Ross was conspicuous by her absence. Reputedly leaving RCA Records for MCA Records, Ross' absence was said to be due to Wilson's comments about her in *Dreamgirl: My Life As A Supreme*. More realistically, Ross preferred to spend her time with her family including her newly-born son. *Echoes* reporter Clifton Miller wrote that when Wilson and Chapman received the award from Little Richard: 'Mary gushed, as she is inclined to do, but no-one minded. She looked radiant, and made some generous remarks about Diana's absence. "I respect the fact that she maybe saw fit to stay with something so personal", an allusion to Ross being in Norway with her husband and family. Wilson expressed sorrow that "Florence could not live to know that what three little girls

dreamt of so many years ago came true." She also paid tribute to Berry Gordy, Holland, Dozier and Holland, and Motown. Chapman, dressed in black, said a few words, but was clearly intimidated by the event. What was most striking about the youngster was her resemblance to her late mother. Little Richard was pleased to give The Supremes their award he said "because they remind me of myself; they dressed like me!"'

In the non-performing category Motown's founder Berry Gordy attended the function to accept his prestigious award from Atlantic Records' chairman and co-founder, Ahmet

Ertegun. Clifton Miller: 'The man behind Motown has a reputation for being very private. During his acceptance speech Gordy said as much – "I still like it better behind the scenes" he admitted. Gordy also spoke about his life – he called it "an embarrassment of riches" – and his homeland – "I would like to thank a country whose form of government makes it possible for someone to have a dream (like mine) come true". He also said "Human potential is the world's most unused resource" and referred to the many Motown artists who demonstrated their potential. "Truest to the arts" Gordy declared "was Mar-vin Gaye. His life was in every song. If he owed taxes, he sang about that. Marvin's music was marvellous work that lives forever". And the Motown founder paid tribute to Smokey Robinson, calling him "probably the finest human being I've ever met". Another graduate from Motown High was there in spirit, if not in body. Gordy read a telegram he received earlier that day: "Congratulations. You deserve it. You are the father of fine music. Love always. Your son, Michael Jackson".'

Perhaps Smokey Robinson was right when he said: 'Once a Motowner, always a Motowner.'

Motown's founder Berry Gordy receives the prestigious Hall of Fame Award during a ceremony in New York. It was a fitting tribute to the man who had the courage and ambition to introduce a new direction in music and create a sound that would become a part of everyone's life for decades. Thank you Berry Gordy for the music.

Motown Discography

Letters at the top of the list next to the label name are the prefix before the individual record numbers.

Note for information 'European system applies' – from 1984 the British listing systems were discontinued and transferred to the European numbering system.

Abbreviations: CD – compact disc; d/s double-sided; ext. – extended; f/s. – film soundtrack; instr. – instrumental; l.v. – long version; s.v. – single version; vers. – version.

Discography compiled by Gordon Frewin.

AMERICAN SINGLES

TAMLA LABEL

MATRIX NO:	ARTIST	SINGLE TITLE	RELEASE DATE
101	Marv Johnson	Come To Me	1.1959
		Whisper	
102	Eddie Holland	Merry-Go-Round	1.1959
		It Moves Me	
5501	Nick & the Jaguars	Ich-I-Bon I	5.1959
		Cool And Crazy	
†54024	Chico Leverette	Solid Sender	6.1959
		I'll Never Love Again	
†54024	The Swinging Tigers	Snake Walk (Part 1) (instr.)	6.1959
		Snake Walk (Part 2) (instr.)	
54025	Ron & Bill	It	8.1959
		Don't Say Bye Bye	
*54026	Satintones	Going To The Hop	10.1959
		Motor City	
54027	Barrett Strong	Money (That's What I Want)	8.1959
		Oh I Apologise	
†54028	The Miracles	The Feeling Is So Fine	3.1960
		You Can Depend On Me	
†54028	The Miracles	The Feeling Is So Fine (2nd vers.)	4.1960
		You Can Depend On Me	
†54028	The Miracles	Way Over There	4.1960
		(You Can) Depend On Me	
†54028	The Miracles	Way Over There (2nd vers.)	6.1960
		Depend On Me	
54029	Barrett Strong & the Rayber Voices	Yes, No, Maybe So	7.1960
		You Knows What To Do	
†54030	Singin' Sammy Ward	Who's The Fool	8.1960
		What Makes You Love Him	
†54030	Singin' Sammy Ward	Who's The Fool	9.1960
		That Child Is Really Wild	
54031	Mable John	Who Wouldn't Love A Man Like That	8.1960
		You Made A Fool Out Of Me	

† When cataloguing first started errors arose in the matrix numbering system hence repeat numbers. This was rectified in 1960 when Billie Jean Brown took charge of Berry Gordy's tape library and unified the numbering system.

* Also listed as Downbeats 'Your Baby's Back/Request Of A Fool'.

54032	Herman Griffin	True Love	10.1960
		It's You	
54033	Barrett Strong	I'm Gonna Cry (If You Quit Me)	8.1960
		Whirlwind	
54034	The Miracles	Shop Around	10.1960
		Who's Loving You	
54035	Barrett Strong	Money And Me	2.1961
		You Got What It Takes	

54036	The Miracles	Ain't It Baby	3.1961
		The Only One I Love	
54037	The Gospel Stars	He Lifed Me	3.1962
		Behold The Saints Of God	
54038	The Supremes	I Want A Guy	3.1961
		Never Again	
54039	Mickey Woods	Poor Sam Jones	3.1961
		They Rode Through The Valley	
54040	Mable John	Looking For A Man	6.1961
		(I Guess There's) No Love	
54041	Marvin Gaye	Let Your Conscience Be Your Guide	5.1961
		Never Let You Go (Sha Lu Bop)	
54042	Gino Parks	Same Thing (Will Happen To You)	6.1961
		That's No Lie	
54043	Barrett Strong	Misery	6.1961
		Two Wrongs Don't Make A Right	
54044	The Miracles	Brokenhearted	6.1961
		Mighty Good Lovin'	
54045	The Supremes	Buttered Popcorn	7.1961
		Who's Lovin' You	
54046	The Marvelettes	Please Mr Postman	8.1961
		So Long Baby	
54047	The Rev. Columbus Mann	(They) Shall Be Mine	3.1962
		Jesus Loves	
54048	The Miracles	Everybody's Gotta Pay Some Dues	9.1961
		I Can't Believe	
54049	Sammy Ward	What Makes You Love Him	11.1961
		Don't Take It Away	
54050	Mable John	Action Speaks Louder Than Words	11.1961
		Take Me	
54051	Bob Kayli	Small Sad Sam	11.1961
		Tie Me Tight	
54052	Mickey Woods	Please Mr. Kennedy	2.1962
		They Call Me Cupid	
54053	The Miracles	What's So Good About Goodbye	12.1961
		I've Been Good to You	
54054	The Marvelettes	Twistin' Postman	12.1961
		I Want A Guy	
54055	Marvin Gaye	Sandman	1.1962
		I'm Yours, You're Mine	
54056	The Downbeats	Your Baby's Back	2.1962
		Request Of A Fool	
54057	Singin' Sammy Ward	Big Joe Moe	3.1962
		Everybody Knew It	
54058	Little Otis	I Out-Duked The Duke	3.1962
		Baby I Need You	
54059	The Miracles	I'll Try Something New	4.1962
		You Never Miss A Good Thing	
54060	The Marvelettes	Playboy	4.1962
		All The Love I've Got	
54061	Little Stevie Wonder	I Call It Pretty Music But The Old People Call It The Blues Part 1	8.1962
		I Call It Pretty Music But The Old People Call It The Blues Part 2	
54062	–	–	–
54063	Marvin Gaye	Soldier's Plea	5.1962
		Taking My Time	
54064	Mickey McCullers	Same Old Story	6.1962
		I'll Cry A Million Tears	
54065	The Marvelettes	Beechwood 4-5789	7.1962
		Some Day, Someway	
54066	Gino Parks	Fire	8.1962
		For This I Thank You	
54067	Saundra Mallett & the Vandellas	Camel Walk	unknown
		It's Gonna Be Hard Times	
54068	Marvin Gaye	Stubborn Kind Of Fellow	7.1962
		It Hurt Me Too	
54069	The Miracles	Way Over There	8.1962
		If Your Mother Only Knew	

54070	Little Stevie Wonder & Clarence Paul	Little Water Boy / La La La La La	10.1962
54071	Singin' Sammy Ward	Someday Pretty Baby / Part Time Love	8.1962
54072	The Marvelettes	Strange I Know / Too Strong To Be Strung Along	10.1962
54073	The Miracles	You've Really Got A Hold On Me / Happy Landing	11.1962
54074	Little Stevie Wonder	Contract On Love / Sunset	12.1962
54075	Marvin Gaye	Hitch Hike / Hello There Angel	12.1962
54076	Kim Weston	It Should Have Been Me / Love Me All The Way	2.1963
54077	The Marvelettes	Locking Up My Heart / Forever	2.1963
54078	The Miracles	A Love She Can Count On / I Can Take A Hint	3.1963
54079	Marvin Gaye	Pride And Joy / One Of These Days	4.1963
54080	Little Stevie Wonder	Fingertips Part 2 / Fingertips Part 1	5.1963
54081	Mable John	Who Wouldn't Love A Man Like That / Say You'll Never Let Me Go	6.1963
54082	The Marvelettes	My Daddy Knows Best / Tie A String Around Your Finger	7.1963
54083	The Miracles	Mickey's Monkey / Whatever Makes You Happy	7.1963
54084	—	—	—
54085	Kim Weston	Just Loving You / Another Train Coming	10.1963
54086	Little Stevie Wonder	Workout Stevie, Workout / Monkey Talk	9.1963
54087	Marvin Gaye	Can I Get A Witness / I'm Crazy 'Bout My Baby	9.1963
54088	The Marvelettes	As Long As I Know He's Mine / Little Girl Blue	10.1963
54089	The Miracles	I Gotta Dance To Keep From Crying / Such Is Love, Such Is Life	10.1963
54090	Little Stevie Wonder	Castles In The Sand / Thank You (For Loving Me All The Way)	1.1964
54091	The Marvelettes	He's A Good Guy (Yes He Is) / Goddess Of Love	1.1964
54092	The Miracles	(You Can't Let The Boy Overpower) The Man In You / Heartbreak Road	1.1964
54093	Marvin Gaye	You're A Wonderful One / When I'm Alone I Cry	2.1964
54094	Brenda Holloway	Every Little Bit Hurts / Land Of A Thousand Boys	3.1964
54095	Marvin Gaye	Try It Baby / If My Heart Could Sing	5.1964
54096	Stevie Wonder	Hey Harmonica Man / This Little Girl	5.1964
54097	The Marvelettes	You're My Remedy / A Little Bit Of Sympathy, A Little Bit Of Love	6.1964
54098	The Miracles	I Like It Like That / You're So Fine And Sweet	7.1964
54099	Brenda Holloway	I'll Always Love You / Sad Song	7.1964
54100	Kim Weston	Looking For The Right Guy / Feel Alright Tonight	8.1964
54101	Marvin Gaye	Baby Don't You Do It / Walk On The Wild Side	9.1964
54102	The Miracles	That's What Love Is Made Of / Would I Love You	8.1964
54103	Stevie Wonder	Happy Street / Sad Boy	9.1964
54104	Marvin Gaye & Kim Weston	What Good Am I Without You / I Want You 'Round	10.1964
54105	The Marvelettes	Too Many Fish In The Sea / A Need For Love	10.1964
54106	Kim Weston	A Little More Love / Go Ahead And Laugh	11.1964
54107	Marvin Gaye	How Sweet It Is (To Be Loved By You) / Forever	11.1964
54108	Stevie Wonder	Pretty Little Angel / Tears In Vain	NR
54109	The Miracles	Come On Do The Jerk / Baby Don't You Go	11.1964
54110	Kim Weston	I'm Still Loving You / Go Ahead And Laugh	1.1965
54111	Brenda Holloway	When I'm Gone / I've Been Good To You	2.1965
54112	Marvin Gaye	I'll Be Doggone / You've Been A Long Time Coming	2.1965
54113	The Miracles	Ooo Baby Baby / All That's Good	3.1965
54114	Stevie Wonder	Kiss Me Baby / Tears In Vain	3.1965
54115	Brenda Holloway	Operator / I'll Be Available	5.1965
54116	The Marvelettes	I'll Keep Holding On / No Time For Tears	5.1965
54117	Marvin Gaye	Pretty Little Baby / Now That You've Won Me	6.1965
54118	The Miracles	The Tracks Of My Tears / A Fork In The Road	6.1965
54119	Stevie Wonder	High Heel Sneakers / Music Talk	8.1965
54120	The Marvelettes	Danger Heartbreak Dead Ahead / Your Cheating Ways	7.1965
54121	Brenda Holloway	You Can Cry On My Shoulder / How Many Times Did You Mean It	8.1965
54122	Marvin Gaye	Ain't That Peculiar / She's Got To Be Real	9.1965
54123	The Miracles	My Girl Has Gone / Since You Won My Heart	9.1965
54124	Stevie Wonder	Uptight (Everything's Alright) / Purple Raindrops	11.1965
54125	Brenda Holloway	Together Till The End Of Time / Sad Song	1.1966
54126	The Marvelettes	Don't Mess With Bill / Anything You Wanna Do	11.1965
54127	The Miracles	Going To A Go-Go / Choosey Beggar	12.1965
54128	The Isley Brothers	This Old Heart Of Mine (Is Weak For You) / There's No Love Left	1.1966
54129	Marvin Gaye	One More Heartache / When I Had Your Love	1.1966
54130	Stevie Wonder	Nothing's Too Good For My Baby / With A Child's Heart	3.1966
54131	The Marvelettes	You're The One / Paper Boy	4.1966
54132	Marvin Gaye	Take This Heart Of Mine / Need Your Lovin' (Want You Back)	5.1966
54133	The Isley Brothers	Take Some Time Out For Love / Who Could Ever Doubt My Love	4.1966
54134	Smokey Robinson & the Miracles	Whole Lot Of Shaking In My Heart (Since I Met You) / Oh Be My Love	5.1966
54135	The Isley Brothers	I Guess I'll Always Love You / I Hear A Symphony	6.1966
54136	Stevie Wonder	Blowing In The Wind / Ain't That Asking For Trouble	6.1966
54137	Brenda Holloway	Hurt A Little Every Day / Where Were You	8.1966

54138	**Marvin Gaye**	*Little Darlin' (I Need You)*	7.1966
		Hey Diddle Diddle	
54139	**Stevie Wonder**	*A Place In The Sun*	10.1966
		Sylvia	
54140	**Smokey Robinson & the Miracles**	*(Come Round Here) I'm The One You Need*	10.1966
		Save Me	
54141	**Marvin Gaye & Kim Weston**	*It Takes Two*	12.1966
		It's Got To Be A Miracle (This Thing Called Love)	
54142	**Stevie Wonder**	*Someday At Christmas*	11.1966
		The Miracles Of Christmas	
54143	**The Marvelettes**	*The Hunter Gets Captured By The Game*	12.1966
		I Think I Can Change You	
54144	**Brenda Holloway**	*'Till Johnny Comes*	NR
		Where Were You	
54145	**Smokey Robinson & the Miracles**	*The Love I Saw In You Was Just A Mirage*	1.1967
		Come Spy With Me	
54146	**The Isley Brothers**	*Got To Have You Back*	3.1967
		Just Ain't Enough Love	
54147	**Stevie Wonder**	*Travelin' Man*	2.1967
		Hey Love	
54148	**Brenda Holloway**	*Just Look What You've Done*	3.1967
		Starting The Hurt All Over Again	
54149	**Marvin Gaye & Tammi Terrell**	*Ain't No Mountain High Enough*	4.1967
		Give A Little Love	
54150	**The Marvelettes**	*When You're Young And In Love*	4.1967
		The Day You Take One (You Have To Take The Other)	
54151	**Stevie Wonder**	*I Was Made To Love Her*	5.1967
		Hold Me	
54152	**Smokey Robinson & the Miracles**	*More Love*	5.1967
		Swept For You Baby	
54153	**Marvin Gaye**	*Your Unchanging Love*	6.1967
		I'll Take Care Of You	
54154	**The Isley Brothers**	*That's The Way Love Is*	6.1967
		One Too Many Heartaches	
54155	**Brenda Holloway**	*You've Made Me So Very Happy*	8.1967
		I've Got To Find It	
54156	**Marvin Gaye & Tammi Terrell**	*Your Precious Love*	8.1967
		Hold Me, Oh My Darling	
54157	**Stevie Wonder**	*I'm Wondering*	9.1967
		Every Time I See You I Go Wild	
54158	**The Marvelettes**	*My Baby Must Be A Magician*	11.1967
		I Need Someone	
54159	**Smokey Robinson & the Miracles**	*I Second That Emotion*	10.1967
		You Must Be Love	
54160	**Marvin Gaye**	*You*	12.1967
		Change What You Can	
54161	**Marvin Gaye & Tammi Terrell**	*If I Could Build My Whole World Around You*	11.1967
		If This World Were Mine	
54162	**Smokey Robinson & the Miracles**	*If You Can Want*	2.1968
		When The Words From Your Heart Get Caught Up In Your Throat	
54163	**Marvin Gaye & Tammi Terrell**	*Ain't Nothing Like The Real Thing*	3.1968
		Little Ole Boy, Little Ole Girl	
54164	**The Isley Brothers**	*Take Me In Your Arms (Rock Me A Little While)*	3.1968
		Why When Love Is Gone	
54165	**Stevie Wonder**	*Shoo-Be-Doo-Be-Doo-Da-Day*	3.1968
		Why Don't You Lead Me To Love	
54166	**The Marvelettes**	*Here I Am Baby*	5.1968
		Keep Off, No Trespassing	
54167	**Smokey Robinson & the Miracles**	*Yester Love*	5.1968
		Much Better Off	
54168	**Stevie Wonder**	*You Met Your Match*	6.1968
		My Girl	
54169	**Marvin Gaye & Tammi Terrell**	*You're All I Need To Get By*	7.1968
		Two Can Have A Party	
54170	**Marvin Gaye**	*Chained*	8.1968
		At Last (I Found A Love)	
54171	**The Marvelettes**	*Destination: Anywhere*	8.1968
		What's Easy For Two Is So Hard For One	
54172	**Smokey Robinson & the Miracles**	*Special Occasion*	7.1968
		Give Her Up	
54173	**Marvin Gaye & Tammi Terrell**	*Keep On Lovin' Me Honey*	9.1968
		You Ain't Livin' Till You're Lovin'	
54174	**Stevie Wonder**	*For Once In My Life*	10.1968
		Angie Girl	
54175	**The Isley Brothers**	*All Because I Love You*	11.1968
		Behind A Painted Smile	
54176	**Marvin Gaye**	*I Heard It Through The Grapevine*	10.1968
		You're What's Happening (In The World Today)	
54177	**The Marvelettes**	*I'm Gonna Hold On Long As I Can*	12.1968
		Don't Make Hurtin' Me A Habit	
54178	**Smokey Robinson & the Miracles**	*Baby Baby Don't Cry*	12.1968
		Your Mother's Only Daughter	
54179	**Marvin Gaye & Tammi Terrell**	*Good Lovin' Ain't Easy To Come By*	1.1969
		Satisfied Feelin'	
54180	**Stevie Wonder**	*I Don't Know Why*	1.1969
		My Cherie Amour	
54181	**Marvin Gaye**	*Too Busy Thinking About My Baby*	4.1969
		Wherever I Lay My Hat (That's My Home)	
54182	**The Isley Brothers**	*Just Ain't Enough Love*	5.1969
		Take Some Time Out For Love	
54183	**Smokey Robinson & the Miracles**	*Doggone Right*	5.1969
		Here I Go Again	
54184	**Smokey Robinson & the Miracles**	*Abraham, Martin And John*	6.1969
		Much Better Off	
54185	**Marvin Gaye**	*That's The Way Love Is*	8.1969
		Gonna Keep On Trying To Win Your Love	
54186	**The Marvelettes**	*That's How Heartaches Are Made*	9.1969
		Rainy Mourning	
54187	**Marvin Gaye & Tammi Terrell**	*What You Gave Me*	11.1969
		How You Gonna Keep It (After You Get It)	
54188	**Stevie Wonder**	*Yester-Me, Yester-You, Yesterday*	9.1969
		I'd Be A Fool Right Now	
54189	**Smokey Robinson & the Miracles**	*Point It Out*	11.1969
		Darling Dear	
54190	**Marvin Gaye**	*How Can I Forget*	12.1969
		Gonna Give Her All The Love I've Got	
54191	**Stevie Wonder**	*Never Had A Dream Come True*	1.1970
		Somebody Knows, Somebody Cares	
54192	**Marvin Gaye & Tammi Terrell**	*The Onion Song*	3.1970
		California Soul	
54193	**Kiki Dee**	*The Day Will Come Between Sunday And Monday*	6.1970
		My Whole World Ended (The Moment You Left Me)	

54194	**Smokey Robinson & the Miracles**	Who's Gonna Take The Blame I Gotta Thing For You	4.1970
54195	**Marvin Gaye**	The End Of Our Road Me And My Lonely Room	5.1970
54196	**Stevie Wonder**	Signed, Sealed, Delivered, I'm Yours I'm More Than Happy (I'm Satisfied)	6.1970
54197	**Bob & Marcia**	Young, Gifted And Black Peace Of Mine	7.1970
54198	**The Marvelettes**	Marionette After All	11.1970
54199	**Smokey Robinson & the Miracles**	The Tears Of A Clown Promise Me	9.1970
54200	**Stevie Wonder**	Heaven Help Us All I Gotta Have A Song	9.1970
54201	**Marvin Gaye**	What's Going On God is Love	1.1971
54202	**Stevie Wonder**	We Can Work It Out Never Dreamed You'd Leave In Summer	2.1971
54203	**Eddie Kendricks**	This Used To Be The Home Of Johnnie Mae It's So Hard For Me To Say Goodbye	3.1971
54204	**Valerie Simpson**	Can't It Wait Until Tomorrow Back To Nowhere	7.1971
54205	**Smokey Robinson & the Miracles**	I Don't Blame You At All That Girl	2.1971
54206	**Smokey Robinson & the Miracles**	Crazy 'Bout The La La La Oh Baby Baby I Love You	6.1971
54207	**Marvin Gaye**	Mercy Mercy Me (The Ecology) Sad Tomorrows	6.1971
54208	**Stevie Wonder**	If You Really Love Me Think Of Me As Your Soldier	7.1971
54209	**Marvin Gaye**	Inner City Blues (Make Me Wanna Holler) Wholy Holy	9.1971
54210	**Eddie Kendricks**	I Did It All For You Can I	7.1971
54211	**Smokey Robinson & the Miracles**	Satisfaction Flower Girl	10.1971
54212	**Virgil Henry**	I Can't Believe You're Really Leaving You Ain't Sayin' Nothin' New	11.1971
54213	**The Marvelettes**	A Breath Taking Guy You're The One For Me Bobby	1.1972
54214	**Stevie Wonder**	What Christmas Means To Me Bedtime For Toys	11.1971
54215	**P.J.**	T.L.C. (Tender Loving Care) It Takes A Man To Teach A Woman How To Love	12.1971
54216	**Stevie Wonder**	Superwoman (Where Were You When I Needed You) I Love Every Little Thing About You	4.1972
54217	**The Courtship**	It's The Same Old Love Last Row, First Balcony	4.1972
54218	**Eddie Kendricks**	Let Me Run Into Your Lonely Heart Eddie's Love	3.1972
54219	**Different Shades Of Brown**	Label Me Love Life's A Ball While It Lasts	5.1972
54220	**Smokey Robinson & the Miracles**	We've Come Too Far To End It Now When Sundown Comes	5.1972
54221	**Marvin Gaye**	You're The Man Part 1 You're The Man Part 2	4.1972
54222	**Eddie Kendricks**	If You Let Me Just Memories	8.1972
54223	**Stevie Wonder**	Keep On Running Evil	8.1972
54224	**Valerie Simpson**	Silly Wasn't I I Believe I'm Gonna Take This Ride	10.1972
54225	**Smokey Robinson & the Miracles**	I Can't Stand To See You Cry With Your Love Came	11.1972
54226	**Stevie Wonder**	Superstition You've Got It Bad Girl	10.1972
54227	**The Courtship**	Love Ain't Love (Till You Give It To Somebody) Oops It Just Slipped Out	NR
54228	**Marvin Gaye**	Trouble Man Don't Mess With Mister 'T'	11.1972
54229	**Marvin Gaye**	I Want To Come Home For Christmas Christmas in The City	NR
54230	**Eddie Kendricks**	Girl You Need A Change Of Mind Part 1 Girl You Need A Change Of Mind Part 2	1.1973
54231	**Valerie Simpson**	Genius II One More Baby Child Born	NR
54232	**Stevie Wonder**	You Are The Sunshine Of My Life Tuesday Heartbreak	2.1973
54233	**Smokey Robinson**	Sweet Harmony Want To Know My Mind	4.1973
54234	**Marvin Gaye**	Let's Get It On I Wish It Would Rain	6.1973
54235	**Stevie Wonder**	Higher Ground Too High	7.1973
54236	**Eddie Kendricks**	Darling Come Back Home Loving You The Second Time Around	4.1973
54237	**The Miracles**	Don't Let It End (Till You Let It Begin) Wigs And Lashes	6.1973
54238	**Eddie Kendricks**	Keep On Truckin' (Part 1) Keep On Truckin' (Part 2)	7.1973
54239	**Smokey Robinson**	Baby Come Close A Silent Partner In A Three-Way Love Affair	10.1973
54240	**The Miracles**	Give Me Just Another Day I Wanna Be With You	11.1973
54241	**Marvin Gaye**	Come Get To This Distant Lover	10.1973
54242	**Stevie Wonder**	Living For The City Visions	10.1973
54243	**Eddie Kendricks**	Boogie Down Can't Help What I Am	12.1973
54244	**Marvin Gaye**	You Sure Love To Ball Just To Keep You Satisfied	1.1974
54245	**Stevie Wonder**	Don't You Worry 'Bout A Thing Blame It On The Sun	3.1974
54246	**Smokey Robinson**	It's Her Turn To Live Just My Soul Responding	4.1974
54247	**Eddie Kendricks**	Son Of Sagittarius Trust Your Heart	4.1974
54248	**The Miracles**	Do It Baby I Wanna Be With You	6.1974
54249	**Eddie Kendricks**	Tell Her Love Has Felt The Need Loving You The Second Time Around	7.1974
54250	**Smokey Robinson**	Virgin Man Fulfill Your Need	7.1974
54251	**Smokey Robinson**	I Am I Am The Family Song	11.1974
54252	**Stevie Wonder**	You Haven't Done Nothin' Big Brother	7.1974
54253	**Marvin Gaye**	Distant Lover (live version) Trouble Man (live version)	9.1974
54254	**Stevie Wonder**	Boogie On Reggae Woman Seems So Long	10.1974
54255	**Eddie Kendricks**	One Tear The Thin Man	11.1974

54256	The Miracles	Don't Cha Love It	11.1974
		Up Again	
54257	Eddie Kendricks	Shoeshine Boy	1.1975
		Hooked on Your Love	
54258	Smokey Robinson	Baby That's Backatcha	2.1975
		Just Passing Through	
54259	The Miracles	Gemini	3.1975
		You Are Love	
54260	Eddie Kendricks	Get The Cream Off The Top	6.1975
		Honey Brown	
54261	Smokey Robinson	The Agony And The Ecstasy	7.1975
		Wedding Song	
54262	The Miracles	Love Machine (Part 1)	9.1975
		Love Machine (Part 2)	
54263	Eddie Kendricks	Happy	9.1975
		Deep And Quiet Love	
54264	Marvin Gaye	I Want You (voc.)	4.1976
		I Want You (instr.)	
54265	Smokey Robinson	Quiet Storm	11.1975
		Asleep On My Love	
54266	Eddie Kendricks	He's A Friend	1.1976
		All Of My Love	
54267	Smokey Robinson	Open	3.1976
		Coincidently	
54268	The Miracles	Night Life	4.1976
		Smog	
54269	Smokey Robinson	When You Came	NR
		Coincidentally	
54270	Eddie Kendricks	Get It While It's Hot	5.1976
		Never Gonna Leave You	
54271	Tata Vega	Full Speed Ahead	7.1976
		Just As Long As There Is You	
54272	Smokey Robinson	An Old-Fashioned Man	NR
	Thelma Houston	One Out Of Every Six (censored)	
54273	Marvin Gaye	After The Dance	7.1976
		Feel All My Love Inside	
54274	Stevie Wonder	I Wish	11.1976
		You And I	
54275	Thelma Houston	One Out Of Every Six (censored)	9.1976
		Pick Of The Week	
54276	Smokey Robinson	An Old-Fashioned Man	9.1976
		Just Passing Through	
54277	Eddie Kendricks	Goin' Up In Smoke	10.1976
		Thanks For The Memories	
54278	Thelma Houston	Don't Leave Me This Way	11.1976
		Today Will Soon Be Yesterday	
54279	Smokey Robinson	There Will Come A Day (I'm Gonna Happen To You)	1.1977
		The Humming Song (Lost For Words)	
54280	Marvin Gaye	Got To Give It Up (Part 1)	3.1977
		Got To Give It Up (Part 2)	
54281	Stevie Wonder	Sir Duke	3.1977
		He's Misstra Know-It-All	
54282	Tata Vega	You'll Never Rock Alone	4.1977
		Just When Things Are Getting Good	
54283	Thelma Houston	If It's The Last Thing I Do	4.1977
		If You Won't Let Me Walk On The Water	
54284	Smokey Robinson	Vitamin U	5.1977
		Holly	
54285	Eddie Kendricks	Born Again	4.1977
		Date With The Rain	
54286	Stevie Wonder	Another Star	8.1977
		Creepin'	
54287	Thelma Houston	I'm Here Again	9.1977
		Sharing Something Perfect Between Ourselves	
54288	Smokey Robinson	Theme From Big Time (Part 1)	8.1977
		Theme From Big Time (Part 2)	
54289	Eddie Kendricks	Baby	NR
		I Want To Live (My Life With You)	
54290	Eddie Kendricks	Intimate Friends	12.1977
		Baby	
54291	Stevie Wonder	As	10.1977
		Contusion	
54292	Thelma Houston	I Can't Go On Living Without Your Love	1.1978
		Any Way You Like It	
54293	Smokey Robinson	Why You Wanna See My Bad Side	2.1978
		Daylight And Darkness	
54294	Kenny Lupper	Passion Flower	3.1978
		Kiss Me Now	
54295	Thelma Houston	I'm Not Strong Enough To Love You Again	8.1978
		Triflin'	
54296	Smokey Robinson	Shoe Soul	9.1978
		I'm Loving You Softly	
54297	Thelma Houston	Saturday Night, Sunday Morning	12.1978
		Come To Me	
54298	Marvin Gaye	A Funky Space Reincarnation (Part 1)	1.1979
		A Funky Space Reincarnation (Part 2)	
54299	Tata Vega	I Just Keep Thinking About You Baby	4.1979
		Music in My Heart	
54300	Marvin Gaye	Anger	NR
		Time To Get It Together	
54301	Smokey Robinson	Get Ready	5.1979
		Ever Had A Dream	
54302	Shadee	I Just Need More Money (Part 1)	6.1979
		I Just Need More Money (Part 2)	
54303	Stevie Wonder	Send One Your Love	10.1979
		Send One Your Love (instr.)	
54304	Tata Vega	I Need You Now	7.1979
		In The Morning	
54305	Marvin Gaye	Ego Tripping Out	9.1979
		Ego Tripping Out (instr.)	
54306	Smokey Robinson	Cruisin'	8.1979
		Ever Had A Dream	
54307	Keith & Darrell	Feel The Fever	10.1979
		The Things You're Made Of	
54308	Stevie Wonder	Outside My Window	2.1980
		Same Old Story	
54309	Keith & Darrell	Kickin' It Around	2.1980
		I Met This Girl	
54310	Quiet Storm	Only You (Part 1)	2.1980
		Only You (Part 2)	
54311	Smokey Robinson	Let Me Be The Clock	2.1980
		Travelin' Through	
54312	Billy Preston & Syreeta	One More Time For Love	5.1980
	Syreeta	Dance For Me Children	
54313	Smokey Robinson	Heavy On Pride (Light on Love)	5.1980
		I Love The Nearness Of You	
54314	Quiet Storm	Heartbreak Graffiti (Part 1)	8.1980
		Heartbreak Graffiti (Part 2)	
54315	Legend	Shake It Lady	8.1980
		Lay Your Body Down	
54316	Tata Vega	You Keep Me Hangin' On	11.1980
		You Better Watch Out	
54317	Stevie Wonder	Master Blaster (Jammin')	9.1980
		Master Blaster (Dub)	
54318	Smokey Robinson	Wine, Women And Song	9.1980
		I Want to Be Your Love	
54319	Billy Preston & Syreeta	Please Stay	9.1980
	Syreeta	Signed, Sealed, Delivered I'm Yours	
54320	Stevie Wonder	I Ain't Gonna Stand For It	12.1980
		Knocks Me Off My Feet	
54321	Smokey Robinson	Being With You	1,1981
		What's In Your Life For Me	
54322	Marvin Gaye	Praise	2.1981
		Funk Me	

Number	Artist	Title	Date
54323	**Stevie Wonder**	*Lately*	3.1981
		If It's Magic	
54324	—		—
54325	**Smokey Robinson**	*Aqui Con Tigo*	4.1981
		Being With You – Aqui Con Tigo	
54326	**Marvin Gaye**	*Heavy Love Affair*	4.1981
		Far Cry	
54327	**Smokey Robinson**	*You Are Forever*	5.1981
		I Hear The Children Singing	
54328	**Stevie Wonder**	*Did I Hear You Say You Love Me*	7.1981
		As If You Read My Mind	
54329	**Keith & Darrell**	*You're My Gardener*	7.1981
		Don't Be Afraid	
54330	**Quiet Storm**	*When You Came*	7.1981
		I Let You Go	
54331	**Stevie Wonder**	*Happy Birthday*	NR
		Happy Birthday (instr.)	
54332	**Smokey Robinson**	*Who's Sad*	7.1981
		Food For Thought	
54333	**Syreeta**	*Quick Slick*	9.1981
		I Don't Know	

MOTOWN LABEL

Number	Artist	Title	Date
*1000	**The Satintones**	*My Beloved*	9.1961
		Sugar Daddy	
*1000	**The Satintones**	*My Beloved*	9.1961
		Sugar Daddy (2nd vers.)	
*1001	**Eugene Remus**	*You Never Miss A Good Thing*	—
		Hold Me Tight	
*1001	**Eugene Remus**	*You Never Miss A Good Thing*	—
		Gotta Have Your Lovin'	
*1001	**Eugene Remus**	*You Never Miss A Good Thing (2nd vers.)*	—
		Gotta Have Your Lovin'	
1002	**Popcorn and the Mohawks**	*Custer's Last Stand*	9.1961
		Shimmy Gully	
1003	**Mary Wells**	*Bye Bye Baby*	2.1961
		Please Forgive Me	
1004	**Sherrie Taylor & Singin' Sammy Ward**	*Oh Lover*	9.1960
		That's Why I Love You So Much	
1005	**Henry Lumpkin**	*I've Got A Notion*	1.1961
		We Really Love Each Other	
*1006	**The Satintones**	*Angel*	4.1961
		A Love That Can Never Be	
*1006	**The Satintones**	*Tomorrow And Always*	4.1961
		A Love That Can Never Be	
1007	**Debbie Dean**	*Don't Let Him Shop Around*	9.1961
		A New Girl	
*1008	**The Supremes**	*I Want A Guy*	transferred
		Never Again	
*1008	**The Contours**	*Whole Lotta Woman*	2.1961
		Come On And Be Mine	
1009	**Richard Wylie & his Band**	*Money (That's What I Want)*	4.1961
	Popcorn Wylie & The Mohawks	*I'll Still Be Around*	
1010	**The Satintones**	*I Know How It Feels*	6.1961
		My Kind Of Love	
1011	**Mary Wells**	*I Don't Want To Take A Chance*	6.1961
		I'm Sorry	
1012	**The Contours**	*The Stretch*	8.1961
		Funny	
1013	**Henry Lumpkin**	*What Is A Man (Without A Woman)*	1.1962
		Don't Leave Me	
1014	**Debbie Dean**	*But I'm Afraid*	8.1961
		Itsy Bity Pity Love	
1015	**The Gospel Harmoniers**	*I'm Bound*	3,1962
		Precious Memories	
1016	**Mary Wells**	*Strange Love*	10.1961
		Come To Me	

Number	Artist	Title	Date
1017	—	—	—
1018	**The All Stars**	*Disintegrated (Part 1)*	NR
		Disintegrated Part 2)	
1019	**Popcorn & the Mohawks**	*Real Good Lovin'*	10.1961
		Have I The Right	
1020	**The Satintones**	*Zing Went The Strings Of My Heart*	10.1961
		Faded Letter	
*1021	**Eddie Holland**	*Jamie*	1.1962
		Take A Chance On Me	
*1021	**Eddie Holland**	*Jamie (2nd vers.)*	1.1962
		Take A Chance On Me	
1022	**The Twistin' Kings**	*Xmas Twist*	11.1961
		White House Twist	
1023	**The Twistin' Kings**	*Congo Twist (Part 1)*	12.1961
		Congo Twist (Part 2)	
1024	**Mary Wells**	*The One Who Really Loves You*	2.1962
		I'm Gonna Stay	
1025	**Debbie Dean**	*Everybody's Talkin' About My Baby*	3.1962
		I Cried All Night	
1026	**Eddie Holland**	*You Deserve What You Got*	4.1962
		Last Night I Had A Vision	
*1027	**The Supremes**	*Your Heart Belongs To Me*	5.1962
		(He's) Seventeen	
*1027	**The Supremes**	*Your Heart Belongs To Me*	5.1962
		(He's) Seventeen (2nd vers.)	

* When cataloging first started errors arose in the matrix numbering system hence repeat numbers. This was rectified in 1960 when Billie Jean Brown took charge of the Berry Gordy's tape library and unified the numbering system.

Number	Artist	Title	Date
1028	**Herman Griffin**	*Sleep (Little One)*	6.1962
		Uptight	
1029	**Henry Lumpkin**	*Mo Jo Hanna*	7.1962
		Break Down And Sing	
1030	**Eddie Holland**	*If Cleopatra Took A Chance*	5.1962
		What About Me	
1031	**Eddie Holland**	*If It's Love (It's Alright)*	8.1962
		It's Not Too Late	
1032	**Mary Wells**	*You Beat Me To The Punch*	7.1962
		Old Love (Let's Try It Again)	
1033	**The Beljeans**	*Camel Walk*	transferred
		The Chaperone	
1034	**The Supremes**	*Let Me Go The Right Way*	11.1962
		Time Changes Things	
1035	**Mary Wells**	*Two Lovers*	10.1962
		Operator	
1036	**Eddie Holland**	*Darling I Hum Our Song*	1.1963
		Just A Few More Days	
1037	**Linda Griner**	*Goodbye Cruel Love*	1.1963
		Envious	
1038	**Amos Milburn**	*I'll Make It Up To You Somehow*	3.1963
		My Baby Gave Me Another Chance	
1039	**Mary Wells**	*Laughing Boy*	2.1963
		Two Wrongs Don't Make A Right	
1040	**The Supremes**	*My Heart Can't Take It No More*	2.1963
		You Bring Back Memories	
1041	**Connie Van Dyke**	*Oh Freddy*	3.1963
		It Hurt Me Too	
1042	**Mary Wells**	*Your Old Stand-By*	4.1963
		What Love Has Joined Together	
1043	**Eddie Holland**	*Baby Shake*	4.1963
		Brenda	
1044	**The Supremes**	*A Breathtaking Guy*	6.1963
		(The Man With The) Rock And Roll Banjo Band	
1045	**Holland & Dozier with the Four Tops & The Andantes**	*What Goes Up Must Come Down*	6.1963
		Come On Home	

1046	The Serenaders	If Your Heart Says Yes	transferred
		I'll Cry Tomorrow	
1047	The Morocco Muzik Makers	Back To School Again	8.1963
		Pig Knuckles	
1048	Mary Wells	You Lost The Sweetest Boy	8.1963
		What's Easy For Two Is So Hard For One	
1049	Eddie Holland	I'm On The Outside Looking In	10.1963
		I Couldn't Cry If I Wanted To	
1050	Carolyn Crawford	Forget About Me	11.1963
		Devil In His Heart	
1051	The Supremes	When The Lovelight Starts Shinin' Thru' His Eyes	10.1963
		Standing At The Crossroads Of Love	
1052	Eddie Holland	Leaving Here	12.1963
		Brenda	
1053	Bobby Breen	Better Late Than Never	1.1964
		How Can We Tell Him	
1054	The Supremes	Run, Run, Run	2.1964
		I'm Giving You Your Freedom	
1055	Sammy Turner	Right Now	2.1964
		Only You	
1056	Mary Wells	My Guy	3.1964
		Oh Little Boy (What Did You Do To Me)	
1057	Marvin Gaye & Mary Wells	Once Upon A Time	4.1964
		What's The Matter With You Baby	
1058	Eddie Holland	Just Ain't Enough Love	4.1964
		Last Night I Had A Vision	
1059	Bobby Breen	You're Just Like You	5.1964
		Here Comes That Heartache	
1060	The Supremes	Where Did Our Love Go	6.1964
		He Means The World To Me	
1061	Mary Wells	When I'm Gone	NR
		Guarantee For A Lifetime	
1062	Four Tops	Baby I Need Your Loving	7.1964
		Call On Me	
1063	Eddie Holland	Candy To Me	7.1964
		If You Don't Want My Love	
1064	Carolyn Crawford	My Smile Is Just A Frown Turned Upside Down	8.1964
		I'll Come Running	
1065	Mary Wells	Whisper You Love Me Boy	NR
		I'll Be Available	
1066	The Supremes	Baby Love	9.1964
		Ask Any Girl	
1067	The Spinners	Sweet Thing	10.1964
		How Can I	
1068	The Supremes	Come See About Me	10.1964
		Always In My Heart	
1069	Four Tops	Without The One You Love (Life's Not Worthwhile)	11.1964
		Love Has Gone	
1070	Carolyn Crawford	When Someone's Good To You	11.1964
		My Heart	
1071	Tony Martin	Talking To Your Picture	11.1964
		Our Rhapsody	
1072	Choker Campbell's 16 Piece Band	Come See About Me	12.1964
		Pride And Joy	
1073	Four Tops	Ask The Lonely	1.1965
		Where Did You Go	
1074	The Supremes	Stop! In The Name Of Love	2.1965
		I'm In Love Again	
1075	The Supremes	Back In My Arms Again	4.1965
		Whisper You Love Me Boy	
1076	Four Tops	I Can't Help Myself	4.1965
		Sad Souvenirs	
1077	Billy Eckstine	Down To Earth	5.1965
		Had You Been Around	
1078	The Spinners	I'll Always Love you	6.1965
		Tomorrow May Never Come	
1079	The Supremes	The Only Time I'm Happy	NR (Promo)
		The Supremes Interview	only

1080	The Supremes	Nothing But Heartaches	7.1965
		He Holds His Own	
1081	Four Tops	It's The Same Old Song	7.1965
		Your Love Is Amazing	
1082	Tony Martin	The Bigger Your Heart Is (The Harder You'll Fall)	8.1965
		The Two Of Us	
1083	The Supremes	I Hear A Symphony	10.1965
		Who Could Ever Doubt My Love	
1084	Four Tops	Something About You	10.1965
		Darling, I Hum Our Song	
1085	The Supremes	Children's Christmas Song	11.1965
		Twinkle Twinkle Little Me	
1086	Tammi Terrell	I Can't Believe You Love Me	11.1965
		Hold Me Oh My Darling	
1087	Barbara McNair	You're Gonna Love My Baby	11.1965
		The Touch Of Time	
1088	Tony Martin	Ask Any Man	12.1965
		Spanish Rose	
1089	The Supremes	My World Is Empty Without You	12.1965
		Everything Is Good About You	
1090	Four Tops	Shake Me Wake Me (When It's Over)	2.1966
		Just As Long As You Need Me	
1091	Billy Eckstine	The Slender Thread	3.1966
		Wish You Were Here	
1092	Connie Haines	What's Easy For Two Is So Hard For One	3.1966
		Walk In Silence	
1093	The Spinners	Truly Yours	3.1966
		Where Is That Girl	
1094	The Supremes	Love Is Like An Itching In My Heart	4.1966
		He's All I Got	
1095	Tammi Terrell	Come On And See Me	4.1966
		Baby Don'tcha Worry	
1096	Four Tops	Loving You Is Sweeter Than Ever	5.1966
		I Like Everything About You	
1097	The Supremes	You Can't Hurry Love	7.1966
		Put Yourself In My Place	
1098	Four Tops	Reach Out I'll Be There	8.1966
		Until You Love Someone	
1099	Barbara McNair	Everything Is Good About You	9.1966
		What A Day	
1100	Billy Eckstine	And There You Were	9.1966
		A Warmer World	
1101	The Supremes	You Keep Me Hangin' On	10.1966
		Remove This Doubt	
1102	Four Tops	Standing In The Shadows Of Love	11.1966
		Since You've Been Gone	
1103	The Supremes	Love Is Here And Now You're Gone	1.1967
		There's No Stopping Us Now	
1104	Four Tops	Bernadette	2.1967
		I Got A Feeling	
1105	Billy Eckstine	I Wonder Why (Nobody Loves Me)	4.1967
		I've Been Blessed	
1106	Barbara McNair	Here I Am Baby	3.1967
		My World Is Empty Without You	
1107	The Supremes	The Happening	3.1967
		All I Know About You	
1108	Paul Petersen	Chained	5.1967
		Don't Let It Happen To Us	
1109	The Spinners	For All We Know	5.1967
		I Cross My Heart	
1110	Four Tops	Seven Rooms Of Gloom	5.1967
		I'll Turn To Stone	
1111	Diana Ross & the Supremes	Reflections	7.1967
		Going Down For The Third Time	

1112	Barbara McNair	Steal Away Tonight	NR
		For Once In My Life	
1113	Four Tops	You Keep Running Away	8.1967
		If You Don't Want My Love	
1114	Chris Clark	From Head To Toe	9.1967
		The Beginning Of The End	
1115	Tammi Terrell	What A Good Man He Is	NR
		There Are Things	
1116	Diana Ross & the Supremes	In And Out Of Love	10.1967
		I Guess I'll Always Love You	
1117	The Ones	You Haven't Seen My Love	11.1967
		Happy Day	
1118	Chuck Jackson	(You Can't Let The Boy Overpower) The Man In You	2.1968
		Girls, Girls, Girls	
1119	Four Tops	Walk Away Renee	1.1968
		Your Love Is Wonderful	
1120	Billy Eckstine	Thank You Love	2.1968
		Is Anybody Here Goin' My Way	
1121	Chris Clark	Whisper You Love Me Boy	2.1968
		The Beginning Of The End	
1122	Diana Ross & the Supremes	Forever Came Today	2.1968
		Time Changes Things	
1123	Barbara McNair	Where Would I Be Without You	3.1968
		For Once In My life	
1124	Four Tops	If I Were A Carpenter	4.1968
		Wonderful Baby	
1125	Diana Ross & the Supremes	What The World Needs Now Is Love	NR
		Your Kiss Of Fire	
1126	Diana Ross & the Supremes	Some Things You Never Get Used To	5.1968
		You've Been So Wonderful To Me	
1127	Four Tops	Yesterday's Dreams	6.1968
		For Once In My Life	
1128	Marvin Gaye Gladys Knight & the Pips	His Eye Is On The Sparrow	9.1968
		Just A Closer Walk With Thee	
1129	Paul Petersen	A Little Bit For Sandy	8.1968
		Your Love's Got Me Burning Alive	
1130	The Ones	Don't Let Me Lose This Dream	8.1968
		I've Been Good To You	
1131	Billy Eckstine	For The Love Of Ivy	8.1968
		A Woman	
1132	Four Tops	I'm In A Different World	9.1968
		Remember When	
1133	Barbara McNair	You Could Never Love Him (Like I Love Him)	10.1968
		Fancy Passes	
1134	Blinky	I Wouldn't Change The Man He Is	11.1968
		I'll Always Love You	
1135	Diana Ross & the Supremes	Love Child	9.1968
		Will This Be The Day	
1136	The Spinners	Bad Bad Weather (Till You Come Home)	10.1968
		I Just Can't Help But Feel The Pain	
1137	Diana Ross & the Supremes & The Temptations	I'm Gonna Make You Love Me	11.1968
		A Place in The Sun	
1138	Tammi Terrell	This Old Heart Of Mine (Is Weak For You)	12.1968
		Just Too Much To Hope For	
1139	Diana Ross & the Supremes	I'm Living' In Shame	1.1969
		I'm So Glad I Got Somebody (Like You Around)	
1140	David Ruffin	My Whole World Ended (The Moment You Left Me)	1.1969
		I've Got To Find Myself A Brand New Baby	
1141	Soupy Sales	Muck-Arty Park	1.1969
		Green Grow The Lilacs	
1142	Diana Ross & the Supremes & The Temptations	I'll Try Something New	2.1969
		The Way You Do The Things You Do	
1143	Billy Eckstine	My Cup Runneth Over	NR
		Ask The Lonely	
1144	Chuck Jackson	Are You Lonely For Me	3.1969
		Your Wonderful Love	
1145	Jonah Jones	For Better Or Worse	NR
		Don't Mess With Bill	
1146	Diana Ross & the Supremes	The Composer	3.1969
		The Beginning Of The End	
1147	Four Tops	What Is A Man	4.1969
		Don't Bring Back Memories	
1148	Diana Ross & the Supremes	No Matter What Sign You Are	5.1969
		The Young Folks	
1149	David Ruffin	I've Lost Everything I've Ever Loved	7.1969
		We'll Have A Good Thing Going On	
1150	Diana Ross & the Supremes & The Temptations	Stubborn Kind Of Fellow	NR
		Try It Baby	
1151	Captain Zap & the Motortown Cut-Ups	The Luney Landing	7.1969
		The Luney Take-Off	
1152	Chuck Jackson	Honey Come Back	8.1969
		What Am I Gonna Do Without You	
1153	Diana Ross & the Supremes & The Temptations	The Weight	8.1969
		For Better Or Worse	
1154	Joe Harnell	Midnight Cowboy	9.1969
		Green Grow The Lilacs	
1155	The Spinners	In My Diary	NR
		(She's Gonna Love Me) At Sundown	
1156	Diana Ross & the Supremes	Someday We'll Be Together	10.1969
		He's My Sunny Boy	
1157	Jackson 5	I Want You Back	10.1969
		Who's Loving You	
1158	David Ruffin	I'm So Glad I Fell For You	11.1969
		I Pray Every Day You Won't Regret Loving Me	
1159	Four Tops	Don't Let Him Take Your Love From Me	11.1969
		The Key	
1160	Chuck Jackson	Baby I'll Get It	NR
		The Day My World Stood Still	
1161	Joe Harnell	My Cherie Amour	1.1970
		Green Grow The Lilacs	
1162	The Supremes	Up The Ladder To The Roof	2.1970
		Bill, When Are You Coming Back	
1163	Jackson 5	ABC	2.1970
		The Young Folks	
1164	Four Tops	It's All In The Game	3.1970
		Love (Is The Answer)	
1165	Diana Ross	Reach Out And Touch (Somebody's Hand)	4.1970
		Dark Side Of The World	
1166	Jackson 5	The Love You Save	5.1970
		I Found That Girl	
1167	The Supremes	Everybody's Got The Right To Love	6.1970
		But I Love You More	
1168	Blinky	How You Gonna Keep It (After You Get It)	NR
		This Time Last Summer	
1169	Diana Ross	Ain't No Mountain High Enough	7.1970
		Can't It Wait Until Tomorrow	
1170	Four Tops	Still Water (Love)	8.1970
		Still Water (Peace)	
1171	Jackson 5	I'll Be There	8.1970
		One More Chance	
1172	The Supremes	Stoned Love	10.1970
		Shine On Me	

1173	The Supremes & Four Tops	River Deep Mountain High	11.1970
		Together We Can Make Such Sweet Music	
1174	Jackson 5	Santa Claus Is Coming To Town	11.1970
		Christmas Won't Be The Same This Year	
1175	Four Tops	Just Seven Numbers (Can Straighten Out My Life)	12.1970
		I Wish I Were Your Mirror	
1176	Diana Ross	Remember Me	12.1970
		How About You	
1177	Jackson 5	Mama's Pearl	1.1971
		Darling Dear	
1178	David Ruffin	Each Day Is A Lifetime	2.1971
		Don't Stop Loving Me	
1179	Jackson 5	Never Can Say Goodbye	3.1971
		She's Good	
1180	Gordon Staples & the Motown Strings	Strung Out	3.1971
		Sounds Of The Zodiac	
1181	The Supremes & Four Tops	You Gotta Have Love In Your Heart	5.1971
		I'm Glad About It	
1182	The Supremes	Nathan Jones	4.1971
		Happy (Is A Bumpy Road)	
1183	Bobby Darin	Melodie	4.1971
		Someday We'll Be Together	
1184	Diana Ross	Reach Out I'll Be There	4.1971
		(They Long To Be) Close To You	
1185	Four Tops	In These Changing Times	5.1971
		Right Before My Eyes	
1186	Jackson 5	Maybe Tomorrow	6.1971
		I Will Find A Way	
1187	David Ruffin	You Can Come Right Back To Me	7.1971
		Dinah	
1188	Diana Ross	Surrender	7.1971
		I'm A Winner	
1189	Four Tops	Macarthur Park (Part 2)	8.1971
		Macarthur Park (Part 1)	
1190	The Supremes	Touch	9.1971
		It's So Hard For Me To Say Goodbye	
1191	Michael Jackson	Got To Be There	10.1971
		Maria (You Were The Only One)	
1192	Diana Ross	I'm Still Waiting	10.1971
		A Simple Thing Like Cry	
1193	Bobby Darin	Simple Song Of Freedom	11.1973
		I'll Be Your Baby Tonight	
1194	Jackson 5	Sugar Daddy	11.1971
		I'm So Happy	
1195	The Supremes	Floy Joy	12.1971
		This Is The Story	
1196	Four Tops	Simple Game	1.1972
		L.A. My Town	
1197	Michael Jackson	Rockin' Robin	2.1972
		Love Is Here And Now You're Gone	
1198	Four Tops	I Can't Quit Your Love	4.1972
		Happy (Is A Bumpy Road)	
1199	Jackson 5	Little Bitty Pretty One	4.1972
		If I Have To Move A Mountain	
1200	The Supremes	Automatically Sunshine	4.1972
		Precious Little Things	
1201	Jermaine Jackson	That's How Love Goes	8.1972
		I Lost My Love In The Big City	
1202	Michael Jackson	I Wanna Be Where You Are	5.1972
		We've Got A Good Thing Going	
1203	Bobby Darin	Sail Away	6.1972
		Hard Headed Woman	
1204	David Ruffin	A Little More Trust	6.1972
		A Day In The Life Of A Working Man	
1205	Jackson 5	Lookin' Through The Windows	6.1972
		Love Song	
1206	The Supremes	Your Wonderful Sweet Sweet Love	7.1972
		The Wisdom Of Time	
1207	Michael Jackson	Ben	7.1982
		You Can Cry On My Shoulder	
1208	The Naturals	The Good Things (Where Was I When Love Came By)	9.1972
		Me And My Brother	
1209	The Jerry Ross Symposium	Duck You Sucker	8.1972
		It Happened On A Sunday Morning	
1210	Four Tops	(It's The Way) Nature Planned It	8.1972
		I'll Never Change	
1211	Diana Ross	Good Morning Heartache	12.1972
		God Bless The Child	
1212	Bobby Darin	Average People	11.1972
		Something In Her Love	
1213	The Supremes	I Guess I'll Miss The Man	9.1972
		Over And Over	
1214	Jackson 5	Corner Of The Sky	10.1972
		To Know	
1215	The Jerry Ross Symposium	Take It Out On Me	NR
		It's The Same Old Love	
1216	Jermaine Jackson	Daddy's Home	11.1972
		Take Me In Your Arms (Rock Me A Little While)	
1217	Bobby Darin	Happy (Love Theme From 'Lady Sings The Blues')	11.1972
		Something In Her Love	
1218	Michael Jackson	With A Child's Heart	4.1973
		Morning Glow	
1219	Michel Legrand	Love Theme From 'Lady Sings The Blues'	1.1973
	Gil Askey	Any Happy Home	
1220	The Gil Askey Orchestra	Don't Explain	2.1973
		C.C. Rider	
1221	Irene 'Granny' Ryan	No Time At All	2.1973
		Time (To Believe in Each Other)	
1222	Willie Hutch	Brother's Gonna Work It Out	2.1973
		I Choose You	
1223	David Ruffin	Blood Donors Needed (Give All You Can)	2.1973
		Go On With Your Bad Self	
1224	Jackson 5	Hallelujah Day	2.1973
		You Made Me What I Am	
1225	The Supremes	Bad Weather	3.1973
		Oh Be My Love	
1226	Vin Cardinal	Shame And Scandal in The Family	NR
		Never Been To Spain	
1227	—	—	—
1228	Reuben Howell	I'll See You Through	4.1973
		Help The People	
1229	Martin & Finley	Thinkin' 'Bout My Baby	NR
		Best Friends	
1230	Jackson 5	The Boogie Man	NR
		Don't Let Your Baby Catch You	
1231	Irene 'Granny' Ryan	See Your Name Up In Lights	NR
		When Yesterday Was Tomorrow	
1232	—	—	—
1233	Blinky	You Get A Tangle In Your Lifeline	5.1973
		This Man Of Mine	
1234	G.C. Cameron	No Matter Where	5.1973
		Have I Lost You	
1235	The Spinners	Together We Can Make Such Sweet Music	4.1973
		Bad Bad Weather (Till You Come Home)	
1236	Stacie Johnson	Woman In My Eyes	7.1973
		Every Little Bit Hurts	

1237	**Suzee Ikeda**	*Time For Me To Go*	4.1973
		Zip-A-Dee-Doo-Dah	
1238	**Celebration**	*Since I Met You There's No Magic*	NR
		The Circle Again	
1239	**Diana Ross**	*Touch Me In The Morning*	5.1973
		I Won't Last A Day Without You	
1240	**Severin Browne**	*Darling Christina*	NR
		The All-American Boy And His Dog	
1241	**Different Shades of Brown**	*When The Hurt Is Put Back On You*	7.1973
		Sending Good Vibrations	
1242	**Martin & Finley**	*It's Another Sunday*	5.1973
		Best Friends	
1243	**Jimmy Randolph**	*Plainsville U.S.A.*	5.1973
		High Road	
1244	**Jermaine Jackson**	*You're in Good Hands*	9.1973
		Does Your Mother Know About Me	
1245	**Thelma Houston**	*Piano Man*	3.1973
		I'm Just A Part Of Yesterday	
1246	**Art & Honey**	*Let's Make Love Now*	7.1973
		(I've Given You) The Best Years Of My Life	
1247	**Marbaya**	*Follow Me – Mother Nature*	7.1973
		And I Thought You Loved Me	
1248	**Stoney**	*Let Me Come Down Easy*	4.1973
		It's Always Me	
1249	**Earthquire**	*Sunshine Man*	7.1973
		Soul Long	
1250	**Third Creation**	*Rolling Down A Mountainside*	7.1973
		It's Just A Phase	
1251	**Frankie Valli**	*You've Got Your Troubles*	5.1973
		Listen To Yesterday	
1252	**Willie Hutch**	*Slick*	6.1973
		Mother's Theme (Mama)	
1253	**Vin Cardinal**	*There'll Be No City on The Hill*	6.1973
		Never Been To Spain	
1254	**Four Tops**	*Hey Man – We Got To Get You A Woman*	NR
		How Will I Forget You	
1255	**Frankie Valli & the Four Seasons**	*How Come*	5.1973
		Life And Breath	
1256	**Gloria Jones**	*Why Can't You Be Mine*	2.1974
		Baby Don'tcha Know (I'm Bleeding For You)	
1257	**Eric & the Vikings**	*I'm Truly Yours*	NR
		Where Do You Go (Baby)	
1258	**Severin Browne**	*Darling Christina*	8.1973
		Snow Flakes	
1259	**David Ruffin**	*Common Man*	7.1973
		I'm Just A Mortal Man	
1260	**Thelma Houston**	*Do You Know Where You're Going To*	NR
		Together	
1261	**G.C. Cameron**	*Let Me Down Easy*	9.1973
		Time	
1262	**Charlene Duncan**	*Relove*	NR
		Give It One More Try	
1263	**The Devastasting Affair**	*That's How It Was (Right From The Start)*	11.1973
		It's So Sad	
1264	**Puzzle**	*Lady*	7.1973
		You Make Me Happy	
1265	**Riot**	*God Bless Conchita*	9.1973
		A Song Of Long Ago	
1266	—	—	—
1267	—	—	—
1268	**Commodores**	*Are You Happy*	8.1973
		There's A Song In My Heart	
1269	**Diana Ross & Marvin Gaye**	*My Mistake (Was To Love You)*	1.1974
		Include Me In Your Life	
1270	**Michael Jackson**	*Doggin' Around*	NR
		Up Again	
1271	**Diahann Carroll**	*To A Gentler Time*	NR
		I Can't Give Back The Love I Feel For You	
1272	**C.P. Spencer**	*Still Holdin' on*	NR
		Say It Like The Children	
1273	—	—	—
1274	**Reuben Howell**	*When You Take Another Chance On Love*	10.1973
		You Can't Stop A Man in Love	
1275	**The Sisters Love**	*My Love Is Yours (Till The End Of Time)*	9.1973
		You've Got My Mind	
1276	**Edwin Starr**	*You've Got My Soul on Fire*	8.1973
		Love (The Lonely People's Prayer)	
1277	**Jackson 5**	*Get It Together*	8.1973
		Touch	
1278	**Diana Ross**	*Last Time I Saw Him*	12.1973
		Save The Children	
1279	**Frankie Valli**	*The Scalawag Song (And I Will Love You)*	10.1973
		Listen to Yesterday	
1280	**Diana Ross & Marvin Gaye**	*You're A Special Part Of Me*	9.1973
		I'm Falling In Love With You	
1281	**Zell Black**	*I'd Hate Myself in The Morning*	NR
		Take My Word	
1282	**Willie Hutch**	*Sunshine Lady*	10.1973
		I Just Wanted To Make Her Happy	
1283	**Puzzle**	*Mary Mary*	11.1973
		On With The Show	
1284	**Edwin Starr**	*Ain't It Hell Up In Harlem*	12.1973
		Don't It Feel Good To Be Free	
1285	**Charlene Duncan**	*All That Love Went To Waste*	1.1974
		Give It One More Try	
1286	**Jackson 5**	*Dancing Machine*	2.1974
		It's Too Late To Change The Time	
1287	**Willie Hutch**	*If You Ain't Got No Money (You Can't Get No Honey) (Part 1)*	1.1974
		If You Ain't Got No Money (You Can't Get No Honey) (Part 2)	
1288	**Frankie Valli & the Four Seasons**	*Hickory*	2.1974
		Charisma	
1289	**Michael Edward Campbell**	*Roxanne (You Sure Got A Fine Design)*	2.1974
		Roll It Over	
1290	**Zell Black**	*I Been Had By The Devil*	2.1974
		Confession (Gotta Get Back To Myself)	
1291	**Bottom & Company**	*You're My Life*	2.1974
		Gonna Find A True Love	
1292	**Willie Hutch**	*Theme Of Foxy Brown*	3.1974
		Give Me Some Of That Good Old Love	
1293	**Dan The Banjo Man**	*Dan The Banjo Man*	2.1974
		Londonderry	
1294	**Martin & Finley**	*White Bird*	4.1974
		He Still Plays On	
1295	**Diana Ross**	*Sleepin'*	4.1974
		You	
1296	**Diana Ross & Marvin Gaye**	*Don't Knock My Love*	6.1974
		Just Say, Just Say	
1297	**Syreeta**	*Come And Get This Stuff*	6.1974
		Black Maybe	
1298	**Dickey & the Poseidons**	*Where Were You When The Ship Went Down*	3.1974
		Tidal Wave	
1299	—	—	—
1300	**Edwin Starr**	*Big Papa*	4.1974
		Like We Used To Do	
1301	**Matrix**	*Streakin' Down The Avenue*	3.1974
		Commercial Break	

1302	Puzzle	Everybody Wants To Be Somebody	5.1974
		State Of Mind	
1303	Severin Browne	Love Song	6.1974
		Snow Flakes	
1304	XIT	I Need Your Love (Give It To Me)	5.1974
		Movin' From The City	
1305	Reuben Howell	Rings	5.1974
		I'll Be Your Brother	
1306	Yvonne Fair	Funky Music Sho Nuff Turns Me On	5.1974
		Let Your Hair Down	
1307	Commodores	Machine Gun	4.1974
		There's A Song In My Heart	
1306	Jackson 5	Whatever You Got, I Want	10.1974
		I Can't Quit Your Love	
1309	Bottom & Company	Spread The News	9.1974
		Love Pains	
1310	Jackson 5	I Am Love	12.1974
		I Am Love Part 2	
1311	G. C. Cameron	If You Don't Love Me	10.1974
		Topics	
1312	Riot	Just Beyond	NR
		It's Been Oh So Long	
1313	Diahann Carroll	I've Been There Before	NR
		I Can't Give Back The Love I Feel For You	
1314	Pat Boone Family	Please Mr. Postman	9.1974
		Friend	
1315	Third Creation	Where Do I Belong	NR
		Penny Annie Fortune Lady	
1316	Thelma Houston	You've Been Doing Wrong For So Long	8.1974
		Pick Of The Week	
1317	Syreeta	I'm Going' Left	8.1974
		Heavy Day	
1318	Riot	Put Down Your Gun Brother	8.1974
		It's Been Oh So Long	
1319	Commodores	I Feel Sanctified	10.1974
		It's As Good As You Make It	
1320	XIT	Renegade	NR
		Cement Prairie	
1321	The Devastating Affair	You Don't Know (How Hard It Is To Make It) (vocal)	8.1974
		You Don't Know (How Hard It Is To Make It) (inst.)	
1322	The Allens	High Tide	NR
		Don't Make Me Wait Too Long	
1323	Yvonne Fair	Walk Out The Door If You Wanna	9.1974
		It Should Have Been Me	
1324	The Dynamic Superiors	Shoe Shoe Shine	8.1974
		Release Me	
1325	Reuben Howell	Constant Disappointment	9.1974
		I Believe (When I Fall In Love It Will Be Forever)	
1326	Edwin Starr	Who's Right Or Wrong	10.1974
		Lonely Rainy Days In San Diego	
1327	David Ruffin	Me & Rock And Roll Are Here To Stay	10.1974
		Smiling Faces Sometimes	
1328	Syreeta	Just A Little Piece Of You	NR
		Spinnin' And Spinnin'	
1329	Jimmy Ruffin	What Becomes Of The Brokenhearted	1.1975
		Baby I've Got It	
1330	Stephen Cohn	Power Is	1.1975
		Take It Now	
1331	Willie Hutch	I'm Gonna Stay	NR
		Woman You Touched Me	
1332	David Ruffin	Take Me Clear From Here	NR
		I Just Want To Celebrate	
1333	Severin Browne	Romance	1.1975
		Sweet Sound Of Your Song	
1334	The Boones	When The Lovelight Starts Shining Thru' His Eyes	2.1975
		Viva Espana (Forever A Song In My Heart)	
1335	Diana Ross	Sorry Doesn't Always Make It Right	2.1975
		Together	
1336	David Ruffin	Superstar (Remember How You Got Where You Are)	1.1975
		No Matter Where	
1337	Bottom & Company	Do You Wanna Do A Thing	4.1975
		Ticket To The Moon	
1338	Commodores	Slippery When Wet	4.1975
		The Bump	
1339	Willie Hutch	Get Ready For The Get Down	1.1975
		Don't You Let Nobody Tell You How To Do Your Thing	
1340	The Allens	A Bird In The Hand	3.1975
		California Music	
1341	Michael Jackson	We're Almost There	2.1975
		Take Me Back	
1342	The Dynamic Superiors	Leave It Alone	2.1975
		One-Nighter	
1343	Su Shifrin	All I Wanna Do	3.1975
		For You	
1344	Yvonne Fair	It's Bad For Me To See You	4.1975
		You Can't Judge A Book By Its Cover	
1345	Bob Horn	You've Gotta Try A Little Love	5.1975
		Static Free	
1346	Kathe Green	Love City	NR
		What Kind Of Man Are You	
1347	G.C. Cameron	If You're Ever Gonna Love Me	4.1975
		Tippin'	
1348	—	—	—
1349	Michael Jackson	Just A Little Bit Of You	4.1975
		Dear Michael	
1350	The Supremes	It's All Been Said Before	NR
		Give Out, But Don't Give Up	
1351	The Allens	High Tide	5.1975
		California Music	
1352	Jr Walker & the All Stars	What Does It Take (To Win Your Love)	5.1975
		Country Boy	
1353	Syreeta	Harmour Love	5.1975
		Cause We've Ended As Lovers	
1354	Yvonne Fair	Love Ain't No Toy	5.1975
		You Can't Judge A Book By Its Cover	
1355	The Originals	Good Lovin' Is Just A Dime Away	5.1975
		Nothing Can Take The Place (Of Your Love)	
1356	Jackson 5	Forever Came Today	6.1975
		All I Do Is Think Of You	
1357	The Dynamic Superiors	Romeo	NR
		I Got Away	
1358	The Supremes	He's My Man	6.1975
		Give Out, But Don't Give Up	
1359	The Dynamic Superiors	Nobody's Gonna Change Me	7.1975
		I Got Away	
1360	Willie Hutch	Love Power	7.1975
		Talk To Me	
1361	Commodores	This Is Your Life	8.1975
		Look What You've Done To Me	
1362	The Magic Disco Machine	Control Tower	7.1975
		Scratchin'	
1363	Bottom & Company	Here For The Party	8.1975
		Ticket To The Moon	
1364	G.C. Cameron	It's So Hard To Say Goodbye To Yesterday	8.1975
		Haulin' – Cold Blooded (instr.)	
1365	The Dynamic Superiors	Deception	9.1975
		One-Nighter	
1366	—	—	—

1367	Chip Hand	Wait Until September	8.1975
		Dreamtime Lover	
1368	Leon Ware	Comfort	NR
		Share Your Love	
1369	Lenny Williams	Since I Met You	9.1975
		Motion	
1370	The Originals	Fifty Years	NR
		Financial Affair	
1371	Willie Hutch	Party Down	1.1976
		Just Another Day	
1372	Kathe Green	Beautiful Changes	10.1975
		What Kind Of Man Are You	
1373	William Goldstein	Spirit Of '76 (A.M.America)	12.1975
		Southern Comfort	
1374	The Supremes	Where Do I Go From Here	NR
		Give Out, But Don't Give Up	
1375	Jackson 5	Body Language	NR
		Call Of The Wild	
1376	David Ruffin	Walk Away From Love	10.1975
		Love Can Be Hazardous To Your Health	
1377	Diana Ross	Theme From Mahogany (Do You Know Where You're Going To)	9.1975
		No-One's Gonna Be A Fool Forever	
1378	Joe Frazier	First Round Knock-Out	9.1975
		Looky Looky (Look At Me Girl)	
1379	The Originals	Everybody's Got To Do Something (vocal)	11.1975
		Everybody's Got To Do Something (instr.)	
1380	Jr Walker	I'm So Glad	NR
		Hot Shot	
1381	Commodores	Sweet Love	11.1975
		Better Never Than Forever	
1382	Stephanie Mills	This Empty Place	12.1975
		I See You For The First Time	
1383	Rose Banks	Whole New Thing	4.1976
		What Am I Gonna Do (With My Life)	
1384	Yvonne Fair	It Should Have Been Me	1.1976
		Tell Me Something Good	
1385	Thelma Houston	The Bingo Long Song (Steal on Home)	6.1976
	William Goldstein	Razzle Dazzle (instr.)	
1386	Jermaine Jackson	She's The Ideal Girl	NR
		I'm So Glad You Chose Me	
1387	Diana Ross	I Thought It Took A Little Time (But Today I Fell In Love)	2.1976
		After You	
1388	David Ruffin	Heavy Love	2.1976
		Love Can Be Hazardous To Your Health	
1389	The Boones	My Guy	2.1976
		When The Lovelight Starts Shining Through His Eyes	
1390	Kathe Green	Love City	2.1976
		What Kind Of Man Are You	
1391	The Supremes	I'm Gonna Let My Heart Do The Walking	5.1976
		Early Morning Love	
1392	Diana Ross	Love Hangover	3.1976
		Kiss Me Now	
1393	David Ruffin	Everything's Coming Up Love	5.1976
		No Matter Where	
1394	Commodores	Come Inside	NR
		Time	
1395	—	—	—
1396	Ronnie McNeir	Selling My Heart To The Junkman	8.1976
		Love Proposition	
1397	G.C. Cameron	Dream Lady	7.1976
		Tippin'	
1398	Diana Ross	One Love In My Lifetime	7.1976
		Smile	
1399	Commodores	High On Sunshine	NR
		Thumpin' Music	
1400	William Goldstein & the Magic Disco Machine	Midnight Rhapsody	7.1976
		Midnight Rhapsody (Part 2)	
1401	Jermaine Jackson	Let's Be Young Tonight	8.1976
		Bass Odyssey	
1402	Commodores	Just To Be Close To You	8.1976
		Thumpin' Music	
1403	Jerry Butler	The Devil in Mrs. Jones	8.1976
		Don't Wanna Be Reminded	
1404	Rose Banks	Right's Alright	9.1976
		Darling Baby	
1405	David Ruffin	On And Off	9.1976
		Statue Of A Fool	
1406	Willie Hutch	Let Me Be The One, Baby	9.1976
		She's Just Doing Her Thing	
1407	The Supremes	You're My Driving Wheel	9.1976
		You're What's Missing In My Life	
1408	Commodores	Fancy Dancer	11.1976
		Cebu	
1409	Jermaine Jackson	You Need To Be Loved	9.1977
		My Touch Of Madness	
1410	Ronnie McNeir	Have You Ever Seen Them Shake (Shake It Baby)	11.1976
		It Won't Be Long (When We're All Gone)	
1411	Willie Hutch	Shake It, Shake It	11.1976
		I Feel Like We Can Make It	
1412	G.C. Cameron	You're What's Missing In My Life	2.1977
		Kiss Me When You Want To	
1413	The Dynamic Superiors	I Can't Stay Away (From Someone I Love)	1.1977
		Supersensuousensation (Try Some Love)	
1414	Jerry Butler	I Wanna Do It To You	1.1977
		Don't Wanna Be Reminded	
1415	The Supremes	Let Yourself Go	1.1977
		You Are The Heart Of Me	
1416	Willie Hutch	We Gonna Have A House Party	3.1977
		I Never Had It So Good	
1417	Jennifer	Do It For Me	4.1977
		Boogie Boogie Love	
1418	Commodores	Easy	5.1977
		Can't Let You Tease Me	
1419	The Dynamic Superiors	Nowhere To Run (Part 1)	6.1977
		Nowhere To Run (Part 2)	
1420	David Ruffin	Just Let Me Hold You For A Night	6.1977
		Rode By The Place (Where We Used To Stay)	
1421	Jerry Butler	Chalk It Up	6.1977
		I Don't Want Nobody To Know	
1422	Thelma Houston & Jerry Butler	It's A Lifetime Thing	7.1977
		Kiss Me Now	
1423	Albert Finney	Those Other Men	6.1977
		What Have They Done (To My Home Town?)	
1424	Willie Hutch	We Gonna Party Tonight	7.1977
		Precious Pearl	
1425	Commodores	Brick House	8.1977
		Captain Quick Draw	
1426	G.C. Cameron & Syreeta	Let's Make A Deal/Love To The Rescue	8.1977
		Let's Make A Deal (Part 1)/ Let's Make A Deal (Part 2)	
1427	Diana Ross	Gettin' Ready For Love	10.1977
		Confide In Me	
1428	The Dynamic Superiors	You're What I Need	9.1977
		Here Comes That Feeling Again	
1429	Mandré	Solar Flight (Opus 1)	9.1977
		Money (That's What I Want)	
1430	Albert Finney	When It's Gone	10.1977
		A State Of Grace	
1431	Scherrie Payne	When I Looked At Your Face	10.1977
		Fly	

1432	Commodores	Too Hot Ta Trot	11.1977
		Funky Situation	
1433	Willie Hutch	What You Gonna Do After The Party	11.1977
		I Feel Like We Can Make It	
1434	Mandré	Keep Tryin'	12.1977
		Third World Calling (Opus II)	
1435	David Ruffin	You're My Peace Of Mind	12.1977
		Rode By The Place (Where We Used To Stay)	
1436	Diana Ross	Your Love Is So Good For Me	1.1978
		Baby It's Me	
1437	5th Dimension	You Are The Reason (I Feel Like Dancing)	1.1978
		Slipping Into Something New	
1438	Carl Bean	I Was Born This Way	3.1978
		I Was Born This Way (instr.)	
1439	3 Ounces Of Love	Star Love	3.1978
		I Found The Feeling	
1440	Cuba Gooding	Mind Pleaser	4.1978
		Where Would I Be Without You	
1441	Jermaine Jackson	Castles Of Sand	4.1978
		I Love Every Little Thing About You	
1442	Diana Ross	You Got It	4.1978
		Too Shy To Say	
1443	Commodores	Three Times A Lady	6.1978
		Look What You've Done To Me	
1444	Prime Time	Good Times Theme	7.1978
		Carter Country Theme	
1445	Finished Touch	Sticks And Stones Will Break Your Bones (But The Funk Will Never Hurt You)	8.1978
		Strokin'	
1446	3 Ounces Of Love	Give Me Some Feeling	7.1978
		Does Your Chewing Gum Lose Its Flavor On The Bedpost Overnight	
1447	Platinum Hook	Hooked For Life	7.1978
		Gotta Find A Woman	
1448	Mandré	Fair Game	7.1978
		Light Years (Opus IV)	
1449	Finished Touch featuring Kenny Stover	I Love To See You Dance	11.1978
	featuring Larry Brown & Harold Johnson	You Danced Into My Life	
1450	Diana Ross	Lovin', Livin' & Givin'	NR
		Baby It's Me	
1451	Bonnie Pointer	Free Me From My Freedom	9.1978
		Free Me From My Freedom (instr.)	
1452	Commodores	Flying High	8.1978
		X-Rated Movie	
1453	5th Dimension	Everybody's Got To Give It Up	4.1979
		You're My Star	
1454	Grover Washington Jr	Do Dat	11.1978
		Reed Seed (Trio Tune)	
1455	Diana Ross, Marvin Gaye, Smokey Robinson & Stevie Wonder	Pops, We Love You	12.1978
		Pops, We Love You (instr.)	
1456	Diana Ross	What You Gave Me	12.1978
		Together	
1457	Commodores	Say Yeah	NR
		Thumpin' Music	
1458	Bloodstone	Just Wanna Get The Feel Of It	4.1979
		It's Been A Long Time	
1459	Bonnie Pointer	Heaven Must Have Sent You	3.1979
		Heaven Must Have Sent You (album vers.)	
1460	Billy Preston & Syreeta	Go For It	4.1979
	Billy Preston	With You I'm Born Again (instr.)	

1461	Mandré	Spirit Groove	4.1979
		M 3000 (Opus VI)	
1462	Diana Ross	The Boss	5.1979
		I'm In The World	
1463	Finished Touch featuring Harold Johnson	The Down Sound (Part 2)	4.1979
		The Down Sound (Part 1)	
1464	Platinum Hook	Give Me Time To Say	6.1979
		Lover What You've Done (To Me)	
1465	Patrick Gammon	Cop An Attitude	5.1979
		My Song In -G-	
1466	Commodores	Sail On	7.1979
		Thumpin' Music	
1467	Mary Wilson	Red Hot	8.1979
		Midnight Dancer	
1468	Sterling	Roll-Her, Skater	8.1979
		Roll-Her, Skater (instr.)	
1469	Jermaine Jackson	Let's Get Serious	2.1980
		Je Vous Aime Beaucoup (I Love You)	
1470	Billy Preston & Syreeta	It Will Come In Time	8.1979
	Billy Preston	All I Wanted Was You	
1471	Diana Ross	It's My House	10.1979
		Sparkle	
1472	Mandré	Freakin's Fine	9.1979
		Spirit Groove	
1473	Scherrie & Susaye	Leaving Me Was The Best Thing You've Ever Done	9.1979
		When The Day Comes Every Night	
1474	Commodores	Still	9.1979
		Such A Woman	
1475	Dr. Strut	Granite Palace	9.1979
		Blow Top	
1476	Cook County	Pinball Playboy (Playboy Theme)	10.1979
		Reach Out For Love	
1477	Billy Preston & Syreeta	With You I'm Born Again	11.1979
	Billy Preston	All I Wanted Was You	
1478	Bonnie Pointer	I Can't Help Myself (Sugar Pie, Honey Bunch)	11.1979
		I Wanna Make It (In Your World)	
1479	Commodores	Wonderland	11.1979
		Lovin' You	
1480	—	—	—
1481	Cook County	Little Girls & Ladies	2.1980
		Olympiad '84	
1482	Clifton Dyson	Body in Motion (Want Your Body In Motion With Mine)	1.1980
		You Gotta Keep Dancin'	
1483	Dr. Strut	Struttin'	3.1980
		Blue Lodge	
1484	Bonnie Pointer	Deep Inside My Soul	3.1980
		I Love To Sing To You	
1485	Planets	Break It To Me Gently	3.1980
		Secret	
1486	Grover Washington Jr.	Snake Eyes	4.1980
		Love	
1487	Ozone	Walk On	5.1980
		This Is Funkin' Insane	
1488	Diana Ross & the Supremes	Medley Of Hits	5.1980
	Diana Ross	Where Did We Go Wrong	
1489	Commodores	Old-Fashion Love	6.1980
		Sexy Lady	
1490	Jermaine Jackson	You're Supposed To Keep Your Love For Me	6.1980
		Let It Ride	
1491	Diana Ross	I'm Coming Out	8.1980
		Give Up (orig: Friend To Friend)	

1492	**Charlene**	*Hungry*	6.1980
		I Won't Remember Ever	
		Loving You	
1493	**Black Russian**	*Leave Me Now*	6.1980
		Love's Enough	
1494	**Diana Ross**	*Upside Down*	6.1980
		Friend To Friend	
1495	**Commodores**	*Heroes*	8.1980
		Funky Situation	
1496	**Diana Ross**	*It's My Turn*	9.1980
		Together	
1497	**Black Russian**	*Mystified*	10.1980
		Move Together	
1498	**Platinum Hook**	*Words Of Love*	9.1980
		Ecstasy Paradise	
1499	**Jermaine**	*Little Girl Don't You Worry*	10.1980
	Jackson	*We Can Put It Back Together*	
1500	**The Dazz Band**	*Shake It Up*	10.1980
		Only Love	
1501	**The Temptations**	*Take Me Away*	10.1980
		There's More Where That	
		Came From	
1502	**Commodores**	*Jesus Is Love*	11.1980
		Mighty Spirit	
1503	**Jermaine**	*You Like Me Don't You*	1.1981
	Jackson	*You Like Me Don't You* (instr.)	
1504	**Joel Diamond**	*Theme From The Raging Bull*	1.1981
		(Cavalleria Rasticana)	
		Joey's Theme	
1505	**Billy Preston**	*Hope*	1.1981
		Sock-It, Rocket	
1506	**Midnight Blue**	*I (Who Have Nothing)*	1.1981
		I (Who Have Nothing) (instr.)	
1507	**The Dazz Band**	*Invitation To Love*	2.1981
		Magnetized	
1508	**Diana Ross**	*One More Chance*	2.1981
		After You	
1509	—	—	—
1510	**Ozone**	*Ozonic Bee Bop*	3.1981
		The Preacher's Gone Home	
		(Tribute To Cannonball	
		Adderly)	
1511	**Billy Preston**	*A Change Is Gonna Come*	3.1981
		You	
1512	**Michael Jackson**	*One Day In Your Life*	3.1981
		Take Me Back	
1513	**Diana Ross**	*Cryin' My Heart Out For You*	5.1981
		To Love Again	
1514	**Commodores**	*Lady (You Bring Me Up)*	6.1981
		Gettin' It	
1515	**The Dazz Band**	*Knock! Knock!*	6.1981
		Sooner Or Later	
1516	**Tommy Hill**	*Flame*	6.1981
		Superstar Of Love (instr.)	
1517	**José Feliciano**	*Everybody Loves Me*	9.1981
		The Drought Is Over	
1518	**Ozone**	*Mighty-Mighty*	6.1981
		Rock And Roll, Pop And Soul	
1519	**Diana Ross &**	*Endless Love*	6.1981
	Lionel Richie	*Endless Love* (instr.)	
1520	**Billy Preston &**	*Searchin'*	7.1981
	Syreeta	*Hey You*	(withdrawn)
1521	**Ozone**	*Gigolette*	8.1981
		Gigolette (instr.)	
1522	**Billy Preston &**	*Just For You (Put The Boogie*	8.1981
	Syreeta	*In Your Body)*	
		Hey You	
1523	**Diana Ross & the**	*Medley Of Hits*	8.1981
	Supremes		
	Diana Ross	*Where Did We Go Wrong*	
1524	**José Feliciano**	*I Second That Emotion*	NR
		The Drought Is Over	
1525	**Jermaine**	*I'm Just Too Shy*	9.1981
	Jackson	*All Because Of You*	
1526	**Lovesmith**	*Shame On You*	9.1981
		Look Out Below	
1527	**Commodores**	*Oh No*	9.1981
		Lovin' You	

1528	**Dazz Band**	*Let The Music Play*	9.1981
		Hello Girl	
1529	**Ozone**	*Over And Over Again*	NR
		Come On In	
1530	**José Feliciano**	*I Wanna Be Where You Are*	11.1981
		Let's Make Love Over The	
		Telephone	
1531	**Diana Ross**	*My Old Piano*	11.1981
		Now That You're Gone	
1532	**Bettye Lavette**	*Right In The Middle (Of Falling*	12.1981
		In Love)	
		You Seen One You Seen 'Em	
		All	

7 INCH SINGLES

New numbering system replacing and including MOTOWN (M), TAMLA (T), GORDY (G), LATINO (L), MOROCCO (C)

1600M	**Jermaine**	*Paradise In Your Eyes*	12.1981
	Jackson	*I'm My Brother's Keeper*	
1601T	**Smokey**	*Tell Me Tomorrow (Part 1)*	12.1981
	Robinson	*Tell Me Tomorrow (Part 2)*	
1602T	**Stevie Wonder**	*That Girl*	12.1981
		All I Do	
1603G	**Switch**	*Call On Me*	1.1982
		Fallin'	
1604M	**Commodores**	*Why You Wanna Try Me*	1.1982
		X-Rated Movie	
1605M	**Ozone**	*Do What Cha Wanna*	2.1982
		Come On In	
1606G	**Nolen & Crossley**	*Chance*	NR
		Because	
1607M	**Lovesmith**	*I Fooled Ya*	3.1982
		You're A Fox (Out The Box)	
1608G	**Nolen & Crossley**	*Ready Or Not*	2.1982
		A Place In My Heart	
1609M	**Dazz Band**	*Let It Whip*	2.1982
		Everyday Love	
1610T	**Syreeta**	*I Must Be In Love*	2.1982
		Wish Upon A Star	
1611M	**Charlene**	*I've Never Been To Me*	2.1982
		Somewhere In My Life	
1612T	**Stevie Wonder**	*Do I Do*	5.1982
		Rocket Love	
1613G	**High Inergy**	*First Impressions*	3.1982
		Could This Be Love	
1614M	**Bettye Lavette**	*I Can't Stop*	4.1982
		Either Way We Lose	
1615T	**Smokey**	*Old Fashioned Love*	3.1982
	Robinson	*Destiny*	
1616G	**The Temptations**	*Standing On The Top (Part 1)*	4.1982
	featuring Rick	*Standing On The Top (Part 2)*	
	James		
1617M	**Ozone**	*Keep On Dancin'*	NR
		Your Love Stays On My Mind	
1618M	**José Feliciano**	*I Second That Emotion*	4.1982
		Free Me From My Freedom	
1619G	**Rick James**	*Dance Wit' Me (Part 1)*	4.1982
		Dance Wit' Me (Part 2)	
1620M	**Jean Carn**	*If You Don't Know Me By*	6.1982
		Now	
		Completeness	
1621M	**Charlene**	*It Ain't Easy Comin' Down*	6.1982
		If I Could See Myself	
1622M	**Dazz Band**	*Keep It Live (On The K.I.L)*	7.1982
		This Time It's Forever	
1623M	**O.C. Smith**	*Love Changes*	5.1982
		Got To Know	
1624L	**Charlene**	*Nunca He Ido A Mi*	5.1982
		If I Could See Myself	
1625M	**Billy Preston**	*I'm Never Gonna Say*	6.1982
		Goodbye	
		I Love You So	
1626M	**Diana Ross**	*We Can Never Light That Old*	6.1982
		Flame Again	
		Old Funky Rolls	
1627M	**Ozone**	*Li'l Suzy*	6.1982
		I'm Not Easy	

1628M	**Jermaine Jackson**	*Let Me Tickle Your Fancy* *Maybe Next Time*	7.1982
1629M	**Regal Funkharmonic Orchestra**	*Strung Out On Motown* *Strung Out On Commodores*	7.1982
1630T	**Smokey Robinson**	*Yes It's You Lady* *Are You Still Here*	6.1982
1631G	**The Temptations**	*More On The Inside* *Money's Hard To Get*	6.1982
1632G	**High Inergy**	*Wrong Man, Right Touch* *Beware*	7.1982
1633L	**Isela Sotelo**	*Angelito (Angel Baby)* *Esta Vez*	7.1982
1634G	**Rick James**	*Hard To Get* *My Love*	7.1982
1635G	**DeBarge**	*Stop! Don't Tease Me* *Hesitated*	7.1982
1636M	**O.C. Smith**	*I Betcha* *That's One For Love*	8.1982
1637M	**Willie Hutch**	*In And Out* *The Girl (Can't Help It)*	8.1982
1638M	**Bill Cosby**	*Just The Slew Of Us* *Put A Little Punk In Your Funk*	NR
1639T	**Stevie Wonder**	*Ribbon In The Sky* *Black Orchid*	8.1982
1640T	**Smokey Robinson**	*Greatest Hits Medley* *The Only Game In Town*	NR
1641G	**High Inergy**	*Journey To Love* *Could This Be Love*	8.1982
1642T	**Gene Van Buren**	*You've Got Me Where I Want You* *One*	12.1982
1643M	**Bobby Nunn**	*She's Just A Groupie* *Never Seen Anything Like You*	8.1982
1644M	**Lionel Richie**	*Truly* *Just Put Some Love in Your Heart*	9.1982
1645G	**DeBarge**	*I Like It* *Hesitated*	10.1982
1646G	**Rick James**	*She Blew My Mind (69 Times)* *She Blew My Mind (69 Times)* (instr.)	9.1982
1647L	**José Feliciano**	*Samba Pa Ti* *Malas Costumbres (Evil Ways)*	9.1982
1648M	**Isela Sotelo**	*Angelito (Angel Baby)* *Esta Vez*	9.1982
1649M	**Jermaine Jackson**	*Very Special Part* *You're Givin' Me The Runaround*	9.1982
1650M	**Charlene & Stevie Wonder**	*Used To Be* *I Want To Come Back As A Song (Charlene Solo)*	10.1982
1651M	**Commodores**	*Painted Picture* *Reach High* (instr.)	11.1982
1652G	**Bobby M featuring Jean Carn***	*Let's Stay Together** *Charlie's Backbeat*	11.1982
1653M	**Bobby Nunn**	*Got To Get Up On It* *You Need Non-Stop Lovin'*	11.1982
1654G	**The Temptations**	*Silent Night* *Everything For Christmas*	12.1982
1655T	**Smokey Robinson**	*I've Made Love To You A Thousand Times* *Into Each Rain Some Life Must Fall*	12.1982
1656G	**High Inergy**	*So Right* *Don't Let Up On The Groove*	NR
1657M	**Lionel Richie**	*You Are* *You Mean More To Me*	12.1982
1658G	**Rick James**	*Teardrops* *Throwdown*	12.1982
1659M	**Dazz Band**	*On The One* *Just Believe In Love*	1.1983
1660G	**DeBarge**	*All This Love* *I'm In Love With You*	3.1983
1661M	**Commodores**	*Reach High* *Sexy Lady*	1.1983
1662G	**High Inergy**	*He's A Pretender* *Don't Let Up On The Groove*	12.1982
1663M	**Charlene**	*I Want To Go Back There Again* *Richie's Song (For Richard Oliver)*	1.1983
1664M	**Robert John**	*Bread And Butter* *If You Don't Want My Love*	1.1983
1665M	**Monalisa Young**	*Dancing Machine* *I'll Be There*	2.1983
1666G	**The Temptations**	*Love On My Mind Tonight* *Bring Your Body Here (Exercise Chant)*	2.1983
1667G	**Bobby M**	*How Do You Feel Tonight* *Redliner*	NR
1668M	**Ozone**	*Strutt My Thang* *Don't Leave Me Now*	3.1983
1669M	**Finis Henderson**	*Skip To My Lou* *I'd Rather Be Gone*	4.1983
1670G	**Mary Jane Girls**	*Candy Man* *Candy Man* (instr.)	2.1983
1671M	**Bobby Nunn**	*Sexy Sassy* *Sexy Sassy* (instr.)	2.1983
1672M	**Kagny & the Dirty Rats**	*At 15* *Dirty Rats*	3.1983
1673L	**José Feliciano**	*Volvere Alguna Vez* *La Balada Del Pianista*	NR
1674M	**José Feliciano**	*Let's Find Each Other Tonight* *Cuidado!*	6.1983
1675T	**Syreeta**	*Forever Is Not Enough* *She's Leaving Home*	3.1983
1676M	**Dazz Band**	*Cheek To Cheek* *Can We Dance*	3.1983
1677M	**Lionel Richie**	*My Love* *Round And Round*	3.1983
1678T	**Smokey Robinson**	*Touch The Sky* *All My Life's A Lie*	3.1983
1679M	**José Feliciano**	*Lonely Teardrops* *Cuidado!*	3.1983
1680M	**Dazz Band**	*Party Right Here* *Gamble With My Love*	5.1983
1681G	**Stone City Band**	*Bad Lady* *Bad Lady* (instr.)	5.1983
1682M	**Bobby Nunn**	*The Party's Over* *Get It While You Can*	4.1983
1683G	**The Temptations**	*Surface Thrills* *Made In America*	5.1983
1684T	**Smokey Robinson with Barbara Mitchell**	*Blame It On Love* *Even Tho (Smokey solo)*	6.1983
1685M	**Michael Lovesmith**	*Baby I Will* *What's The Bottom Line*	6.1983
1686T	**Gene Van Buren**	*When Is My Turn* *When Is My Turn* (instr.)	NR
1687G	**Rick James**	*Cold Blooded* *Cold Blooded* (instr.)	7.1983
1688G	**High Inergy**	*Back In My Arms Again* *So Right*	7.1983
1689M	**Jr Walker**	*Blow The House Down* *Ball Baby* (instr.)	7.1983
1690G	**Mary Jane Girls**	*All Night Long* *Musical Love*	6.1983
1691M	**Ozone**	*Our Hearts (Will Always Shine)* *Here I Go Again*	7.1983
1692C	**Sparks Malcolm McDowell**	*Get Crazy* *Hot Shot*	8.1983
1693G	**Stone City Band**	*Ladies Choice* *Ladies Choice* (instr.)	8.1983
1694M	**Commodores**	*Only You* *Cebu*	8.1983

286

No.	Artist	Title	Date
1695M	**Bobby Nunn**	*Private Party*	8.1983
		Get It While You Can	
1696M	**Finis Henderson**	*Lovers*	8.1983
		Schoolgirl	
1697M	**The Motor City Crew**	*Let's Break* (later *Scratch Break*)	8.1983
		Let's Break (instr.)	
1698M	**Lionel Richie**	*All Night Long (All Night)*	8.1983
		Wandering Stranger	
1699M	**Michael Lovesmith**	*A Promise Is A Promise*	NR
		Just Say The Word	
1700T	**Smokey Robinson**	*Don't Play Another Love Song*	10.1983
		Wouldn't You Like To Know	
1701M	**Dazz Band**	*Joystick*	10.1983
		Don't Get Caught In The Middle	
1702M	**Rockwell**	*Somebody's Watching Me*	12.1983
		Somebody's Watching Me (instr.)	
1703G	**Rick James**	*U Bring The Freak Out*	9.1983
		Money Talks	
1704G	**Mary Jane Girls**	*Boys*	9.1983
		Boys (instr.)	
1705G	**DeBarge**	*Time Will Reveal*	9.1983
		I'll Never Fall In Love Again	
1706M	**Four Tops**	*I Just Can't Walk Away*	9.1983
		Hang	
1707G	**The Temptations**	*Miss Busy Body (Part 1)*	9.1983
		Miss Busy Body (Part 2)	
1708M	**Jr Walker**	*Closer Than Close*	NR
		Rise And Shine	
1709M	**Monalisa Young**	*Sweet Remedy*	2.1984
		Don't Mess With Bill	
1710M	**Lionel Richie**	*Running With The Night*	11.1983
		Serves You Right	
1711M	**Bobby Nunn**	*Hangin' Out At The Mall*	11.1983
		The Lady Killer	
1712T	**Keith & Darrell**	*Work That Body*	12.1983
		The Things You're Made Of	
1713G	**The Temptations**	*Silent Night*	11.1983
		Everything For Christmas	
1714G	**Rick James & Friend**	*Ebony Eyes*	11.1983
		1,2,3 (U, Her And Me)	
1715G	**Dennis Edwards *featuring Siedah Garrett**	*Don't Look Any Further*	1.1984
		I Thought I Could Handle It	
1716C	**Tiggi Clay**	*Flashes*	1.1984
		Roses For Lydia	
1717C	**Kidd Glove**	*Good Clean Fun*	3.1984
		Street Angel	
1718M	**Four Tops**	*Make Yourself Right At Home*	3.1984
		Sing A Song Of Yesterday	
1719M	**Commodores**	*Turn Off The Lights*	12.1983
		Been Loving You	
1720G	**The Temptations**	*Sail Away*	1.1984
		Isn't The Night Fantastic	
1721G	**Mary Jane Girls**	*Jealousy*	1.1984
		You Are My Heaven	
1722M	**Lionel Richie**	*Hello*	2.1984
		You Mean More To Me	
1723G	**DeBarge**	*Love In A Special Way*	2.1984
		Dance The Night Away	
1724M	**Bobby Nunn**	*Do You Look That Good In The Morning*	2.1984
		Sex Maniac	
1725M	**Dazz Band**	*Swoop (I'm Yours)*	3.1984
		Bad Girl	
1726M	**Bobby King**	*Lovequake*	3.1984
		Fall In Love	
1727T	**Gene Van Buren**	*You Excite Me*	7.1984
		I Love You More (Than I Hate What You Do)	
1728C	**Tiggi Clay**	*The Winner Gets The Heart*	3.1984
		Who Shot Zorro?	
1729C	**Wolf & Wolf**	*Don't Take The Candy*	4.1984
		War Of Nerves	
1730G	**Rick James**	*17*	6.1984
		17 (instr.)	
1731M	**Rockwell**	*Obscene Phone Caller*	4.1984
		Obscene Phone Caller (instr.)	
1732M	**Michael Lovesmith**	*Gotta Get Out Tonight*	4.1984
		Sorry Won't Get It	
1733M	**KokoPop**	*Baby Sister*	5.1984
		Baby Sister (instr.)	
1734M	**Charlene**	*We're Both In Love With You*	6.1984
		I Want The World To Know He's Mine	
1735T	**Smokey Robinson**	*And I Don't Love You*	4.1984
		Dynamite	
1736C	**Duke Jupiter**	*Little Lady*	4.1984
		(I've Got A) Little Black Book	
1737G	**Dennis Edwards**	*(You're My) Aphrodisiac*	4.1984
		Shake Hands (Come Out Dancin')	
1738M	**Sammy Davis Jr**	*Hello Detroit*	5.1984
		Hello Detroit (instr.)	
1739M	**Michael Jackson**	*Farewell My Summer Love*	4.1984
		Call On Me	
1740C	**Kidd Glove**	*Killer Instinct*	NR
		Hellzarockin'	
1741G	**Mary Jane Girls**	*In My House*	1.985
		In My House (instr.)	
1742C	**Coyote Sisters**	*Straight From The Heart (Into Your Life)*	6.1984
		Echo	
1743M	**Sam Harris**	*Sugar Don't Bite*	8.1984
		You Keep Me Hangin' On	
1744M	**Kagny**	*Sundown On Sunset*	8.1984
		Nothin' But Pocket	
1745M	**Stevie Wonder**	*I Just Called To Say I Love You*	8.1984
		I Just Called To Say I Love You (instr.)	
1746M	**Lionel Richie**	*Stuck On You*	6.1984
		Round And Round	
1747M	**Bobby King *featuring Alfie Silas**	*Close To Me**	6.1984
		Love In The Fire	
1748C	**Duke Jupiter**	*Rescue Me*	7.1984
		Me And Michelle	
1749M	**Michael Lovesmith**	*I Can't Give Her Up*	6.1984
		He Only Looks The Part	
1750C	**Jakata**	*Hell Is On The Run*	8.1984
		Don't Ever Let Go	
1751M	**Willie Hutch**	*She's Making A Game Out Of Love*	NR
		(B side not selected)	
1752M	**Vanity**	*Pretty Mess*	8.1984
		Pretty Mess (instr.)	
1753	—	—	—
1754C	**Wolf & Wolf**	*Talk Of The Town*	9.1984
		War Of Nerves	
1755G	**Dennis Edwards**	*Another Place In Time*	7.1984
		Let's Go Up	
1756T	**Smokey Robinson**	*I Can't Find*	7.1984
		Gimme What You Want	
1757M	**Michael Jackson**	*Girl You're So Together*	8.1984
		Touch The One You Love	
1758M	**Phyllis St. James**	*Candlelight Afternoon*	8.1984
		Back In The Race	
1759M	**Koko-Pop**	*I'm In Love With You*	8.1984
		On The Beach	
1760M	**Dazz Band**	*Let It All Blow*	9.1984
		Now That I Have You	
1761M	**Charlene**	*Hit And Run Lover*	9.1984
		The Last Song	
1762M	**Lionel Richie**	*Penny Lover*	9.1984
		Tell Me	
1763G	**Rick James**	*You Turn Me On*	9.1984
		Fire And Desire	
1764M	**Bobby King**	*Midnight Shine*	NR
		Ain't Never Met A Woman Like You	

Cat.	Artist	Titles	Date
1765G	The Temptations	Treat Her Like A Lady / Isn't The Night Fantastic	10.1984
1766C	The Coyote Sisters	I've Got A Radio / I'll Do It	10.1984
1767M	Vanity	Mechanical Emotion / Crazy Maybe	11.1984
1768M	Thomas McClary	Thin Walls / Love Will Find A Way (instr.)	11.1984
1769M	Stevie Wonder	Love Light In Flight / It's More Than You (instr.)	11.1984
1770G	DeBarge	Rhythm Of The Night / Queen Of My Heart	1.1985
1771M	Sam Harris	Hearts On Fire / I Will Not Wait For You	11.1984
1772M	Rockwell	He's A Cobra / Change Your Ways	12.1984
1773M	Commodores	Nightshift / I Keep Running	12.1984
1774M	Stevie Wonder	Don't Drive Drunk / Don't Drive Drunk (instr.)	NR
1775M	Dazz Band	Heartbeat / Rock With Me	1.1985
1776G	Rick James	Can't Stop / Oh What A Night (4 Luv)	3.1985
1777M	Alfie Silas	Star / Keep On Smilin'	2.1985
1778M	Jakata	Golden Girl / Light At The End Of The Tunnel	3.1985
1779M	Thomas McClary	Man In The Middle / Man In The Middle (instr.)	2.1985
1780M	Sam Harris	Over The Rainbow / I've Heard It All Before	2.1985
1781G	The Temptations	My Love Is True (Truly For You) / Set Your Love Right	2.1985
1782M	Rockwell	Peeping Tom / Tokyo (instr.)	2.1985
1783	—	—	—
1784M	The Emotions	Miss Your Love / I Can't Wait To Make You Mine	3.1985
1785M	Dwight David	The Last Dragon (title song from Berry Gordy's 'The Last Dragon') / The Last Dragon (instr.)	2.1985
1786	—	—	—
1787M	Maureen Steele	Save The Night For Me / Boys Will Be Boys	4.1985
1788M	Commodores	Animal Instinct / Lightin' Up The Night	4.1985
1789G	The Temptations	How Can You Say That It's Over / I'll Keep My Light In My Window	4.1985
1790M	Four Tops	Sexy Ways / Body And Soul	4.1985
1791M	Michael Lovesmith	Love In The Combat Zone / Diamond In The Raw	NR
1792M	The Emotions	If I Only Knew Then (What I Know Now) / Eternally	5.1985
1793G	DeBarge	Who's Holding Donna Now / Be My Lady	5.1985
1794M	Michael Lovesmith	Break The Ice / Lucky In Love	5.1985
1795G	Val Young	Mind Games / Mind Games (instr.)	6.1985
1796G	Rick James	Glow / Glow (instr.)	5.1985
1797M	Willie Hutch	Keep On Jammin' / The Glow	5.1985
1798G	Mary Jane Girls	Wild And Crazy Love / Wild And Crazy Love (instr.)	6.1985
1799G	Dennis Edwards	Amanda / I'm Up For You	6.1985
1800M	Dazz Band	Hot Spot / I've Been Waiting	6.1985
1801M	Lushus Daim & the Pretty Vain	More Than You Can Handle / More Than You Can Handle (instr.)	8.1985
1802M	Commodores	Janet / I'm In Love	7.1985
1803M	Koko-Pop	Brand New Beat / Brand New Beat (Part 2)	7.1985
1804G	El DeBarge with DeBarge	You Wear It Well / Baby, Won't Cha Come Quick	8.1985
1805G	Dennis Edwards	Coolin' Out / I Thought I Could Handle It	8.1985
1806G	Rick James	Spend The Night With Me / Spend The Night With Me (instr.)	8.1985
1807M	Maureen Steele	Boys Will Be Boys / Rock My Heart	8.1985
1808T	Stevie Wonder	Part-Time Lover / Part-Time Lover (instr.)	8.1985
1809	—	—	—
1810M	Pal	Panic / Panic (instr.)	NR
1811M	Four Tops	Don't Tell Me That It's Over / I'm Ready For Love	9.1985
1812G	Val Young	Seduction / Seduction (instr.)	9.1985
1813M	Warp 9	Skips A Beat / Skips A Beat (dub vers.)	12.1985
1814M	Mello-Mackin-D & Mr. Stretch	Back To School / Back To School (instr.)	9.1985
1815M	Duke Jupiter	The Line Of Your Fire / Sounds Like Love	9.1985
1816G	Mary Jane Girls	Break It Up / Break It Up (instr.)	9.1985
1817T	Stevie Wonder	Go Home / Go Home (instr.)	11.1985
1818G	The Temptations	Do You Really Love Your Baby / I'll Keep My Light In My Window	10.1985
1819M	Lionel Richie	Say You, Say Me / Can't Slow Down	10.1985
1820	—	—	—
1821	—	—	—
1822G	El DeBarge with DeBarge	The Heart Is Not So Smart / Share My World	10.1985
1823	—	—	—
1824M	Koko-Pop	Lonely Girl, Lonely Boy / Make Up Your Mind	NR
1825M	Roq-In' Zoo	Frig-o-rator / Frig-o-rator (dub vers.)	11.1985
1826M	Lushus Daim & the Pretty Vain	The One You Love / The One You Love (instr.)	12.1985
1827M	Alfie	Just Gets Better With Time / Keep On Smilin'	12.1985
1828T	Smokey Robinson	Hold On To Your Love / Train Of Thought	12.1985
1829M	Sam Harris	I'd Do It All Again / The Rescue	12.1985
1830G	Val Young	If You Should Ever Be Lonely / If You Should Ever Be Lonely (instr.)	12.1985
1831M	Troy Johnson	It's You / It's You (instr.)	2.1986
1832T	Stevie Wonder	Overjoyed / Overjoyed (instr.)	1.1986
1833M	Vanity	Under The Influence / Wild Animal	2.1986
1834G	The Temptations	Touch Me / Set Your Love Right	1.1986
1835M	Guinn Family	Dreamin' / Dreamin' (instr.)	1.1986
1836T	Marvin Gaye	The World Is Rated X / No Greater Love	5.1986
1837M	The Temptations Smokey Robinson	A Fine Mess / Wishful Thinking	4.1986

1838M	**Fizzy Quick**	*Hangin' Out*	5.1986
		Angels in The Snow	
1839T	**Smokey Robinson**	*Sleepless Nights*	4.1986
		Close Encounters Of The First Kind	
1840M	**Sam Harris**	*Forever For You*	4.1986
		The Storm	
1841	**—**		**—**
1842GF	**El DeBarge**	*Who's Johnny*	4.1986
	El DeBarge with DeBarge	*Love Me In A Special Way*	
1843MF	**Lionel Richie**	*Dancing On The Ceiling*	6.1986
		Love Will Find A Way	
1844GF	**Rick James**	*Sweet And Sexy Thing*	4.1986
		Sweet And Sexy Thing (instr.)	
1845MF	**Rockwell**	*Carmé (Part 1)*	5.1986
		Carmé (Part 2)	
1846TF	**Stevie Wonder**	*Land Of La La*	5.1986
		Land Of La La (instr.)	
1847MF	**Maureen Steele**	*One More Saturday Night*	NR
		Rock My Heart	
1848MF	**Vanity**	*Animals*	6.1986
		Gun Shy	
1849MF	**Alfie**	*That Look*	NR
		(B side not selected)	
1850MF	**Guinn**	*Open Your Door*	6.1986
		Sincerely	
1851MF	**Mary Jane Girls**	*Walk Like A Man*	6.1986
		Shadow Lover	
1852MF	**Burston & Littlejohn**	*Rich And Famous*	6.1986
		Rich And Famous (instr.)	
1853MF	**Nick Jameson**	*Weatherman*	6.1986
		Casco Bay (instr.)	
1854MF	**Four Tops**	*Hot Nights*	6.1986
		Again	
1855TF	**Smokey Robinson**	*Because Of You (It's The Best It's Ever Been)*	7.1986
		Girl I'm Standing There	
1856GF	**The Temptations**	*Lady Soul*	7.1986
		Put Us Together Again	
1857GF	**El DeBarge**	*Love Always*	7.1986
	El DeBarge with DeBarge	*The Walls (Came Tumbling Down)*	
1858MF	**Chico DeBarge**	*Talk To Me*	8.1986
		If It Takes All Night	
1859MF	**Stacy Lattisaw**	*Nail It To The Wall*	8.1986
		Nail It To The Wall (instr.)	
1860MF	**Jakata**	*Nothing Lasts Forever*	NR
		Silver Lining	
1861TF	**Stevie Wonder**	*Spiritual Walkers*	NR
		Spiritual Walkers (instr.)	
1862GF	**Rick James**	*Forever And A Day*	8.1986
		Forever And A Day (instr.)	
1863MF	**Rockwell**	*Grow Up*	8.1986
		Grow Up (instr.)	
1864MF	**Fizzy Quick**	*You Want It Your Way*	8.1986
		Always	
		Young, Single And Tough	
1865GF	**General Kane**	*Crack Killed Applejack*	8.1986
		Applejack's Theme	
1866MF	**Lionel Richie**	*Love Will Conquer All*	9.1986
		The Only One	
1867GF	**El DeBarge**	*Someone*	10.1986
		Stop! Don't Tease Me	
1868TF	**Smokey Robinson**	*Love Will Set You Free*	10.1986
		Love Will Set You Free (instr.)	
1869MF	**Bunny DeBarge**	*Save The Best For Me*	12.1986
	Bunny DeBarge with DeBarge	*Life Begins With You*	
1870MF	**Billy Preston**	*Since I Held You Close*	10.1986
		It Don't Get Better Than This	
1871GF	**The Temptations**	*To Be Continued . . .*	11.1986
		You're The One	
1872GF	**General Kane**	*Hairdooz*	11.1986
		Cuttin' It Up	
1873MF	**Lionel Richie**	*Deep River Woman*	11.1986
		Ballerina Girl	
1874MF	**Stacy Lattisaw**	*Jump Into My Life*	12.1986
		Long Shot	
1875MF	**Chico DeBarge**	*The Girl Next Door*	2.1987
		You're Much Too Fast	
1876MF	**Bruce Willis**	*Respect Yourself*	12.1986
		Fun Time	
1877TF	**Smokey Robinson**	*Just To See Her*	2.1987
		I'm Gonna Love You Like There's No Tomorrow	
1878MF	**Blake & Hines**	*Sherry*	1.1987
		Movie Queen	
1879GF	**General Kane**	*Can't Let Go*	2.1987
		Cuttin' It Up	
1880MF	**F.G.O.**	*Nice Girls*	NR
		That's The One Who Loves You	
1881GF	**The Temptations**	*Someone*	3.1987
		Love Me Right	
1882MF	**Georgio**	*Sexappeal*	2.1987
		Sexappeal (instr.)	
1883MF	**Lionel Richie**	*Se La*	3.1987
		Serves You Right	
1884MF	**Angela Cole**	*L-O-V-E (Love)*	5.1987
		Turn Up The Beat	
1885MF	**Carrie McDowell**	*Casual Sex*	3.1987
		Prove It	
1886MF	**Bruce Willis**	*Young Blood*	3.1987
		Flirting With Disaster	
1887MF	**Darryl Duncan**	*Rock The House*	4.1987
		Rock The House (instr.)	
1888MF	**F.G.O.**	*I'll Be Around*	NR
		That's The One Who Loves You	
1889MF	**Kim O'Leary**	*Put The Pieces Back*	4.1987
		The Kids Downtown	
1890M	**Chico DeBarge**	*I Like My Body*	4.1987
		You're Much Too Fast	
1891M	**Stacy Lattisaw**	*Take Me All The Way*	NR
		(B side not selected)	
1892M	**Georgio**	*Tina Cherry*	5.1987
		Menage À Trois	
1893M	**Blake & Hines**	*Road Dog*	4.1987
		Big Beat	
1894M	**Family Dream**	*Rescue Me*	4.1987
		Rescue Me (instr.)	
1895M	**The Superiors**	*Step By Step*	6.1987
		Step By Step (instr.)	
1896M	**Bruce Willis**	*Under The Boardwalk*	5.1987
		Jackpot (Bruno's Bop)	
1897M	**Smokey Robinson**	*One Heartbeat*	5.1987
		Love Will Set You Free (Theme from 'Solarbabies')	
1898M	**Wilson Pickett**	*Don't Turn Away*	6.1987
		Can't Stop Now	
1899M	**Gung Ho**	*Play To Win*	7.1987
		Ike Gung Ho	
1900M	**Chris Rea**	*Let's Dance*	7.1987
		I Don't Care Any More	
1901M	**General Kane**	*Girl Pulled The Dog*	6.1987
		Cuttin' It Up	
1902M	**Bruce Willis**	*Secret Agent Man (James Bond Is Back)*	NR
		Lose Myself	
1903M	**Carrie McDowell**	*Uh, Uh, No No Casual Sex (Part 1)*	6.1987
		Uh Uh, No No Casual Sex (Part 2)	
1904M	**Garry Glenn**	*Do You Have To Go*	7.1987
		Lonely Night	
1905M	**Ada Dyer**	*I Bet Ya, I'll Let Ya*	8.1987
		I Bet Ya, I'll Let Ya (instr.)	
1906M	**Georgio**	*Lover's Lane*	8.1987
		I Won't Change	
1907M	**Stevie Wonder**	*Skeletons* (CD: 1907-MD)	
		Skeletons (instr.)	9.1987
1908M	**Temptations**	*I Wonder Who She's Seeing Now*	8.1987
		Girls (They Like It)	

1909M	Chico DeBarge	I've Been Watching You	8.1987
		If It Takes All Night	
1910M	Carrie McDowell	When A Woman Loves A Man	9.1987
		The Tracks Of My Tears	
1911M	Smokey Robinson	What's Too Much	9.1987
		I've Made Love To You A Thousand Times	
1912M	Stacy Lattisaw	Every Drop Of Your Love	12.1987
		Longshot	
1913M	El DeBarge	Real Love	TBA
	El DeBarge with DeBarge	Love Me In A Special Way	
1914M	Michael Jackson	Twenty-Five Miles	10.1987
	Michael Jackson with Jackson 5	Up On The House Top	
1915M	General Kane	House Party	10.1987
		Can't Let Go	
1916M	Wilson Pickett	In The Midnight Hour	10.1987
		Just Let Her Know	
1917	—	—	—
1918M	Garry Glenn *featuring Sheila Hutchinson	Feels Good To Feel Good*	11.1987
		You Don't Even Know	
1919M	Stevie Wonder	You Will Know	12.1987
		You Will Know (instr.)	
1920M	The Temptations	Look What You Started	12.1987
		More Love, Your Love	
1921M	Georgio	Bedrock	NR
		¼ 2 9	
1922M	Chico DeBarge	Rainy Night	12.1987
		Desperate	
1923M	Brownmark	Next Time	12.1987
		Stakeout	
1924M	Darryl Duncan	James Brown (Part 1)	12.1987
		James Brown (Part 2)	
1925M	Smokey Robinson	Love Don't Give No Reason	12.1987
		Hanging On By A Thread	
1926M	Magic Lady	Wait A Minute	NR
		Wait A Minute (instr.)	

12 INCH SINGLES (M)

00001	The Originals	Down To Love Town	11.1976
	Jermaine Jackson	Let's Be Young Tonight	
00002	Thelma Houston	Don't Leave Me This Way	12.1976
	Commodores	Fancy Dancer	
00003	Eddie Kendricks	Goin' Up In Smoke	12.1976
	Willie Hutch	Shake It, Shake It	
00004	Smokey Robinson	Vitamin U	6.1977
	Jerry Butler	Chalk It Up	
00005	Syreeta	One To One	4.1977
	Jennifer	Do It For Me	
00006	Eddie Kendricks	Born Again	4.1977
	21st Creation	Tailgate	
00007	Commodores	Brick House (d/s)	9.1977
00008	Carl Bean	I Was Born This Way	12.1977
		I Was Born This Way (instr.)	
00009	Ernie Fields Jr	Ride A Wild Horse	2.1978
		As	
00010	Diana Ross	Your Love Is So Good For Me	2.1978
	Thelma Houston	I Can't Go On Living Without Your Love	
00011	Diana Ross	What You Gave Me	12.1978
	Bonnie Pointer	Free Me From My Freedom	
00012	Rick James	High On Your Love Suite	3.1979
		You And I	

00013	Thelma Houston	Saturday Night, Sunday Morning	3.1979
		Saturday Night, Sunday Morning (instr.)	
00014	Marvin Gaye	A Funky Space Reincarnation	3.1979
		A Funky Space Reincarnation (instr.)	
00015	Diana Ross, Marvin Gaye, Smokey Robinson, Stevie Wonder	Pops, We Love You (d/s)	3.1979
00016	Billy Preston & Syreeta	Go For It	3.1979
		Go For It (instr.)	
00017	Bloodstone	Just Wanna Get The Feel Of It	4.1979
		Just Wanna Get The Feel Of It (instr.)	
00018	Apollo	Astro Disco	3.1979
		Astro Disco (instr.)	
00019	High Inergy	Shoulda Gone Dancin'	3.1979
		Shoulda Gone Dancin' (instr.)	
00020	Bonnie Pointer	Heaven Must Have Sent You (revised vers.)	4.1979
		Heaven Must Have Sent You (album vers.)	
00021	Tata Vega	I Just Keep Thinking About You Baby	4.1979
		Get It Up For Love	
00022	Mandré	Spirit Groove	4.1979
		Freakin's Fine	
00023	Finished Touch	The Down Sound	5.1979
		Need To Know You Better	
00024	Teena Marie	I'm A Sucker For Your Love	5.1979
		I'm A Sucker For Your Love (instr.)	
00025	Switch	Best Beat In Town	5.1979
		We Like To Party . . . Come On	
00026	Diana Ross	The Boss	5.1979
		Lovin', Livin' And Givin'	
00027	Smokey Robinson	Get Ready	5.1979
		Get Ready (instr.)	
00028	Shadee	I Just Need More Money	6.1979
		I Just Need More Money (instr.)	
00029	Platinum Hook	Give Me Time To Say	6.1979
		Standing On The Verge (Of Gettin' It On)	
00030	Mira Waters	You Have Inspired Me (d/s)	6.1979
00031	Kenny Lupper	Heartache	NR
		—	
00032	Sterling	Roll-Her, Skater	8.1979
		Roll-Her, Skater (instr.)	
00033	Mary Wilson	Red Hot	10.1979
		Midnight Dancer	
00034	Clifton Dyson	Body In Motion (Want Your Body In Motion With Mine)	2.1980
		You Gotta Keep Dancin'	
00035	Diana Ross & the Supremes	Medley Of Hits	2.1980
	Diana Ross	No-one Gets The Prize/The Boss	
00036	Gary Byrd	(You Wear) The Crown	NR
		(You Wear) The Crown (instr.)	

M3500 Series:

35000	Teena Marie	Square Biz	7.1981
		Square Biz (instr.)	
35001	Rick James	Give It To Me Baby	7.1981
		Give It To Me Baby (instr.)	
35002	Rick James	Super Freak (ext. vers.)	10.1981
		Super Freak (album vers.)	

Suffix MG unless otherwise stated

| 4500 | Captain Funkercise | Funkercise | NR |
| | | Funkercise (instr.) | |

4501	**Willie Hutch**	*In And Out*	9.1982
		Brother's Gonna Work It Out	
4502	**Bobby Nunn**	*She's Just A Groupie*	9.1982
		She's Just A Groupie (instr.)	
4503	**Dazz Band**	*Let It Whip*	9.1982
		Let It Whip (instr.)	
4504	**Ozone**	*Li'l Suzy*	9.1982
		Li'l Suzy (instr.)	
4505	**Smokey Robinson**	*Greatest Hits Medley*	10.1982
		The Only Game In Town	
4506	**High Inergy**	*He's A Pretender*	2.1983
		He's A Pretender (instr.)	
4507WG	**Gary Byrd & the G.B. Experience**	*You Wear The Crown*	6.1983
		You Wear The Crown (instr.)	
4508	**Stone City Band**	*Bad Lady*	5.1983
		Bad Lady (instr.)	
4509	**Mary Jane Girls**	*Candy Man* (ext. vers.)	6.1983
		Candy Man (short vers./instr.)	
4510	**Four Tops & The Temptations Jackson 5**	*Medley Of Hits*	6.1983
		Medley Of Hits	
4511	**Rick James**	*Cold Blooded*	7.1983
		Cold Blooded (instr.)	
4512	**Jr Walker**	*Blow The House Down*	8.1983
		Blow The House Down (instr.)	
4513	**The Motor City Crew**	*Let's Break*	8.1983
		Let's Break (instr.)/*Scratch Break (Glove Style)*	
4514	**Lionel Richie**	*All Night Long (All Night)*	10.1983
		All Night Long (All Night) (instr.)	
4515	**Rockwell**	*Somebody's Watching Me*	12.1983
		Somebody's Watching Me (instr.)	
4516	**Keith & Darrell**	*Work That Body*	12.1983
		Work That Body (instr.)	
4517	**Stevie Wonder Rev. Martin Luther King**	*Happy Birthday*	11.1983
		Greatest Excerpts From His Speeches	
4518	**Bobby King**	*Lovequake*	2.1984
		Midnight Shine	
4519	**Sammy Davis Jr**	*Hello Detroit*	5.1984
		Hello Detroit (instr.)	
4520	**Dazz Band**	*Swoop (I'm Yours)*	4.1984
		Joystick	
4521	**Smokey Robinson**	*And I Don't Love You*	6.1984
		And I Don't Love You (instr.)	
4522	**Rick James**	*17*	7.1984
		17 (instr.)	
4523	**Sam Harris**	*Sugar Don't Bite* (revised dance mix)	9.1984
		Sugar Don't Bite (dance mix/instr.)	
4524	**Dazz Band**	*Let It All Blow* (ext. vers.)	9.1984
		Let It All Blow (instr.)	
4525	**Bruni Pagan**	*You Turn Me On*	12.1984
		You Turn Me On (instr.)	
4526	**Vanity**	*Pretty Mess* (ext. vers.)	10.1984
		Mechanical Emotion (ext. vers.) (picture disc)	
4527	**Stevie Wonder**	*Don't Drive Drunk*	12.1984
		Don't Drive Drunk (instr.)/*Did I Hear You Say You Love Me*	
4528	**Rick James**	*Can't Stop*	3.1985
		Oh What A Night (4 luv)	
4529	**Mary Jane Girls**	*In My House*	2.1985
		In My House (instr.)	
4530	**Alfie**	*Star*	2.1985
		Keep On Smilin'	
4531	**Rockwell**	*Peeping Tom*	2.1985
		Tokyo (instr.)	
4532	**DeBarge**	*Rhythm Of The Night*	2.1985
		Queen Of My Heart	
4533	**Commodores**	*Nightshift* (edited mix)	2.1985
		Nightshift (club mix/instr.)	

4534	**Willie Hutch**	*The Glow*	4.1985
		Keep On Jammin'	
4535	**Commodores**	*Animal Instinct* (club mix)	4.1985
		Lightin' Up The Night	
4536	**Michael Lovesmith**	*Love In The Combat Zone*	NR
		Diamond In The Raw	
4537	**Michael Lovesmith**	*Break The Ice* (dance mix)	5.1985
		Lucky in Love	
4538GG	**Val Young**	*Mind Games*	NR
		Mind Games (instr.)	
4539GG	**Rick James**	*Glow*	5.1985
		Glow (reprise)/*Glow* (instr.)	
4540GG	**Mary Jane Girls**	*Wild And Crazy Love*	NR
		Wild And Crazy Love (instr.)	
4541GG	**Mary Jane Girls**	*Wild And Crazy Love* (club mix)	6.1985
		Wild And Crazy Love (ext. vocal/instr.)	
4542	**Maureen Steele**	*Boys Will Be Boys* (club mix)	6.1985
		Rock My Heart (dub mix)/*Boys Will Be Boys* (edit)	
4543	**Dazz Band**	*Hot Spot* (club mix)	6.1985
		I've Been Waiting	
4544GG	**Val Young**	*Seduction*	9.1985
		Seduction (instr.)	
4545GG	**El DeBarge with DeBarge**	*You Wear It Well*	8.1985
		Baby Won't Cha Come Quick	
4546	**Mello-Mackin-D & Mr. Stretch**	*Back To School* (dance mix)	9.1985
		Back To School (ext. mix/instr.)	
4547GG	**Mary Jane Girls**	*Break It Up*	9.1985
		Break It Up (instr.)	
4548TG	**Stevie Wonder**	*Part-Time Lover*	9.1985
		Part-Time Lover (instr.)	
4549	**Michael Lovesmith**	*Ain't Nothin' Like It*	NR
		—	
4550GG	**The Temptations**	*Do You Really Love Your Baby* (club mix/radio edit)	10.1985
		I'll Keep My Light In My Window	
4551TG	**Smokey Robinson**	*Love Got In The Way*	NR
		—	
4552GG	**El DeBarge with DeBarge**	*The Heart Is Not So Smart* (club mix/radio edit)	10.1985
		Share My World	
4553TG	**Stevie Wonder**	*Go Home*	11.1985
		Go Home (instr.)	
4554	**Roq-in'Zoo**	*Frig-o-rator* (club mix)	11.1985
		Frig-o-rator (dub mix/edit)	
4555	**Warp 9**	*Skips A Beat* (club mix/radio edit)	12.1985
		Skips A Beat (dub/fly dub)	
4556	**Sam Harris**	*I'd Do It All Again* (head mix)	12.1985
		I'd Do It All Again (foot mix)/*The Rescue*	
4557GG	**Val Young**	*If You Should Ever Be Lonely* (club mix)	12.1985
		If You Should Ever Be Lonely (edit/street mix)	
4558	**Vanity**	*Under The Influence* (mid-day mix/vocal)	2.1986
		Under The Influence (early morning/late night mix/vocal)/*Wild Animal*	
4559GG	**El DeBarge**	*Who's Johnny*	NR
		—	
4560	**Sam Harris**	*The Bells*	5.1986
		Forever For You	
4561GG	**Rick James**	*Sweet And Sexy Thing*	6.1986
		Sweet And Sexy Thing (instr./vocal)	
4562	**Burston & Littlejohn**	*Rich And Famous*	6.1986
		Rich And Famous (7" vers./instr.)	
4563	**Stacy Lattisaw**	*Nail It To The Wall*	8.1986
		Nail It To The Wall (instr./edit)	
4564	**Lionel Richie**	*Dancing On The Ceiling*	6.1986
		Love Will Find A Way	

4565GG	Rick James	Forever And A Day	8.1986
		Forever And A Day (instr.)	
4566	Rockwell	Grow Up	8.1986
		Grow Up (dub/rhythm mix)	
4567	Chico DeBarge	Talk To Me	8.1986
		If It Takes All Night	
4568GG	General Kane	Crack Killed Applejack	8.1986
		Applejack's Theme (club mix)	
4569	Lionel Richie	Love Will Conquer All	10.1986
		The Only One	
4570	Billy Preston	Since I Held You Close	10.1986
		Since I Held You Close (instr.)/It Don't Get Better Than This	
4571GG	General Kane	Hairdooz	11.1986
		Hairdooz (7"/instr.)/Cuttin' It Up	
4572	Chico DeBarge	The Girl Next Door	2.1987
		The Girl Next Door (7"/dub)/You're Much Too Fast	
4573	—	—	—
4574	Stacy Lattisaw	Jump Into My Life	12.1986
		Jump Into My Life (7"/dub)/Long Shot	
4575	Bunny DeBarge	Save The Best For Me	1.1987
		Save The Best For Me (7"/dub)/Life Begins With You	
4576	Blake & Hines	Sherry	1.1987
		Sherry (7"/dub)/Movie Queen	
4577	F.G.O.	Nice Girls	3.1987
		Nice Girls (12"/dub/a capella/That's The One Who Loves You	
4578	Lionel Richie	Se La	NR
		Se La/Serves You Right	
4579MG	Georgio	Sex Appeal	NR
		Sex Appeal (instr.)	
4580MG	Carrie McDowell	Casual Sex (12 & 7")	3.1987
		Casual Sex (instr.)/Prove It	
4581MG	Darryl Duncan	Rock The House	4.1987
		Rock The House (instr.)	
4582MG	Chico DeBarge	I Like My Body (ex. vers./movie mix)	4.1987
		I Like My Body (dub mix)/You're Much Too Fast	
4583MG	The Superiors	Step By Step	6.1987
		Step By Step (dub vers./s.v.)	
4584MG	Catch	—	NR
4585MG	Family Dream	Rescue Me (l.v./s.v.)	4.1987
		Rescue Me (dub/club mix)	
4586MG	Georgio	Tina Cherry (club/dub mix)	5.1987
		Tina Cherry (radio mix/bonus beats)–Menage A Trois	
4587MG	Voyage	Strange Situation	NR
4588MG	General Kane	Girl Pulled The Dog	6.1987
		Girl Pulled The Dog (s.v./ext. and dub)/Cuttin' It Up	
4589MG	Gung Ho	Play To Win	NR
		Ike Gung Ho	
4590MG	The Temptations	Papa Was A Rollin' Stone (vocal remix)	NR
		Papa Was A Rollin' Stone (dub remix)	
4591MG	Bruce Willis	Secret Agent Man (James Bond Is Back)	NR
		—	
4592MG	Georgio	Lover's Lane (club/dub mix)	8.1987
		Georgio's Love Dance Mix (after hours mix)/I Won't Change	
4593MG	Stevie Wonder	Skeletons	10.1987
		Skeletons (instr.)	
4594MG	Chico DeBarge	I've Been Watching You (ext./dub mix)	9.1987
		If It Takes All Night/I've Been Watching You (s.v.)	

4595MG	—	—	—
4596MG	Wilson Pickett	In The Midnight Hour (7" dub mix)	NR
		In The Midnight Hour (7")/Straight Pass	
4597MG	General Kane	House Party (ext./dub vers.)	11.1987
		Can't Let Go/House Party (7" vers.)	
4598MG	The Temptations	Look What You Started (12" vocal/radio edit)	12.1987
		Look What You Started (12" Piano dub/12" beat Acapella)/More Love Your Love	
4599MG	Darryl Duncan	James Brown	12.1987
		J-J-J-Ja-Ja James Brown	
4600MG	Smokey Robinson	Love Don't Give No Reason (4 versions)	2.1988
		Hangin' On By A Thread	
4601MG	Brownmark	Next Time (5 versions)	2.1988
		Stakeout	
4602MG	Ada Dyer	I Bet Ya, I'll Let Ya (4 mixes)	2.1988
4603MG	Georgio	Bedrock (3 versions)	2.1988

GORDY LABEL

7001	The Temptations	Dream Come True	3.1962
		Isn't She Pretty	
7002	Lee & the Leopards	Come Into My Palace	4.1962
		Trying To Make It	
7003	Valadiers	Because I Love Her	5.1962
		While I'm Away	
7004	Hattie Littles	Back in My Arms Again	NR
		Is It Love	
7005	The Contours	Do You Love Me	6.1962
		Move Mr Man	
7006	Mike & the Modifiers	I Found Myself A Brand New Baby	7.1962
		It's Too Bad	
7007	Hattie Littles	Here You Come	1.1963
		Your Love Is Wonderful	
7008	Bob Kayli	Hold On Pearl	—
		Toodle Loo	
7009	LaBrenda Ben & the Beljeans	Camel Walk	NR
		The Chaperone	
7010	The Temptations	Paradise	10.1962
		Slow Down Heart	
7011	Martha & the Vandellas	I'll Have To Let Him Go	9.1962
		My Baby Won't Come Back	
7012	The Contours	Shake Sherry	11.1962
		You Better Get In Line	
7013	The Valadiers	I Found A Girl	1.1963
		You'll Be Sorry Someday	
7014	Martha & the Vandellas	Come And Get These Memories	2.1963
		Jealous Lover	
7015	The Temptations	I Want A Love I Can See	3.1963
		The Further You Look, The Less You See	
7016	The Contours	Don't Let Her Be Your Baby	3.1963
		It Must Be Love	
7017	Bunny Paul	I'm Hooked	5.1963
		We're Only Young Once	
7018	The Stylers	Going Steady Anniversary	5.1963
		Pushing Up Daisies	
7019	The Contours	You Get Ugly	6.1963
		Pa, I Need A Car	
7020	The Temptations	Farewell My Love	6.1963
		May I Have This Dance	
7021	LaBrenda Ben	Just Be Yourself	8.1963
		I Can't Help It, I've Got To Dance	
7022	Martha & the Vandellas	Heatwave	7.1963
		A Love Like Yours (Don't Come Knocking Every Day)	

No.	Artist	Titles	Date
7023	Liz Lands & the Voices Of Salvation / Rev Martin Luther King	We Shall Overcome / I Have A Dream	12.1963
7024	The Darnells	Too Hurt To Cry, Too Much In Love To Say Goodbye / Come On Home	11.1963
7025	Martha & the Vandellas	Quicksand / Darling I Hum Our Song	11.1963
7026	Liz Lands	May What He Live For, Live / He's Got The Whole World In His Hands	12.1963
7027	Martha & the Vandellas	Livewire / Old Love (Let's Try It Again)	1.1964
7028	The Temptations	The Way You Do The Things You Do / Just Let Me Know	1.1964
7029	The Contours	Can You Do It? / I'll Stand By You	2.1964
7030	Liz Lands & The Temptations	Keep Me / Midnight Johnny	3.1964
7031	Martha & the Vandellas	In My Lonely Room / A Tear For The Girl	3.1964
7032	The Temptations	I'll Be In Trouble / The Girl's Alright With Me	4.1964
7033	Martha & the Vandellas	Dancing In The Street / There He Is (At My Door)	7.1964
7034	Tommy Good	Baby I Miss You / Leaving Here	7.1964
7035	The Temptations	(Girl) Why You Wanna Make Me Blue / Baby Baby, I Need You	8.1964
7036	Martha & the Vandellas	Wild One / Dancing Slow	11.1964
7037	The Contours	Can You Jerk Like Me? / That Day When She Needed Me	11.1964
7038	The Temptations	My Girl / (Talking 'Bout) Nobody But My Baby	12.1964
7039	Martha & the Vandellas	Nowhere To Run / Motoring	2.1965
7040	The Temptations	It's Growing / What Love Has Joined Together	3.1965
7041	Kim Weston	A Thrill A Moment / I'll Never See My Love Again	4.1965
7042	Marv Johnson	Why Do You Want To Let Me Go / I'm Not A Plaything	5.1965
7043	The Temptations	Since I Lost My Baby / You've Got To Earn It	6.1965
7044	The Contours	First I Look At The Purse / Searching For A Girl	6.1965
7045	Martha & the Vandellas	You've Been In Love Too Long / Love (Makes Me Do Foolish Things)	7.1965
7046	Kim Weston	Take Me In Your Arms (Rock Me A Little While) / Don't Compare Me With Her	9.1965
7047	The Temptations	My Baby / Don't Look Back	9.1965
7048	Martha & the Vandellas	My Baby Loves Me / Never Leave Your Baby's Side	1.1966
7049	The Temptations	Get Ready / Fading Away	2.1966
7050	Kim Weston	Helpless / A Love Like Yours (Don't Come Knocking Every Day)	2.1966
7051	Marv Johnson	I Miss You Baby (How I Miss You) / Just The Way You Are	3.1966
7052	The Contours	Just a Little Misunderstanding / Determination	4.1966
7053	Martha & the Vandellas	What Am I Going To Do Without Your Love / Go Ahead And Laugh	5.1966
7054	The Temptations	Ain't Too Proud To Beg / You'll Lose A Precious Love	5.1966
7055	The Temptations	Beauty Is Only Skin Deep / You're Not An Ordinary Girl	8.1966
7056	Martha & the Vandellas	I'm Ready For Love / He Doesn't Love Her Anymore	10.1966
7057	The Temptations	(I Know) I'm Losing You / I Couldn't Cry If I Wanted To	11.1966
7058	Martha & the Vandellas	Jimmy Mack / Third Finger, Left Hand	2.1967
7059	The Contours	It's So Hard Being A Loser / Your Love Grows More Precious Every Day	3.1967
7060	The San Remo Golden Strings	Festival Time / Joy Road	4.1967
7061	The Temptations	All I Need / Sorry Is A Sorry Word	4.1967
7062	Martha Reeves & the Vandellas	Love Bug Leave My Heart Alone / One Way Out	8.1967
7063	The Temptations	You're My Everything / I've Been Good To You	6.1967
7064	Rita Wright	I Can't Give Back The Love I Feel For You / Something On My Mind	1.1968
7065	The Temptations	(Loneliness Made Me Realise) It's You That I Need / Don't Send Me Away	9.1967
7066	Edwin Starr	I Want My Baby Back / Gonna Keep On Trying Till I Win Your Love	10.1967
7067	Martha Reeves & the Vandellas	Honey Chile / Show Me The Way	10.1967
7068	The Temptations	I Wish It Would Rain / I Truly, Truly Believe	12.1967
7069	Bobby Taylor & the Vancouvers	Does Your Mama Know About Me / Fading Away	2.1968
7070	Martha Reeves & the Vandellas	I Promise To Wait My Love / Forget Me Not	4.1968
7071	Edwin Starr	I Am The Man For You Baby / My Weakness Is You	3.1968
7072	The Temptations	I Could Never Love Another (After Loving You) / Gonna Give Her All The Love I've Got	4.1968
7073	Bobby Taylor & the Vancouvers	I Am Your Man / If You Love Her	6.1968
7074	The Temptations	Please Return Your Love To Me / How Can I Forget	7.1968
7075	Martha Reeves & the Vandellas	I Can't Dance To That Music Your Playing / I Tried	7.1968
7076	Eivets Rednow	Alfie / More Than A Dream	8.1968
7077	Marv Johnson	I'll Pick A Rose For My Rose / You Got The Love I Love	10.1968
7078	Edwin Starr	Way Over There / If My Heart Could Tell The Story	10.1968
7079	Bobby Taylor & the Vancouvers	Malinda / It's Growing	10.1968
7080	Martha Reeves & the Vandellas	Sweet Darlin' / Without You	10.1968
7081	The Temptations	Cloud Nine / Why Did She Have To Leave Me (Why Did She Have To Go)	10.1968
7082	The Temptations	Rudolph The Red-Nose Reindeer / Silent Night	11.1968
7083	Edwin Starr	Twenty Five Miles / Love Is My Destination	1.1969
7084	The Temptations	Runaway Child, Running Wild / I Need Your Lovin'	1.1969
7085	Martha Reeves & the Vandellas	(We've Got) Honey Love / I'm In Love (And I Know It)	3.1969

7086	The Temptations	Don't Let The Joneses Get You Down	5.1969
		Since I've Lost You	
7087	Edwin Starr	I'm Still A Struggling Man	5.1969
		Pretty Little Angel	
7088	Bobby Taylor	Oh I've Been Blessed	NR
		It Should Have Been Me Loving Her	
7089	—	—	—
7090	Blinky & Edwin Starr	Oh How Happy	7.1969
		Ooo Baby Baby	
7091	—	—	—
7092	Bobby Taylor	My Girl Has Gone	7.1969
		It Should Have Been Me Loving Her	
7093	The Temptations	I Can't Get Next To You	7.1969
		Running Away (Ain't Gonna Help You)	
7094	Martha Reeves & the Vandellas	Taking My Love (And Leaving Me)	8.1969
		Heartless	
7095	Terry Johnson	What'cha Gonna Do	1.1970
		Suzie	
7096	The Temptations	Psychedelic Shack	12.1969
		That's The Way Love Is	
7097	Edwin Starr	Time	1.1970
		Running Back And Forth	
7098	Martha Reeves & the Vandellas	I Should Be Proud	2.1970
		Love, Guess Who	
7099	The Temptations	Ball Of Confusion (That's What The World Is Today)	5.1970
		It's Summer	
7100	Buzzie	Stone Soul Booster	8.1970
		Sandy	
7101	Edwin Starr	War	6.1970
		He Who Picks A Rose	
7102	The Temptations	Ugena Za Ulimwengu (Unite The World)	9.1970
		Hum Along And Dance	
7103	Martha Reeves & the Vandellas	I Gotta Let You Go	10.1970
		You're The Loser Now	
7104	Edwin Starr	Stop The War Now	11.1970
		Gonna Keep On Trying Till I Win Your Love	
7105	The Temptations	Just My Imagination (Running Away With Me)	1.1971
		You Make Your Own Heaven And Hell Right Here On Earth	
7106	The Undisputed Truth	Save My Love For A Rainy Day	2.1971
		Since I've Lost You	
7107	Edwin Starr	Funky Music Sho Nuff Turns Me On	3.1971
		Cloud Nine	
7108	The Undisputed Truth	Smiling Faces Sometimes	5.1971
		You Got The Love I Need	
7109	The Temptations	It's Summer	6.1971
		I'm The Exception To The Rule	
7110	Martha Reeves & the Vandellas	Bless You	9.1971
		Hope I Don't Get My Heart Broke	
7111	The Temptations	Superstar (Remember How You Got Where You Are)	10.1971
		Gonna Keep On Trying Till I Win Your Love	
7112	The Undisputed Truth	You Make Your Own Heaven And Hell Right Here On Earth	11.1971
		Ball Of Confusion (That's What The World Is Today)	
7113	Martha Reeves & the Vandellas	In And Out Of My Life	12.1971
		Your Love Makes It All Worthwhile	
7114	The Undisputed Truth	What It Is	1.1972
		California Soul	
7115	The Temptations	Take A Look Around	2.1972
		Smooth Sailing From Now On	
7116	Eric & the Vikings	It's Too Much For Man To Take Too Long	4.1972
		Time Don't Wait	
7117	The Undisputed Truth	Papa Was A Rollin' Stone	5.1972
		Friendship Train	
7118	Martha Reeves & the Vandellas	Tear It On Down	5.1972
		I Want You Back	
7119	The Temptations	Mother Nature	6.1972
		Funky Music Sho Nuff Turns Me On	
7120	The Festivals	Green Grow The Lilacs	7.1972
		So In Love	
7121	The Temptations	Papa Was A Rollin' Stone (vocal)	9.1972
		Papa Was A Rollin' Stone (instr.)	
7122	The Undisputed Truth	Girl You're Alright	10.1972
		With A Little Help From My Friends	
7123	Jay & Techniques	Robot Man	11.1972
		I'll Be Here	
7124	The Undisputed Truth	Mama I Got A Brand New Thing (Don't Say No)	2.1973
		Gonna Keep On Trying Till I Win Your Love	
7125	Paul Williams	Feel Like Givin' Up	NR
		Once You Had A Heart	
7126	The Temptations	Masterpiece (vocal)	2.1973
		Masterpiece (instr.)	
7127	Martha Reeves	I Won't Be The Fool I've Been Again	NR
		Baby (Don't You Leave Me)	
7128	Luther Allison	The Little Red Rooster	NR
		Raggedy And Dirty	
7129	The Temptations	Plastic Man	5.1973
		Hurry Tomorrow	
7130	The Undisputed Truth	Law Of The Land	6.1973
		Just My Imagination (Running Away With Me)	
7131	The Temptations	Hey Girl (I Like Your Style)	7.1973
		Ma	
7132	Eric & the Vikings	I'm Truly Yours	10.1973
		Where Do You Go (Baby)	
7133	The Temptations	Let Your Hair Down	11.1973
		Ain't No Justice	
7134	The Undisputed Truth	Help Yourself	2.1974
		What's Going On	
7135	The Temptations	Heavenly	2.1974
		Zoom	
7136	The Temptations	You've Got My Soul on Fire	5.1974
		I Need You	
7137	Luther Allison	Now You Got It	5.1974
		Part Time Love	
7138	The Temptations / The Temptations Band	Happy People (vocal)	11.1974
		Happy People (instr.)	
7139	The Undisputed Truth	I'm A Fool For You	6.1974
		The Girl's Alright With Me	
7140	The Undisputed Truth	Lil' Red Ridin' Hood	10.1974
		Big John Is My Name	
7141	The Undisputed Truth	Earthquake Shake	NR
		Spaced Out	
7142	The Temptations	Shakey Ground	2.1975
		I'm A Bachelor	
7143	The Undisputed Truth	UFO's	3.1975
		Got To Get My Hands On Some Lovin'	
7144	The Temptations	Glasshouse	6.1975
		The Prophet	
7145	The Undisputed Truth	Higher Than High	8.1975
		Spaced Out	
7146	The Temptations	Keep Holding On	1.1976
		What You Need Most (I Do Best Of All)	
7147	The Undisputed Truth	Boogie Bump Boogie	10.1975
		I Saw You When You Met Her	
7148	Leon Ware	Comfort	NR
		Share Your Love	

No.	Artist	Title	Date
7149	**Leslie Uggams**	*I Want To Make It Easy For You* / *Two Shoes*	4.1976
7150	**The Temptations**	*Up The Creek (Without A Paddle)* / *Darling, Stand By Me (Song For My Woman)*	4.1976
7151	**The Temptations**	*I'll Take You In* / *Let Me Count The Ways (I Love You)*	NR
7152	**The Temptations**	*Who Are You* / *Let Me Count The Ways (I Love You)*	9.1976
7153	**Franki Kah'rl**	*I'm In Love* / *Don't Fan The Flame*	11.1976
7154	**21st Creation**	*Tailgate* / *Mr Disco Radio*	4.1977
7155	**High Inergy**	*You Can't Turn Me Off (In The Middle Of Turning Me On)* / *Let Me Get Close To You* (originally: *Save It For A Rainy Day*)	8.1977
7156	**Rick James**	*You And I* / *Hollywood*	3.1978
7157	**High Inergy**	*Love Is All You Need* / *Some Kinda Magic*	1.1978
7158	**21st Creation**	*Girls Let's Keep Dancing Close* / *Funk Machine*	3.1978
7159	**Switch**	*There'll Never Be* / *You Pulled A Switch*	6.1978
7160	**High Inergy**	*We Are The Future* / *High School*	4.1978
7161	**High Inergy**	*Lovin' Fever* / *Beware*	8.1978
7162	**Rick James**	*Mary Jane* / *Dream Maker*	9.1978
7163	**Switch**	*I Wanna Be Closer* / *Somebody's Watchin' You*	12.1978
7164	**Rick James**	*High On Your Love Suite* / *Stone City Band, Hi!*	2.1979
7165	**Apollo**	*Astro Disco (Part 1)* / *Astro Disco (Part 2)*	3.1979
7166	**High Inergy**	*Shoulda Gone Dancin'* / *Peaceland*	4.1979
7167	**Rick James**	*Bustin' Out* / *Sexy Lady*	4.1979
7168	**Switch**	*Best Beat in Town* / *It's So Real*	4.1979
7169	**Teena Marie**	*I'm A Sucker For Your Love* / *De Ja Vu (I've Been Here Before)*	4.1979
7170	**Mira Waters**	*You Have Inspired Me* (d/s)	6.1979
7171	**Rick James**	*Fool On The Street* / *Jefferson Ball*	7.1979
7172	**High Inergy**	*Come And Get It* / *Midnight Music Man*	7.1979
7173	**Teena Marie**	*Don't Look Back* / *I'm Gonna Have My Cake (And Eat It Too)*	8.1979
7174	**High Inergy**	*Skate To The Rhythm* / *Midnight Music Man*	9.1979
7175	**Switch**	*I Call Your Name* / *Best Beat In Town* (re-pressed with B-side) *Next To You*	9.1979 / 10.1979
7176	**Rick James**	*Love Gun* / *Stormy Love*	10.1979
7177	**Rick James**	*Come Into My Life (Part 1)* / *Come Into My Live (Part 2)*	1.1980
7178	**High Inergy**	*I Love Makin' Love (To The Music)* / *Somebody, Somewhere*	1.1980
7179	**Stone City Band**	*Strut Your Stuff* / *F.I.M.A. (Funk in Mama Afrika)*	1.1980
7180	**Teena Marie**	*Can It Be Love* / *Too Many Colors (Tee's Interlude)*	1.1980
7181	**Switch**	*Don't Take My Love Away* / *Don't Take My Love Away (instr.)*	4.1980
7182	**Stone City Band**	*Little Runaway* / *South American Sneeze*	4.1980
7183	**The Temptations**	*Power (vocal)* / *Power (instr.)*	4.1980
7184	**Teena Marie**	*Behind The Groove* / *You're All The Boogie I Need*	4.1980
7185	**Rick James**	*Big Time* / *Island Lady*	6.1980
7186	**Mira Waters**	*Rock And Roll Me* / *You're Moving Out Today*	9.1980
7187	**High Inergy**	*Make Me Yours* / *I Love Makin' Love (To The Music)*	6.1980
7188	**The Temptations**	*Struck By Lightning Twice* / *I'm Coming Home*	6.1980
7189	**Teena Marie**	*I Need Your Lovin'* / *Irons In The Fire*	8.1980
7190	**Switch**	*My Friend In The Sky* / *Next To You*	NR
7191	**Rick James**	*Summer Love* / *Gettin' It On (In The Sunshine)*	9.1980
7192	**High Inergy**	*Hold On To My Love* / *If I Love You Tonight*	10.1980
7193	**Switch**	*Love Over And Over Again* / *Keep Movin' On*	10.1980
7194	**Teena Marie**	*Young Love* / *First Class Love*	1.1981
7195	**Stone City Band**	*All Day And All Of The Night* / *All Day And All Of The Night (vamp vers.)*	1.1981
7196	**Nolen & Crossley**	*Messin' Up A Good Thing* / *Face On The Photograph*	3.1981
7197	**Rick James**	*Give It To Me Baby* / *Don't Give Up On Love*	3.1981
7198	**The DeBarges**	*Dance The Night Away*	NR
7199	**Switch**	*You And I* / *Get Back With You*	3.1981
7200	**Stone City Band**	*Freaky* / *Party Girls*	4.1981
7201	**High Inergy**	*I Just Wanna Dance With You* / *Take My Life*	4.1981
7202	**Teena Marie**	*Square Biz* / *Opus III (Does Anybody Care)*	5.1981
7203	**The DeBarges**	*What's Your Name* / *You're So Gentle, So Kind*	5.1981
7204	**Tony Travalini**	*This Is It (This Is My Love)* / *Again*	6.1981
7205	**Rick James**	*Super Freak (Part 1)* / *Super Freak (Part 2)*	7.1981
7206	**Stone City Band**	*Funky Reggae* / *Ganja*	NR
7207	**High Inergy**	*Goin' Thru The Motions* / *I Just Can't Help Myself*	7.1981
7208	**The Temptations**	*Aiming At Your Heart* / *The Life Of A Cowboy*	7.1981
7209	**Nolan & Crossley**	*Chance* / *Into The Groove*	NR
7210	—		—
7211	**High Inergy**	*Don't Park Your Lovin'* / *Now That There's You*	9.1981
7212	**Teena Marie**	*It Must Be Magic* / *Yes Indeed*	9.1981
7213	**The Temptations**	*Oh What A Night* / *Isn't The Night Fantastic*	10.1981
7214	**Switch**	*I Do Love You* / *Without You In My Life*	10.1981
7215	**Rick James**	*Ghetto Life* / *Below The Funk (Pass The J)*	10.1981
7216	**Teena Marie**	*Portuguese Love* / *The Ballad Of Cradle Rob And Me*	10.1981

SOUL LABEL

Cat #	Artist	Titles	Date
35001	**Shorty Long**	Devil With The Blue Dress / Wind It Up	3.1964
35002	**Jimmy Ruffin**	Since I've Lost You / I Want Her Love	7.1964
35003	**Jr Walker & the All Stars**	Satan's Blues / Monkey Jump	8.1964
35004	**Sammy Ward**	You've Got To Change / Bread Winner	8.1964
35005	**Shorty Long**	Out To Get You / It's A Crying Shame (The Way You Treat A Good Man Like Me)	8.1964
35006	**Earl Van Dyke & The Soul Brothers**	Soul Stomp / Hot'n'Tot	9.1964
35007	**Merced Blue Notes**	Thumpin' / Do The Pig	NR
35008	**Jr Walker & the All Stars**	Shotgun / Hot Cha	1.1965
35009	**Earl Van Dyke & The Soul Brothers**	All For You / Too Many Fish In The Sea	2.1965
35010	**Hit Pack**	Never Say No To Your Baby / Let's Dance	3.1965
35011	**The Freeman Brothers**	My Baby / Beautiful Brown Eyes	3.1965
35012	**Jr Walker & the All Stars**	Do The Boomerang / Tune Up	5.1965
35013	**Jr Walker & the All Stars**	Shake And Fingerpop / Cleo's Back	7.1965
35014	**Earl Van Dyke & The Soul Brothers**	I Can't Help Myself / How Sweet It Is (To Be Loved By You)	9.1965
35015	**Jr Walker & the All Stars**	Road Runner / Shoot Your Shot	3.1966
35016	**Jimmy Ruffin**	As Long As There is L-O-V-E Love / How Can I Say I'm Sorry	10.1965
35017	**Jr Walker & the All Stars**	Cleo's Mood / Baby You Know You Ain't Right	12.1965
35018	**Earl Van Dyke & The Soul Brothers**	The Flick (Part 1) / The Flick (Part 2)	11.1965
35019	**Frank Wilson**	Do I Love You (Indeed I Do) / Sweeter As The Days Go By	12.1965
35020	**Frances Nero**	Keep On Loving Me / Fight Fire With Fire	3.1966
35021	**Shorty Long**	Function At The Junction / Call On Me	3.1966
35022	**Jimmy Ruffin**	What Becomes Of The Brokenhearted / Baby I've Got It	6.1966
35023	**Gladys Knight & the Pips**	Just Walk in My Shoes / Stepping Closer to Your Heart	6.1966
35024	**Jr Walker & the All Stars**	How Sweet It Is (To Be Loved By You) / Nothing But Soul	7.1966
35025	**The Velvelettes**	These Things Will Keep Me Loving You / Since You've Been Loving Me	8.1966
35026	**Jr Walker & the All Stars**	Money (That's What I Want) (Part 2) / Money (That's What I Want) (Part 1)	10.1966
35027	**Jimmy Ruffin**	I've Passed This Way Before / Tomorrow's Tears	11.1966
35028	**Earl Van Dyke & the Motown Brass**	Six By Six / There Is No Greater Love	12.1966
35029	**The Originals**	Goodnight Irene / Need Your Lovin' (Want You Back)	12.1966
35030	**Jr Walker & the All Stars**	Pucker Up Buttercup / (Dance) Anyway You Wanna	1.1967
35031	**Shorty Long**	Chantilly Lace / Your Love Is Amazing	1.1967
35032	**Jimmy Ruffin**	Gonna Give Her All The Love I've Got / World So Wide, Nowhere To Hide (From Your Heart)	2.1967
35033	**Gladys Knight & the Pips**	Take Me In Your Arms And Love Me / Do You Love Me Just A Little Honey	3.1967
35034	**Gladys Knight & the Pips**	Everybody Needs Love / Stepping Closer To Your Heart	6.1967
35035	**Jimmy Ruffin**	Don't You Miss Me Just A Little Bit Baby / I Want Her Love	6.1967
35036	**Jr Walker & the All Stars**	Shoot Your Shot / Ain't That The Truth	6.1967
35037	**Messengers**	Window Shopping / California Soul	9.1967
35038	**Barbara Randolph**	I Got A Feeling / You Got Me Hurtin' All Over	9.1967
35039	**Gladys Knight & the Pips**	I Heard It Through The Grapevine / It's Time To Go Now	9.1967
35040	**Shorty Long**	Night Fo' Last (vocal) / Night Fo' Last (instr.)	1.1968
35041	**Jr Walker & the All Stars**	Come See About Me / Sweet Soul	11.1967
35042	**Gladys Knight & the Pips**	The End Of Our Road / Don't Let Her Take Your Love From Me	1.1968
35043	**Jimmy Ruffin**	I'll Say Forever My Love / Everybody Needs Love	2.1968
35044	**Shorty Long**	Here Comes The Judge / Sing What You Wanna	5.1968
35045	**Gladys Knight & the Pips**	It Should Have Been Me / You Don't Love Me No More	5.1968
35046	**Jimmy Ruffin**	Don't Let Him Take Your Love From Me / Lonely Lonely Man Am I	6.1968
35047	**Gladys Knight & the Pips**	I Wish It Would Rain / It's Summer	8.1968
35048	**Jr Walker & the All Stars**	Hip City (Part 2) / Hip City (Part 1)	7.1968
35049	**The Monitors**	Step By Step (Hand In Hand) / Time Is Passin' By	8.1968
35050	**Barbara Randolph**	Can I Get A Witness / You Got Me Hurtin' All Over	8.1968
35051	**Abdullah**	I Comma Zimba Zio (Here I Stand The Mighty One) / Why Them, Why Me?	10.1968
35052	**The Fantastic Four**	I Love You Madly (vocal) / I Love You Madly (instr.)	9.1968
35053	**Jimmy Ruffin**	Gonna Keep On Trying Till I Win Your Love / Sad And Lonesome Feeling	11.1968
35054	**Shorty Long**	I Had A Dream / Ain't No Justice	2.1969
35055	**Jr Walker & the All Stars**	Home Cookin' / Mutiny	12.1968
35056	**The Originals**	We've Got A Way Out Love / You're The One	1.1969
35057	**Gladys Knight & the Pips**	Didn't You Know (You'd Have To Cry Sometime) / Keep An Eye	2.1969
35058	**The Fantastic Four**	I Feel Like I'm Falling In Love / Pin Point It Down	3.1969
35059	**Earl Van Dyke**	Runaway Child, Running Wild / Gonna Give Her All The Love I've Got	3.1969
35060	**Jimmy Ruffin**	If You Will Let Me, I Know I Can / Farewell Is A Lonely Sound	10.1969
35061	**The Originals**	Green Grow The Lilacs / You're The One	5.1969
35062	**Jr Walker & the All Stars**	What Does It Take (To Win Your Love) / Brainwasher Part 1	4.1969

35063	**Gladys Knight & the Pips**	*The Nitty Gritty*	6.1969
		Got Myself A Good Man	
35064	**Shorty Long**	*A Whiter Shade Of Pale*	8.1969
		When You Are Available	
35065	**The Fantastic Four**	*Just Another Lonely Night*	9.1969
		Don't Care Why You Want Me (Long As You Want Me)	
35066	**The Originals**	*Baby I'm For Real*	8.1969
		The Moment Of Truth	
35067	**Jr Walker & the All Stars**	*These Eyes*	10.1969
		Got To Find A Way to Win Maria Back	
35068	**Gladys Knight & the Pips**	*Friendship Train*	10.1969
		Cloud Nine	
35069	**The Originals**	*The Bells*	1.1970
		I'll Wait For You	
35070	**Jr Walker & the All Stars**	*Gotta Hold On To This Feeling*	1.1970
		Clinging To The Thought She's Coming Back	
35071	**Gladys Knight & the Pips**	*You Need Love Like I Do (Don't You)*	3.1970
		You're My Everything	
35072	**The Fantastic Four**	*On The Brighter Side Of A Blue World*	4.1970
		I'm Gonna Carry On	
35073	**Jr Walker & the All Stars**	*Do You See My Love (For You Growing)*	6.1970
		Groove And Move	
35074	**The Originals**	*We Can Make It Baby*	7.1970
		I Like Your Style	
35075	**Yvonne Fair**	*Stay A Little Longer*	7.1970
		We Shall Never Be Lonely My Love	
35076	**David & Jimmy Ruffin**	*Stand By Me*	9.1970
		Your Love Was Worth Waiting For	
35077	**Jimmy Ruffin**	*Maria (You Were The Only One)*	12.1970
		Living In A World I Created For Myself	
35078	**Gladys Knight & the Pips**	*If I Were Your Woman*	10.1970
		The Tracks Of My Tears	
35079	**The Originals**	*God Bless Whoever Sent You*	11.1970
		Desperate Young Man	
35080	**Joe Hilton**	*Let's All Save The Children*	1.1971
		You Are Blue	
35081	**Jr Walker & the All Stars**	*Holly Holy*	11.1970
		Carry Your Own Load	
35082	**David & Jimmy Ruffin**	*When My Love Hand Comes Down*	3.1971
		Steppin' On A Dream	
35083	**Gladys Knight & the Pips**	*I Don't Want To Do Wrong*	5.1971
		Is There A Place In His Heart For Me	
35084	**Jr Walker & the All Stars**	*Take Me Girl I'm Ready*	7.1971
		Right On Brothers And Sisters	
35085	**The Originals**	*Keep Me*	7.1971
		A Man Without Love	
35086	**David & Jimmy Ruffin**	*Lo And Behold*	NR
		The Things We Have To Do	
35087	**Popcorn Wylie**	*Funky Rubber Band* (vocal)	8.1971
		Funky Rubber Band (instr.)	
35088	**Jack Hamer**	*Color Combination*	9.1971
		Swim	
35089	**Blinky**	*How You Gonna Keep It (After You Get It)*	NR
		This Time Last Summer	
35090	**Jr Walker & the All Stars**	*Way Back Home* (vocal)	11.1971
		Way Back Home (instr.)	
35091	**Gladys Knight & the Pips**	*Make Me The Woman That You Go Home To*	11.1971
		It's All Over But The Shoutin'	
35092	**Jimmy Ruffin**	*Our Favorite Melody*	1.1972
		You Gave Me Love	
35093	**The Originals**	*I'm Someone Who Cares*	1.1972
		Once I Have You (I Will Never Let You Go)	
35094	**Gladys Knight & the Pips**	*Help Me Make It Through The Night*	3.1972
		If You Gonna Leave (Just Leave)	
35095	**Jr Walker & the All Stars**	*Walk In The Night*	2.1972
		I Don't Want To Do Wrong	
35096	**Edwin Starr**	*Take Me Clear From Here*	3.1972
		Ball Of Confusion (That's What The World Is Today)	
35097	**Jr Walker & the All Stars**	*Groove Thang*	6.1972
		Me And My Family	
35098	**Gladys Knight & the Pips**	*Neither One Of Us (Wants To Be The First To Say Goodbye)*	12.1972
		Can't Give Up No More	
35099	**Billy Proctor**	*What Is Black*	7.1972
		I Can Take It All	
35100	**Edwin Starr**	*Who Is The Leader Of The People*	8.1972
		Don't Tell Me I'm Crazy	
35101	**Bob Babbit**	*Gospel Truth*	NR
		Running Like A Rabbit	
35102	**The Originals**	*Be My Love*	4.1973
		Endlessly Love	
35103	**Edwin Starr**	*There You Go* (vocal)	3.1973
		There You Go (instr.)	
35104	**Jr Walker & the All Stars**	*Gimme That Beat (Part 1)*	1.1973
		Gimme That Beat (Part 2)	
35105	**Gladys Knight & the Pips**	*Daddy Could Swear (I Declare)*	4.1973
		For Once In My Life	
35106	**Jr Walker & the All Stars**	*I Don't Need No Reason*	5.1973
		Country Boy	
35107	**Gladys Knight & the Pips**	*All I Need Is Time*	7.1973
		The Only Time You Love Me Is When You're Losing Me	
35108	**Jr Walker & the All Stars**	*Peace And Understanding Is Hard To Find*	7.1973
		Soul Clappin'	
35109	**The Originals**	*There's A Chance When You Love You'll Lose*	9.1973
		First Lady (Sweet Mother's Love)	
35110	**Jr Walker & the All Stars**	*Dancin' Like They Do On Soul Train*	5.1974
		I Ain't That Easy to Lose	
35111	**Gladys Knight & the Pips**	*Between Her Goodbye And My Hello*	5.1974
		This Child Needs Its Father	
35112	**The Originals**	*Supernatural Voodoo Woman (Part 1)*	1.1974
		Supernatural Voodoo Woman (Part 2)	
35113	**The Originals**	*Game Called Love*	5.1974
		Ooh You (Put A Crush On Me)	
35114	**Jr Walker**	*You Are The Sunshine Of My Life*	NR
		Until You Come Back To Me	
35115	**The Originals**	*You're My Only World*	11.1974
		So Near (And Yet So Far)	
35116	**Jr Walker**	*I'm So Glad*	1.1976
		Soul Clappin'	
35117	**The Originals**	*Touch*	4.1976
		Ooh You (Put A Crush On Me)	
35118	**Jr Walker**	*You Ain't No Ordinary Woman*	5.1976
		Hot Shot	
35119	**The Originals**	*Down To Love Town*	7.1976
		Just To Be Close To You	
35120	**Jamal Trice**	*If Love Is Not The Answer (Baby Right Ain't Right)*	11.1976
		Nothing Is Too Good (For You Baby)	
35121	**The Originals**	*Call On Your Six-Million Dollar Man*	NR
		Mother Nature's Best	
35122	**Jr Walker**	*Hard Love*	8.1977
		Whopper Bopper Show Stopper	

35123	**Major Lance**	*I Never Thought I'd Be Losing You*	3.1978
		Chicago Disco	

VIP LABEL

25002	**The Serenaders**	*If Your Heart Says Yes*	1.1964
		I'll Cry Tomorrow	
25003	**Joanne & The Triangles**	*After The Showers Come Flowers*	2.1964
		Don't Be A Cry Baby	
25004	**The Hornets**	*Give Me A Kiss*	2.1964
		She's My Baby	
25005	—	—	—
25006	**Andantes**	*(Like A) Nightmare*	NR
		If You Were Mine	
25007	**The Velvelettes**	*Needle In A Haystack*	9.1964
		Should I Tell Them	
25008	**Oma Heard**	*Lifetime Man*	NR
		My Lonely Heart	
25009	**Mickey McCullers**	*Who You Gonna Run To*	10.1964
		Same Old Story	
25010	—	—	—
25011	**The Headliners**	*Tonight's The Night*	10.1964
		You're Bad News	
25012	**Ray Oddis**	*Randy The Newspaper Boy*	11.1964
		Happy Ghoul Tide	
25013	**The Velvelettes**	*He Was Really Saying Something*	12.1964
		Throw A Farewell Kiss	
25014	—	—	—
25015	—	—	—
25016	**The Vows**	*Buttered Popcorn*	5.1965
		Tell Me	
25017	**The Velvelettes**	*Lonely Lonely Girl Am I*	5.1965
		I'm The Exception To The Rule	
25018	**The Lewis Sisters**	*He's An Oddball*	5.1965
		By Some Chance	
25019	**Danny Day**	*This Time Last Summer*	NR
		Please Don't Turn The Lights Out	
25020	**The Isley Brothers**	*I Hear A Symphony*	NR
		Who Could Ever Doubt My Love	
25021	**The Velvelettes**	*A Bird In The Hand (Is Worth Two In The Bush)*	NR
		Since You've Been Loving Me	
25022	**Richard Anthony**	*I Don't Know What To Do*	8.1965
		What Now My Love	
25023	**Little Lisa**	*Hang On Bill*	8.1965
		Puppet On A String	
25024	**The Lewis Sisters**	*You Need Me*	8.1965
		Moonlight On The Beach	
25025	**The Dalton Boys**	*I've Been Cheated*	10.1965
		Something's Bothering You	
25026	**The Headliners**	*We Call It Fun*	10.1965
		Voodoo Plan	
25027	**R. Dean Taylor**	*Let's Go Somewhere*	10.1965
		Poor Girl	
25028	**The Monitors**	*Say You*	11.1965
		All For Someone	
25029	**The Elgins**	*Put Yourself In My Place*	12.1965
		Darling Baby	
25030	**The Velvelettes**	*A Bird In The Hand (Is Worth Two In The Bush)*	11.1965
		Since You've Been Loving Me	
25031	**Chris Clark**	*Do Right Baby, Do Right*	12.1965
		Don't Be Too Long	
25032	**The Monitors**	*Greetings (This Is Uncle Sam)*	2.1966
		Number One In Your Heart	
25033	—	—	—
25034	**The Velvelettes**	*These Things Will Keep Me Loving You*	NR
		Since You've Been Loving Me	
25035	**Rick, Robin & Him**	*Three Choruses of Despair*	6.1966
		'Cause You Know Me	

25036	**The LaSalles**	*This Is True*	6.1966
		La La La La La	
25037	**The Elgins**	*Heaven Must Have Sent You*	8.1966
		Stay In My Lonely Arms	
25038	**Chris Clark**	*Love's Gone Bad*	7.1966
		Put Yourself In My Place	
25039	**The Monitors**	*Since I Lost You Girl*	12.1966
		Don't Put Off Till Tomorrow What You Can Do Today	
25040	**The Underdogs**	*Love's Gone Bad*	1.1967
		Mo Jo Hanna	
25041	**Chris Clark**	*I Want To Go Back There Again*	2.1967
		I Love You	
25042	**R. Dean Taylor**	*There's A Ghost In My House*	3.1967
		Don't Fool Around	
25043	**The Elgins**	*It's Been A Long Long Time*	6.1967
		I Understand My Man	
25044	**Debbie Dean**	*Why Am I Loving You*	2.1968
		Stay My Love	
25045	**R. Dean Taylor**	*Gotta See Jane*	4.1968
		Don't Fool Around	
25046	**The Monitors**	*Bring Back The Love*	4.1968
		The Further You Look The Less You See	
25047	**The Honest Men**	*Cherie*	4.1969
		Baby	
25048	—	—	—
25049	—	—	—
25050	**The Spinners**	*In My Diary*	10.1969
		(She's Gonna Love Me) At Sundown	
25051	**The Lollipops**	*Cheating Is Telling On You*	10.1969
		Need Your Love	
25052	**Chuck Jackson**	*Baby I'll Get It*	11.1969
		The Day My World Stood Still	
25053	**Bobby Taylor**	*Blackmail*	1.1970
		Oh I've Been Blessed	
25054	**The Spinners**	*Message From A Blackman*	2.1970
		(She's Gonna Love Me) At Sundown	
25055	**Ivy Jo**	*I Remember When (Dedicated To Beverly)*	3.1970
		Sorry Is A Sorry Word	
25056	**Chuck Jackson**	*Let Somebody Love Me*	5.1970
		Two Feet From Happiness	
25057	**The Spinners**	*It's A Shame*	6.1970
		Together We Can Make Such Sweet Music	
25058	**Hearts Of Stone**	*It's A Lonesome Road*	9.1970
		Yesterday's Love Is Over	
25059	**Chuck Jackson**	*Pet Names*	1.1971
		Is There Anything Love Can't Do	
25060	**The Spinners**	*We'll Have It Made*	12.1970
		My Whole World Ended (The Moment You Left Me)	
25061	**King Floyd**	*Heartaches*	4.1971
		Together We Can Do Anything	
25062	**P.J.**	*(I've Given You) The Best Years Of My Life*	4.1971
		It Takes A Man To Teach A Woman How To Love	
25063	**Ivy Joe**	*I'd Still Love You*	5.1971
		I Can Feel The Pain	
25064	**Hearts Of Stone**	*If I Could Give You The World*	6.1971
		You Gotta Sacrifice (We Gotta Sacrifice)	
25065	**The Elgins**	*Heaven Must Have Sent You*	9.1971
		Stay In My Lonely Arms	
25066	**The Stylists**	*What Is Love*	7.1971
		Where Did The Children Go	
25067	**Chuck Jackson**	*Who You Gonna Run To*	NR
		Forgive My Jealousy	
25068	**Tony & Carolyn**	*We've Only Just Begun – I'll Be There*	11.1971
		I Can Get Away From You (But I Can't Get Over You)	

| 25069 | **Posse** | Feel Like Giving Up | 2.1972 |
| | | Take Somebody Like You | |

RARE EARTH LABEL

5005	**Pretty Things**	Private Sorrow	7.1969
		Balloon Burning	
5006	**Virgil Brothers**	Temptation 'Bout To Get Me	8.1969
		Look Away	
5007	**Wes Henderson**	In Bed	8.1969
		Reality	
5008	**Sounds Nice**	Love At First Sight	9.1969
		Love You Too	
5009	**Easybeats**	St. Louis	9.1969
		Can't Find Love	
5010	**Rare Earth**	Generation, Light Up The Sky	11.1969
		Magic Key	
5011	**Rustix**	Can't You Hear The Music Play	11.1969
		I Guess This Is Goodbye	
5012	**Rare Earth**	Get Ready	2.1970
		Magic Key	
5013	**R. Dean Taylor**	Indiana Wants Me	4.1970
		Love's Your Name	
5014	**Rustix**	Come On People	4.1970
		Free Again (Non . . . C'est Rien)	
5015	**Michael Denton**	Just Another Morning	5.1970
		Arma'geden	
5016	**Cats**	Marianne	6.1970
		Somewhere Up There	
5017	**Rare Earth**	(I Know) I'm Losing You	7.1970
		When Joannie Smiles	
5018	**Danny Hernandez and the Ones**	As Long As I've Got You	9.1970
		One Little Teardrop	
5019	**Toe Fat**	Just Like Me	10.1970
		Bad Side Of The Moon	
5020	**Allan Nicholls**	Coming Apart	11.1970
		Let The Music Play	
5021	**Rare Earth**	Born To Wander	11.1970
		Here Comes The Night	
5022	**Brass Monkey**	Sweet Water	1.1971
		You Keep Me Hanging On	
5023	**R. Dean Taylor**	Ain't It A Sad Thing	1.1971
		Back Street	
5024	**Ken Christie & the Sunday People**	Don't Pay Me No Mind	2.1971
		Listen To Your Soul	
5025	**Kiki Dee**	Love Makes The World Go Round	2.1971
		Jimmy	
5026	**R. Dean Taylor**	Gotta See Jane	3.1971
		Back Street	
5027	**Stoney & Meatloaf**	What You See Is What You Get	4.1971
		Lady Be Mine	
5028	**Impact Of Brass**	Never Can Say Goodbye	4.1971
		So Far, So Good	
5029	**Ken Christie & the Sunday People**	The Rev. John B. Daniels	6.1971
		Jesus Is The Key	
5030	**R. Dean Taylor**	Candy Apple Red	6.1971
		Woman Alive	
5031	**Rare Earth**	I Just Want To Celebrate	6.1971
		The Seed	
5032	**The Messengers**	That's The Way A Woman Is	7.1971
		In The Jungle	
5033	**Stoney & Meatloaf**	It Takes All Kinds Of People	7.1971
		The Way You Do The Things You Do	
5034	**Rustix**	My Piece Of Heaven	NR
		Down Down	
5035	**The Sunday Funnies**	Walk Down The Path of Freedom	9.1971
		It's Just A Dream	
5036	**My Friends**	I'm An Easy Rider	8.1971
		Concrete And Clay	
5037	**Rustix**	We All End Up In Boxes	11.1971
		Down Down	
5038	**Rare Earth**	Hey Big Brother	11.1971
		Under God's Light	
5039	**Dave Prince**	The Greatest Man Whoever Lived	11.1971
		A Child Is Waiting	
5040	**Blue Scepter**	Out In The Night	1.1972
		Gypsy Eyes	
5041	**R. Dean Taylor**	Taos New Mexico	3.1972
		Shadow	
5042	**Vincent DiMirco**	I Can Make It Alone	4.1972
		Come Clean	
5043	**Rare Earth**	What'd I Say	3.1972
		Nice To Be With You	
5044	**XIT**	Nihaa Shil Hozho (I Am Happy About You)	4.1972
		End	
5045	**Howl The Good**	Long Way From Home	4.1972
		Why Do You Cry	
5046	**Chris Holland & T Bone**	Get Me Some Help	5.1972
		If Time Could Stand Still	
5047	**Crystal Mansion**	Somebody Oughta' Turn Your Head Around	7.1972
		Earth People	
5048	**Rare Earth**	Good Time Sally	10.1972
		Love Shines Down	
5049	**Wolfe**	Ballad Of The Unloved	NR
		Tale Of Two Cities	
5050	**Puzzle**	It's Not The Last Time	NR
		On With The Show	
5051	**John Wagner Coalition**	The Battle Is Over	1.1973
		Take Time To Love Me	
5052	**Rare Earth**	We're Gonna Have A Good Time	12.1972
		Would You Like To Come Along	
5053	**Rare Earth**	Ma (vocal)	3.1973
		Ma (instr.)	
5054	**Rare Earth**	Hum Along And Dance	8.1973
		Come With Me	
5055	**XIT**	Reservation Of Education	9.1973
		Color Nature Gone	
5056	**Rare Earth**	Big John Is My Name	10.1973
		Ma (vocal)	
5057	**Rare Earth**	Chained	5.1974
		Fresh From The Can	
5058	**Rare Earth**	It Makes You Happy	10.1975
		Boogie With Me Children	
5059	**Rare Earth**	Keepin' Me Out Of The Storm	8.1975
		Let Me Be Your Sunshine	
5060	**Rare Earth**	Midnight Lady	5.1976
		Wallking Schtick	

MOWEST LABEL

5001	**The Devastating Affair**	I Want To Be Humble	1.1972
		My Place	
5002	**Tom Clay**	What The World Needs Now Is Love – Abraham, Martin And John	6.1971
		The Victors	
5003	**Lodi**	Happiness	8.1971
		I Hope I See It In My Lifetime	
5004	**Suzee Ikeda**	Zip-A-Dee-Doo-Dah	10.1971
		Bah-Bah-Bah	
5005	**G.C. Cameron**	Act Like A Shotgun	8.1971
		Girl I Really Love You	
5006	**Bobby Taylor**	Hey Lordy	11.1971
		Just A Little Bit Closer	
5007	**Tom Clay**	Whatever Happened To Love	10.1971
		Baby I Need Your Loving	
5008	**Thelma Houston**	I Want To Go Back There Again	11.1971
		Pick Of The Week	
5009	**Commodores**	The Zoo (The Human Zoo)	3.1972
		I'm Looking For Love	
5010	—	—	—
5011	**Frankie Valli**	Love Isn't Here (Like It Used To Be)	2.1972
		Poor Fool	

5012	G.C. Cameron	I'm Gonna Get You (Part 2)	NR
		I'm Gonna Get You (Part 1)	
5013	Thelma Houston	Me And Bobby McGee	3.1972
		No One's Gonna Be A Fool Forever	
5014	The Sisters Love	Mr. Fix-It Man	3.1972
		You've Got To Make The Choice	
5015	G.C. Cameron	What It Is, What It Is	3.1972
		You Are That Special One	
5016	Syreeta	I Love Every Little Thing About You	9.1972
		Black Maybe	
5017	Suzee Ikeda	I Can't Give Back The Love I Feel For You	6.1972
		Mind, Body And Soul	
*5018	Michelle Aller	The Morning After	8.1972
		Spend Some Time Together	

* Original A-side: The Morning After (withdrawn). Replacement A-side: Just Not Gonna Make It

5019	Blinky	Money (That's What I Want)	6.1972
		For Your Precious Love	
5020	The Blackberries	Somebody Up There	NR
		But I Love Him	
5021	Syreeta	To Know You Is To Love You	7.1972
		Happiness	
5022	Odyssey	Our Lives Are Shaped By What We Love	8.1972
		Broken Road	
5023	Devastating Affair	—	NR
5024	—	—	—
5025	The Four Seasons	The Night	NR
		Sun Country	
5026	Frankie Valli & The Four Seasons	Walk On, Don't Look Back	8.1972
		Sun Country	
5027	Thelma Houston	What If	NR
		There Is A God	
5028	The Crusaders	Spanish Harlem	10.1972
		Papa Hooper's Barrelhouse Groove	
5029	Lesley Gore	She Said That	10.1972
		The Road I Walk	
5030	Sisters Love	You've Got My Mind	NR
		Try It, You'll Like It	
5031	Repairs	Songwriter	NR
		Fiddler	
5032	Kubie	Glad That You're Not Me	NR
		Child He Die	
5033	Blinky	T'Ain't Nobody's Bizness If I Do	1.1973
		What More Can I Do	
5034	Celebration	Since I Met You There's No Magic	NR
		The Circle Again	
5035	G.C. Cameron & Willie Hutch	Come Get This Thang	NR
		My Woman	
5036	G.C. Cameron	Don't Wanna Play Pajama Games	1.1973
		Jesus Help Me Find Another Way	
5037	The Nu Page	When The Brothers Come Marching Home	2.1973
		A Heart Is A House	
5038	Commodores	Don't You Be Worried	1.1973
		Determination	
5039	Martin & Finley	Long Life And Success To The Farmer	11.1972
		Half Crazed	
5040	Mike Campbell	Angel Got A Book Today	1.1973
		The People In The Valley	
5041	The Sisters Love	(I Could Never Make) A Better Man Than You	1.1973
		Give Me Your Love	
5042	Lesley Gore	Give It To Me Sweet Thing	NR
		Don't Want To Be The One	
5043	Martin & Finley	Thinkin' 'Bout My Baby	NR
		Best Friends	

5044	The Music Makers	Follow Me – Mother Nature	NR
		And I Thought You Loved Me	
5045	Stoney	Let Me Down Easy	NR
		It's Always Me	
5046	Thelma Houston	If It's The Last Thing I Do	NR
		And I Never Did	
5047	Stacie Johnson	Woman In My Eyes	NR
		A Carbon Copy	
5048	Art & Honey	Let's Make Love Now	NR
		(I've Given You) The Best Years Of My Life	
5049	—	—	—
5050	Thelma Houston	Piano Man	3.1973
		I'm Just A Part Of Yesterday	

PRODIGAL LABEL

611	Shirley Alston	I Hear Those Church Bells Ringing – Chapel Of Love	12.1974
		I Do Love You	
612	Gary U.S. Bonds	Grandma's Washboard Band	1.1975
		Believing You	
613	—	—	—
614	Ronnie McNeir	Wendy Is Gone	3.1975
		Give Me A Sign	
615	Fox Fire	Bump In Your Jeans	3.1975
		Such A Long Time	
616	Shirley Alston	I'd Rather Not Be Loving You	5.1975
		Can't Stop Singin' ('Bout The Boy I Love)	
617	Eddie Parker	Body Chains (vocal)	11.1975
		Body Chains (instr.)	
618	Softouch	After You Give Your All (What Else Is There To Give)	7.1975
		Say That You Love Me Boy	
619	Ronnie McNeir	For Your Love	8.1975
		You Better Come On Down	
620	Ronnie McNeir	Saggitarian Affair	11.1975
		You Better Come On Down	
621	Orange Sunshine	Who's Cheating On Who	12.1975
		I'm In Love	
622	Gaylord & Holiday	Eh! Cumpari	12.1975
		The Little Shoemaker	
623	Joe Frazier	Little Dog Heaven	1.1976
		What Ya Gonna Do When The Rain Starts Fallin'	
624	Disco Stan	Funky Cocktail (Part 1)	4.1976
		Funky Cocktail (Part 2)	
625	Chip Hand	Wait Until September	NR
		Dreamtime Lover	
626	Rita Graham	Rich Man, Poor Man	6.1976
		I'll Hold Out My Hand	
627	Fantacy Hill	Minnie Ha Ha	6.1976
		Stay With Me	
628	Michael Quatro	The Stripper	NR
		Children Of Tomorrow	
629	Dunn & Rubini	Imaginary Girl	1.1977
		Two	
630	Dunn & Rubini	Diggin' It	6.1976
		Just Keep Laughin'	
631	Michael Quatro	Pure Chopin	10.1976
		One By One	
632	Charlene	It Ain't Easy Comin' Down	11.1976
		On My Way To You	
633	Charlene	Freddie	3.1977
		Freddie (instr.)	
634	Don Dunn	Ruby	NR
		Ruby (instr.)	
635	The Graffiti Orchestra	Star Wars Theme	7.1977
		Star Wars Theme (long vers.)	
636	Charlene	I've Never Been To Me	7.1977
		It's Really Nice To Be In Love Again	
637	Rare Earth	Is Your Teacher Cool?	9.1977
		Crazy Love	
638	Phillip Jarrell	I'm Dyin'	11.1977
		Wings Of Time	

639	**Fresh**	Just How Does It Feel	3.1978
		Feelin' Fresh	
640	**Rare Earth**	Warm Ride	3.1978
		Would You Like To Come Along	
641	**Fantacy Hill**	Sanity Baby	6.1978
		Your Mama	
642	**Fresh**	Summertime	6.1978
		Feelin' Fresh	
643	**Rare Earth**	I Can Feel My Love Risin'	11.1978
		Stop Her On Sight (S.O.S.)	
644	**Stylus**	Look At Me	2.1979
		Natural Feeling	
645	**Fresh**	You Never Cared	3.1979
		When The Winter Comes	
646	**Stylus**	Bushwalkin'	5.1979
		Sweetness	

MIRACLE LABEL

1	**Jimmy Ruffin**	Don't Feel Sorry For Me	1.1961
		Heart	
2	**Little Iva & Her Band**	When I Need You	4.1961
		Continental Strut	
3	**Gino Parks**	Blibber Blabber	5.1961
		Don't Say Bye Bye	
4	**Andre Williams**	Rosa Lee	6.1961
		Shoo Oo	
5	**The Temptations**	Oh, Mother Of Mine	7.1961
		Romance Without Finance	
6	**The Valadiers**	Greetings (This Is Uncle Sam)	10.1961
		Take A Chance	
7	**The Equadors**	Someone To Call My Own	9.1961
		You're My Desire	
8	**Pete Hartfield**	Love Me	9.1961
		Darling Tonight	
9	**Joel Sebastian**	Angel In Blue	10.1961
		Blue Cinderella	
10	**Don McKenzie**	Whose Heart (Are You Gonna Break Now)	11.1961
		I'll Call You	
11	**Freddie Gorman**	The Day Will Come	10.1961
		Just For You	
12	**The Temptations**	Check Yourself	11.1961
		Your Wonderful Love	

HARVEY LABEL

111	**Eddie Burns**	Orange Driver	11.1961
		Hard Hearted Woman	
112	**Loe & Joe**	Little Ole Boy, Little Ole Girl	—
		That's How I Am Without You	
113	**Jr Walker & the All Stars**	Twist Lackawanna	10.1962
		Willie's Blues	
114	**Five Quails**	Get To School On Time	9.1962
		Been A Long Time	
115	**Eddie Burns**	The Thing To Do	—
		Mean And Evil (Baby)	
116	**The Quails**	Never Felt Like This Before	9.1962
		My Love	
117	**Jr Walker & the All Stars**	Cleo's Mood	9.1962
		Brain Washer	
118	**Eddie Burns**	(Don't Be) Messing With My Bread	11.1962
		Orange Driver	
119	**Jr Walker & the All Stars**	Good Rockin'	1.1963
		Brain Washer Part 2	
120	**The Quails**	Over The Hump	4.1963
		I Thought	
121	**Harvey & Ann**	What Can You Do Now	5.1963
		Will I Do	

WORKSHOP JAZZ LABEL

2001	**Hank & Carol Diamond**	Exodus	5.1962
		I Remember You	
2002	**Earl Washington**	Opus 2	5.1962
		March Lightly	

2003	**Paula Greer**	I Want To Talk About You	—
		So In Love	
2004	**Dave Hamilton**	Late Freight	5.1962
		Mellow In Coli	
2005	**The Johnny Griffith Trio**	I'mi See You Later	5.1962
		I Did	
2006	**The George Bohannon Quartet**	Bobbie	5.1962
		El Rig	
2007	**Paula Greer**	I Did	5.1962
		Falling In Love With Love	

DIVINITY LABEL

99004	**The Wright Specials**	That's What He Is To Me	7.1962
		Pilgrim Of Sorrow	
99005	**The Wright Specials**	Ninety-Nine And A Half Won't Do	6.1963
		I Won't Go Back	
99006	**The Gospel Stars**	Give God A Chance	7.1963
		Have You Any Time For Jesus	
99007	**Burnadettes**	First, You've Got To Recognise God	5.1963
		I'm Going Home	
99008	**Liz Lands**	We Shall Overcome	—
		Trouble In This Land	

MELODY LABEL

101	**Creations**	This Is Our Night	7.1962
		My Inspiration	
102	**Lamont Dozier**	Fortune Teller Tell Me	6.1962
		Dearest One	
103	**The Vells**	You'll Never Cherish A Love So True (Till You Lose It)	10.1962
		There He Is (At My Door)	
104	**—**	—	—
105	**The Pirates**	Mind Over Matter (I'm Gonna Make You Mine)	9.1962
		I'll Love You Till I Die	
106	**Chuck-A-Lucks**	Sugar Cane Curtain	2.1963
		Ding Bat Diller	
107	**Jack Haney & Nikiter Armstrong**	Peaceful	—
		Summit Chanted Meeting	
108	**—**	—	—
109	**Howard Crockett**	The Big Wheel	12.1963
		That Silver Haired Daddy Of Mine	
110	**Gene Henslee**	Shambles	1.1964
		Beautiful Women	
111	**Howard Crockett**	Bringing In The Gold	3.1964
		I've Been A Long Time Leaving	
112	**Bruce Channel**	Satisfied Mind	3.1964
		That's What's Happenin'	
113	**Dorsey Burnette**	Little Acorn	5.1964
		Cold As Usual	
114	**Bruce Channel**	You Make Me Happy	7.1964
		You Never Looked Better	
115	**Howard Crockett**	My Lil's Run Off	—
		Spanish Lace And Memories	
116	**Dorsey Burnette**	Jimmy Brown	6.1964
		Everybody's Angel	
117	**Dee Mullins**	Love Makes The World Go Round But Money Greases The Wheel	1.1965
		Come Back (And Be My Love Again)	
118	**Dorsey Burnette**	Ever Since The World Began	11.1964
		Long Long Time Ago	
119	**Howard Crockett**	Put Me In Your Pocket	12.1964
		The Miles	
120	**The Hillsiders**	You Only Pass This Way One Time	3.1965
		Rain Is A Lonesome Thing	
121	**Howard Crockett**	All The Good Times Are Gone	4.1965
		The Great Titanic	

INFERNO LABEL

5001	**The Volumes**	Ain't That Loving You	5.1968
		I Love You Baby	
5002	**The Detroit Wheels**	Linda Sue Dixon	4.1968
		Tally Ho	
5003	**The Detroit Wheels**	Think (About The Good Things)	9.1968
		For The Love Of A Stranger	

CHISA LABEL

8001	**Stu Gardner**	Home On The Range (Everybody Needs A Home)	9.1969
		It's A Family Thang	
		Mend This Generation (alt. B-side)	
8002	**Monk Montgomery**	A Place In The Sun	9.1969
		Your Love	
8003	**Arthur Adams**	It's Private Tonight	10.1969
		Let's Make Some Love	
8004	**Anonymous Children Of Today**	Can We Talk To You? (For A Little While)	11.1969
		Love And Peace	
8005	**Dorothy, Oma & Zelpha**	Gonna Put in On Your Mind	11.1969
		Henry Blake	
8006	**The Five Smooth Stones**	I Will Never Love Another	12.1969
		Love Unto Me	
8007	**Stu Gardner**	Expressin' My Love	2.1970
		I Don't Dream No More	
8008	**Arthur Adams**	My Baby's Love	4.1970
		Loving You	
8009	**Hugh Masekela**	You Keep Me Hangin' On	10.1970
		Make Me A Potion	
8010	**The Jazz Crusaders**	Way Back Home	9.1970
		Jackson!	
8011	**Arthur Adams**	Can't Wait To See You	2.1971
		It's Private Tonight	
8012	**Letta**	I Won't Weep No More	3.1971
		You Touched Me	
8013	**The Jazz Crusaders**	Pass The Plate	6.1971
		Greasy Spoon	
8014	**Hugh Masekela & Union Of South Africa**	Dyambo (Dee-Yambo) Weary Day Is Over	6.1971
		Shebeen	
8015	**Arthur Adams**	Uncle Tom	NR
		Mornin' Train	

ECOLOGY LABEL

| 1000 | **Sammy Davis Jr** | In My Own Lifetime | 3.1971 |
| | | I'll Begin Again | |

BLACK FORUM LABEL

| 20000 | **Elaine Brown** | No Time | 4.1973 |
| | | Until We're Free | |

MELODYLAND LABEL

6001	**Pat Boone**	Candy Lips	10.1974
		Young Girls	
6002	**T. G. Sheppard**	Devil In The Bottle	11.1974
		Rollin' With The Flow	
6003	**Jerry Naylor**	Is This All There Is to Honky Tonk?	11.1974
		You're The One	
6004	**Ronnie Dove**	Please Come To Nashville	2.1975
		Pictures On Paper	
6005	**Pat Boone**	Indiana Girl	2.1975
		Young Girl	
6006	**T. G. Sheppard**	Tryin' To Beat The Morning Home	3.1975
		I'll Be Satisfied	
6007	**Dorsey Burnette**	Molly (I Ain't Gettin' Any Younger)	4.1975
		She's Feelin' Low	
6008	**Karen Kelly**	The Dessert	4.1975
		Annie	
6009	**Terry Stafford**	Darling Think It Over	4.1975
		I Can't Find It	
6010	**Barbara Wyrick**	Baby, I Love You Too Much	5.1975
		You've Been Doing Wrong For So Long	
6011	**Ronnie Dove**	Things	5.1975
		Here We Go Again	
6012	**Jerry Naylor**	He'll Have To Go	5.1975
		Once Again	
6013	**Sheila Taylor**	She Satisfies	5.1975
		How Important Can It Be?	
6014	**Kenny Seratt**	If I Could Have It Any Way	5.1975
		Not Too Old To Cry	
6015	**Jud Strunk**	The Biggest Parakeets In Town	5.1975
		I Wasn't Wrong About You	
6016	**T. G. Sheppard**	Another Woman	7.1975
		I Can't Help Myself (Sugar Pie Honey Bunch)	
6017	**Darla Foster**	Say Love (Or Don't Say Anything At All)	9.1975
		He Makes The Wrong Seem Right	
6018	**Pat Boone & Shirley Boone**	I'd Do It With You	8.1975
	Pat Boone	Yester-me, Yester-you, Yesterday	
6019	**Dorsey Burnette**	Lyin' In Her Arms Again	8.1975
		Doggone The Dogs	
6020	**Jerry Naylor**	Prayin' For My Mind	9.1975
		What's A Nice Girl Like You Doing In A Honkey Tonk	
6021	**Ronnie Dove**	Drina (Take Your Lady Off For Me)	9.1975
		Your Sweet Love	
6022	**Terry Stafford**	Reba	—
		(She's A) Fire Out Of Control	
6023	**Barbara Wyrick**	Pity Little Billy Jo	9.1975
		Crazy Love	
6024	**Kenny Seratt**	Let's Hold On To What We've Got	9.1975
		Truly Great American Blues	
6025	**Joey Martin**	Anything To Keep From Going Home	10.1975
		Ruby Is A Groupie	
6026	**Ernie Payne**	Take Me (The Way That I Am)	12.1975
		Talk To Jeanette	
6027	**Jud Strunk**	Pamela Brown	12.1975
		They're Tearing Down A Town	
6028	**T. G. Sheppard**	Motels And Memories	12.1975
		Pigskin Charade	
6029	**Pat Boone**	Glory Train	2.1976
		U.F.O.	
6030	**Ronnie Dove**	Right Or Wrong	3.1976
		Guns	
6031	**Dorsey Burnette**	Ain't No Heartbreak	3.1976
		I Dreamed I Saw	

GAIEE LABEL

| 90001 | **Valentino** | I Was Born This Way | 4.1975 |
| | | Liberation | |

BLAZE LABEL

| 1107 | **Jack Ashford & the Sound Of New Detroit** | Do The Choo Choo Part 1 (vocal) | 9.1975 |
| | | Do The Choo Choo Part 2 (instr.) | |

The Blaze label was previously owned by Barney Ales who sold it to Motown in 1975 as a subsidiary of the Prodigal label.

HITSVILLE LABEL

6032	**T. G. Sheppard**	Solitary Man	5.1976
		Shame	
6033	—	—	—
6034	—	—	—
6035	**Rick Tucker**	I Heard A Song	6.1976
		Plans That We Made	
6036	—	—	—
6037	**Pat Boone**	Texas Woman	6.1976
		It's Gone	
6038	**Ronnie Dove**	Tragedy	7.1976
		Songs We Sang As Children	
6039	**Kenney Seratt**	I've Been There Too	7.1976
		She Made Me Love You More	
6040	**T. G. Sheppard**	Show Me A Man	8.1976
		We Just Live Here (We Don't Love Here Anymore)	
6041	**Jerry Naylor**	The Bad Part Of Me	8.1976
		I Hate To Drink Alone	
6042	**Pat Boone**	Oklahoma Sunshine	9.1976
		Won't Be Home Tonight	
6043	**Jerry Foster**	I Knew You When	10.1976
		One	
6044	**Marty Mitchell**	My Eyes Adored You	10.1976
		Devil Woman	
6045	**Ronnie Dove**	Why Daddy	11.1976
		The Morning After The Night Before	
6046	**Jerry Naylor**	The Last Time You Love Me	11.1976
		Born To Fool Around	
6047	**Pat Boone**	Lovelight Comes A Shining	11.1976
		Country Days And Country Nights	
6048	**T. G. Sheppard**	May I Spend Every New Year's With You	11.1976
		I'll Always Remember That Song	
6049	**Kenny Seratt**	Daddy, They're Playin' A Song About You	1.1977
		I Threw Away A Rose	
6050	**Wendel Adkins**	I Will	1.1977
		Show Me The Way	
6051	**Lloyd Schoonmaker**	She Gives Me Love	1.1977
		Little Sister	
6052	**Jerry Foster**	Family Man	1.1977
		Just Another Song Away	
6053	**T. G. Sheppard**	Lovin' On	2.1977
		I'll Always Remember That Song	
6054	**Pat Boone**	Colorado Country Morning	2.1977
		Don't Want to Fall Away From You	
6055	**Wendel Adkins**	Texas Moon	3.1977
		Laid Back Country Picker	

NATURAL RESOURCES LABEL

6001	**Gaylord & Holiday**	Angelina (The Waitress At The Pizzeria)	12.1976
		Ramona	

JU-PAR LABEL

8001	**Flavor**	Don't Freeze Up	2.1977
		Don't Freeze Up (instr.)	
8002	**Ju-Par Universal Orchestra**	Funky Music	4.1977
		Time	

MC RECORDS

5001	**Pat Boone**	Whatever Happened To The Good Old Honky Tonk	9.1977
		Ain't Going Down In The Ground Before My Time	
5002	**Wendel Adkins**	Julieanne (Where Are You Tonight)	10.1977
		She Gives Me Love	
5003	**Marty Cooper**	Like A Gypsy	10.1977
		$10 Room	
5004	**Jerry Naylor**	If You Don't Want To Love Her	1.1978
		Love Away Her Memory Tonight	
5005	**Marty Mitchell**	You Are The Sunshine Of My Life	1.1978
		Yester-me, Yester-you, Yesterday	
5006	**Porter Jordan**	What We Do Two By Two	2.1978
		Broken Bones	
5007	**Kenny Seratt**	She's The Trip I've Been On (Since You've Been Gone)	2.1978
		She Made Me Love You More	
5008	**Wendel Adkins**	You've Lost That Lovin' Feeling	3.1978
		Show Me The Way	
5009	**Ernie Payne**	Neon Riders And Sawdust Gliders	4.1978
		The Very Last Love Letter	
5010	**Jerry Naylor**	Rave On	4.1978
		Lady, Would You Like To Dance	
5011	**Marty Mitchell**	All Alone In Austin	5.1978
		Virginia	
5012	**E. D. Wofford**	Baby, I Need Your Lovin'	5.1978
		Why Not Try Lovin' Me	
5013	**Ronnie Dove**	Angel In Your Eyes (Brings Out The Devil In Me)	8.1978
		Songs We Sang As Children	
5014	**Kay Austin**	Try Me	7.1978
		Big Red Roses (And Little White Lies)	
5015	**Arthur Blanch**	The Little Man's Got The Biggest Smile In Town	7.1978
		Another Pretty Country Song	
5016	**Joey Click**	California Girl	NR
		I Married You To Be With You	

ANNA RECORDS

101	**Voice Masters**	Oops I'm Sorry	5.1959
		Hope And Pray	
102	**Voice Masters**	Needed	
		Needed (For Lovers Only)	
1103	**Hill Sisters**	Hit And Run Away Love	
		Advertising For Love	
1104	**Bob Kayli**	Never More	
		You Knows What To Do	
1105	**Wreg Tracey**	Take Me Back (I Was Wrong)	10.1959
		All I Want Is You	
1106	**Paul Gayten**	The Hunch	9.1959
		Hot Cross Buns	
1107	—	—	—
1108	**Johnny & Jackey**	Lonely & Blue	3.1960
		Let's Go To A Movie Baby	
1109	—	—	—
1110	**Falcons**	This Heart Of Mine	
		Just For Your Love	
1111	**Barrett Strong**	Money (That's What I Want)	8.1959
		Oh! I Apologise	
1112	**Paul Gayten**	Beatnik Beat	3.1960
		Scratch Back	
1113	**Letha Jones**	I Need You	
		—	
1114	**Ty Hunter & Voice Masters**	Orphan Boy	7.1960
		Everything About You	
1115	**Herman Griffin & Mello-Dees**	Hurry Up And Marry Me	
		Do You Want To See My Baby	
1116	**Barrett Strong**	Yes, No, Maybe So	
		You Knows What To Do	
1117	**Ruben Fort**	So Good	
		I Feel It	

1118	Allan (Bo) Story	Blue Moon	
		Don't	
1119	Joe Tex	All I Could Do Was Cry (Part 1)	
		All I Could Do Was Cry (Part 2)	
1120	Johnnie & Jackie	Hoy Hoy	10.1960
		No One Else But You	
1121	Bill (Winehead Willie) Murray & George (Sweet Lucy) Copeland	The Big Time Spender (Part 1)	
		The Big Time Spender (Part 2)	
1122	Cap-Tans	Tight Skirts And Crazy Sweaters	10.1960
		I'm Afraid	
1123	Ty Hunter & Voice Masters	Everytime	
		Free	
1124	Joe Tex & the Vibrators	I'll Never Break Your Heart (Part 1)	
		I'll Never Break Your Heart (Part 2)	
1125	Lamont Anthony	Let's Talk It Over	11.1960
		Benny The Skinny Man	
1126	Wreg Tracey	All I Want For Christmas (Is Your Love)	
		Take Me Back (I Was Wrong)	
1127	David Ruffin	I'm In Love	
		One Of These Days	
1128	Joe Tex	Baby You're Right	1.1961
		Ain't It A Mess	

TRI-PHI RECORDS

1001	The Spinners	That's What Girls Are Made For	5.1961
		Heebie Jeebies	
1002	Johnnie & Jackie	Carry Your Own Load	
		So Disappointing	
1003	Lorri Rudolph	Don't Let Them Tell Me (Tell Me Yourself)	
		Grieving About A Love	
1004	The Spinners	I'm So Glad (Love I Found You)	
	Playmates	Sud Duster	
1005	Johnny & Jackie	Someday We'll Be Together	
		Sho – Don't Play	
1006	Shorty Long	I'll Be Here	1.1962
		Bad Willie	
1007	The Spinners	What Did She Use	
		Itchin' For My Baby (But I Don't Know What To Scratch)	
1008	Davenport Sisters	You've Got Me Cyring Again	
		Hoy Hoy	
1009	—	—	—
1010	Harvey	Whistling About You	
		She Loves Me So	
1011	The Merced Blue Notes	Midnite Session (Part 1)	
		Midnite Session (Part 2)	
1012	The Challengers	Honey Honey Honey	
		Stay With Me	
1013	The Spinners	I've Been Hurt	
		I Got Your Water Boiling Baby	
1014	The Ervin Sisters	Changing Baby	
		Do It Right	
1015	Shorty Long	I'll Be Here	
		Too Smart	
1016	—	—	—
1017	Harvey	She Loves Me So	
		Any Way You Wanta	
1018	Bobby Smith & the Spinners	She Don't Love Me	12.1962
		Too Young, Too Much, Too Soon	
1019	Johnny & Jackie	Baby Don't Cha Worry	
		Stop What You're Saying	
1020	Challengers 3 featuring Ann Bogan and Ann & Harvey Fuqua	Everday	
		I Hear An Echo	
1021	—	—	—
1022	—	—	—
1023	The Merced Blue Notes	Whole Lotta Nothing	
		Fragile	
1024	Harvey	Come On And Answer Me	5.1963
		Memories Of You	

RIC TIC RECORDS

100	Gino Washington	Gino Is A Coward	7.1964
		Puppet On A String	
101	Freddie Gorman	In A Bad Way	
		There Can Be Too Much (Of Everything I Do)	
102	Freddie Gorman	Can't Get It Out Of My Mind	
		Take Me Back	
103	Edwin Starr	Agent Double-O-Soul	
		Agent Double-O-Soul (instr.)	
104	San Remo Golden Strings	Hungry For Love	
	Bob Wilson & San Remo Quartet	All Turned On	
105	Rose Battiste	That's What He Told Me	
		Holding Hands	
106	J. J. Barnes	Please Let Me In	1965
		I Think I Found A Love	
107	Edwin Starr	Back Street	6.1965
		Back Street (instr.)	
108	San Remo Golden Strings	Blueberry Hill	6.1965
		I'm Satisfied	
109	Edwin Starr	Stop Her On Sight (S.O.S.)	1.1966
		I Have Faith In You	
110	J. J. Barnes	Real Humdinger	1965
		I Ain't Gonna Do It	
111	Laura Lee	To Win Your Heart	2.1966
		So Will I	
112	San Remo Golden Strings	Festival Time	
		Joy Road	
113	—	—	—
114	Edwin Starr	Headline News	
		Harlem	
115	J. J. Barnes	Day Tripper	
		Don't Bring Me Bad News	
116	San Remo Golden Strings	Quanto Sei Bella (You Are So Beautiful)	
		International Love Theme	
117	J. J. Barnes	Say It	
		Deeper In Love	
118	Edwin Starr	It's My Turn Now	
		Girls Are Gettin' Prettier	
119	The Fantastic Four	Girl Have Pity	
		(I'm Gonna) Live Up To What She Thinks	
120	Edwin Starr	My Kind Of Woman	
		You're My Mellow	
121	—	—	—
122	The Fantastic Four	Ain't Love Wonderful	
		The Whole World Is A Stage	
123	Al Kent	The Way You Been Acting Lately	
		The Way You Been Acting Lately (instr.)	
124	Andre Williams	You Got It And I Want It	
		I Can't Stop Crying	
125	—	—	—
126	—	—	—
127	Al Kent	You've Got To Pay The Price	
		Where Do I Go From Here	
128	The Fantastic Four	You Gave Me Something (And Everything's Alright)	
		Romeo & Juliet's 'I Don't Want To Live Without You' (play)	
129	The Flaming Embers	Let's Have A Love-In (Cause Everybody Needs Love)	
	Wingate's Love-In Strings	Let's Have A Love-In (instr.)	
130	The Fantastic Four	As Long As I Live (I Live For You)	
		To Share Your Love	

131	Wingate's Love-In Strings	Let's Have A Love-In	
	The Flaming Embers	She's A Real Live Wire	
132	The Flaming Embers	Let's Have A Love-In (Cause Everybody Needs Love)	
		Hey Mama (What'cha Got For Daddy)	
133	Al Kent Orchestra	Ooh! Pretty Lady	
		Finders Keepers	
134	The Fantastic Four	As Long As The Feeling Is There	
		Goddess Of Love	
135	The Detroit Emeralds	Showtime	1.1968
		Showtime (instr.)	
136	The Fantastic Four	Goddess Of Love	
		Love Is A Many Splendored Thing	
137	The Fantastic Four	Man In Love	
		No Love Like Your Love	
138	The Detroit Emeralds	Shades Down	
		Ode To Billy Joe	
139	The Fantastic Four	I've Got To Have You	
		Win Or Lose (I'm Gonna Love You)	
140	The Flaming Embers	Bless You (My Love)	
	Al Kent	Bless You (My Love) (instr.)	
141	The Detroit Emeralds	(I'm An Ordinary Man) Take Me The Way I Am	
		I'll Keep On Coming Back	
142	Little Ann	Going Down A One-Way Street (The Wrong Way)	
		I'd Like To Know You Better	
143	The Flaming Embers	Children	
		Children (instr.)	
†144	The Fantastic Four	I Love You Madly	8.1968
		I Love You Madly (instr.)	
145	The Flaming Embers	Just Like Children	
		Tell It Like It Is	

GOLDEN WORLD RECORDS

1	Willie Kendrick	Stop This Train	11.1963
		Fine As Wine	
2	Sue Perrin	Candy Store Man	2.1964
		Recipe Of Love	
3	—	—	—
4/5	The Adorables	Deep Freeze	3.1964
		Daddy Please	
6	Patti Gilson	Pulling Petals (From A Daisy)	
		Don't You Tell A Lie	
7	—	—	—
8/9	Reflections	(Just Like) Romeo & Juliet	3.1964
		Can't You Tell By The Look In My Eyes	
10	The Adorables	School's All Over	5.1964
		Be	
11	Elliot Baron	Man To Man	
		The Spare Rib	
12	The Reflections	Like Columbus Did	6.1964
		Lonely Girl	
13	—	—	—
14	The Manhattans	Just A Little Loving	
		Beautiful Brown Eyes	
15	The Reflections	Talkin' About My Girl	
		Oowee Now Now	
16	The Reflections	(I'm Just) A Henpecked Guy	
		Don't Do That To Me	
17	The Debonaires	Please Don't Say We're Through	10.1964
		A Little Too Long	
18	Juanita Williams	Baby Boy	9.1964
		You Knew What You Was Getting	

19	The Reflections	Shabby Little Hut	
		You're My Baby (And Don't You Forget It)	
20	The Reflections	Poor Man's Son	2.1965
		Comin' At You	
21	Barbara Mercer	Hey!	7.1965
		Can't Stop Loving You Baby	
22	The Reflections	Wheelin' and Dealin'	6.1965
		Deborah Ann	
23	Carl Carlton (12 Year Wonder)	Nothin' No Sweeter Than Love	7.1965
		I Love True Love	
24	The Reflections	Out Of The Picture	7.1965
		June Bride	
25	The Adorables	Oh! Boy	
		Devil In His Eyes	
26	The Debonaires	Eenie Meenie Gypsaleenie	8.1965
		Please Don't Say We're Through	
27	Barbara Mercer	The Things We Do Together	
		Hungry For Love (instr.)	
28	Barbara Mercer	Doin' Things Together With You	
		Nobody Loves You Like Me	
29	The Reflections	Girl In The Candy Store	9.1965
		Your Kind Of Love	
30	—	—	—
31	The Sunliners	The Swingin' Kind	
		All Alone	
32	Gino Parks	My Sophisticated Lady	1.1966
		Talkin' About My Baby	
33	Rose Battiste	Sweetheart Darling	1.1966
		That's What He Told Me	
34	—	—	—
35	—	—	—
36	The Holidays	I'll Love You Forever	4.1966
		Makin' Up Time	
37	Larry Knight & the Upsetters	Hurt Me	2.1966
		Everything's Gone Wrong	
38	The Debonaires	How's Your New Love Treating You	
		Big-Time Fun	
39	—	—	—
40	Tamiko Jones	I'm Spellbound	
		Am I Glad Now	
41	Tony Michaels	Picture Me And You	
		I Love The Life I Live (And Live The Life I Love)	
42	Pat Lewis	Can't Shake It Loose	3.1966
		Let's Go Together	
43	Theresa Lindsay	Daddy-O	
		I'll Bet You	
44	The Debonaires	C.O.D. (Collect on Delivery)	
		How's Your New Love Treating You	
45	Dickie & the Ebbtides	One Boy, One Girl	
		I've Got A Shadow	
46	The Parliaments	That Was My Girl	
		Heart Trouble	
47	The Holidays	No Greater Love	
		Watch Out Girl	

WINGATE RECORDS

001	—	—	
002	Sam Bowie & Blue Feelings	Think Of The Times We Had Together	
		Swoop Swoop	
003	—	—	
004	Al Kent	You Know I Love You	
		Country Boy	
005	—	—	
006	Sonny Stitt	The Double-O-Soul Of Sonny Stitt (Part 1)	
		The Double-O-Soul Of Sonny Stitt (Part 2)	

007	—	—	
008	**Juanita Williams**	*Some Things You Never Get Used To*	
		You Knew What You Were Gettin'	
009			
010	**Sonny Stitt**	*Stitt's Groove*	
	Hank Marr	*Marr's Groove*	
011	—	—	
012	—	—	
013	—	—	
014	**Andre Williams Orchestra**	*Loose Juice*	
		Sweet Little Pussycat	
015	**Mark III Trio**	*G'wan*	
		Good Grease	
016	—		—
017	—		—
018	—	—	
019	—	—	
020	—	—	
021	—	—	
022	**The Dramatics**	*Inky Dinky Wang Dang Doo*	
		Baby I Need You	
023	—	—	
024	—	—	
025	—	—	

AMERICAN ALBUMS

TAMLA LABEL

220	**The Miracles**	*Hi! We're The Miracles*	6.1961
221	**Marvin Gaye**	*The Soulful Moods Of Marvin Gaye*	6.1961
222	**The Great Gospel Stars**	*The Great Gospel Stars*	11.1961
223	**The Miracles**	*Cookin' With The Miracles*	11.1961
224	**Various**	*Tamla Special No. 1*	6.1961
225	—	—	—
226	—	—	—
227	**The Rev. Columbus Mann**	*They Shall Be Mine*	12.1961
228	**The Marvelettes**	*Please Mr. Postman*	11.1961
229	**The Marvelettes**	*The Marvelettes Sing*	4.1962
230	**The Miracles**	*I'll Try Something New*	7.1962
231	**The Marvelettes**	*Playboy*	7.1962
232	**Little Stevie Wonder**	*Tribute To Uncle Ray*	10.1962
233	**Little Stevie Wonder**	*The Jazz Soul Of Little Stevie*	9.1962
234	—	—	—
235	—	—	—
236	**The Miracles**	*Christmas With The Miracles*	10.1963
237	**The Marvelettes**	*The Marvelous Marvelettes*	2.1963
238	**The Miracles**	*The Fabulous Miracles – You've Really Got A Hold On Me*	2.1963
239	**Marvin Gaye**	*That Stubborn Kinda Fellow*	1.1963
240	**Little Stevie Wonder**	*Recorded Live! – The 12 Year Old Genius*	6.1963
241	**The Miracles**	*Recorded Live! On Stage*	6.1963
242	**Marvin Gaye**	*Recorded Live! On Stage*	9.1963
243	**The Marvelettes**	*Recorded Live! On Stage*	6.1963
244	**Various**	*Recorded Live! At The Regal*	NR
245	**The Miracles**	*Doin' Mickey's Monkey*	11.1963
246	—	—	—
247	—	—	—
248	**Little Stevie Wonder**	*Workout Stevie Workout*	NR
249	—	—	—
250	**Stevie Wonder**	*With A Song In My Heart*	12.1963
251	**Marvin Gaye**	*When I'm Alone I Cry*	6.1964
252	**Marvin Gaye**	*Greatest Hits*	4.1964
253	**The Marvelettes**	*Greatest Hits*	2.1966
254	**The Miracles**	*Greatest Hits – From The Beginning*	3.1965
255	**Stevie Wonder**	*Stevie At The Beach*	6.1964
256	**Various**	*16 Big Hits Vol. 2*	7.1964

257	**Brenda Holloway**	*Every Little Bit Hurts*	9.1964
258	**Marvin Gaye**	*How Sweet it Is To Be Loved By You*	1.1965
259	**Marvin Gaye**	*Hello Broadway*	11.1964
260	**Marvin Gaye & Kim Weston**	*Side By Side*	NR
261	**Marvin Gaye**	*A Tribute To The Great Nat King Cole*	11.1965
262	—	—	—
263	—	—	—
264	**Various**	*Motortown Revue Recorded Live In Paris*	11.1965
265	**Willie Tyler & Lester**	*Hello Dummy*	11.1965
266	**Marvin Gaye**	*Moods Of Marvin Gaye*	5.1966
267	**Smokey Robinson & the Miracles**	*Going To A Go-Go*	11.1965
268	**Stevie Wonder**	*Uptight*	5.1966
269	**The Isley Brothers**	*This Old Heart Of Mine*	5.1966
270	**Marvin Gaye & Kim Weston**	*Take Two*	8.1966
271	**Smokey Robinson & the Miracles**	*Away We A Go-Go*	11.1966
272	**Stevie Wonder**	*Down To Earth*	12.1966
273	—	—	—
274	**The Marvelettes**	*The Marvelettes*	3.1967
275	**Ths Isley Brothers**	*Soul On The Rocks*	8.1967
276	**Smokey Robinson & the Miracles**	*Make It Happen (The Tears Of A Clown)*	8.1967
277	**Marvin Gaye & Tammi Terrell**	*United*	8.1967
278	**Marvin Gaye**	*Greatest Hits Vol. 2*	6.1967
279	**Stevie Wonder**	*I Was Made To Love Her*	8.1967
280	**Smokey Robinson & the Miracles**	*Greatest Hits Vol. 2*	1.1968
281	**Stevie Wonder**	*Someday At Christmas*	11.1967
282	**Stevie Wonder**	*Greatest Hits*	3.1968
283	—	—	—
284	**Marvin Gaye & Tammi Terrell**	*You're All I Need*	8.1968
285	**Marvin Gaye**	*In The Groove (I Heard It Through The Grapevine)*	8.1968
286	**The Marvelettes**	*Sophisticated Soul*	8.1968
287	**The Isley Brothers**	*Doin' Their Thing*	4.1969
288	**The Marvelettes**	*In Full Bloom*	9.1969
289	**Smokey Robinson & the Miracles**	*Live!*	1.1969
290	**Smokey Robinson & the Miracles**	*Special Occasion*	8.1968
291	**Stevie Wonder**	*For Once In My Life*	11.1968
292	**Marvin Gaye**	*MPG*	5.1969
293	**Marvin Gaye & His Girls**	*Marvin Gaye And His Girls*	5.1969
294	**Marvin Gaye & Tammi Terrell**	*Easy*	9.1969
295	**Smokey Robinson & the Miracles**	*Time Out*	7.1969
296	**Stevie Wonder**	*My Cherie Amour*	8.1969
297	**Smokey Robinson & the Miracles**	*Four In Blue*	11.1969
298	**Stevie Wonder**	*Live!*	3.1970
299	**Marvin Gaye**	*That's The Way Love Is*	1.1970
300	**Marvin Gaye**	*Super Hits*	9.1970
301	**Smokey Robinson & the Miracles**	*What Love Has Joined Together*	4.1970
302	**Marvin Gaye & Tammi Terrell**	*Greatest Hits*	5.1970
303	**Kiki Dee**	*Great Expectations*	7.1970
304	**Stevie Wonder**	*Signed, Sealed & Delivered*	8.1970
305	**The Marvelettes**	*Return Of The Marvelettes*	9.1970
306	**Smokey Robinson & the Miracles**	*Pocketful Of Miracles*	9.1970
307	**Smokey Robinson & the Miracles**	*The Season For Miracles*	11.1970
308	**Stevie Wonder**	*Where I'm Coming From*	4.1971
309	**Eddie Kendricks**	*All By Myself*	4.1971
310	**Marvin Gaye**	*What's Going On*	5.1971

311	**Valerie Simpson**	*Exposed*	5.1971
312	**Smokey Robinson & the Miracles**	*One Dozen Roses*	8.1971
313	**Stevie Wonder**	*Greatest Hits Vol. 2*	10.1971
314	**Stevie Wonder**	*Music Of My Mind*	3.1972
315	**Eddie Kendricks**	*People Hold On*	5.1972
316	—		
317	**Valerie Simpson**	*Valerie Simpson*	7.1972
318	**Smokey Robinson & the Miracles**	*Flying High Together*	8.1972
319	**Stevie Wonder**	*Talking Book*	10.1972
320	**Smokey Robinson & the Miracles**	*1957-1972 (Live!)*	12.1972
321	—	—	—
322	**Marvin Gaye**	*Trouble Man*	12.1972
323	**Ashford & Simpson**	*Nick And Val*	NR
324	—	—	—
325	**The Miracles**	*Renaissance*	4.1973
326	**Stevie Wonder**	*Innervisions*	8.1973
327	**Eddie Kendricks**	*Eddie Kendricks*	5.1973
328	**Smokey Robinson**	*Smokey*	6.1973
329	**Marvin Gaye**	*Let's Get It On*	8.1973
330	**Eddie Kendricks**	*Boogie Down*	2.1974
331	**Smokey Robinson**	*Pure Smokey*	3.1974
332	**Stevie Wonder**	*Fulfillingness' First Finale*	7.1974
333	**Marvin Gaye**	*Live!*	6.1974
334	**The Miracles**	*Do It Baby*	8.1974
335	**Eddie Kendricks**	*For You*	11.1974
336	**The Miracles**	*Don't Cha Love It*	1.1975
337	**Smokey Robinson**	*A Quiet Storm*	3.1975
338	**Eddie Kendricks**	*The Hit Man*	6.1975
339	**The Miracles**	*City Of Angels*	9.1975
340	**Stevie Wonder**	*Songs In The Key Of Life*	9.1976
341	**Smokey Robinson**	*Smokey's Family Robinson*	2.1976
342	**Marvin Gaye**	*I Want You*	3.1976
343	**Eddie Kendricks**	*He's A Friend*	1.1976
344	**The Miracles**	*The Power Of Music*	9.1976
345	**Thelma Houston**	*Anyway You Like It*	10.1976
346	**Eddie Kendricks**	*Goin' Up In Smoke*	9.1976
347	**Tata Vega**	*Full Speed Ahead*	8.1976
348	**Marvin Gaye**	*Greatest Hits*	9.1976
349	**Syreeta**	*One To One*	1.1977
350	**Smokey Robinson**	*Deep In My Soul*	1.1977
351	**Valerie Simpson**	*Keep It Coming*	1.1977
352	**Marvin Gaye**	*Live! At The London Palladium*	3.1977
353	**Tata Vega**	*Totally Tata*	2.1977
354	**Eddie Kendricks**	*At His Best*	1.1978
355	**Smokey Robinson**	*Big Time*	6.1977
356	**Eddie Kendricks**	*Slick*	8.1977
357	**The Miracles**	*Greatest Hits*	7.1977
358	**Thelma Houston**	*The Devil In Me*	10.1977
359	**Smokey Robinson**	*Love Breeze*	2.1978
360	**Tata Vega**	*Try My Love*	2.1979
361	**Thelma Houston**	*Ready To Roll*	10.1978
362	**Stevie Wonder**	*Someday At Christmas*	10.1978
363	**Smokey Robinson**	*Smokin' Live!*	10.1978
364	**Marvin Gaye**	*Here, My Dear*	12.1978
365	**Thelma Houston**	*Ride To The Rainbow*	5.1979
366	**Smokey Robinson**	*Where There's Smoke*	5.1979
367	**Smokey Robinson**	*Warm Thoughts*	2.1980
368	**Shadee**	*I Just Need More Money*	7.1979
369	**Marvin Gaye**	*Love Man*	NR
370	**Tata Vega**	*Givin' All My Love*	NR
371	**Stevie Wonder**	*Stevie Wonder's Journey Through The Secret Life Of Plants*	10.1979
372	**Syreeta**	*Syreeta*	4.1980
373	**Stevie Wonder**	*Hotter Than July*	10.1980
374	**Marvin Gaye**	*In Our Lifetime*	1.1981
375	**Smokey Robinson**	*Being With You*	2.1981
376	**Syreeta**	*Set My Love In Motion*	10.1981
377	**Stevie Wonder**	*Stevie Wonder's Original Musiquarium*	NR
378	**Smokey Robinson**	*Yes, It's You Lady*	NR

MOTOWN LABEL

600	**Mary Wells**	*Bye Bye Baby – I Don't Want To Take A Chance*	8.1961
601	**The Twistin' Kings**	*Twistin' The World Around*	11.1961
602	—		
603	**Various**	*Motown Special Vol. 1*	5.1962
604	**Eddie Holland**	*Eddie Holland*	5.1962
605	**Mary Wells**	*The One Who Really Loves You*	6.1962
606	**The Supremes**	*Meet The Supremes*	12.1963
607	**Mary Wells**	*Two Lovers*	1.1963
608	**Amos Milburn**	*The Return of Amos Milburn: The Blues Boss*	4.1963
609	**Various**	*The Motown Review Vol. 1 Recorded Live At The Apollo in New York*	4.1963
610	**The Supremes**	*Sing Ballads And Blues*	NR
611	**Mary Wells**	*Live! On Stage*	9.1963
612	**Mary Wells**	*Second Time Around*	NR
613	**Marvin Gaye & Mary Wells**	*Together*	4.1964
614	**Various**	*A Package Of 16 Big Hits*	10.1963
615	**Various**	*The Motortown Review Vol. 2 Recorded Live!*	4.1964
616	**Mary Wells**	*Greatest Hits*	4.1964
617	**Mary Wells**	*My Guy*	6.1964
618	—	—	—
619	**Stepin Fetchit**	*My Son The Sit-In*	1964
620	**The Choker Campbell Band**	*Hits Of The Sixties*	2.1965
621	**The Supremes**	*Where Did Out Love Go*	8.1964
622	**Four Tops**	*Four Tops*	1.1965
623	**The Supremes**	*A Bit Of Liverpool*	10.1964
624	**Various**	*16 Hits Vol. 3*	12.1964
625	**The Supremes**	*Sing Country & Western And Pop*	2.1965
626	**The Supremes**	*Live! Live! Live!*	NR
627	**The Supremes**	*More Hits*	7.1965
628	**The Supremes**	*There's A Place For Us*	NR
629	**The Supremes**	*We Remember Sam Cooke*	5.1965
630	**Various**	*Nothing But A Man*	4.1965
631	**Earl Van Dyke & the Soul Brothers**	*That Motown Sound*	5.1965
632	**Billy Eckstine**	*The Prime Of My Life*	11.1965
633	**Various**	*16 Big Hits Vol. 4*	11.1965
634	**Four Tops**	*Second Album*	11.1965
635	—	—	—
636	**The Supremes**	*At The Copa*	11.1965
637	**The Supremes**	*A Tribute To The Girls*	NR
638	**The Supremes**	*Merry Christmas*	11.1965
639	**The Spinners**	*The Original Spinners*	8.1967
640	**Billy Eckstine**	*Live At Lake Tahoe*	NR
641	—	—	—
642	**Various**	*In Loving Memory*	8.1968
643	**The Supremes**	*I Hear A Symphony*	2.1966
644	**Barbara McNair**	*Here I Am*	11.1966
645	**Tony Martin**	*Live! At The Americana*	NR
646	**Billy Eckstine**	*My Way*	11.1966
647	**Four Tops**	*On Top*	7.1966
648	**The Supremes**	*The Supremes Pure Gold*	NR
649	**The Supremes**	*A Go Go*	8.1966
650	**The Supremes**	*Sing Holland, Dozier, Holland*	1.1967
651	**Various**	*16 Big Hits Vol. 5*	8.1966
652	**Tammi Terrell**	*Irresistible*	1.1969
653	**Mary Wells**	*Vintage Stock*	11.1966
654	**Four Tops**	*Live*	11.1966
655	**Various**	*16 Big Hits Vol. 6*	1.1967
656	—	—	—
657	**Four Tops**	*On Broadway*	3.1967
658	—	—	—
659	**The Supremes**	*Sing Rodgers And Hart*	5.1967
660	**Four Tops**	*Reach Out*	7.1967
661	**Various**	*16 Big Hits Vol. 7*	8.1967
662	**Four Tops**	*Greatest Hits*	8.1967

No.	Artist	Title	Date
663	Diana Ross & the Supremes	Greatest Hits	8.1967
664	Chris Clark	Soul Sounds	8.1967
665	Diana Ross & the Supremes	Reflectioins	3.1968
666	Various	16 Big Hits Vol. 8	11.1967
667	Chuck Jackson	Arrives	2.1968
668	Various	16 Big Hits Vol. 9	8.1968
669	Four Tops	Yesterday's Dreams	8.1968
670	Diana Ross & the Supremes	Love Child	11.1968
671	—	—	—
672	Diana Ross & the Supremes	Sing And Perform Funny Girl	8.1968
673	—	—	—
674	—	—	—
675	Four Tops	Now	5.1969
676	Diana Ross & the Supremes	Live At London's Talk Of The Town	8.1968
677	Billy Eckstine	For The Love Of Ivy	11.1968
678	—	—	—
679	Diana Ross & the Supremes & The Temptations	Diana Ross & The Supremes Join The Temptations	11.1968
680	Barbara McNair	The Real Barbara McNair	4.1969
681	Various	Merry Christmas From Motown	12.1968
682	Diana Ross & the Supremes & The Temptations	TCB	12.1968
683	Jonah Jones	Along Came Jonah	1.1969
684	Various	16 Big Hits Vol. 10	4.1969
685	David Ruffin	My Whole World Ended	5.1969
686	Soupy Sales	A Bag Of Soup	4.1969
687	Chuck Jackson	Going Back To Chuck Jackson	5.1969
688	Various	Motortown Review Live!	7.1969
689	Diana Ross & the Supremes	Let The Sunshine In	5.1969
690	Jonah Jones	A Little Dis, A Little Dat	3.1970
691	Red Jones	Strikes Back	8.1969
692	Diana Ross & the Supremes & The Temptations	Together	9.1969
693	Various	16 Big Hits Vol. 11	9.1969
694	Diana Ross & the Supremes	Cream Of The Crop	11.1969
695	Four Tops	Soul Spin	11.1969
696	David Ruffin	Doin' His Thing	11.1969
697	—	—	—
698	Joe Harnell	Moving On	11.1969
699	Diana Ross & the Supremes & The Temptations	On Broadway	11.1969
700	Jackson 5	Diana Ross Presents The Jackson 5	12.1969
701	Various	Shades Of Gospel Soul	3.1970
702	Diana Ross & the Supremes	Greatest Hits Vol. 3	12.1969
703	Various	Motown At The Hollywood Palace	3.1970
704	Four Tops	Still Waters Run Deep	3.1970
705	The Supremes	Right On	5.1970
706	—	—	—
707	Various	Motown Chartbusters Vol. 1	9.1970
708	Diana Ross & the Supremes	Farewell	4.1970
709	Jackson 5	ABC	5.1970
710	Sammy Davis Jr	Something For Everyone	5.1970
711	Diana Ross	Diana Ross	5.1970
712	Blinky	Sunny And Warm	NR
713	Jackson 5	Christmas Album	10.1970
714	—	—	—
715	Various	Motown Chartbusters Vol. 2	9.1970
716	Ding Dongs	Gimme Dat Ding	7.1970
717	The Supremes & Four Tops	Magnificent Seven	9.1970
718	Jackson 5	Third Album	9.1970
719	Diana Ross	Diana! (TV Special)	3.1971
720	The Supremes	New Ways But Love Stays	9.1970
721	Four Tops	Changing Times	9.1970
722	Gordon Staples & the Motown Strings	Strung Out	9.1970
723	Diana Ross	Surrender	7.1971
724	Diana Ross	Everything Is Everything	10.1970
725	Various	Christmas Gift Rap	10.1970
726	Various	The Motown Story (box set)	2.1971
*727			
*728	Various	The Motown Story	
*729		* numbers not released separately	
*730			
*731			
732	Various	Motown Chartbusters Vol. 3	5.1971
733	—		
734	Various	Motown Chartbusters Vol. 4	5.1971
735	Jackson 5	Maybe Tomorrow	4.1971
736	The Supremes & Four Tops	Return Of The Magnificent Seven	5.1971
737	The Supremes	Touch	5.1971
738	Bobby Darin	Live At The Desert Inn Finally	NR
739	Various	Promotional Album	NR
740	Four Tops	Greatest Hits Vol. 2	8.1971
741	Jackson 5	Greatest Hits	12.1971
742	Jackson 5	Goin' Back To Indiana	9.1971
743	Various	The Key To The Kingdom	9.1971
744	Various	Motown Chartbusters Vol. 5	12.1971
745	The Supremes & Four Tops	Dynamite	12.1971
746	The Supremes	Promises Kept	NR
747	Michael Jackson	Got To Be There	1.1972
748	Four Tops	Nature Planned It	4.1972
749	—	—	—
750	Jackson 5	Lookin' Through The Windows	5.1972
751	The Supremes	Floy Joy	5.1972
752	Jermaine Jackson	Jermaine	7.1972
753	Bobby Darin	Bobby Darin	7.1972
754	Jerry Ross Symposium	Jerry Ross Symposium	8.1972
755	Michael Jackson	Ben	8.1972
756	The Supremes	Produced And Arranged By Jimmy Webb	10.1972
757	Jackie Jackson	Jackie Jackson	NR
758	Diana Ross	Lady Sings The Blues	12.1972
759	—		
760	Various	Pippin (Orig. Cast Album)	12.1972
761	Jackson 5	Skywriter	3.1973
762	David Ruffin	David Ruffin	2.1973
763	Various	Promotional 'Lady Sings The Blues' LP	—
764	Four Tops	The Best Of The Four Tops	4.1973
765	—		
766	Willie Hutch	The Mack	4.1973
767	Michael Jackson	Music And Me	4.1973
768	Puzzle	Puzzle	4.1973
769	The Spinners	The Best Of The Spinners	4.1973
770	Blinky	Softly	NR
771	Reuben Howell	Reuben Howell	4.1973
772	Diana Ross	Touch Me In The Morning	6.1973
773	—	—	—
774	Severin Browne	Severin Browne	5.1973
775	Jermaine Jackson	Come Into My Life	5.1973
776	Stacie Johnson	Stacie	NR
777	Scatman Crothers	Big Ben Sings	6.1973
778	Martha Reeves & the Vandellas	Anthology	6.1974
779	Severin Browne	The New Improved	11.1974
780	Jackson 5	Dancing Machine	9.1974
781	The Devastating Affair	The Devastating Affair	NR

782	The Temptations	Anthology – 10th Anniversary Special	8.1973
783	Jackson 5	Get It Together	9.1973
784	Willie Hutch	Fully Exposed	9.1973
785	Jackie Jackson	Jackie Jackson	10.1973
786	Jr Walker & the All Stars	Anthology	7.1974
787	XIT	Relocation	NR
788	Frankie Valli & the Four Seasons	Inside Out	NR
789	Stephen Cohn	Stephen Cohn	9.1973
790	Gloria Jones	Share My Love	9.1973
791	Marvin Gaye	Anthology	4.1974
792	Gladys Knight & the Pips	Anthology	1.1974
793	Smokey Robinson & the Miracles	Anthology	1.1974
794	Diana Ross & the Supremes	Anthology	5.1974
795	Various	A Motown Christmas	9.1973
796	The Crusaders	At Their Best	9.1973
797	Martin & Finley	Dazzle 'Em With Footwork	6.1974
798	Commodores	Machine Gun	7.1974
799	Reuben Howell	Rings	6.1974
800	Various	Save The Children (Live!)	4.1974
801	Diana Ross	Live! At The Caesar's Palace	5.1974
802	Edwin Starr	Hell Up in Harlem	1.1974
803	Diana Ross & Marvin Gaye	Diana & Marvin	10.1973
804	Stevie Wonder	Anthology/Looking Back	12.1977
805	Diahann Carroll	Diahann Carroll	4.1974
806	Riot	Welcome To The World Of Riot	5.1974
807	Puzzle	Second Album	2.1974
808	Syreeta	Stevie Wonder Presents Syreeta	6.1974
809	Four Tops	Anthology	7.1974
810	Michael Edward Campbell	Michael Edward Campbell	4.1974
811	Willie Hutch	Foxy Brown	4.1974
812	Diana Ross	Last Time I Saw Him	12.1973
813	Bobby Darin	Darin 1936-1973	2.1974
814	Caston & Majors	Caston & Majors	11.1974
815	Willie Hutch	Mark Of The Beast	11.1974
816	Puzzle	How Do We Get Out Of The Business Alive	NR
817	Rickenstein	Rickenstein	NR
818	David Ruffin	Me & Rock 'n' Roll Are Here To Stay	11.1974
819	G. C. Cameron	Love Songs And Other Tragedies	11.1974
820	Commodores	Caught In The Act	2.1975
821	Magic Disco Machine	Discotech	5.1975
822	The Dynamic Superiors	The Dynamic Superiors	1.1975
823	—	—	—
824	Various	Discotech No. 1	5.1975
825	Michael Jackson	Forever, Michael	1.1975
826	The Originals	California Sunset	2.1975
827	The Marvelettes	Anthology	5.1975
828	The Supremes	The Supremes	5.1975
829	Jackson 5	Moving Violation	5.1975
830	—	—	—
831	Various	Discotech No. 2	5.1975
832	Yvonne Fair	The Bitch Is Black	5.1975
833	Various	Discotech No. 3	NR
834	Sonny Burke	Free Delivery	NR
835	Various	Motortown Revue Groups	NR
836	Various	Love Ballads	NR
837	Various	Mellow Moods	NR
838	Willie Hutch	Ode To My Lady	6.1975
839	Soundtrack Album	Murph The Surph	6.1975
840	Various	Cooley High	6.1975
841	The Dynamic Superiors	Pure Pleasure	7.1975
842	Jermaine Jackson	My Name Is Jermaine	8.1976
843	Lenny Williams	Rise Sleeping Beauty	7.1975
844	Syreeta	Syreeta	NR
845	Rose Banks	Rose	5.1976
846	Leslie Uggams	Leslie Uggams	8.1975
847	Libra	Libra	8.1975
848	Commodores	Movin' On	10.1975
849	David Ruffin	Who I Am	10.1975
850	Jerry Butler	Love's On The Menu	6.1976
851	Michael Jackson	The Best Of Michael Jackson	8.1975
852	Frankie Valli	Inside You	9.1975
853	Various	Motown Discotech 3	1.1976
854	Willie Hutch	Concert In Blues	2.1976
855	G. C. Cameron	G. C. Cameron	5.1976
856	Kathe Green	Kathe Green	NR
857	Magic Disco Machine	Motown Magic Disco Machine Vol. 2	5.1976
858	Diana Ross	Mahogany (f/s.)	10.1975
859	Stephanie Mills	For The First Time	11.1975
860	Various	Motown Original Versions	2.1976
861	Diana Ross	Diana Ross	2.1976
862	The Dynamic Superiors	Sky's The Limit	NR
863	The Supremes	High Energy	4.1976
864	Libra	Winter's Day Nightmare	5.1976
865	Jackson 5	Joyful Jukebox Music	10.1976
866	David Ruffin	Everything's Coming Up Love	5.1976
867	Commodores	Hot On The Tracks	6.1976
868	Jackson 5	Anthology	6.1976
869	Diana Ross	Greatest Hits	7.1976
870	Ronnie McNeir	Love's Coming Down	8.1976
871	Willie Hutch	Color Her Sunshine	9.1976
872	Various	Motown Discotech 4	8.1976
873	The Supremes	Mary, Scherrie And Susaye	10.1976
874	Willie Hutch	Havin' A House Party	5.1977
875	The Dynamic Superiors	You Name It	10.1976
876	Various	Guys And Dolls Original Cast Album	12.1976
877	Diana Ross	An Evening With Diana Ross	1.1977
878	Jerry Butler	Suite For The Single Girl	1.1977
879	The Dynamic Superiors	Give And Take	5.1977
880	G. C. Cameron	You're What's Missing In My Life	1.1977
881	Various	Motown's Preferred Stock – Stock Option No. 1	2.1977
882	Various	Motown's Preferred Stock – Stock Option No. 2	2.1977
883	Various	Motown's Preferred Stock – Stock Option No. 3	2.1977
884	Commodores	Commodores	3.1977
885	David Ruffin	In My Stride	5.1977
886	Mandré	Mandré	4.1977
887	Thelma Houston & Jerry Butler	Thelma & Jerry	5.1977
888	Jermaine Jackson	Feel The Fire	6.1977
889	Albert Finney	Albert Finney's Album	6.1977
890	Diana Ross	Baby It's Me	9.1977
891	Syreeta & G. C. Cameron	Rich Love, Poor Love	8.1977
892	Jerry Butler	It All Comes Out In My Song	10.1977
893	—	—	—
894	Commodores	Live!	10.1977
895	David Ruffin	At His Best	1.1978
896	5th Dimension	Star Dancing	1.1978
897	Cuba Gooding	The 1st Cuba Gooding Album	2.1978
898	Jermaine Jackson	Frontiers	2.1978
899	Platinum Hook	Platinum Hook	3.1978
900	Mandré	Mandré II	3.1978
901	Three Ounces Of Love	Three Ounces Of Love	4.1978
902	Commodores	Natural High	5.1978

903	Thelma Houston & Jerry Butler	Two To One	6.1978
904	The Supremes	At Their Best	6.1978
905	Prime Time	Motown Presents Prime Time	7.1978
906	Finished Touch	Need To Know You Better	7.1978
907	Diana Ross	Ross	9.1978
908	Motown Sounds	Space Dance	1.1979
909	Bloodstone	Don't Stop!	1.1979
910	Grover Washington Jr	Reed Seed	9.1978
911	Bonnie Pointer	Bonnie Pointer	10.1978
912	Commodores	Greatest Hits	10.1978
913	T. Boy Ross	Changes	2.1979
914	The 5th Dimension	High On Sunshine	1.1979
915	Billy Preston & Syreeta	Music From The Motion Picture Fast Break	3.1979
916	Finished Touch	Finished Touch	NR
917	Mandré	M3000	2.1979
918	Platinum Hook	It's Time	3,1979
919	Cuba Gooding	Love Dancer	4.1979
920	Scherrie & Susaye	Partners	10.1979
921	Various	Pops We Love You . . . The Album	4.1979
922	Patrick Gammon	Don't Touch Me	5.1979
923	Diana Ross	The Boss	5.1979
924	Dr Strut	Dr Strut	5.1979
925	Billy Preston	Late At Night	7.1979
926	Commodores	Midnight Magic	7.1979
927	Mary Wilson	Mary Wilson	8.1979
928	Jermaine Jackson	Let's Get Serious	3.1980
929	Bonnie Pointer	Bonnie Pointer	11.1979
930	Cook County	Pinball Playboy (Playboy Theme)	11.1979
931	Dr Strut	Struttin'	2.1980
932	Flight	Excursion Beyond	2.1980
933	Grover Washington Jr	Skylarkin'	2.1980
934	The Planets	The Planets	2.1980
935	—	—	—
936	Diana Ross	Diana	5.1980
937	Various	20/20-Twenty No. 1 Hits From Twenty Years At Motown	3.1980
938	Ozone	Walk On	4.1980
939	Commodores	Heroes	6.1980
940	Grover Washington Jr	Baddest	8.1980
941	Billy Preston	The Way I Am	2.1981
942	Black Russian	Black Russian	5.1980
943	Platinum Hook	Ecstasy Paradise	NR
944	Michal Urbaniak	Serenade For The City	8.1980
945	Ahmad Jamal	Night Song	10.1980
946	The Dazz Band	Invitation To Love	10.1980
947	Various	It's My Turn (f/s.)	10.1980
948	Jermaine Jackson	Jermaine	11.1980
949	Various	Loving Couples (f/s.)	11.1980
950	Ozone	Jump On It	1.1981
951	Diana Ross	To Love Again	2.1981
952	Jermaine Jackson	I Like Your Style	8.1981
953	José Feliciano	José Feliciano	10.1981
954	Commodores	Anthology	NR
955	Commodores	In The Pocket	6.1981
956	Michael Jackson	One Day In Your Life	3.1981
957	Dazz Band	Let The Music Play	5.1981
958	Billy Preston & Syreeta	Billy Preston & Syreeta	7.1981
959	Lovesmith	Lovesmith	8.1981
960	Diana Ross	All The Great Hits	10.1981
961	Grover Washington Jr	Anthology	9.1981
962	Ozone	Send It	9.1981

6000 Series (incorporating all American labels. Includes Compact Discs.)

* Compact disc only.   † Cassette only.

‡ American and Canadian release only.

6000M	Bettye Lavette	Tell Me A Lie	1.1982
6001T	Smokey Robinson	Yes, It's You Lady	1.1982
6002T	Stevie Wonder	Stevie Wonder's Original Musiquarium	5.1982
6003G	Nolen & Crossley	Ambience	2.1982
6004M	Dazz Band	Keep It Live	2.1982
6005G	Rick James	Throwin' Down	5.1982
6006G	High Inergy	So Right	4.1982
6007M	Lionel Richie	Lionel Richie (CD: 2.1984)	9.1982
6008G	The Temptations	Reunion	4.1982
6009M	Charlene	I've Never Been To Me	3.1982
6010M	Jean Carn	Trust Me	5.1982
6011M	Ozone	Li'l Suzy	7.1982
6012G	DeBarge	All This Love	7.1982
6013M	Lawanda Page	Watch It Sucker	NR
6014M	Regal Funkharmonic Orchestra	Strung Out On Motown	7.1982
6015T	Gene Van Buren	What's Your Pleasure	12.1982
6016	—	—	—
6017M	Jermaine Jackson	Let Me Tickle Your Fancy	7.1982
6018L	Jose Feliciano	Escenas De Amor (Love Scenes)	7.1982
6019M	O.C. Smith	Love Changes	5.1982
6020M	Billy Preston	Pressin' on	8.1982
6021L	Pedro Montero	Amor Secreto	8.1982
6022M	Bobby Nunn	Second To Nunn	8.1982
6023G	Bobby Militello	Blow – Rick James Presents	10.1982
6024M	Charlene	The Sky Is The Limit	12.1982
6025	—	—	—
6026M	Bill Cosby	Himself (CD: 5.1986)	11.1982
6027M	Charlene	Used To Be	10.1982
6028M	Commodores	All The Great Hits	11.1982
6029G	Monalisa Young	Knife	11.1983
6030T	Smokey Robinson	Touch The Sky	1.1983
6031M	Dazz Band	On The One	1.1983
6032G	The Temptations	Surface Thrills	2.1983
6033M	Stephanie Mills	Love Has Lifted Me	11.1982
6034M	Thelma Houston	Reachin' All Around	11.1982
6035M	Jose Feliciano	Romance In The Night	3.1983
6036M	Finis Henderson	Finis	4.1983
6037M	Ozone	Glasses	3.1983
6038M	Kagny & the Dirty Rats	Kagny And The Dirty Rats	3.1983
6039T	Syreeta	The Spell	4.1983
6040G	Mary Jane Girls	Mary Jane Girls	4.1983
6041G	High Inergy	Groove Patrol	4.1983
6042G	Stone City Band	Out Of The Shadows: Meet The Stone City Band	7.1983
6043G	Rick James	Cold Blooded	8.1983
6044M	Commodores	Anthology	5.1983
6045M	Michael Lovesmith	I Can Make It Happen	6.1983
6046C	Wolf & Wolf	Wolf And Wolf	5.1984
6047T	Stevie Wonder	People Move, Human Plays	NR
6048M	Various	The Motown Story (box set)	5.1983
6049M	Diana Ross	Anthology	5.1983
6050T	Smokey Robinson	Untitled	NR
6051M	Bobby Nunn	Private Party	9.1983
6052M	Rockwell	Somebody's Watching Me	1.1984
6053M	Junior Walker	Blow The House Down	8.1983
6054M	Commodores	13	9.1983
6055L	Jose Feliciano	Me Enamore	NR
6056C	Kidd Glove	Killer Instinct	2.1984
6057G	Dennis Edwards	Don't Look Any Further	1.1984
6058M	Marvin Gaye	Every Great Motown Hit: 15 Spectacular Performances	9.1983
6059M	Lionel Richie	Can't Slow Down (CD: 2.1984)	10.1983
6060C	Jakata	Light The Night	8.1984
6061G	DeBarge	in A Special Way	9.1983
6062M	Various	The Big Chill (f/s.)	9.1983
6063C	The Coyote Sisters	The Coyote Sisters	7.1984
6064T	Smokey Robinson	Blame It On Love And All The Great Hits	8.1983
6065C	Various	Get Crazy (f/s.)	8.1983
6066M	Four Tops	Back Where I Belong	10.1983
6067C	Tiggi Clay	Tiggi Clay	1.1984

Cat. No.	Artist	Title	Date
*6068M	**Commodores**	*Compact Command Performances: 14 Greatest Hits*	2.1984
*6069T	**Marvin Gaye**	*Compact Command Performances: 15 Greatest Hits*	2.1984
*6070M	**Michael Jackson & Jackson 5**	*Compact Command Performances: 18 Greatest Hits*	2.1984
*6071T	**Smokey Robinson & the Miracles**	*Compact Command Performances: 18 Greatest Hits*	2.1984
*6072M	**Diana Ross**	*Compact Command Performances: 14 Greatest Hits*	2.1984
*6073M	**Diana Ross & the Supremes**	*Compact Command Performances: 20 Greatest Hits*	2.1984
†6074M	**Commodores**	*Machine Gun / Movin' On*	9.1983
†6075M	**Four Tops**	*Four Tops / Reach Out*	9.1983
†6076M	**Marvin Gaye**	*Live! / Let's Get It On*	9.1983
†6077M	**Michael Jackson**	*Got To Be There / Ben*	9.1983
†6078M	**Rick James**	*Come Get It / Fire It Up*	9.1983
†6079M	**The Temptations**	*Meet The Temptations / Masterpiece*	9.1983
†6080M	**Grover Washington Jr**	*Mister Magic / Feels So Good*	9.1983
†6081M	**Stevie Wonder**	*Signed Sealed Delivered / My Cherie Amour*	9.1983
†6082M	**Diana Ross**	*Touch Me In The Morning / Live! At Caesar's Palace*	9.1983
†6083M	**Marvin Gaye & Tammi Terrell**	*You're All I Need / United*	9.1983
6084M	**Dazz Band**	*Joystick*	11.1983
6085G	**The Temptations**	*Back To Basics*	10.1983
6086M	**Various**	*Christine (f/s.)*	11.1983
6087G	**Teena Marie**	*You Got The Love*	NR
6088M	**Bobby King**	*Love In The Fire*	3.1984
6089T	**Gene Van Buren**	*Love Never Dies*	NR
6090M	**Charlene**	*Hit And Run Lover*	7.1984
6091M	**Various**	*Making Trax: The Great Instrumentals*	3.1984
6092G	**Mary Jane Girls**	*Only Four You (CD: 9.1985)*	2.1985
6093M	**Michael Lovesmith**	*Diamond In The Raw*	4.1984
6094M	**Various**	*More Songs From The Original Soundtrack: 'The Big Chill'*	4.1984
6095G	**Rick James**	*Reflections Of Rick James (CD: 9.1984)*	8.1984
6096M	**Koko-Pop**	*Koko-Pop*	5.1984
6097C	**Duke Jupiter**	*White Knuckle Ride*	4.1984
6098T	**Smokey Robinson**	*Essar*	5.1984
6099M	**Michael Jackson & Jackson 5**	*14 Greatest Hits (pic. disc)*	5.1984
†6100M	**Michael Jackson & Jackson 5**	*16 Greatest Hits*	5.1984
6101M	**Michael Jackson**	*Farewell My Summer Love*	5.1984
6102M	**Vanity**	*Wild Animal*	8.1984
6103M	**Sam Harris**	*Sam Harris (CD: 2.1985)*	8.1984
6104M	**Kagny**	*Mind Control*	NR
*6105M	**Diana Ross**	*All The Great Love Songs*	9.1984
*6106M	**Four Tops**	*Compact Command Performances (19 Greatest Hits)*	9.1984
*6107M	**Commodores**	*All The Great Love Songs*	9.1984
6108M	**Stevie Wonder**	*Woman In Red (f/s., album) (CD: 12.1984)*	8.1984
*6109M	**Gladys Knight & the Pips**	*Compact Command Performances: 17 Greatest Hits*	9.1984
*6110M	**Various**	*Motown Grammy R&B Performances Of The 1960s And 1970s*	9.1984
*6111M	**Al Green**	*Compact Command Performances: 14 Greatest Hits*	8.1984
6112M	**Phyllis St. James**	*Ain't No Turnin' Back*	8.1984
*6113T	**Stevie Wonder**	*Original Musiquarium Vol. 1 and Vol. 2*	1.1985
6114	—	—	—
*6115T	**Stevie Wonder**	*Songs In The Key Of Life Vol. 1 and Vol. 2*	12.1984
6116	—	—	—
6117M	**Dazz Band**	*Jukebox*	9.1984
6118M	**Bobby Nunn**	*Fresh*	NR
6119G	**The Temptations**	*Truly For You*	10.1984
*6120M	**Various**	*The Bill Chill*	11.1984
6121M	**Thomas McClary**	*Thomas McClary*	11.1984
6122M	**Rockwell**	*Captured*	1.1985
6123G	**DeBarge**	*Rhythm Of The Night (CD: 4.1985)*	2.1985
6124M	**Commodores**	*Nightshift (CD: 4.1985)*	1.1985
*6125G	**The Temptations**	*Compact Command Performances: 17 Greatest Hits*	3.1985
*6126M	**Grover Washington Jr**	*At His Best*	3.1985
*6127T	**Stevie Wonder**	*Stevie Wonder's Journey Through The Secret Life Of Plants*	3.1985
6128M	**Various**	*Berry Gordy's 'The Last Dragon' (f/s.)*	2.1985
6129	—	—	—
6130M	**Four Tops**	*Magic*	5.1985
6131M	**Various**	*The Flamingo Kid (f/s.)*	1.1985
*6132M	**Various**	*25# 1 Hits From Twenty-Five Years*	4.1985
*6133M	**Diana Ross**	*Lady Sings The Blues (f/s.)*	4.1985
6134T	**Stevie Wonder**	*In Square Circle (CD: 10.1985)*	9.1985
6135G	**Rick James**	*Glow*	4.1985
6136M	**The Emotions**	*If I Only Knew*	3.1985
*6137M	**Various**	*20 Greatest Songs In Motown History*	8.1985
*6138M	**Various**	*The Composer Series – The Greatest Songs Written By Holland-Dozier-Holland*	9.1985
*6139M	**Various**	*The Composer Series – The Greatest Songs Written By Smokey Robinson*	8.1985
*6140M	**Various**	*The Composer Series – The Greatest Songs Written By Ashford & Simpson*	8.1985
6141M	**Maureen Steele**	*Nature Of The Beast*	4.1985
6142M	**Willie Hutch**	*Making A Game Out Of Love*	6.1985
*6143M	**Lionel Richie: The Composer Various Artists**	*Great Love Songs With The Commodores And Diana Ross*	8.1985
*6144T	**Stevie Wonder**	*Love Songs – 20 Classic Hits*	8.1985
6145M	**Michael Lovesmith**	*Rhymes Of Passion*	6.1985
6156M	**Alfie**	*That Look*	1.1986
6147G	**Val Young**	*Seduction*	7.1985
6148G	**Dennis Edwards**	*Coolin' Out*	6.1985
6149M	**Dazz Band**	*Hot Spot*	7.1985
6150M	**Lushus Daim & the Pretty Vain**	*More Than You Can Handle*	9.1985
*6151T	**Stevie Wonder**	*Talking Book*	11.1985
*6152T	**Stevie Wonder**	*Innervisions*	11.1985
*6153T	**Marvin Gaye**	*Marvin Gaye & His Women – Classic Duets*	10.1985
6154M	**Nick Jameson**	*A Crowd Of One*	NR
6155M	**Koko-Pop**	*Secrets Of Lonely Boys*	8.1985
6156T	**Smokey Robinson**	*Smoke Signals (CD: 3.1986)*	1.1986
6157M	**Pal**	*Truth For The Moment*	NR

Cat. No.	Artist	Title	Date
6158M	Lionel Richie	Dancing On The Ceiling (CD: 8.1986)	8.1986
‡6159	Various	Good Feeling Music of The Big Chill Generation Vol. 1	12.1985
‡6160	Various	Good Feeling Music of The Big Chill Generation Vol. 2	12.1985
‡6161	Various	Good Feeling Music of The Big Chill Generation Vol. 3	12.1985
6162M	Duke Jupiter	The Line Of Your Fire	9.1985
6163M	Warp 9	Fade In, Fade Out	1.1986
6164G	The Temptations	Touch Me	11.1985
6165M	Sam Harris	Sam-I-Am	1.1986
6166M	Troy Johnson	Getting A Grip On Love	3.1986
6167M	Vanity	Skin On Skin	2.1986
6168M	Guinn	Guinn	3.1986
*6169T	The Marvelettes	Compact Command Performances: 23 Greatest Hits	3.1986
*6170G	Martha Reeves & the Vandellas	Compact Command Performances: 24 Greatest Hits	3.1986
*6171M	Mary Wells	Compact Command Performances: 22 Greatest Hits	5.1986
6172T	Marvin Gaye	Motown Remembers Marvin Gaye	3.1986
*6173G	DeBarge	Greatest Hits	5.1986
*6174M	Various	Motown's Biggest Pop Hits	5.1986
*6175T	Stevie Wonder	Original Musiquarium Vol. 1	NR
*6176T	Stevie Wonder	Original Musiquarium Vol. 2	NR
*6177M	Various	Endless Love – 15 Of Motown's Greatest Love Songs	4.1986
6178M	Rockwell	The Genie	5.1986
6179M	Fizzy Qwick	Fizzy Qwick	6.1986
6180M	Various	A Fine Mess (f/s)	7.1986
6181G	El DeBarge	El DeBarge (CD: 7.1986)	5.1986
*6182G	Teena Marie	Compact Command Performances	9.1986
*6183M	Various	20 Hard To Find Motown Classics Vol. 1	5.1986
*6184M	Various	20 Hard To Find Motown Classics Vol. 2	5.1986
6185G	Rick James	The Flag (CD: 5.1986)	5.1986
*6186M	Various	Pippin (Original Cast)	6.1986
*6187M	Various	Guys And Dolls (Original Cast)	NR
*6188M	Four Tops	Anthology	10.1986
*6189G	The Temptations	Anthology	10.1986
*6190M	Various	The Motown Story – The First 25 Years	11.1986
*6191T	Marvin Gaye	Live! At The London Palladium	10.1986
*6192M	Various	You Can't Hurry Love	8.1986
*6193M	Diana Ross & the Supremes	25th Anniversary	10.1986
*6194M	Jackson 5	Anthology	10.1986
*6195M	Michael Jackson		10.1986
*6196T	Smokey Robinson & the Miracles	Anthology	10.1986
*6197M	Diana Ross	Anthology	10.1986
*6198M	Diana Ross & the Supremes	Anthology	10.1986
*6199T	Marvin Gaye	Anthology	10.1986
*6200M	Gladys Knight & the Pips	Anthology	10.1986
*6201T	Marvin Gaye	Compact Command Performances: Vol. 2	9.1986
*6202T	Smokey Robinson & the Miracles	Compact Command Performances: Vol. 2	9.1986
*6203M	Jr Walker & the All Stars	Compact Command Performances	9.1986
*6204M	The Temptations	25th Anniversary	10.1986
*6205T	Stevie Wonder	Hotter Than July	9.1986
‡*6206M	Jimmy Reed	Compact Command Performances	9.1986
6207G	The Temptations	To Be Continued (CD: 12.1986)	6.1986
‡*6208M	Little Richard	Compact Command Performances	9.1986
6209M	Jakata	Designs Of The Heart	NR
6210M	Nick Jameson	A Crowd of One	7.1986
6211M	Four Tops	Hot Nights	NR
6212M	Stacy Lattisaw	Take Me All The Way	9.1986
6213G	Mary Jane Girls	Conversation	NR
6214M	Chico DeBarge	Chico DeBarge	9.1986
‡*6215M	Various	Hits From The Legendary Vee-Jay Records	11.1986
6216G	General Kane	In Full Chill	10.1986
6217M	Bunny DeBarge	In Love	1.1987
*6218M	Duane Eddy	Compact Command Performances	1.1987
*6219M	Various	25 Hard-To-Find Motown Classics: Vol. 3	1.1987
*6220G	Dr Martin Luther King	Compact Command Performances (His Greatest Speeches In Their Original And Complete Form)	12.1986
*6221M	Various	24 Enduring Classics From The Small Label Era Of Rock Music Including Mortown Rarities	NR
6222M	Bruce Willis	The Return Of Bruno (CD: 1.1987)	1.1987
6223M	Carrie McDowell	Carrie McDowell	7.1987
6224M	Blake & Hines	Blake & Hines	3.1987
6225M	F.G.O.	Give Her What She Wants	NR
6226M	Smokey Robinson	One Heartbeat (CD: 4.1987)	2.1987
*6227M	Bobby Darin	Live! At The Desert Inn	4.1987
6228M	Angela Cole	Turn Up The Beat	NR
6229M	Georgio	Sexappeal (CD: 3.1988)	3.1987
*6230M	Various	Motown Dance Party Vol. 1	4.1987
*6231M	Various	Motown Dance Party Vol. 2	4.1987
*6232M	Various	Motown Around The World	4.1987
*6233M	Diana Ross & the Supremes	The Rodgers & Hart Collection	4.1987
6234M	Garry Glenn	Feels Good To Feel Good (CD: 9.1987)	6.1987
6235M	Various Artists	Music From The Motion Picture Soundtrack Police Acadamy IV 'Citizens on Patrol'	3.1987
6236M	Kim O'Leary	Kim O'Leary	NR
6237M	Darryl Duncan	Heaven	2,1988
6238M	General Kane	Wide Open	7.1987
6239M	Various Artists	Motown Dance Party '88	NR
6240M	El DeBarge	Real Love	TBA
6241M	Ada Dyer	Meant To Be	4.1988
6242M	Family Dream	—	NR
6243M	Superiors	—	NR
6244M	Wilson Pickett	American Soul Man	8.1987
‡6245M	Chris Rea	Dancing With Strangers (CD: 9.1987)	9.1987
6246M	Temptations	Together Again (CD: 9.1987)	9.1987
6247M	Stacy Lattisaw	Personal Attention (CD: 2.1988)	2.1988
6248M	Stevie Wonder	Characters (CD: 11.1987)	11.1987
6249M	Chco DeBarge	Kiss Serious	9.1987
6250M	Michael Jackson	The Original Soul Of . . . (CD: 11.1987)	11.1987
6251M	Brownmark	Just Like That (CD: 2.1988)	2.1988
6252M	Magic Lady	Magic Lady (CD: 4.1988)	4.1988

U.S.A. MID-LINE SERIES (1987)

This series supercedes the 5000 Series and is for albums only. The 5000 Series is now used for cassettes only; CDs on 9000 Series.

2801	**Various**	Motown Grammy R&B Performances Of The 60's	3.1987
2802	**Dazz Band**	Greatest Hits	3.1987
2803	**Various**	25 Years Of Motown Classics – The Grammy Award Winners	3.1987
2804	**Four Tops**	Great Songs And Performances That Inspired The Motown 25th Anniversary TV Special	3.1987
2805	**Diana Ross & the Supremes**	I Hear A Symphony	3.1987
2806	**Various**	Lionel Richie: The Composer – Great Love Songs With The Commodores – Diana Ross	3.1987
2807	**Marvin Gaye**	Super Hits	3.1987
2808	**Rick James**	Greatest Hits	3.1987
2809	**Various**	Endless Love: Motown's Greatest Love Songs	3.1987
2810	**Stevie Wonder**	Signed, Sealed, Delivered	3.1987
2811	**Al Green**	Greatest Hits	3.1987
2812	**Marvin Gaye**	Greatest Hits	3.1987
2813	**Bill Cosby**	Himself	3.1987
2814	**Marvin Gaye & Tammi Terrell**	United	3.1987
2815	**Marvin Gaye**	What's Going On	3.1987
2816	**The Temptations**	All The Million Sellers	3.1987
2617	**Michael Jackson**	Motown Superstar Series Vol. 7	3.1987
2818	**Four Tops**	Greatest Hits	3.1987
‡2819	**Various Artists**	Good Feeling Music Of The Big Chill Generation Vol. 1	3.1987
2820	**Al Green**	Greatest Hits Vol. 2	3.1987
2821	**Al Green**	I'm Still In Love With You	3.1987
2822	**Stevie Wonder**	My Cherie Amour	3.1987
2823	**Gladys Knight & the Pips**	All The Greatest Hits	3.1987
2824	**Smokey Robinson & the Miracles**	Great Songs And Performances That Inspired The Motown 25th Anniversary TV Special	3.1987
2825	**Jackson 5**	Motown Superstar Series Vol. 12	3.1987
2826	**Mary Wells**	Greatest Hits	3.1987
2827	**Smokey Robinson & the Miracles**	Greatest Hits Vol. 2	3.1987
2828	**Martha Reeves & the Vandellas**	Greatest Hits	3.1987
2829	**Various Artists**	16 #1 Hits From The Late 60s	3.1987
2830	**The Temptations**	. . . Sing Smokey	3.1987
2831	**Commodores**	Movin' On	5.1987
2832	**Commodores**	Midnight Magic	5.1987
2833	**Diana Ross**	Diana Ross (1976 LP)	5.1987
2834	**Marvin Gaye**	Let's Get It On	5.1987
2835	**Diana Ross & the Supremes**	Great Songs And Performances That Inspired The Motown 25th Anniversary TV Special	5.1987
2836	**Teena Marie**	Greatest Hits	5.1987
2837	**Jackson 5**	Greatest Hits	5.1987
2838	**Al Green**	Lets Stay Together	5.1987
2839	**Various Artists**	16 #1 Hits From The Early 60s	5.1987
2840	**Rare Earth**	Get Ready	5.1987
2841	**Marvin Gaye**	Live!	5.1987
2842	**The Temptations**	Give Love At Christmas	7.1987
2843	**Jackson 5**	Christmas Album	10.1987
2844	**Rick James**	Street Songs	2.1988
2845	**Mary Jane Girls**	Mary Jane Girls	2.1988

AMERICAN MID-PRICE SERIES
(Albums &Cassettes)

PREFIX M5-no-V1 unless stated otherwise

101	**Diana Ross & the Supremes**	Motown Superstar Series Vol. 1	9.1980
102	**Marvin Gaye & Tammi Terrell**	Motown Superstar Series Vol. 2	8.1980
103	**Edwin Starr**	Motown Superstar Series Vol. 3	8.1980
104	**Frankie Valli & the Four Seasons**	Motown Superstar Series Vol. 4	8.1980
105	**Jr Walker & the All Stars**	Motown Superstar Series Vol. 5	8.1980
106	**The Isley Brothers**	Motown Superstar Series Vol. 6	8.1980
107	**Michael Jackson**	Motown Superstar Series Vol. 7	8.1980
108	**Jimmy & David Ruffin**	Motown Superstar Series Vol. 8	8.1980
109	**The Spinners**	Motown Superstar Series Vol. 9	8.1980
110	**The Originals**	Motown Superstar Series Vol. 10	8.1980
111	**Martha Reeves & the Vandellas**	Motown Superstar Series Vol. 11	9.1980
112	**Jackson 5**	Motown Superstar Series Vol. 12	9.1980
113	**Gladys Knight & the Pips**	Motown Superstar Series Vol. 13	9.1980
114	**Four Tops**	Motown Superstar Series Vol. 14	9.1980
115	**Marvin Gaye**	Motown Superstar Series Vol. 15	9.1980
116	**Rare Earth**	Motown Superstar Series Vol. 16	4.1981
117	**Jermaine Jackson**	Motown Superstar Series Vol. 17	4.1981
118	**Smokey Robinson**	Motown Superstar Series Vol. 18	4.1981
119	**Eddie Kendricks**	Motown Superstar Series Vol. 19	4.1981
120	**Thelma Houston**	Motown Superstar Series Vol. 20	4.1981
121	**Commodores**	Machine Gun	6.1981
122	**Four Tops**	Four Tops	6.1981
123	**The Supremes & Four Tops**	Magnificent Seven	7.1981
124	**Diana Ross & Marvin Gaye**	Diana & Marvin	6.1981
125	**Marvin Gaye**	MPG	6.1981
126	**Gladys Knight & the Pips**	Everybody Needs Love	6.1981
127	**Thelma Houston**	Sunshower	6.1981
128	**The Isley Brothers**	This Old Heart Of Mine	6.1981
129	**Jackson 5**	Diana Ross Presents The Jackson 5	6.1981
130	**Michael Jackson**	Got To Be There	6.1981
131	**Stevie Wonder**	12 Year Old Genius Recorded Live!	6.1981
132	**The Spinners**	The Original Spinners	6.1981
133	**The Miracles**	Do It Baby	6.1981
134	**Smokey Robinson**	Smokey	6.1981
135	**Diana Ross**	Diana Ross	6.1981
136	**Smokey Robinson & the Miracles**	Away We A Go Go	6.1981
137	**The Originals**	Baby I'm For Real	6.1981
138	**Diana Ross & the Supremes**	The Supremes A Go Go	6.1981
139	**Diana Ross & the Supremes with The Temptations**	Diana Ross and the Supremes Join The Temptations	6.1981
140	**The Temptations**	Meet The Temptations	6.1981
141	**Jr Walker & the All Stars**	Shotgun	6.1981
142	**Marvin Gaye & Tammi Terrell**	You're All I Need	6.1981

143	The Isley Brothers	Doin' Their Thing	6.1981
144	The Temptations	Masterpiece	6.1981
145	Martha Reeves & the Vandellas	Heatwave	6.1981
146	David Ruffin	My Whole World Ended	6.1981
147	Diana Ross & the Supremes	I Hear A Symphony	6.1981
148	Gladys Knight & the Pips	The Nitty Gritty	6.1981
149	Four Tops	Reach Out	6.1981
150	Stevie Wonder	With A Song In My Heart	6.1981
151	Eddie Kendricks	Eddie Kendricks	6.1981
152	Jackson 5	ABC	6.1981
153	Michael Jackson	Ben	6.1981
154	Smokey Robinson	Deep In My Soul	6.1981
155	Diana Ross	Diana! (TV Special)	6.1981
156	Smokey Robinson & the Miracles	The Tears Of A Clown	6.1981
157	Jackson 5	Third Album	6.1981
158	Diana Ross & the Supremes	Sing Country Western And Pop	NR
159	The Temptations	Cloud Nine	6.1981
160	Smokey Robinson & the Miracles	Hi! We're The Miracles	6.1981
161	Mary Wells	Bye Bye Baby	6.1981
162	Diana Ross & the Supremes	At The Copa	6.1981
163	Diana Ross	Touch Me In The Morning	6.1981
164	The Temptations	Psychedelic Shack	6.1981
165	Grover Washington Jr	A Secret Place	6.1981
166	Stevie Wonder	Down To Earth	6.1981
167	Mary Wells	My Guy	6.1981
168	Smokey Robinson	Pure Smokey	6.1981
169	Diana Ross	Live! At Caesar's Palace	6.1981
170	Edwin Starr	War And Peace	6.1981
171	Daiana Ross & the Supremes & The Temptations	TCB	6.1981
172	The Temptations	Puzzle People	6.1981
173	Stevie Wonder	Tribute To Uncle Ray	6.1981
174	Various	Motortown Revue	6.1981
175	Grover Washington Jr	Mr. Magic	6.1981
176	Stevie Wonder	Signed, Sealed, Delivered	6.1981
177	Grover Washington Jr	Feels So Good	6.1981
178	Commodores	Movin' On	6.1981
179	Stevie Wonder	My Cherie Amour	6.1981
180	The Marvelettes	Greatest Hits	6.1981
181	Marvin Gaye	Live!	6.1981
182	Diana Ross & the Supremes	Diana Ross And The Supremes Sing Holland-Dozier-Holland	6.1981
183	Stevie Wonder	Uptight	6.1981
184	Grover Washington Jr	Soul Box Vol. 1	7.1981
185	Bobby Darin	1936-1973	7.1981
186	Grover Washington Jr	All The Kings Horses	7.1981
187	Grover Washington Jr	Soul Box Vol. 2	7.1981
188	The Contours	Do You Love Me	7.1981
189	Grover Washington Jr	Inner City Blues	7.1981
190	Various	From The Vaults	9.1981
191	Marvin Gaye	Greatest Hits	9.1981
192	Marvin Gaye	Let's Get It On	9.1981
193	Gladys Knight & the Pips	Neither One Of Us	9.1981
194	Michael Jackson	The Best Of Michael Jackson	9.1981
195	The Crusaders	At Their Best	9.1981
196	Eddie Kendricks	He's A Friend	9.1981
197	Smokey Robinson	A Quiet Storm	9.1981
198	Diana Ross	The Boss	9.1981
199	The Spinners	The Best Of The Spinners	9.1981

200	Marvin Gaye & Tammi Terrell	United	9.1981
201	Jackson 5	Greatest Hits	9.1981
202	Rare Earth	Ecology	9.1981
203	Diana Ross & the Supremes	Greatest Hits Vol. 3	9.1981
204	Martha Reeves & the Vandellas	Greatest Hits	9.1981
205	The Temptations	The Temptations Sing Smokey	9.1981
206	Various	Motor Town Revue Vol. 2	9.1981
207	Various	In Loving Memory	9.1981
208	Jr Walker & the All Stars	Greatest Hits	9.1981
209	Four Tops	Greatest Hits	9.1981
210	Smokey Robinson & the Miracles	Greatest Hits Vol. 2	9.1981
211	David Ruffin	At His Best	9.1981
212	The Temptations	All The Million Sellers	9.1981
213	Diana Ross	From The Vaults	NR
214	Diana Ross	Diana's Duets	9.1981
215	Various	Motor Town Revue Vol. 1: Recorded Live At The Apollo	9.1981
216	Marvin Gaye	A Tribute To The Great Nat King Cole	9.1981
217	The Miracles	Doin' Mickey's Monkey	9.1981
218	Marvin Gaye	That Stubborn Kind Of Fellow	9.1981
219	Stevie Wonder	The Jazz Soul Of Little Stevie	9.1981
220	The Miracles	Recorded Live! On Stage	9.1981
221	Mary Wells	Two Lovers	9.1981
222	Commodores	Commodores	1.1982
223	Diana Ross & the Supremes	Meet The Supremes	1.1982
224	Four Tops	Still Waters Run Deep	1.1982
225	Marvin Gaye & Tammi Terrell	Greatest Hits	1.1982
226	Thelma Houston	Any Way You Like It	1.1982
227	Stephanie Mills	For The First Time	1.1982
228	Jackson 5	Maybe Tomorrow	1.1982
229	Rare Earth	Get Ready	1.1982
230	Smokey Robinson	Love Breeze	1.1982
231	Tammi Terrell	Irresistible	1.1982
232	Grover Washington Jr	Skylarkin'	1.1982
233	Mary Wells	Greatest Hits	1.1982
234	Stevie Wonder	For Once In My Life	1.1982
235	The Temptations	In A Mellow Mood	1.1982
236	Grover Washington Jr	Reed Seed	1.1982
M8-237-M2	Diana Ross & the Supremes	Greatest Hits Vol. 1 & 2	1.1982
M8-238-M2	Smokey Robinson & the Miracles	Greatest Hits From The Beginning	1.1982
M8-239-M2	Grover Washington Jr	Live At The Bijou	1.1982

SUFFIX ML (unless stated otherwise)

5240	Commodores	Caught In The Act	4.1982
5241	Marvin Gaye	Trouble Man	4.1982
5242	Brenda Holloway	Every Little Bit Hurts	4.1982
5243	Various	Pippin (Original Cast)	4.1982
5244	Diana Ross	Last Time I Saw Him	4.1982
5245	Diana Ross & the Supremes	Love Child	4.1982
5246	Marvin Gaye, Kim Weston, Mary Wells, Tammi Terrell	Marvin Gaye And His Girls	4.1982
5247	Stevie Wonder	Where I'm Coming From	4.1982
5248	Various	16 No. 1 Hits Vol. 1 – Early 60s	4.1982
5249	Various	16 No. 1 Hits Vol. 2 – Late 60s	4.1982
5250	Jackson 5	Christmas Album	7.1982
5251	The Temptations	Christmas Card	7.1982

5252	**The Supremes**	*Merry Christmas*	7.1982
5253	**Smokey Robinson & the Miracles**	*The Season For Miracles*	7.1982
5254	**Smokey Robinson & the Miracles**	*Christmas With The Miracles*	7.1982
5255	**Stevie Wonder**	*Someday At Christmas*	7.1982
5256M2	**Various**	*A Motown Christmas*	7.1982
5257	**Commodores**	*Hot on The Tracks*	7.1982
5258	**Four Tops**	*Live!*	7.1982
5259 ML2	**Marvin Gaye**	*Live At The London Palladium*	7.1982
5260	**Marvin Gaye & Mary Wells**	*Together*	9.1982
5261	**Jackson 5**	*Goin' Back To Indiana*	7.1982
5262	**Jackson 5**	*Looking Through The Windows*	9.1982
5263	**Rick James**	*Come And Get It*	7.1982
5264	**Four Tops**	*Second Album*	9.1982
5265	**Martha & the Vandellas**	*Watch Out*	9.1982
5266	**The Marvelettes**	*Please Mr. Postman*	9.1982
5267	**Smokey Robinson**	*Where There's Smoke*	7.1982
5268 ML2	**Diana Ross**	*An Evening With Diana Ross*	7.1982
5269	**Smokey Robinson & the Miracles**	*Going To A Go Go*	7.1982
5270	**The Supremes**	*Where Did Our Love Go*	9.1982
5271	**Teena Marie**	*Wild And Peaceful*	9.1982
5272	**The Temptations**	*A Song For You*	7.1982
5273	**Stevie Wonder**	*I Was Made To Love Her*	9.1982
5274	**Various**	*Tamla Special No. 1*	9.1982
5275	**Various**	*12 No. 1 Hits From The 70s*	9.1982
5276	**The Temptations**	*I Wish It Would Rain*	9.1982
5277	**Various**	*Guys And Dolls (Original Cast)*	7.1982
5278 ML2	**Diana Ross & the Supremes**	*Diana Ross And The Supremes Captured Live On Stage*	7.1982
5279	**The Temptations**	*Give Love At Christmas*	7.1982
5280	**Eddie Kendricks**	*People Hold On*	9.1982
5281	**Willie Hutch**	*The Mack*	9.1982
5282	**Smokey Robinson & the Miracles**	*What Love Has Joined Together*	9.1982
‡5283	**Al Green**	*Greatest Hits Vol. 1*	10.1982
‡5284	**Al Green**	*I'm Still In Love With You*	10.1982
‡5285	**Al Green**	*Full Of Fire*	10.1982
‡5286	**Al Green**	*Call Me*	10.1982
‡5287	**Al Green**	*Explores Your Mind*	10.1982
‡5288	**Ann Peebles**	*I Can't Stand The Rain*	10.1982
‡5289 ML2	**Willie Mitchell**	*Best Of Willie Mitchell*	10.1982
‡5290	**Al Green**	*Let's Stay Together*	10.1982
‡5291	**Al Green**	*Greatest Hits Vol. II*	10.1982
5292	**Marvin Gaye**	*I Want You*	1.1983
5293	**Commodores**	*Natural High*	1.1983
5294	**Diana Ross**	*Diana Ross*	1.1983
5295	**Marvin Gaye**	*Here, My Dear*	4.1984
5296	**Marvin Gaye**	*The Moods Of Marvin Gaye*	2.1983
5297	**Jr Walker & the All Stars**	*All The Great Hits*	2.1983
5298	**Eivets Rednow**	*Alfie*	2.1983
5299	**The Temptations**	*With A Lot Of Soul*	2.1983
‡5300	**Ace Cannon**	*Memphis Golden Hits*	4.1983
5301	**Marvin Gaye**	*Super Hits*	12.1982
‡5302 ML2	**Al Green**	*Tokyo Live!*	4.1983
5303	**Gladys Knight & the Pips**	*All The Great Hits*	4.1983
‡5304	**Al Green**	*Livin' For You*	4.1983
5305	**Diana Ross & the Supremes**	*Let The Sunshine In*	4.1983
5306	**The Temptations**	*Live!*	4.1983
5307	**Grover Washington Jr**	*Greatest Performances*	4.1983
5308 ML2	**Various**	*25 No. 1 Hits From 25 Years*	5.1983
5309	**Various**	*25 Years Of Grammy Greats*	5.1983
5310	**Various**	*Motown Superstars Sing Motown Superstars*	5.1983
5311	**Marvin Gaye**	*Great Songs And Performances That Inspired The Motown 25th Anniversary TV Show*	8.1983
5312	**Michael Jackson & Jackson 5**	*Great Songs And Performances That Inspired The Motown 25th Anniversary TV Show*	8.1983
5313	**Diana Ross & the Supremes**	*Great Songs And Performances That Inspired The Motown 25th Anniversary TV Show*	8.1983
5314	**Four Tops**	*Great Songs And Performances That Inspired The Motown 25th Anniversary TV Show*	8.1983
5315	**The Temptations**	*Great Songs And Performances That Inspired The Motown 25th Anniversary TV Show*	8.1983
5316	**Smokey Robinson & the Miracles**	*Great Songs And Performances That Inspired The Motown 25th Anniversary TV Show*	8.1983
‡5317	**Al Green**	*Truth 'N' Time*	9.1983
‡5318	**Al Green**	*Belle*	9.1983
‡5319	**Al Green**	*Al Green Sings The Gospel*	9.1983
5320	**Bill Black Combo**	*Greatest Hits*	NR
5321	**Various**	*The Incredible Medleys*	6.1983
5322	**Various**	*Girl Groups: The Story Of A Sound*	11.1983
5323	**Various**	*Motown Solo Stars: Top 10 With A Bullet*	2.1984
5324	**Various**	*Motown Love Songs: Top 10 With A Bullet*	2.1984
5325	**Various**	*Motown Girl Groups: Top 10 With A Bullet*	2.1984
5326	**Various**	*Motown Dance: Top 10 With A Bullet*	2.1984
5327	**Various**	*Motown Male Groups: Top 10 With A Bullet*	2.1984
5328	—	—	—
5329	**Various**	*Motown Grammy R&B Performances Of The 60s*	3.1984
5330	**Various**	*Motown Grammy R&B Performances Of The 70s*	3.1984
5331	**Michael Jackson**	*Forever, Michael*	5.1984
5332	**Michael Jackson**	*Music And Me*	5.1984
5333	**Jackson 5**	*Skywriter*	5.1984
5334	**Jackson 5**	*Dancing Machine*	5.1984
5335	**DeBarges**	*The DeBarges*	2.1985
5336	**Jackson 5**	*Get It Together*	5.1984
5337	**Jackson 5**	*Moving Violation*	5.1984
5338	**Jackson 5**	*Joyful Jukebox Music*	5.1984
5339	**Marvin Gaye**	*What's Going On*	4.1984
5340	**Rev. Martin Luther King**	*Free At Last*	6.1984
5341	**Rev. Martin Luther King**	*Great March On Washington*	6.1984
5342	**Rev. Martin Luther King**	*Great March To Freedom*	6.1984
5343	**Various**	*Every Great Motown Song: Vol. 1 – The 1960s*	6.1984
5344	**Various**	*Every Great Motown Song: Vol. 2 – The 1970s*	6.1984
5345	**Michael Jackson**	*The Great Love Songs*	6.1984
5346	**Jackson 5**	*The Great Love Songs*	6.1984
5347	**Commodores**	*Live!*	8.1984
5348	**Commodores**	*Midnight Magic*	6.1984
5349	**Smokey Robinson**	*Being With You*	8.1984
5350	**Dazz Band**	*Keep It Live*	8.1984
5351	**Various**	*The Best Of The Beatles Songs Sung By Motown's Greatest Stars*	8.1984
5352	**Michael Jackson**	*One Day In Your Life*	2.1985
5353	**Commodores**	*Heroes*	2.1985

5354	**Jermaine Jackson**	Let's Get Serious	2.1985
5355	**Teena Marie**	It Must Be Magic	2.1985
5356	**Various**	All The Great Motown Love Song Duets	2.1985
*5357	**Diana Ross & the Supremes**	Greatest Hits Vol. 1	3.1985
*5358	**Diana Ross & the Supremes**	Greatest Hits Vol. 2	3.1985
5359	**Marvin Gaye**	Motown Legends	3.1985
5360	**Smokey Robinson & the Miracles**	Motown Legends	3.1985
5361	**Diana Ross & the Supremes**	Motown Legends	3.1985
5362	**Stevie Wonder**	Motown Legends	3.1985
5363	**Four Tops**	Motown Legends	3.1985
5364	**Bill Cosby**	Himself	10.1985
5365	**Jackson 5 featuring Michael Jackson**	Motown Legends	6.1985
5366	**Gladys Knight & the Pips**	Motown Legends	6.1985
5367	**Various**	Motown Legends – Love Songs	6.1985
5368	**Diana Ross & the Supremes & The Temptations**	Motown Legends	6.1985
5369	**Michael Jackson**	Motown Legends	6.1985
5370	**Teena Marie**	Greatest Hits	9.1985
5371	**Diana Ross & the Supremes**	Diana Ross And The Supremes Sing Motown	9.1985
5372	**Teena Marie**	Irons In The Fire	9.1985
5373	**The Temptations**	Gettin' Ready	9.1985
5374	**The Temptations**	The Temptin' Temptations	9.1985
‡5375	**Various**	Good Feeling Music Of The Big Chill Generation Vol. 1	9.1985
‡5376	**Various**	Good Feeling Music Of The Big Chill Generation Vol. 2	9.1985
‡5377	**Various**	Good Feeling Music Of The Big Chill Generation Vol. 3	9.1985
‡5378	**Various**	Good Feeling Music Of The Big Chill Generation Vol. 4	9.1985
‡5379	**Various**	Good Feeling Music Of The Big Chill Generation Vol. 5	9.1985
5380	**Various**	Never-Before-Released Masters From Motown's Brightest Stars – The 1960s	2.1986
5381	**Diana Ross & the Supremes**	25th Anniversary	4.1986
5382	**Rick James**	Greatest Hits	2.1986
5383	**Diana Ross**	Diana	2.1986
5384	**Michael Jackson**	Looking Back To Yesterday – Never-Before-Released Masters	2.1986
5385	**Various**	Endless Love: Motown's Great Love Songs	5.1986
5386	**Various**	The Composer Series: Lionel Richie – Great Love Songs With The Commodores And Diana Ross	3.1986
5387	**Dazz Band**	Greatest Hits	3.1986
5388	**Gladys Knight & the Pips**	If I were Your Woman	3.1986
5389	**The Temptations**	25th Anniversary	4.1986
5390	**Various**	Hard To Find Motown Classics Vol. 1	3.1986
5391	**Various**	Hard To Find Motown Classics Vol. 2	3.1986
*5392	**DeBarge**	All This Love	5.1986
*5393	**DeBarge**	In A Special Way	5.1986
5394	**Marvin Gaye & Tammi Terrell**	Easy	5.1986
*5395	**Marvin Gaye**	I Heard It Through The Grapevine	7.1986
*5396	**Gladys Knight & the Pips**	All I Need Is Time	7.1986

*5397	**Various**	Motown's Mustangs	7.1986
*5398	**Various**	Motown Time Capsule Vol. 1 – 1960s	8.1986
*5399	**Various**	Motown Time Capsule Vol. 2 – 1970s	8.1986
*5400	**Commodores**	Nightshift	9.1986
*5401	**Smokey Robinson**	Blame It On Love And All The Great Hits	9.1986
*5402	**Michael Jackson**	Anthology	9.1986
*5403	**Various**	The Last Radio Station	9.1986
*5404	**Dennis Edwards**	Don't Look Any Further	2.1988
*5405	**Rick James**	Street Songs	2.1988
*5406	**Mary Jane Girls**	Only Four You	2.1988
*5407	**Mary Jane Girls**	Mary Jane Girls	2.1988
*5408	**Sam Harris**	Sam Harris	2.1988
*5409	**Various Artists**	Motown Memories Vol. 1	2.1988
*5410	**Various Artists**	Motown Memories Vol. 2	2.1988

* Cassettes only

COMPACT DISC 8000 SERIES

2 on 1 CD Series introduced during 1986 (full-price)

8000MD	**Michael Jackson**	Got To Be There Ben	7.1986
8001TD	**Smokey Robinson**	Being With You Where There's Smoke	7.1986
8002MD	**Diana Ross**	Diana The Boss	7.1986
8003GD	**Teena Marie**	Irons In The Fire It Must Be Magic	7.1986
8004TD	**Smokey Robinson & the Miracles**	Going To A Go Go The Tears Of A Clown	7.1986
8005MD	**Diana Ross & the Supremes**	Where Did Our Love Go I Hear A Symphony	7.1986
8006TD	**Stevie Wonder**	My Cherie Amour Signed, Sealed, Delivered	7.1986
8007MD	**Four Tops**	Reach Out Still Waters Run Deep	7.1986
8008MD	**Gladys Knight & the Pips**	Neither One Of Us All I Need Is Time	7.1986
8009MD	**Grover Washington Jr**	Mister Magic Feels So Good	7.1986
8010TD	**Marvin Gaye**	I Heard It Through The Grapevine I Want You	7.1986
8011MD	**Jackson 5**	Third Album Maybe Tomorrow	9.1986
8012GD	**Rick James**	Street Songs Throwin' Down	7.1986
8013TD	**Marvin Gaye**	What's Going On Let's Get It On	7.1986
8014MD	**Commodores**	Natural High Midnight Magic	7.1986
8015TD	**Marvin Gaye & Tammi Terrell** **Diana Ross & Marvin Gaye**	Greatest Hits Diana & Marvin	7.1986
8016GD	**The Temptations**	Cloud Nine Puzzle People	7.1986
8017GD	**The Temptations**	Christmas Card Give Love At Christmas	7.1986
8018MD	**Al Green**	Let's Stay Together I'm Still In Love With You	9.1986
8019MD	**Jackson 5**	Diana Ross Presents The Jackson 5 ABC	8.1986
8020GD	**Edwin Starr**	25 Miles War And Peace	8.1986
8021MD	**Diana Ross & the Supremes**	Love Child Supremes A Go Go	8.1986
8022GD	**The Temptations**	Psychedelic Shack All Directions	8.1986
8023MD	**Jr Walker & the All Stars**	Shotgun Road Runner	9.1986
8024MD	**Mary Wells**	Two Lovers My Guy	8.1986

8025TD	**Stevie Wonder**	*For Once in My Life* Uptight	8.1986
8026MD	**Diana Ross**	*Touch Me in The Morning* Baby It's Me	9.1986
8027MD	**Four Tops**	*Four Tops* Second Album	8.1986
8028TD	**Smokey Robinson**	*Smokey* A Quiet Storm	8.1986
8029MD	**Diana Ross & the Supremes**	*Greatest Hits Vols. 1 & 2*	9.1986
8030MD	**Grover Washington Jr**	*A Secret Place* All The King's Horses	8.1986
8031MD	**Gladys Knight & the Pips**	*Everybody Needs Love* If I Were Your Woman	8.1986
8032MD	**Diana Ross & the Supremes**	*Let The Sunshine In* Cream Of The Crop	8.1986
8033MD	**Rare Earth**	*Get Ready* Ecology	9.1986
8034MD	**Various**	*Every Great Motown Song – The First 25 Years As Originally Recorded Vol. 1 – 60s* Vol. 2 – 70s	8.1986
8035GD	**The Temptations**	*A Song For You* Masterpiece	9.1986
8036TD	**Marvin Gaye**	*Trouble Man* M.P.G.	9.1986
8037MD	**The Temptations**	*Live! At The Copa* With A Lot O'Soul	9.1986
8038MD	**Diana Ross & the Supremes with The Temptations**	*Diana Ross And The Supremes Join The Temptations* Together	9.1986
8039MD	**Commodores**	*Heroes* Commodores	9.1986
8040MD	**Al Green**	*Call Me* Livin' For You	8.1986
8041MD	**Diana Ross & the Supremes Stevie Wonder**	*Merry Christmas* Someday At Christmas	8.1986
8042M	**Diana Ross**	*Ain't No Mountain High Enough* Surrender	1.1987
8043T	**Smokey Robinson & the Miracles**	*Time Out For The Miracles* Special Occasion	1.1987
8044M	**Commodores**	*Hot On The Tracks* In The Pocket	1.1987
8045G	**DeBarge**	*All This Love* In A Special Way	1.1987
8046M	**Four Tops**	*Nature Planned It* Keeper Of The Castle	2.1987
8047T	**Marvin Gaye & Tammi Terrell**	*You're All I Need* United	1.1987
8048M	**Al Green**	*Al Green Is Love* Full Of Fire	1.1987
8049G	**Martha Reeves & the Vandellas**	*Heatwave* Dance Party	1.1987
8050T	**Smokey Robinson & the Miracles**	*Doin' Mickey's Monkey* Away We A Go Go	1.1987
8051M	**Diana Ross & the Supremes**	*More Hits* The Supremes Sing Holland-Dozier-Holland	1.1987
8052M	**Diana Ross & the Supremes (with the Temptations)**	*A Bit Of Liverpool* TCB**	1.1987
8053T	**Stevie Wonder**	*Down To Earth* I Was Made To Love Her	1.1987
8054G	**The Temptations**	*Wish It Would Rain* In A Mellow Mood	1.1987
8055T	**The Marvelettes**	*The Marvelettes* Sophisticated Soul	1.1987
8056T	**The Isley Brothers**	*This Old Heart Of Mine* Soul On The Rocks	1.1987
8057T	**Marvin Gaye**	*Stubborn Kind Of Fellow* How Sweet It Is	1.1987
8058M	**Duane Eddy**	*Have Twangy Guitar Will Travel* $1,000,000 Worth Of Twang	1.1987

*8159M	**Diana Ross & the Supremes**	*We Remember Sam Cooke* At The Copa	NR
*8160M	**The Temptations**	*Meet The Temptations* Sing Smokey	6.1987
*8161M	**Marvin Gaye**	*Moods Of Marvin Gaye* Thats The Way Love Is	6.1987
*8162M	**Mary Wells**	*Bye Bye Baby* The One Who Really Loves You	6.1987

* On 8100 Series from start, not 8000

** The Temptations do not appear on *A Bit Of Liverpool* – only on *TCB*

MID-LINE SERIES

COMPACT DISCS (Prefix MD)

0900	**Various**	*An Introduction To The Motown Elite 9000 Series*	5.1987
9000	**Gladys Knight & the Pips**	*Motown Superstar Series Vol. 13*	5.1987
9001	**Diana Ross**	*Touch Me In The Morning*	5.1987
9002	**Grover Washington Jr**	*Mister Magic*	5.1987
9003	**The Marvelettes**	*Greatest Hits*	5.1987
9004	**Marvin Gaye**	*Live!*	5.1987
9005	**Marvin Gaye**	*Greatest Hits*	5.1987
9006	**Marvin Gaye**	*Let's Get It On*	5.1987
9007	**Diana Ross**	*The Boss*	5.1987
9008	**The Spinners**	*The Best Of The Spinners*	5.1987
9009	**Marvin Gaye & Tammi Terrell**	*United*	5.1987
9010	**Jackson 5**	*Greatest Hits*	5.1987
9011	**Martha Reeves & the Vandellas**	*Greatest Hits*	5.1987
9012	**Jr Walker & the All Stars**	*Greatest Hits*	5.1987
9013	**Four Tops**	*Greatest Hits*	5.1987
9014	**Smokey Robinson & the Miracles**	*Greatest Hits Vol. 2*	5.1987
9015	**The Temptations**	*All The Million Sellers*	5.1987
9016	**Mary Wells**	*Greatest Hits*	5.1987
9017	**Various**	*16 #1 Hits From The Early 60s*	5.1987
9018	**Various**	*16 # Hits From The Late 60s*	5.1987
9019	**Al Green**	*Greatest Hits*	5.1987
9020	**Al Green**	*Greatest Hits Vol. 2*	5.1987
9021	**Various**	*25 Years Of Grammy Greats*	5.1987
9022	**Four Tops**	*Great Songs And Performances That Inspired The Motown 25th Anniversary TV Special*	5.1987
9023	**Commodores**	*Midnight Magic*	5.1987
9024	**Teena Marie**	*Greatest Hits*	5.1987
9025	**Rick James**	*Greatest Hits*	5.1987
9026	**Diana Ross**	*Diana* (Chic LP)	5.1987
9027	**Diana Ross & the Supremes**	*I Hear A Symphony*	6.1987
9028	**Grover Washington Jr**	*A Secret Place*	6.1987
9029	**Stevie Wonder**	*Signed Sealed Delivered*	6.1987
9030	**Grover Washington Jr**	*Feels So Good*	6.1987
9031	**Various**	*Diana's Duets*	6.1987
9032	**Stevie Wonder**	*For Once In My Life*	6.1987
9033	**The Temptations**	*Great Songs And Performances That Inspired The Motown 25th Anniversary TV Special*	6.1987
9034	**Smokey Robinson & the Miracles**	*Great Songs And Performances That Inspired The Motown 25th Anniversary TV Special*	6.1987

9035	**Various**	Motown Love Songs (Top 10 With A Bullet)	6.1987
9036	**Marvin Gaye**	What's Going On	6.1987
‡9037	**Various**	Good Feeling Music Of The Big Chill Generation Vol. 3	6.1987
9038	**Diana Ross & the Supremes**	Every Great No. 1 Hit	6.1987
9039	**Commodores**	Compact Command Performances/Greatest Hits	6.1987
9040	**Michael Jackson & Jackson 5**	Compact Command Performances/Greatest Hits	6.1987
9041	**Smokey Robinson & the Miracles**	Compact Command Performances/Greatest Hits	6.1987
9042	**Four Tops**	Compact Command Performances/Greatest Hits	6.1987
9043	**Stevie Wonder**	The Woman In Red (f/s.)	6.1987
9044	**Gladys Knight & the Pips**	Compact Command Performances/Greatest Hits	6.1987
9045	**Grover Washington Jr**	At His Best	6.1987
9046	**Diana Ross**	Lady Sings The Blues (f/s.)	6.1987
9047	**Various**	The Composer Series: Great Songs By Holland-Dozier-Holland	6.1987
9048	**Various**	The Composer Series: Great Songs By Smokey Robinson	6.1987
9049	**Various**	The Composer Series: Great Songs By Ashford & Simpson	6.1987
9050	**Stevie Wonder**	Love Songs	6.1987
9051	**Stevie Wonder**	Talking Book	6.1987
9052	**Stevie Wonder**	Innervisions	6.1987
9053	**Marvin Gaye**	Marvin Gaye & His Women (duets)	6.1987
‡9054	**Various**	Big Chill Generation Vol. 1	6.1987
‡9055	**Various**	Big Chill Generation Vol. 2	6.1987
9056	**The Marvelettes**	Compact Command Performances/Greatest Hits	6.1987
9057	**Martha Reeves & the Vandellas**	Compact Command Performances/Greatest Hits	6.1987
9058	**Mary Wells**	Compact Command Performances/Greatest Hits	6.1987
9059	**DeBarge**	Greatest Hits	6.1987
9060	**Various**	Motowns Biggest Pop Hits	6.1987
9061	**Various**	20 Hard-To-Find Motown Classics Vol. 1	6.1987
9062	**Various**	20 Hard-To-Find Motown Classics Vol. 2	6.1987
9063	**Teena Marie**	Compact Command Performances/Greatest Hits	6.1987
9064	**Stevie Wonder**	Hotter Than July	6.1987
‡9065	**Jimmy Reed**	Compact Command Performances/Greatest Hits	6.1987
‡9066	**Little Richard**	Compact Command Performances/Greatest Hits	6.1987
‡9067	**Various**	Legendary Masters From Vee Jay Records	6.1987
9068	**Duane Eddy**	Compact Command Performances/Greatest Hits	6.1987
9069	**Various**	25 Hard-To-Find Motown Classics Vol. 3	6.1987
9070	**Bobby Darin**	Live! At The Desert Inn	6.1987
9071	**Various**	Motown Dance Party Vol. 1	6.1987
9072	**Various**	Motown Dance Party Vol. 2	6.1987
9073	**Various**	Motown Around The World	6.1987
9074	**Diana Ross & the Supremes**	The Rodgers & Hart Collection	6.1987
9075	**Diana Ross & the Supremes**	The Never-Before-Released Masters	7.1987
9076	**Stevie Wonder**	Music Of My Mind	7.1987
9077	**Stevie Wonder**	Fullfillingness' First Finale	7.1987
9078	**The Temptations**	Give Love At Christmas	7.1987
9079	**Michael Jackson**	The Best Of Michael Jackson	7.1987
9080	**Jackson 5**	Christmas Album	7.1987
9081	**Stevie Wonder**	Someday At Christmas	7.1987
9082	**Various**	Three Times A Lady: Motown's Greatest Love Songs	7.1987
9083	**Stevie Wonder**	My Cherie Amour	7.1987
9084	**Marvin Gaye**	Motown Legends	7.1987
9085	**Diana Ross & the Supremes**	Merry Christmas	7.1987
9086	**Gladys Knight & the Pips**	All The Great Hits	7.1987
9087	**Various**	Girl Groups: The Story Of A Sound	7.1987
9088	**Various**	Pippin (Original Cast Recording)	7.1987
9089	**Marvin Gaye & Tammi Terrell**	Greatest Hits	7.1987
9090	**Diana Ross & Marvin Gaye**	Diana & Marvin	7.1987
9091	**Smokey Robinson & the Miracles**	Christmas With The Miracles	7.1987
9092	**Smokey Robinson & the Miracles**	The Tears Of A Clown	7.1987
9093	**Grover Washington Jr**	Inner City Blues	7.1987
9094	**Rare Earth**	Get Ready	7.1987
9095	**Various**	Motown Girl Groups: Top 10 With A Bullet	7.1987
9096	**The Temptations**	Cloud Nine	7.1987
9097	**Various**	The Most Played Oldies On America's Jukeboxes	7.1987
9098	**Various**	Radio's #1 Hits – Records That Have Been Played Over 15M Times On Radio (The Most Requested Music Of Our Time)	7.1987
9099	**Dennis Edwards**	Don't Look Any Further	2.1988
9100	**Rick James**	Street Songs	2.1988
9101	**Mary Jane Girls**	Only Four You	2.1988
9102	**Mary Jane Girls**	Mary Jane Girls	2.1988
9103	**Sam Harris**	Sam Harris	2.1988
9104	**Various**	Motown Memories Vol. 1	2.1988
9105	**Various**	Motown Memories Vol. 2	2.1988

GORDY LABEL

901	**The Contours**	Do You Love Me	10.1962
902	**Martha & the Vandellas**	Come And Get These Memories	6.1963
903	**Ralph Sharon**	Modern Innovations On Country And Western Themes	6.1963
904	—	—	—
905	—	—	—
906	**Rev. Martin Luther King**	The Great March To Freedom	8.1963
907	**Martha & The Vandellas**	Heatwave	9.1963
908	**Rev. Martin Luther King**	The Great March On Washington	10.1963
909	—	—	—
910	—	—	—
911	**The Temptations**	Meet The Temptations	3.1964
912	**The Temptations**	Sing Smokey	2.1965

913	—	—	—
914	**The Temptations**	*The Temptin' Temptations*	11.1965
915	**Martha & The Vandellas**	*Dance Party*	4.1965
916	—	—	—
917	**Martha & The Vandellas**	*Greatest Hits*	5.1966
918	**The Temptations**	*Getting' Ready*	6.1966
919	**The Temptations**	*Greatest Hits*	11.1966
920	**Martha & the Vandellas**	*Watchout*	12.1966
921	**The Temptations**	*Live!*	3.1967
922	**The Temptations**	*With A Lot O'Soul*	7.1967
923	**San Remo Golden Strings**	*Hungry For Love*	8.1967
924	**The Temptations**	*In A Mellow Mood*	8.1967
925	**Martha Reeves & the Vandellas**	*Live!*	8.1867
926	**Martha Reeves & the Vandellas**	*Ridin' High*	4.1968
927	**The Temptations**	*Wish It Would Rain*	4.1968
928	**San Remo Golden Strings**	*Swing*	6.1968
929	**Rev. Martin Luther King**	*Free At Last*	6.1968
930	**Bobby Taylor & the Vancouvers**	*Bobby Taylor & the Vancouvers*	8.1968
931	**Edwin Starr**	*Soul Master*	8.1968
932	**Eivets Rednow**	*Alfie*	11.1968
933	**The Temptations**	*The Temptations Show*	7.1969
934	—	—	—
935	**Various**	*Motown Winners Circle Vol. 1*	1.1969
936	**Various**	*Motown Winners Circle Vol. 2*	1.1969
937	—	—	—
938	**The Temptations**	*Live At The Copa*	12.1968
939	**The Temptations**	*Cloud Nine*	2.1969
940	**Edwin Starr**	*25 Miles*	4.1969
941	—	—	—
942	**Bobby Taylor**	*Taylor Made Soul*	7.1969
943	**Various**	*Motown Winners Circle Vol. 3*	7.1969
944	**Martha & the Vandellas**	*Sugar 'n' Spice*	9.1969
945	**Edwin Starr & Blinky**	*Just We Two*	9.1969
946	**Various**	*Motown Winners Circle Vol. 4*	10.1969
947	**The Temptations**	*Psychedelic Shack*	3.1970
948	**Edwin Starr**	*War And Peace*	8.1970
949	**The Temptations**	*Puzzle People*	9.1969
950	**Various**	*Motown Winners Circle Vol. 5*	3.1970
951	**The Temptations**	*Christmas Card*	10.1970
952	**Martha Reeves & the Vandellas**	*Natural Resources*	9.1970
953	**The Temptations**	*Live At London's Talk Of The Town*	7.1970
954	**The Temptations**	*Greatest Hits Vol. 2*	9.1970
955	**The Undisputed Truth**	*The Undisputed Truth*	6.1971
956	**Edwin Starr**	*Involved*	6.1971
957	**The Temptations**	*Sky's The Limit*	4.1971
958	**Martha Reeves & the Vandellas**	*Black Magic*	3.1972
959	**The Undisputed Truth**	*Face To Face With The Truth*	1.1972
960	—	—	—
961	**The Temptations**	*Solid Rock*	1.1972
962	**The Temptations**	*All Directions*	7.1972
963	**The Undisputed Truth**	*Law Of The Land*	6.1973
964	**Luther Allison**	*Bad News Is Coming*	12.1972
965	**The Temptations**	*Masterpiece*	2.1973
966	**The Temptations**	*1990*	12.1973
967	**Luther Allison**	*Luther's Blues*	2.1974

968	**The Undisputed Truth**	*Down To Earth*	7.1974
969	**The Temptations**	*A Song For You*	1.1975
970	**The Undisputed Truth**	*Cosmic Truth*	2.1975
971	**The Temptations**	*Wings Of Love*	3.1976
972	**The Undisputed Truth**	*Higher Than High*	9.1975
973	**The Temptations**	*House Party*	11.1975
974	**Luther Allison**	*Night Life*	2.1976
975	**The Temptations**	*The Temptations Do The Temptations*	8.1976
976	**Leon Ware**	*Musical Massage*	9.1976
977	**Bottom & Co**	*Rock Bottom*	11.1976
978	**High Inergy**	*Turning' On*	9.1977
979	**21st Creation**	*Break Thru'*	1.1978
980	**Switch**	*Switch*	7.1978
981	**Rick James**	*Come Get It*	4.1978
982	**High Inergy**	*Steppin' Out*	6.1978
983	**21st Creation**	*21st Creation*	NR
984	**Rick James**	*Bustin' Out Of L Seven*	1.1979
985	**Apollo**	*Apollo*	3.1979
986	**Teena Marie**	*Wild & Peaceful*	3.1979
987	**High Inergy**	*Shoulda Gone Dancin'*	4.1979
988	**Switch**	*Switch II*	4.1979
989	**High Inergy**	*Frenzy*	10.1979
990	**Rick James**	*Fire It Up*	10.1979
991	**The Stone City Band**	*Rick James Presents The Stone City Band In 'n' Out*	2.1980
992	**Teena Marie**	*Lady T*	2.1980
993	**Switch**	*Reaching For Tomorrow*	3.1980
994	**The Temptations**	*Power*	4.1980
995	**Rick James**	*Garden Of Love*	6.1980
996	**High Inergy**	*Hold On*	8.1980
997	**Teena Marie**	*Irons In The Fire*	8.1980
998	**The Temptations**	*Give Love At Christmas*	8.1980
999	**Switch**	*This Is My Dream*	10.1980
1000	**Nolen & Crossley**	*Nolen & Crossley*	1.1981
1001	**The Stone City Band**	*The Boys Are Back*	1.1981
1002	**Rick James**	*Street Songs*	4.1981
1003	**The DeBarges**	*The DeBarges*	4.1981
1004	**Teena Marie**	*It Must Be Magic*	5.1981
1005	**High Inergy**	*High Inergy*	5.1981
1006	**The Temptations**	*The Temptations*	8.1981
1007	**Switch**	*Switch 5*	10.1981
1008	**Nolen & Crossley**	*Ambience*	NR

WORKSHOP JAZZ LABEL

202	**Earl Washington**	*All Star Jazz*	11.1963
203	**Paula Greer**	*Introducing Paula Greer*	2.1963
204	**Paula Greer & the Johnny Griffith Trio**	*Detroit Jazz*	1963
205	**Johnny Griffith Trio**	*Jazz*	2.1963
206	**Dave Hamilton**	*Blue Vibrations*	3.1963
207	**George Bohannon Quartet**	*Boss Bosso Nova*	2.1963
212	**Lefty Edwards**	*The Right Side Of Lefty Edwards*	6.1964
213	**Earl Washington**	*Reflections*	6.1964
214	**George Bohannon Quartet**	*Bold Bohannon*	1964
215	—	—	—
216	**Herbie Williams**	*The Soul And Sound Of Herbie Williams*	1964
217	**Four Tops**	*Breaking Through*	1964
218	—	—	—
219	**Pepper Adams**	*Compositions Of Charlie Mingus*	8.1964
220	**Roy Brooks**	*Beat*	8.1964

SOUL LABEL

701	**Jr Walker & the All Stars**	*Shotgun*	5.1965

702	Jr Walker & the All Stars	Soul Sessioin	2.1966
703	Jr Walker & the All Stars	Road Runner	7.1966
704	Jimmy Ruffin	Sings Top Ten	1.1967
705	Jr Walker & the All Stars	Live!	8.1867
706	Gladys Knight & the Pips	Everybody Needs Love	8.1967
707	Gladys Knight & the Pips	Feelin' Bluesy	4.1968
708	Jimmy Ruffin	Ruff 'n' Ready	2.1969
709	Shorty Long	Here Comes The Judge	8.1968
710	Jr Walker & the All Stars	Home Cookin'	1.1969
711	Gladys Knight & the Pips	Silk 'n' Soul	12.1968
712	—	—	—
713	Gladys Knight & the Pips	Nitty Gritty	9.1969
714	The Monitors	Greetings! We're The Monitors	11.1968
715	Earl Van Dyke	The Earl Of Funk (Live)	9.1970
716	The Originals	Green Grow The Lilacs/ Baby I'm For Real	7.1969
717	The Fantastic Four	Best Of The Fantastic Four	2.1969
718	Jr Walker & the All Stars	Greatest Hits	5.1969
719	Shorty Long	The Prime Of Shorty Long	11.1969
720	Various	Switched On Blues	11.1969
721	Jr Walker & the All Stars	What Does It Take To Win Your Love (Gotta Hold On To This Feeling)	11.1969
722	The Fantastic Four	How Sweet He Is	NR
723	Gladys Knight & the Pips	Greatest Hits	3.1970
724	The Originals	Portrait Of The Originals	5.1970
725	Jr Walker & the All Stars	Live!	4.1970
726	Jr Walker & the All Stars	A Gasssss	9.1970
727	Jimmy Ruffin	The Groove Governer	9.1970
728	David & Jimmy Ruffin	I Am My Brother's Keeper	9.1970
729	The Originals	Naturally Together	9.1970
730	Gladys Knight & the Pips	All In A Knight's Work (Live!)	9.1970
731	Gladys Knight & the Pips	If I Were Your Woman	4.1971
732	Jr Walker & the All Stars	Rainbow Funk	6.1971
733	Jr Walker & the All Stars	Moody Jr.	12.1971
734	The Originals	Definitions	1.1972
735	Blinky	Sunny And Warm	NR
736	Gladys Knight & the Pips	Standing Ovation	12.1971
737	Gladys Knight & the Pips	Neither One Of Us	2.1973
738	Jr Walker & the All Stars	Peace And Understanding Is Hard To Find	4.1973
739	Gladys Knight & the Pips	All I Need Is Time	6.1973
740	The Originals	Game Called Love	5.1974
741	Gladys Knight & the Pips	Knight Time	2.1974
742	Jr Walker & the All Stars	Jr Walker & The All Stars	NR
743	The Originals	California Sunset	—
744	Gladys Knight & the Pips	A Little Knight Music	3.1975
745	Jr Walker & the All Stars	Hot Shot	1.1976
746	The Originals	Communique	5.1976
747	Jr Walker & the All Stars	Sax Appeal	6.1976
748	Jr Walker & the All Stars	Whopper, Bopper Show Stopper	10.1976

749	The Originals	Down To Love Town	1.1977
750	Jr Walker & the All Stars	Smooth	4.1978
751	Major Lance	Now Arriving	7.1978

V.I.P. LABEL

400	The Elgins	Darling Baby	8.1966
401	The Monitors	Greetings! We're The Monitors	NR
402	Abbey Tavern Singers	We're Off To Dublin in The Green	2.1967
403	Chuck Jackson	Teardrops Keep Falling On My Heart	9.1970
404	Hearts Of Stone	Stop The World – We Wanna Get On	9.1970
405	The Spinners	The Second Time Around	9.1970
406	Ivo Jo	Is In This Bag	NR
407	King Floyd	Heart Of The Matter	4.1971

RARE EARTH LABEL

505	Love Sculpture	Blues Helping	6.1969
506	The Pretty Things	S. F. Sorrow	6.1969
507	Rare Earth	Get Ready	9.1969
508	Rustix	Bedlam	9.1969
509	The Messengers	The Messengers	9.1969
510	Rare Earth	Generation	NR
511	Toe Fat	Toe Fat	7.1970
512	Sounds Nice	Love At First Sight	9.1970
513	Rustix	Come on People	7.1970
514	Rare Earth	Ecology	6.1970
515	The Pretty Things	Parachute	9.1970
516	Power Of Zeus	The Gospel According To Zeus	9.1970
517	The Easybeats	Easy Ridin'	9.1970
518	Lost Nation	Paradise Lost	9.1970
519	The Poor Boys	Ain't Nothin' In Our Pocket But Love	9.1970
520	Rare Earth	One World	6.1971
521	The Cats	45 Lives	9.1970
522	R. Dean Taylor	I Think Therefore I Am	12.1970
523	Brass Monkey	Brass Monkey	4.1971
524	UFO	UFO 1	4.1971
525	Toe Fat	Toe Fat Two	3.1971
526	The Sunday Funnies	The Sunday Funnies	5.1971
527	Magic	Magic	9.1971
528	Stoney & Meatloaf	Stoney and Meatloaf	9.1971
529	The Impact Of Brass	Down At The Brassworks	9.1971
530	Dennis Stoner	Dennis Stoner	11.1971
531	The God Squad featuring Leonard Caston	JC Greatest Hits	1.1972
532	Repairs	Already A Household Word	11.1971
533	Other People	Head To Head	NR
534	Rare Earth	In Concert	12.1971
535	—	—	—
536	XIT	Plight Of The Redman	2.1972
537	Howl The Good	Howl The Good	2.1972
538	The Sunday Funnies	Benediction	5.1972
539	Keef James	One Tree Or Another	5.1972
540	Crystal Mansion	Crystal Mansion	4.1972
541	Wolfe	Wolfe	7.1972
542	Matrix	Matrix	10.1972
543	Rare Earth	Willie Remembers	10.1972
544	Puzzle	Puzzle	NR
545	XIT	Silent Warrior	4.1973
546	Rare Earth	Ma	5.1973
547	Rare Earth	Live! In Chicago	NR
548	Rare Earth	Back To Earth	6.1975
549	The Pretty Things	Real Pretty	2.1976
550	Rare Earth	Midnight Lady	3.1976

WEED LABEL

801	**Chris Clark**	*CC Rides Again*	11.1969

BLACK FORUM LABEL

451	**Dr Martin Luther King**	*Why I Oppose The War in Vietnam*	10.1970
452	**Stokley Carmichael**	*Free Huey*	10.1970
453	**Langston Hughes & Margaret Danner**	*Writers Of The Revolution*	10.1970
454	**Black Fighting Men Recorded Live In Vietnam**	*Guess Who's Coming Home (Narrated By Wallace Terry)*	2.1972
455	**Ossie Davis And Bill Cosby**	*The Congressional Black Caucus*	4.1972
456	**Emamu Amiri Baraka, The Original Last Poets**	*Black Spirits*	4.1972
457	**Imamu Amiri Baraka**	*Its Nation Time – African Visionary Music*	4.1972
458	**Elaine Brown**	*Elaine Brown*	4.1973

CHISA LABEL

801	**Monk Montgomery**	*Its Never Too Late*	1.1970
802	—	—	—
803	**Hugh Masekela**	*Reconstruction*	7.1970
804	**The Jazz Crusaders**	*Old Socks New Shoes, New Socks Old Shoes*	7.1970
805	**Letta**	*Letta*	10.1970
806	**Monk Montgomery**	*Bass Odyssey*	5.1971
807	**The Jazz Crusaders**	*Pass The Plate*	5.1971
808	**Hugh Masekela & the Union Of South Africa**	*Hugh Masekela & The Union Of South Africa*	5.1971
809	**Letta**	*Mosadi*	NR

NATURAL RESOURCES LABEL

101	**Two Friends**	*Two Friends*	5.1972
102	**Heart**	*Heart*	5.1972
103	**Corliss**	*Corliss*	5.1972
104	**Gotham**	*Pass The Butter*	7.1972
105	**Road**	*Road*	7.1972
106	**Earthquire**	*Earthquire*	1.1973
107	**Northern Lights**	*Vancouver Dreaming*	1.1973
108	**Gaylord & Holiday**	*Wine, Women & Song*	10.1976
4001	**Various**	*Motown's Great Interpretations*	3.1978
4002	**Various**	*Motown Instrumentals*	3.1978
4003	**Various**	*Motown Show Tunes*	3.1978
4004	**Gladys Knight & the Pips**	*Silk 'N' Soul*	9.1978
4005	**The Temptations**	*In A Mellow Mood*	9.1978
4006	**Diana Ross & the Supremes**	*Where Did Our Love Go*	9.1978
4007	**Marvin Gaye**	*The Soulful Moods Of Marvin Gaye*	9.1978
4008	**Four Tops**	*Reach Out*	9.1978
4009	**Smokey Robinson & the Miracles**	*I'll Try Something New*	9.1978
4010	**Diana Ross & the Supremes**	*Merry Christmas*	10.1978
4011	**Various**	*We Wish You A Merry Christmas*	10.1978
4012	**Various**	*It Takes Two*	1.1979
4013	**Jackson 5**	*Boogie*	NR
4014	**Various**	*From The Vaults*	1.1979
4015	**Various**	*Mighty Motown*	5.1979
4016	**Various**	*Motown Disco Party*	5.1979
4017	**Various**	*Motown's Parade Of Song Hits*	5.1979
4018	**Various**	*Motown's Love Songs Vol. 1 – In Love*	8.1979
4019	**Various**	*Motown's Love Songs Vol. 2 – Broken Hearted*	8.1979
4020	**Diana Ross & the Supremes & The Temptations**	*TCB*	8.1979

MOWEST LABEL

101	**Lodi**	*Happiness*	10.1972
102	**Thelma Houston**	*Thelma Houston*	7.1972
103	**Tom Clay**	*What The World Needs Now Is Love*	7.1971
104	—	—	—
105	—	—	—
106	**The Blackberries**	*Blackberries*	NR
107	**G. C. Cameron**	*7th Son*	NR
108	**Frankie Valli & the Four Seasons**	*Chameleon*	5.1972
109	—	—	—
110	—	—	—
111	—	—	—
112	—	—	—
113	**Syreeta**	*Syreeta*	6.1972
114	—	—	—
115	**Odyssey**	*Odyssey*	5.1972
116	—	—	—
117	**Lesley Gore**	*Someplace Else Now*	7.1972
118	**The Crusaders**	*Hollywood*	7.1972
119	**Celebration**	*Celebration*	7.1972
120	**Martin & Finley**	*Dazzle 'Em With Footwork*	NR
121	**Repairs**	*Repairs*	10.1972
122	**Kubie**	*Kubie*	NR

MELODYLAND LABEL & HITSVILLE LABEL

*401	**T. G. Sheppard**	*T. G. Sheppard*	5.1975
*402	—	—	—
*403	**T. G. Sheppard**	*Motels And Memories*	3.1976
404	**T. G. Sheppard**	*Solitary Man*	9.1976
405	**Pat Boone**	*Texas Woman*	9.1976
406	**Wendel Adkins**	*Sundowners*	1.1977

* 401-3 Melodyland; 404-6 Hitsville

PRODIGAL LABEL

10007	**Ronnie McNeir**	*Ronnie McNeir*	11.1975
10008	**Shirley Alston**	*With A Little Help From My Friends*	11.1975
10009	**Gaylord & Holiday**	*Second Generation*	11.1975
10010	**Michael Quatro**	*Dancers, Romancers, Dreamers And Schemers*	6.1976
10011	**Kathe Green**	*Kathe Green*	8.1976
10012	**Fantacy Hill**	*Fantacy Hill*	8.1976
10013	**Dunn & Rubini**	*Diggin' It*	8.1976
10014	**Tattoo**	*Tattoo*	11.1976
10015	**Charlene**	*Charlene*	11.1976
10014	**Tattoo**	*Tattoo*	11.1976
10016	**Michael Quatro**	*Gettin' Ready*	1.1977
10017	**Delaney Bramlett**	*Delaney And Friends – Class Reunion*	2.1977
10018	**Charlene**	*Songs Of Love*	5.1977
10019	**Rare Earth**	*Rarearth*	7.1977
10020	**Phillip Jarrell**	*I Sing My Songs For You*	9.1977
10021	—	—	—
10022	**Fantacy Hill**	*First Step*	1.1978
10023	**Phil Cordell**	*Born Again*	NR
10024	**Fresh**	*Feelin' Fresh*	1.1978
10025	**Rare Earth**	*Band Together*	4.1978
10026	**Friendly Enemies**	*Round One*	4.1978
10027	**Rare Earth**	*Grand Slam*	9.1978
10028	**Fresh**	*Omniverse*	10.1978

10029	**Meatloaf**	_Meatloaf Featuring Stoney And Meatloaf_	10.1978
10030	**Stylus**	_Stylus_	10.1978
10031	**Stylus**	_Part Of It All_	NR
10032	**Fresh**	_Fresh_	NR

JU-PAR LABEL

1001	**Ju-Par Universal Orchestra**	_Moods And Grooves_	1.1977
1002	**Flavor**	_In Good Taste_	5.1977
1003	**Sly, Slick & Wicked**	_Sly, Slick And Wicked_	8.1977

MC RECORDS LABEL

501	**Pat Booone**	_The Country Side Of Pat Boone_	8.1977
502	**Jerry Naylor**	_Love Away Her Memory Tonight_	NR
503	**Jerry Naylor**	_Once Again_	NR
504	**Porter Jordan**	_Sings_	NR
505	**Pat Boone**	_Country Days And Country Nights_	NR
506	—	—	—
507	**Bob & Penny**	_Presenting_	NR
508	**Kenny Seratt**	_Kenny Seratt_	NR
509	—	—	—
510	—	—	—
511	**Marty Mitchell**	_You Are The Sunshine Of My Life_	11.1977
512	**Wendel Adkins**	_Wendel Adkins_	NR
513	**Tucker & Schoonmaker**	_Tucker And Schoonmaker_	NR
514	—	—	—
515	**Larry Groce**	_Please Take Me Back_	12.1977

BRITISH SINGLES

The following initials indicate which label was used on a particular record.
TM – Tamla Motown; G – Gordy; L – Latino.

7 INCH SINGLES

LONDON-AMERICAN

*HLT 8856	**Marv Johnson**	_Come To Me_ _Whisper_	5.1959
HLM 8998	**Paul Gayten**	_The Hunch_ _Hot Cross Buns_	11.1959
*HLT 9013	**Marv Johnson**	_You Got What It Takes_ _Don't Leave Me_	12.1959
HLU 9088	**Barrett Strong**	_Money (That's What I Want)_ _Oh I Apologise_	3.1960
*HLT 9109	**Marv Johnson**	_I Love The Way You Love_ _Let Me Love You_	4.1960
*HLT 9165	**Marv Johnson**	_All The Love I've Got_ _Ain't Gonna Be That Way_	7.1960
*HLT 9187	**Marv Johnson**	_(You've Got To) Move Two Mountains_ _I Need You_	9.1960
*HLT 9265	**Marv Johnson**	_Happy Days_ _Baby Baby_	1.1961
HLU 9276	**The Miracles**	_Shop Around_ _Who's Loving You_	2.1961
*HLT 9311	**Marv Johnson**	_Merry-Go-Round_ _Tell Me That You Love Me_	3.1961
HLU 9366	**The Miracles**	_Ain't It Baby_ _The Only One I Love_	6.1961

*Masters made by, but not now owned by, Motown Record Corp. because leased to the US United Artists Record Co.

FONTANA

| H 355 | **The Marvelettes** | _Please Mr. Postman_ _So Long Baby_ | 11.1961 |

H 384	**The Miracles**	_What's So Good About Goodbye_ _I've Been Good To You_	2.1962
H 386	**The Marvelettes**	_Twistin' Postman_ _I Want A Guy_	3.1962
H 387	**Eddie Holland**	_Jamie_ _Take A Chance On Me_	3.1962

ORIOLE (Prefix: CBA)

1762	**Mary Wells**	_You Beat Me To The Punch_ _Old Love (Let's Try It Again)_	9.1962
1763	**The Contours**	_Do You Love Me?_ _Move Mr. Man_	9.1962
1764	**The Marvelettes**	_Beechwood 4-5789_ _Someday, Some Way_	9.1962
1775	**Mike & the Modifiers**	_I Found Myself A Brand New Baby_ _It's Too Bad_	10.1962
1795	**The Miracles**	_You've Really Got A Hold On Me_ _Happy Landing_	1.1963
1796	**Mary Wells**	_Two Lovers_ _Operator_	1.1963
1799	**The Contours**	_Shake Sherry_ _You Better Get In Line_	2.1963
1803	**Marvin Gaye**	_Stubborn Kind Of Fellow_ _It Hurt Me Too_	2.1963
1808	**Eddie Holland**	_If It's Love (It's Alright)_ _It's Not Too Late_	3.1963
1809	**The Valadiers**	_I Found A Girl_ _You'll Be Sorry Someday_	3.1963
1814	**Martha & the Vandellas**	_I'll Have To Let Him Go_ _My Baby Won't Come Back_	3.1963
1817	**The Marvelettes**	_Locking Up My Heart_ _Forever_	4.1963
1819	**Martha & the Vandellas**	_Come And Get These Memories_ _Jealous Lover_	4.1963
1829	**Mary Wells**	_Laughing Boy_ _Two Wrongs Don't Make A Right_	5.1963
1831	**The Contours**	_Don't Let Her Be Your Baby_ _It Must Be Love_	5.1963
1846	**Marvin Gaye**	_Pride And Joy_ _One Of These Days_	7.1963
1847	**Mary Wells**	_Your Old Standby_ _What Love Has Joined Together_	7.1963
1853	**Little Stevie Wonder**	_Fingertips (Part 2)_ _Fingertips (Part 1)_	8.1963
1863	**The Miracles**	_Mickey's Monkey_ _Whatever Makes You Happy_	9.1963

STATESIDE (Prefix: SS)

228	**Martha & the Vandellas**	_Heatwave_ _A Love Like Yours (Don't Come Knocking Every Day)_	10.1963
238	**Little Stevie Wonder**	_Workout, Stevie Workout_ _Monkey Talk_	11.1963
242	**Mary Wells**	_You Lost The Sweetest Boy_ _What's Easy For Two (Is So Hard For One)_	11.1963
243	**Marvin Gaye**	_Can I Get A Witness_ _I'm Crazy 'Bout My Baby_	11.1963
250	**Martha & the Vandellas**	_Quicksand_ _Darling I Hum Our Song_	1.1964
251	**The Marvelettes**	_As Long As I Know He's Mine_ _Little Girl Blue_	1.1964

257	The Supremes	When The Lovelight Starts Shining Thru His Eyes	1.1964
		Standing At The Crossroads Of Love	
263	The Miracles	I Gotta Dance To Keep From Crying	2.1964
		Such Is Love, Such Is Life	
272	Martha & the Vandellas	Live Wire	3.1964
		Old Love (Let's Try It Again)	
273	The Marvelettes	He's A Good Guy, Yes He Is	3.1964
		Goddess Of Love	
278	The Temptations	The Way You Do The Things You Do	4.1964
		Just Let Me Know	
282	The Miracles	(You Can't Let The Boy Overpower) The Man In You	4.1964
		Heartbreak Road	
284	Marvin Gaye	You're A Wonderful One	4.1964
		When I'm Alone I Cry	
285	Little Stevie Wonder	Castles In The Sand	4.1964
		Thank You (For Loving Me All The Way)	
288	Mary Wells	My Guy	5.1964
		Oh Little Boy (What Did You Do To Me?)	
299	The Contours	Can You Do It?	5.1964
		I'll Stand By You	
305	Martha & the Vandellas	In My Lonely Room	6.1964
		A Tear For The Girl	
307	Brenda Holloway	Every Little Bit Hurts	6.1964
		Land Of A Thousand Boys	
316	Mary Wells & Marvin Gaye	Once Upon A Time	7.1964
		What's The Matter With You Baby?	
319	The Temptations	I'll Be In Trouble	7.1964
		The Girl's Alright With Me	
323	Stevie Wonder	Hey Harmonica Man	8.1964
		This Little Girl	
324	The Miracles	I Like It Like That	8.1964
		You're So Fine And Sweet	
326	Marvin Gaye	Try It Baby	8.1964
		If My Heart Could Sing	
327	The Supremes	Where Did Our Love Go?	8.1964
		He Means The World To Me	
334	The Marvelettes	You're My Remedy	9.1964
		A Little Bit of Sympathy, A Little Bit Of Love	
336	Four Tops	Baby, I Need Your Loving	9.1964
		Call On Me	
345	Martha & the Vandellas	Dancing In The Street	10.1964
		There He Is (At My Door)	
348	The Temptations	(Girl) Why You Wanna Make Me Blue?	10.1964
		Baby, Baby I Need You	
350	The Supremes	Baby Love	10.1964
		Ask Any Girl	
353	The Miracles	That's What Love Is Made Of	11.1964
		Would I Love You	
357	Earl Van Dyke & The Soul Brothers	Soul Stomp	11.1964
		Hot 'n' Tot	
359	Kim Weston	A Little More Love	11.1964
		Go Ahead And Laugh	
360	Marvin Gaye	How Sweet It Is (To Be Loved By You)	11.1964
		Forever	
361	The Velvelettes	Needle In A Haystack	11.1964
		Should I Tell Them?	
363	Marvin Gaye & Kim Weston	What Good Am I Without You?	12.1964
		I Want You 'round	
369	The Marvelettes	Too Many Fish In The Sea	1.1965
		A Need For Love	
371	Four Tops	Without The One You Love (Life's Not Worthwhile)	1.1965
		Love Has Gone	
376	The Supremes	Come See About Me	1.1965
		Always In My Heart	
377	The Miracles	Come On Do The Jerk	1.1965
		Baby Don't You Go	
378	The Temptations	My Girl	1.1965
		Talkin' 'Bout Nobody But My Baby	
381	The Contours	Can You Jerk Like Me?	1.1965
		That Day When She Needed Me	
383	Martha & the Vandellas	Wild One	1.1965
		Dancing Slow	
384	Carolyn Crawford	When Someone's Good To You	2.1965
		My Heart	
387	The Velvelettes	He Was Really Sayin' Somethin'	2.1965
		Throw A Farewell Kiss	
394	Tony Martin	Talking To Your Picture	3.1965
		Our Rhapsody	

TAMLA MOTOWN (Prefix: TMG)

501	The Supremes	Stop! In The Name Of Love	3.1965
		I'm In Love Again	
502	Martha & the Vandellas	Nowhere To Run	3.1965
		Motoring	
503	The Miracles	Ooo Baby Baby	3.1965
		All That's Good	
504	The Temptations	It's Growing	3.1965
		What Love Has Joined Together	
505	Stevie Wonder	Kiss Me Baby	3.1965
		Tears In Vain	
506	Earl Van Dyke & The Soul Brothers	All For You	3.1965
		Too Many Fish In The Sea	
507	Four Tops	Ask The Lonely	3.1965
		Where Did You Go?	
508	Brenda Holloway	When I'm Gone	4.1965
		I've Been Good To You	
509	Jr Walker & the All Stars	Shotgun	4.1965
		Hot Cha	
510	Marvin Gaye	I'll Be Doggone	4.1965
		You've Been A Long Time Coming	
511	Kim Weston	I'm Still Loving You	4.1965
		Just Loving You	
512	Shorty Long	Out To Get You	4.1965
		It's A Crying Shame	
513	The Hit Pack	Never Say No To Your Baby	5.1965
		Let's Dance	
514	The Detroit Spinners	Sweet Thing	5.1965
		How Can I?	
515	Four Tops	I Can't Help Myself	5.1965
		Sad Souvenirs	
516	The Supremes	Back In My Arms Again	5.1965
		Whisper You Love Me Boy	
517	Choker Campbell & His Band	Mickey's Monkey	6.1965
		Pride And Joy	
518	The Marvelettes	I'll Keep Holding On	6.1965
		No Time For Tears	
519	Brenda Holloway	Operator	6.1965
		I'll Be Available	
520	Jr Walker & the All Stars	Do The Boomerang	7.1965
		Tune Up	
521	The Velvelettes	Lonely, Lonely Girl Am I	7.1965
		I'm The Exception To The Rule	
522	The Miracles	The Tracks Of My Tears	7.1965
		Fork In The Road	
523	The Detroit Spinners	I'll Always Love You	7.1965
		Tomorrow May Never Come	
524	Marvin Gaye	Pretty Little Baby	8.1965
		Now That You've Won Me	
525	Marv Johnson	Why Do You Want To Let Me Go?	8.1965
		I'm Not A Plaything	

526	The Temptations	Since I Lost My Baby	8.1965
		You've Got To Earn It	
527	The Supremes	Nothing But Heartaches	8.1965
		He Holds His Own	
528	Four Tops	It's The Same Old Song	8.1965
		Your Love Is Amazing	
529	Jr Walker & the All Stars	Shake And Fingerpop	9.1965
		Cleo's Back	
530	Martha & the Vandellas	You've Been In Love Too Long	9.1965
		Love (Makes Me Do Foolish Things)	
531	The Contours	First I Look At The Purse	9.1965
		Searching For A Girl	
532	Stevie Wonder	High Heel Sneakers	9.1965
		Music Talk	
533	Billy Eckstine	Had You Been Around	10.1965
		Down to Earth	
534	Dorsey Burnette	Jimmy Brown	10.1965
		Everybody's Angel	
535	The Marvelettes	Danger Heartbreak Dead Ahead	10.1965
		Your Cheating Ways	
536	The Lewis Sisters	You Need Me	10.1965
		Moonlight On The Beach	
537	Tony Martin	The Bigger Your Heart Is	10.1965
		The Two Of Us	
538	Kim Weston	Take Me In Your Arms (Rock Me A Little While)	10.1965
		Don't Compare Me With Her	
539	Marvin Gaye	Ain't That Peculiar	11.1965
		She's Got To Be Real	
540	The Miracles	My Girl Has Gone	11.1965
		Since You Won My Heart	
541	The Temptations	My Baby	11.1965
		Don't Look Back	
542	Four Tops	Something About You	11.1965
		Darling I Hum Our Song	
543	The Supremes	I Hear A Symphony	11.1965
		Who Could Ever Doubt My Love	
544	Barbara McNair	You're Gonna Love My Baby	1.1966
		The Touch Of Time	
545	Stevie Wonder	Uptight (Everything's Alright)	1.1966
		Purple Raindrops	
546	The Marvelettes	Don't Mess With Bill	1.1966
		Anything You Wanna Do	
547	The Miracles	Going To A Go-Go	2.1966
		Choosey Beggar	
548	The Supremes	My World Is Empty Without You	2.1966
		Everything Is Good About You	
549	Martha & the Vandellas	My Baby Loves Me	2.1966
		Never Leave Your Baby's Side	
550	Jr Walker & the All Stars	Cleo's Mood	2.1966
		Baby, You Know You Ain't Right	
551	The Elgins	Put Yourself In My Place	2.1966
		Darling Baby	
552	Marvin Gaye	One More Heartache	3.1966
		When I Had Your Love	
553	Four Tops	Shake Me, Wake Me (When It's Over)	3.1966
		Just As Long As You Need Me	
554	Kim Weston	Helpless	3.1966
		A Love Like Yours (Don't Come Knockin' Every Day)	
555	The Isley Brothers	This Old Heart Of Mine (Is Weak For Me)	3.1966
		There's No Love Left	
556	Brenda Holloway	Together 'Till The End Of Time	3.1966
		Sad Song	

557	The Temptations	Get Ready	4.1966
		Fading Away	
558	Stevie Wonder	Nothing's Too Good For My Baby	4.1966
		With A Child's Heart	
559	Jr Walker & the All Stars	Road Runner	5.1966
		Shoot Your Shot	
560	The Supremes	Love Is Like An Itching In My Heart	5.1966
		He's All I Got	
561	Tammi Terrell	Come On And See Me	5.1966
		Baby, Don'tcha Worry	
562	The Marvelettes	You're The One	5.1966
		Paper Boy	
563	Marvin Gaye	Take This Heart Of Mine	6.1966
		Need Your Lovin' (Want You Back)	
564	The Contours	Determination	6.1966
		Just a Little Misunderstanding	
565	The Temptations	Ain't Too Proud To Beg	6.1966
		You'll Lose A Precious Love	
566	The Isley Brothers	Take Some Time Out For Love	6.1966
		Who Could Ever Doubt My Love?	
567	Martha & the Vandellas	What Am I Going To Do Without Your Love	7.1966
		Go Ahead And Laugh	
568	Four Tops	Loving You Is Sweeter Than Ever	7.1966
		I Like Everything About You	
569	The Miracles	Whole Lotta Shakin' In My Heart (Since I Met You Girl)	7.1966
		Oh Be My Love	
570	Stevie Wonder	Blowin' In The Wind	8.1966
		Ain't That Asking For Trouble	
571	Jr Walker & the All Stars	How Sweet It Is (To Be Loved By You)	8.1966
		Nothing But Soul	
572	The Isley Brothers	I Guess I'll Always Love You	8.1966
		I Hear A Symphony	
573	Shorty Long	Function At The Junction	8.1966
		Call On Me	
574	Marvin Gaye	Little Darling (I Need You)	9.1966
		Hey Diddle Diddle	
575	The Supremes	You Can't Hurry Love	9.1966
		Put Yourself In My Place	
576	Gladys Knight & the Pips	Just Walk In My Shoes	9.1966
		Stepping Closer To Your Heart	
577	Jimmy Ruffin	What Becomes Of The Brokenhearted	9.1966
		Baby I've Got It	
578	The Temptations	Beauty Is Only Skin Deep	9.1966
		You're Not An Ordinary Girl	
579	Four Tops	Reach Out, I'll Be There	10.1966
		Until You Love Someone	
580	The Velvelettes	These Things Will Keep Me Loving You	10.1966
		Since You've Been Loving Me	
581	Brenda Holloway	Hurt A Little Everyday	11.1966
		Where Were You?	
582	Martha & the Vandellas	I'm Ready For Love	11.1966
		He Doesn't Love Her Anymore	
583	The Elgins	Heaven Must Have Sent You	11.1966
		Stay In My Lonely Arms	
584	The Miracles	(Come Round Here) I'm The One You Need	11.1966
		Save Me	
585	The Supremes	You Keep Me Hangin' On	11.1966
		Remove This Doubt	
586	Jr Walker & the All Stars	Money (Part 1)	12.1966
		Money (Part 2)	

587	The Temptations	(I Know) I'm Losing You	12.1966
		Little Miss Sweetness	
588	Stevie Wonder	A Place In The Sun	12.1966
		Sylvia	
589	Four Tops	Standing In The Shadows Of	!.1967
		Love	
		Since You've Been Gone	
590	Marvin Gaye &	It Takes Two	1.1967
	Kim Weston	It's Gotta Be A Miracle (This	
		Thing Called Love)	
591	Chris Clark	Love's Gone Bad	1.1967
		Put Yourself In My Place	
592	The Originals	Goodnight Irene	1.1967
		Need Your Lovin' (Want You	
		Back)	
593	Jimmy Ruffin	I've Passed This Way Before	2.1967
		Tomorrow's Tears	
594	The Marvelettes	The Hunter Gets Captured	2.1967
		By The Game	
		I Think I Can Change You	
595	The Velvelettes	Needle In A Haystack	2.1967
		He Was Really Sayin'	
		Something	
596	Jr Walker & the	Pucker Up Buttercup	2.1967
	All Stars	Any Way You Wanta	
597	The Supremes	Love Is Here And Now You're	2.1967
		Gone	
		There's No Stopping Us Now	
598	Smokey	The Love I Saw In You Was	3.1967
	Robinson & the	Just A Mirage	
	Miracles	Swept For You Baby	
599	Martha & the	Jimmy Mack	3.1967
	Vandellas	Third Finger, Left Hand	
600	Shorty Long	Chantilly Lace	3.1967
		Your Love Is Amazing	
601	Four Tops	Bernadette	3.1967
		I Got A Feeling	
602	Stevie Wonder	Travelin' Man	3.1967
		Hey Love	
603	Jimmy Ruffin	Gonna Give Her All The Love	4.1967
		I've Got	
		World So Wide, Nowhere To	
		Hide (From Your Heart)	
604	Gladys Knight &	Take Me In Your Arms And	4.1967
	the Pips	Love Me	
		Do You Love Me Just A Little	
		Honey?	
605	The Contours	It's So Hard Being A Loser	5.1967
		Your Love Grows More	
		Precious Every Day	
606	The Isley	Got To Have You Back	5.1967
	Brothers	Just Ain't Enough Love	
607	The Supremes	The Happening	5.1967
		All I Know About You	
608	Brenda Holloway	Just Look What You've Done	5.1967
		Starting The Hurt All Over	
		Again	
609	The Marvelettes	When You're Young And In	5.1967
		Love	
		The Day You Take One (You	
		Have To Take The Other)	
610	The Temptations	All I Need	5.1967
		Sorry Is A Sorry Word	
611	Marvin Gaye &	Ain't No Mountain High	6.1967
	Tammi Terrell	Enough	
		Give A Little Love	
612	Four Tops	Seven Rooms Of Gloom	6.1967
		I'll Turn To Stone	
613	Stevie Wonder	I Was Made To Love Her	6.1967
		Hold Me	
614	Smokey	More Love	7.1967
	Robinson & the	Come Spy With Me (Orig. 'B'	
	Miracles	side Swept For You Baby)	
615	The Elgins	It's Been A Long Long Time	7.1967
		I Understand My Man	
616	Diana Ross & the	Reflections	8.1967
	Supremes	Going Down For The Third	
		Time	

617	Jimmy Ruffin	Don't You Miss Me A Little	8.1967
		Bit Baby?	
		I Want Her Love	
618	Marvin Gaye	Your Unchanging Love	8.1967
		I'll Take Care Of You	
619	Gladys Knight &	Everybody Needs Love	9.1967
	the Pips	Since I've Lost You	
620	The Temptations	You're My Everything	9.1967
		I've Been Good To You	
621	Martha Reeves &	Love Bug Leave My Heart	9.1967
	the Vandellas	Alone	
		One Way Out	
622	Brenda Holloway	You've Made Me So Very	9.1967
		Happy	
		I've Got To Find It	
623	Four Tops	You Keep Running Away	10.1967
		If You Don't Want My Love	
624	Chris Clark	From Head To Toe	10.1967
		Beginning Of The End	
625	Marvin Gaye &	Your Precious Love	10.1967
	Tammi Terrell	Hold Me Oh My Darling	
626	Stevie Wonder	I'm Wondering	10.1967
		Every Time I See You I Go	
		Wild	
627	The Spinners	For All We Know	10.1967
		I'll Always Love You	
628	Barbara	I Got A Feeling	11.1967
	Randolph	You Got Me Hurtin' All Over	
629	Gladys Knight &	I Heard It Through The	11.1967
	the Pips	Grapevine	
		It's Time To Go Now	
630	Edwin Starr	I Want My Baby Back	11.1967
		Gonna Keep On Trying Till I	
		Win Your Love	
631	Smokey	I Second That Emotion	11.1967
	Robinson & the	You Must Be Love	
	Miracles		
632	Diana Ross & the	In And Out Of Love	11.1967
	Supremes	I Guess I'll Always Love You	
633	The Temptations	(Loneliness Made Me	12.1967
		Realise) It's You That I Need	
		I Want A Love I Can See	
634	Four Tops	Walk Away Renée	12.1967
		Mame	
635	Marvin Gaye &	If I Could Build My Whole	12.1967
	Tammi Terrell	World Around You	
		If This World Were Mine	
636	Martha Reeves &	Honey Chile	1.1968
	the Vandellas	Show Me The Way	
637	Jr Walker & the	Come See About Me	1.1968
	All Stars	Sweet Soul	
638	Chris Clark	I Want To Go Back There	1.1968
		Again	
		I Love You	
639	The Marvelettes	My Baby Must Be A Magician	1.1968
		I Need Someone	
640	Marvin Gaye	You	1.1968
		Change What You Can	
641	The Temptations	I Wish It Would Rain	2.1968
		I Truly Truly Believe	
642	The Elgins	Put Yourself In My Place	2.1968
		Darling Baby	
643	Rita Wright	I Can't Give Back The Love I	2.1968
		Feel For You	
		Something On My Mind	
644	Shorty Long	Night Fo' Last (vocal)	2.1968
		Night Fo' Last (instr.)	
645	Glady Knight &	The End Of Our Road	3.1968
	the Pips	Don't Let Her Take Your	
		Love From Me	
646	Edwin Starr	I Am The Man For You Baby	2.1968
		My Weakness Is You	
647	Four Tops	If I Were A Carpenter	3.1968
		Your Love Is Wonderful	
648	Smokey	If You Can Want	3.1968
	Robinson & the	When The Words From Your	
	Miracles	Heart Get Caught Up In	
		Your Throat	

649	**Jimmy Ruffin**	*I'll Say Forever My Love*	3.1968
		Everybody Needs Love	
650	**Diana Ross & the**	*Forever Came Today*	4.1968
	Supremes	*Time Changes Things*	
651	**Chuck Jackson**	*Girls, Girls, Girls*	4.1968
		(You Can't Let The Boy	
		Overpower) The Man In You	
652	**The Isley**	*Take Me In Your Arms (Rock*	4.1968
	Brothers	*Me A Little While)*	
		Why, When Love Is Gone	
653	**Stevie Wonder**	*Shoo-Be-Doo-Be-Doo-Da-*	4.1968
		Day	
		Why Don't You Lead Me To	
		Love?	
654	**Bobby Taylor &**	*Does Your Mama Know*	5.1968
	the Vancouvers	*About Me?*	
		Fading Away	
655	**Marvin Gaye &**	*Ain't Nothing Like The Real*	5.1968
	Tammi Terrell	*Thing*	
		Little Ole Boy, Little Ole Girl	
656	**R. Dean Taylor**	*Gotta See Jane*	5.1968
		Don't Fool Around	
657	**Martha Reeves &**	*I Promise To Wait My Love*	5.1968
	the Vandellas	*Forget Me Not*	
658	**The Temptations**	*I Could Never Love Another*	5.1968
		(After Loving You)	
		Gonna Give Her All The Love	
		I've Got	
659	**The Marvelettes**	*Here I Am Baby*	6.1968
		Keep Off, No Trespassing	
660	**Gladys Knight &**	*It Should Have Been Me*	6.1968
	the Pips	*You Don't Love Me No More*	
661	**Smokey**	*Yesterlove*	6.1968
	Robinson & the	*Much Better Off*	
	Miracles		
662	**Diana Ross & the**	*Some Things You Never Get*	6.1968
	Supremes	*Used To*	
		You've Been So Wonderful	
		To Me	
663	**Shorty Long**	*Here Comes The Judge*	7.1968
		Sing What You Wanna	
664	**Jimmy Ruffin**	*Don't Let Him Take Your*	7.1968
		Love From Me	
		Lonely, Lonely Man Am I	
665	**Four Tops**	*Yesterday's Dreams*	8.1968
		For Once In My Life	
666	**Stevie Wonder**	*You Met Your Match*	8.1968
		My Girl	
667	**Jr. Walker & the**	*Hip City (Part 1)*	9.1968
	All Stars	*Hip City (Part 2)*	
668	**Marvin Gaye &**	*You're All I Need To Get By*	9.1968
	Tammi Terrell	*Two Can Have A Party*	
669	**Martha Reeves &**	*I Can't Dance To That Music*	9.1968
	the Vandellas	*You're Playin'*	
		I Tried	
670	**Paul Petersen**	*A Little Bit For Sandy*	9.1968
		Your Love's Got Me Burning	
		Alive	
671	**The Temptations**	*Why Did You Leave Me*	10.1968
		Darling?	
		How Can I Forget	
672	**Edwin Starr**	*25 Miles*	9. 1968
		Mighty Good Lovin'	
673	**Smokey**	*Special Occasion*	10.1968
	Robinson & the	*Give Her Up*	
	Miracles		
674	**Gladys Knight &**	*I Wish It Would Rain*	10.1968
	the Pips	*It's Summer*	
675	**Four Tops**	*I'm In A Different World*	11.1968
		Remember When	
676	**Marvin Gaye**	*Chained*	11.1968
		At Last (I Found A Love)	
677	**Diana Ross & the**	*Love Child*	11.1968
	Supremes	*Will This Be The Day?*	
678	**The Fantastic**	*I Love You Madly (vocal)*	11.1968
	Four	*I Love You Madly (instr.)*	
679	**Stevie Wonder**	*For Once In My Life*	11.1968
		Angie Girl	
680	**Marv Johnson**	*I'll Pick A Rose For My Rose*	12.1968
		You Got The Love I Love	
681	**Marvin Gaye &**	*You Ain't Livin' Til You're*	1.1969
	Tammi Terrell	*Lovin'*	
		Oh How I'd Miss You	
682	**Jr Walker & the**	*Home Cookin'*	1.1969
	All Stars	*Mutiny*	
683	**The Isley**	*I Guess I'll Always Love You*	1.1969
	Brothers	*It's Out Of The Question*	
684	**Martha Reeves &**	*Dancing In The Street*	1.1969
	the Vandellas	*Quicksand*	
685	**Diana Ross & the**	*I'm Gonna Make You Love*	1.1969
	Supremes & The	*Me*	
	Temptations	*A Place In The Sun*	
686	**Marvin Gaye**	*I Heard It Through The*	2.1969
		Grapevine	
		Need Somebody	
687	**Smokey**	*Baby, Baby Don't Cry*	2.1969
	Robinson & the	*Your Mother's Only Daughter*	
	Miracles		
688	**The Temptations**	*Get Ready*	2.1969
		My Girl	
689	**David Ruffin**	*My Whole World Ended (The*	3.1969
		Moment You Left Me)	
		I've Got To Find Myself A	
		Brand New Baby	
690	**Stevie Wonder**	*I Don't Know Why*	3.1969
		My Cherie Amour	
691	**Jr Walker & the**	*Road Runner*	3.1969
	All Stars	*Shotgun*	
692	**Edwin Starr**	*Way Over There*	3.1969
		If My Heart Could Tell The	
		Story	
693	**The Isley**	*Behind A Painted Smile*	4.1969
	Brothers	*One Too Many Heartaches*	
694	**Martha Reeves &**	*Nowhere To Run*	3.1969
	the Vandellas	*Live Wire*	
695	**Diana Ross & the**	*I'm Livin' In Shame*	4.1969
	Supremes	*I'm So Glad I Got Somebody*	
		(Like You Around)	
696	**Smokey**	*The Tracks Of My Tears*	4.1969
	Robinson & the	*Come On Do The Jerk*	
	Miracles		
697	**Marvin Gaye &**	*Good Lovin' Ain't Easy To*	5.1969
	Tammi Terrell	*Come By*	
		Satisfied Feelin'	
698	**Four Tops**	*What Is A Man?*	5.1969
		Don't Bring Back Memories	
699	**The Temptations**	*Ain't Too Proud To Beg*	5.1969
		Fading Away	
700	**Brenda Holloway**	*Just Look What You've Done*	6.1969
		You've Made Me So Very	
		Happy	
701	**The Marvelettes**	*Reachin' For Something I*	6.1969
		Can't Have	
		Destination: Anywhere	
702	**The Originals**	*Green Grow The Lilacs*	6.1969
		You're The One	
703	**Jimmy Ruffin**	*I've Passed This Way Before*	7.1969
		Tomorrow's Tears	
704	**Diana Ross & the**	*No Matter What Sign You Are*	7.1969
	Supremes	*The Young Folks*	
705	**Marvin Gaye**	*Too Busy Thinkin' 'Bout My*	7.1969
		Baby	
		Wherever I Lay My Hat	
		(That's My Home)	
706	**The Honest Men**	*Cherie*	8.1969
		Baby	
707	**The Temptations**	*Cloud Nine*	8.1969
		Why Did She Have To Leave	
		Me (Why Did She Have To	
		Go?)	
708	**The Isley**	*Put Yourself In My Place*	8.1969
	Brothers	*Little Miss Sweetness*	
709	**Diana Ross & the**	*I Second That Emotion*	9.1969
	Supremes & The	*The Way You Do The Things*	
	Temptations	*You Do*	

710	**Four Tops**	Do What You Gotta Do	9.1969
		Can't Seem To Get You Out Of My Mind	
711	**David Ruffin**	I've Lost Everything I've Ever Loved	9.1969
		We'll Have A Good Thing Going On	
712	**Jr Walker & the All Stars**	What Does It Take (To Win Your Love)	10.1969
		Brainwasher	
713	**Marv Johnson**	I Miss You Baby (How I Miss You)	10.1969
		Bad Girl	
714	**Gladys Knight & the Pips**	The Nitty Gritty	10.1969
		Got Myself A Good Man	
715	**Marvin Gaye & Tammi Terrell**	The Onion Song	10.1969
		I Can't Believe You Love Me	
716	**The Temptations**	Runaway Child, Running Wild	10.1969
		I Need Your Lovin'	
717	**Stevie Wonder**	Yester-me, Yester-you, Yesterday	11.1969
		I'd Be A Fool Right Now	
718	**Marvin Gaye**	That's The Way Love Is	11.1969
		Gonna Keep On Tryin' 'Til I Win Your Love	
719	**The Isley Brothers**	Take Some Time Out For Love	11.1969
		Who Could Ever Doubt My Love	
720	**Blinky & Edwin Starr**	Oh How Happy	NR
		Ooo Baby Baby	
721	**Diana Ross & the Supremes**	Someday We'll Be Together	11.1969
		He's My Sunny Boy	
722	**The Temptations**	I Can't Get Next To You	1.1970
		Running Away (Ain't Gonna Help You)	
723	**The Contours**	Just A Little Misunderstanding	1.1970
		First I Look At The Purse	
724	**Jackson 5**	I Want You Back	1.1970
		Who's Loving You?	
725	**Edwin Starr**	Time	1.1970
		Running Back And Forth	
726	**Jimmy Ruffin**	Farewell Is A Lonely Sound	2.1970
		If You Will Let Me I Know I Can	
727	**Jr Walker & the All Stars**	These Eyes	2.1970
		I've Got To Find A Way To Win Maria Back	
728	**Gladys Knight & the Pips**	Didn't You Know (You'd Have To Cry Sometime)	2.1970
		Keep An Eye	
729	**Chuck Jackson**	Honey Come Back	3.1970
		What Am I Gonna Do Without You?	
730	**Diana Ross & the Supremes & The Temptations**	Why (Must We Fall In Love)	3.1970
		Uptight (Everything's Alright)	
731	**Stevie Wonder**	Never Had A Dream Come True	3.1970
		Somebody Knows, Somebody Cares	
732	**Four Tops**	I Can't Help Myself	3.1970
		Baby I Need Your Loving	
733	**The Originals**	Baby I'm For Real	3.1970
		The Moment Of Truth	
734	**Marvin Gaye**	Abraham, Martin And John	4.1970
		How Can I Forget?	
735	**The Supremes**	Up The Ladder To The Roof	4.1970
		Bill, When Are You Coming Back	
736	**Four Tops**	It's All In The Game	5.1970
		Love (Is The Answer)	
737	**Marv Johnson**	So Glad You Chose Me	5.1970
		I'm Not A Plaything	
738	**Jackson 5**	ABC	5.1970
		The Young Folks	

739	**Kiki Dee**	The Day Will Come Between Sunday And Monday	5.1970
		My Whole World Ended (The Moment You Left Me)	
740	**Jimmy Ruffin**	I'll Say Forever My Love	5.1970
		Everybody Needs Love	
741	**The Temptations**	Psychedelic Shack	6.1970
		That's The Way Love Is	
742	**Rare Earth**	Get Ready	6.1970
		Magic Key	
743	**Diana Ross**	Reach Out And Touch (Somebody's Hand)	6.1970
		Dark Side Of The World	
744	**Stevie Wonder**	Signed, Sealed, Delivered I'm Yours	6.1970
		I'm More Than Happy (I'm Satisfied)	
745	**Smokey Robinson & the Miracles**	The Tears Of A Clown	7.1970
		You Must Be Love or Who's Gonna Take The Blame	
746	**Jackson 5**	The Love You Save	7.1970
		I Found That Girl	
747	**The Supremes**	Everybody's Got The Right To Love	7.1970
		But I Love You More	
748	**Blinky & Edwin Starr**	Oh How Happy	8.1970
		Ooo Baby Baby	
749	**The Temptations**	Ball Of Confusion (That's What The World Is Today)	9.1970
		It's Summer	
750	**Jr Walker & the All Stars**	Do You See My Love (For You Growing)	9.1970
		Groove And Move	
751	**Diana Ross**	Ain't No Mountain High Enough	8.1970
		Can't It Wait Until Tomorrow	
752	**Four Tops**	Still Water (Love)	9.1970
		Still Water (Peace)	
753	**Jimmy Ruffin**	It's Wonderful (To Be Loved By You)	10.1970
		Maria (You Were The Only One)	
754	**Edwin Starr**	War	10.1970
		He Who Picks A Rose	
755	**The Motown Spinners**	It's A Shame	10.1970
		Sweet Thing	
756	**Gladys Knight & the Pips**	Friendship Train	10.1970
		You Need Love Like I Do (Don't You)	
757	**Stevie Wonder**	Heaven Help Us All	10.1970
		I Gotta Have A Song	
758	**Jackson 5**	I'll Be There	11.1970
		One More Chance	
759	**Earl Van Dyke**	Six By Six	11.1970
		All For You	
760	**The Supremes**	Stoned Love	1.1971
		Shine On Me	
761	**Smokey Robinson & the Miracles**	(Come Round Here) I'm The One You Need	1.1971
		We Can Make It We Can	
762	**Martha Reeves & the Vandellas**	Forget Me Not	1.1971
		I Gotta Let You Go	
763	**R. Dean Taylor**	Indiana Wants Me	2.1971
		Love's Your Name	
764	**Edwin Starr**	Stop The War Now!	1.1971
		Gonna Keep On Tryin' Till I Win Your Love	
765	**Gladys Knight & the Pips**	If I Were Your Woman	6.1971
		The Tracks Of My Tears	
766	**The Motown Spinners**	Together We Can Make Such Sweet Music	3.1971
		Truly Yours	
767	**Jimmy Ruffin**	Let's Say Goodbye Tomorrow	3.1971
		Living In A World I Created For Myself	

768	Diana Ross	Remember Me	3.1971
		How About You	
769	Jackson 5	Mama's Pearl	4.1971
		Darling Dear	
770	Four Tops	Just Seven Numbers (Can Straighten Out My Life)	4.1971
		I Wish I Were Your Mirror	
771	The Elgins	Heaven Must Have Sent You	4.1971
		Stay In My Lonely Arms	
772	Stevie Wonder	We Can Work It Out	4.1971
		Don't Wonder Why	
773	The Temptations	Just My Imagination (Running Away With Me)	5.1971
		You Make Your Own Heaven And Hell Right Here On Earth	
774	Smokey Robinson & the Miracles	I Don't Blame You At All	5.1971
		That Girl	
775	Marvin Gaye	What's Going On	5.1971
		God Is Love	
776	The Undisputed Truth	Save My Love For A Rainy Day	6.1971
		Since I've Lost You	
777	The Supremes & Four Tops	River Deep, Mountain High	6.1971
		It's Gotta Be A Miracle (This Thing Called Love)	
778	Jackson 5	Never Can Say Goodbye	7.1971
		She's Good	
779	Stevie Wonder	Never Dreamed You'd Leave In Summer	7.1971
		If You Really Love Me	
780	The Velvelettes	These Things Will Keep Me Loving You	7.1971
		Since You've Been Loving Me	
781	Diana Ross	I'm Still Waiting	7.1971
		Reach Out I'll Be There	
782	The Supremes	Nathan Jones	8.1971
		Happy (Is A Bumpy Road)	
783	The Temptations	It's Summer	8.1971
		Unite The World (Ungena Za Ulimwengu)	
784	Jimmy Ruffin	On The Way Out (On The Way In)	8.1971
		Honey Come Back	
785	Four Tops	Simple Game	9.1971
		You Stole My Love	
786	R. Dean Taylor	Ain't It A Sad Thing	NR on TMG
		Back Street	
787	The Elgins	Put Yourself In My Place	9.1971
		It's Gonna Be Hard Times	
788	Barbara Randolph	I Got A Feeling	9.1971
		You Got Me Hurtin' All Over	
789	The Undisputed Truth	Smiling Faces Sometimes	10.1971
		You Got The Love I Need	
790	Edwin Starr	Agent Double O Soul	10.1971
		Back Street	
791	Rita Wright	I Can't Give Back The Love I Feel For You	10.1971
		Something On My Mind	
792	Diana Ross	Surrender	10.1971
		I'm A Winner	
793	The Supremes & Four Tops	You Gotta Have Love In Your Heart	11.1971
		I'm Glad About It	
794	Martha Reeves & the Vandellas	Bless You	11.1971
		Hope I Don't Get My Heart Broke	
795	The San Remo Strings	Festival Time	11.1971
		All Turned On	
796	Marvin Gaye	Save The Children	11.1971
		Little Darling (I Need You)	
797	Michael Jackson	Got To Be There	1.1972
		Maria (You Were The Only One)	
798	Stevie Wonder	If You Really Love Me	1.1972
		Think Of Me As Your Soldier	

799	Thelma Houston	I Want To Go Back There Again	1.1972
		Pick Of The Week	
800	The Temptations	Superstar (Remember How You Got Where You Are)	1.1972
		Gonna Keep On Tryin' Till I Win Your Love	
801	Tom Clay	What The World Needs Now Is Love	2.1972
		Abraham, Martin and John	
		The Victors	
802	Marvin Gaye	Mercy Mercy Me (The Ecology)	2.1972
		Sad Tomorrows	
803	Four Tops	Bernadette	2.1972
		I Got The Feeling/It's The Same Old Song	
804	The Supremes	Floy Joy	2.1972
		This Is The Story	
805	Gladys Knight & the Pips	Make Me The Woman That You Go Home To	3.1972
		I Don't Want To Do Wrong	
806	The Velvelettes	Needle In A Haystack	3.1972
		I'm The Exception To The Rule	
807	The San Remo Strings	Reach Out I'll Be There	3.1972
		Hungry For Love	
808	The Temptations	Take A Look Around	3.1972
		Smooth Sailing From Now On	
809	Jackson 5	Sugar Daddy	3.1972
		I'm So Happy	
810	Edwin Starr	Funky Music Sho Nuff Turns Me On	4.1972
		Cloud Nine	
811	Smokey Robinson	My Girl Has Gone	4.1972
		Crazy 'Bout The La La La	
812	Diana Ross	Doobedood'ndoobe, Doobedood'ndoobe, Doobedood'ndoo	4.1972
		Keep An Eye	
813	Gladys Knight & the Pips	Just Walk In My Shoes	6.1972
		(I Know) I'm Losing You	
814	Earl Van Dyke & the Soul Brothers	I Can't Help Myself	5.1972
		How Sweet It Is (To Be Loved By You)	
815	The Supremes & Four Tops	Without The One You Love	5.1972
		Let's Make Love Now	
816	Michael Jackson	Rockin' Robin	5.1972
		Love Is Here And Now You're Gone	
817	Marvin Gaye	Inner City Blues (Make Me Wanna Holler)	5.1972
		Wholy Holy	
818	The Undisputed Truth	Superstar (Remember How You Got Where You Are)	6.1972
		Ain't No Sun Since You've Been Gone	
819	Frankie Valli & the Four Seasons	You're A Song (That I Can't Sing)	6.1972
		Sun Country	
820	Mary Wells	My Guy	6.1972
		You Lost The Sweetest Boy/ Two Lovers	
821	The Supremes	Automatically Sunshine	6.1972
		Precious Little Things	
822	The Originals	God Bless Whoever Sent You	6.1972
		I Like Your Style/Baby I'm For Real	
823	Four Tops	Walk With Me, Talk With Me Darling	7.1972
		L.A. (My Town)	
824	Jr Walker & the All Stars	Walk In The Night	7.1972
		Right On Brothers And Sisters	
		Gotta Hold On To This Feeling	
825	Jackson 5	Little Bitty Pretty One	9.1972
		Maybe Tomorrow	

826	**Michael Jackson**	*Ain't No Sunshine*	7.1972
		I Wanna Be Where You Are	
827	**Stevie Wonder**	*Superwoman*	9.1972
		Seems So Long	
828	**Sisters Love**	*Mr. Fix-It Man*	9.1972
		You've Got To Make Your Choice	
829	**Four Tops**	*I'll Turn To Stone*	9.1972
		Love Feels Like Fire	
830	**Gladys Knight & the Pips**	*Help Me Make It Through The Night*	10.1972
		If You Gonna Leave (Just Leave)	
831	**Laura Lee**	*To Win Your Heart*	9.1972
		So Will I	
832	**The Temptations**	*Smiling Faces Sometimes*	10.1972
		Mother Nature	
833	**Jackson 5**	*Lookin' Through The Windows*	10.1972
		Love Song	
834	**Michael Jackson**	*Ben*	11.1972
		You Can Cry On My Shoulder	
835	**The Supremes**	*Your Wonderful Sweet, Sweet Love*	11.1972
		Love It Came To Me This Time	
836	**The Supremes & Four Tops**	*Reach Out And Touch (Somebody's Hand)*	11.1972
		Where Would I Be Without You Baby	
837	**Jackson 5**	*Santa Claus Is Coming To Town/Someday At Christmas*	12.1972
		Christmas Won't Be The Same This Year	
838	**Jermaine Jackson**	*That's How Love Goes*	12.1972
		I Lost My Love In The Big City	
839	**The Temptations**	*Papa Was A Rollin' Stone (vocal)*	1.1973
		Papa Was A Rollin' Stone (instr.)	
840	**Jr Walker & the All Stars**	*Take Me Girl I'm Ready*	1.1973
		I Don't Want To Do Wrong	
841	**Stevie Wonder**	*Superstition*	1.1973
		You've Got It Bad Girl	
842	**Jackson 5**	*Doctor My Eyes*	2.1973
		My Little Baby	
843	**Martha Reeves**	*No One There*	2.1973
		(I've Given You) The Best Years Of My Life	
844	**Gladys Knight & the Pips**	*The Look Of Love*	2.1973
		You're My Everything	
845	**Eddie Kendricks**	*If You Let Me*	2.1973
		Just Memories	
846	**Marvin Gaye**	*Trouble Man*	3.1973
		Don't Mess With Mister 'T'	
847	**The Supremes**	*Bad Weather*	3.1973
		It's So Hard For Me To Say Goodbye	
848	**Michel Legrand**	*Love Theme from 'Lady Sings The Blues'*	3.1973
	Gil Askey	*Any Happy Home*	
849	**Diana Ross**	*Good Morning Heartache*	3.1973
		God Bless The Child	
850	**Four Tops**	*So Deep Within You*	3.1973
		Happy (Is A Bumpy Road)	
851	**Jermaine Jackson**	*Daddy's Home*	4.1973
		Take Me In Your Arms (Rock Me A Little While)	
852	**Stevie Wonder**	*You Are The Sunshine Of My Life*	5.1973
		Look Around	
853	**Smokey Robinson & the Miracles**	*Going To Go-Go/Whole Lot Of Shakin' In My Heart (Since I Met You)/Yester Love*	4.1973
854	**The Temptations**	*Masterpiece (vocal)*	4.1973
		Masterpiece (instr.)	
855	**Gladys Knight & the Pips**	*Neither One Of Us (Wants To Be The First To Say Goodbye)*	5.1973
		Can't Give It Up No More	
856	**Jackson 5**	*Hallelujah Day*	5.1973
		To Know	
857	**Jr Walker & the All Stars**	*Way Back Home (vocal)*	6.1973
		Way Back Home (instr.)	
		Country Boy	
858	**Four Tops**	*I Can't Quit Your Love*	6.1973
		I Am Your Man	
859	**The Supremes**	*Tossin' And Turnin'*	6.1973
		Oh Be My Love	
860	**The Marvelettes**	*Reachin' For Something I Can't Have*	9.1973
		Here I Am Baby	
861	**Diana Ross**	*Touch Me In The Morning*	7.1973
		Baby It's Love	
862	**Willie Hutch**	*Brother's Gonna Work It Out*	8.1973
		I Choose You	
863	**Michael Jackson**	*Morning Glow*	7.1973
		My Girl	
864	**Gladys Knight & the Pips**	*Take Me In Your Arms And Love Me*	7.1973
		No One Could Love You More	
865	**Jackson 5**	*Skywriter*	8.1973
		Ain't Nothing Like The Real Thing	
866	**The Temptations**	*Law Of The Land*	8.1973
		Funky Music Sho Nuff Turns Me on	
867	**Martin & Finley**	*It's Another Sunday*	NR
		Best Friends	
868	**Marvin Gaye**	*Let's Get It On*	8.1973
		I Wish It Would Rain	
869	**Stevie Wonder**	*Higher Ground*	9.1973
		Too High	
870	**J. J. Barnes**	*Real Humdinger*	9.1973
		Please Let Me In/I Ain't Gonna Do It	
871	**The Detroit Spinners**	*Together We Can Make Such Sweet Music*	12.1973
		Bad Bad Weather (Till You Come Home)	
872	**Jr Walker & the All Stars**	*Holly Holy*	9.1973
		Peace and Understanding Is Hard To Find	
873	**Eddie Kendricks**	*Keep On Truckin' (Part 1)*	10.1973
		Keep On Truckin' (Part 2)	
874	**Jermaine Jackson**	*The Bigger You Love (The Harder You Fall)*	10.1973
		I'm In A Different World	
875	**Edwin Starr**	*You've Got My Soul On Fire*	10.1973
		Love (The Lonely People's Prayer)	
876	**Gladys Knight & the Pips**	*Daddy Could Swear, I Declare*	9.1973
		For Once In My Life	
877	**The Isley Brothers**	*Tell Me It's Just A Rumour Baby*	10.1973
		Save Me From This Misery	
878	**Jackson 5**	*Get It Together*	11.1973
		Touch	
879	**Diana Ross & Marvin Gaye**	*You're A Special Part Of Me*	11.1973
		I'm Falling In Love With You	
880	**Diana Ross**	*All Of My Life*	11.1973
		A Simple Thing Like Cry	
881	**Stevie Wonder**	*Living For The City*	11.1973
		Visions	
882	**Marvin Gaye**	*Come Get To This*	1.1974
		Distant Lover	
883	**Smokey Robinson**	*Just My Soul Responding*	1.1974
		Sweet Harmony	

884	The Supremes	I Guess I'll Miss The Man	1.1974
		Over and Over	
885	Willie Hutch	Tell Me Why Has Our Love Turned Cold	NR
		Mother's Theme (Mama)	
886	The Contours	Baby Hit And Run	2.1974
		Can You Jerk Like Me	
887	The Temptations	I Need You	3.1974
		Hey Girl (I Like Your Style)	
888	Eddie Kendricks	Boogie Down	2.1974
		Eddie's Love	
889	Jr Walker & the All Stars	Don't Blame The Children	2.1974
		Soul Clappin'	
890	Diana Ross & Marvin Gaye	You Are Everything	3.1974
		Include Me In Your Life	
891	The Miracles	Don't Let It End (Till You Let It Begin)	3.1974
		I Wanna Be With You	
892	Stevie Wonder	He's Misstra Know-It-All	4.1974
		You Can't Judge A Book By Its Cover	
893	Diana Ross	Last Time I Saw Him	4.1974
		Everything Is Everything	
894	Jr Walker & the All Stars	Gotta Hold On To This Feeling	4.1974
		I Ain't Going Nowhere	
895	Jackson 5	The Boogie Man	4.1974
		Don't Let Your Baby Catch You	
896	R. Dean Taylor	There's A Ghost In My House	5.1974
		Let's Go Somewhere	
897	The Undisputed Truth	Help Yourself	5.1974
		What It Is	
898	Smokey Robinson	A Silent Partner In A Three Way Love Affair	5.1974
		Baby Come Close	
899	The Contours	Do You Love Me	6.1974
		Determination	
900	Michael Jackson	Music And Me	5.1974
		Johnny Raven	
901	Eddie Kendricks	Son Of Sagittarius	6.1974
		Can't Help What I Am	
902	Commodores	Machine Gun	7.1974
		There's A Song In My Heart	
903	Gladys Knight & the Pips	Didn't You Know (You'd Have To Cry Sometime)	6.1974
		Cloud Nine	
904	Jackson 5	Dancing Machine	6.1974
		It's Too Late To Change The Time	
905	Edwin Starr	Stop Her On Sight (SOS)	6.1974
		Headline News	
906	Diana Ross & Marvin Gaye	Stop, Look, Listen (To Your Heart)	6.1974
		Love Twins	
907	The Reflections	(Just Like) Romeo And Juliet	6.1974
		Can't You Tell By The Look In My Eyes	
908	Stevie Wonder	Don't You Worry 'Bout A Thing	7.1974
		Do Yourself A Favour	
909	R. Dean Taylor	Don't Fool Around	6.1974
		Poor Girl	
910	Gloria Jones	Tin Can People	7.1974
		So Tired (Of The Way You're Treating Our Love Baby)	
911	Jimmy Ruffin	What Becomes Of The Brokenhearted	7.1974
		Don't You Miss Me A Little Bit Baby	
912	Syreeta	Spinnin' And Spinnin'	8.1974
		Black Maybe	
913	Yvonne Fair	Funky Music Sho Nuff Turns Me On	8.1974
		Let Your Hair Down	
914	The Miracles	Do It Baby	8.1974
		Wigs And Lashes	

915	Diana Ross & the Supremes	Baby Love	8.1974
		Ask Any Girl	
916	Eddie Kendricks	Girl You Need A Change Of Mind (Part 1)	9.1974
		Girl You Need A Change Of Mind (Part 2)	
917	Diana Ross	Love Me	9.1974
		Save The Children	
918	R. Dean Taylor	Gotta See Jane	9.1974
		Candy Apple Red	
919	The Undisputed Truth	I'm A Fool For You	9.1974
		Mama I Gotta Brand New Thing (Don't Say No)	
920	Diana Ross & Marvin Gaye	My Mistake (Was To Love You)	10.1974
		Just Say, Just Say	
921	Stevie Wonder	You Haven't Done Nothin'	10.1974
		Happier Than The Morning Sun	
922	Jimmy Ruffin	Farewell Is A Lonely Sound	10.1974
		I Will Never Let You Get Away	
923	Marvin Gaye	I Heard It Through The Grapevine	11.1974
		Chained	
924	Commodores	The Zoo (The Human Zoo)	11.1974
		I'm Looking For Love	
925	Diana Ross & the Supremes	Where Did Our Love Go	11.1974
		Nothing But Heartaches	
926	Syreeta	I'm Goin' Left	11.1974
		Heavy Day	
927	Jackson 5	The Life Of The Party	11.1974
		Whatever You Got, I Want	
928	Stevie Wonder	Boogie On Reggae Woman	12.1974
		Evil	
929	The Dynamic Superiors	Shoe Shoe Shine	1.1975
		Release Me	
930	Edwin Starr	Who's Right Or Wrong?	12.1974
		Ain't It Hell Up In Harlem	
931	The Temptations	Happy People	1.1975
	The Temptations Band	Happy People (instr.)	
932	Popcorn Wylie	Funky Rubber Band (vocal)	2.1975
		Funky Rubber Band (instr.)	
933	Syreeta	Your Kiss Is Sweet	1.1975
		How Many Days	
934	Jimmy Ruffin	I've Passed This Way Before	1.1975
		Sad And Lonesome Feeling	
935	Commodores	Superman	2.1975
		It Is As Good As You Make It	
936	David Ruffin	Take Me Clear From Here	1.1975
		Blood Donors Needed (Give All You Can)	
937	The Isley Brothers	This Old Heart of Mine (Is Weak For You)	1.1975
		There's No Love Left	
938	Caston & Majors	Child Of Love	2.1975
		No One Will Know	
939	The Marvelettes	When You're Young And In Love	2.1975
		The Day You Take One (You Have To Take The Other)	
940	The Miracles	Where Are You Going To My Love?	2.1975
		Up Again	
941	Diana Ross	Sorry Doesn't Always Make It Right	2.1975
		Together	
942	Jackson 5	I Am Love (Part 1)	3.1975
		I Am Love (Part 2)	
943	The Undisputed Truth	Law Of The Land	3.1975
		Lil' Red Ridin' Hood	
944	Commodores	I Feel Sanctified	3.1975
		Determination	
945	Gladys Knight & the Pips	You've Lost That Lovin' Feeling	4.1975
		This Child Needs Its Father	

946	**Michael Jackson**	One Day In Your Life With A Child's Heart	4.1975
947	**Eddie Kendricks**	Shoeshine Boy Hooked On Your Love	5.1975
948	**The Temptations**	Memories Ain't No Justice	5.1975
949	**Smokey Robinson**	Baby That's Backatcha Just Passing Through	5.1975
950	**The Supremes**	He's My Man Give Out But Don't Give Up	8.1975
951	**Caston & Majors**	Sing There's Fear	6.1975
952	**Commodores**	Slippery When Wet The Bump	6.1975
953	**Diana Ross & Marvin Gaye**	Don't Knock My Love I'm Falling In Love With You	7.1975
954	**Syreeta**	Harmour Love What Love Has Joined Together	6.1975
955	**Gladys Knight & the Pips**	If I Were Your Woman The Only Time You Love Me Is When You're Losing Me	6.1975
956	**Diana Ross & the Supremes**	You Can't Hurry Love The Happening	10.1980
957	**Smokey Robinson & the Miracles**	(Come Round Here) I'm The One You Need I Second That Emotion	10.1980
958	**Four Tops**	Seven Rooms Of Gloom If I Were A Carpenter	10.1980
959	**Stevie Wonder**	I Was Made To Love Her Never Had A Dream Come True	10.1980
960	**Diana Ross & The Supremes**	Reflections Love Child	10.1980
961	**Jimmy Ruffin**	I'll Say Forever My Love It's Wonderful (To Be Loved By You)	10.1980
962	**Jr Walker & the All Stars**	What Does It Take (To Win Your Love) Take Me Girl, I'm Ready	10.1980
963	**Jackson 5**	I Want You Back The Love You Save	10.1980
964	**The Supremes**	Up The Ladder To The Roof Automatically Sunshine	10.1980
965	**Four Tops**	It's All In The Game Bernadette	10.1980
966	**Stevie Wonder**	Signed, Sealed, Delivered I'm Yours Fingertips (Part 2)	10.1980
967	**The Temptations**	Ball Of Confusion (That's What The World Is Today) Take A Look Around	10.1980
968	**Edwin Starr** **R. Dean Taylor**	War Indiana Wants Me	10.1980
969	**Jackson 5**	I'll Be There ABC	10.1980
970	**Diana Ross**	Remember Me Surrender	10.1980
971	**The Supremes & Four Tops**	River Deep, Mountain High You Gotta Have Love In Your Heart	10.1980
972	**Four Tops**	Simple Game Still Water (Love)	10.1980
973	**Michael Jackson** **Marv Johnson**	Got To Be There I Miss You Baby (How I Miss You)	10.1980
974	**The Supremes**	Floy Joy Bad Weather	10.1980
975	**Jackson 5**	Lookin' Through The Windows Doctor My Eyes	10.1980
976	**Michael Jackson**	One Day In Your Life Take Me Back	4.1981
977	**Michael Jackson**	We're Almost There We've Got A Good Thing Going	7.1981
978	**Four Tops**	Baby I Need Your Loving Yesterday's Dreams	4.1982
979	**The Isley Brothers**	I Guess I'll Always Love You Take Some Time Out For Love	2.1983
980	**Smokey Robinson & the Miracles**	I Don't Blame You At All Ooo Baby Baby	2.1983
981	**Diana Ross & the Supremes**	Back In My Arms Again Love Is Here And Now You're Gone	2.1983
982	**The Temptations**	Cloud Nine Psychedelic Shack	2.1983
983	**Martha Reeves & the Vandellas**	I'm Ready For Love Forget Me Not	2.1983
984	**Marvin Gaye**	What's Going On God Is Love	2.1983
985	**Eddie Kendricks**	Keep On Truckin' (Part 1) Keep On Truckin' (Part 2)	5.1983
986	**Michael Jackson**	Happy (Love Theme From Lady Sings The Blues) We're Almost There	7.1983
987	**Marvin Gaye**	What's Going On I Heard It Through The Grapevine	11.1983
988	**Diana Ross**	Reach Out And Touch (Somebody's Hand)	7.1984
	The Supremes & Four Tops	Reach Out And Touch (Somebody's Hand)	
989	**Stevie Wonder**	For Once In My Life I Was Made To Love Her	4.1985
990	**The Temptations**	Law Of The Land Beauty Is Only Skin Deep	4.1985
991	**Diana Ross & the Supremes & The Temptations**	I'm Gonna Make You Love Me I Second That Emotion	4.1985
992	**Diana Ross & the Supremes**	You Keep Me Hangin' On Come See About Me	4.1985
993	**Marvin Gaye & Tammi Terrell**	The Onion Song You Ain't Livin' Till You're Lovin'	4.1985
994	**Michael Jackson**	Got To Be There Rockin' Robin	4.1985
995	**Four Tops**	Bernadette If I Were A Carpenter	4.1985
996	**Jimmy Ruffin**	Gonna Give Her All The Love I've Got I've Passed This Way Before	4.1985
997	**The Temptations**	Ball Of Confusion (That's What The World Is Today) Ain't Too Proud To Beg	4.1985
998	**Diana Ross & Marvin Gaye**	You Are Everything Stop, Look, Listen (To Your Heart)	4.1985
999	**Diana Ross & the Supremes**	The Composer Take Me Where You Go	4.1985
1000	**The Marvelettes**	Finders Keepers, Losers Weepers	9.1980
	Kim Weston	Do Like I Do	
1001	**Jackson 5**	Forever Came Today I Can't Quit Your Love	9.1975
1002	**Sisters Love**	I'm Learning To Trust My Man Try It, You'll Like It	9.1975
1003	**Eddie Kendricks**	If Anyone Can Get The Cream Off The Top	9.1975
1004	**Magic Disco Machine**	Control Tower Scratchin'	9.1975
1005	**Caston & Majors**	I'll Keep My Light In My Window Say You Love Me True	9.1975
1006	**Michael Jackson**	Just A Little Bit Of You Dear Michael	10.1975
1007	**Commodores**	Let's Do It Right This Is Your Life	10.1975
1008	**Willie Hutch**	Love Power Get Ready For The Get Down	10.1975

1009	Gladys Knight & the Pips	Neither One Of Us (Wants To Be The First To Say Goodbye)	10.1975
		Everybody Needs Love/I Wish It Would Rain	
1010	Diana Ross	Theme From Mahogany 'Do You Know Where You're Going To'	10.1975
		No One's Gonna Be A Fool Forever	
1011	Four Tops	Walk Away Renee	10.1975
		You Keep Running Away	
1012	The Supremes	Early Morning Love	11.1975
		Where Is It I Belong	
1013	Yvonne Fair	It Should Have Been Me	11.1975
		You Can't Judge A Book By Its Cover	
1014	The Undisputed Truth	Higher Than High	11.1975
		Spaced Out	
1015	The Miracles	Love Machine (Part 1)	11.1975
		Love Machine (Part 2)	
1016	The Dynamic Superiors	Deception	11.1975
		One-Nighter	
1017	David Ruffin	Walk Away From Love	12.1975
		Love Can Be Hazardous To Your Health	
1018	Commodores	Sweet Love	1.1976
		Better Never Than Forever	
1019	Smokey Robinson	Quiet Storm	1.1976
		Asleep On My Love	
1020	Stephanie Mills	This Empty Place	2.1976
		If You Can Learn How To Cry	
1021	Eddie Kendricks	He's A Friend	2.1976
		All Of My Love	
1022	David Ruffin	Heavy Love	3.1976
		Me & Rock 'n' Roll (Are Here To Stay)	
1023	The Miracles	Night Life	3.1976
		Miracle Workers – Overture	
1024	Diana Ross	Love Hangover	4.1976
		Kiss Me Now	
1025	Yvonne Fair	It's Bad For Me To See You	5.1976
		Walk Out The Door If You Wanna	
1026	Marvin Gaye	I Want You	4.1976
		I Want You (instr.)	
1027	Jr Walker	I'm So Glad	4.1976
		Dancing Like They Do On Soul Train	
1028	Edwin Starr	Time	4.1976
		Running Back And Forth	
1029	The Supremes	I'm Gonna Let My Heart Do The Walking	5.1976
		Colour My World Blue	
1030	The Boones	My Guy	6.1976
		When The Lovelight Starts Shining Thru His Eyes	
1031	Eddie Kendricks	The Sweeter You Treat Her	7.1976
		Happy	
1032	Diana Ross	I Thought It Took A Little Time (But Today I Fell In Love)	6.1976
		After You	
1033	G. C. Cameron	Me And My Life	7.1976
		Act Like A Shotgun	
1034	Commodores	High On Sunshine	8.1976
		Thumpin' Music	
1035	Marvin Gaye	After The Dance	8.1976
		Feel All My Love Inside	
1036	David Ruffin	Discover Me	8.1976
		Smiling Faces Sometimes	
1037	Rose Banks	Darling Baby	8.1976
		Whole New Thing	
1038	The Originals	Down To Love Town	9.1976
		Just To Be Closer To You	
1039	Jerry Butler	The Devil In Mrs Jones	9.1976
		Don't Wanna Be Reminded	
1040	Jermaine Jackson	Let's Be Young Tonight	10.1976
		Bass Odyssey	
1041	Diana Ross	I'm Still Waiting	9.1976
		Touch Me In The Morning	
1042	Stevie Wonder	Yester-me, Yester-you, Yesterday	9.1976
		Uptight (Everything's Alright)	
1043	The Temptations	Just My Imagination (Running Away With Me)	9.1976
		Get Ready	
1044	Diana Ross & the Supremes	Baby Love	9.1976
		Stop! In The Name Of Love	
1045	Diana Ross & the Supremes & The Temptations	I'm Gonna Make You Love Me	9.1976
	Marvin Gaye	I Heard It Through The Grapevine	
1046	The Supremes	Stoned Love	9.1976
		Nathan Jones	
1047	Diana Ross & Marvin Gaye	You Are Everything	9.1976
	Marvin Gaye & Tammi Terrell	The Onion Song	
1048	Smokey Robinson & the Miracles	The Tears Of A Clown	9.1976
		The Tracks Of My Tears	
1049	Four Tops	Reach Out, I'll Be There	9.1976
		Standing In The Shadows Of Love	
1050	The Isley Brothers	This Old Heart Of Mine (Is Weak For You)	9.1976
		Behind A Painted Smile	
1051	Martha Reeves & the Vandellas	Dancing In The Street	9.1976
		Jimmy Mack	
1052	Jimmy Ruffin	What Becomes Of The Brokenhearted	9.1976
	Marv Johnson	I'll Pick A Rose For My Rose	
1053	Táta Vega	Try Love From The Inside	10.1976
		Just As Long As There Is You	
1054	Stevie Wonder	I Wish	12.1976
		You And I	
1055	William Goldstein & the Magic Disco Machine	Midnight Rhapsody	10.1976
		Midnight Rhapsody (Part 2)	
1056	Diana Ross	One Love In My Lifetime	10.1976
		You're Good My Child	
1057	The Temptations	Who Are You	10.1976
		Let Me Count The Ways (I Love You)	
1058	Commodores	Just To Be Close To You	10.1976
		Look What You've Done To Me	
1059	Thelma Houston	The Bingo Long Song (Steal On Home)	11.1976
	William Goldstein	Razzle Dazzle (instr.)	
1060	Thelma Houston	Don't Leave Me This Way	1.1977
		Today Will Soon Be Yesterday	
1061	Eddie Kendricks	Goin' Up In Smoke	1.1977
		Get It While It's Hot	
1062	Commodores	Fancy Dancer	1.1977
		Cebu	
1063	The Temptations featuring Dennis Edwards	Shakey Ground	2.1977
		I'm A Bachelor	
1064	The Supremes	Love I Never Knew You Could Feel So Good	3.1977
		This Is Why I Believe In You	
1065	Smokey Robinson	There Will Come A Day (I'm Gonna Happen To You)	3.1977
		An Old-Fashioned Man	
1066	The Originals	Call On Your Six-Million Dollar Man	NR
		Mother Nature's Best	
1067	Jennifer	Do It For Me	4.1977
		Boogie Boogie Love	

1068	**Stevie Wonder**	*Sir Duke* *Tuesday Heartbreak*	3.1977
1069	**Marvin Gaye**	*Got To Give It Up (Part 1)* *Got To Give It Up (Part2)*	4.1977
1070	**Jr Walker & the All Stars**	*I Ain't Going Nowhere/What Does It Take (To Win Your Love)* *Take Me Girl, I'm Ready*	5.1977
1071	**The Dynamic Superiors**	*Stay Away* *Supersensuousensation (Try Some Love)*	5.1977
1072	**Tata Vega**	*You'll Never Rock Alone* *Just When Things Are Getting Good*	5.1977
1073	**Commodores**	*Easy – Machine Gun* *I Feel Sanctified*	5.1977
1074	**Thelma Houston & Jerry Butler**	*It's A Lifetime Thing* *Only The Beginning*	7.1977
1075	**21st Creation**	*Tailgate* *Mr Disco Radio*	6.1977
1076	**Smokey Robinson**	*Vitamin U* *Holly*	6.1977
1077	**The Dynamic Superiors**	*Nowhere To Run* *Nowhere To Run (Part 2)*	7.1977
1078	**David Ruffin**	*I Can't Stop The Rain* *My Whole World Ended (The Moment You Left Me)*	7.1977
1079	**Flavor**	*Don't Freeze Up (vocal)* *Don't Freeze Up (instr.)*	7.1977
1080	**Diana Ross & the Supremes**	*Someday We'll Be Together* *You Keep Me Hangin' On*	8.1977
1081	**Jackson 5**	*Skywriter/I Want You Back* *The Love You Save*	8.1977
1082	**Jerry Butler**	*Chalk It Up* *I Don't Want Nobody To Know*	8.1977
1083	**Stevie Wonder**	*Another Star* *Creepin'*	8.1977
1084	**Albert Finney**	*Those Other Men* *What Have They Done (To My Home Town?)*	9.1977
1085	**Smokey Robinson**	*Theme From Big Time (Part 1)* *Theme From Big Time (Part 2)*	9.1977
1086	**Commodores**	*Brick House* *Sweet Love*	9.1977
1087	**High Inergy**	*You Can't Turn Me Off (In The Middle Of Turning Me On)* *Let Me Get Close To You*	10.1977
1088	**Thelma Houston**	*I'm Here Again* *Sharing Something Perfect Between Ourselves*	10.1977
1089	**Mandré**	*Solar Flight (Opus 1)* *Keep Tryin'*	10.1977
1090	**Diana Ross**	*Gettin' Ready For Love* *Stone Liberty*	10.1977
1091	**Stevie Wonder**	*As* *Contusion*	11.1977
1092	**Jermaine Jackson**	*Take Time* *You Need To Be Loved*	11.1977
1093	**David Ruffin**	*You're My Peace Of Mind* *Rode By The Place (Where We Used To Stay)*	11.1977
1094	**Syreeta G. C. Cameron**	*Let's Make A Deal (Part 1)* *Let's Make A Deal (Part 2)*	11.1977
1095	**Gladys Knight & the Pips**	*Help Me Make It Through The Night* *Daddy Could Swear, I Declare*	11.1977
1096	**Commodores**	*Zoom* *Too Hot Ta Trot*	1.1978
1097	**Jerry Butler**	*I Wanna Do It To You* *Let's Go Get Out Of Town*	1.1978
1098	**Scherrie Payne**	*Fly* *When I Looked At Your Face*	1.1978
1099	**Diana Ross**	*Top Of The World* *Too Shy To Say*	2.1978
1100	**Mary Wells**	*My Guy* *What's Easy For Two Is So Hard For One*	2.1978
1101	**5th Dimension**	*You Are The Reason (I Feel Like Dancing)* *Slipping Into Something New*	3.1978
1102	**Thelma Houston**	*I Can't Go On Living Without Your Love* *Any Way You Like It*	3.1978
1103	**High Inergy**	*Love Is All You Need* *Save It For A Rainy Day*	3.1978
1104	**Diana Ross**	*Your Love Is So Good For Me* *Baby It's Me*	4.1978
1105	**Three Ounces Of Love**	*Star Love* *I Found The Feeling*	3.1978
1106	**Smokey Robinson**	*Madam X* *The Agony And The Ecstasy*	4.1978
1107	**Cuba Gooding**	*Mind Pleaser* *Ain't Nothing To It*	4.1978
1108	**Carl Bean**	*I Was Born This Way* *I Was Born This Way (instr.)*	5.1978
1109	**Major Lance**	*I Never Though I'd Be Losing You* *Chicago Disco*	5.1978
1110	**Rick James**	*You And I* *Hollywood*	5.1978
1111	**Commodores**	*Flying High* *Funky Situation*	6.1978
1112	**Diana Ross**	*Lovin' Livin' And Givin'* *You Got It*	7.1978
1113	**Commodores**	*Three Times A Lady* *Can't Let You Tease Me*	7.1978
1114	**Smokey Robinson**	*Daylight And Darkness* *Why You Wanna See My Bad Side*	7.1978
1115	**Platinum Hook**	*Standing On The Verge (Of Gettin' It On)* *'Til I Met You*	8.1978
1116	**Mandré**	*Fair Game* *Light Years (Opus IV)*	9.1978
1117	**Thelma Houston**	*Don't Pity Me* *It's Just Me Feeling Good*	9.1978
1118	**Jr Walker (*with Thelma Houston)**	*Walk In The Night* **I Need You Right Now*	9.1978
1119	**Three Ounces Of Love**	*Give Me Some Feeling* *Don't Worry 'Bout My Love*	9.1978
1120	**Four Tops**	*I Can't Help Myself* *It's The Same Old Song*	9.1978
1121	**Rick James**	*Mary Jane* *Dream Maker*	10.1978
1122	**High Inergy**	*Lovin' Fever* *Beware*	10.1978
1123	**Switch**	*There'll Never Be* *You Pulled A Switch*	10.1978
1124	**The Velvelettes**	*Needle In A Haystack* *He Was Really Saying Somethin'*	10.1978
1125	**Bonnie Pointer**	*Free Me From My Freedom – Tie Me To A Tree (Handcuff Me)* *Free Me From My Freedom – Tie Me To A Tree (Handcuff Me) (instr.)*	10.1978
1126	**Finished Touch**	*I Love To See You Dance* *Sticks And Stones (But The Funk Won't Never Hurt You)*	11.1978
1127	**Commodores**	*Just To Be Close To You* *X-Rated Movie*	11.1978
1128	**Platinum Hook**	*Gotta Find A Woman* *Hooked For Life*	11.1978
1129	**Smokey Robinson**	*Shoe Soul* *I'm Loving You Softly*	11.1978

!130	**Thelma Houston**	*Saturday Night, Sunday Morning*	1.1979
		I'm Not Strong Enough (To Love You Again)	
1131	**Grover Washington Jr**	*Do Dat*	1.1979
		Reed Seed (Trio Tune)	
1132	**Switch**	*We Like To Party . . . Come On*	1.1979
		Somebody's Watchin' You	
1133	**Barbara Randolph**	*I Got A Feeling*	2.1979
		Can I Get A Witness	
		You Got Me Hurtin' All Over	
1134	**Bonnie Pointer**	*Heaven Must Have Sent You*	1.1979
		I Wanna Make It (In Your World)	
1135	**Diana Ross**	*What You Gave Me*	2.1979
		Ain't No Mountain High Enough	
1136	**Diana Ross/ Marvin Gaye/ Smokey Robinson/ Stevie Wonder**	*Pops, We Love You*	2.1979
		Pops, We Love You (instr.)	
1137	**Rick James**	*High On Your Love Suite*	3.1979
		Stone City Band, Hi	
1138	**Marvin Gaye**	*A Funky Space Reincarnation (Part 1)*	2.1979
		A Funky Space Reincarnation (Part 2)	
1139	**Billy Preston & Syreeta**	*Go For It*	4.1979
		With You I'm Born Again (instr.)	
1140	**Tata Vega**	*Get It Up For Love*	4.1979
		I Just Keep Thinking About You Baby	
1141	**Apollo**	*Astro Disco (Part 1)*	5.1979
		Astro Disco (Part 2)	
1142	**High Inergy**	*Shoulda Gone Dancin'*	5.1979
		Peaceland	
1143	**Motown Sounds**	*Space Dance*	5.1979
		Bad Mouthin'	
1144	**Mandré**	*Swang*	5.1979
		Spirit Groove	
1145	**Bonnie Pointer**	*Heaven Must Have Sent You (New Version)*	7.1979
		My Everything	
1146	**Teena Marie**	*I'm A Sucker For Your Love*	6.1979
		De Ja Vu (I've Been Here Before)	
1147	**Rick James**	*Bustin' Out*	6.1979
		Sexy Lady	
1148	**Switch**	*Best Beat In Town*	6.1979
		It's So Real	
1149	**Stevie Wonder**	*Send One Your Love*	11.1979
		Send One Your Love (instr.)	
1150	**Diana Ross**	*The Boss*	6.1979
		I'm In The World	
1151	**Finished Touch**	*The Down Sound (Part 1)*	7.1979
		The Down Sound (Part 2)	
1152	**Smokey Robinson**	*Get Ready*	7.1979
		Ever Had A Dream	
1153	**Grover Washington Jr**	*Just The Way You Are*	7.1979
		Loran's Dance	
1154	**Mira Waters**	*You Have Inspired Me*	8.1979
		You Have Inspired Me (long vers.)	
1155	**Commodores**	*Sail On*	8.1979
		Captain Quick Draw	
1156	**Rick James**	*Fool On The Street*	9.1979
		Jefferson Ball	
1157	**Tata Vega**	*If Love Must Go*	8.1979
		Come In Heaven (Earth Is Calling) (Part 2)	
1158	**Teena Marie**	*Don't Look Back*	9.1979
		I'm Gonna Have My Cake (And Eat It Too)	
1159	**Belly Preston & Syreeta**	*With You I'm Born Again* (vocal)	8.1979
	Billy Preston	*Sock-It, Rocket*	
1160	**Diana Ross**	*No One Gets The Prize*	9.1979
		Never Say I Don't Love You	
1161	**Patrick Gammon**	*Cop An Attitude*	9.1979
		My Song In -G-	
1162	**Sterling**	*Roll Her, Skater*	9.1979
		Roll Her, Skater (instr.)	
1163	**Mary Wilson**	*Red Hot*	9.1979
		Midnight Dancer	
1164	**Smokey Robinson**	*Cruisin'*	9.1979
		The Humming Song (Lost For Words)	
1165	**Michael Jackson**	*Ben*	2.1980
	Marvin Gaye	*Abraham, Martin And John*	
1166	**Commodores**	*Still*	10.1979
		Such A Woman	
1167	**Scherrie and Susaye**	*Leaving Me Was The Best Thing You've Ever Done*	11.1979
		When The Day Comes Every Night	
1168	**Marvin Gaye**	*Ego Tripping Out*	11.1979
		Ego Tripping Out (instr.)	
1169	**Diana Ross**	*It's My House*	11.1979
		Sparkle	
1170	**Frank Wilson**	*Do I Love You (Indeed I Do)*	11.1979
		Sweeter As The Days Go By	
1171	**Bonnie Pointer**	*I Can't Help Myself (Sugar Pie Honey Bunch)*	1.1980
		When I'm Gone	
1172	**Commodores**	*Wonderland*	1.1980
		Lovin' You	
1173	**Stevie Wonder**	*Black Orchid*	1.1980
		Blame It On The Sun	
1174	**Rick James**	*Love Gun*	1.1980
		Stormy Love	
1175	**Billy Preston & Syreeta**	*It Will Come In Time*	2.1980
	Billy Preston	*All I Wanted Was You*	
1176	**Martha Reeves & the Vandellas**	*Heatwave*	1.1980
		Dancing In The Street	
1177	**Mary Wilson**	*Pick Up The Pieces*	3.1980
		You're The Light That Guides My Way	
1178	**Teena Marie**	*Can It Be Love*	3.1980
		Too Many Colours (Tee's Interlude)	
1179	**Stevie Wonder**	*Outside My Window*	3.1980
		Same Old Story	
1180	**Diana Ross & the Supremes**	*Supremes' Medley (Part 1)*	4.1980
		Supremes' Medley (Part 2)	
1181	**Stone City Band**	*Strut Your Stuff*	4.1980
		F.I.M.A. (Funk In Mama Afrika)	
1182	**Smokey Robinson**	*Let Me Be The Clock*	4.1980
		Travelin' Through	
1183	**Jermaine Jackson**	*Let's Get Serious*	4.1980
		Je Vous Aime Beaucoup (I Love You)	
1184	**Bonnie Pointer**	*Deep Inside My Soul*	4.1980
		I Love To Sing To You	
1185	**Teena Marie**	*Behind The Groove*	5.1980
		You're All The Boogie I Need	
1186	**The Temptations**	*Power*	5.1980
		Power (instr.)	
1187	**Switch**	*Don't Take My Love Away*	5.1980
		Don't Take My Love Away (instr.)	
1188	**Billy Preston & Syreeta**	*One More Time For Love*	5.1980
	Syreeta	*Dance For Me Children*	
1189	**The Detroit Spinners**	*It's A Shame*	6.1980
		Sweet Thing	
1190	**Dr. Strut**	*Struttin'*	6.1980
		Blue Lodge	

1191	**Smokey Robinson**	Heavy On Pride (Light On Love)	6.1980
		I Love The Nearness Of You	
1192	**Ozone**	Walk On	7.1980
		This Is Funkin' Insane	
1193	**Commodores**	Old-Fashion Love	6.1980
		Sexy Lady	
1194	**Jermaine Jackson**	Burnin' Hot	7.1980
		Castles Of Sand	
1195	**Diana Ross**	Upside Down	7.1980
		Friend To Friend	
1196	**Teena Marie**	Lonely Desire	7.1980
		Aladdin's Lamp	
1197	**The Temptations**	Struck By Lightning Twice	8.1980
		I'm Coming Home	
1198	**Rick James**	Big Time	8.1980
		Island Lady	
1199	**Black Russian**	Mystified	8.1980
		Love's Enough	
1200	**Syreeta**	He's Gone	
		Here's My Love	
1201	**Jermaine Jackson**	You're Supposed To Keep Your Love For Me	9.1980
		Lit It Ride	
1202	**Diana Ross**	My Old Piano	9.1980
		Where Did We Go Wrong	
1203	**Teena Marie**	I Need Your Lovin'	9.1980
		Irons In The Fire	
1204	**Stevie Wonder**	Master Blaster (Jammin')	9.1980
		Master Blaster (dub ver.)	
1205	**High Inergy**	Make Me Yours	10.1980
		I Love Makin' Love (To The Music)	
1206	**Commodores**	Heroes	9.1980
		Don't You Be Worried	
1207	**Lynda Carter**	The Last Song	9.1980
		What's A Little Love Between Friends	
1208	**Michal Urbaniak**	Nanava	11.1980
		Joy	
1209	**Rick James**	Summer Love	10.1980
		Gettin' It On (In The Sunshine)	
1210	**Diana Ross**	I'm Coming Out	11.1980
		Give Up	
1211	**Billy Preston & Syreeta**	Please Stay	11.1980
	Syreeta	Signed, Sealed, Delivered I'm Yours	
1212	**Jermaine Jackson**	Little Girl Don't You Worry	11.1980
		We Can Put It Back Together	
1213	**The Dazz Band**	Shake It Up	12.1980
		Only Love	
1214	**High Inergy**	Hold On To My Love	12.1980
		If I Love You Tonight	
1215	**Stevie Wonder**	I Ain't Gonna Stand For It	12.1980
		Knocks Me Off My Feet	
1216	**The Temptations**	Take Me Away	1.1981
		There's More Where That Came From	
1217	**Diana Ross**	It's My Turn	1.1981
		Sleepin'	
1218	**Commodores**	Jesus Is Love	12.1980
		Mighty Spirit	
1219	**Táta Vega**	You Keep Me Hangin' On	1.1981
		You Better Watch Out	
1220	**Black Russian**	Leave Me Now	1.1981
		Move Together	
1221	**Stone City Band**	All Day And All Of The Night	2.1981
		All Day And All Of The Night (vamp vers.)	
1222	**Jermaine Jackson**	You Like Me Don't You	2.1981
		You Like Me Don't You (instr.)	
1223	**Smokey Robinson**	Being With You	2.1981
		What's In Your Life For Me	
1224	**Billy Preston**	Hope	2.1981
		Give It Up, Hot	
1225	**Marvin Gaye**	Praise	3.1981
		Funk Me	
1226	**Stevie Wonder**	Lately	2.1981
		If It's Magic	
1227	**Diana Ross**	One More Chance	3.1981
		Confide In Me	
1228	**Syreeta**	Love Fire	NR
		'Cause We've Ended As Lovers	
1229	**Rick James**	Give It To Me Baby	4.1981
		Don't Give Up On Love	
1230	**Táta Vega**	Love Your Neighbor	4.1981
		There's Love In The World	
1231	**Billy Preston**	A Change Is Gonna Come	4.1981
		You	
1232	**Marvin Gaye**	Heavy Love Affair	5.1981
		Far Cry	
1233	**Diana Ross**	Cryin' My Heart Out For You	6.1981
		To Love Again	
1234	**High Inergy**	I Just Wanna Dance With You	6.1981
		Take My Life	
1235	**Stevie Wonder**	Happy Birthday	7.1981
		Happy Birthday (Sing-A-Long)	
1236	**Teena Marie**	Square Biz	7.1981
		Opus III (Does Anybody Care)	
1237	**Smokey Robinson**	You Are Forever	7.1981
		I Hear The Children Singing	
1238	**Commodores**	Lady (You Bring Me Up)	7.1981
		Gettin' It	
1239	**Stone City Band**	Funky Reggae	8.1981
		Ganja	
1240	**Diana Ross & Lionel Richie**	Endless Love	9.1981
		Endless Love (instr.)	
1241	**Rick James**	Super Freak (Part 1)	8.1981
		Super Freak (Part 2)	
1242	**Jermaine Jackson**	I'm Just Too Shy	11.1981
		All Because Of You	
1243	**The Temptations**	Aiming At Your Heart	10.1981
		The Life Of A Cowboy	
1244	**José Feliciano**	Everybody Loves Me	10.1981
		The Drought Is Over	
1245	**Commodores**	Oh No	10.1981
		Are You Happy	
1246	**Teena Marie**	It Must Be Magic	10.1981
		Yes Indeed	
1247	**Syreeta**	Quick Slick	10.1981
		I Don't Know	
1248	**Diana Ross**	Tenderness	12.1981
	Diana Ross & the Supremes	Medley	
1249	**Ozone**	Gigolette	11.1981
		Gigolette (instr.)	
1250	**Rick James**	Ghetto Life	1.1982
		Below The Funk (Pass The J)	
1251	**Teena Marie**	Portuguese Love	1.1982
		The Ballad Of Cradle Rob And Me	
1252	**José Feliciano**	I Wanna Be Where You Are	1.1982
		Let's Make Love Over The Telephone	
1253	**Jermaine Jackson**	Paradise In Your Eyes	2.1982
		I'm My Brother's Keeper	
1254	**Stevie Wonder**	That Girl	1.1982
		All I Do	
1255	**Smokey Robinson**	Tell Me Tomorrow (Part 1)	2.1982
		Tell Me Tomorrow (Part 2)	
1256	**Commodores**	Why You Wanna Try Me	3.1982
		Celebrate	
1257	**Betty LaVette**	You Seen One You Seen 'Em All	3.1982
		Right In The Middle (Of Falling In Love)	
1258	**Syreeta**	I Must Be In Love	4.1982
		Out Of The Box	

335

1259	Ozone	Do What Cha Wanna	4.1982
		Come On In	
1260	Charlene	I've Never Been To Me	3.1982
		Somewhere In My Life	
1261	Nolen & Crossley	Ready Or Not	4.1982
		A Place In My Heart	
1262	Smokey Robinson	Old Fashioned Love	5.1982
		Destiny	
1263	The Temptations featuring Rick James	Standing On The Top (Part 1)	5.1982
		Standing On The Top (Part 2)	
1264	José Feliciano	I Second That Emotion	5.1982
		Free Me From My Freedom	
1265	Betty LaVette	I Can't Stop	7.1982
		Either Way We Lose	
1266	Rick James	Dance Wit' Me (Part 1)	6.1982
		Dance Wit' Me (Part 2)	
1267	Bobby Womack	So Many Sides Of You	6.1982
		Just My Imagination	
1268	High Inergy	First Impressions	7.1982
		Could This Be Love	
1269	Stevie Wonder	Do I Do	5.1982
		Rocket Love	
1270	Dazz Band	Let It Whip	6.1982
		Everyday Love	
1271	Jean Carn	If You Don't Know Me By Now	7.1982
		Completeness	
1272	Charlene	It Ain't Easy Comin' Down	7.1982
		Nunca He Ido A Mi – If I Could See Myself	
1273	Diana Ross	Old Funky Rolls	9.1982
		The Boss	
1274	Smokey Robinson	Cruisin'	8.1982
		The Only Game In Town	
1275	Syreeta	Can't Shake Your Love	8.1982
		Wish Upon A Star	
1276	Jermaine Jackson	Let Me Tickle Your Fancy	8.1982
		Maybe Next Time	
1277	Rick James	Hard To Get	8.1982
		My Love	
1278	Bobby Womack	Secrets	9.1982
		Stand Up	
1279	Dazz Band	Keep It Live (On The K.I.L.)	NR
		This Time It's Forever	
1280	Stevie Wonder	Ribbon In The Sky	10.1982
		The Secret Life Of Plants	
1281L	José Feliciano	Samba Pa Ti	10.1982
		No Hay Sombre Que Me Cubra	
1282	Commodores	Lucy	10.1982
		Heaven Knows	
1283	Billy Preston	I'm Never Gonna Say Goodbye	10.1982
		I Love You So	
1284	Lionel Richie	Truly	11.1982
		Just Put Some Love In Your Heart	
1285	Willie Hutch	In And Out	11.1982
		The Girl (Can't Help It)	
1286	Jermaine Jackson	Very Special Part	12.1982
		You're Giving Me The Runaround	
1287	Charlene & Stevie Wonder	Used To Be	11.1982
	Charlene	I Want To Come Back As A Song	
1288G	Bobby M featuring Jean Carn	Let's Stay Together	1.1983
	Bobby M	Charlie's Backbeat	
1289	Stevie Wonder	Front Line	1.1983
		Front Line (instr.)	
1290	Lionel Richie	You Are	1.1983
		You Mean More To Me	
1291	Billy Preston & Syreeta	A New Way To Say I Love You	2.1983
		Hey You	

1292	Commodores	Reach High (vocal)	2.1983
		Reach High (instr.)	
1293	Willie Hutch	Party Down	2.1983
		Slick	
1294G	High Inergy	He's A Pretender	3.1983
		Don't Let Up On The Groove	
1295	Smokey Robinson	I've Made Love To You A Thousand Times	3.1983
		Into Each Rain Some Life Must Fall	
1296G	DeBarge	I Like It	3.1983
		Hesitated	
1297	The Temptations	Love On My Mind Tonight	3.1983
		Bring Your Body Here (Exercise Chant)	
1298	Robert John	Bread and Butter	3.1983
		If You Don't Want My Love	
1299	Dazz Band	On The One	3.1983
		Just Believe In Love	
1300	Lionel Richie	My Love	4.1983
		Round and Round	
1301G	Mary Jane Girls	Candy Man	4.1983
		Candy Man (instr.)	
1302	Monalisa Young	Dancing Machine	4.1983
		I'll Be There	
1303	Jermaine Jackson	You Moved A Mountain	4.1983
		Running	
1304	Finis Henderson	Skip To My Lou	7.1983
		I'd Rather Be Gone	
1305	José Feliciano	Lonely Teardrops	5.1983
		Cuidado	
1306	Syreeta	Forever Is Not Enough	5.1983
		She's Leaving Home	
1307	Smokey Robinson	Touch The Sky	5.1983
		All My Life's A Lie	
1308G	DeBarge	All This Love	7.1983
		I'm In Love With You	
1309G	Mary Jane Girls	All Night Long	6.1983
		Musical Love	
1310	Charlene	If You Take Away The Pain Until The Morning	8.1983
		Richie's Song (For Richard Oliver)	
1311	Michael Lovesmith	Baby I Will	8.1983
		What's The Bottom Line	
*1312	Gary Byrd & the GB Experience	The Crown	NR
		The Crown (instr.)	
1313	Smokey Robinson & Barbara Mitchell	Blame It On Love	9.1983
	Smokey Robinson	Even Tho'	
1314G	Rick James	Cold Blooded	8.1983
		Cold Blooded (instr.)	
1315G	Mary Jane Girls	Boys	9.1983
		You Are My Heaven	
1316G	Stone City Band	Ladies Choice	10.1983
		Ladies Choice (instr.)	
1317	Commodores	Only You	9.1983
		Cebu	
1318	Junior Walker	Blow The House Down	10.1983
		Ball Baby (instr.)	
1319	Lionel Richie	All Night Long (All Night)	9.1983
		Wandering Stranger	
1320TM	The Temptations & the Four Tops	Medley	10.1983
	The Temptations	Papa Was A Rollin' Stone	
1321	Four Tops	I Just Can't Walk Away	10.1983
		Hang	
1322	Commodores	Turn Off The Lights	11.1983
		Painted Picture	
1323	Bobby Nunn	Don't Knock It (Until You Try It)	1.1984
		Private Party	
1324	Lionel Richie	Running With The Night	11.1983
		Serves You Right	

No.	Artist	A-side / B-side	Date
*1325	Motor City Crew	Scratch Break (Glove Style) / Let's Break (instr.)	NR
*1326	Stevie Wonder / The Rev. Martin Luther King	Happy Birthday / I Have A Dream	NR
1327G	Rick James & Friend	Ebony Eyes	1.1984
	Rick James	1, 2, 3 (You, Her And Me)	
*1328	The Dazz Band	Joystick / Don't Get Caught In The Middle	NR
1329G	DeBarge	Time Will Reveal / I'll Never Fall In Love Again	3.1984
1330	Lionel Richie	Hello / All Night Long (All Night) (instr.)	3.1984
1331	Rockwell	Somebody's Watching Me / Somebody's Watching Me (instr.)	1.1984
1332	Keith & Darrell	Work That Body / The Things You're Made Of	2.1984
1333C	Tiggi Clay	The Winner Gets The Heart / Who Shot Zorro?	4.1984
1334G	Dennis Edwards featuring Siedah Garrett	Don't Look Any Further	3.1984
	Dennis Edwards	I Thought I Could Handle It	
1335	Bobby King	Lovequake / Fall In Love	4.1984
1336	Rockwell	(Obscene) Phone Caller / (Obscene) Phone Caller (instr.)	3.1984
1337C	Kidd Glove	Good Clean Fun / Street Angel	4.1984
1338	Dazz Band	Swoop (I'm Yours) / Bad Girl	4.1984
1339	Bobby Womack	Tell My Why	6.1984
	Bobby Womack & Patti Labelle	Through The Eyes Of A Child	
1340G	Dennis Edwards	(You're My) Aphrodisiac / Shake Hands (Come Out Dancing)	5.1984
1341	Lionel Richie	Stuck On You / Round And Round	6.1984
1342	Michael Jackson	Farewell My Summer Love / Call On Me	5.1984
1343C	Duke Jupiter	Little Lady / (I've Got A) Little Black Book	6.1984
1344	Smokey Robinson	And I Don't Love You / Dynamite	6.1984
1345	Rockwell	Taxman / Wasting Away	8.1984
1346C	Wolf & Wolf	Don't Take The Candy / War Of Nerves	7.1984
1347	Bobby King featuring Alfie Silas	Close To Me	8.1984
	Bobby King	Love In The Fire	
1348G	Rick James	17 / 17 (instr.)	8.1984
1349	Stevie Wonder	I Just Called To Say I Love You / I Just Called To Say I Love You (instr.)	8.1984

*Released on 12-inch format only.

No.	Artist	A-side / B-side	Date
1350C	The Coyote Sisters	Straight From The Heart (Into Your Life) / Echo	7.1984
1351	Sammy Davis Jr	Hello Detroit / Hello Detroit (instr.)	9.1984
1352	Charlene	We're Both In Love With You / Richie's Song (For Richard Oliver)	9.1984
1353	Bobby Womack	Surprise, Surprise / American Dream	9.1984
1354	Sam Harris	Sugar Don't Bite / You Keep Me Hangin' On	11.1984
1355	Michael Jackson	Girl You're So Together / Touch The One You Love	8.1984
1356	Lionel Richie	Penny Lover / You Are	10.1984
1357C	Jakata	Hell Is On The Run / Don't Ever Let Go	10.1984
1358	Phyllis St James	Candlelight Afternoon / Back In The Race	9.1984
1359G	Rick James	You Turn Me On / Fire And Desire	10.1984
1360	Vanity	Pretty Mess / Pretty Mess (instr.)	10.1984
1361	Dazz Band	Let It All Blow / Now That I Have You	10.1984
1362C	The Coyote Sisters	I've Got A Radio / I'll Do It	NR
1363	Koko-Pop	I'm In Love With You / On The Beach	12.1984
1364	Stevie Wonder	Love Light In Flight / It's More Than You (instr.)	11.1984
1365	The Temptations	Treat Her Like A Lady / Isn't The Night Fantastic	11.1984
1366	Thomas McClary	Thin Walls / Love Will Find A Way (instr.)	1.1985
1367	Phyllis St James	Ain't No Turnin' Back / Ruler Of The Hunt	NR
1368	Dazz Band	Heartbeat / Rock With Me	2.1985
1369	Vanity	Mechanical Emotion / Crazy Maybe	1.1985
1370	Sam Harris	Hearts On Fire / Over The Rainbow	1.1985
1371	Commodores	Nightshift / I Keep Running	1.1985
1372	Stevie Wonder	Don't Drive Drunk / Don't Drive Drunk (instr.)	12.1984
1373	The Temptations	My Love Is True (Truly For You) / I'll Keep My Light In My Window	3.1985
1374	Rockwell	He's A Cobra / Change Your Ways	3.1985
1375	Thomas McClary	Man In The Middle / Man In The Middle (instr.)	NR
1376G	DeBarge	Rhythm Of The Night / Queen Of My Heart	3.1985
1377G	Mary Jane Girls	In My House / In My House (instr.)	2.1985
1378G	Rick James	Can't Stop / On What A Night (4 Luv)	4.1985
1379	Jakata	Golden Girl / Light At The End Of The Tunnel	4.1985
1380TM	Diana Ross	Love Hangover / Remember Me	4.1985
1381TM	Marvin Gaye	Got To Give It Up (Part 1) / How Sweet It Is (To Be Loved By You)	4.1985
1382	Thelma Houston	Don't Leave Me This Way / Jumpin' Jack Flash	4.1985
1383	Bonnie Pointer	Heaven Must Have Sent You / Deep Inside My Soul	4.1985
1384	Stevie Wonder	I Wish / Sir Duke	4.1985
1385	Teena Marie	Behind The Groove / I Need Your Lovin'	4.1985
1386	Stevie Wonder	Do I Do / I Ain't Gonna Stand For It	4.1985
1387	Diana Ross	My Old Piano / I'm Coming Out	4.1985
1388TM	Stevie Wonder	He's Misstra Know-It-All / Boogie On Reggae Woman	4.1985

| 1389 | **Stevie Wonder** | *Upset Stomach* (B side not selected) | NR |
| 1390 | **Alfie Silas** | *Star* *Keep On Smilin'* | 7.1985 |

EUROPEAN SERIES INTRODUCED

PREFIX ZB

40097	**Commodores**	*Animal Instinct* *Lightin' Up The Night*	5.1985
40099	**Rockwell**	*Peeping Tom* *Tokyo* (instr.)	5.1985
40113	**The Emotions**	*Miss Your Love* *I Can't Wait To Make You Mine*	5.1985
40159	**Maureen Steele**	*Save The Night For Me* *Rock My Heart*	6.1985
40173	**Willie Hutch**	*Keep On Jammin'* *The Glow*	6.1985
40201	**Jake Jacas**	*Hold Me* *Hold Me* (instr.)	6.1985
40213G	**DeBarge**	*Who's Holding Donna Now* *Be My Lady*	6.1985
40223G	**Rick James**	*Glow* *Glow* (instr.)	6.1985
40271G	**Mary Jane Girls**	*Wild And Crazy Love* *Wild And Crazy Love* (instr.)	8.1985
40273	**Michael Lovesmith**	*Break The Ice* *Lucky In Love*	7.1985
40307	**Dazz Band**	*Hot Spot* *I've Been Waiting*	8.1985
40311	**Commodores**	*Janet* *I'm In Love*	8.1985
40343	**Maureen Steele**	*Boys Will Be Boys* *Rock My Heart*	9.1985
40345G	**El DeBarge with DeBarge** **DeBarge**	*You Wear It Well* *Baby Won't Cha Come Quick*	9.1985
40351	**Stevie Wonder**	*Part-Time Lover* *Part-Time Lover* (instr.)	9.1985
40369	**Michael Lovesmith**	*Ain't Nothin' Like It* *Fast Girls*	9.1985
40401	**KoKo Pop**	*Brand New Beat (Part 1)* *Brand New Beat (Part 2)*	11.1985
40419G*	**Val Young**	*Seduction* *Seduction* (instr.)	NR
40421	**Lionel Richie**	*Say You, Say Me* *Can't Slow Down*	11.1985
40453	**The Temptations**	*Do You Really Love Your Baby* *I'll Keep My Light In My Window*	11.1985
40497G	**El DeBarge with DeBarge** **DeBarge**	*The Heart Is Not So Smart* *Share My World*	12.1985
40501	**Stevie Wonder**	*Go Home* *Go Home* (instr.)	11.1985
40503	**Warp 9**	*Skips A Beat* *Skips A Beat* (dub ver.)	2.1986
40553	**Smokey Robinson**	*Hold On To Your Love* *Train Of Thought*	1.1986
40561	**Pal**	*Talk We Don't* *Talk We Don't* (instr.)	3.1986
40567	**Stevie Wonder**	*Overjoyed* *Overjoyed* (instr.)	2.1986
40571	**Sam Harris**	*I'd Do It All Again* *The Rescue*	trans.
40577G	**Val Young**	*If You Should Ever Be Lonely* *If You Should Ever Be Lonely* (instr.)	2.1986
40609	**Vanity**	*Under The Influence* *Wild Animal*	4.1986

40621	**The Temptations**	*I'm Fascinated* *How Can You Say That It's Over*	4.1986
40701TM	**Marvin Gaye**	*I Heard It Through The Grapevine* *Can I Get A Witness*	4.1986
40709TM	**Diana Ross & the Supremes**	*You Keep Me Hangin' On* *Come See About Me*	4.1986
40717	**Smokey Robinson**	*Sleepless Nights* *Close Encounters Of The First Kind*	6.1986
40721	**Lionel Richie**	*Dancing On The Ceiling* *Love Will Find A Way*	trans.
40723	**El DeBarge** **El DeBarge with DeBarge**	*Who's Johnny* *Love Me In A Special Way*	trans.

*Available on 12-inch format only.

40743 TM	**The Temptations**	*My Girl* *Wherever I Lay My Hat (That's My Home)*	6.1986
40747	**Stevie Wonder**	*Land Of La La* *Land Of La La* (instr.)	trans.
40755G	**Rick James**	*Sweet And Sexy Thing* *Sweet And Sexy Thing* (instr.)	7.1986
40757	**Marvin Gaye**	*The World Is Rated X* *Lonely Lover*	6.1986
40777	**Rockwell**	*Carmé (Part 1)* *Carmé (Part 2)*	7.1986
40795	**Mary Jane Girls**	*Walk Like A Man* *Shadow Lover*	8.1986
40803 TM	**Diana Ross**	*Ain't No Mountain High Enough* *It's My House*	7.1986
40845	**El DeBarge** **El DeBarge with DeBarge**	*Love Always* *The Walls (Come Tumbling Down)*	trans.
40847	**Four Tops**	*Hot Nights* *Again*	8.1986
40849	**The Temptations**	*Lady Soul* *A Fine Mess*	9.1986
40885	**Stacy Lattisaw**	*Nail It To The Wall* *Nail It To The Wall* (instr.)	10.1986
40887	**Chico DeBarge**	*Talk To Me* *If It Takes All Night*	10.1986
41033	**General Kane**	*Hairdooz* *Crack Killed Applejack*	1.1987
41109	**Stacy Lattisaw**	*Jump Into My Life* *Longshot*	2.1987
41117	**Bruce Willis**	*Respect Yourself* *Fun Time*	2.1987
41123	**Chico DeBarge**	*The Girl Next Door* *You're Much Too Fast*	3.1987
41147	**Smokey Robinson**	*Just To See Her* *I'm Gonna Love You Like There's No Tomorrow*	3.1987
41147M	**Smokey Robinson**	*As 41147 & additional track* *The Tracks Of My Tears*	6.1987
41209	**Georgio**	*Sexappeal* *Sexappeal* (instr.)	3.1987
41273	**Bruce Willis**	*Young Blood* *Flirting With Disaster*	4.1988
41277	**Darryl Duncan**	*Rock The House* *Rock The House* (instr.)	6.1987
41349	**Bruce Willis**	*Under The Boardwalk* *Jackpot (Bruno's Bop)*	5.1987
41373	**Smokey Robinson & the Miracles**	*The Tracks Of My Tears* *I Second That Emotion*	7.1987
41411	**Kim O'Leary**	*Put The Pieces Back* *The Kids Downtown*	NR
41431	**The Temptations**	*Papa Was A Rollin' Stone* (re-mix) *Ain't Too Proud To Beg*	8.1987
41433	**General Kane**	*Girl Pulled The Dog* *Cuttin' It Up*	7.1987

41437	**Bruce Willis**	*Secret Agent Man – James Bond Is Back*	9.1987
		Lose Myself	
41439	**Stevie Wonder**	*Skeletons*	10.1987
		Skeletons (instr.)	
41501	**Carrie McDowell**	*Uh Uh, No No Casual Sex (Part 1)*	9.1987
		Uh Uh, No No Casual Sex (Part 2)	
41525	**Smokey Robinson**	*One Heartbeat*	9.1987
		Love Will Set You Free	
41547	**Temptations**	*I Wonder Who She's Seeing Now*	11.1987
		Girls (They Like It)	
41555	**Georgio**	*Tina Cherry*	10.1987
		Tina Cherry (Bonus Beats)	
41583	**Wilson Pickett**	*In The Midnight Hour*	11.1987
		In The Midnight Hour (edit of dub mix)	
41611	**Georgio**	*Lover's Lane*	2.1988
		Lover's Lane (edit of After Hours mix)	
**41651	**Carrie McDowell**	*When A Woman Loves A Man*	11.1987
		The Tracks Of My Tears	
41653	**Bruce Willis**	*Comin' Right Up*	12.1987
		Down In Hollywood	
41655	**Michael Jackson with the Jackson 5**	*I Saw Mommy Kissing Santa Claus – Frosty the Snowman – Santa Claus Is Comin' To Town – Up On The Housetop*	11.1987
41723	**Stevie Wonder**	*You Will Know*	1.1988
		You Will Know (instr.)	
41733	**The Temptations**	*Look What You Started*	1.1988
		Look What You Started (radio edit. of 12-inch)	
41739	**Darryl Duncan**	*James Brown (Part 1)*	2.1988
		James Brown (Part 2)	

**12-inch not scheduled.

PERSONALIZED SERIES: 7 inch Singles:

Sammy 1	**Sam Harris**	*I'd Do It All Again*	5.1986
		The Rescue	
Wond 1	**Stevie Wonder**	*Land Of La La*	6.1986
		Land Of La La (instr.)	
Wond 2	**Stevie Wonder**	*Stranger On The Shore Of Love*	1.1987
		Did I Hear You Say You Love Me	
Lio 1	**Lionel Richie**	*Dancing On The Ceiling*	7.1986
		Love Will Find A Way	
Lio 2	**Lionel Richie**	*Love Will Conquer All*	9.1986
		The Only One	
Lio 3	**Lionel Richie**	*Ballerina Girl*	12.1986
		Deep River Woman	
Lio 4	**Lionel Richie**	*Se La*	3.1987
		Serves You Right	
Guinn 1	**Guinn**	*Open Your Door*	5.1986
		Sincerely	
Guinn 2	**Guinn**	*People Will Be People*	7.1986
		Dreamin'	
Eld 1	**El DeBarge**	*Who's Johnny*	5.1986
	El DeBarge with DeBarge	*Love Me In A Special Way*	
Eld 2	**El DeBarge**	*Love Always*	8.1986
	El DeBarge with DeBarge	*The Walls (Come Tumbling Down)*	

12-INCH SINGLES: 12TMG

| TMG 977 | **Michael Jackson** | *We're Almost There* | 7.1981 |
| | | *We've Got A Good Thing Going* | |

TMGT 978	**Four Tops**	*Baby I Need Your Loving – Yesterday's Dreams/Four Tops Medley*	4.1982
TMGT 987	**Marvin Gaye**	*What's Going On*	11.1983
		I Heard It Through The Grapevine (ext. version)	
		Wherever I Lay My Hat (That's My Home)	
1096	**Commodores**	*Zoom*	2.1978
		Too Hot Ta Trot	
1104	**Diana Ross**	*Your Love Is So Good For Me*	4.1978
		Baby It's Me	
1110	**Rick James**	*You And I*	7.1978
		Hollywood	
1111	**Commodores**	*Flying High*	6.1978
		Funky Situation	
1115	**Platinum Hook**	*Standing On The Verge (Of Gettin' It On)*	8.1978
		'Til I Met You	
1123	**Switch**	*There'll Never Be*	10.1978
		You Pulled The Switch	
1132	**Switch**	*We Like To Party . . . Come On*	1.1979
		Somebody's Watchin' You	
1134	**Bonnie Pointer**	*Heaven Must Have Sent You*	1.1979
		I Wanna Make It (In Your World)	
1135	**Diana Ross**	*What You Gave Me*	2.1979
		Ain't No Mountain High Enough	
1136	**Diana Ross, Marvin Gaye, Smokey Robinson, Stevie Wonder**	*Pops, We Love You*	3.1979
		Pops, We Love You (instr.)	
1137	**Rick James**	*High On Your Love Suite – One Mo' Hit (Of Your Love)*	3.1979
		You And I	
1138	**Marvin Gaye**	*A Funky Space Reincarnation*	2.1979
		Got To Give It Up	
1139	**Billy Preston & Syreeta**	*Go For It*	4.1979
		Go For It (instr.)	
1140	**Tata Vega**	*Get It Up For Love*	4.1979
		I Just Keep Thinking About You Baby	
1141	**Apollo**	*Astro Disco*	5.1979
		Astro Disco (instr.)	
1142	**High Inergy**	*Shoulda Gone Dancin'*	5.1979
		Shoulda Gone Dancin' (instr.)	
1143	**Motown Sounds**	*Space Dance*	5.1979
		Bad Mouthin'	
1144	**Mandré**	*Swang*	5.1979
		Spirit Groove	
1145	**Bonnie Pointer**	*Heaven Must Have Sent You (new version)*	NR
		My Everything	
1146	**Teena Marie**	*I'm A Sucker For Your Love*	6.1979
		I'm A Sucker For Your Love (instr.)	
1147	**Rick James**	*Bustin' Out*	6.1979
		Bustin' Out (instr.)	
1148	**Switch**	*Best Beat In Town*	6.1979
		It's So Real	
1150	**Diana Ross**	*The Boss*	7.1979
		Lovin', Livin' And Givin'	
1158	**Teena Marie**	*Don't Look Back*	9.1979
		I'm Gonna Have My Cake (And Eat It Too)	
1162	**Sterling**	*Roll Her, Skater*	9.1979
		Roll Her, Skater (instr.)	
1168	**Marvin Gaye**	*Ego Tripping Out*	11.1979
		What's Going On – What's Happening Brother	
1169	**Diana Ross**	*It's My House*	11.1979
		No One Gets The Prize – The Boss	

1180TM	**Diana Ross & the Supremes**	*The Supremes Medley*	4.1980
	Diana Ross	*Love Hangover*	
1183	**Jermaine Jackson**	*Let's Get Serious*	5.1980
		Je Vous Aime Beaucoup (I Love You)	
1185	**Teena Marie**	*Behind The Groove*	5.1980
		You're All The Boogie I Need	
1186	**The Temptations**	*Power*	5.1980
		Power (instr.)	
1194	**Jermaine Jackson**	*Burnin' Hot*	7.1980
		Castles Of Sand	
1195	**Diana Ross**	*Upside Down*	7.1980
		Friend To Friend	
1196	**Teena Marie**	*Lonely Desire*	7.1980
		I'm A Sucker For Your Love (instr.)	
1198	**Rick James**	*Big Time*	8.1980
		Island Lady	
1202	**Diana Ross**	*My Old Piano*	9.1980
		Where Did We Go Wrong	
1203	**Teena Marie**	*I Need Your Lovin'*	9.1980
		Behind The Groove/I Need Your Lovin' (instr.-vocal re-mix)	
1204	**Stevie Wonder**	*Master Blaster (Jammin')*	9.1980
		Master Blaster (dub ver.)	
1208	**Michal Urbaniak**	*Nanava*	11.1980
		Joy	
1209	**Rick James**	*Summer Love*	10.1980
		Gettin' It On (In The Sunshine)	
1210	**Diana Ross**	*I'm Coming Out*	11.1980
		Give Up	
1212	**Jermaine Jackson**	*Little Girl Don't You Worry*	12.1980
		We Can Put It Back Together	
1213	**The Dazz Band**	*Shake It Up*	1.1981
		Only Love	
1215	**Stevie Wonder**	*I Ain't Gonna Stand For It*	NR
		Knocks Me Off My Feet	
1219	**Táta Vega**	*You Keep Me Hangin' On*	1.1981
		You Better Watch Out	
1221	**Stone City Band**	*All Day And All Of The Night*	2.1981
		All Day And All Of The Night (vamp vers.)	
1222	**Jermaine Jackson**	*You Like Me Don't You*	5.1981
		You Like Me Don't You (instr.-vocal re-mix)	
1224	**Billy Preston**	*Hope*	2.1981
		Give It Up, Hot	
1225	**Marvin Gaye**	*Praise*	3.1981
		Funk Me	
1229	**Rick James**	*Give It To Me Baby*	4.1981
		Don't Give Up On Love	
1230	**Tata Vega**	*Love Your Neighbor*	4.1981
		There's Love In The World	
1232	**Marvin Gaye**	*Heavy Love Affair*	5.1981
		Far Cry	
1235	**Stevie Wonder**	*Happy Birthday*	8.1981
		Happy Birthday (sing-a-long vers.)	
1236	**Teena Marie**	*Square Biz*	7.1981
		Square Biz (instr.)	
1238	**Commodores**	*Lady (You Bring Me Up)*	7.1981
		Gettin' It	

TMGT:

1241	**Rick James**	*Super Freak*	10.1981
		Fire And Desire/Super Freak (short vers.; B-Side altered)	
1243	**The Temptations**	*Aiming At Your Heart*	10.1981
		The Life Of A Cowboy	
1246	**Teena Marie**	*It Must Be Magic*	11.1981
		Yes Indeed	
1247	**Syreeta**	*Quick Slick*	12.1981
		Quick Slick (instr.)	

1248	**Diana Ross**	*Tenderness*	12.1981
	Diana Ross & the Supremes	*The Supremes Medley*	
1249	**Ozone**	*Gigolette*	1.1982
		Gigolette (instr.)	
1250	**Rick James**	*Ghetto Life*	1.1982
		Below The Funk (Pass the J)	
1251	**Teena Marie**	*Portuguese Love*	1.1982
		The Ballad Of Cradle Rob And Me	
1255	**Smokey Robinson**	*Tell Me Tomorrow*	2.1982
		Being With You/Aqui Con Tigo	
1256	**Commodores**	*Why You Wanna Try Me*	3.1982
		Celebrate	
1258	**Syreeta**	*I Must Be In Love*	4.1982
		Out The Box	
1259	**Ozone**	*Do What Cha Wanna*	4.1982
		Come On In	
1261	**Nolen & Crossley**	*Ready Or Not*	4.1982
		A Place In My Heart	
1262	**Smokey Robinson**	*Old Fashioned Love*	5.1982
		Destiny	
1263	**The Temptations featuring Rick James**	*Standing On The Top*	5.1982
		Standing On The Top (Part 1)	
1266	**Rick James**	*Dance Wit' Me*	6.1982
		Dance Wit' Me (Part 1)	
1267	**Bobby Womack**	*So Many Sides Of You*	7.1982
		Just My Imagination	
1269	**Stevie Wonder**	*Do I Do*	5.1982
		Rocket Love	
1270	**Dazz Band**	*Let It Whip*	6.1982
		Everyday Love	
1273	**Diana Ross**	*Old Funky Rolls*	9.1982
		The Boss	
1274	**Smokey Robinson**	*Cruisin'*	8.1982
		The Only Game In Town	
1275	**Syreeta**	*Can't Shake Your Love*	8.1982
		Can't Shake Your Love (instr.)	
1276	**Jermaine Jackson**	*Let Me Tickle Your Fancy*	8.1982
		Let Me Ticle Your Fancy (instr.)	
1277	**Rick James**	*Hard To Get*	8.1982
		Hard To Get (instr.) – *Give It To Me Baby* (instr.)	
1279	**Dazz Band**	*Keep It Live (On The K.I.L.)*	NR
		This Time It's Forever	
1280	**Stevie Wonder**	*Ribbon In The Sky*	10.1982
		The Secret Life Of Plants	
1282	**Commodores**	*Lucy*	10.1982
		Heaven Knows	
1284	**Lionel Richie**	*Truly*	11.1982
		Just Put Some Love In Your Heart	
1285	**Willie Hutch**	*In And Out*	10.1982
		Brother's Gonna Work It Out	
1286	**Jermaine Jackson**	*Very Special Part*	12.1982
		Very Special Part (instr.)	
1288G	**Bobby M featuring Jean Carn**	*Let's Stay Together*	1.1983
	Bobby M	*Charlie's Backbeat*	
1289	**Stevie Wonder**	*Front Line*	1.1983
		Front Line (instr.)	
1290	**Lionel Richie**	*You Are*	2.1983
		You Mean More To Me/Truly (instr.)	
1291	**Billy Preston & Syreeta**	*A New Way To Say I Love You*	2.1983
		Hey You/One More Time For Love/Please Stay	
1292	**Commodores**	*Reach High*	2.1983
		Reach High (instr.)	
1293	**Willie Hutch**	*Party Down*	2.1983
		Slick – Get Ready For The Get Down	

1294G	High Inergy	He's A Pretender	3.1983
		He's A Pretender (instr.)	
1295	Smokey Robinson	I've Made Love To You A Thousand Times	3.1983
		Greatest Hits Medley	
1296G	DeBarge	I Like It	3.1983
		Hesitated	
1297	The Temptations	Love On My Mind Tonight	3.1983
		Bring Your Body Here (exercise chant)	
1298	Robert John	Bread And Butter	NR
		If You Don't Want My Love	
1299	Dazz Band	On The One	3.1983
		On The One (instr.)	
1300	Lionel Richie	My Love	4.1983
		Round And Round	
1301G	Mary Jane Girls	Candy Man	4.1983
		Candy Man (instr.)	
1302	Monalisa Young	Dancing Machine	4.1983
		Dancing Machine (instr.)	
1304	Finis Henderson	Skip To My Lou	6.1983
		Peraission Intro./I'd Rather Be Gone/Vina Del Mar	
1306	Syreeta	Forever Is Not Enough	6.1983
		She's Leaving Home	
1308G	DeBarge	All This Love	7.1983
		I'm In Love With You	
1309G	Mary Jane Girls	All Night Long	6.1983
		Musical Love	
1311	Michael Lovesmith	Baby I Will	7.1983
		What's The Bottom Line	
1312	Gary Byrd & the G.B. Experience	(You Wear) The Crown	7.1983
		(You Wear) The Crown (instr.)	
1314G	Rick James	Cold Blooded	8.1983
		Cold Blooded (instr.)	
1315G	Mary Jane Girls	Boys	9.1983
		All Night Long (instr.)/Candy Man (instr.)	
1316G	Stone City Band	Ladies Choice	9.1983
		Ladies Choice (instr.)	
1318	Jr Walker	Blow The House Down	10.1983
		Blow The House Down (instr.)	
1319	Lionel Richie	All Night Long (All Night)	10.1983
		Wandering Stranger	
1320TM	The Temptations & the Four Tops	Medley Of Hits	10.1983
	The Temptations	Papa Was A Rollin' Stone	
1321	Four Tops	I Just Can't Walk Away	10.1983
		Hang	
1322	Commodores	Turn Off The Lights	11.1983
		Painted Picture	
1323	Bobby Nunn	Don't Knock It (Until You Try It)	1.1984
		Private Party	
1324	Lionel Richie	Running With The Night	11.1983
		Serves You Right	
1325	Motor City Crew	Scratch Break (Glove Style)	11.1983
		Let's Break (vocal/instr.)	
1326	Stevie Wonder, Rev. Martin Luther King	Happy Birthday	12.1983
		I Have A Dream/Drum Major Instinct Sermon/Dr King's Desired Eulogy/I've Been to The Mountaintop	
1327G	Rick James & Friend	Ebony Eyes	1.1984
	Rick James	1-2-3 (You Her And Me)	
	Rick James & the Temptations	Standing On The Top	
1328	Dazz Band	Joystick	1.1984
		Don't Get Caught In The Middle	
1329G	DeBarge	Time Will Reveal	3.1984
		I'll Never Fall In Love Again – I Like It – All This Love	
1330	Lionel Richie	Hello	3.1984
		Running With The Night (instr.)/All Night Long (All Night) (instr.)	
1331	Rockwell	Somebody's Watching Me	1.1984
		Somebody's Watching Me (instr.)	
1332	Keith & Darrell	Work That Body	2.1984
		Work That Body (instr.)	
1334G	Dennis Edwards featuring Siedah Garrett	Don't Look Any Further	3.1984
1334R	Dennis Edwards Dennis Edwards (4 tracks)	I Thought I Could Handle It (1) featuring Siedah Garrett – Don't Look Any Further (orig. 12-inch mix) (2) I Thought I Could Handle It (3) featuring Siedah Garrett – Don't Look Any Further (new mix) (4) Don't Look Any Further (instr.)	6.1987
1335	Bobby King	Lovequake	4.1984
		Fall In Love	
1336	Rockwell	(Obscene) Phone Caller	3.1984
		(Obscene) Phone Caller (instr.)	
1337	Kidd Glove	Good Clean Fun	4.1984
		Street Angel	
1338	Dazz Band	Swoop (I'm Yours)	4.1984
		Bad Girl	
1339	Bobby Womack Bobby Womack & Patti LaBelle	Tell Me Why Through The Eyes Of A Child	6.1984
1340G	Dennis Edwards	(You're My) Aphrodisiac Shake Hands (Come Out Dancing)	5.1984
1341	Lionel Richie	Stuck On You	6.1984
		Round And Round/Tell Me	
1342	Michael Jackson	Farewell My Summer Love	5.1984
		Call On Me	
1343C	Duke Jupiter	Little Lady	6.1984
		Don't Turn Your Back/I've Got A Little Black Book	
1344	Smokey Robinson	And I Don't Love You	6.1984
		Dynamite	
1345	Rockwell	Taxman	8.1984
		Wasting Away/Change Your Ways	
1347	Bobby King featuring Alfie Silas	Close To Me	8.1984
	Bobby King	Love In The Fire – Midnight Shine	
1348G	Rick James	17	8.1984
		17 (instr.)	
1349	Stevie Wonder	I Just Called To Say I Love You	9.1984
		I Just Called To Say I Love You (instr.)	
1350C	Coyote Sisters	Straight From The Heart (Into Your Life)	7.1984
		Echo	
1351	Sammy Davis Jr	Hello Detroit	9.1984
		Hello Detroit (instr.)	
1352	Charlene	We're Both In Love With You	9.1984
		Richie's song (For Richard Oliver)/I Want To Go Back There Again	
1354	Bobby Womack	Surprise Surprise	10.1984
		American Queen – If You Think You're Lonely Now	
1355	Michael Jackson	Girl You're So Together	8.1984
		Touch The One You Love/Ben/Ain't No Sunshine	
1356	Lionel Richie	Penny Lover	10.1984
		You Are/My Love	

Cat.	Artist	Titles	Date
1357C	Jakata	Hell Is On The Run / Hell Is On The Run (instr.)/ Don't Ever Let Go	10.1984
1358	Phyllis St. James	Candlelight Afternoon / Candlelight Afternoon (short vers.)/ Back In The Race	9.1984
1359G	Rick James	You Turn Me On / You Turn Me On (instr.)/ Fire And Desire	10.1984
1360	Vanity	Pretty Mess / Pretty Mess (instr.)	10.1984
1361	Dazz Band	Let It All Blow / Let It Blow (instr.)/ Now That I Have You	10.1984
1363	Koko Pop	I'm In Love With You / On The Beach	12.1984
1364	Stevie Wonder	Love Light In Flight / It's More Than You (instr.)	11.1984
1365	The Temptations	Treat Her Like A Lady / Isn't The Night Fantastic	11.1984
1366	Thomas McClary	Thin Walls / Love Will Find A Way (instr.)	11.1985
1367	Phyllis St James	Ain't No Turnin' Back / Ruler Of The Hunt	NR
1368	Dazz Band	Heartbeat / Let It All Blow (disco mix)/ Rock With Me	2.1985
1369	Vanity	Mechanical Emotion / Mechanical Emotion (instr.)/ Crazy Maybe	1.1985
1370	Sam Harris	Hearts On Fire (dance mix) / Over The Rainbow/Hearts On Fire (psycho mix)	1.1985
1371	Commodores	Nightshift / I Keep Running	1.1985
1372	Stevie Wonder	Don't Drive Drunk / Don't Drive Drunk (instr.)	12.1984
1373	The Temptations	My Love Is True (Truly For You) / Treat Her Like A Lady (club mix)/I'll Keep My Light In My Window	3.1985
1374	Rockwell	He's A Cobra / He's A Cobra (instr.)/Change Your Ways	3.1985
1375	Thomas McClary	Man In The Middle / Man In The Middle (instr.)	NR
1376G	DeBarge	Rhythm Of The Night / Queen Of My Heart	3.1985
1377G	Mary Jane Girls	In My House / In My House (instr.)	2.1985
1378G	Rick James	Can't Stop / Can't Stop (instr.)	4.1985
1379	Jakata	Golden Girl / Golden Girl (instr.)/Light At The End Of The Tunnel	4.1985
1383	Bonnie Pointer	Heaven Must Have Sent You / Deep Inside My Soul	NR
1389	Stevie Wonder	Upset Stomach / (B side not selected)	NR
1390	Alfie	Star / Keep On Smilin'	7.1985

EUROPEAN SERIES: 12-inch Singles

ZT:

Cat.	Artist	Titles	Date
40098	Commodores	Animal Instinct (club-dub mix/M&M mix) / Lightin' Up The Night	5.1985
40100	Rockwell	Peeping Tom / Tokyo (instr.)	5.1985
40114	The Emotions	Miss Your Love / I Can't Wait To Make You Mine	5.1985
40160	Maureen Steele	Save The Night For Me (M&M mix) / Rock My Heart	6.1985
40174	Willie Hutch	Keep On Jammin' / In And Out – The Glow	6.1985
40202	Jake Jacas	Hold Me / Hold Me (instr.)	6.1985
40214G	DeBarge	Who's Holding Donna Now / Be My Lady	6.1985
40224G	Rick James	Glow/Glow (Reprise) / Glow (instr.)	6.1985
40272G	Mary Jane Girls	Wild And Crazy Love / All Night Long/Wild and Crazy Love (instr.)	8.1985
40274	Michael Lovesmith	Break The Ice (dance mix) / Baby I Will – Lucky In Love	7.1985
40308	Dazz Band	Hot Spot (club mix) / I've Been Waiting	8.1985
40312	Commodores	Janet/I'm In Love / Nightshift (instr.) (M&M)	8.1985
40342G	Dennis Edwards	Coolin' Out / Another Place In Time	NR
40344	Maureen Steele	Boys Will Be Boys (M&M) (club mix) / Rock My Heart	9.1985
40346G	El DeBarge with DeBarge	You Wear It Well / Baby, Won't Cha Come Quick	9.1985
40352	Stevie Wonder	Part-Time Lover / Part-Time Lover (instr.)	9.1985
40370	Michael Lovesmith	Ain't Nothing Like It (M&M) (club mix) / Ain't Nothing Like It (dub vers.)/Fast Girls	9.1985
40402	KoKo Pop	Brand New Beat (Part 1) (M&M mix) (club mix) / Brand New Beat (Part 2) (M&M mix) (club mix)	11.1985
40420G	Val Young	Seduction / Seduction (instr.)	11.1985
40422	Lionel Richie	Say You, Say Me / Can't Slow Dow	11.1985
40454	The Temptations	Do You Really Love Your Baby (M&M club mix/radio edit) / Do You Really Love Your Baby (M&M mix) (dub mix)/ I'll Keep My Light In My Window	11.1985
40498G	El DeBarge with DeBarge	The Heart Is Not So Smart (M&M club mix/dub mix) / You Wear It Well (dub mix)/ Share My World	12.1985
40502	Stevie Wonder	Go Home / Go Home (instr.)	11.1985
40502R	Stevie Wonder	Go Home / Go Home (instr.)	11.1985
40504	Warp 9	Skips A Beat (M&M club mix)/radio edit of club mix / Skips A Beat (dub vers.)/(Fly dub mix)	2.1986
40554	Smokey Robinson	Hold On To Your Love / Train Of Thought	1.1986
40562	Pal	Talk We Don't (M&M club mix/tribal mix – instr.) / Talk We Don't (safari mix/ jungle talk mix)	3.1986
40568	Stevie Wonder	Overjoyed / Overjoyed (single vers.) (instr.)	2.1986
40572	Sam Harris	I'd Do It All Again (club mix) / I'd Do It All Again (s.v.)/The Rescue	
40578G	Val Young	If You Should Ever Be Lonely (M&M club mix)/(radio edit) / If You Should Ever Be Lonely (street mix)	2.1986

40610	**Vanity**	*Under The Influence* (M&M mid-day mix–voc./early morning mix-dub)	4.1986
		Under The Influence (late night mix-voc.)/*Wild Animal*	4.1986
40622	**The Temptations**	*I'm Fascinated*	4.1986
		Treat Her Like A Lady (M&M club mix)	
		How Can You Say That It's Over	
40702TM	**Marvin Gaye**	*I Heard It Through The Grapevine/That's The Way Love Is*	4.1986
		Can I Get A Witness/You're A Wonderful One	
40710TM	**Diana Ross & the Supremes**	*You Keep Me Hangin' On/ Love's Like An Itching In My Heart*	4.1986
		Come See About Me/I Hear A Symphony	
*40718	**Smokey Robinson**	*Sleepless Nights – Close Encounters Of The First Kind*	6.1986
	Smokey Robinson & the Miracles	*Mickey's Monkey/I Gotta Dance To Keep From Crying*	
40744TM	**The Temptations**	*My Girl/The Way You Do The Things You Do*	6.1986
		Wherever I Lay My Hat (That's My Home)/My Baby	
40756G	**Rick James**	*Sweet And Sexy Thing* (12" vers.)	7.1986
		Super Freak/Sweet And Sexy Thing (instr.)	
40758	**Marvin Gaye**	*The World Is Rated X*	6.1986
		Lonely Lover/The World Is Rated X (instr.)	
40778	**Rockwell**	*Carmé*	7.1986
		Somebody's Watching Me/ Carmé (instr.)	
40796	**Mary Jane Girls**	*Walk Like A Man*	8.1986
		All Night Long/Shadow Lover	
40804TM	**Diana Ross**	*Ain't No Mountain High Enough/It's My House*	7.1986
		The Boss/Remember Me	
*40848	**Four Tops**	*Hot Nights/Again*	8.1986
		Medley of Hits	
*40850	**The Temptations**	*Lady Soul/A Fine Mess*	9.1986
		Papa Was A Rollin' Stone	
40886	**Stacy Lattisaw**	*Nail It To The Wall* (12" vers.)	10.1986
		Nail It To The Wall (instr.)/edit of 12" vers.	
40888	**Chico DeBarge**	*Talk To Me* (12" vers.)	10.1986
		If It Takes All Night/Talk To Me (LP vers.)/*If It Takes All Night*	
40986	**General Kane**	*Crack Killed Applejack* Promo only	
		Applejack's Theme/Crack Killed Applejack (club mix)	
41034	**General Kane**	*Hairdooz*	1.1987
		Crack Killed Applejack	
41110	**Stacy Lattisaw**	*Jump Into My Life* (12" dance mix)/7" vers.	2.1987
		Jump Into My Life (dub)/ *Longshot*	
41118	**Bruce Willis**	*Respect Yourself* (12" dance mix)	2.1987
		Fun Time/Respect Yourself (7" s.v.)	
41124	**Chico DeBarge**	*The Girl Next Door* (12" mix)/(7" vers.)	3.1987
		The Girl Next Door (dub)/ *You're Much Too Fast*	
*41148	**Smokey Robinson**	*Just To See Her/I'm Gonna Love You Like There's No Tomorrow*	3.1987
	Smokey	*You've Really Got A Hold On*	

	Robinson & the Miracles	*Me/That's What Love Is Made Of/Ooo Baby Baby*	

*Motown label on A-side, Tamla Motown on B-side.

41148A	**Smokey Robinson & the Miracles**	Tracks as original except *That's What Love Is Made Of* (dropped to line up with 4 track maximum for UK Gallup Chart rules)	6.1987
41210	**Georgio**	*Sexappeal* (new mix)	3.1987
		Sexappeal (orig. mix)/ *Sexappeal* (instr.)	
41264	**Carrie McDowell**	*Uh Uh, No No Casual Sex* (s.v.)/(club dub) (promo only)	
		Uh Uh, No No Casual Sex (sunrise mix)/(emu dub)	
41274	**Bruce Willis**	*Young Blood* (ext. dance mix)	4.1988
		Flirting With Disaster/Young Blood (7" single mix)	
41278	**Darryl Duncan**	*Rock The House*	6.1987
		Rock The House (instr.)	
41350	**Bruce Willis**	*Under The Boardwalk/ Respect Yourself* (instr.)	5.1987
		Jackpot (Bruno's Bop)	
41374	**Smokey Robinson & the Miracles**	*The Tracks Of My Tears/I Second That Emotion*	7.1987
		Going To A Go Go/Shop Around	
41412	**Kim O'Leary**	*Put The Pieces Back*	NR
		Put The Pieces Back (instr.)/ *The Kids Downtown*	
41432	**The Temptations**	*Papa Was A Rollin' Stone* (vocal re-mix)	8.1987
		Ain't Too Proud To Beg/Papa Was A Rollin' Stone (dub)	
41434	**General Kane**	*Girl Pulled The Dog* (ext. vers./dub)	7.1987
		Girl Pulled The Dog(s.v.)/ *Cuttin' It Up*	
41438	**Bruce Willis**	*Secret Agent Man – James Bond Is Back*	9.1987
		Lose Myself – Under The Boardwalk (instr.)	
41440	**Stevie Wonder**	*Skeletons*	10.1987
		Skeletons (instr.)	
41502	**Carrie McDowell**	*Uh Uh, No No Casual Sex* (s.v.)/(club dub)	9.1987
		Uh Uh, No No Casual Sex (sunrise mix)	
41526	**Smokey Robinson**	*One Heartbeat/Just To See Her* (instr.)	9.1987
		Love Will Set You Free (voc. & instr.)	
41548	**The Temptations**	*I Wonder Who She's Seeing Now* (ext. mix)	11.1987
		I Wonder Who She's Seeing Now (s.v.)/*Girls (They Like It)*	
41556	**Georgio**	*Tina Cherry* (club mix)	10.1987
		Tina Cherry (dub mix)/(radio mix)	
41584	**Wilson Pickett**	*In The Midnight Hourr* (midnight mix)	11.1987
		In The Midnight Hour (dub/ radio edit)	
41612	**Georgio**	*Lover's Lane* (new After Hours vocal mix)/(club mix)	2.1988
		Lover's Lane (Georgio's love dance mix)	
41654	**Bruce Willis**	*Comin' Right Up/Under The Boardwalk*	12.1987
		Down In Hollywood/Comin' Right Up (instr.)	

41656	**Michael Jackson with the Jackson 5**	*I Saw Mommy Kissing Santa Claus/Frosty The Snowman Santa Claus Is Comin' To Town/Up On The House Top*	11.1987
41724	**Stevie Wonder**	*You Will Know You Will Know* (s.v./instr.)	1.1988
41734	**The Temptations**	*Look What You Started* (12" vocal) *Look What You Started* (piano dub)/*Beat A Cappella*	1.1988
41740	**Darryl Duncan**	*J-J-J-Ja-Ja James Brown James Brown* (edit.)/*James Brown* (s.v.)	2.1988

PERSONALIZED SERIES: 12-inch Singles

SammyT 1	**Sam Harris**	*I'd Do It All Again I'd Do It All Again* (7" vers.)/*The Rescue*	5.1986
WondT 1	**Stevie Wonder**	*Land Of La La Land Of La La* (instr.)	6.1986
WondT 1R	**Stevie Wonder**	*Land Of La La* (re-mix) *Land Of La La* (instr. re-mix)	6.1986
WondT 2	**Stevie Wonder**	*Stranger On The Shore Of Love Did I Hear You Say You Love Me*	12.1986
LioT 1	**Lionel Richie**	*Dancing On The Ceiling Love Will Find A Way*	7.1986
LioT 1R	**Lionel Richie**	*Dancing On The Ceiling* (ext. re-mix)/*Love Will Find A Way*	8.1986
LioT 2	**Lionel Richie**	*Love Will Conquer All The Only One*	9.1986
LioT 2R	**Lionel Richie**	*Love Will Conquer All* (12" voc.) (istr.)/*Love Will Conquer All* (radio edit)/*The Only One*	10.1986
LioT 3	**Lionel Richie**	*Ballerina Girl/Deep River Woman Dancing On The Ceiling* (instr.)	12.1986
LioT 4	**Lionel Richie**	*Se La Se La* (edit)/*Serves You Right*	3.1987
GuinnT 1	**Guinn**	*Open Your Door Sincerely*	5.1986
GuinnT 2	**Guinn**	*People Will Be People Dreamin'* (vocal)/(instr.)	7.1986
EldT 1	**El DeBarge El DeBarge with DeBarge**	*Who's Johnny – Love Me In A Special Way/ Rhythm Of The Night*	5.1986
EldT 2	**El DeBarge El DeBarge with Debarge**	*Love Always – The Walls (Came Tumbling Down) You Wear It Well/All This Love*	8.1986

CASSETTE SINGLES:

TC-TMG 1226	**Stevie Wonder**	*Lately If It's Magic*	2.1981
CTMGT 1312	**Gary Byrd & G.B. Experience**	*(You Wear) The Crown (You Wear) The Crown* (instr.)	7.1983
ZV 40702	**Marvin Gaye**	*I Heard It Through The Grapevine That's The Way Love Is/Can I Get A Witness/You're A Wonderful One*	4.1986
ZB 41349C	**Bruce Willis**	*Under The Boardwalk Respect Yourself* (instr.)/ *Jackpot (Bruno's Bop)/ Under The Boardwalk* (instr.)	6.1987

ZB 41431C	**The Temptations**	*Papa Was A Rollin' Stone* (re-mix) *Ain't Too Proud To Beg/Papa Was A Rollin' Stone* (dub re-mix)	7.1987
ZB 41437C	**Bruce Willis**	*Secret Agent Man – James Bond Is Back Lose Myself/Under The Boardwalk* (voc.)	9.1987
ZB 41439C	**Stevie Wonder**	*Skeletons Skeletons* (instr.)	10.1987
ZB 41501C	**Carrie McDowell**	*Uh Uh, No No Casual Sex* (club mix)/(emu dub/sunset mix)	NR

CD SINGLES:

LIOCD 4	**Lionel Richie**	*Se La/Se La* (edit. vers.) *Serves You Right*	4.1987
ZD 41654	**Bruce Willis**	*Comin' Right Up Under The Boardwalk/Down In Hollywood/Respect Yourself*	1.1988
ZD 41724	**Stevie Wonder**	*You Will Know/You Will Know* (instr.) *You Will Know – Stevie Wonder Interview*	1.1988

RARE EARTH: RES

101	**R. Dean Taylor**	*Ain't It A Sad Thing Back Street*	9.1971
102	**Rare Earth**	*The Seed I Just Want To Celebrate*	9.1971
103	**Stoney & Meatloaf**	*What You See Is What You Get The Way You Do The Things You Do*	10.1971
104	**Rare Earth**	*Hey Big Brother Under God's Light*	1.1972
105	**Rare Earth**	*Born To Wander Here Comes The Night*	4.1972
106	**R. Dean Taylor**	*Taos New Mexico Shadow*	7.1972
107	**XIT**	*I Was Raised End*	9.1972
*108	**Wolfe**	*Dancing In The Moonlight Snarlin' Mama Lion*	2.1973
109	**Rare Earth**	*Good Time Sally Love Shines Down*	8.1973
*110	**Dan The Banjo Man**	*Dan The Banjo Man Everything Will Rhyme*	8.1973
111	**XIT**	*Reservation Of Education Young Warrior*	1.1974
*112	**David Alexander**	*Love, Love, Love Missy*	3.1974
*113	**Dan The Banjo Man**	*Black Magic Londonderry* (instr.)	6.1974
114	**Rare Earth**	*(I Know) I'm Losing You When Joannie Smiles*	5.1974
115	**Michael Edward Campbell**	*Roxanne (You Sure Got A Fine Design) Roll It Over*	5.1974
*116	**Slowbone the Wonder Boys**	*Happy Birthday Sweet Sixteen Tales Of A Crooked Man*	5.1974
*117	**Sonny and the Sovereigns**	*School Is Out Warm Jetz*	7.1974
*118	**The Rough Riders**	*Hot California Beach Do You See Me*	9.1974
*119	**Slowbone**	*Oh Man Get What You're Given*	10.1974
*120	**Friendly Persuasion**	*Remember (Sha La La) I'll Always Do The Best I Can*	11.1974
*121	**Dan The Banjo Man**	*Red River Valley Theme Of Love*	7.1975

*British production.

MOWEST:

3001	**Thelma Houston**	*No One's Gonna Be A Fool Forever*	10.1972
		What If	
3002	**Frankie Valli & the Four Seasons**	*The Night*	10.1972
		When The Morning Comes	
3003	**Frankie Valli & the Four Seasons**	*Walk On, Don't Look Back*	3.1973
		Touch The Rainchild	
3004	**Thelma Houston**	*Black California*	NR
		I'm Letting Go	
3005	**Thelma Houston**	*Piano Man*	10.1973
		I'm Just A Part Of Yesterday	
3006	**Syreeta**	*To Know You Is To Love You*	6.1973
		Happiness	
3007	**Hetherington**	*Teenage Love Song*	7.1973
		That Girl's Alright	
3008	**Phil Cordell**	*Close To You*	7.1973
		Londonderry	
3009	**The Sisters Love**	*I'm Learning To Trust My Man*	9.1973
		Try It, You'll Like It	
3010	**The Devastating Affair**	*That's How It Was (Right From The Start)*	9.1973
		It's So Sad	
3011	**Phil Cordell**	*Roadie For The Band*	9.1973
		Twistin' and Jivin'	
3012	**The Rockits**	*Livin' Without You*	11.1973
		Love My Love	
3013	**Tom Clay**	*What The World Needs Now Is Love/Abraham, Martin And John*	12.1973
		The Victors	
3014	**Bobby Darin**	*Blue Monday*	4.1974
		Moritat (Mack The Knife)	
3015	**Phil Cordell**	*Laughter In The Rain*	5.1974
		If I Don't Get All The Luck	
3016	**The Rockits**	*I'm Losing You*	7.1974
		Gimme True Love	
3017	**Leo Bendix**	*Holdin' On You*	NR
		Don't Take Your Love From A Clown	
3018	**Riverhead**	*I Can't Let Maggie Go*	8.1974
		This Time Around	
3019	**Reuben Howell**	*Rings*	8.1974
		I Believe (When I Fall In Love It Will Be Forever)	
3020	**Severin Browne**	*Love Song*	9.1974
		Snow Flakes	
3021	**Phil Cordell**	*Cool Clear Water*	9.1974
		Everywhere I Go	
3022	**Boone Family**	*Please Mr Postman*	11.1974
		Friends	
3023	**Severin Browne**	*Romance*	3.1975
		The Sweet Sound Of Your Song	
*3024	**Frankie Valli & the Four Seasons**	*The Night*	3.1975
		When The Morning Comes	
3025	**The Boones**	*When The Lovelight Starts Shining Thru' His Eyes*	4.1975
		Friends	
3026	**Phil Cordell**	*Chevy Van*	NR
		Strange Things	
3027	**T. G. Sheppard**	*Tryin' To Beat The Morning Home*	5.1975
		I'll Be Satisfied	
3028	**Frankie Valli & the Four Seasons**	*Touch The Rainchild*	6.1975
		Poor Fool	
3029	**The Allens**	*High Tide*	7.1975
		California Music	
3030	**Franki Valli**	*And I Will Love You*	8.1975
		Sun Country	
3031	**T. G. Sheppard**	*Another Woman*	10.1975
		I Can't Help Myself	
3032	**Jud Strunk**	*The Biggest Parakeets In Town*	10.1975
		I Wasn't Wrong About You	
3033	**T. G. Sheppard**	*Motels And Memories*	3.1976
		Pigskin Charade	
3034	**Franki Valli**	*Life And Breath*	6.1976
		Thank You	
3035	**T. G. Sheppard**	*Solitary Man*	7.1976
		Pigskin Charade	

* Transferred to Tamla Motown

GAIEE RECORDS

GAE: 101	**Valentino**	*I Was Born This Way*	6.1975
		Liberation	

PRODIGAL RECORDS

PROD: 1	**Dunn & Rubini**	*Diggin' It*	11.1976
		Just Keep Laughin'	
2	**Charlene**	*It Ain't Easy Comin' Down*	2.1977
		On My Way To You	
3	**Phil Cordell**	*Back In Your Arms*	8.1977
		One Man Show	
4	**Charlene**	*I've Never Been To Me*	8.1977
		Freddie	
5	**Graffiti Orchestra**	*Theme From 'Star Wars'*	8.1977
		Theme From 'Star Wars' (l.v.)	
6	**Phil Cordell**	*Doin' The Best I Can*	10.1977
		Cheatin' In The Dark	
7	**Rare Earth**	*Is Your Teacher Cool?*	11.1977
		Crazy Love	
8	**Fresh**	*Just How Does It Feel*	3.1978
		Let Yourself Go	
9	**Rare Earth**	*Warm Ride*	5.1978
		Would You Like To Come Along	
10	**Stoney & Meatloaf**	*What You See Is What You Get*	3.1979
		The Way You Do The Things You Do	

HITSVILLE RECORDS

HV: 101	**T. G. Sheppard**	*Lovin' On*	4.1977
		We Just Live Here (We Don't Love Here Anymore)	
102	**Wendel Adkins**	*Texas Moon*	5.1977
		Laid Back Country Picker	

MC RECORDS

MC: 7001	**Marty Mitchell**	*You Are The Sunshine Of My Life*	3.1978
		Yester-Me, Yester-You, Yesterday	
7002	**Jerry Naylor**	*Rave On*	5.1978
		Lady, Would You Like To Dance	

BRITISH EPS (Extended Play)

LONDON-AMERICAN

RE: 1295	**The Miracles**	*Shop Around*	10.1961

STATESIDE

SE: 1009	**Various**	*R&B Chartmakers No. 1*	1.1964
1014	**Little Stevie Wonder**	*I Call It Pretty Music But The Old People Call It The Blues*	1.1964
1018	**Various**	*R&B Chartmakers No. 2*	4.1964
1022	**Various**	*R&B Chartmakers No. 3*	6.1964
1025	**Various**	*R&B Chartmakers No. 4*	9.1964

TAMLA MOTOWN

TME: 2001	**Various**	*Hitsville USA No. 1*	3.1965
2002	**The Contours**	*The Contours*	3.1965
2003	**The Marvelettes**	*The Marvelettes*	3.1965
2004	**The Temptations**	*The Temptations*	3.1965
2005	**Kim Weston**	*Kim Weston*	3.1965
2006	**Stevie Wonder**	*Stevie Wonder*	3.1965
2007	**Mary Wells**	*Mary Wells*	5.1965
2008	**The Supremes**	*The Supremes Hits*	5.1965
2009	**Martha & the Vandellas**	*Martha & the Vandellas*	5.1965
2010	**The Temptations**	*It's The Temptations*	2.1966
2011	**The Supremes**	*Shake*	2.1966
2012	**Four Tops**	*The Four Tops*	2.1966
2013	**Jr Walker & the All Stars**	*Shake And Fingerpop*	2.1966
2014	**Various**	*New Faces From Hitsville*	4.1966
2015	**Kim Weston**	*Rock Me A Little While*	4.1966
2016	**Marvin Gaye**	*Marvin Gaye*	4.1966
2017	**Martha & the Vandellas**	*Hittin'*	10.1966
2018	**Four Tops**	*Four Tops Hits*	3.1967
2019	**Marvin Gaye**	*Originals From Marvin Gaye*	3.1967
STME: 2020	**Stevie Wonder**	*A Something's Extra* bonus record for *Songs in The Key Of Life'* (7" 33rpm)	9.1976

EPs ON CASSETTE ONLY

CTME: 2021	**Diana Ross**	*Motown Flip Hits (Cass)*	4.1983
2022	**Stevie Wonder**	*Motown Flip Hits* (cass)	4.1983
2023	**Four Tops**	*Motown Flip Hits* (cass)	4.1983
2024	**Temptations**	*Motown Flip Hits* (cass)	4.1983
2025	**Jimmy Ruffin**	*Motown Flip Hits* (cass) *What Becomes Of The Brokenhearted* *Its Wonderful (To Be Loved By You)* *Farewell Is A Lovely Sound* *I'll Say Forever My Love*	4.1983
2026	**Jr Walker & the All Stars**	*Motown Flip Hits* (cass) *(I'm A) Road Runner* *Take Me Girl I'm Ready* *Walk In The Night* *What Does It Take (To Win Your Love)*	4.1983
2027	**Smokey Robinson & the Miracles**	*Motown Flip Hits* (cass) *The Tears Of A Clown* *(Come 'Round Here) I'm The One You Need* *The Tracks Of My Tears* *I Don't Blame You At All*	4.1983
2028	**Martha Reeves & the Vandellas**	*Motown Flip Hits* (cass) *Dancing In The Street* *Forget Me Not* *Jimmy Mack* *I'm Ready For Love*	4.1983
2029	**Various Artists**	*Four Motown Number 1 Hits Vol. 1* (cass) Smokey Robinson – *Being With You* Charlene – *I've Never Been To Me* Commodores – *Three Times A Lady* Diana Ross – *I'm Still Waiting*	4.1983
2030	**Various Artists**	*Four Motown Number 1 Hits Vol 2* (cass) Michael Jackson – *One Day In Your Life* Smokey Robinson & the Miracles – *The Tears Of A Clown* Four Tops – *Reach Out I'll Be There* Diana Ross & the Supremes – *Baby Love*	4.1983
2031	**Commodores**	*Motown Flip Hits* (cass) *Three Times A Lady* *Sail On* *Still* *Easy*	7.1983
2032	**Four Tops**	*Motown Flip Hits* (cass) *It's All In The Game* *Bernadette* *Standing In The Shadows Of Love* *If I Were A Carpenter*	7.1983
2033	**Isley Brothers**	*Motown Flip Hits* (cass) *This Old Heart Of Mine* *I Guess I'll Always Love You* *Behind A Painted Smile* *Put Yourself In My Place*	7.1983
2034	**Jackson 5**	*Motown Flip Hits* (cass) *I Want You Back* *I'll Be There* *Lookin' Through The Windows* *ABC*	7.1983
2035	**Michael Jackson**	*Motown Flip Hits* (cass) *One Day In Your Life* *Ben* *Got To Be There* *Ain't No Sunshine*	7.1983
2036	**Gladys Knight & the Pips**	*Motown Flip Hits* (cass) *Help Me Make It Through The Night* *Just Walk, In My Shoes* *The Look Of Love* *Take Me In Your Arms And Love Me*	7.1983
2037	**Diana Ross**	*Motown Flip Hits* (cass) *Ain't No Mountain High Enough* *Remember Me* *I'm Still Waiting* *Doobedood'ndoobe* etc.	NR
2038	**Diana Ross & the Supremes**	*Motown Flip Hits* (cass) *You Can't Hurry Love* *Where Did Our Love Go* *Stop! In The Name Of Love* *I'm Livin' In Shame*	NR
2039	**Various Artists**	*Four Motown Smash Hits Vol. 1* (cass) Jermaine Jackson – *Let's Get Serious* Thelma Houston – *Don't Leave Me This Way* David Ruffin – *Walk Away From Love* Teena Marie – *Behind The Groove*	NR
2040	**Various Artists**	*Four Motown Smash Hits Vol. 2* (cass) Mary Wells – *My Guy* Elgins – *Heaven Must Have Sent You* Marv Johnson – *I'll Pick A Rose For My Rose* Detroit Spinners – *It's A Shame*	NR

2041	**Marvin Gaye**	Motown Flip Hits (cass)	NR
		I Heard It Through The Grapevine	
		Got To Give It Up (Part 1)	
		Too Busy Thinking About My Baby	
		Abraham, Martin And John	
2042	**Marvin Gaye & Tammi Terrell**	Motown Flip Hits (cass)	
		You're All I Need to Get By	
		The Onion Song	
		You Ain't Livin' Till You're Lovin'	
		Good Lovin' Ain't Easy To Come By	

BRITISH ALBUMS

ORIOLE: PS

40043	**The Contours**	Do You Love Me	7.1963
40044	**The Miracles**	Hi! We're The Miracles	7.1963
40045	**Mary Wells**	Two Lovers	7.1963
40049	**Little Stevie Wonder**	Tribute To Uncle Ray	8.1963
40050	**Little Stevie Wonder**	The 12 Year Old Genius Recorded Live	8.1963
40051	**Mary Wells**	Bye Bye Baby	8.1963
40052	**Martha & the Vandellas**	Come And Get These Memories	8.1963

STATESIDE: SL

10065	**Various**	On Stage Live!	3.1964
10077	**Various**	The Sound Of The R&B Hits	5.1964
10078	**Little Stevie Wonder**	The Jazz Soul Of Little Stevie	5.1964
10095	**Mary Wells**	My Guy	9.1964
10097	**Marvin Gaye & Mary Wells**	Together	10.1964
10099	**The Miracles**	The Fabulous Miracles	11.1964
10100	**Marvin Gaye**	Marvin Gaye	11.1964
10108	**Stevie Wonder**	Hey Harmonica Man	1.1965
10109	**The Supremes**	Meet The Supremes	12.1964

TAMLA MOTOWN: TML (Mono)/STML (Stereo)

11001	**Various**	A Collection Of 16 Big Tamla Motown Hits	3.1965
11002	**The Supremes**	With Love (From Us To You)	3.1965
11003	**The Miracles**	I Like It Like That	3.1965
11004	**Marvin Gaye**	How Sweet It Is	3.1965
11005	**Martha & the Vandellas**	Heatwave	3.1965
11006	**Mary Wells**	My Baby Just Cares For Me	3.1965
11007	**Various**	The Motortown Revue Live	4.1965
11008	**The Marvelettes**	The Marvellous Marvelettes	4.1965
11009	**The Temptations**	Meet The Temptations	4.1965
11010	**Four Tops**	Four Tops	6.1965
11011	**Choker Campbell & His 16-Piece Band**	Hits Of The Sixties	6.1965
11012	**The Supremes**	We Remember Sam Cooke	7.1965
11013	**Martha & the Vandellas**	Dance Party	9.1965
11014	**Earl Van Dyke & the Soul Brothers**	That Motown Sound	9.1965
11015	**Marvin Gaye**	Hello Broadway	9.1965
11016	**The Temptations**	The Temptations Sing Smokey	10.1965
11017	**Jr Walker & the All Stars**	Shotgun	10.1965
11018	**The Supremes**	The Supremes Sing Country & Western & Pop	10.1965
11019	**Various**	Hitsville USA	12.1965
11020	**The Supremes**	More Hits By The Supremes	12.1965

STML:

| 11021 | **Four Tops** | Second Album | 3.1966 |

11022	**Marvin Gaye**	A Tribute To The Great Nat King Cole	2.1966
11023	**The Temptations**	The Temptin' Temptations	3.1966
11024	**Smokey Robinson & the Miracles**	Going To A Go-Go	2.1966
11025	**Billy Eckstine**	The Prime Of My Life	2.1966
11026	**The Supremes**	The Supremes At The Copa	2.1966
11027 (TML)	**Various**	Motortown Revue Live In Paris	2.1966
11028	**The Supremes**	I Hear A Symphony	6.1966
11029	**Jr Walker & the All Stars**	Soul Session	6.1966
11030 (TML)	**Various**	Motown Magic	6.1966
11031 (TML)	**The Miracles**	From The Beginning	7.1966
11032 (TML)	**Mary Wells**	Greatest Hits	7.1966
11033	**Marvin Gaye**	Moods Of Marvin Gaye	10.1966
11034	**The Isley Brothers**	This Old Heart Of Mine	10.1966
11035	**The Temptations**	Gettin' Ready	10.1966
11036	**Stevie Wonder**	Uptight	9.1966
11037	**Four Tops**	On Top	11.1966
11038	**Jr Walker & the All Stars**	Road Runner	12.1966
11039	**The Supremes**	Supremes A Go-Go	12.1966
11040	**Martha & the Vandellas**	Greatest Hits	2.1967
11041	**Four Tops**	Live!	2.1967
11042	**The Temptations**	Greatest Hits	2.1967
11043 (TML)	**Various**	A Collection Of 16 Original Big Hits Vol. 4	3.1967
11044	**Smokey Robinson & the Miracles**	Away We A Go Go	3.1967
11045	**Stevie Wonder**	Down To Earth	4.1967
11046	**Billy Eckstine**	My Way	4.1967
11047	**The Supremes**	Supremes Sing Motown	5.1967
11048	**Jimmy Ruffin**	The Jimmy Ruffin Way	5.1967
11049	**Marvin Gaye & Kim Weston**	Take Two	5.1967
11050	**Various**	A Collection Of 16 Original Big Hits Vol. 5	6.1967
11051	**Martha & the Vandellas**	Watchout!	6.1967
11052	**The Marvelettes**	The Marvelettes	7.1967
11053	**The Temptations**	Live!	7.1967
11054	**The Supremes**	Sing Rogers And Hart	9.1967
11055	**Various**	British Motown Charbusters	10.1967
11056	**Four Tops**	Reach Out	11.1967
11057	**The Temptations**	With A Lot O' Soul	11.1967
11058	**Gladys Knight & the Pips**	Everybody Needs Love	1.1968
11059	**Stevie Wonder**	I Was Made To Love Her	12.1967
11060	**The Detroit Spinners**	The Detroit Spinners	1.1968
11061	**Four Tops**	Greatest Hits	1.1968
11062	**Marvin Gaye & Tammi Terrell**	United	1.1968
11063	**Diana Ross & the Supremes**	Greatest Hits	1.1968
11064	**Various**	Motown Memories	1.1968
11065	**Marvin Gaye**	Greatest Hits	2.1968
11066	**The Isley Brothers**	Soul On The Rocks	2.1968
11067	**Smokey Robinson & the Miracles**	Make It Happen	2.1968
11068	**The Temptations**	In A Mellow Mood	3.1968
11069	**Chris Clark**	Soul Sounds	2.1968
11070	**Diana Ross & the Supremes**	Live! At The Talk Of The Town	3.1968
11071	**Chuck Jackson**	Arrives	6.1968
11072	**Smokey Robinson & the Miracles**	Greatest Hits	6.1968
11073	**Diana Ross & the Supremes**	Reflections	7.1968
11074	**Various**	A Collection Of 16 Original Big Hits Vol. 6	7.1968
11075	**Stevie Wonder**	Greatest Hits	8.1968

Cat. No.	Artist	Title	Date
11076 (TML)	Dr Martin Luther King	The Great March To Freedom	7.1968
11077 (TML)	Various	Motown Memories Vol. 2	10.1968
11078	Martha Reeves & the Vandellas	Ridin' High	8.1968
11079	The Temptations	Wish It Would Rain	8.1968
11080	Gladys Knight & the Pips	Feelin' Bluesy	9.1968
11081	The Elgins	Darling Baby	9.1968
11082	Various	British Motown Chartbusters Vol. 2	11.1968
11083	Brenda Holloway	The Artistry Of Brenda Holloway	10.1968
11084	Marvin Gaye & Tammi Terrell	You're All I Need	10.1968
11085	Stevie Wonder	Someday At Christmas	12.1968
11086	Shorty Long	Here Comes The Judge	12.1968
11087	Four Tops	Yesterday's Dreams	1.1969
11088	Diana Ross & the Supremes	Sing And Perform Funny Girl	2.1969
11089	Smokey Robinson & the Miracles	Special Occasion	1.1969
11090	The Marvelettes	Sophisticated Soul	1.1969
11091	Marvin Gaye	In The Groove	1.1969
11092	Various	The Motown Sound-Collection Of 16 Original Big Hits Vol. 7	5.1969
11093	Bobby Taylor & the Vancouvers	Bobby Taylor & the Vancouvers	2.1969
11094	Edwin Starr	Soul Master	2.1969
11095	Diana Ross & the Supremes	Love Child	1.1969
11096	Diana Ross & the Supremes & The Temptations	Diana Ross & The Supremes Join The Temptations	1.1969
11097	Jr Walker & the All Stars	Home Cookin'	2.1969
11098	Stevie Wonder	For Once In My Life	2.1969
11099	Martha Reeves & the Vandellas	Dancing In The Street	4.1969
11100	Gladys Knight & the Pips	Silk 'N Soul	4.1969
11101	Billy Eckstine	Gentle On My Mind	7.1969
11102	Mary Wells	Vintage Stock	NR
11103	Tammi Terrell	Irresistible	5.1969
11104	The Temptations	Live At The Copa	5.1969
11105	The Fantastic Four	The Fantastic Four	6.1969
11106	Jimmy Ruffin	Ruff 'N' Ready	5.1969
11107	Smokey Robinson & the Miracles	Live	6.1969
11108	The Monitors	Greetings! We're The Monitors	6.1969
11109	The Temptations	Cloud Nine	9.1969
11110	Diana Ross & the Supremes & The Temptations	TCB	7.1969
11111	Marv Johnson	I'll Pick A Rose For My Rose	8.1969
11112	The Isley Brothers	Behind A Painted Smile	9.1969
11113	Four Tops	Four Tops Now	9.1969
11114	Diana Ross & the Supremes	Let The Sunshine In	9.1969
11115	Edwin Starr	25 Miles	9.1969
11116	The Originals	Green Grow The Lilacs	11.1969
11117	Chuck Jackson	Going Back To . . .	9.1969
11118	David Ruffin	My Whole World Ended	9.1969
11119	Marvin Gaye	MPG	9.1969
11120	Jr Walker & the All Stars	Greatest Hits	11.1969
11121	Various	Motown Chartbusters Vol. 3	11.1969
11122	Diana Ross & the Supremes & The Temptations	Together	2.1970
11123	Marvin Gaye & His Girls (Mary Wells, Kim Weston, Tammi Terrell)	Marvin Gaye And His Girls	1.1970
11124 (TML)	Various	In Loving Memory	11.1969
11125	Bobby Taylor	Taylor Made Soul	1.1970
11126	Various	Merry Christmas From Motown	11.1969
11127	Various	Motortown Revue – Live	1.1970
11128	Stevie Wonder	My Cherie Amour	1.1970
11129	Smokey Robinson & the Miracles	Take Some Time Out For . . .	1.1970
11130	Various	A Collection Of 16 Big Hits Vol. 8	1.1970
11131	Edwin Starr & Blinky	Just We Two	1.1970
11132	Marvin Gaye & Tammi Terrell	Easy	1.1970
11133	The Temptations	Puzzle People	2.1970
11134	Martha Reeves & the Vandellas	Sugar 'N' Spice	12.1969
11135	Gladys Knight & the Pips	Nitty Gritty	12.1969
11136	Marvin Gaye	That's The Way Love Is	4.1970
11137	Diana Ross & the Supremes	Cream Of The Crop	1.1970
11138	Four Tops	Soul Spin	1.1970
11139	David Ruffin	Feelin' Good	3.1970
11140	Jr Walker & the All Stars	These Eyes	4.1970
11141	The Temptations	Live! At London's Talk Of The Town	4.1970
11142	Jackson 5	Diana Ross Presents	4.1970
11143	Various	Motown Memories Vol. 3	5.1970
11144	Shorty Long	The Prime Of . . .	5.1970
11145	The Marvelettes	In Full Bloom	5.1970
11146	Diana Ross & the Supremes	Greatest Hits Vol. 2	5.1970
11147	The Temptations	Psychedelic Shack	6.1970
11148	Gladys Knight & the Pips	Greatest Hits	6.1970
11149	Four Tops	Still Waters Run Deep	6.1970
11150	Stevie Wonder	Live	6.1970
11151	Smokey Robinson & the Miracles	Four In Blue	7.1970
11152	Jr Walker & the All Stars	Live	7.1970
11153	Marvin Gaye & Tammi Terrell	Greatest Hits	8.1970
11154 } 11155 }	Diana Ross & The Supremes	Farewell (2LP set)	8.1970
11156	Jackson 5	ABC	8.1970
11157	The Supremes	Right On	8.1970
11158	Kiki Dee	Great Expectations	8.1970
11159	Diana Ross	Diana Ross	10.1970
11160	Sammy Davis Jr	Something For Everyone	9.1970
11161	Jimmy Ruffin	Jimmy Ruffin . . . Forever	10.1970
11162	Various	Motown Chartbusters Vol. 4	10.1970
11163	Smokey Robinson & the Miracles	What Love Has Joined Together	NR
11164	Stevie Wonder	Live! At The Talk Of The Town	10.1970
11165	Rare Earth	Get Ready	11.1970
11166	Martha Reeves & the Vandellas	Natural Resources	11.1970
11167	Jr Walker & the All Stars	A Gassss	11.1970
11168	Jackson 5	The Jackson 5 Christmas Album	12.1970
11169	Stevie Wonder	Signed, Sealed And Delivered	12.1970
11170	The Temptations	Greatest Hits Vol. 2	12.1970
11171	Edwin Starr	War And Peace	1.1971
11172	Smokey Robinson and the Miracles	Smokey Robinson And The Miracles	2.1971
11173	Four Tops	Changing Times	3.1971
11174	Jackson 5	Third Album	2.1971
11175	The Supremes	New Ways But Love Stays	2.1971
11176	David & Jimmy Ruffin	I Am My Brother's Keeper	5.1971

11177	The Marvelettes	The Return Of The Marvelettes	NR
11178	Diana Ross	Everything Is Everything	4.1971
11179	The Supremes & Four Tops	The Magnificent Seven	5.1971
11180	Rare Earth	Ecology	3.1971
11181	Various	Motown Chartbusters Vol. 5	4.1971
11182	The Motown Spinners	Second Time Around	4.1971
11183	Stevie Wonder	Where I'm Coming From	6.1971
11184	The Temptations	The Sky's The Limit	8.1971
11185	R. Dean Taylor	Indiana Wants Me	8.1971
11186	Eddie Kendricks	All By Myself	9.1971
11187	Gladys Knight & the Pips	If I Were Your Woman	9.1971
11188	Jackson 5	Maybe Tomorrow	10.1971
11189	The Supremes	Touch	9.1971
11190	Marvin Gaye	What's Going On	9.1971
11191	Various	Motown Chartbusters Vol. 6	10.1971
11192	The Supremes & Four Tops	The Return Of The Magnificent 7	11.1971
11193	Diana Ross	I'm Still Waiting	10.1971
11194	Valerie Simpson	Valerie Simpson Exposed	4.1972
11195	Four Tops	Greatest Hits Vol. 2	11.1971
11196	Stevie Wonder	Greatest Hits Vol. 2	12.1971
11197	The Undisputed Truth	The Undisputed Truth	2.1972
11198	Jr Walker & the All Stars	Rainbow Funk	2.1972
11199	Edwin Starr	Involved	1.1972
11200	Various	Motown Memories (16 Non-Stop Tamla Hits)	2.1972
11201	Marvin Gaye	The Hits Of Marvin Gaye	2.1972
11202	The Temptations	Solid Rock	4.1972
11203	The Supremes & Four Tops	Dynamite	4.1972
11204	Martha Reeves & the Vandellas	Black Magic	5.1972
11205	Michael Jackson	Got To Be There	4.1972
11206	Four Tops	Nature Planned It	6.1972
11207	Various	Motown Disco Classic Vol. 2	trans.
11208	Gladys Knight & the Pips	Standing Ovation	7.1972
11209	Edwin Starr	The Hits Of Edwin Starr	9.1972
11210	The Supremes	Floy Joy	9.1972
11211	Jr Walker & the All Stars	Moody Junior	8.1972
11212	Jackson 5	Greatest Hits	8.1972
11213	Eddie Kendricks	People . . . Hold On	2.1973
11214	Jackson 5	Lookin' Through The Windows	10.1972
11215	Various	Motown Chartbusters Vol. 7	11.1972
11216	San Remo Strings	San Remo Strings Swing	1.1973
11217	Various	The Motown Sound Vol. 1	2.1973
11218	The Temptations	All Directions	11.1972
11219	Valerie Simpson	Valerie Simpson	1.1973
11220	Michael Jackson	Ben	12.1972
11221	Jermaine Jackson	Jermaine	1.1973
11222	The Supremes	Produced And Arranged By Jimmy Webb	3.1973
11223	Martha Reeves & the Vandellas	Greatest Hits Vol. 2	2.1973
11224	Jr Walker & the All Stars	Greatest Hits Vol. 2	3.1973
11125	Marvin Gaye	Trouble Man	2.1973
11226	Gladys Knight & the Pips	Help Me Make It Through The Night	2.1973
11227	Various	Motown Disco Classics Vol. 3	4.1973
11228	David Ruffin	David Ruffin	5.1973
11229	The Temptations	Masterpiece	6.1973
11230	Gladys Knight & The Pips	Neither One Of Us	6.1973
11231	Jackson 5	Skywriter	6.1973
11232	Various	Ric Tic Relics	8.1973
11233	Smokey Robinson & the Miracles	Greatest Hits Vol. 2	7.1973
11234	Jr Walker & the All Stars	Peace And Understanding Is Hard To Find	7.1973
11235	Michael Jackson	Music And Me	7.1973
11236	The Detroit Spinners	The Best Of	8.1973
11237	Various	The Motown Sound Vol. 2	8.1973
11238	Jermaine Jackson	Come Into My Life	9.1973
11239	Diana Ross	Touch Me In The Morning	8.1973
11240	The Undisputed Truth	Law Of The Land	9.1973
*11241	Four Tops	Four Tops Story 1964-1972	—
*11242			
11243	Jackson 5	Get It Together	11.1973
11244	Various	Motown Disco Classics Vol. 4	4.1974
**11245	Eddie Kendricks	Eddie Kendricks	10.1973
11246	Various	Motown Chartbusters Vol. 8	10.1973
11247	Willie Hutch	Fully Exposed	1.1974
11248	Diana Ross	Live!	5.1974
11249	Jackie Jackson	Jackie Jackson	1.1974
11250	Various	The Motown Sound Vol. 3	NR
***11251	Diana Ross & the Supremes	Anthology	—
***11252	Diana Ross & the Supremes	Anthology	—
11253	—	—	—
11254	Gloria Jones	Share My Love	1.1974
11255	Diana Ross	Last Time I Saw Him	2.1974
11256	The Supremes	Greatest Hits	3.1974
11257	Diahann Carroll	Diahann Carroll	7.1974
11258	The Marvelettes	The Best Of The Marvelettes	1.1975
11259	Jimmy Ruffin	Greatest Hits	5.1974
11260	Edwin Starr	Hell Up In Harlem	5.1974

*Individual LP numbers for 2 record set TMSP1124.
**Title changed on Cassette/8-track Cartridge to Keep On Truckin'.
***Individual LP numbers for 2 record set TMSP1125 (subsequently changed to TMSP6001).

*11261	The Temptations	Anthology – 10th Anniversary	—
*11262			
*11263			
11264	Gladys Knight & the Pips	All I Need Is Time	4.1974
11265	Smokey Robinson	Pure Smokey	6.1974
11266	Eddie Kendricks	Boogie Down	3.1974
11267	Marvin Gaye	Live!	trans.
11268	Syreeta	Stevie Wonder Presents	7.1974
11269	Willie Hutch	Foxy Brown	8.1974
11270	Various	Motown Chartbusters Vol. 9	10.1974
**11271	Gladys Knight & the Pips	Anthology	—
**11272			
11273	Commodores	Machine Gun	10.1974
11274	Jr Walker & the All Stars	Jr Walker And The All Stars	7.1975
11275	Jackson 5	Dancing Machine	11.1974
11276	The Miracles	Do It Baby	12.1974
11277	The Undisputed Truth	Down To Earth	1.1975
11278	Various	Motown Disco Classics Vol. 5	12.1974
11279	Gladys Knight & the Pips	Knight Time	3.1975
11280	Willie Hutch	The Mark Of The Beast	1.1975
***11281	Marvin Gaye	Anthology	—
***11282	—	—	—
11283	David Ruffin	Me 'N Rock 'N Roll Are Here To Stay	1.1975
11284	Caston & Majors	Caston & Majors	3.1975
11285	The Isley Brothers	Super Hits	trans.
11286	Commodores	Caught In The Act	5.1975
11287	The Originals	California Sunset	6.1975
11288	Smokey Robinson	A Quiet Storm	6.1975
11289	Various	The Magic Disco Machine	7.1975
11290	Jackson 5	Moving Violation	7.1975

†11291 †11292	**Jr Walker & the All Stars**	*Anthology*	—
11293	**The Supremes**	*The Supremes*	7.1975

Continues at 12001 except for:

†††11301 †††11302 †††11303 †††11304 †††11305	**Various**	*The Motown Story*	—
††11311 ††11312	**Diana Ross**	*Lady Sings The Blues*	—
‡11321 ‡11322	**Stevie Wonder**	*Anthology*	—
‡‡11331 ‡‡11332	**Various**	*Save The Children*	—

TMSP series multiple LP sets – individual cat. numbers for:
*TMSP 1126 (NR)
**TMSP 1127
***TMSP 1128
†TMSP 1129
††TMSP 1131
†††TMSP 1130
‡TMSP 1132 (NR)
‡‡TMSP 1133
See also TMSP series.

12001	**Eddie Kendricks**	*The Hit Man*	9.1975
12002	**Various**	*Discotech*	9.1975
12003	**Various**	*Motown Gold*	10.1975
12004	**Diana Ross**	*Mahogany*	11.1975
12005	**Michael Jackson**	*The Best Of Michael Jackson*	9.1975
12006	**The Temptations**	*House Party*	12.1975
12007	**The Dynamic Superiors**	*Pure Pleasure*	2.1976
12008	**Yvonne Fair**	*The Bitch Is Black*	11.1975
12009	**The Undisputed Truth**	*Higher Than High*	11.1975
12010	**The Miracles**	*City Of Angels*	11.1975
12011	**Commodores**	*Movin' On*	11.1975
12012	**David Ruffin**	*Who I Am*	1.1976
12013	**Gladys Knight & the Pips**	*A Little Knight Music*	1.1976
12014	**The Isley Brothers**	*Super Hits*	trans.
12015	**Willie Hutch**	*Ode To My Lady*	1.1976
12016	**Eddie Kendricks**	*He's A Friend*	2.1976
12017	**Stephanie Mills**	*For The First Time*	3.1976
12018	**Jr Walker & the All Stars**	*Hot Shot*	3.1976
12019	**Various**	*Motown Discotech No. 2*	3.1976
12020	**The Miracles**	*Love Machine*	2.1976
12021	**Smokey Robinson**	*Smokey's Family Robinson*	4.1976
12022	**Diana Ross**	*Diana Ross*	3.1976
12023	**Willie Hutch**	*Concert In Blues*	5.1976
12024	**Rose Banks**	*Rose*	7.1976
12025	**Marvin Gaye**	*I Want You*	4.1976
12026	**Various**	*Motown Songbook – The Original Versions*	8.1976
12027	**The Supremes**	*High Energy*	5.1976
12028	**Various**	*Motown Magic Disco Machine Vol. 2*	7.1976
12029	**G. C. Cameron**	*G. C. Cameron*	8.1976
12030	**David Ruffin**	*Everything's Coming Up Love*	6.1976
12031	**Commodores**	*Hot On The Tracks*	7.1976
12032	**Jerry Butler**	*Love's On The Menu*	7.1976
12033	**Jr Walker**	*Sax Appeal*	8.1976
12034	**The Originals**	*Communique*	9.1976
12035	**Ronnie McNair**	*Ronnie McNair*	9.1976
12036	**Diana Ross**	*Greatest Hits Vol. 2*	7.1976
12037	**Various**	*The Motown Christmas Album*	11.1977
12038	**The Miracles**	*The Power Of Music*	10.1976
12039	**Tata Vega**	*Full Speed Ahead*	10.1976
12040	**The Temptations**	*The Temptations Do The Temptations*	10.1976

12041	**Ronnie McNair**	*Love's Comin' Down*	11.1976
12042	**Marvin Gaye**	*The Best Of Marvin Gaye*	9.1976
12043	**Eddie Kendricks**	*Goin' Up In Smoke*	11.1976
12044	**Various**	*Motown Discotech No. 3*	12.1976
12045	**Various**	*Cooley High* (soundtrack)	12.1976
12046	**Jackson 5**	*Joyful Jukebox Music*	12.1976
12047	**The Supremes**	*Mary, Scherrie And Susaye*	12.1976
12048	**Jr Walker**	*Whopper Bopper Show Stopper*	1.1977
12049	**Thelma Houston**	*Any Way You Like It*	1.1977
12050	**Leon Ware**	*Musical Massage*	2.1977
12051	**The Dynamic Superiors**	*You Name It*	2.1977
12052	**Jerry Butler**	*Suite For The Single Girl*	3.1977
12053	**Syreeta**	*One To One*	3.1977
12054	**The Originals**	*Down To Love Town*	4.1977
12055	**Smokey Robinson**	*Deep In My Soul*	4.1977
12056	**G. C. Cameron**	*You're What's Missing In My Life*	4.1977
12057	**Commodores**	*Zoom*	3.1977
12058	**Tata Vega**	*Totally Tata*	5.1977
12059	**Various**	*A Motown Special Disco Album*	5.1977
12060	**Martha Reeves & the Vandellas**	*Anthology*	6.1977
12061	**The Temptations**	*Greatest Hits Vol. 3*	8.1977
12062	**Mandré**	*Mandré*	7.1977
12063	**Thelma Houston & Jerry Butler**	*Thelma & Jerry*	7.1977
12064	**David Ruffin**	*In My Stride*	7.1977
12065	**The Dynamic Superiors**	*Nowhere To Run*	9.1977
12066	**Flavor**	*In Good Taste*	8.1977
12067	**Jermaine Jackson**	*Feel The Fire*	9.1977
12068	**Smokey Robinson**	*Big Time*	9.1977
12069	**Willie Hutch**	*Havin' A House Party*	9.1977
12070	**Various**	*Motown Gold Vol. 2*	10.1977
12071	**Eddie Kendricks**	*Slick*	11.1977
12072	**Jerry Butler**	*It All Comes Out In My Song*	12.1977
12073	**Syreeta & G. C. Cameron**	*Rich Love, Poor Love*	11.1977
12074	**High Inergy**	*Turnin' On*	12.1977
12075	**Thelma Houston**	*The Devil In Me*	12.1977
12076	**Smokey Robinson**	*Smokey's World*	2.1978
12077	**5th Dimension**	*Star Dancing*	3.1978
12078	**21st Creation**	*Break Thru*	3.1978
12079	**David Ruffin**	*At His Best*	4.1978
12080	**Eddie Kendricks**	*At His Best*	4.1978
12081	**Smokey Robinson**	*Love Breeze*	5.1978
12082	**Jermaine Jackson**	*Frontiers*	4.1978
12083	**Cuba Gooding**	*The First Cuba Gooding Album*	5.1978
12084	**Mandré**	*Mandré Two*	6.1978
12085	**Rick James**	*Come Get It*	7.1978
12086	**Platinum Hook**	*Platinum Hook*	6.1978
12087	**Commodores**	*Natural High*	5.1978
12088	**Three Ounces Of Love**	*Three Ounces Of Love*	8.1978
12089	**Jr Walker**	*Smooth Soul*	8.1978
12090	**High Inergy**	*Steppin' Out*	8.1978
12091	**The Supremes**	*At Their Best*	9.1978
12092	**Thelma Houston & Jerry Butler**	*Two To One*	9.1978
12093	**Diana Ross**	*Ross*	10.1978
12094	**Major Lance**	*Now Arriving*	10.1978
12095	**Finished Touch**	*Need To Know You Better*	10.1978
12096	**Switch**	*Switch*	10.1978
12097	**Bloodstone**	*Don't Stop*	4.1979
12098	**Thelma Houston**	*Ready To Roll*	11.1978
12099	**Grover Washington Jr**	*Reed Seed*	11.1978
12100	**Commodores**	*Greatest Hits*	11.1978
12101	**Bonnie Pointer**	*Bonnie Pointer*	1.1979
12102	**Various**	*A Special Motown Disco Album Vol. 2*	2.1979
12103	**Tata Vega**	*Try My Love*	4.1979
12104	**Rick James**	*Bustin' Out Of L Seven*	3.1979
12105	**Motown Sounds**	*Space Dance*	3.1979

12106	5th Dimension	High On Sunshine	5.1979
12107	Billy Preston & Syreeta	Music From Fast Break	5.1979
12108	Apollo	Apollo	6.1979
12109	Teena Marie	Wild And Peaceful	6.1979
12110	Platinum Hook	It's Time	8.1979
12111	High Inergy	Shoulda Gone Dancin'	6.1979
12112	Switch	Switch II	7.1979
12113	Cuba Gooding	Love Dancer	8.1979
12114	Various	Pops, We Love You . . . The Album	6.1979
12115	Smokey Robinson	Where There's Smoke	8.1979
12116	Billy Preston	Late At Night	9.1979
12117	Thelma Houston	Ride To The Rainbow	7.1979
12118	Diana Ross	The Boss	6.1979
12119	Patrick Gammon	Don't Touch Me	9.1979
12120	Dr Strut	Dr Strut	10.1979
12121	Jackson 5	20 Golden Greats	10.1979
12122	Gladys Knight & the Pips	20 Golden Greats	10.1979
12123	Various	Motown Chartbusters Vol. 10	11.1979
12124	Mary Wilson	Mary Wilson	10.1979
12125	Various	20 Mod Classics	11.1979
12126	Marvin Gaye	Love Man	NR
12127	Jermaine Jackson	Let's Get Serious	4.1980
12128	Rick James	Fire It Up	12.1979
12129	Bonnie Pointer	Bonnie Pointer/2	2.1980
12130	Teena Marie	Lady T	3.1980
12131	Grover Washington Jr	Skylarkin'	3.1980
12132	Dr Strut	Struttin'	4.1980
12133	Various	20 Mod Classic Vol 2	4.1980
12134	Smokey Robinson	Warm Thoughts	4.1980
12135	Switch	Reaching For Tomorrow	5.1980
12136	The Temptations	Power	6.1980
12137	Syreeta	Syreeta	6.1980
12138	Tata Vega	Givin' All My Love	3.1981
12139	Various	Motown Chartbusters '80	12.1980
12140	The Temptations	20 Golden Greats	10.1980
12141	Rick James	Garden Of Love	9.1980
12142	Black Russian	Black Russian	9.1980
12143	Teena Marie	Irons In The Fire	10.1980
12144	High Inergy	Hold On	11.1980
12145	Ahmad Jamal	Night Song	12.1980
12146	The Dazz Band	Invitation To Love	12.1980
12147	Jermaine Jackson	Jermaine	12.1980
12148	Billy Preston	The Way I Am	4.1981
12149	Marvin Gaye	In Our Lifetime	2.1981
12150	Stone City Band	The Boys Are Back	3.1981
12151	Smokey Robinson	Being With You	4.1981
12152	Diana Ross	To Love Again	3.1981
12153	Rick James	Street Songs	5.1981
12154	Teena Marie	It Must Be Magic	8.1981
12155	Billy Preston & Syreeta	Billy Preston & Syreeta	9.1981
12156	Commodores	In The Pocket	7.1981
12157	High Inergy	High Inergy	7.1981
12158	Michael Jackson	One Day In Your Life	7.1981
12159	The Temptations	The Temptations	10.1981
12160	Jermaine Jackson	I Like Your Style	10.1981
12161	José Feliciano	José Feliciano	11.1981
12162	Syreeta	Set My Love In Motion	12.1981
12163	Diana Ross	Diana's Duets	1.1982
12164	Various	Motown Chartbusters Vol. 12	7.1982
12165	Smokey Robinson	Yes, It's You Lady	3.1982
12166	Bettye Lavette	Tell Me A Lie	4.1982
12167	Rick James	Throwin' Down	6.1982
12168	Bobby Womack	The Poet	5.1982
12169	The Temptations	Reunion	6.1982
12170	High Inergy	So Right	8.1982
12171	Charlene	I've Never Been To Me	6.1982
12172	Jean Carn	Trust Me	8.1982
12173	Dazz Band	Keep It Live!	9.1982
12174	Jermaine Jackson	Let Me Tickle Your Fancy	8.1982
12175	Smokey Robinson	Touch The Sky	3.1982

12176L	José Feliciano	Escanas De Amor – Love Songs	10.1982
12177	Billy Preston	Pressin' On	11.1982
12178	Michael Jackson	20 Greatest Hits	NR
12179	Charlene	Used To Be	12.1982
12180G	Bobby M	Rick James Presents . . . Blow	12.1982
12181	Dazz Band	On The One	3.1983
12182	The Temptations	Surface Thrills	3.1983
12183	Commodores	All The Great Hits	3.1983
12184	Syreeta	The Spell	5.1983
12185L	Jose Feliciano	Romance In The Night	5.1983
12186G	DeBarge	All This Love	7.1983
12187	Kagny & the Dirty Rats	Kagny & The Dirty Rats	NR
12188	Ozone	Glasses	NR
12189G	Mary Jane Girls	Mary Jane Girls	5.1983
12190	Stone City Band	Out From The Shadow	10.1983
12191	Finis Henderson	Finis	7.1983
12192	Michael Lovesmith	I Can Make It Happen	9.1983
12193	Smokey Robinson	Blame It On Love & All The Great Hits	10.1983
12194	Jr Walker	Blow The House Down	10.1983
12195C	Various	Get Crazy (f/s)	10.1983
12196	The Temptations	Back To Basics	11.1983
12197	Four Tops	Back Where I Belong	11.1983
12198G	Teena Marie	You Got The Love	NR
12199	Bobby Nunn	Private Party	1.1984
12200G	DeBarge	In A Special Way	3.1984
12201	Dazz Band	Joystick	4.1984

TMSP SERIES

1124	Four Tops	Four Tops Story: 1964-1972	10.1973
1125	Diana Ross & the Supremes	Anthology	NM
1126	The Temptations	Anthology – 10th Anniversary Special	NM
1127	Gladys Knight & the Pips	Anthology	3.1974
1128	Marvin Gaye	Anthology	5.1974
1129	Jr Walker & the All Stars	Anthology	10.1974
1130	Various	The Motown Story	2.1972
1131	Diana Ross	Lady Sings The Blues	3.1973
1132	Stevie Wonder	Anthology	NM
1133	Various	Save The Children (Live)	7.1974
6001	Diana Ross & the Supremes	Anthology	10.1975
6002	Stevie Wonder	Songs In The Key Of Life	9.1976
6003	The Temptations	Anthology	5.1978
6004	Jackson 5	Anthology	1.1977
6005	Diana Ross	An Evening With Diana Ross	2.1977
6006	Marvin Gaye	Live! At The London Palladium	4.1977
6007	Commodores	Live!	11.1977
6008	Marvin Gaye	Here, My Dear	12.1978
6009	Stevie Wonder	Stevie Wonder's Journey Through The Secret Life Of Plants	10.1979
6010	Various	The Motown 20th Anniversary Album	6.1980
6011	Grover Washington Jr	Baddest	2.1981
6012	Stevie Wonder	Stevie Wonder's Original Musiquarium 1	5.1982
6013	Four Tops	Anthology	9.1982
6014	Smokey Robinson & the Miracles	Anthology	9.1982
6015	Grover Washington Jr	Anthology	9.1982
6016	Various	Cruisin' With Motown 1 (tape only)	9.1983
6017	Diana Ross	Anthology/The Very Best Of Diana Ross	10.1983
6018	Various	25 US No. 1 Hits From 25 Years	10.1983

6019	**Various**	The Motown Story: The First 25 Years	10.1983
6020	**Commodores**	Anthology	NM
6021	**Various**	M25 TV Soundtrack Special	NM
6022	**Various**	Cruisin' With Motown 2 (tape only)	9.1983

RARE EARTH: SRE

3001	**Crusaders**	Old Socks New Shoes, New Socks Old Shoes	10.1971
3002	**Hugh Masekela & the Union Of South Africa**	Hugh Masekela & The Union Of South Africa	11.1971
3003	**Letta Mbulu**	Letta	NM
3004	**Sunday Funnies**	Sunday Funnies	11.1971
3005	**Stoney & Meatloaf**	Stoney & Meatloaf	10.1972
3006	**Road**	Road	1.1973
3007	**Keef James**	One Tree Or Another	2.1973
3008	**Rare Earth**	Willie Remembers	3.1973
3009	**Corliss**	Corliss	4.1973
3010	**Rare Earth**	Ma	9.1973
*3011	**Rare Earth**	In Concert	5.1972
*3012		(released SRESP 301)	
3013	**Rare Earth**	Midnight Lady	5.1976

SREA:

| 4001 | **Rare Earth** | One World | 10.1971 |
| 4002 | **XIT** | Plight Of The Red Man | 9.1972 |

SRESP:

| 301 | **Rare Earth** | In Concert | 5.1972 |

*Individual LP catalogue numbers for multiple LP set SRESP 301.

PRODIGAL: PDL

2001	**Michael Quatro**	Dancers, Romancers, Dreamers & Schemers	10.1976
2002	**Dunn & Rubini**	Diggin' It	11.1976
2003	**Tattoo**	Tattoo	1.1977
2004	**Charlene**	Charlene	5.1977
2005	**Delaney Bramlett**	Delaney And Friends – Class Reunion	5.1977
2006	**Phil Cordell**	Born Again	10.1977
2007	**Rare Earth**	Rarearth	10.1977
2008	**Rare Earth**	Band Together	7.1978
2009	**Rare Earth**	Grand Slam	11.1978
2010	**Meatloaf**	Meatloaf . . . Featuring Stoney & Meatloaf	3.1979
2011	**Stylus**	Stylus	7.1979

HITSVILLE: HVS

3001	**Various**	Hitsville – The New Direction In Country Music	4.1977
3002	**T.G. Sheppard**	Nashville Hitmaker	4.1977
3003	**Pat Boone**	Texas Women/The Country Side Of Pat Boone	4.1977

MOWEST: MWS

7001	**Syreeta**	Syreeta	11.1972
7002	**Odyssey**	Odyssey	2.1973
7003	**Thelma Houston**	Thelma Houston	1.1973
7004	**Crusaders**	Hollywood	7.1973
7005	**Severin Browne**	Love Songs	7.1975
7006	**Frankie Valli & the Four Seasons**	Chameleon	5.1975
7007	**Frankie Valli**	Inside You	5.1976
7008	**Gaylord & Holiday**	Second Generation	4.1977

MWSA:

| 5501 | **Frankie Valli & the Four Seasons** | Chameleon | 11.1972 |

US SERIES: M

782A3	**The Temptations**	Anthology 10th Anniversary	12.1973
793R3	**Smokey Robinson & the Miracles**	Anthology	2.1974
794A3	**Diana Ross & the Supremes**	Anthology	7.1974
M9804	**Stevie Wonder**	Anthology	12.1977
M8949	**Various**	Loving Couples (f/s.)	12.1981

EMTV/MTV SERIES

5	**Diana Ross & the Supremes**	20 Golden Greats	8.1977
12	**Various**	The Big Wheels Of Motown	9.1978
20	**Various**	The Last Dance	1.1980
21	**Diana Ross**	20 Golden Greats	11.1979
26	**Four Tops**	Reach Out! 20 Golden Greats	2.1981
29	**Various**	Heart And Soul	NR

STMF SERIES

| 7001 | **Various** | The Motown Sound – 16 Big Hits – The Late 60s | 10.1982 |
| 7002 | **Various** | The Motown Sound – 16 Big Hits – The Early 60s | 10.1982 |

STARLINE SERIES: SRS

5040	**Mary Wells**	My Guy	10.1970
5043	**Isley Brothers**	Greatest Hits	10.1970
5078	**Marv Johnson**	I'll Pick A Rose For My Rose	9.1971
5098	**Isley Brothers**	Isley Brothers	2.1972

SOUNDS SUPERB SERIES: SPR

90001	**Diana Ross & the Supremes**	Baby Love	9.1973
90002	**Four Tops**	I Can't Help Myself	9.1973
90003	**Stevie Wonder**	Uptight	9.1973
90004	**The Temptations**	Get Ready	9.1973
90005	**Martha Reeves & the Vandellas**	Dancing In The Street	9.1973
90006	**Marvin Gaye**	How Sweet It Is	9.1973
90007	**R. Dean Taylor**	Gotta See Jane/Indiana Wants Me	9.1973
90008	**Mary Wells**	Greatest Hits including 'My Guy'	9.1973
90009	**Smokey Robinson & the Miracles**	I Heard It Through The Grapevine	9.1973
90010	**Various**	It's Christmas In Motown	9.1973
90030	**Kiki Dee**	Kiki Dee	5.1974
90037	**Marvin Gaye and Tammi Terrell**	The Onion Song	3.1974
90041	**Jimmy Ruffin**	I've Passed This Way Before	8.1974
90055	**Jr Walker & the All Stars**	Shotgun	8.1974

MUSIC FOR PLEASURE: MFP

50014	**Isley Brothers**	Tamla Motown Presents	5.1972
50054	**The Contours**	Baby Hit And Run	5.1974
50291	**Diana Ross & the Supremes**	Stop! In The Name Of Love	7.1976
50304	**Gladys Knight & the Pips**	The Fabulous Gladys Knight And The Pips	10.1976
50395	**Various**	Motown Magic	10.1978
50416	**Four Tops**	It's All In The Game	1.1979
50417	**Gladys Knight & the Pips**	The Look Of Love	1.1979
50418	**Jackson 5**	Zip A Dee Doo Dah	1.1979
50419	**The Temptations**	Live! At London's 'Talk Of The Town'	1.1979
50420	**Stevie Wonder**	Light My Fire	1.1979
50421	**The Supremes**	Stoned Love	1.1979

50422	**Smokey Robinson & the Miracles**	*The Tears Of A Clown*	1.1979
50423	**Marvin Gaye**	*How Sweet It Is (To Be Loved By You)*	1.1979
50447	**Diana Ross & the Supremes**	*Live! At London's 'Talk Of The Town'*	8.1979
50448	**Various**	*Motown Disco Magic*	8.1979
50536	**Various**	*More Motown Magic Vol. 1*	9.1981
50537	**Various**	*More Motown Magic Vol. 2*	9.1981

STMA SERIES: STMA

8001	**Diana Ross**	*Diana! (TV Sountrack)*	11.1971
8002	**Stevie Wonder**	*Music Of My Mind*	5.1972
8003	**Various**	*Motown Sound Vol. 1*	trans.
8004	**The Undisputed Truth**	*Face To Face With The Truth*	7.1972
8005	**Various**	*Motown Disco Classics Vol. 2*	8.1972
8006	**Diana Ross**	*Greatest Hits*	10.1972
8007	**Stevie Wonder**	*Talking Book*	1.1973
8008	**Smokey Robinson & the Miracles**	*1957-1972 Live!*	4.1973
8009	**Willie Hutch**	*The Mack (f/s.)*	8.1973
8010	**The Miracles**	*Renaissance*	10.1973
8011	**Stevie Wonder**	*Innervisions*	8.1973
8012	**Smokey Robinson**	*Smokey*	11.1973
8013	**Marvin Gaye**	*Let's Get It On*	9.1973
8014	**Various**	*Pippin (orig. cast album)*	11.1973
8015	**Diana Ross & Marvin Gaye**	*Diana & Marvin*	12.1973
8016	**The Temptations**	*1990*	2.1974
8017	**Diana Ross**	*Live!*	trans.
8018	**Marvin Gaye**	*Live!*	7.1974
8019	**Stevie Wonder**	*Fulfillingness' First Finale*	7.1974
8020	**Eddie Kendricks**	*For You*	12.1974
8021	**The Temptations**	*A Song For You*	1.1975
8022	**Michael Jackson**	*Forever, Michael*	2.1975
8023	**The Undisputed Truth**	*Cosmic Truth*	6.1975
8024	**Isley Brothers**	*Super Hits*	2.1976
8025	**The Temptations**	*Wings Of Love*	4.1976
8026	**Gladys Knight & the Pips**	*Super Hits*	9.1976
8027	**Jermaine Jackson**	*My Name Is Jermaine*	10.1976
8028	**Four Tops**	*Super Hits*	11.1976
8029	**The Undisputed Truth**	*The Best Of The Undisputed Truth*	9.1977
8030	**Albert Finney**	*Albert Finney's Album*	9.1977
8031	**Diana Ross**	*Baby It's Me*	10.1977
8032	**Commodores**	*Midnight Magic*	7.1979
8033	**Diana Ross**	*Diana!*	6.1980
8034	**Commodores**	*Heroes*	6.1980
8035	**Stevie Wonder**	*Hotter Than July*	9.1080
8036	**Diana Ross**	*All The Great Hits*	1.1981
8037	**Lionel Richie**	*Lionel Richie*	11.1982
8038G	**Rick James**	*Cold Blooded*	9.1983
8039	**Commodores**	*13*	9.1983
8040	**Stevie Wonder**	*People Move, Human Plays*	NR
8041	**Lionel Richie**	*Can't Slow Down*	10.1983

(European system applies).

PICKWICK SERIES: TMS

3501	**Smokey Robinson & the Miracles**	*Tears Of A Clown*	6.1982
3502	**Four Tops**	*The Fabulous Four Tops*	6.1982
3503	**Jackson 5 featuring Michael Jackson**	*The Jackson 5 Featuring Michael Jackson*	6.1982
3504	**Stevie Wonder**	*The Special Magic Of Stevie Wonder*	6.1982
3505	**Diana Ross & the Supremes**	*Dynamic Diana*	6.1982
3506	**Gladys Knight & the Pips**	*Every Beat Of My Heart*	6.1982
3507	**The Temptations**	*Get Ready*	6.1982

3508	**Marvin Gaye**	*The Magic Of Marvin Gaye*	6.1982
3509	**Various**	*Motown Love Songs*	9.1982
3510	**Smokey Robinson**	*Hot Smokey*	9.1982
3511	**Michael Jackson**	*Ain't No Sunshine*	9.1982
3512	**Various**	*Motown Dance Machine*	9.1982
3513	**Diana Ross & the Supremes & The Temptations**	*Diana Ross And The Supremes With The Temptations*	9.1982
3514	**Four Tops**	*Hits Of Gold*	9.1982

STMS SERIES: STMS

5001	**Diana Ross & Marvin Gaye**	*Diana & Marvin*	8.1981
5002	**Commodores**	*Machine Gun*	8.1981
5003	**Commodores**	*Movin' On*	8.1981
5004	**Four Tops**	*Reach Out*	8.1981
5005	**Marvin Gaye & Tammi Terrell**	*You're All I Need*	8.1981
5006	**Jackson 5**	*Diana Ross Presents*	8.1981
5007	**Michael Jackson**	*Got To Be There*	8.1981
5008	**Michael Jackson**	*Ben*	8.1981
5009	**Martha Reeves & the Vandellas**	*Heatwave*	8.1981
5010	**Smokey Robinson & the Miracles**	*The Tears Of A Clown*	8.1981
5011	**Smokey Robinson**	*Smokey*	8.1981
5012	**Diana Ross & the Supremes**	*I Hear A Symphony*	8.1981
5013	**Diana Ross & the Supremes**	*A Go Go*	8.1981
5014	**Diana Ross & the Supremes**	*Sing Motown*	8.1981
5015	**Diana Ross & the Supremes & The Temptations**	*Diana Ross And The Supremes Join The Temptations*	8.1981
5016	**The Supremes & Four Tops**	*Magnificent Seven*	8.1981
5017	**Diana Ross**	*Diana Ross*	8.1981
5018	**Diana Ross**	*Touch Me In The Morning*	8.1981
5019	**Diana Ross**	*Live!*	8.1981
5020	**The Temptations**	*Cloud Nine*	8.1981
5021	**The Temptations**	*Masterpiece*	8.1981
5022	**Stevie Wonder**	*Down To Earth*	8.1981
5023	**Stevie Wonder**	*Uptight*	8.1981
5024	**Stevie Wonder**	*My Cherie Amour*	8.1981
5025	**Stevie Wonder**	*Signed, Sealed & Delivered*	8.1981
5026	**The Isley Brothers**	*This Old Heart Of Mine*	8.1981
5027	**Grover Washington Jr**	*Mr. Magic*	8.1981
5028	**Grover Washington Jr**	*Feels So Good*	8.1981
5029	**Grover Washington Jr**	*A Secret Place*	8.1981
5030	**Thelma Houston**	*Sunshower*	8.1981
5031	**Diana Ross**	*I'm Still Waiting*	3.1982
5032	**Commodores**	*Caught In The Act*	3.1982
5033	**Four Tops**	*Four Tops*	3.1982
5034	**Marvin Gaye**	*Let's Get It On*	3.1982
5035	**Marvin Gaye**	*Live!*	3.1982
5036	**Marvin Gaye & Tammi Terrell**	*United*	3.1982
5037	**Jackson 5**	*Third Album*	3.1982
5038	**Jackson 5**	*Greatest Hits*	3.1982
5039	**Gladys Knight & the Pips**	*Everybody Needs Love*	3.1982
5040	**Gladys Knight & and the Pips**	*Nitty Gritty*	3.1982
5041	**Gladys Knight & the Pips**	*Neither One Of Us*	3.1982
5042	**Martha Reeves & the Vandellas**	*Greatest Hits*	3.1982
5043	**Smokey Robinson**	*Pure Smokey*	3.1982
5044	**Smokey Robinson**	*A Quiet Storm*	3.1982
5045	**Diana Ross & and the Supremes**	*At The Copa*	3.1982

5046	Diana Ross & the Supremes & The Temptations	TCB	3.1982
5047	Diana Ross	Everything Is Everything	3.1982
5048	Diana Ross	Diana! (orig. tv soundtrack)	3.1982
5049	Diana Ross	The Boss	3.1982
5050	The Temptations	Puzzle People	3.1982
5051	The Temptations	Psychedelic Shack	3.1982
5052	The Temptations	All Directions	3.1982
5053	The Temptations	All The Million Sellers	3.1982
5054	Jr Walker & the All Stars	Greatest Hits	3.1982
5055	Grover Washington Jr	Inner City Blues	3.1982
5056	Grover Washington Jr	All The King's Horses	3.1982
5057	Mary Wells	My Guy	3.1982
5058	Stevie Wonder	The Jazz Soul Of Little Stevie	3.1982
5059	Stevie Wonder	Tribute To Uncle Ray	3.1982
5060	Stevie Wonder	With A Song In My Heart	3.1982
5061	Commodores	Zoom	6.1982
5062	Bobby Darin	1936-1973	8.1982
5063	Four Tops	Still Waters Run Deep	6.1982
5064	Marvin Gaye	MPG	8.1982
5065	Marvin Gaye	Trouble Man	7.1982
5066	Marvin Gaye & Tammi Terrell	Greatest Hits	7.1982
5067	Thelma Houston	Any Way You Like It	8.1982
5068	Jackson 5	ABC	6.1982
5069	Stephanie Mills	For The First Time	7.1982
5070	Diana Ross & the Supremes	Love Child	8.1982
5071	Diana Ross	Last Time I Saw Him	8.1982
5072	Grover Washington Jr	Reed Seed	6.1982
5073	Grover Washington Jr	Skylarkin'	7.1982
5074	Stevie Wonder	For Once In My Life	6.1982
5075	Stevie Wonder	Where I'm Coming From	7.1982
5076	Commodores	Hot On The Tracks	10.1982
5077	Four Tops	Second Album	10.1982
5078	Rick James	Come Get It!	10.1982
5079	Syreeta	Stevie Wonder Presents	10.1982
5080	Various	From The Vaults	11.1982
5081	Commodores	Natural High	11.1982
5082	Diana Ross	Mahogany (f/s.)	11.1982
5083	Jackson 5	Christmas Album	11.1982
5084	Diana Ross & the Supremes	Merry Christmas	11.1982
5085	The Temptations	Give Love At Christmas	11.1982
5086	Stevie Wonder	Someday At Christmas	11.1982
5087	Four Tops	Live!	2.1983
5088	Marvin Gaye	Marvin Gaye & His Girls	2.1983
5089	Jackson 5	Lookin' Through The Windows	2.1983
5090	Diana Ross & the Supremes	More Hits	4.1983
5091	The Temptations	. . . Sing Smokey	NR
5092	Various	Original Motortown Revue – Live!	4.1983
5093	Mary Wells	Greatest Hits	2.1983
5094	Stevie Wonder	I Was Made To Love Her	2.1983
5095	Michael Jackson	Forever Michael	6.1983
5096	Gladys Knight & the Pips	Help Me Make It Through The Night	6.1983
5097	Diana Ross	Baby It's Me	6.1983
5098	The Supremes	Greatest Hits	6.1983
5099	Grover Washington Jr	Greatest Performances	6.1983
5100	Various	Motown Superstars Sing Motown Superstars	8.1983
5101	Jackson 5	Skywriter	NR
5102	Stevie Wonder	Live! At The Talk Of The Town	NR
5103	Diana Ross & the Supremes	Reflections	NR
5104	Edwin Starr	The Hits Of Edwin Starr	NR

5105	Various	25 Years Of Motown Classics – The Grammy Award Winners	10.1983
5106	Various	The Incredible Medleys	10.1983

(European system applies).

STMX SERIES

6001	Diana Ross & the Supremes	Motown Special	3.1977
6002	The Temptations	Motown Special	3.1977
6003	Diana Ross & the Supremes & The Temptations	Motown Special	3.1977
6004	Four Tops	Motown Special	3.1977
6005	Jr Walker & the All Stars	Motown Special	3.1977
6006	Jackson 5	Motown Special	3.1977
6007	Various	Motown Extra Special	3.1977
6008	Gladys Knight & the Pips	Motown Special	NR
6009	The Supremes & Four Tops	Motown Special	NR

STMR SERIES

9001	Various Artists	From the Vaults	5.1979
9002	Various Artists	It Takes Two	6.1979
9003	Little Stevie Wonder	12-Year-Old Genius, Recorded Live!	4.1980
9004	Marvin Gaye	Early Years: 1961-1964	10.1980
9005	The Temptations	The Temptations Sing Smokey	2.1980
9006	Diana Ross & the Supremes	More Hits	9.1979
9007	Four Tops	Second Album	2.1980
9008	Diana Ross & the Supremes	Early Years: 1961-1964	10.1980
9009	Michael Jackson	The Best Of Michael Jackson	3.1980
9010	The Supremes featuring Mary Wilson	Greatest Hits	4.1980
9011	Detroit Spinners	20 Golden Classics	6.1980
9012	Jimmy Ruffin	20 Golden Classics	7.1980
9013	Various Artists	20 Christmas Classics	11.1980
9014	Syreeta	The Best Of Syreeta	4.1981
9015	Stevie Wonder	Early Years: 1962-1966	NR
9016	Smokey Robinson & the Miracles	Early Years: 1958-1964	NR
9017	Martha Reeves & the Vandellas	Anthology (re-issue STML 12060)	9.1982
9018	The Marvelettes	Anthology	9.1982
9019	Willie Hutch	In And Out	2.1983
9020	Various	Girl Groups: Story Of A Sound (f/s.)	1.1984
9021	Various	The Big Chill (f/s.)	2.1984
9022	Various	Christine (f/s.)	2.1984

European numbers apply from here (European system applies).

EUROPEAN SERIES

ZL/ZK/ZD – full price; WL/WK/WD – mid price; TL/TK/TD – budget price; ZL/WL/TL – albums; ZK/WK/TK – cassettes; ZD/WD/TD – compact discs; NM – not manufactured.
Bracketed figures are the original numbers allocated on the UK listing. All new European numbers start from 1984 onwards and conversions are made when new stock is ordered.

72001 ZL	Stevie Wonder	Characters (ZD: 11.1987)	11.1987
72002 ZL	Bobby Nunn	Private Party (STML 12199)	
72003 ZL	The Dazz Band	Joystick (STML 12201)	
72004 ZL	DeBarge	In A Special Way (STML 12200)	

72005 ZL	**Stevie Wonder**	*In Square Circle* (ZD: 11.1985)	9.1985
72006 ZL	**Various**	*Big Wheels Of Motown* (MTV 12)	
72007 ZL	**Various**	*The Last Dance* (MTV 20)	
72008 ZL	**Diana Ross**	*20 Golden Greats* (MTV 21)	
72009 ZL	**Diana Ross & the Supremes**	*20 Golden Greats* (MTV 5)	
72010 ZL	**Diana Ross**	*Greatest Hits* (STMA 8006)	
72011 ZL	**Stevie Wonder**	*Talking Book* (ZD: 3.1986) (STMA 8007)	
72012 ZL	**Stevie Wonder**	*Innervisions* (ZD: 3.1986) (STMA 8011)	
72013 ZL	**Stevie Wonder**	*Fulfillingness First Finale* (STMA 8019)	
72014 ZL	**Diana Ross**	*Diana* (STMA 8033)	
72015 ZL	**Stevie Wonder**	*Hotter Than July* (ZD: 12.1986) (STMA 8035)	
72016 ZL	**Diana Ross**	*All The Great Hits* (STMA 8036)	
72017 ZL	**Lionel Richie**	*Lionel* (ZD: 8.1986) (STMA 8037)	
72018 ZL	**Rick James**	*Cold Blooded* (STMA 8038)	
72019 ZL	**Commodores**	*13* (STMA 8039)	
72020 ZL	**Lionel Richie**	*Can't Slow Down* (ZD: 8.1986) (STMA 8041)	
72021 WL	**Various**	*The Motown Sound: 16 Big Hits From The Late 60s* (STMF 7001) NM – trans. to WL72385	
72022 ZL	**Various**	*British Motown Chartbusters* (STML 11055)	
72023 ZL	**Stevie Wonder**	*Greatest Hits* (STML 11075)	
72024 ZL	**Various**	*Motown Chartbusters Vol. 3* (STML 11121)	
72025 ZL	**Marvin Gaye**	*What's Going On* (STML 11190)	
72026 ZL	**Stevie Wonder**	*Greatest Hits Vol. 2* (STML 11196)	
72027 WL	**Marvin Gaye**	*I Want You* (STML 12025)	
72028 ZL	**Diana Ross**	*Greatest Hits/2* (STML 12036)	
72029 ZL	**Marvin Gaye**	*The Best Of . . .* (STML 12042)	
72030 ZL	**Commodores**	*Greatest Hits* (STML 12100)	
72031 ZL	**Jackson 5**	*20 Golden Greats* (STML 12121)	
72032 ZL	**Various**	*20 Mod Classics* (STML 12125)	
72033 ZL	**Various**	*20 Mod Classics Vol. 2* (STML 12133)	
72034 ZL	**Various**	*Motown Chartbusters 80 (Vol. 11)* (STML 12139)	
72035 ZL	**Diana Ross**	*To Love Again* (STML 12152)	
72036 ZL	**Rick James**	*Street Songs* (STML 12153)	
72037 ZL	**Teena Marie**	*It Must Be Magic* (STML 12154)	
72038 ZL	**Michael Jackson**	*One Day In Your Life* (STML 12158)	
72039 ZL	**Jermaine Jackson**	*I Like Your Style* (STML 12160)	
72040 ZL	**José Feliciano**	*José Feliciano* (STML 12161)	
72041 WL	**Diana Ross**	*Diana's Duets* (STML 12163)	

72042 ZL	**Various**	*Motown Chartbusters Vol. 12* (STML 12164)
72043 ZL	**Smokey Robinson**	*Yes It's You Lady* (STML 12165)
72044 ZL	**Rick James**	*Throwin' Down* (STML 12167)
72045 ZL	**Bobby Womack**	*The Poet* (STML 12168)
72046 ZL	**Charlene**	*I've Never Been To Me* (STML 12171)
72047 ZL	**Smokey Robinson**	*Touch The Sky* (STML 12175)
72048 ZL	**Bobby M**	*Blow . . . Rick James Presents* (STML 12180)
72049 ZL	**The Dazz Band**	*On The One* (STML 12181)
72050 ZL	**The Temptations**	*Surface Thrills* (STML 12182)
72051 ZL	**Commodores**	*All The Great Hits* (STML 12183)
72052 ZL	**Syreeta**	*The Spell* (STML 12184)
72053 ZL	**José Feliciano**	*Romance In The Night* (STML 12185)
72054 ZL	**DeBarge**	*All This Love* (STML 12186)
72055 ZL	**Mary Jane Girls**	*Mary Jane Girls* (STML 12189)
72056 ZL	**Stone City Band**	*Out From the Shadow Meet The . . .* (STML 12190)
72057 ZL	**Finis Henderson**	*Finis* (STML 12191)
72058 ZL	**Michael Lovesmith**	*I Can Make It Happen* (STML 12192)
72059 ZL	**Smokey Robinson**	*Blame It On Love All The Great Hits* (STML 12193)
72060 ZL	**Jr Walker**	*Blow The House Down* (STML 12194)
72061 ZL	**The Temptations**	*Back To Basics* (STML 12196)
72062 ZL	**Four Tops**	*Back Where I Belong* (STML 12197)
72063 WL	**Michael Jackson**	*The Best Of . . .* (STMR 9009)
72064 ZL	**Various**	*20 Christmas Classics* (STMR 9013)
72065 ZL	**Willie Hutch**	*In And Out* (STMR 9019)
72066 WL	**Diana Ross & Marvin Gaye**	*Diana & Marvin* (STMS 5001)
72067 WL	**Four Tops**	*Reach Out* (STMS 5004)
72068 WL	**Michael Jackson**	*Got To Be There* (STMS 5007)
72069 WL	**Michael Jackson**	*Ben* (STMS 5008)
72070 WL	**Martha Reeves & the Vandellas**	*Heatwave* (STMS 5009)
72071 WL	**Smokey Robinson & the Miracles**	*The Tears Of A Clown* (STMS 5010)
72072 WL	**Diana Ross & the Supremes**	*Supremes A Go-Go* (STMS 5013)
72073 WL	**Diana Ross**	*Diana Ross* (STMS 5017)
72074 WL	**Diana Ross**	*Touch Me In The Morning* (STMS 5018)
72075 WL	**Diana Ross**	*Live!* (STMS 5019)
72076 WL	**The Temptations**	*Masterpiece* (STMS 5021)
72077 WL	**Stevie Wonder**	*My Cherie Amour* (STMS 50234)
72078 WL	**Isley Brothers**	*This Old Heart Of Mine* (STMS 5026)

72079 WL	**Grover Washington Jr**	*Mister Magic* (STMS 5027)	
72080 WL	**Grover Washington Jr**	*Feels So Good* (STMS 5028)	
72081 WL	**Grover Washington Jr**	*A Secret Place* (STMS 5029)	
72082 WL	**Diana Ross**	*I'm Still Waiting* (STMS 5031)	
72083 WL	**Commodores**	*Caught In The Act* (STMS 5032)	
72084 WL	**Four Tops**	*Four Tops* (STMS 5033)	
72085 WL	**Marvin Gaye**	*Let's Get It On* (WD: 4.1988) (STMS 5034)	
72086 WL	**Marvin Gaye**	*Live!* (WD: 3.1988) (STMS 5035)	
72087 WL	**Jackson 5**	*Greatest Hits* (WD: 2.1988) (STMS 5038)	
72088 WL	**Gladys Knight & the Pips**	*Everybody Needs Love* (STMS 5039)	
72089 WL	**Martha Reeves & the Vandellas**	*Greatest Hits* (STMS 5042)	
72090 WL	**Smokey Robinson**	*Pure Smokey* (STMS 5043)	
72091 WL	**Diana Ross & the Supremes**	*Live! At The Copa* (STMS 5045)	
72092 WL	**Diana Ross & the Supremes & the Temptations**	*T.C.B.* (STMS 5046)	
72093 WL	**Diana Ross**	*Everything Is Everything* (STMS 5047)	
72094 WL	**Diana Ross**	*Diana! (TV soundtrack)* (STMS 5048)	
72095 WL	**Diana Ross**	*The Boss* (STMS 5049)	
72096 WL	**The Temptations**	*All The Million Sellers* (WD: 2.1988) (STMS 5053)	
72097 WL	**Jr Walker & the All Stars**	*Greatest Hits* (STMS 5054)	
72098 WL	**Grover Washington Jr**	*Inner City Blues* (WD: 2.1988) (STMS 5055)	
72099 WL	**Grover Washington Jr**	*All The Kings Horses* (STMS 5056)	
72100 WL	**Stevie Wonder**	*With A Song In My Heart* (STMS 5060)	
72101 WL	**Commodores**	*Zoom* (STMS 5061)	
72102 WL	**Bobby Darin**	*1936-1973* (STMS 5062)	
72103 WL	**Marvin Gaye & Tammi Terrell**	*Greatest Hits* (STMS 5066)	
72104 WL	**Jackson 5**	*ABC* (STMS 5068)	
72105 WL	**Diana Ross & the Supremes**	*Love Child* (STMS 5070)	
72106 WL	**Grover Washington Jr**	*Reed Seed* (STMS 5072)	
72107 WL	**Grover Washington Jr**	*Skylarkin'* (STMS 5073)	
72108 WL	**Stevie Wonder**	*Where I'm Coming From* (STMS 5075)	
72109 WL	**Rick James**	*Come Get It* (STMS 5078)	
72110 WL	**Various**	*From The Vaults* (STMS 5080)	
72111 WL	**Commodores**	*Natural High* (STMS 5081)	
72112 WL	**Jackson 5**	*Christmas Album* (STMS 5083)	
72113 WL	**Diana Ross & the Supremes**	*Merry Christmas* (STMS 5084)	
72114 WL	**Four Tops**	*Live!* (STMS 5087)	
72115 WL	**Marvin Gaye**	*Marvin Gaye And His Girls* (STMS 5088)	
72116 WL	**Jackson 5**	*Lookin' Through The Windows* (STMS 5089)	
72117 WL	**Diana Ross & the Supremes**	*More Hits* (STMS 5090)	
72118 WL	**Various**	*Motortown Revue Recorded Live!* (STMS 5092)	
72119 WL	**Mary Wells**	*Greatest Hits* (STMS 5093)	
72120 WL	**Stevie Wonder**	*I Was Made To Love Her* (STMS 5094)	
72121 WL	**Michael Jackson**	*Forever, Michael* (STMS 5095)	
72122 WL	**Gladys Knight & the Pips**	*Help Me Make It Through The Night* (STMS 5096)	
72123 WL	**Diana Ross**	*Baby It's Me* (STMS 5097)	
72124 WL	**The Supremes**	*Greatest Hits* (STMS 5098)	
72125 WL	**Grover Washington Jr**	*Greatest Performances* (STMS 5099)	
72126 WL	**Various**	*Motown Superstars Sing Motown Superstars* (STMS 5100)	
72127 WL	**Various**	*25 Years Of Grammy Award Winners* (STMS 5105)	
72128 WL	**Various**	*The Incredible Medleys* (STMS 5106)	
72129 ZL	**Diana Ross**	*Lady Sings The Blues* (2-LP) (ZD: 5.1986) (TMSP 1131)	
72130 ZL	**Diana Ross & the Supremes**	*Anthology* (2-LP) (TMSP 6001)	
72131 ZL	**Stevie Wonder**	*Songs In The Key Of Life* (2-LP) (ZD: 6.1985) (TMSP 6002)	
72132 ZL	**Various**	*20th Anniversary Album* (2-LP) (TMSP 6010)	
72133 ZL	**Stevie Wonder**	*Original Musiquarium 1* (2-LP) (ZD: 6.1985) (TMSP 6012)	
72134 ZL	**Smokey Robinson & the Miracles**	*Anthology* (2-LP) (TMSP 6014)	
72135 WL	**Diana Ross**	*Anthology* *The Very Best Of . . .* (2-LP) (TMSP 6017)	
72136 WL/ZD	**Various**	*20 US No. 1 Hits From 25 Years* (2-LP) (ZD: 12.1985) (TMSP 6018)	
72137 ZL	**Various**	*The Motown Story* (5-LP) (ZD: 2.1987) (TMSP 6019)	
72138 ZL	**Various**	*The Big Chill* (f/s.) (STMR 9021)	
72139 ZL	**Various**	*Christine* (f/s.) (STMR 9022)	
72140 WL	**Various**	*Girl Groups: Story Of A Sound* (f/s.) (STMR 9020)	
72141 ZL	**Commodores**	*Anthology* (2-LP)	Eur only
72142 ZL	**Commodores**	*'Live'* (2-LP)	Eur only
72143 WL	**Rare Earth**	*Get Ready*	Eur only
72144 WL	**Various**	*Top 10 With A Bullet – Motown Girl Groups*	6.1984
72145 ZL	**Stevie Wonder**	*The Secret Life Of Plants* (2-LP) (ZD: 3.1986) (TMSP 6009)	
72146 ZL	**Stevie Wonder**	*Music Of My Mind* (STMA 8002)	
72147 ZL	**Rockwell**	*Somebody's Watching Me*	2.1984
72148 ZL	**Dennis Edwards**	*Don't Look Any Further*	4.1984
72149 ZL	**Kidd Glove**	*Kidd Glove*	4.1984

Cat. No.	Artist	Title	Date/Status
72150 ZL	**Tiggi Clay**	*Tiggi Clay*	4.1984
72151 ZL	**Bobby King**	*Love In The Fire*	4.1984
72152 ZL	**Smokey Robinson**	*Essar*	8.1984
72153 ZL	**Marvelettes**	*Anthology* (STMR 9018)	
72154 WL	**Diana Ross & the Supremes & The Temptations**	*Diana Ross & The Supremes Join The Temptations* (STMS 5015)	
72155 WL	**Smokey Robinson**	*Smokey* (STMS 5011)	
72156 ZL	**Marvin Gaye**	*Anthology* (2-LP) (TMSP 1128)	
72157 ZL	**Jackson 5**	*Anthology* (2-LP) (TMSP 6004)	
72158 ZL	**Michael Jackson & Jackson 5**	*18 Greatest Hits* (TELSTAR 2232)	Eur only
72159 ZL	**Marvin Gaye**	*20 Golden Greats*	Eur only
72160 ZL	**The Temptations**	*20 Golden Greats* (STML 12140)	
72161 ZL	**Various**	*Motown Gold Vol. 1*	Eur only
72162 ZL	**Various**	*The Duet Album*	Eur only
72163 ZL	**Various**	*Motown's Dream Girls*	Eur only
72164 ZL	**Isley Brothers**	*Super Hits* (STMA 8024)	
72165 ZL	**Various**	*Motown Chartbusters Vol. 2* (STML 11082)	
72166 ZL	**Martha Reeves & the Vandellas**	*Anthology* (STMR 9017)	
72167 WL	**Diana Ross & the Supremes**	*I Hear A Symphony* (STMS 5012)	
72168 ZL	**Grover Washington Jr**	*Anthology* (2-LP) (TMSP 6015)	
72169 WL	**Various**	*Top 10 With A Bullet – Motown Love Songs*	6.1984
72170 WL	**Various**	*Top 10 With A Bullet – Motown Dance*	6.1984
72171 WL	**Various**	*Top 10 With A Bullet – Motown Male Groups*	6.1984
72172 WL	**Various**	*Top 10 With A Bullet – Motown Solo Stars*	6.1984
72173 ZL	**The Coyote Sisters**	*Coyote Sisters*	10.1984
72174 ZL	**Rick James**	*Reflections* (ZD: 2.1985)	8.1984
72175 ZL	**Gene Van Buren**	*Love Never Dies*	NM
72176 ZL	**Charlene**	*Hit And Run Lover*	10.1984
72177 ZL	**Wolf & Wolf**	*Wolf And Wolf*	8.1984
72178 ZL	**The Temptations**	*Anthology* (2-LP) (TMSP 6003)	
72179 ZL	**Stevie Wonder**	*Wonderland*	NM
72180 WL	**Stevie Wonder**	*Down To Earth*	Eur only
72181 WL	**Stevie Wonder**	*Tribute To Uncle Ray* (STMS 5059)	
72182 WL	**Stevie Wonder**	*Jazz Soul Of Little Stevie* (STMS 5058)	
72183 WL	**Stevie Wonder**	*For Once In My Life* (STMS 5074)	
72184 ZL	**Stevie Wonder**	*12 Year Old Genius Live!* (STMR 9003)	
72185 WL	**Stevie Wonder**	*Uptight* (STMS 5023)	
72186 WL	**Stevie Wonder**	*Signed, Sealed, Delivered* (STMS 5025)	
72187 ZL	**Various**	*Making Trax: The Great Instrumentals*	10.1984
72188 ZL	**Various**	*More Songs That Inspired 'The Big Chill'*	NM
72189 WL	**Various**	*Great Grammy R&B Performances Of The 70s*	NM
72190 WL	**Various**	*Great Grammy R&B Performances of the 60s*	NM
72191 ZL	**KoKo-Pop**	*KoKo-Pop*	NM
72192 ZL	**Michael Lovesmith**	*Diamond In The Raw*	Eur only
72193 ZL	**Duke Jupiter**	*White Knuckle Ride*	10.1984
72194 WL	**Diana Ross & Marvin Gaye**	*Diana & Marvin* (WL 72066)	NM
72195 WL	**Jackson 5**	*Greatest Hits* (WL 72087)	NM
72196 WL	**Marvin Gaye**	*Let's Get It On* (WL 72085)	NM
72197 WL	**Diana Ross**	*I'm Still Waiting* (WL 72082)	NM
72198 WL	**Diana Ross**	*Touch Me In The Morning* (WL 72074)	NM
72199 WL	**Michael Jackson**	*Ben* (WL 72069)	NM
72200 WL	**Commodores**	*Zoom* (WL 72101)	NM
72201 WL	**The Temptations**	*All The Million Sellers* (WL 72096)	NM
72202 WL	**Grover Washington Jr**	*Skylarkin'* (WL 72107)	NM
72203 WL	**Stevie Wonder**	*My Cherie Amour* (WL 72077)	NM
72204 WL	**Various**	*Top 10 With A Bullet – This Is Motown*	6.1984
72205 ZL	**Bobby Womack**	*Poet II*	4.1984
72206 WL	**Marvin Gaye**	*M.P.G.* (STMS 5064)	
72207 WL	**Marvin Gaye**	*That Stubborn Kind Of Fellow*	Eur only
72208 WL	**Marvin Gaye & Tammi Terrell**	*You're All I Need* (STMS 5005)	
72209 ZL	**Marvin Gaye**	*The Best Of . . .* (ZL 72029)	NM
72210 WL	**Marvin Gaye**	*Tribute To Nat King Cole*	Eur only
72211 WL	**Marvin Gaye & Tammi Terrell**	*United* (STMS 5036)	
72212 ZL	**Marvin Gaye**	*In Our Lifetime* (STMS 12149)	
72213 WL/WK/ZD	**Marvin Gaye**	*Live! At The London Palladium* (2-LP) (ZD: 3.1987)	8.1986
72214 WL	**Marvin Gaye & Mary Wells**	*Together*	Eur only
72215 WL	**Marvin Gaye**	*Trouble Man* (STMS 5065)	
72216 ZL	**Marvin Gaye**	*The Hits Of . . .* (STML 11201)	
72217 ZL	**Meatloaf**	*Featuring Stoney & Meatloaf* (PDL 2010)	
72218 WL	**Various**	*Motown Gold Vol. 2*	Eur only
72219 WL	**Rare Earth**	*Ecology*	Eur only
72220 ZD	**Four Tops**	*Compact Command Performances: 19 Greatest Hits* (WD: 10.1987)	10.1984
72221 ZD	**Diana Ross**	*All The Great Love Songs*	10.1984
72222 ZD	**Commodores**	*All The Great Love Songs*	10.1984
72223 ZD	**Stevie Wonder**	*Songs In The Key Of Life Vol. 1*	NM
72224 ZD	**Stevie Wonder**	*Songs In The Key Of Life Vol. 2*	NM

72225 ZD	**Stevie Wonder**	*Original Musiquarium Vol. 1*	NM
72226 ZD	**Stevie Wonder**	*Original Musiquarium Vol. 2*	NM
72227 ZL	**Michael Jackson**	*Farewell My Summer Love*	5.1984
72228 WL	**Various**	*Motown's Love Songs* (COMP-NL)	Eur only
72229 ZL	**Marvin Gaye**	*Every Great Motown Hit*	Eur only
72230 ZL	**Kagny**	*Mind Control*	NM
72231 ZL	**The Coyote Sisters**	*The Coyote Sisters* (trans. to ZL 72173)	NM
72232 WL	**Martin Luther King**	*Free At Last*	NM
72233 WL	**Martin Luther King**	*Great March On Washington*	NM
72234 WL	**Martin Luther King**	*Great March To Freedom*	NM
72235 WL	**Various**	*Every Great Motown Song – The First 25 Years – Vol. 1 The 1960s*	3.1988
72236 WL	**Various**	*Every Great Motown Song – The First 25 Years – Vol. 2 The 1970s*	3.1988
72237 ZL	**Sam Harris**	*Sam Harris* (ZD: NM)	10.1984
72238 WL	**Diana Ross & the Supremes**	*. . . Sing Motown* (STMS 5014)	
72239 WL	**Jackson 5**	*Third Album* (STMS 5037)	
72240 ZL	**Michal Jackson & Jackson 5**	*16 Greatest Hits* (trans. to ZL 72293)	NM
72241 ZK	**Various**	*15 Succes De L'Eté* (cassette only)	Eur only
72242 WL	**Commodores**	*Hot On The Tracks* (STMS 5076)	
72243 WL	**The Temptations**	*A Song For You*	Eur only
72244 WL	**Diana Ross & the Supremes**	*Motown Superstar Series Vol. 1*	Eur only
72245 WL	**Four Tops**	*Motown Superstar Series Vol. 14*	Eur only
72246 WL	**Isley Brothers**	*Motown Superstar Series Vol. 6*	Eur only
72247 WL	**Michael Jackson**	*Motown Superstar Series Vol. 7*	Eur only
72248 WL	**Rare Earth**	*Motown Superstar Series Vol. 16*	Eur only
72249 WL	**Commodores**	*Midnight Magic*	4.1985
72250 ZL	**Commodores**	*Heroes*	Eur only
72251 ZL	**Rick James**	*Fire It Up*	Eur only
72252 ZL	**Rick James**	*Garden Of Love*	Eur only
72253 ZL	**Billy Preston**	*Late At Night*	Eur only
72254 WL	**The Temptations**	*Greatest Hits*	Eur only
72255 WL	**Jermaine Jackson**	*Let's Get Serious*	4.1985
72256 WL	**Smokey Robinson**	*Being With You*	4.1985
72257 ZL	**Jermaine Jackson**	*Jermaine*	Eur only
72258 ZL	**Billy Preston**	*The Way I Am*	Eur only
72259 WL	**The Dazz Band**	*Let The Music Play*	Eur only
72260 ZL	**Commodores**	*In The Pocket*	Eur only
72261 ZL	**Billy Preston & Syreeta**	*Billy Preston & Syreeta*	Eur only
72262 ZL	**The Temptations**	*The Temptations*	Eur only

72263 ZL	**Syreeta**	*Set My Love In Motion*	Eur only
72264 ZL	**Dazz Band**	*Keep It Live*	Eur only
72265 ZL	**Bobby Nunn**	*Second To Nunn*	Eur only
72266 ZL	**High Inergy**	*Groove Patrol*	Eur only
72267 WL	**Grover Washington Jr**	*Live! At The Bijou* (2-LP)	5.1986
72268 WL	**Diana Ross**	*An Evening With . . .* (2-LP)	9.1985
72269 WL	**Grover Washington Jr**	*Baddest* (2-LP) (TMSP 6011)	
72270 WL	**Diana Ross & the Supremes**	*Greatest Hits Vol 1 & 2* (2-LP)	Eur only
72271 WL	**Jackson 5**	*Diana Ross Presents . . .*	
72272 WL	**The Temptations**	*Psychedelic Shack* (STMS 5051)	
72273 WL	**The Temptations**	*Cloud Nine* (STMS 5020)	
72274 WL	**Grover Washington Jr**	*Soul Box Vol. 1*	Eur only
72275 WL	**The Temptations**	*Puzzle People* (STMS 5050)	
72276 WL	**Diana Ross & the Supremes**	*. . . Sing Holland-Dozier-Holland*	Eur only
72277 WL	**Marvin Gaye**	*Greatest Hits*	Eur only
72278 WL	**Diana Ross & the Supremes**	*Greatest Hits Vol. 3*	Eur only
72279 WL	**Grover Washington Jr**	*Soul Box Vol.2*	Eur only
72280 WL	**Four Tops**	*Greatest Hits* (WD: 2.1988)	4.1985
72281 WL	**Commodores**	*Movin' On* (STMS 5003)	
72282 WL	**Commodores**	*Machine Gun* (STMS 5002)	
72283 ZL	**Vanity**	*Wild Animal*	10.1984
72284 ZL	**Jakata**	*Light The Night*	10.1984
72285 ZL	**Stevie Wonder**	*Woman In Red* (f/s.) (ZD: 12.1984)	9.1984
72286 WL	**Rare Earth**	*Ma*	Eur only
72287 WL	**Rare Earth**	*Rarearth*	Eur only
72288 WL	**Rare Earth**	*Rare Earth In Concert* (2-LP)	Eur only
72289 WL	**Michael Jackson**	*The Great Love Songs Of*	11.1984
72290 WL	**Jackson 5**	*The Great Love Songs Of . . .*	11.1984
72291 WL	**Michael Jackson**	*Music And Me*	11.1984
72292 WL	**Jackson 5**	*Skywriter*	11.1984
72293 ZL	**Michael Jackson & Jackson 5**	*14 Greatest Hits*	NM
72294 ZK	**Michael Jackson & Jackson 5**	*16 Greatest Hits* (cassette only)	NM
72295 ZL	**Ada Dyer**	*—*	NM
72296 ZL	**José Feliciano**	*Los Exitos De José Feliciano*	Eur only
72297 ZD	**Various**	*Great Grammy R&B Performances Of The 1960s, and 1970s*	2.1985
72298 ZL	**Phyllis St James**	*Ain't No Turnin' Back*	11.1984
72299 ZD	**Gladys Knight & the Pips**	*Compact Command Performances: 17 Greatest Hits*	2.1985
72300 TL	**Jackson 5 featuring Michael Jackson**	*Motown Legends*	Eur only

Cat. no.	Artist	Title	Date
72301 TL	Stevie Wonder	*Motown Legends*	Eur only
72302 TL	Diana Ross & the Supremes	*Motown Legends*	Eur only
72303 TL	Gladys Knight & the Pips	*Motown Legends*	Eur only
72304 TL	Smokey Robinson & the Miracles	*Motown Legends*	Eur only
72305 TL	Marvin Gaye	*Motown Legends*	Eur only
72306 TL	Various	*Motown Legends-Love Songs*	Eur only
72307 TL	Diana Ross & the Supremes & the Temptations	*Motown Legends*	Eur only
72308 TL	Michael Jackson	*Motown Legends*	Eur only
72309 TL	Four Tops	*Motown Legends*	Eur only
72310 ZL/ZK/ZD	Stevie Wonder	*La Fille En Rouge*	Eur only
72311 WL	Various	*The Legendary Long Versions Album*	Eur only
72312 WL	Jackson 5	*Motown Superstars Series Vol. 12*	Eur only
72313 WL	Gladys Knight & the Pips	*Motown Superstars Series Vol. 13*	Eur only
72314 WL	Martha Reeves & the Vandellas	*Motown Superstars Series Vol. 11*	Eur only
72315 WL	Smokey Robinson	*Motown Superstars Series Vol. 18*	Eur only
72316 WL	Edwin Starr	*Motown Superstars Series Vol. 3*	Eur only
72317 WL	Diana Ross & the Supremes	*Greatest Hits Vol. 2*	Eur only
72318 WL	The Marvelettes	*Greatest Hits*	Eur only

*Transferred from . . . (orig. UK cat. no.)

Cat. no.	Artist	Title	Date
72319 ZL	Rick James	*Bustin' Out*	Eur only
72320 ZL	The Temptations	*Greatest Hits Vol. 3*	Eur only
*72321 WL	The Temptations	*All Directions* (*STMS 5052)	—
72322 ZL	The Temptations	*Power*	Eur only
72323 ZL	The Temptations	*Reunion*	Eur only
72324 ZL	José Feliciano	*Escenas De Amor*	Eur only
72325 ZL	Jermaine Jackson	*Let Me Tickle Your Fancy*	Eur only
72326 ZL	Billy Preston	*Pressin' On*	Eur only
72327 ZL	José Feliciano	*Me Enamore*	Eur only
72328 ZL	Diana Ross	*Portrait*	Eur only
72329 ZL	Four Tops	*Portrait*	Eur only
72330 ZL	Jackson 5	*Portrait*	Eur only
72331 ZL	Diana Ross & the Supremes	*Portrait*	Eur only
72332 ZL	The Temptations	*Portrait*	Eur only
72333 ZL	Bobby Nunn	*Fresh*	NM
72334 ZL	Process & the Doo Rags	*Process And The Doo Rags*	NM
72335 ZL	Dazz Band	*Jukebox*	11.1984
72336 ZD	Diana Ross	*Compact Command Performances: 14 Greatest Hits*	1988
72337 ZL	Diana Ross	*All The Great Hits*	Eur only
72338 WL	Various	*Motown Gold Vol. 3*	Eur only
72339 ZL	Rockwell	*Captured*	6.1985
72340 ZL	DeBarge	*Rhythm Of The Night* (ZD: 11.1985)	5.1985
72341 ZL	Mary Jane Girls	*Only Four You* (ZD: 9.1986)	4.1985
72342 ZL	The Temptations	*Truly For You*	11.1984
72343 ZL	Commodores	*Nightshift* (ZD: 6.1985)	2.1985
72344 WL	Michael Jackson	*Michael Jackson* (box set)	Eur only
72345 WL	Marvin Gaye	*Marvin Gaye* (box set)	Eur only
72346 WL	Diana Ross	*Diana Ross* (box set)	Eur only
72347 ZD	Various	*Music From The Original Motion Soundtrack 'The Big Chill'*	6.1985
72348 WL	Various	*20 Golden Greats – Motown Sings The Beatles*	12.1984
72349 ZL	Thomas McClary	*Thomas McClary*	2.1985
*72350 ZL	Jimmy Ruffin	*20 Golden Classic* (*STMR 9012)	—
*72351 ZL	Gladys Knight & the Pips	*Anthology* (*TMSP 1127)	—
*72352 WL	Four Tops	*Anthology* (*TMSP 6013)	—
*72353 WL	Diana Ross	*Last Time I Saw Him* (*STMS 5071)	—
*72354 WL	Four Tops	*Second Album* (*STMS 5077)	—
*72355 WL	Diana Ross	*Mahogany* (f/s.) (*STMS 5082)	—
*72356 WL	The Temptations	*Give Love At Christmas* (*STMS 5085)	—
*72357 WL	Stevie Wonder	*Someday At Christmas* (*STMS 5086)	—
*72358 ZK	Various	*Cruisin' With Motown Vol. 1* (cassette only) (*CTMSP 6016)	—
*72359 ZK	Various	*Cruisin' With Motown Vol. 2* (cassette only) (*CTMSP 6022)	—
*72360 ZL	Various	*Get Crazy* (f/s.) (*STML 12195)	—
72361 ZL	Four Tops	*Magic*	7.1985

* Transferred from . . . (orig. UK cat. no.)

Cat. no.	Artist	Title	Date
72362 ZL	Rick James	*Glow*	5.1985
72363 ZL	Various	*Berry Gordy's 'The Last Dragon'* (f/s.) (ZD: 11.1985)	5.1985
72364 ZL	Syreeta	*Untitled*	NM
72365 ZD	The Temptations	*Compact Command Performances: 17 Greatest Hits*	7.1985
72366 ZD	Grover Washington Jr	*At His Best*	11.1985
72367 WL	Various	*All The Great Motown Love Song Duets*	4.1985
72368 WL	Diana Ross & the Supremes	*Reflections*	4.1985
72369 WL	Stevie Wonder	*Live! At The Talk Of The Town*	4.1985
72370 ZL	Various	*The Flamingo Kid* (f/s.)	10.1985
72371 ZL	The Emotions	*If I Only Knew*	6.1985

72372 ZL	**Maureen Steele**	*Nature Of The Beast*	7.1985
72373 WL	**Gladys Knight & the Pips**	*All The Greatest Hits*	4.1985
72374 WL	**Marvin Gaye**	*I Heard It Through The Grapevine*	4.1985
72375 WL	**Diana Ross**	*Diana Ross*	4.1985
72376 ZL	**Michael Lovesmith**	*Rhymes Of Passion*	8.1985
72377 WL	**Various**	*The Songs Of Ashford & Simpson*	NM
72378 ZL	**Willie Hutch**	*Making A Game Out Of Love*	7.1985
72379 ZD	**Various**	*The Songs Of Smokey Robinson*	3.1986
72380 ZD	**Various**	*The Songs Of Holland-Dozier-Holland*	3.1986
72381 WL	**Bill Cosby**	*Himself*	NM
72382 WL	**Diahann Carroll**	*Diahann Carroll*	8.1986
72383 ZD	**Various**	*The Greatest Songs Written By Ashford & Simpson*	3.1986
72384 WL	**Billy Preston & Syreeta**	*The Most Beautiful Songs*	Eur only
72385 WL	**Various**	*The Motown Sound – 16 Big Hits – The Late 60s*	6.1988
72386 WL	**Various**	*The Motown Sound – 16 Big Hits – The Early 60s*	6.1988
72387 ZL	**Val Young**	*Seduction*	3.1986
72388 ZD	**Various**	*The Composer: Great Love Song With Commodores And Diana Ross*	12.1985
72389 ZD	**Stevie Wonder**	*Love Songs – 20 Classic Hits (WD: 10. 1987)*	3.1986
72390 ZL	**Dennis Edwards**	*Coolin' Out*	8.1985
72391 ZL	**Dazz Band**	*Hot Spot*	9.1985
72392 ZL	**Lushus Daim & the Pretty Vain**	*More Than You Can Handle*	Eur only
72393 ZL	**Various**	*Ready, Steady Go! The Sounds Of Motown*	NM
72394 ZL	**Smokey Robinson**	*Smoke Signals (ZD: 9.1986)*	3.1986
72395 ZL	**Nick Jameson**	*A Crowd Of One*	Eur only
72396 ZL	**Koko-Pop**	*Secrets Of Lonely Boys*	NM
72397 ZD	**Marvin Gaye**	*Marvin Gaye & His Women – Classic Duets (WD: 10.1987)*	7.1986
72398 ZL	**Pal**	*Truth For The Moment*	4.1986
72399 ZL	**Vanity**	*Skin On Skin*	5.1986
72400 ZD	**Various**	*20 Greatest Songs In Motown History*	3.1986
72401 WL	**Various**	*Motown Hits Of Gold Vol. 1*	10.1985
72402 WL	**Various**	*Motown Hits Of Gold Vol. 2*	10.1985
72403 WL	**Various**	*Motown Hits Of Gold Vol. 3*	10.1985
72404 WL	**Various**	*Motown Hits Of Gold Vol. 4*	10.1985
72405 WL	**Various**	*Motown Hits Of Gold Vol. 5*	10.1985
72406 WL	**Various**	*Motown Hits Of Gold Vol. 6*	10.1985
72407 WL	**Various**	*Motown Hits Of Gold Vol. 7*	10.1985
72408 WL	**Various**	*Motown Hits Of Gold Vol 8*	10.1985
72409 WL	**Various**	*Motown: Today And Forever (promo. only)*	10.1985
72410 WL	**Various**	*150 Motown Hits Of Gold (9-LP box set)*	10.1985
72411 ZL	**Duke Jupiter**	*The Line Of Your Fire*	Eur only
72412 ZL/ZD	**Lionel Richie**	*Dancing On The Ceiling*	8.1986
72413 ZL	**The Temptations**	*Touch Me*	12.1985
72414 ZL	**Warp 9**	*Fade In, Fade Out*	3.1986
72415 ZL	**Sam Harris**	*Sam-I-Am*	5.1986
72416 ZL	**Troy Johnson**	*Getting A Grip On Love*	6.1986
72417 ZL	**Alfie**	*That Look*	NM
72418 ZL	**Guinn**	*Guinn*	4.1986
72419 ZD	**Smokey Robinson & the Miracles**	*Compact Command Performances: 18 Greatest Hits (WD: 10.1983)*	12.1986
72420 WD	**Michael Jackson & the Jackson 5**	*Compact Command Performances: 18 Greatest Hits*	10.1987
72421 ZD	**Commodores**	*Compact Command Performances: 14 Greatest Hits (WD: 10.1987)*	12.1986
72422 ZD	**Marvin Gaye**	*Compact Command Performances: 15 Greatest Hits*	8.1986
72423 ZD	**Diana Ross & the Supremes**	*Compact Command Performances: 20 Greatest Hits*	9.1986
72424 WL	**Michael Jackson**	*Looking Back To Yesterday Never-Before-Released Masters*	5.1986
72425 WL	**Various**	*Never-Before-Released Masters From Motown's Brightest Stars – The 1960s*	5.1986
72426 ZL	**Marvin Gaye**	*Motown Remembers Marvin Gaye*	Eur only
72427 WL	**Rick James**	*Greatest Hits*	8.1986
72428 WL	**Teena Marie**	*Greatest Hits And More*	11.1986
72429 WL	**Edwin Starr**	*The Hits Of Edwin Starr: 20 Greatest Motown Hits*	2.1987
72430 WL	**Diana Ross**	*Diana (Chic LP)*	3.1987
72431 WL	**Various**	*Big Motown Hits & Hard To Find Classics Vol. 1*	6.1986
72432 WL	**Various**	*Big Motown Hits & Hard To Find Classics Vol.2*	6.1986
72433 WL	**Dazz Band**	*Greatest Hits*	6.1986
72434 WL	**Gladys Knight & the Pips**	*If I Were Your Woman*	NM
72435 WL	**The Temptations**	*25th Anniversary (2-LP)*	6.1986
72436 WL	**Diana Ross & the Supremes**	*25th Anniversary (3-LP)*	6.1986
72437 WL	**Various**	*Lionel Richie: The Composer: Great Love Song With The Commodores & Diana Ross*	5.1986
72438 WL	**Diana Ross & the Supremes**	*Captured Live! On Stage*	2.1987
72439 WL	**Commodores**	*Live!*	5.1986
72440 ZL	**Various**	*A Fine Mess (f/s.)*	9.1986
72441 ZL	**El DeBarge**	*El DeBarge (ZD: 3.1987)*	7.1986
72442 ZL	**Rockwell**	*The Genie*	7.1986
72443 ZL	**Rick James**	*The Flag (ZD: 3.1987)*	7.1986

Cat.	Artist	Title	Date
72444 ZL	Fizzy Qwick	Fizzy Qwick	NM
72445 WL	Diana Ross & the Supremes	We Remember Sam Cooke	5.1986
*72446 ZD	The Marvelettes	Compact Command Performances: 23 Greatest Hits (WD: 10.1987)	3.1987
*72447 ZD	Martha Reeves & the Vandellas	Compact Command Performances: 24 Greatest Hits (WD: 10.1987)	3.1987
*72448 ZD	Mary Wells	Compact Command Performances: 22 Greatest Hits (WD: 10.1987)	3.1987
*72449 ZD	DeBarge	Greatest Hits (WD: 2.1987)	12.1986
*72450 ZD	Various	Motown's Biggest Pop Hits (WD: 10.1987)	3.1987
*72451 ZD	Various	Endless Love: 15 Of Motown's Greatest Love Songs	12.1986
*72452 ZD	Grover Washington Jr	Mister Magic / Feel So Good	11.1986
*72453 ZD	Stevie Wonder	My Cherie Amour / Signed, Sealed, Delivered	10.1986
*72454 ZD	Marvin Gaye & Tammi Terrell / Diana Ross & Marvin Gaye	Greatest Hits / Diana And Marvin	10.1986
*72455 ZD	Commodores	Natural High / Midnight Magic	10.1986
*72456 ZD	Marvin Gaye	What's Going On / Let's Get It On	11.1986
*72457 ZD	Marvin Gaye	I Heard I Through The Grapevine / I Want You	11.1986
*72458 ZD	Smokey Robinson & the Miracles	Going To A Go Go / The Tears Of A Clown	10.1986
*72459 ZD	Diana Ross & the Supremes	Where Did Our Love Go / I Hear A Symphony	12.1986
*72460 ZD	The Temptations	Cloud Nine / Puzzle People	10.1986
*72461 ZD	Gladys Knight & the Pips	Neither One Of Us / All I Need Is Time	11.1986
72462 ZL	Various	R&B Hits Of The 1960s	Eur only
72463 ZL	Marvin Gaye	Motown Remembers Marvin Gaye: Never Before Released Masters plus I Heard It Through The Grapevine	5.1986
*72464 ZD	Al Green	Compact Command Performances	Eur only
*72467 ZD	Various	Good Feeling Music Of The Big Chill Generation Vol. 1	NM

*Compact disc only

Cat.	Artist	Title	Date
*72466 ZD	Various	Good Feeling Music Of The Big Chill Generation Vol. 2	NM
*72467 ZD	Various	Good Feeling Music Of The Big Chill Generation Vol. 3	NM
*72468 ZD	Michael Jackson	Got To Be There / Ben	11.1986
*72469 ZD	Smokey Robinson	Being With You / Where There's Smoke	NM
*72470 ZD	Diana Ross	Diana / The Boss	10.1986
*72471 ZD	Teena Marie	Irons In The Fire / It Must Be Magic	NM
*72472 ZD	Four Tops	Reach Out / Still Waters Run Deep	2.1987
*72473 ZD	Jackson 5	Third Album / Maybe Tomorrow	NM
*72474 ZD	Rick James	Street Songs / Throwin' Down	12.1986

Cat.	Artist	Title	Date
*72475 ZD	The Temptations	Christmas Card / Give Love At Christmas	NM
*72476 ZD	Various	Pippin (original cast recording)	NM
*72477 ZD	Various	Guys And Dolls (original cast recording)	NM
72478 WL	Diana Ross	Greatest Hits Vol. 1	9.1986
72479 ZL	Stacy Lattisaw	Take Me All The Way	11.1986
72480 ZL	Four Tops	Hot Nights	NM
72481 WL	Various	Endless Love: Motown's Greatest Love Songs	NM
*72482 ZD	Al Green	Let's Stay Together / I'm Still In Love With You	NM
*72483 ZD	Jackson 5	Diana Ross Presents The Jackson 5 / ABC	11.1986
*72484 ZD	Edwin Starr	25 Miles / War And Peace	12.1986
*72485 ZD	Diana Ross & the Supremes	Love Child / Supremes A Go Go	11.1986
*72486 ZD	The Temptations	Psychedelic Shack / All Directions	11.1986
*72487 ZD	Jr Walker & the All Stars	Shotgun / Road Runner	12.1986
*72488 ZD	Mary Wells	Two Lovers / My Guy	NM
*72489 ZD	Stevie Wonder	For Once In My Life / Uptight	10.1986
*72490 ZD	Diana Ross	Touch Me In The Morning / Baby It's Me	12.1986
*72491 ZD	Four Tops	Four Tops / Second Album	3.1987
*72492 ZD	Smokey Robinson	Smokey / A Quiet Storm	NM
*72493 ZD	Diana Ross & the Supremes	Greatest Hits Vol. 1 and 2	11.1986
*72494 ZD	Grover Washington Jr	A Secret Place / All The King's Horses	12.1986
*72495 ZD	Gladys Knight & the Pips	Everybody Needs Love / If I Were Your Woman	NM
*72496 ZD	Diana Ross & the Supremes	Let The Sunshine In / Cream Of The Crop	2.1987
*72497 ZD	Rare Earth	Get Ready / Ecology	Eur only
*72498 ZD	Various	Every Great Motown Hit Vol. 1 and Vol. 2	11.1986
*72499 ZD	The Temptations	A Song For You / Masterpiece	12.1986
*72500 ZD	Marvin Gaye	Trouble Man / M.P.G.	2.1987
*72501 ZD	The Temptations	Live! / With A Lot O' Soul	2.1987
*72502 ZD	Diana Ross & the Supremes & The Temptations	Diana Ross And The Supremes Join The Temptations / Together	12.1986
*72503 ZD	Commodores	Heroes	NM

*Compact disc only.

Cat.	Artist	Title	Date
*72504 ZD	Al Green	Call Me / Livin' For You	NM
72505 WK	DeBarge	In A Special Way (cassette only)	NM
72506 WK	DeBarge	All This Love (cassette only)	NM
72507 WL	Marvin Gaye & Tammi Terrell	Easy	9.1986
*72508 ZD	Marvin Gaye	Compact Command Performances Vol. 2	3.1987
*72509 ZD	Various	You Can't Hurry Love	3.1987
*72510 ZD	Smokey Robinson & the Miracles	Compact Command Performances Vol. 2	3.1987

Cat. No.	Artist	Title	Date
*72511 ZD	Jr Walker & the All Stars	Compact Command Performances	3.1987
*72512 ZD	Diana Ross & the Supremes	25th Anniversary	3.1987
*72513 ZD	Various	Big Motown Hits + Hard To Find Motown Classics Vol. 1 (WD: 10.1987)	4.1987
*72514 ZD	Various	Big Motown Hits + Hard To Find Motown Classics Vol. 2 (WD: 12.1987)	6.1987
72515 ZL	The Temptations	To Be Continued	9.1986
72516 WL	The Isley Brothers	Greatest Motown Hits	2.1987
72517 WL	Marvin Gaye	Untitled	NM
72518 WL	Various	Motown Trackin'	9.1986
72519 WK	Various	Motown's Mustangs	NM
72520 WK	Marvin Gaye	Marvin Gaye In The Groove	NM
72521 WK	Gladys Knight & the Pips	All I Need Is Time	NM
72522 ZL	Mary Jane Girls	Conversation	NM
72523 ZL	Jakata	Designs Of The Heart	NM
72524 ZL	Chico DeBarge	Chico DeBarge	11.1986
*72525 ZD	The Temptations	Anthology	4.1987
*72526 ZD	Diana Ross & the Supremes / Stevie Wonder	Merry Christmas / Someday At Christmas	NM
*72527 ZD	Teena Marie	Compact Command Performances	NM
*72528 ZD	Four Tops	Anthology	4.1987
*72529 ZD	Jackson 5	Anthology	6.1987
*72530 ZD	Michael Jackson	Anthology	4.1987
*72531 ZD	Smokey Robinson & the Miracles	Anthology	6.1987
*72532 ZD	Diana Ross	Anthology	4.1987
*72533 ZD	Diana Ross & the Supremes	Anthology	6.9187
*72534 ZD	Marvin Gaye	Anthology	4.1987
*72535 ZD	Gladys Knight & the Pips	Anthology	6.1987
*72536 ZD	Jimmy Reed	Compact Command Performances	NM
*72537 ZD	Little Richard	Compact Command Performances	NM
72538 ZL	General Kane	In Full Chill	2.1987
*72539 ZD	The Temptations	25th Anniversary	NM

*Compact disc only.

Cat. No.	Artist	Title	Date
72540 WK	Various	Motown Time Capsule Vol. 1	NM
72541 WK	Various	Motown Time Capsule Vol. 2	NM
72542 WK	Smokey Robinson	Blame It On Love And All The Great Hits	NM
72543 WK	Various	The Last Radio Station	NM
72544 WK	Michael Jackson	Anthology (cassette only)	NM
72545 WL	Various	Legendary Long Versions Vol. 1	Eur only
72546 WK	Various	20 Motown Christmas Classics	11.1986

Cat. No.	Artist	Title	Date
*72547 WD	Duane Eddy	Compact Command Performances	2.1988
72548 WD	Various	Big Motown Hits And Hard To Find Classics Vol 3	2.1988
72549 ZD	Diana Ross	Ain't No Mountain High Enough / Surrender	7.1987
*72550 ZD	Smokey Robinson & the Miracles	Time Out For Special Occasion	NM
*72551 ZD	Commodores	Hot On The Tracks / In The Pocket	7.1987
*72552 ZD	DeBarge	All This Love / In A Special Way	Eur only
*72553 ZD	Marvin Gaye & Tammi Terrell	You're All I Need / United	NM
*72554 ZD	Martha Reeves & the Vandellas	Heatwave / Dance Party	NM
*72555 ZD	Smokey Robinson & the Miracles	Doin' Mickey's Monkey / Away We A Go Go	NM
*72556 ZD	Diana Ross & the Supremes	More Hits/ The Supremes Sing Holland-Dozier-Holland	NM
*72557 ZD	Diana Ross & the Supremes	A Bit Of Liverpool	NM
	Diana Ross & the Supremes & The Temptations	TCB	
*72558 ZD	Stevie Wonder	Down To Earth / I Was Made To Love Her	7.1987
*72559 ZD	The Temptations	Wish It Would Rain / In A Mellow Mood	NM
*72560 ZD	The Marvelettes	The Marvelettes / Sophisticated Soul	NM
*72561 ZD	The Isley Brothers	This Old Heart Of Mine / Soul On The Rocks	NM
*72562 ZD	Marvin Gaye	That Stubborn Kind Of Fellow / How Sweet It Is	7.1987
*72563 ZD	Duane Eddy	Have Twangy Guitar, Will Travel / $1,000,000 Worth Of Twangy	NM
*72564 ZD	Four Tops	Live! / Keeper Of The Castle	NM
*72565 ZD	Al Green	Al Green Is Love / Full Of Fire	NM
*72566 ZD	Various	Rock Gems – 24 Enduring Classics	NM
*72567 ZD	Various	Hits From The Legendary Vee Jay Records	NM
*72568 ZD	Dr Martin Luther King	Compact Command Performances	NM
72569 ZL	Various	Coast To Coast	NM
72570 ZL	Bunny DeBarge	In Love	4.1987
72571 ZL	Bruce Willis	The Return Of Bruno (ZD: 4.1987)	4.1987
72572 ZL	Billy Preston	Untitled	NM
72573 ZL	Blake & Hines	Blake & Hines	NM
72574 ZL	Four Tops	(originally ZL72480)	NM
72575 ZL	F.G.O.	Give Her What She Wants	NM
72576 WL	Marvin Gaye	Super Hits	Eur only

*Compact disc only.

Cat. No.	Artist	Title	Date
72577 ZL	Marvin Gaye	Every Great Motown Hit	Eur only
72578 WL	Smokey Robinson & the Miracles	Greatest Hits Vol. 2	Eur only
72579 WL	Diana Ross & the Supremes	Greatest Hits Vol. 1 and 2	Eur only
72580 ZL	Smokey Robinson	One Heartbeat (ZD: 4.1984)	4.1987

72581 ZL	**Angela Cole**	Turn Up The Beat	NM
72582 ZL	**Kim O'Leary**	Kim O'Leary	NM
72583 ZL	**Georgio**	Sexappeal	12.1987
72584 ZL	**Voyage**	Untitled	NM
72585 WL	**Stevie Wonder**	Essential Stevie Wonder (WD: 4.1988)	7.1987
72586 ZL	**Various**	Music From The Motion Picture Soundtrack, 'Police Academy IV' 'Citizens On Patrol'	7.1987
72587 ZK	**Michael Jackson**	Ben Got To Be There (cassette only)	Eur only
72588 ZK	**Jose Feliciano**	Esecnas De Amore Me Enamore (cassette only)	Eur only
72589 ZL/K	**General Kane**	Wide Open	NM
72590 ZL/K	**Carrie McDowell**	Carrie McDowell	11.1987
72591 WD	**Various**	Motown Dance Party Vol. 1	12.1987
72592 WD	**Various**	Motown Dance Party Vol. 2	12.1987
72593 WD	**Various**	Motown Around The World	NM
72594 WD	**Diana Ross & the Supremes**	The Rodgers & Hart Collection	12.1987
72595 WL/WK	**Smokey Robinson**	Smokey Robinson Story	Eur only
72596 WD	**Detroit Spinners**	The Best of . . .	NM
72597 WD	**Diana Ross & the Supremes**	Every Great Number 1 Hit	2.1988
72598 WD	**Bobby Darin**	Live! At The Desert Inn	NM
72599 WD	**Smokey Robinson & the Miracles**	Christmas With The Miracles	NM
72600 WD	**Diana Ross & the Supremes**	The Never-Before-Released Masters	2.1988
72601 WD	**Various**	The Most Played Oldies On America's Jukeboxes	12.1987
72602 WD	**Various**	Radio's Number 1 Hits Records That Have Been Played Over 15M Times On Radio	2.1988
72603 WL/WK/WD	**Various**	Three Times A Lady – Great Motown Love Songs (CD: 12.1987)	3.1988
72604 WD	**Stevie Wonder**	Music Of My Mind	12.1987
72605 WD	**Stevie Wonder**	Talking Book	10.1987
72606 WD	**Stevie Wonder**	Innervisions	10.1987
72607 WD	**Stevie Wonder**	Fulfillingness' First Finale	10.1987
72608 WD	**Stevie Wonder**	Hotter Than July	10.1987
72609 WD	**Stevie Wonder**	The Woman In Red	10.1987
72610 WD	**Diana Ross**	Lady Sings The Blues	12.1987
72611 WD	**Marvin Gaye**	What's Going On (CD: 4.1988)	4.1988
72612 WD	**Marvin Gaye**	The Best Of . . .	TBA
72613 ZL/K/D	**Stevie Wonder**	Characters (trans. to 72001)	NM
72614 WD	**Smokey Robinson & the Miracles**	Greatest Hits	TBA
72615 ZL/K	**Wilson Pickett**	American Soul Man	10.1987
72616 ZL/K/D	**Temptations**	Together Again (CD: 11.1987)	11.1987

72617 ZL/K/D	**Garry Glenn**	Feels Good To Feel Good (CD: NM)	10.1987
72618 ZL/K	**Ada Dyer**	Meant To Be	TBA
72619 ZL/K	**Chico DeBarge**	Kiss Serious	TBA
72620 ZL/K/D	**Stacy Lattisaw**	Personal Attention (CD: 3.1988)	3.1988
72621 ZL/K	**El DeBarge**	Real Love	TBA
72622 ZL/K/D	**Michael Jackson**	The Original Soul Of . . . (CD: 2.1988)	2.1988
72623 ZL/K/D	**Brownmark**	Just Like That (CD: 3.1988)	3.1988
72624 ZL/K	**Darryl Duncan**	Heaven	3.1988
72625 WD	**Dennis Edwards**	Don't Look Any Further (CD: 6.1988)	TBA
72626 WD	**Mary Jane Girls**	Mary Jane Girls	TBA
72627 WD	**Various**	Motown Memories Vol. 1	6.1988
72628 WD	**Various**	Motown Memories Vol. 2	6.1988
72629 WL/K	**Michael Jackson**	18 Greatest Hits	6.1988
72630	**Michael Jackson**	Farewell My Summer Love	6.1988

INDEX

Due to restricted page space, this index does not include all the singles and albums mentioned in the History, only those given significant coverage. The Discography content is not included in the Index. Page numbers in bold indicate either a colour or black and white illustration.

Picture Acknowledgements

Picture acknowledgements: We would like to thank the following for supplying us with photographs for the book: Motown Record Corporation; Motown/EMI Records; Motown/BMG Records; Peter Vernon; David Tufney; Jim Hegarty Collection; Gill Trodd Collection; Paramount Pictures; Dave Godin Collection; Sharon Davis Collection; Joe Bangay; Nightmare Records; 10 Records; CBS/Epic Records; Capitol Records; A & M Records.

Editor: **Honor Head**
Design and Layout: **Rob Burt**
Picture Editor: **Alex Goldberg**

© Sharon Davis and Guinness Publishing Ltd, 1988

Published in Great Britain by Guinness Publishing Ltd,
33 London Road, Enfield, Middlesex

Typeset in Novarese
by SX Composing Limited, Rayleigh, England
Printed and bound in Italy by New Interlitho SpA, Milan

'Guinness' is a registered trade mark of Guinness Superlatives Ltd

British Library Cataloguing in Publication Data

Davis, Sharon
    Motown: the history.
    1. United States. Pop music recording
    industries. Motown Corporation, to 1987
    I. Title
    338.7'6178991'0973

    ISBN 0-85112-894-7